Real World SQL Server
Administration with Perl

LINCHI SHEA

Apress™

Real World SQL Server Administration with Perl
Copyright ©2003 by Linchi Shea

ISBN (pbk): 1-59059-097-X

Printed and bound in the United States of America 12345678910

Trademarked names may appear in this book. Rather than use a trademark symbol with every occurrence of a trademarked name, we use the names only in an editorial fashion and to the benefit of the trademark owner, with no intention of infringement of the trademark.

Technical Reviewer: Mark Allison

Editorial Board: Dan Appleman, Craig Berry, Gary Cornell, Tony Davis, Steven Rycroft, Julian Skinner, Martin Streicher, Jim Sumser, Karen Watterson, Gavin Wright, John Zukowski

Assistant Publisher: Grace Wong

Project Manager: Tracy Brown Collins

Copy Editor: Kim Wimpsett

Production Manager: Kari Brooks

Production Editor: Janet Vail

Compositor: Argosy Publishing

Indexer: Carol Burbo

Artist and Cover Designer: Kurt Krames

Manufacturing Manager: Tom Debolski

Distributed to the book trade in the United States by Springer-Verlag New York, Inc., 175 Fifth Avenue, New York, NY, 10010 and outside the United States by Springer-Verlag GmbH & Co. KG, Tiergartenstr. 17, 69112 Heidelberg, Germany.

In the United States, phone 1-800-SPRINGER, email orders@springer-ny.com, or visit http://www.springer-ny.com. Outside the United States, fax +49 6221 345229, email orders@springer.de, or visit http://www.springer.de.

For information on translations, please contact Apress directly at 2560 Ninth Street, Suite 219, Berkeley, CA 94710. Phone 510-549-5930, fax 510-549-5939, email info@apress.com, or visit http://www.apress.com.

The information in this book is distributed on an "as is" basis, without warranty. Although every precaution has been taken in the preparation of this work, neither the author(s) nor Apress shall have any liability to any person or entity with respect to any loss or damage caused or alleged to be caused directly or indirectly by the information contained in this work.

The source code for this book is available to readers at http://www.apress.com in the Downloads section.

To Shirley, Monica, Christine, and Victor!

Contents at a Glance

Contents

Appendix B Getting Started with Perl 721

About the Author

Linchi Shea has been working with Microsoft SQL Server since version 4.2 for both the government and the financial services industry. He's currently a SQL Server technical lead at a major Wall Street firm in the New York City area.

Linchi is passionate about creating robust and automated infrastructures for managing SQL Server. He derives enormous joy in writing tools and utilities to compensate for what he sees as deficiencies in off-the-shelf packages.

Linchi has written articles for SQL Server Professional and has spoken at conferences on SQL Server/Perl topics. He's also a Microsoft MVP.
When not chanting "Automation leads to relaxation" Linchi spends time playing tennis and reading newspaper bridge columns.

About the Technical Reviewer

Mark Allison is a freelance database consultant working for various blue-chip organizations in London. Mark likes to work both as a development database administrator/database architect and as a production database administrator. Mark is also cofounder of Allison Mitchell Database Consultants Ltd, a successful database-consulting firm based in southeast England. Mark is a SQL Server MCP and was awarded the title of MVP by Microsoft in 2002.

Acknowledgments

WRITING A BOOK IS HARD WORK. Often, it appears to be a rather lonely endeavor. But in fact it requires sustained teamwork for the efforts to come to fruition. Although my name is listed as the author, this book couldn't have been published without significant contributions from many people.

First and foremost, I'd like to thank my editor, Karen Watterson. Without her encouragement, guidance, and contagious enthusiasm, I wouldn't have written this book. I had always felt a need for a book on managing SQL Server with Perl, but I didn't start writing until I met Karen in Denver at the close of the Professional Association for SQL Server (PASS) Conference in February 2002. A brief conversation with her in the hotel lobby set this book in motion. Thank you, Karen!

Second, I'm indebted to my technical reviewer, Microsoft MVP Mark Allison, whose comments significantly improved the quality and relevance of this book. Any remaining technical inaccuracies are all mine. By the way, Mark, if I remember one thing from this process, it's "Don't talk to me, talk to your reader!"

I can't thank my family enough, especially my wife, Shirley, for putting up with my repeated disappearing act on evenings and weekends to work on the book.

I'm also grateful to Bruce Bott and Hilary Cotter, both Microsoft MVPs, for their excellent feedback.

The Apress team, including Tracy Brown Collins, Kim Wimpsett, Janet Vail, Sofia Marchant, and Beth Christmas, did a fantastic job in guiding the entire project from the chapter drafts to the final production. Without your efforts, this book couldn't have been completed. In particular, I'd like to thank Tracy and Kim. Tracy Brown Collins is an excellent project manager, who knows how to keep the pressure on and get the chapters in. If not for her regular "nagging," I would still be at the start of the final lap. Thank you, Tracy! Kim Wimpsett is the copy editor for this book. I've learned a great deal about writing consistently simply by reading Kim's edits.

I'd like to extend my gratitude to my colleagues at work and to numerous participants on various SQL Server discussion groups for fruitful knowledge exchange. Indeed, the best way to gain knowledge is to share it!

Special thanks to my friend, Ara Barsegian, a SQL Server extraordinaire and techno-gadget aficionado, for his support and simply being a friend. My day job would feel much less complete without chatting with him over coffee and lunch breaks. He has a knack for derailing an otherwise serious but nevertheless nonsensical discussion.

Much of this book was written at various Starbucks coffee shops and at Modern Bagel Café in Fair Lawn, New Jersey. I'd like to thank the friendly folks at these coffee shops for allowing me to take up their spaces for an extended time.

Finally, thank you, Larry Wall, for creating Perl and guiding it to such a phenomenal success. You've made the world a much better place to live for many people, including the SQL Server database administrators and developers.

Introduction

THIS BOOK IS ABOUT SOLVING **SQL SERVER** administrative problems with Perl. My goal is to super-charge your SQL Server administrative skills by adding the power of Perl scripting to your toolset and to take you to the next level of SQL Server administration, far beyond what you can accomplish with the tools available in point-and-clicking interfaces or ordinary Transact-SQL (T-SQL) scripting.

I've designed this book to consist of a series of scenarios covering a wide range of SQL Server administrative topics. These are real-world scenarios that professional SQL Server Database Administrators (DBAs) encounter in their day-to-day development or production environments. The scenarios are grouped into the following areas:

- Assisting in data migration

- Comparing and sorting database objects

- Analyzing databases

- Analyzing SQL code

- Generating SQL code

- Analyzing log files

- Managing SQL Server security

- Monitoring SQL Server

- Managing SQL Server in the enterprise

You'll be able to walk away from this book with the following:

- A SQL Server DBA toolkit—SQLDBA Toolkit—with more than 150 Perl scripts that you can either use right away or customize easily to meet your particular requirements.

- Useful Perl problem solving techniques you can apply to create more tools for tackling SQL Server administrative problems not covered in this book.

The focus of the book isn't just how to access SQL Server from Perl but how to use Perl to solve SQL Server administration problems.

The Changing Landscape of SQL Server Administration

Recent years have witnessed rapid changes in the SQL Server technologies and database market forces. Consequently, several trends in SQL Server administration are significant and worth noting.

First, the rapid improvement in SQL Server has introduced a real shift in the nature of SQL Server administration. Traditionally, for production support, DBAs had to devote a large portion of their time to a few servers performing routine tasks such as installing and configuring SQL Server, creating databases, backing up and restoring databases, creating logins and users, granting permissions, scheduling jobs, and monitoring server performance and activities.

A DBA is now expected to manage many servers efficiently and effectively. Because of this expectation, the demand for the DBAs having only traditional skill sets has declined.

The demand, however, is on the rise for DBAs who can work on a larger scale in terms of more servers, more and bigger databases, and more complex database objects and environments.

This new era of SQL Server administration requires different approaches and tools. The tasks that used to be done manually are now becoming impossible or ineffective to do manually. It's not uncommon for a midsize company to have more than 100 SQL Servers. This isn't even factoring in the increasingly popular Microsoft Database Engine (MSDE). Automation in many cases is the only viable option to meet the demands placed on the modern DBA.

Second, the demand is also on the rise for DBAs to go beyond SQL Server because of SQL Server's integration with other technologies and tools. The days when a DBA was only expected to be proficient in database constructs such as tables, indexes, and stored procedures are fading away.

For instance, DBAs may need to reach into various parts of the Windows environment to retrieve such administrative information as the hardware configurations, operating system configurations, and system error conditions. In an enterprise environment, SQL Server administration generally must conform to the established enterprise-wide system management frameworks and is often required to interface with or take advantage of the existing technology infrastructures beyond the traditional boundaries of SQL Server.

These changes have contributed to the tremendous increase in information overload on many SQL Server DBAs. Not only does the amount of administrative information grow exponentially when compared with the number of servers or the number of databases, the information also comes from increasingly diverse sources other than SQL Server itself.

To meet the challenges brought on by these changes, SQL Server DBAs need expanded skill sets and good tools to perform their jobs effectively in a much larger scale and to interoperate with the related technologies and processes of Windows system administration.

SQL Server Administration with Perl

As a SQL Server DBA, you've always had the luxury of powerful out-of-the-box administrative tools such as Enterprise Manager or the Data Transformation Services Wizard—the Data Import and Export applets you can find in your Microsoft SQL Server program group. When these aren't enough, you can find more off-the-shelf tools from third-party vendors. Inevitably, though, you'll come to find holes in a tool or gaps among the available tools and discover that none of them quite solves your problem by itself. Perhaps you're working with the latest SQL Server version and the vendors haven't caught up with the releases of their tools. Throughout this book, I'll illustrate scenarios where you can quickly fill the holes or plug the gaps with Perl scripts.

It's common and annoying to find a tool that almost does what you want but yet doesn't do exactly what you want. For instance, a tool may do everything else right, but its output isn't exactly what you want. It may give you too little or overwhelmingly too much. You need to be able to extend the tool a little.

Other times, you may need to get two or more tools to automatically work together to get the job done, perhaps feeding the data out of one tool into another. In this book, I've included numerous Perl scripts that help address the problem of tool deficiency or help glue tools together.

Comprehensive as the available SQL Server DBA tools are, eventually you'll run into a problem that you can't solve with any tool. Perhaps you're able to find an off-the-shelf tool, but it's not uncommon that you need only about 10 percent of the tool and don't really want to pay for the 90 percent you don't need. Convincing your management to pay for such a tool can be a tough challenge. With Perl skills, you may find it both quicker and cheaper to write your own tools than search out, evaluate, understand, and buy them.

In fact, this book contains many Perl scripts that I've developed because I couldn't find the right tools for the DBA problems I was trying to solve. If I purchased all the tools I needed, I would have ended up spending a fortune with much of the money wasted on duplicate features.

Unfortunately, although many tools are great when used on a small scale, many of the available DBA tools haven't kept up with the increasing need to administrate SQL Server in the context of modern enterprises.

In that sense, I'd like to caution you that this book contains Perl scripts that may not seem worth discussing when framed in the context of a small SQL Server environment. But as the server environment becomes larger and more complex, the value of these scripts becomes more and more evident.

A case in point is the script for summarizing SQL Server errorlogs (see Chapter 9, "Analyzing Log Files"). If you only have a few SQL Server instances, it's not obvious such a script would add significant value to your job. Another example is the enforcement of the local SQL Server administrative standards. I've dedicated significant space in this book to discuss Perl scripts that automate best practice audit and standards enforcement.

It's good to have tools that can help solve your specific SQL Server administrative problems. It's even better to have a tool such as Perl that you can use to quickly create exactly the tools you need and when you need them.

Notice the key word is *quickly*. If you have to spend too much time writing your own tools, you aren't going to be able to do your job as a DBA. After all, your job title is likely not Professional Tool Developer. All too often and all too easily, DBAs give up on automating a task because they think it would take too long or it simply never occurs to them that it's feasible. What's missing is something quick and powerful such as Perl.

Once you get the hang of it, you'll find that Perl enables you to do things so quickly that you can start automating tasks that would otherwise not be practical. This is efficiency resulting in effectiveness.

You'll see plenty of such examples in this book.

A Personal Note

I came across Perl by accident around late 1995 when one day I picked up a Perl script written by a colleague to help manage SQL Server database upgrade. I was totally taken by the power of that simple script. I've since used Perl to tackle numerous SQL Server administrative problems including the ones presented in this book.

It's unfortunate that the SQL Server DBA community in general isn't familiar with Perl as a powerful scripting tool that can dramatically enhance the productivity of a SQL Server DBA. I've run into many SQL Server DBAs who think that Perl is something of a niche tool or something more in tune with the Unix environment. This is a complete misconception. They don't know what they have missed. It's my hope that this book will help rectify the situation.

Why Not Transact-SQL or Visual Basic?

Most SQL Server DBAs are well versed in T-SQL. Some can really push T-SQL to do amazing things. However, if you're content with using T-SQL alone for all your DBA scripting needs, you're severely limiting yourself within the confines of SQL Server.

Although T-SQL does provide ways to reach out of SQL Server, they're quite limited and aren't built to give you unbridled access to administrative facilities outside SQL Server. Another limitation of T-SQL is its lack of support for text processing. This isn't an indictment of T-SQL—it wasn't designed for processing text. But text processing is critical to solving many SQL Server administrative problems, as you'll see throughout this book. Moreover, T-SQL has no built-in mechanism to implement complex data structures, making it cumbersome to represent non-set-oriented problems.

T-SQL is nevertheless a powerful administrative tool, especially when the problem can be solved within SQL Server and is set oriented in nature. Having had extensive experience in writing both T-SQL scripts and Perl scripts, I found T-SQL plus Perl to be an extremely potent combination in supporting SQL Server administration. With Perl added to your arsenal of tools, you no longer have to squeeze a problem into the round hole of T-SQL. Instead, you can use T-SQL to deal with the facets of the problem that are suitable for T-SQL and leave the rest to Perl. Many Perl scripts in this book contain embedded T-SQL scripts.

Visual Basic is ubiquitous within the Windows environment and is a powerful language for building user applications. It's also a good scripting language for administrative purposes within the Windows environment. However, for many SQL Server administrative problems, Visual Basic isn't as convenient as Perl in several respects.

One is text processing. Although you can use a regular expression object in Visual Basic, pattern matching isn't fully integrated with other constructs of the Visual Basic language. In addition, Visual Basic isn't a convenient tool to help "stretch" an existing tool or to help glue multiple tools together. Compared with Perl, its lack of support for high-level dynamic data structures often makes Visual Basic scripts verbose and cumbersome in representing administrative information.

However, I should reiterate that this book is about solving SQL Server administrative problems with Perl. I didn't write this book to convince you that Perl is necessarily better than some other language. For certain problems, it's natural that you find you can as easily solve the same problem with a different language. After all, as the Perl motto goes, there's more than one way to do it!

Who This Book Is For

This book isn't an introductory Perl tutorial or a SQL Server administration tutorial. You can find the shelves already crowded with introductory books on both Perl and SQL Server administration in any computer bookstore.

You don't have to be a Perl expert to read this book. However, to get the most out of it, you should be conversant with the essentials of Perl, including its syntax, its data structure elements (scalars, arrays, hashes, and references), and its basic string operations. You also need to know the basics of file Input/Output (I/O), subroutines, and regular expressions. For your convenience, I've included a short review of the Perl essentials in Appendix B.

In addition, you should be familiar with the basics of SQL Server administration, and you should be comfortable with T-SQL scripting.

This book is for lazy, impatient, and cheap SQL Server DBAs.[1] If you're tired of having to deal with the same boring routines repetitively and want to have the routines automated, this book is for you. In particular, if you always have an urge to streamline multiple existing tools and make them work together automatically, this book is for you.

If instead of patiently waiting for the management approval process to eventually get you the tool you want for an urgent problem and you'd rather create a tool yourself, this book is for you.

You like a feature you see in an expensive tool but don't want to spend money or don't have the money to spend. Instead, you want to quickly write your own tool to get the job done. This book is for you.

This book is also written for SQL Server DBAs who know they have better things to do than waste their time on repetitive chores and who simply can't bring themselves to perform an administrative task more than twice without asking "How do I automate this darn thing so that I don't have to do it again?"

This book is for the SQL Server DBAs who want to break free from being constrained inside SQL Server and who want to have the freedom to access and use the administrative information wherever it may be kept.

Finally, this book is for those who want to acquire the ability to fill the holes in existing tools, stop the gaps among these tools, and extend existing tools to cover new problems.

Structure of the Book

With the exception of the first three chapters, you can read the book either randomly or sequentially.

---

1. Not that I'm knocking lazy, impatient, and cheap DBAs. These are good qualities in a DBA. Laziness can drive you to write scripts to make your life easier. Impatience can drive you to respond faster to critical problems or to anticipate them. Cheapness can lead you to get more bang for your budget dollars.

The first three chapters don't cover SQL Server specific topics; they cover basic Perl programming constructs and modules, common problem solving techniques, and the Perl routines to be used throughout the rest of the book. I've extracted the common elements from the Perl scripts and present them in these three chapters so that the rest of the book can focus on discussing SQL Server administrative issues instead of Perl issues. If you aren't familiar with Perl, you should read these three chapters thoroughly. If you're already familiar with Perl, you should at least skim through them to become acquainted with the techniques and routines to be used later in the book.

Starting with Chapter 4, "Migrating Data," the book consists of a series of discrete SQL Server administrative scenarios, loosely clustered around common SQL Server administrative topics. Each scenario focuses on a specific SQL Server administrative problem. Some scenarios are simple and can be addressed with a short Perl script. Others are more substantial and require significant Perl scripting.

Chapter 1, "Introducing Perl Basics," covers accessing command-line arguments, checking file attributes, working with file I/O, and using simple regular expressions. This chapter also discusses the use of arrays, hashes, references, and complex data structures as well as how to wrap Perl around other tools and make use of their results. It's important to get a firm grasp of these basic Perl constructs because they're used repeatedly throughout the rest of the book.

Chapter 2, "Working with Commonly Used Perl Modules," discusses the Perl modules that are used later in the book. These modules enable you to access various sources of administrative information (for example, Windows event logs, registries, services, and databases) or provide a simplified interface to the Component Object Model (COM). The chapter also covers miscellaneous utility modules that dump complex data structures to a string, access command-line arguments, and send Simple Mail Transfer Protocol (SMTP) email.

Chapter 3, "Working with Commonly Used Perl Routines," covers the routines that form the building blocks of many of the Perl scripts in this book. These routines deal with a wide range of programming tasks such as reading from a configuration file, getting the common elements of two arrays, working with directory trees, running SQL queries or scripts, and persisting data structures.

Chapter 4, "Migrating Data," presents the Perl scripts that help ease the pain in moving data between different systems or different formats. The scripts address issues such as validating the bulk copy processes, massaging data for import, checking data quality before import, and importing and exporting performance counter data.

Chapter 5, "Comparing and Sorting Database Objects," discusses comparing table columns, indexes, and constraints with Perl scripts. It also includes the scripts for comparing two stored procedures and database schemas. In addition, the chapter has the scripts for producing the call tree for a stored procedure and sorting the database objects by dependency.

Chapter 6, "Analyzing Databases," covers the interesting topic of using Perl to help understand the SQL Server storage internals and locking behavior. It also discusses the Perl scripts for analyzing indexes, constraints, and fragmentation.

Chapter 7, "Analyzing SQL Code," taps into the text processing power of Perl and its ability to conveniently represent extracted data with dynamic high-level data structures. This chapter includes the Perl scripts for cleaning up SQL trace output, identifying excessive joins and queries that contain excessive joins, summarizing index usage, and finding updates on clustered indexes. The chapter also discusses the Perl scripts that help identify poor coding practices for stored procedures.

Chapter 8, "Generating SQL Code," is about using Perl to help generate SQL code. The discussions include generating code from a template with limited variable replacement, generating data conversion SQL code, adding and removing code fragments from a SQL script, generating audit tables and triggers, generating insert statements from the data in a table, and merging and splitting SQL scripts. This chapter also illustrates how Perl can work with SQL-DMO to script the database objects.

Chapter 9, "Analyzing Log Files," covers the important topic of analyzing various types of log files generated daily in SQL Server environments. The Perl scripts discussed in this chapter help SQL Server DBAs mine information out of the log files and help reduce the information overload caused by the explosion of these log files. The chapter focuses on the Windows event logs, SQL Server errorlogs, SQL Server trace flag output, and ODBC trace logs.

Chapter 10, "Managing SQL Server Security," includes the Perl scripts that identify all the individual user accounts of the sysadmin role, scan for SQL Servers on the network, track SQL Server service accounts, track important security changes, and summarize security logs.

Chapter 11, "Monitoring SQL Servers," covers the Perl scripts that you can deploy to monitor disk space usage, errors in the errorlogs, the availability of SQL Server services, and the state changes of SQL Server clusters.

Chapter 12, "Managing SQL Servers in the Enterprise," includes an assortment of SQL Server administrative scenarios that are multiserver in nature. The chapter shows how to use Perl to address such issues as finding memory configurations in your SQL Server environment, locating the errorlogs for all your SQL Server instances, identifying missing database backups in your SQL Server environment, finding basic server information for all your SQL Server instances, finding the configured SQL Server listening ports, and purging old backup files from your SQL Server environment.

Finally, Appendix A, "Perl Resources," shows you where you can find more information about Perl. Appendix B, "Getting Started with Perl," gives you a quick review of the basic concepts of Perl. It also covers how to download and install Perl and how to run Perl scripts in the Windows environment.

Perl and SQL Server Versions

I've developed and tested all the scripts in this book with Perl 5.6.1
using the binary build 631 provided by ActiveState Tool Corporation
(http://www.ActiveState.com).

All the T-SQL queries, stand-alone or embedded in Perl scripts, have been
developed and tested in Microsoft SQL Server 2000 Service Pack 3.

Downloading the Code

To follow along with the examples, you can download the code from the
Downloads section of the Apress Web site (http://www.apress.com).

CHAPTER 1

Introducing Perl Basics

IF YOU WANT TO DO A JOB WELL, you must first sharpen your tools. In this case, the job is SQL Server administration, and the tool is the Perl programming language. This chapter and the next two help sharpen your skills with Perl before you use it to solve SQL Server administrative problems.

Fortunately, Perl is a rich language. Instead of being a minimalist language in pursuit of theoretical elegancy, Perl provides many built-in features and shortcuts for the convenience of the programmer.

Perl is also an easy-to-use language although some may not agree. I've heard from many people many times that Perl looks like C. That's a completely mistaken impression. When it comes to solving problems, Perl and C operate at levels that are far apart. Instead of dealing with computer-oriented memory allocation and pointers, Perl hides the low-level elements and allows you to work with constructs such as scalars, lists, references, and reference-based dynamic structures. You can more conveniently use these constructs to model real-world problems than you could with memory allocation and pointers.

Most important, Perl is a powerful language for text processing. Its text processing features are inherently integrated with the language and blended into all the language constructs. They're not additional utilities, functions, or objects later stuffed into the language to enhance its processing power.

This chapter focuses on the most basic Perl programming concepts. The objective of this chapter and the next two is to make you comfortable with common Perl programming techniques, idioms, modules, and routines. You'll see them being used frequently later in the book and, for that matter, in practically any real-world Perl scripts.

If you're already familiar with Perl to some extent, this chapter reacquaints you with such tasks as accessing command-line arguments, reading from files, working with arrays and hashes, using references, and getting results from other command-line utilities. However, this isn't a Perl primer or a Perl tutorial, and it doesn't systematically cover Perl's rich features from the ground up. You should know how to run a Perl script in Windows, and you should understand the most elementary Perl concepts such as scalars, lists, file handles, and contexts. If you don't, first spend some time with one of the excellent Perl books listed in Appendix A, "Perl Resources."

Accessing the Command-Line Arguments

SCENARIO
You want to access the command-line arguments in your Perl scripts.

The command-line arguments reside in the predefined array @ARGV. Because the index of a Perl array starts with zero, the first argument is in $ARGV[0], the second is in $ARGV[1], and so on. Note that the script name is, however, not in @ARGV.

> **NOTE** *In case you can't contain your curiosity, Perl stores the name of the script in the predefined variable $0. Also, note that Perl is case sensitive. Thus, @ARGV is different from @Argv. It's customary to use all uppercase letters for a predefined Perl construct.*

The following script accepts two command-line arguments:

```
($param1, $param2) = @ARGV;
print "First arg = $param1, Second arg = $param2\n";
```

To see what this two-line script produces, place it in the file test.pl and execute the following on the command line:

```
cmd>perl test.pl John Adam Smith
First arg = John, Second arg = Adam
```

Note that the script doesn't use the third command-line parameter, Smith, but it's still in the array @ARGV. You can specify an arbitrary number of parameters on the command line, and they'll all be stored in @ARGV. It's then up to your script to decide which command-line arguments to use.

Like anything Perl, there's more than one way to do it. In addition, there's often an implicit shortcut to do it! In the code that follows, you access the command-line arguments using the built-in Perl function shift(), which accepts an array, removes its first element, and returns this element. The output is the same as in the previous example:

```
($param1, $param2) = (shift, shift);
print "First arg = $param1, Second arg = $param2\n";
```

At file scopes, when you don't supply a parameter, the shift() function gets the first element of @ARGV, which is $ARGV[0], and removes the element from the array. Therefore, the array is shortened by 1. The previous $ARGV[1] now becomes $ARGV[0], $ARGV[2] becomes $ARGV[1], and so on. Thus, in the previous example, the first shift() function returns $ARGV[0], and the second shift() function returns $ARGV[1]. In Perl, when it's not ambiguous, the parentheses following a function are optional.

When the script expects only one argument on the command line, it's a common Perl idiom to get the argument with the shift() function.

You need to be careful about what constitutes a command-line argument. In general, you separate command-line arguments with a space. If you're running the Windows 2000/NT command shell, an argument can contain a space if the argument is surrounded by double quotation marks. Thus, in the following example, the number of arguments is two, not three:

```
cmd>perl test.pl  "John Adam" Smith
```

and the output is as follows:

```
First arg = John Adam, Second arg = Smith
```

In addition, an argument can have an embedded double quote if you escape it with a backslash. Therefore, the following code:

```
cmd>perl test.pl  "John \"Adam\"" Smith
```

prints the following:

```
First arg = John "Adam", Second arg = Smith
```

If you're unfortunate enough to have to deal with embedded double quotation marks in the command-line arguments, make sure to carefully escape each embedded double quote. You may not receive any error when you don't escape a double quote, but the ensuing experience can be quite frustrating.

Checking File Attributes

SCENARIO
You want to find a file's size and the last time it was modified.

The most straightforward way to retrieve these two file attributes is to use the built-in Perl function stat(), which returns the file size in bytes and the last-modified time in epoch seconds. The other items returned by the stat() function are of less use in the Windows environment.

NOTE *In Windows, epoch seconds are the number of non-leap seconds since 00:00:00 January 1, 1970, Greenwich mean time (GMT).*

Listing 1-1 retrieves the file size and the last-modified date.

Listing 1-1. Getting the Size of a File and Its Last-Modified Time

```
$fileName = shift;
($size, $mdate) = (stat($fileName))[7,  9];
$timeStr = localtime($mdate);
print "Size = $size, ModifyDate = $timeStr\n";
```

Save this script to the file getFileAttributes.pl and then run the script against a test.txt file to produce the following:

```
cmd>perl getFileAttributes.pl test.txt
Size = 114, ModifyDate=Thu Dec 12 00:18:40 2002
```

The eighth element of the array returned by stat($fileName)—in other words, (stat($fileName)[7] in Listing 1-1 because the array index is zero based—is the total file size in bytes. Alternatively, you can use the -s file test operator to return the size of a file:

```
$fileSize = -s $filename;
```

Beware that in the earlier releases of Perl, these methods have problems dealing with large files (2 gigabytes or larger).

The 10th element of the array returned by the function stat($fileName), which is (stat($fileName))[9], is the last-modified time in seconds since the epoch.

As mentioned, the epoch was at 00:00:00 January 1, 1970, GMT on Windows. In Listing 1-1, the localtime() function, when used in a scalar context, converts the epoch seconds to a more readable date/time string. The result is already adjusted for the local time zone. In a list context, localtime() returns an array of nine numeric elements, including such items as seconds, minutes, hours, date, and so on.

Note that localtime(0) may return Wed Dec 31 19:00:00 1969—or some other date/time depending on your computer's time zone setting—instead of the expected Thu Jan 1 00:00:00 1970.[1] If this puzzles you, remember that the starting

---

1. You'll get this date/time string if your computer is set to U.S. eastern standard time (EST).

time of the epoch seconds is in GMT, whereas `localtime()` expects a local time in epoch seconds.

Beyond the file's size and the last-modified time, a file comes with many more attributes, such as whether it's read only or compressed. To access these and other file attributes, you'll need to study various standard Win32 modules such as Win32::File and Win32::FileSecurity. Chapter 2, "Working with Commonly Used Perl Modules," covers Perl modules.

Finding Patterns in a String

SCENARIO
You want to test whether a pattern can be matched in a string.

To search a string for a pattern match, use the `=~` or `!~` operator, immediately followed by a regular expression pattern in the `m//` matching operator. In a scalar context, the `=~` operator returns true if the pattern on the left side matches the string on the right side.

> **NOTE** *Briefly, every Perl expression is evaluated in a context. Perl has two major contexts: scalar and list. In scalar context, the expression is expected to return a single value; in list context, it's expected to return a list. The same Perl expression may return different results in different contexts.*

For instance, the regular expression in the following statement tests whether the string in the `$log` variable contains the words `TradeDB` or `StockDB`:

```
$log =~ /\b(TradeDB|StockDB)\b/;
```

When a forward slash (`/`) is the delimiter, the initial letter `m` in the `m//` matching operator is optional. In other words, `m/PATTERN/` is the same as `/PATTERN/`. This matching operator accepts various modifiers; `/i` and `/x` are the most common. The `/i` modifier tells the regular-expression engine that the pattern matching is case insensitive, and the `/x` modifier permits whitespaces and comments inside the regular expression. Thus, if you decide that the string pattern should be case insensitive, you can rewrite the previous statement as follows:

```
$log =~ /\b ( TradeDB  |     # matching TradeDB
              StockDB  )     # or matching StockDB
            \b/ix;
```

Note that \b matches the word *boundary*, which is an imaginary position between a word character (alphanumeric plus an underscore) and a nonword character. This example doesn't do justice to the usefulness of the /x modifier. If you're specifying a complex regular expression, you should always use this modifier to make the regular expression more readable and therefore more maintainable. As you'll see, the rest of this book uses the /x modifier heavily.

CAUTION   *If you add the /x modifier to a regular expression, make sure you replace any whitespace with an explicit* \s. *Otherwise, your original whitespaces that are effectively part of the matching pattern will be ignored.*

If you're not new to Perl, chances are you've seen the m// matching operator used by itself in a statement as follows (remember that the letter m is optional in the m// operator when the regular expression is delimited with a pair of forward slashes):

```
/\b(TradeDB|StockDB)\b/;
```

This is one of Perl's most popular idioms, which is shorthand for the following:

```
$_ =~ /\b(TradeDB|StockDB)\b/;
```

In Perl, you typically don't have to explicitly use the predefined $_ variable, which is the default input and pattern-searching space. This omission is quintessentially Perl. The reasoning is that if it's done often, there should be an easy way to do it. The easy way is often a Perl idiom in the form of a shortcut. People new to Perl may not like the heavily idiomatic nature of Perl. But after you've gotten the hang of it, it comes rather naturally.

TIP   *See the online Perl core documentation* perlvar *for a complete description of the cases where Perl assumes $_ even when you don't use it explicitly. You can either use the Hypertext Markup Language (HTML) documentation distributed with ActivePerl from ActiveState or type* perldoc perlvar *at the command prompt. After you're used to it, you'll find* perldoc *to be one of the most useful Perl command-line utilities.*

Opening and Reading from a File

SCENARIO
You want to open a file and read in all the lines for further processing.

Listing 1-2 shows the Perl code for reading from a file specified on the command line and then looping through all the lines to apply the dummy() function.

Listing 1-2. Opening and Reading from a File

```
use strict;
my $log = shift or die "***Err: a file is expected on the command line.";
open(LOG, "$log") or die "***Err: couldn't open $log.";
while(<LOG>) {
    dummy($_);
}
close(LOG);

sub dummy {
    my $line = shift or die "***Err: function dummy() expects a string.";
    print $line;
} # dummy
```

Listing 1-2 shows several commonly used Perl programming constructs. The first thing to note is the use strict pragma at the top of the script. It imposes restrictions on what Perl considers unsafe programming practices. Among other things, it forces all variables to be explicitly declared before they're first used, which reduces the risk of a typo in a variable name producing unintended and hard-to-debug results. In spirit, this pragma is similar to Option Explicit in Visual Basic.

NOTE *Like a pragma in many other programming languages such as C, a Perl pragma is a compiler directive that changes the compilation behavior of a script. A Perl pragma is treated as a special kind of module and is invoked with a* use *declaration. Examples of Perl pragmas are* use strict *and* use warnings.

If you want to restrict a variable to a particular scope such as a file or a block of code, you declare that variable with my(). For instance, Listing 1-2 declared the $log variable to be visible to the entire file, and the $line variable is visible only within the dummy() function.

NOTE *The concept of scope is not the easiest to grasp in any serious programming language. Perl is no exception. To make it easier, remember that in the majority of cases, you should use* my() *to confine a variable to a scope. To learn more about declaring and scoping a variable, read the documentation on Perl subroutines,* perlsub, *which has detailed discussions on using the* my() *operator.*

TIP *Always include* use strict *at the beginning of every script unless it's a throwaway one liner. This practice will save you loads of agony.*

In Perl, you manipulate files through file handles. Before a file can be processed, you must first obtain a handle to it. Successfully obtaining a file handle tells you that the file is ready for processing. Often, failure to obtain a handle to a key file means that there's no longer a need for the script to go on; thus, the following Perl idiom is common:

```
open ... or die ...;
```

This aborts the script if open() fails. The die() function prints the concatenation of its arguments to STDERR and exits the script. Because a script that doesn't need to communicate with a file is rarely useful, you'll see this idiom in almost every script throughout this book.

Also in Listing 1-2 is another common Perl idiom, which is the combination of the while block and the line input operator, <> (also known as the *angle operator*):

```
while(<LOG>) {
    dummy($_);
}
```

In this case, <LOG> reads one line from the file handle LOG and implicitly assigns the line to the variable $_. When it reaches the end of the file, the line input operator returns the undefined value, which is false in Perl, and thus causes the while block to exit. In other words, this while block applies the function dummy() to each line in the file whose file handle is LOG. You'll see this idiom in every script in this book.

Finding Lines Matching a Pattern in a File

SCENARIO

You want to single out the lines matching a particular pattern from a file.

Now that you understand the script in Listing 1-2, finding the lines that match a pattern is easy to accomplish. Simply replace the dummy() function with a function that searches the line for the pattern match, and you have the script shown in Listing 1-3.

Listing 1-3. Finding Lines Matching a Pattern in a File

```
1.   use strict;
2.
3.   Main: {
4.     my $log = shift or die "***Err: $0 expects a file name.";
5.     open(LOG, "$log") or die "***Err: couldn't open $log.";
6.     while (<LOG>) {
7.         findPattern($_);
8.     }
9.     close(LOG);
10. } # Main
11.
12. ################
13. sub findPattern {
14.     my $line = shift or die "***Err: findPattern() expects a string.";
15.     if ($line =~ / Error:\s+\d+,          # error number
16.                     \s+                   # whitespace
17.                     Severity:\s+(\d+)     # severity level
18.                   /ix) {
19.         print $line if $1 >= 17;
20.     }
21. } # findPattern
```

This script has a clean structure that other scripts throughout the book follow. Using best practices, it starts with the ubiquitous pragma use strict. Then comes the Main block, where the key steps of the script are performed. The script then defines zero or more functions, or *subroutines*. Listing 1-3 defines one subroutine, `findPattern()`.

Perl allows you to label a block of code enclosed in a pair of braces. I customarily label the main body of a script as `Main`. Although this isn't required, it's a practice that helps highlight the main steps of the script. Typically, the main body of a script—even a complex one—consists of only a few lines of code. The bulk of the code is in the functions defined after the main body.

Now, let's see what the script in Listing 1-3 actually does. The following example feeds a SQL Server errorlog to the Perl script (saved to the file `findError.pl`). It prints all the lines containing SQL Server errors with a severity level of 17 or higher:

```
cmd>perl findError.pl d:\mssql\log\errorlog
2002-12-14 13:38:55.30 spid51    Error: 50000, Severity: 17, State: 1
2002-12-14 13:39:01.28 spid51    Error: 50000, Severity: 20, State: 1
```

You should note several additional points. On line 4 in Listing 1-3, the predefined variable `$0` is used in the error message. This variable contains the filename of the Perl script being executed.

In the `while` block, there's only a single statement. If you don't expect any other statements in the `while` loop, you can replace lines 6 through 8 with a single line:

```
findPattern($_) while <LOG>;
```

In the function `findPattern()`, note how the script takes advantage of the `/x` modifier to split the regular expression onto three lines (lines 15, 16, and 17), each corresponding to a conceptually meaningful element. Each line in this regular expression is also annotated with a comment. This makes the regular expression more readable.

Finally, on line 17 a pair of parentheses captures a substring inside `$line`, which matches the pattern defined in the parentheses. In this case, the pattern is `\d+` for one or more digits, and the matched substring is captured in the variable `$1` for the first pair of parentheses. You can specify an arbitrary number of parentheses in a regular expression to capture as many substrings. The substring for the second pair is recorded with `$2`, the third with `$3`, and so on. It's important to remember that the capturing pairs of parentheses are counted from left to right by the left parenthesis.

Storing and Accessing Data in an Array

SCENARIO
You want to store and access data in an array.

There are three basic data types in Perl: scalars, arrays, and hashes. A *scalar* value
in Perl is a single value that can be a number, a string, or a reference. In Perl, there's
no such thing as declaring a variable to be of type number, type string, or type reference. However, you can declare a variable to be a scalar, an array, or a hash. In
Perl, you always prefix a scalar variable with a $ sign.

An *array* is a named list of scalars indexed with numbers that start at 0. A *hash*
is also a named list of scalars but indexed with strings. And because the indexes are
strings, a hash is considered a list of key/value pairs whose keys are the index
strings and whose values are always scalars. You'll learn more about hashes in the
"Storing and Accessing Data in a Hash" section.

Using the Type Identifiers

Every variable in Perl is prefixed with a type identifier corresponding to one of
the three basic types: scalar, array, or hash:

- $ identifies the variable name as representing a scalar.

- @ identifies the variable name as representing an array.

- % identifies the variable name as representing a hash.

It's important to remember that the type identifier of a variable name may
change depending on what's expected. For instance, after declaring the array
@tables, you can use an expression such as $tables[2] to refer to a scalar value in
the array.

To get a scalar into an array, you can use the functions push() or unshift() or
simply put the scalar into a list that's assigned to the array. The following are four
different ways of putting the string 'master' into the array @databases:

```
1. push @databases, 'master';              # add to the end
2. unshift @databases, 'master';           # add to the beginning
3. @databases = (@databases, 'master');    # add to the end
4. @databases = ('master', @databases);    # add to the beginning
```

Let's assume that @databases is assigned the list ('tempdb', 'pubs') prior to each example. In the first example on line 1, the push() function adds 'master' to the end of the array, which produces ('tempdb', 'pubs', 'master'), and the unshift() function on line 2 puts 'master' at the beginning of the array, which produces ('master', 'tempdb', 'pubs').

The last two examples on lines 3 and 4 use the array @databases and the string 'master' to construct a new list and then assign the new list to @databases. This method is versatile. You can mix lists and scalars in a pair of parentheses in an arbitrary manner. For instance, you can append an array to another as follows:

```
@databases = (@databases, @newDatabases);
```

You can also use this method to replace an array element. The following example replaces the first element of the array with the string 'master':

```
@databases = ('master', @databases[1..$#databases]);
```

This example first uses the range operator (..) to generate a list of indexes from 1 through $#databases, which is the last valid index of the array @databases. Therefore, @databases[1..$#databases] returns all the elements of the array @databases except the first one.

In case you didn't notice, you must prefix the name of a Perl array variable with the character @ when referring to an array as a whole.

Perl provides a rich "array" of means to access the elements in an array. The following are four different ways of retrieving data from an array:

```
$db1 = $databases[1];         # get the second element
$db2 = pop @databases;        # get the one at the end
$db3 = shift @databases;      # get the one at the beginning
@other_dbs = @databases[1, 2]; # get two at the indexes
```

Assume that the value of @databases is ('master', 'tempdb', 'pubs') before each example. The variable $db1 will have the string 'tempdb'. To access an element via its array index, you must prefix the array name with a scalar $ sign, which signifies you're dealing with a scalar, not an array or a hash.

The next two variables are assigned values returned by two Perl functions, pop() and unshift(). As their names imply, the function pop() does the opposite of the function push(), and the function shift() is the opposite of the function unshift(). In other words, pop() removes the last element from a list and returns that element, and shift() removes the first element from a list and returns that element. As such, the variable $db2 will have the string 'pubs', which is the last element in @databases, and the variable $db3 will have the string 'master', which is the first element in @databases.

Finally, the array `@other_dbs` will have the list (`'tempdb'`, `'pubs'`). In this case, on the right side of the assignment, the array name is prefixed with an array @ sign. You must use this symbol when you're *slicing* an array—in other words, taking a sublist out of an array.

As you'll see later, there are many more ways of accessing the elements of an array. One of the most popular methods is to use a `foreach` loop to iterate through the array elements and perform some operations on each element. For example, the following is a common code snippet:

```
foreach my $db (@databases) {
    print "$db\n";
}
```

This prints each database name in `@databases` on a separate line. If you don't specify the iterator variable (also called the *loop* variable), you imply the predefined variable $_. In real-world scenarios, neither the array nor the code block is this simple. However, don't worry! You'll see plenty of complex `foreach` loops throughout this book.

Storing and Accessing Data in a Hash

SCENARIO
You want to store and access data in a hash.

If you think scalars and arrays aren't particularly special, wait until you see hashes. Hashes are special arrays. But unlike regular arrays whose elements are indexed by integer and are nicely ordered by numeric index, hash values can be indexed by arbitrary strings and aren't ordered in any meaningful way. You prefix hash variables with the % sign.

If you're not yet familiar with hashes, they may look deceptively innocuous. But that impression couldn't be further from truth. You'll see repeatedly that hashes coupled with references—to be introduced in the section "Using References and Nested Data Structures" later in this chapter—give you powerful yet easy-to-use dynamic data structures for modeling problems and recording structured information. In other commonly used programming languages such C, C++, and Visual Basic, you don't really see anything similar that has been promoted to the level of visibility of being one of the three basic data types of the language.

The following are three ways to add elements to a hash:

```
%dbSize = ('master', 20, 'tempdb', 15);
%dbSize = ( master => 20, tempdb => 15);
$dbSize{pubs} = 4;
```

The first two examples initialize the hash %dbSize, overwriting whatever might be in %dbSize at the time. They accomplish the same result. The former uses a regular list on the right side, and the latter uses the => operator, making it clear which element is the index and which is the value. The left side of the => operator is called the *key*, and the right side is called the *value*. A hash consists of a list of such key/value pairs.

The third example is different from the first two. It sets the value of the key 'pubs' to 4. If the 'pubs' key doesn't already exist, it adds a new key/value pair to the hash while keeping the other key/value pairs, if any, intact. Moreover, if the hash itself doesn't exist, this results in the hash being created. Note that the string index is enclosed in a pair of braces in contrast to a pair of square brackets used to enclose an array index.

It's common to use the elements of an array of strings as the keys of a hash. The following code goes through each database name in the array @databases and adds a new key/value pair to the hash %dbSize to record the size of that database. The function getDBSize(), which you can ignore because it's not relevant to the current discussion, obtains the database size:

```
foreach my $db (@databases) {
    $dbSize{$db} = getDBSize($db);
}
```

Just as with accessing array elements, there are multiple ways to access data in a hash. The following are two common approaches:

```
$size = $dbSize{'master'};
($db, $size) = each %dbSize;
```

The first example retrieves the value of the key 'master'. Because it's accessing a scalar value, not the hash as a whole, the hash name is prefixed with a $ sign. In the second example, the built-in function each() retrieves a key/value pair from the hash, which is then assigned to the variables $db and $size. Note that the each() function operates on the whole hash.

If you play with each(), you'll notice you have no control over which key/value pair it'll first return. If you keep applying each() to the same hash, all the key/value pairs will eventually be returned. This makes each() a good candidate to be used in a loop where you can perform actions on every pair. The following code is common for looping through all the hash elements:

```
while(($db, $size) = each %dbSize) {
    # perform some action on $db or $size
}
```

Often, you want to control the order in which the key/value pairs are returned. The typical approach is to sort the keys returned by the keys() function before accessing the values:

```
foreach my $db (sort keys %dbSize) {
    print "$db = $dbSize{$db}\n";
    # do something else
}
```

This prints the database names in alphabetical order. You'll see the shadow of this example in almost every script where hashes are accessed. It's really used that often!

 CAUTION   *The function* keys() *returns all the keys of the hash in a list, and this list takes up separate memory space. Thus, if your hash is large, the memory requirement of the function* keys() *can be substantial. You may want to consider trading its convenience for the resource advantages of the function* each().

Finally, the story wouldn't be complete without knowing how to remove a key/value pair from a hash. You do that using the delete() function. The following statement removes the pair whose key is 'master' from the hash %dbSize:

```
delete $dbSize{master};
```

You can also use delete() to remove multiple key/value pairs from a hash. Naturally, you may try one of the following to remove two key/value pairs from the hash %dbSize at once:

```
1.  delete $dbSize{'master', 'tempdb'};
2.  delete %dbSize{'master', 'tempdb'};
3.  delete @dbSize{'master', 'tempdb'};
```

Which one is correct? Only the third one deletes two pairs with the given keys. The first two attempts fail miserably without producing what you want. Specifically, the first example doesn't delete any element from the hash, and the second one gives you a syntactic error. Using the type identifiers ($, @, and %) may look rather quirky, but it's actually quite consistent. The consistency lies in that the type identifier matches what's being returned.

Finding Array Elements Matching a Pattern

> **SCENARIO**
> *You want to single out those elements of an array that match a pattern.*

Use the foreach loop and apply the =~ operator with the match operator to the loop variable. The following example finds any database name containing a character that's not an alphanumeric or an underscore:

```
foreach my $db (sort @databases) {
    print "$db\n" if $db =~ /\W/;
}
```

Note that \W matches a nonword character—in other words, a character that's not alphanumeric or an underscore. \W is the opposite of \w, which matches an alphanumeric plus an underline. With the knowledge from the past several sections, this code fragment should be trivial to you. So let's move on to a different method of finding the array elements:

```
map { print "$_\n"; } grep { /\W/ } @db;
```

That's right! This single line replaces all the looping and branching, and it accomplishes the same result. Because this is another common idiom, let's dissect it a bit.

The evaluation goes from right to left. The function grep() actually performs an implicit loop through the array, applies the code block specified with its first parameter to each element in $_, and returns a list of those elements for which the code block is evaluated to true. Similarly, the function map() iterates through an array and applies the code block to each element. It returns a list consisting of the values returned from the code block.

In the previous example, I wasn't interested in the results of map(), but I did take advantage of the side effect of its code block, which prints the element returned from the grep() function. In general, though, you want to use the result returned from map() instead of its side effect.

 TIP *If you're new to* map() *and* grep() *and aren't exactly clear about their differences, remember that* grep() *filters and* map() *transforms. It pays to become comfortable with these two functions.*

Printing to a File

SCENARIO
You want to output data to a file.

As mentioned in the "Opening and Reading from a File" section earlier in this chapter, before you can work with a file, you must first get a file handle to that file.

If you think a file handle is too abstract, look at it from three perspectives: First, you can consider it shorthand or a special name given to a file. Second, file handles aren't only for regular files in a file system. You can give file handles to many different Input/Output (I/O) devices such as sockets and pipes; however, this book stays with regular text or binary files. File handles provide a level of uniformity over the diversity of I/O devices and help hide the lower-level complexities. Third and most important, you can consider obtaining a file handle as a promise or a commitment from Perl that the lower-level mechanisms have done their preparations and the file is ready for you to use.

In Perl, you'll use four file operations most often. They are the open() function, the line input operator (<>), the print() function, and the close() function. Typically, you first open a file to get a file handle. Then, you either read from the file, often with the <> operator, or write to the file with the print() function—or do both. When you're done, you close the file.

Listing 1-4 shows an example of writing to a log file.

Listing 1-4. Writing to a Log File

```
1.  use strict;
2.  my $log = shift or die "***Err: $0 expects a file name.";
3.  open(LOG, "> $log")  or die "***Err: could not open $log for write.";
4.  print LOG "Logging starts at ", scalar localtime(), "\n";
5.  #
6.  # do other things
7.  #
8.  close(LOG);
```

The open(LOG, "> $log") function call opens the file $log for write and associates the file handle LOG with the file. You can use the angle sign (either > or <) in front of the filename to specify the access mode. Table 1-1 describes the various access modes you can direct the open() function to use.

Table 1-1. File Access Modes

MODE	DESCRIPTION
open(FH, "< $fileName");	Read only.
open(FH, "$fileName");	Read only. Same as open(FH, "< $fileName");.
open(FH, "> $fileName");	Write only. This creates a new file if one doesn't exist. Otherwise, it truncates the file.
open(FH, ">> $fileName");	Write only. This appends to a file if one exists. Otherwise, it creates a new file.
open(FH, "+< $fileName");	Read/write.
open(FH, "+> $fileName");	Read/write. This creates a new file if one doesn't exist. Otherwise, it truncates the file.
open(FH, "+>> $fileName");	Read/write. This appends to the file if one exists. Otherwise, it creates a new file.

NOTE *I've never found a good case to use any of the last three file access modes in Table 1-1 (+<, +>, and +>>). These modes allow both reads and writes. Things can become confusing when you mix reads with writes on the same file.*

The function to write a string or a list of strings to a file handle is print(). Thus, in Listing 1-4, line 4 prints the list ("Logging starts at ", scalar localtime(), "\n") to the file handle LOG. In the print() function, it's not customary to enclose the list in a pair of parentheses; however, you could if you so choose.

When the file handle is omitted, the function writes to the default file handle, which is usually STDOUT. Perl allows you to set any file handle as the default with the function select(). I don't usually set the default file handle to anything other than STDOUT. Explicitly specifying the file handle makes the code more readable.

As is typically Perl, there's always a convenient default for everything. The function print() accepts $_ as the default when the list is omitted. Thus, you could actually say the following:

```
print;
```

to print $_ to the default file handle.

> **CAUTION**   *There's no comma between the file handle and the list. This is easy to forget because there aren't any parentheses around the list.*

Using the Here Document

> **SCENARIO**
> *You want to use a handy little mechanism you heard about called the here document.*

The name *here document* comes from the Unix shell. In Perl, it's a convenient way to quote a large chunk of text that spans multiple lines. It's particularly useful when you need to blend SQL queries within the Perl code.

A here document begins with << immediately followed by a string, called the *terminating identifier*. The quoted text starts from the next line and runs until Perl sees the terminating identifier on a separate line by itself—without even a comment. Listing 1-5 shows how to use a here document.

Listing 1-5. Using a Here Document

```
1.  my $db = 'master';
2.  my $sql = <<END_SQL;            # there is no space between << and END_SQL
3.  USE $db
4.  GO
5.  SELECT * FROM sysobjects
6.  GO
7.  END_SQL
8.  print $sql;
```

The here document, introduced by <<END_SQL on line 2, terminates with END_SQL on line 7. This assigns the SQL code between lines 3 and 6 to the variable $sql. When the terminating identifier END_SQL isn't quoted, it's the same as being double quoted, and the Perl variables embedded in the here document interpolate before the here document is used. In this case, the output of the script in Listing 1-5 is as follows:

```
USE master
GO
SELECT * FROM sysobjects
GO
```

NOTE *When a variable or an expression embedded in a string interpolates or is interpolated, the variable or the expression is evaluated and replaced with the result of the evaluation—in other words, its value.*

Note that you can use <<END_SQL in any expression as if it were a variable whose value is the here document. The following statement, for instance, is perfectly acceptable:

```
my @sql = split /\n/, <<END_SQL;
```

Using References and Nested Data Structures

SCENARIO
You want to use more sophisticated data structures beyond scalars, arrays, and hashes.

Of all the topics covered in this chapter, this section is probably the most important. You must be comfortable building nested data structures before you can get the most out of the Perl scripts presented throughout this book.

If you program in Perl at all, you'll find references indispensable. But prior to Perl 5, references didn't exist as a language feature. Frankly, I find it hard to believe that I managed to survive all those years programming Perl without using references.

A Perl *reference* is a scalar whose value isn't a string or a number but instead is a pointer or an entry that refers to some other thing. This other thing, often called a *referent*, can be any of Perl's built-in types including the three basic types—scalars, arrays, and hashes. The reference can also refer to another reference, a subroutine, or, for completeness, a typeglob.

NOTE *I won't belabor what a typeglob is. In short, it's a Perl internal type that's seldom used since Perl 5 and that's not used at all in this book.*

Because you don't really use the value of a reference directly, there's no need to see exactly what that value might be. But it's critically important to know how to obtain a reference and how to use a reference to get the value of its referent—in other words, how to dereference a reference.

Obtaining References

There are two ways to obtain a reference depending on whether the referent is named. For a named referent, you can apply the backslash operator (\) on the referent to obtain a reference to it. For an unnamed referent, it depends on the data type. Table 1-2 summarizes different ways to obtain a reference. Note that in Perl, the terms *subroutine* and *function* are synonymous.

Table 1-2. Obtaining References to Different Data Types

DATA TYPE	NAMED REFERENT	ANONYMOUS REFERENT
Scalar	\$myScalar	\SCALAR
Array	\@myArray	[LIST]
Hash	\%myHash	{ LIST }
Subroutine	\&myFunction	sub { CODE }

Listing 1-6 shows some examples of obtaining references to the referents of various data types.

Listing 1-6. Obtaining References

```
$ref1 = \$db;              # reference to a scalar variable
$ref2 = \@databases;       # reference to an array variable
$ref3 = \%dbSize;          # reference to a hash variable
$ref4 = \&getSize;         # reference to a subroutine (i.e. function)
$ref5 = \0.25              # reference to an anonymous scalar
$ref6 = [ 'master', 'tempdb', 'pubs' ];    # reference to an anonymous array
$ref7 = { master => 12, tempdb => 20 };    # reference to an anonymous hash
$ref8 = sub { return shift() + 3; };       # reference to an anonymous subroutine
```

Dereferencing

Now, assuming you already have the references obtained in Listing 1-6, how do you get the values of the referents? The following are some examples:

```
$db1 = $$ref1;              # same as $db1 = $db;
foreach (@$ref2) { ...}     # same as foreach (@databases) { ...}
foreach (keys %$ref3) { ... }  # same as foreach (keys %dbSize) { ... }
$ref4->($db)                # same as getSize($db)
$$ref5                      # returns the number of 0.25
$ref6->[1];                 # returns 'tempdb'
$ref7->{tempdb}             # returns 20
$ref8->(4)                  # returns 7 (i.e. 4+3)
```

According to *Programming Perl, 3rd Edition* by Larry Wall, Tom Christiansen, and Jon Orwant (O'Reilly, 2000), the rule to dereference a reference is surprisingly simple: "Anywhere you'd put an alphanumeric identifier as part of a variable or subroutine name, you can replace the identifier with a BLOCK returning a reference of the correct type." If it's just a single scalar reference in the code block, then you can omit the braces. Thus, ${$ref1} becomes $$ref1, @{$ref2} becomes @$ref2, and %{$ref3} becomes %$ref3.

The arrow operator used in dereferencing is a form of syntactic sugar to make the code more readable. Thus, ${$ref4}[1] is replaced with $ref4->[1] where $ref4 is a reference to an array, ${$ref5}{tempdb} is replaced with $ref5->{tempdb} where $ref5 is a reference to a hash, and &{$ref6}(4) is replaced with $ref6->(4) where $ref6 is a reference to a function.

OK, now you know how to reference and dereference. But what does all this have to do with building nested data structures? So far, there hasn't been any sign of the fantastic importance of Perl references promised at the beginning of this section. The following are the key points to note:

- A reference is a scalar.

- An array consists of a list of scalars.

- The values of a hash are scalars.

- A reference can be an element in an array or a value in a hash.

Therefore, you can have an array of references, each of which points to another array or another hash. Alternatively, you can have a hash whose values are references, each of which points to a hash or an array. The array elements or hash values don't even have to point the same data type. One array element can point to an array, and another element can point to a piece of code or any other data type. The possibilities go on and on. By putting a reference where a scalar is expected, you can create arbitrary data structures in Perl. And the great thing is that this is all dynamic; you don't need to worry about allocating or freeing the memory space. This is the key conceptual difference between a Perl reference and a C-style pointer. With the latter, you must be deeply involved in taking care of memory allocation.

 TIP *Perl nested data structures are extremely well documented. You should read* perlref, *which documents Perl references and nested data structures;* perllol, *which documents how to manipulate arrays of arrays; and* perldsc, *which is an excellent Perl data structure cookbook. To refresh your memory, you can read* perlref *from the command line by executing* perldoc perlref, *or you can read the online HTML documentation.*

Next, the following sections show a few examples of how to populate and access Perl nested data structures. But you really should refer to the perldsc documentation, which is the Perl data structure cookbook that comes with Perl. Furthermore, *Programming Perl, 3rd Edition* by Larry Wall, Tom Christiansen, and Jon Orwant (O'Reilly, 2000) devotes an entire chapter to working with various nested data structures. If you're serious about Perl, you should have a copy of this book on your shelf. These two invaluable reference materials contain far more examples than could fit into this section.

Using an Array of Arrays

Assume that the function getProperties() accepts a database name and returns a reference to an array consisting of a list of values about such properties as database name, size, and created date:

```
foreach my $db (@databases) {
    push @properties, getProperties($db);
}
```

The array @properties may end up with the following elements:

```
@properties = ( ['master', 12, '20020528'],
                ['tempdb', 20, '20020712'],
                ['pubs', 3, '20020528'] );
```

To print all the properties, you need to iterate through the arrays at both levels of the nested arrays:

```
foreach my $dbRef (@properties) {
    foreach my $value (@$dbRef) {
        print "$value  ";
    }
    print "\n";
}
```

Make sure that while you iterate through a nested data structure, you're clearly aware of when you're dealing with a reference and when you're dealing with a nonreference scalar value.

Using a Hash of Arrays

Let's continue with the example of database properties. Conceptually, a list of property values is always associated with a specific database. So, why not make this association explicit as follows:

```
foreach my $db (@databases) {
    $properties{$db} = getProperties($db);
}
```

Now, you have a hash of arrays:

```
%properties = ( master => [ 'master', 12, '20020528' ],
                tempdb => [ 'tempdb', 20, '20020712' ],
                pubs =>   [ 'pubs', 3, '20020528' ] );
```

This is not ideal because the database names are repeated in both the key and the array referenced by the value of that key. Let's eliminate that unnecessary redundancy:

```
foreach my $db (@databases) {
    my $ref = getProperties($db);
    shift @$ref;    # remove the first element from the array
    $properties{$db} = $ref;
}
```

The result, as shown in Listing 1-7, is now more pleasant. It applies `shift @$ref` to remove the first element from the array. It would be incorrect to apply `shift $ref`. Again, it's important to be clear about whether an operator expects a reference or its referent.

Listing 1-7. A Hash of Arrays

```
%properties = ( master => [ 12, '20020528' ],
                tempdb => [ 20, '20020712' ],
                pubs   => [ 3, '20020528' ] );
```

Let's print all the elements from this last hash:

```
foreach my $db (sort keys %properties) {  # sort database names alphabetically
    print "Database: $db, ";
    map { print "$_ " }  @{$properties{$db}};
    print "\n";
}
```

Because $properties{$db} is a reference to an array, @{$properties{$db}} is the referent array.

Using an Array of Hashes

Let's use the hash of arrays generated in Listing 1-7 to populate an array of hashes:

```
my @prop;
foreach my $db (keys %properties) {
    push @prop, { name => $db,
                  size => $properties{$db}->[0],
                  date => $properties{$db}->[1]  };
}
```

Because $properties{$db} is a reference to an array, $properties{$db}->[0] returns the first element of the array. Recall that a pair of braces ({...}) around a list of hash elements returns a reference to a new anonymous hash. Thus, the reference is pushed into the array @prop. The array of hashes in @prop looks like this:

```
@prop = ( { date => '20020712',
            size => 20,
            name => 'tempdb' },
          { date => '20020528',
            size => 3,
            name => 'pubs'    },
          { date => '20020528',
            size => 12,
            name => 'master'  }
        );
```

The code to print all the elements of this data structure is straightforward. At each level, make sure you know whether you're dealing with a reference or a regular value:

```
foreach my $h (@prop) {                    # $h is a reference to a hash
    foreach my $k (sort keys %$h) {    # $k is a scalar hash key, a string
        print "$k = $h->{$k}\n";
    }
    print "\n";
}
```

Using a Hash of Hashes

Let's again use the hash of arrays from Listing 1-7, but this time let's populate a hash of hashes instead:

```
my %prop;
foreach my $db (keys %properties) {
    $prop{$db} = { size => $properties{$db}->[0],
                   date => $properties{$db}->[1] };
}
```

This code produces the following hash of hashes:

```
%prop = (
        tempdb => {
                    date => '20020712',
                    size => 20 },
        master => {
                    date => '20020528',
                    size => 12 },
        pubs => {
                    date => '20020528',
                    size => 3 }
      );
```

Now you need two nested loops to visit all the elements of this hash of hashes:

```
foreach my $db (sort keys %prop) {
   print "Database: $db ";
   foreach my $p (sort keys %{$prop{$db}}) {
      print "$p = $prop{$db}->{$p} ";
   }
   print "\n";
}
```

The expression $prop{$db}->{$p} needs some clarification. Note that $db is the key of the outer hash. Thus, $prop{$db} is the corresponding value of the outer hash and is a reference to another hash. The variable $p is a key of the inner hash; thus, ${$prop{$db}}{$p} is the value of the inner hash, which can be rewritten using the -> operator as $prop{$db}->{$p}.

As you can see from these examples, if you peel the nested layers systematically using the dereferencing rule introduced earlier, and you pay close attention to whether you're dealing with a regular scalar or a reference at each step, then it isn't difficult to unravel a Perl nested data structure.

Working with Command-Line Utilities

> **SCENARIO**
> *You want to get the result of a command-line utility into a Perl script for further processing.*

One of the Perl's strengths is the ease with which it glues other programs together. This is evident in the large number of ways you can obtain the result of a program from your Perl scripts.

The simplest way to gather the output from a program is to use the so-called *backtick* operator (`). The following two examples show how you typically use the backtick operator:

```
$result = `net user`;
@result = `net user`;
```

It's important to point out that the command net user isn't quoted with a pair of single quotation marks. Rather, it's quoted with a pair of backticks (`), which is the symbol typically located on the same key as the tilde (~) on your computer keyboard.

In the first example, the backticks are used in a scalar context, and the result from net user will be stored in $result as a single string that may have embedded newlines. In the second example, the backtick operator is used in a list context. The result from net user is split by newline, and each line is a separate element in the array @result.

Note that in these two examples, Perl will get back what the command sends to its STDOUT. If the command runs into trouble and sends error messages to its STDERR, you won't see any of the error messages in $result or @result. If capturing the error message is important, you need to redirect the STDERR of the command to its STDOUT.

In Windows 2000/NT, the command in the backticks runs in the cmd.exe command shell, which redirects STDERR to STDOUT if you specify 2>&1 on the command line. Therefore, you can use the following:

```
$result = `net user 2>&1`;
```

Now, you must prepare your Perl script to handle any net user error messages redirected to $result.

Summary

This chapter covered some of the most fundamental Perl language features. You need to become comfortable with these features before you proceed to the Perl scripts that solve SQL Server administrative problems.

I've omitted one critical Perl feature—the concept of a *module*, which is Perl's basic unit for code reuse. As you journey through this book, you'll come across many useful modules developed by various individuals in the Perl community. The next chapter presents a collection of modules that address common scripting tasks that you'll often encounter when solving SQL Server administrative problems. The chapter walks you through each of the modules using examples to help make the rest of your journey easier.

CHAPTER 2

Working with Commonly Used Perl Modules

PERL HAS A LARGE USER COMMUNITY. In this community is a group of talented volunteer and professional developers actively contributing to make programming Perl a more pleasant experience. Their contributions often come in the form of writing new modules to solve specific problems and making the modules publicly available for free via the Comprehensive Perl Archive Network (CPAN), which is *the* central repository for the Perl community. Anything Perl that's useful and worth sharing is probably available on the CPAN site (http://www.cpan.org). Many excellent CPAN modules have withstood public scrutiny and have gone through numerous releases of refinement, eventually making their way into the Perl standard distribution.

So, what's a Perl module? It's similar to the library in many other programming languages. A Perl module abides by a set of interface rules, making it convenient to distribute and use. In a nutshell, the module is Perl's unit of software reuse. To the module user—as opposed to the module developer—it's a collection of functions in a file with the .pm file extension, somewhere under the directory lib or site\lib in the Perl root.

Typically, a module performs a specific programming task, and the CPAN modules cover a wide range of programming tasks, including parsing command-line arguments, manipulating files, and accessing databases—to name a few tasks that are relevant to a SQL Server Database Administrator (DBA). When using a module, your script makes calls to the functions exported by that module, therefore letting the module do the dirty work. You don't need to care how the module accomplishes the programming task inside its functions. As the user of the module, you care about what functions to call, how to call the functions, what the function returns, and whether the functions have performed the programming tasks they're documented to perform.

On the Windows platform, a significant collection of Win32-specific modules is bundled with ActivePerl from ActiveState (http://www.activestate.com). You can find many more Win32 modules on the CPAN site.

In Chapter 4 through Chapter 12, the Perl scripts for solving SQL Server administration problems use many modules that you'll not only find indispensable in these scripts but also useful in writing your own scripts. Instead of introducing them as you're using them throughout the book, this chapter discusses them all at once. Therefore, the subsequent chapters focus on SQL Server administration issues rather than on Perl modules.

However, this chapter doesn't serve as the condensed documentation for these modules, and it doesn't seek to replace their original documentation. Rather, the chapter illustrates how each module can be used and shows examples resembling the scenarios in the later chapters.

 TIP *You can get to the CPAN site from various Web addresses. A convenient place to start is* http://www.perl.com, *the official Perl Web site where you can find Perl news, announcements, and articles by Perl luminaries, as well as stay informed on Perl development.*

Table 2-1 describes the modules covered in this chapter. The following sections discuss each module.

Table 2-1. Commonly Used Perl Modules

MODULE	DESCRIPTION
Getopt::Std	This module parses the command-line arguments introduced with single-letter switches and sets the argument of each switch to a hash value with the switch letter being the key.
Time::Local	This module converts a time string to the corresponding epoch seconds.
Data::Dumper	This is one of the most popular modules in this book. It allows you to print an arbitrarily nested data structure as a string that assigns the data structure to a reference variable. It's useful for both debugging and persisting data structures.
Win32::Lanman	This is a large module encompassing a comprehensive set of network management functions including enumerating the shares on a remote machine.
Win32::NetAdmin	This module provides functions to manage network groups and users and to enumerate domains and machines.
Win32::TieRegistry	This module makes available a highly simplified hash-like interface to access and manipulate registry entries.
Win32::EventLog	You can use this module to access the entries in a Windows event log.

Table 2-1. Commonly Used Perl Modules (Continued)

MODULE	DESCRIPTION
Win32::Service	This module provides functions to enumerate Windows services and to check their status.
Win32::OLE	If you want to control OLE Automation objects from your Perl scripts, this is the module.
Win32::ODBC	This module has all the functions that allow your Perl script to talk to a SQL Server via Open Database Connectivity (ODBC).
File::Find	Given a directory, you can use this module to recursively enumerate all its files and directories.
Net::SMTP	This module enables your Perl scripts to send email using a Simple Mail Transfer Protocol (SMTP) server.
Parse::RecDescent	This module reads a grammar and generates a recursive descent parser for the grammar. You can then use the parser to parse strings and access the grammatical components.

Using a Perl Module

SCENARIO
You want to use a module in a Perl script.

To highlight the steps you should take in using a module, this section walks you through an example with the simple module File::Copy, which is bundled with Perl.

If the module isn't installed, you need to download the module and install it. The Perl documentation explains the generic process of downloading and installing a module. A module also often comes with its own installation instructions. If you're using ActivePerl, you can use its wonderful Programmer's Package Manager (PPM), formerly known as the Perl Package Manager, to download and install modules in a few simple steps. Refer to the PPM documentation that comes with ActivePerl.

Verifying the Installation of a Module

In the case of File::Copy, installation is already complete when you finish installing Perl. But it's still reassuring to verify that it's indeed installed. You can go about this in two ways. First, you can check the subdirectories under the Perl root to see whether the module file (Copy.pm in this case) is actually present. Assuming that

Perl is installed in d:\Perl, which is the so-called Perl root, you should find the module file in either of two folders: d:\Perl\lib\File or d:\Perl\site\lib\File. For File::Copy, the module file is in d:\perl\lib\File. The File subfolder under d:\Perl\lib corresponds to File in File::Copy. By the same token, if the module is Win32::EventLog, you should then look for the file EventLog.pm in either d:\Perl\lib\Win32 or d:\Perl\site\lib\Win32. It happens to be the latter for Win32::EventLog.

Alternatively and more authoritatively, you can just try to use the module. The most straightforward way is to execute the following on the command line, which tries to load the module:

```
cmd>perl -e "use File::Copy;"
```

The -e switch introduces and executes a Perl one liner on the command line. If the module—for example, File::Copy—is properly installed, nothing will be returned. Indeed, no news is good news. Otherwise, you may get something like this:

```
Can't locate File/Copy.pm in @INC (@INC contains: d:/Perl/lib d:/Perl/site/lib .)
at -e line 1.
BEGIN failed--compilation aborted at -e line 1.
```

This indicates a potential problem with the installation of File::Copy, which you must fix before using the module in your script.

Reviewing the Module Documentation

Usually, Perl modules come with their own documentation. To review the documentation of an ActivePerl module, scroll down the table of contents of the ActivePerl online Hypertext Markup Language (HTML) documentation. You'll find the documentation for the module listed in alphabetic order under the "Modules" heading. Alternatively, you can review the documentation of a module at the command prompt using the venerable perldoc utility:

```
cmd>perldoc File::Copy
```

This causes the perldoc utility to search the Perl directories for the file Copy.pm in the subfolder File and extract the documentation out of the module file. If you open the file Copy.pm, you'll find that the documentation for this module is embedded in the code itself in the POD format. POD stands for *plain old documentation* and is a simple text markup format used by Perl programmers. Perl comes with several utilities to extract the POD entries from a script and format them into a number of other popular file formats such as HTML.

When you study the documentation of a module, pay attention to its exported functions. Some functions are exported into your script by default, and others are exported by request only. I explain the impact of this in the later "Using a Module" section.

It's always worthwhile to study carefully the interface of a module defined in its .pm file. This helps clarify exactly what modules your script can use and how you use them, especially if you find that the documentation isn't clear (as you'll soon find with some of the modules discussed later in the chapter).

NOTE *Checking the actual code may appear to be less than ideal, and ideally, one should just read the documentation and start to use a module. However, Perl modules are contributed by a community of individuals. Although there are guidelines, a single central authority to police the documentation details of the modules doesn't exist. Considering how many times I've run into inconsistent documentation for a commercial product, I view the openness of the interface definition as a boon rather than a bane.*

Exporting Functions

Let's continue to use the File::Copy module as an example. Listing 2-1 shows the interface of the File::Copy module from the file Copy.pm. This example has several new constructs. A thorough explanation of every new construct in this example is beyond the scope of this section. Instead, this section focuses on the arrays @EXPORT and @EXPORT_OK and shows how their values affect the ways functions and other symbols are imported into your scripts.

Listing 2-1. Exporting Functions by Default and by Request

```
# inside Copy.pm
require Exporter;
@ISA = qw(Exporter);
@EXPORT = qw(copy move);
@EXPORT_OK = qw(cp mv);
```

In this module, the functions copy() and move() are exported to your script by default because they're in the special array @EXPORT, and the functions cp() and mv() are exported by request because they're in the array @EXPORT_OK. To see what this difference means, turn your attention to how you can use these functions in your scripts.

Using a Module

You typically include a module in your script with the use declaration:

```
use File::Copy;
```

This loads the File::Copy module and imports into your script its functions, variables, and constants (if any) in the special array @EXPORT. If the module is already loaded, Perl knows not to load it again. To be more precise about exactly what's imported, recall that the functions copy() and move() are exported by default and the functions cp() and mv() are exported by request. As a result, this use statement imports copy() and move(), which means your script can use them as if they were declared in your script.

The following code illustrates how you import the functions from a module by request:

```
use File::Copy qw( cp );
cp('errors.log', 'errors1.log') or die "cp failed.\n";
File::Copy::mv('output.log', '.\log\output.log') or die "mv failed.\n";
```

Both the cp() and mv() functions are exported by request. Because the import of the function cp() is requested in the use declaration, it's used simply as cp() in the script. On the other hand, the mv() function isn't requested and therefore isn't imported. Still, as shown, you can use the function mv() in your script, but it has to be fully qualified with the module name File::Copy. (Technically, the qualifier isn't the module but is the module's package.)

Note that qw(cp) is the same as 'cp'. I customarily use the quote word operator qw because it's more convenient—in other words, it requires less typing—when there are more functions to import.

For completeness, the following code demonstrates the use of functions exported by default:

```
use File::Copy;
copy('errors.log', 'errors1.log') or die "copy failed.\n";
move('output.log', '.\log\output.log') or die "move failed.\n";
```

As you saw in Listing 2-1, because the functions copy() and move() are both exported by default, you don't need to list them on the use declaration in your script, and you don't need to qualify them with their module name.

Finally, if a module is constructed following the rules of Perl's object-oriented interface, the object methods are implemented as functions. These functions automatically become accessible to your script by virtue of their objects. You don't export them explicitly via @EXPORT or @EXPORT_OK.

For the Curious Minds: Learning More

The previous section briefly introduced using a module. It didn't discuss the mechanisms that make a module work. Though it's enough to get you started using a module, for curious minds this scant coverage may have raised more questions than it did raising your comfort level with Perl modules.

To be thoroughly comfortable with a module, you need to understand how the module is constructed and understand the exact process Perl goes through to make the module available to your script. In addition, sometimes you need to study the code of the module. Luckily, there's an abundance of excellent resources on constructing and using Perl modules.

First, you can start with the Perl online documentation: perlmod for Perl modules and perlmodlib for constructing new Perl modules and finding existing ones. In addition to their HTML versions, you can always type perldoc perlmod and perldoc perlmodlib on the command line.

You can find another excellent introduction to Perl modules in *Perl Cookbook* by Tom Christiansen and Nathan Torkinton (O'Reilly, 1998), which devotes Chapter 12 to the various issues of working with Perl modules.

Finally, of course, you should consult *Programming Perl, 3rd Edition* by Larry Wall, Tom Christiansen, and Jon Orwant (O'Reilly, 2000). Incidentally, Larry Wall is the creator of Perl.

Getting Command-Line Arguments

SCENARIO
You want to specify command-line arguments with single-letter switches.

Chapter 1, "Introducing Perl Basics," introduced you to the command-line arguments stored in the Perl predefined array @ARGV. Directly retrieving the arguments from @ARGV works fine when you have only one or two arguments. Beyond that, to keep them manageable, you need to structure your command-line arguments, and your script isn't the right place to parse and enforce that structure.

Several modules hide the processing of command-line arguments. The simplest of them all is the module Getopt::Std, which is bundled with Perl. Using this module in your script, you can specify single-character switches on the command line such as these:

```
cmd>perl yourScript.pl -o -p -i error.log -S NYSQL01
cmd>perl yourScript.pl -op -ierror.log -S NYSQL01
```

In the first example, Boolean switches -o and -p are specified separately; in the second example, they're clustered together. Also, note that in the first example there's a space between the switch -i and its argument error.log, and in the second example there's no space. All these syntactic variations are acceptable to Getopt::Std and don't change the meaning of the command-line arguments.

The module Getopt::Std exports two functions by default: getopt() and getopts(). The former expects an argument for each of the switches, and the latter allows Boolean switches that don't expect any arguments. I like the versatility of getopts() and use it almost exclusively. Listing 2-2 shows an example.

Listing 2-2. Processing Single-Character Command-Line Switches

```perl
use strict;
use Getopt::Std;

my %opts;
getopts('oi:p:', \%opts);

if (exists $opts{o}) {
    print "-o switch is: $opts{o}\n";
} else {
    print "-o not specified.\n";
}
if (exists $opts{i}) {        # if the switch is present
    if (defined $opts{i}) {  # if the argument is present
        print "-i switch: $opts{i}\n";
    } else {
        print "-i switch: undef\n";
    }
} else {
    print "-i not specified.\n";
}
if (exists $opts{p}) {
    if (defined $opts{p}) {  # if the argument is present
        print "-p switch: $opts{p}\n";
```

```
    } else {
        print "-p switch: undef\n";
    }
} else {
    print "-p not specified.\n";
}
```

The key to using the module Getopt::Std is to correctly specify the function getopts() (or the function getopt() if you like) in your script. The function getopts() accepts two parameters. The first one is a string of all the switches. A colon must follow each of the switches that expect an argument. The second parameter is a reference to a hash whose values correspond to the command-line arguments and whose keys are the switch letters.

Thus, in Listing 2-2, the function getopts('oi:p:', \%opts) expects a Boolean switch -o, a switch -i followed by an argument, and a switch -p followed by an argument. Let's go through several examples to clarify what the hash %opts will contain in each case, assuming that the script in Listing 2-2 is saved to the file argTest.pl:

```
cmd>perl argTest.pl -o -i error.log -p output.log
-o siwtch is: 1
-i switch: error.log
-p switch: output.log

cmd>perl argTest.pl -o -i error.log -p
-o siwtch is: 1
-i switch: error.log
-p switch: undef

cmd>perl argTest.pl -o -i error.log
-o siwtch is: 1
-i switch: error.log
-p not specified.
```

As you can see from these examples and from Listing 2-2, for each command line switch, you may need to test two conditions:

- Is the switch specified? In your script, check whether the corresponding hash element exists—for instance, if (exists $opts{p}).

- Is the argument for the switch specified? In your script, check whether the value of the corresponding hash element is defined—for instance, if (defined $opts{p}).

Let me present a word of caution. If you specify the following:

```
cmd>perl argTest.pl  -o -i -p output.log
```

the %opts hash will be as follows:

```
%opts = (
            'o' => 1,
            'i' => '-p'
);
```

Because the switch -i expects an argument, Getopt::Std slurps up -p as the argument for -i and completely discards output.log. This probably isn't what you had in mind.

I'll leave you with a question before moving on to the next topic: What will the keys and values of the hash %opts be if the command line is as follows?

```
cmd>perl argTest.pl -o -i "-p output.log"
```

Working with Dates and Times

SCENARIO
You want to manipulate dates and times in your script.

In Chapter 1, "Introducing Perl Basics," you briefly worked with dates and times in Perl. However, because dates and times are critical to writing almost any Perl script, you need to study in detail how Perl handles them.

Perl represents dates and times in two formats; one format is convenient for calculation, and the other format is good for presentation to the human users. The first format is called *epoch seconds*, which are the number of non-leap seconds since the epoch. In Windows, the epoch was at 00:00:00 January 1, 1970, Greenwich mean time (GMT).

NOTE   *GMT is often referred to as Universal Time Coordinate (UTC).*

The second format is more readable and is made up of an eight-element (or nine-element in some cases) list including values for days, months, years, hours, minutes, and seconds. Some of the Perl date and time functions return values in the first format, and some return values in the second format.

The functions described in Table 2-2 are commonly used to manipulate dates and times.

Table 2-2. Perl Functions for Dates and Times

FUNCTION	DESCRIPTION
time()	This built-in Perl function returns the number of non-leap seconds since the epoch. It doesn't expect any input parameter.
gmtime()	This built-in Perl function accepts as input a time in epoch seconds and converts it to an eight-element list identifying seconds, minutes, hours, days, month, year, and so on. The input time is expected to be GMT, as is the returned value. It returns the current GMT when no input parameter is specified.
localtime()	This is similar to gmtime() except that it's adjusted for the local time. The input time is expected to be local, as is the returned time. Note that locatime() returns a nine-element list, and gmtime() returns an eight-element list. The ninth element indicates whether it's daylight savings. It returns the current local time when no input parameter is specified.
timelocal()	This is a function exported by the module Time::Local. This is the opposite of localtime() converting a list of the date and time elements to epoch seconds.
timegm()	This is a function exported by the module Time::Local. This is the opposite of gmtime() converting a list to the epoch seconds.

Now, what are these date and time elements? Table 2-3 summarizes the elements of the following localtime() function:

```
($sec, $min, $hours, $mday, $mon, $year, $wday, $yday, $isdst) = localtime();
```

Table 2-3. Elements of Dates and Times

ELEMENT	DESCRIPTION	VALID RANGE
$sec	Seconds	0–59
$min	Minutes	0–59
$hours	Hours	0–23
$mday	Day of month	1–31 (note that it starts from 1)
$month	Month	0–11 (note that January is 0)
$year	Number of years since 1900	1–138
$wday	Day of week	0–6 (note that Sunday is 0)
$yday	Day of year	1–366
$isdst	1 if daylight savings is in effect	0 or 1

With Perl's date and time functions explained, let's try two examples of converting dates and times between the two formats.

Printing the Current Time as YYYY/MM/DD hh:mm:ss

Listing 2-3 uses the function `localtime()`, which returns the current date and time when no parameter is supplied.

Listing 2-3. Printing the Current Time as YYYY/MM/DD hh:mm:ss

```
my($sec, $min, $hour, $mday, $mon, $year, $wday, $yday, $isdst)
                = localtime();
printf("%04d\/%02d\/%02d %02d:%02d:%02d ", $year+1900, ++$mon, $mday,
                $hour, $min, $sec);
```

Thus, with the date and time separated into discrete elements of a list, you have the convenience of printing the date and time in any string format you want with the function `printf()`. I ran the script in Listing 2-3, which was saved to the file `printLocaltime.pl` on my computer, and it printed the following:

```
cmd>perl printLocaltime.pl
2003/02/10 01:54:40
```

Converting YYYY/MM/DD hh:mm:ss to Epoch Seconds

Listing 2-4 uses the function `timelocal()` from the module Time::Local to convert a
date/time string into epoch seconds.

Listing 2-4. Converting YYYY/MM/DD hh:mm:ss to Epoch Seconds

```
use Time::Local;

my $timestr = shift or die "***Err: $0 expects a date time string.\n";
# validate the input string
if ($timestr =~ /(\d\d\d\d)(\/|-)(\d\d)(\/|-)(\d\d)          # date portion
                (\s+(\d\d):(\d\d):(\d\d))?                   # time portion
              /x) {
    ($year, $mon, $day, $hour, $min, $sec) = ($1, $3, $5, $7, $8, $9);
    print "Epoch seconds = ",
            timelocal($sec, $min, $hour, $day, $mon - 1, $year - 1900);
}
else {
    print "$timestr is not in the YYYY/MM/DD hh:mm:ss format.\n";
}
```

To test this script, you need to enclose the entire date/time string in double
quotes on the command line. Otherwise, the script picks up only the YYYY/MM/
DD part of string and treats it as YYYY/MM/DD 00:00:00 by default. Save the script
in Listing 2-4 to the file `printEpochSeconds.pl` and run it on the command line as
follows to see the result:

```
cmd>perl printEpochSeconds.pl "2003/02/10 01:54:40"
Epoch seconds = 1044860080
```

In Listing 2-4, the following `if` statement validates the input string:

```
if ($timestr =~ /(\d\d\d\d)(\/|-)(\d\d)(\/|-)(\d\d)      # date portion
                (\s+(\d\d):(\d\d):(\d\d))?               # time portion
              /x) {
```

This regular expression expects a string with four digits followed by a hyphen
or a slash, followed by two digits, followed by a hyphen or a slash, and then followed by two digits. This is the pattern expected of the date portion of the input
string. The regular expression for the time portion of the input string is similar.
Note that the entire time portion goes inside a pair of parentheses, which is quan-
tified with a question mark (?) that indicates the time portion is optional.

To make the code in Listing 2-4 more robust, you should further validate the ranges of $year, $mon, $day, $hour, $min, and $sec after you've obtained their values from the regular-expression matching of the string $timestr and before you feed them to the function timelocal(). In Listing 2-4, the script lets the timelocal() function report any out-of-range error.

Dumping a Perl Data Structure

> **SCENARIO**
> *As you start to work with more complex data structures, you often want to "see" what's currently in a data structure.*

Despite various fancy debugging features that you may like, one of the most popular methods for debugging a piece of Perl code or a data structure is still to print the variables in the code. If a variable happens to represent a complex data structure, the module to use is Data::Dumper, which is bundled with Perl. As you'll see later, this module is for much more than debugging your data structures; you can use it to persist the data structures as well. For now, this section focuses on using it to peek into a data structure.

At the beginning of this chapter, the "Getting Command-Line Arguments" section mentioned that the key to understanding the module Getopt::Std is to know how the hash %opts is populated. What you need to do is test various ways you can specify arguments on the command line and check what ends up in the hash %opts in each case. Let's see how the Data::Dumper module can help in your tests. Listing 2-2 checked various conditions, repetitively using the if statement to print the contents of %opts. As you can imagine, if %opts had been more complex, Listing 2-2 would have been utterly ugly.

Fortunately, there's a much better way using the module Data::Dumper, as demonstrated in Listing 2-5. Note how tidy and short Listing 2-5 is compared to Listing 2-2.

Listing 2-5. Testing the Module Getopt::Std with Data::Dumper

```
use strict;
use Getopt::Std;
use Data::Dumper;

my %opts;
getopts('oi:p:', \%opts);
print Dumper(\%opts);
```

Listing 2-6 shows the same test scenarios you went through with the script in Listing 2-2. Note the differences in the printed outcome. For testing, the script in Listing 2-5 is saved in the file argTest.pl.

Listing 2-6. Testing %opts *with Various Command-Line Scenarios*

```
cmd>perl argTest.pl -o -i error.log -p output.log
$VAR1 = [
            'o' => 1,
            'i' => 'error.log',
            'p' => 'output.log'
];

cmd>perl argTest.pl -o -i error.log -p
$VAR1 = [
            'o' => 1,
            'i' => 'error.log',
            'p' => undef
];

cmd>perl argTest.pl -o -i error.log
$VAR1 = [
            'o' => 1,
            'i' => 'error.log'
];
```

In the second test in Listing 2-6, you can see that the value of the hash key 'p' is undef because no argument is specified for the switch -p. In the third test, the key for the switch -p is not even present in the hash because the switch isn't specified on the command line at all.

The beauty of Data::Dumper is that no matter how complex a data structure may become internally, calling the Dumper() function remains extremely succinct. All the function needs is the reference to the top level of the data structure:

```
print Dumper($ref);    # $ref is the reference to the the data structure
```

Additionally, for each data structure, the output of Dumper($ref) is a simple string, representing a valid Perl statement. The documentation of this module is thorough on the additional functions, variables, and methods it exports to control how the data structure is dumped and how it's formatted.

This is an indispensable module when you're dealing with nested data structures. When you're confused with a nested data structure whose reference is $ref, just insert a print Dumper($ref) statement to see the contents of the data structure.

Instead of trying to traverse the data structure in your head, which is inevitably error prone, traversing through the structure printed on paper or in a file makes you feel like passing through a minefield with all the mines clearly marked.

Data::Dumper is truly one of those Perl modules that make you want to tilt your chair backward, put your feet on the desk, and say, "Cool!"

Finding Network Shares

SCENARIO
You want to find the shared folders on a remote SQL Server machine.

Forget about Perl for a moment. How would you find all the shares on a remote Windows 2000 machine?

I can immediately think of four approaches: First, you can remote control the machine with one of many tools such as Radmin or Terminal Services Client and check the shares locally. Once you're local through a remote control tool, you can issue `net share` at the command prompt or navigate the Computer Management screen to Shares under System Tools.

Second, you can use the Server Manager. You can invoke the Server Manager from Start ➤ Run by executing `srvmgr \\computerName`. When the Server Manager shows up, click Computer to see a list of drop-down menus, and select Shared Directories to see the shares on that computer.

Third, you can use `net view \\computerName`. This prints the resources shared by that machine. This command works with the shares on a remote computer. The main drawback is that it doesn't report all the shares. In particular, it doesn't report the administrative shares.

Finally, my favorite is to use the Windows Resource Kit tool `rmtshare.exe`:

```
cmd>rmtshare \\NYSQL1
```

This lists the shares on machine NYSQL1 just as if you issued `net share` locally on that machine.

All these methods are fine for the ad-hoc checking of one or two machines. They become cumbersome when you have many servers to check or when you want to perform additional actions based on what you've found.

To enumerate the shares on a remote machine programmatically in Perl, you need the module Win32::Lanman. Win32::Lanman is a large module implementing the Microsoft LAN Manager functions that include enumerating network shares among many other things. Listing 2-7 uses Win32::Lanman to enumerate the shares on a remote machine.

Listing 2-7. Enumerating the Shares on a Remote Machine

```perl
use strict;
use Win32;
use Win32::Lanman;

my @servers = ('NYSQL1', 'NJSQL2');  # list of machines
foreach my $server (@servers) {
   my $shareRef = dbaGetShares($server);
   print "Server = $server\n";
   foreach my $share (@$shareRef) {
        print "\t$share\n";
   }
}


###################
sub dbaGetShares {
   my ($server) = shift or
        die "***Err: dbaGetShares() expects a server name.";

   my @shares;
   Win32::Lanman::NetShareEnum($server, \@shares) or
        do { print Win32::FormatMessage(Win32::Lanman::GetLastError());
            return;
        };
   my $shareRef;
   foreach my $share (@shares) {
      push @{$shareRef}, $share->{netname};
   }
   return $shareRef;
} # dbaGetShares
```

Because this script primarily illustrates using the NetShareEnum() function
from the module Win32::Lanman, the server names are hard-coded in the list
@servers. In a real-world scenario, you'd want to modify the script to read the
server names from some external source such as a configuration file.

The Win32::Lanman module doesn't export the function NetShareEnum(). In
fact, Win32::Lanman doesn't export any functions at all. To use this or other functions, you need to fully qualify it with the module name (more accurately, the
module's package name).

Shares enable network users to access a folder and its contents. They're important security objects. On your SQL Server machines, you need to be aware of the status of the shares. Chapter 10, "Managing SQL Server Security," builds on the knowledge gained in this section about the module Win32::Lanman and shows you how to create a script that helps you track changes to the shares on multiple machines.

Listing 2-7 includes the function `dbaGetShares()` for illustration purposes because it's a generally useful function and will be used later in the book. The function is exported by SQLDBA::Security, which is a custom-developed module that is part of the SQLDBA Toolkit included with this book. (You'll learn more about the SQLDBA Toolkit throughout the rest of the book.)

Using the Win32 Module

As you may have noticed, the script in Listing 2-7 uses a module that hasn't been introduced. The module is simply Win32, which is bundled with ActivePerl. It provides a number of useful functions to query and manipulate the Win32 environment that's local to the script.

Some of the most popular functions from this module include the following: `Win32::GetLastError()` to retrieve the most recent error number returned by the Win32 subsystem, `Win32::FormatMessage()` to convert an error number returned from `Win32::GetLastError()` into a readable message text, `Win32::IsWinNT()` to check whether the script is running on a Windows 2000/NT machine, and `Win32::GetCwd()` to return the current working directory.

Three points are worth noting about this module. First, many of its functions are built into the ActivePerl core. That means you can use them without first declaring use Win32. I prefer to explicitly load the module for clarity. Second, the Win32 module doesn't export any of these functions, so you must always qualify them with Win32. Finally, I should reiterate that the functions from this module all work on the Win32 environment *local* to the script. As such, they're useful in managing the interaction of the script with its local environment. They're not useful in interacting with a remote machine. For instance, this isn't the module to use if you want to check whether a remote machine is running Windows NT.

Enumerating Windows Domains and Machines

SCENARIO

You want to enumerate the domains in your network and enumerate the Windows 2000/NT machines in each domain.

The module to use is Win32::NetAdmin, which exports a number of functions to work on Windows domains, users, and groups.

To enumerate domains and machines, you can use the function GetServers(SERVER, DOMAIN, FLAGS, REF). The third argument, FLAGS, controls what this function returns in the fourth argument, REF, which is always a reference. If you're enumerating domains, you don't specify the first two parameters. If you're enumerating servers in a domain, you specify the domain—in other words, the second parameter but not the first one.

The module exports a large number of constants that can modify the behavior of its functions. Listing 2-8 uses the following two constants to set the FLAGS argument in the function GetServers():

- SV_TYPE_DOMAIN_ENUM instructs GetServers() to enumerate domains.

- SV_TYPE_NT tells GetServers() to enumerate the machines running Windows 2000/NT.

Unfortunately, the online documentation for the module Win32::NetAdmin doesn't describe these SV_TYPE_* constants. You can browse NetAdmin.pm to find a complete list of them, and you can intuitively guess their functionality by their names.

NOTE *If you want more information on the constants exported by Win32::NetAdmin, you can find a brief description for each constant in* Win32 Perl Programming: The Standard Extensions, *Second Edition by Dave Roth (New Riders, 2001). You can also search for them at the Microsoft Developer Network (MSDN) site* (http://msdn.microsoft.com). *They appear with brief descriptions under the Windows network Application Programming Interface (API) function* NetServerEnum() *as part of the Win32 Platform Software Development Kit (SDK) documentation.*

Listing 2-8. Enumerating Domains and Windows 2000/NT Machines

```
1.   use strict;
2.   use Win32::NetAdmin;
3.
4.   $| = 1;
5.
6.   my @domains;
7.   my @servers;
8.
9.   # now enumerate domains
10.  Win32::NetAdmin::GetServers( '', '', SV_TYPE_DOMAIN_ENUM, \@domains);
11.
12.  foreach my $domain (sort @domains) {
13.     print "   *** Domain: $domain";
14.
15.     # now enumerate machines in the domain
16.     Win32::NetAdmin::GetServers( '', $domain, SV_TYPE_NT, \@servers);
17.     print "\t\t Found ", scalar @servers, " NT machines in this domain\n";
18.
19.     foreach my $server (sort @servers) {
20.           print "\t\t $server\n";
21.     }
22. }
```

This script first retrieves all the domains into the array @domains on line 10 with the flag SV_TYPE_DOMAIN_ENUM; then, for each domain, it enumerates the Windows 2000/NT machines, again using the function GetServers() on line 16 but with the flag SV_TYPE_NT. It places the enumerated server names in the array @servers. On both line 10 and line 16, the parameter that's not specified is assigned an empty string. Note that it's a pair of single quotation marks, not a single double quote.

Listing 2-8 doesn't really do anything useful with the domains and servers it finds except print their names. This is fine for now because the purpose is to familiarize you with the module Win32::NetAdmin. In Chapter 10, "Managing SQL Server Security," I further develop the script in Listing 2-8 and perform additional work in each domain or on each machine.

Listing 2-8 also introduces the following Perl idiom:

```
$| = 1;
```

This flushes the current file handle's output buffer after every print(), printf(), and write(). By default, $| is false, and the output may be buffered after a print(), printf(), or write().

Forcing the output buffer to flush is particularly useful in this script because the script may run for an extended time and the probability of its being interrupted is high. After the interruption, you may want to know exactly where it stopped. You could potentially get the wrong information if the output buffer isn't flushed.

Using the Predefined Variables

Perl comes with a large number of predefined variables. Most of them are scalar variables, such as $| used in this section, but some are arrays and hashes, such as @ARGV for the command-line arguments and %ENV for the current environment variables.

The predefined variables serve two purposes: to simplify the access to commonly used information such as $_ and @ARGV and to configure the behavior of how Perl executes your scripts such as $|. Some of the most commonly used predefined variables are as follows (for detailed explanation and a complete list, see the Perl documentation perlvar):

- $_: This is the default input and pattern-searching space. For some operators, when you ignore the argument, Perl assumes that the operator should get its argument from $_.

- $1, …, $<N>: $1 is assigned the substring corresponding to the first pair of capturing parentheses in the regular expression used in the last match.

- $/: This is the input record separator, defining what a newline is when Perl reads a record using operators such as <>.

- $|: When this variable is set to a nonzero value, Perl flushes the output after each write or print to the current output channel.

- $@: The Perl syntax error from the last eval() operator is assigned to this variable.

- $0: The name of the Perl script being executed is assigned to this variable.

- @ARGV: This array has the command-line arguments for the executing script.

- @_: This array is used inside a subroutine and stores the arguments passed to the subroutine.

- %ENV: This hash contains the current environment variables and their values with the variable names being the hash keys. To see exactly what's in %ENV, execute use Data::Dumper; print Dumper(\%ENV);.

Finally, from the documentation, it's not clear how the module exports its functions. It becomes clear as soon as you open the `NetAdmin.pm` file: All the functions are exported by request. Once again, make reviewing the module code part of the process of learning the module. You seldom need to study the module code in detail. But you should at least study its interface to be certain how the functions and other symbols are exported or whether they're exported at all.

Accessing the Windows Registry

SCENARIO
You want to retrieve data from a Windows registry value or key.

To retrieve data from a Windows registry value or key, use either Win32::Registry or Win32::TieRegistry.

TIP *In addition, you could use the module WinAPI::Registry, which is bundled with ActivePerl as well. This module provides low-level access to the registry. I don't recommend it if your primary reason for accessing the registry is to solve SQL Server administrative problems.*

Both these modules are bundled with ActivePerl. In this section, I focus on Win32::TieRegistry, which is a high-level and Perl-ish interface.

The Win32::TieRegistry module provides both an object-oriented interface and a so-called *tied hash* interface. This section covers the tied hash interface, which is the easier of the two.

The beauty of the Win32::TieRegistry module is that you can conceptualize the registry as a giant hash where the hash key corresponds to a registry key or a registry value and the hash value is either a reference to one of the direct subkeys or the data of a registry value. But it's even better than working with a regular hash because you don't have to navigate the registry one level a time. You can directly open any registry key from a registry root by constructing a *registry path*, which is a string containing all the keys in between.

For instance, the following code opens the `Microsoft SQL Server` key; this is assuming that the delimiter, which separates the components (either registry keys or registry values) on a registry path, has been set to `/`:

```
$sqlKey = $Registry->{'LMachine/Software/Microsoft/Microsoft SQL Server/'};
```

The variable `$Registry` is the most important object exported by Win32::TieRegistry to your script. It's the virtual root of everything you do with

Win32::TieRegistry. Recall that the Windows registry doesn't have a single root. Instead, it has seven discrete registry roots, which are considered by Win32::TieRegistry to be the direct subkeys of the virtual root $Registry. Table 2-4 describes the seven registry roots along with the shorthand names that module Win32::TieRegistry accepts. You can still use the original names in all uppercase if you so choose.

Table 2-4. Registry Roots and Their TieRegistry Shorthand Names

REGISTRY ROOT	TIEREGISTRY SHORTHAND NAME
HKEY_CLASS_ROOT	Classes
HKEY_CURRENT_USER	CUser
HKEY_LOCAL_MACHINE	LMachine
HKEY_USERS	Users
HKEY_PERFORMANCE_DATA	PerfData
HKEY_CURRENT_CONFIG	CConfig
HKEY_DYN_DATA	DynData

There's one more thing to note before you go crazy with Win32::TieRegistry. As you know, in the Windows registry, there are keys and there are values. When you specify a registry path, you need to explicitly tell Win32::TieRegistry whether the last component in the path is a key or a value to avoid ambiguity. The module follows these two simple rules (which are applicable only to the last component in a registry path):

- Put a delimiter after each key name.

- Put a delimiter in front of each value name.

To see these rules in practice, the following code shows how to retrieve the default domain of the SQL Server named instance APOLLO:

```
use Win32::TieRegistry (Delimiter => '/');
$sqlKey = $Registry->{'LMachine/Software/Microsoft/Microsoft SQL Server/'};
print $sqlKey->{'APOLLO/MSSQLServer//DefaultDomain'};
```

Microsoft SQL Server is a registry key (thus the postfix /). DefaultDomain is a registry value (thus the prefix /). There are two forward slashes in front of DefaultDomain because the first one is the delimiter and the second one is the value prefix. The registry path delimiter is specified to be / in the use declaration that loads the module.

Note that the variable $sqlKey references an intermediate key. You don't have to use it in this example. You can specify the registry path from LMachine all the way to DefaultDomain in a single string. With moderation, using intermediate keys helps improve the readability of your code and limits its width.

Now, let's look at a more useful example. In Listing 2-9, the script queries the registry of a server, whose name is specified on the command line, to report its Central Processing Unit (CPU) speed, the number of CPUs, and the vendor of the CPU.

Listing 2-9. Finding CPU Speed, Number of CPUs, and Vendor ID

```
use strict;
use Win32::TieRegistry( Delimiter=>"/" );

my $server = shift or die "***Err: $0 expects a server name.";
my ($reg, $key, $speed, $numProc, $vendorID);

# prepare the registry paths
my %reg_keys = (
        cpu     => "//$server/HKEY_LOCAL_MACHINE/HARDWARE/DESCRIPTION/" .
                   "System/CentralProcessor/0/",
        numProc => "//$server/LMachine/SYSTEM/CurrentControlSet/" .
                   "Control/Session Manager/Environment/"
    );

# query cpu speed
$reg = $reg_keys{cpu};
$key = $Registry->{$reg} or die "***Err: Can't open key $reg on $server.";
$speed = $key->{'/~MHZ'} or die "***Err: Can't read ${reg}~MHZ on $server.";
$speed = int (((int(hex ($speed) /5) + 1) * 5));

# query number of cpu's
$reg = $reg_keys{numProc};
$key = $Registry->{$reg} or die "***Err: Can't open key $reg on $server.";
$numProc = $key->{'/NUMBER_OF_PROCESSORS'} or
      die "***Err: Can't read ${reg}NUMBER_OF_PROCESSORS on $server.";

# query vendor of cpu
$reg = $reg_keys{cpu};
$key = $Registry->{$reg} or die "***Err: Can't open key $reg of $server.";
$vendorID = $key->{'/VendorIdentifier'} or
```

```
        die "***Err: Can't read ${reg}VendorIdentifier on $server.";
```

```
print "Speed:     $speed\n";
print "Processors: $numProc\n";
print "VendorID:   $vendorID\n";
```

Listing 2-9 should have convinced you that the Win32::TieRegistry module significantly simplifies the task of interacting with the Windows registry. With this module, you can concentrate on constructing the correct registry path to the key or the value of interest.

 TIP *You may wonder what* ${reg} *is in Listing 2-9. This is the same as* $reg. *The braces separate this variable from the text that immediately follows.*

One task you'll perform often is to loop through all the direct subkeys or values under a key. Fortunately, the normal operation of enumerating the hash elements works seamlessly with the Win32::TieRegistry module. The following example retrieves all startup parameters of the SQL Server instance APOLLO on the server NYSQL1:

```
1.  use strict;
2.  use Win32::TieRegistry (Delimiter => '/');
3.  my $server = 'NYSQL1';
4.  my $instance = 'APOLLO';
5.  my $sqlRoot = "//$server/LMachine/Software/Microsoft/Microsoft SQL Server/";
6.  my $sqlKey = $Registry->{$sqlRoot};
7.  my $pkey = $sqlKey->{$instance . '/MSSQLServer/Parameters/'};
8.  foreach my $value (keys %{$pkey}) {
9.      print "$value = $pkey->{$value}\n";
10. }
```

Note the use of the keys() function and the foreach loop on line 8. The variable $pkey is used as if it were a regular hash reference.

Finally, although the ActivePerl documentation considers the module Win32::Registry to be obsolete and recommends Win32::TieRegistry instead, Win32::Registry is still worth studying because it's widely used in the scripts you may find on the CPAN site or other Perl-related Web sites.

You can access the registry through a wide range of means. You may have tried the unsupported T-SQL extended stored procedures xp_regread and xp_regwrite. If you've written scripts using SQL Distributed Management Objects (SQL-DMO), you may have used the SQLDMO.Registry or SQLDMO.Registry2 object. These aren't good methods to use from a Perl script because of their dependency on SQL Server. The SQLDMO.Registry and SQLDMO.Registry2 objects are really misnomers. They don't expose the registry in general. And they don't expose any registry functionality such as traversing the registry tree and adding/deleting registry keys. These objects map only the SQL Server–related registry entries to their properties.

Reading the Windows Event Logs

> **SCENARIO**
> *You want to read the event log records from a Perl script.*

To read the event log records from a Perl script, use the Win32::EventLog module.

On a Windows 2000/NT machine, there are three separate event logs: the system event log, the application event log, and the security event log. An event log consists of a series of records, each of which is structured with a number of fields such as event type, category, event ID, and event message. The file format of the event log is proprietary and not published, meaning you can't directly access an event log file. Instead, you must use the event log API functions supplied by Microsoft. The Win32::EventLog module is a Perl wrapper around the event log API.

The Win32::EventLog module is implemented in an object-oriented style. You'll therefore be dealing with objects and methods. You typically go through the following steps to access the event log records with this module:

1. You first use the new() method to create a new event log object. In the new() method, you specify the event log source—system, application, or security—and the computer name if you're accessing an event log on a remote machine.

2. Then, you loop through the event log records to apply the Read() method to the event log object. You can control what records to access in the loop by setting the flags or setting the record offset in the Read() method.

3. The Read() function returns with a reference to the hash of the event log record being read. The hash keys correspond to the fields of the event log record. Table 2-5 describes some of the hash keys along with their brief descriptions.

4. Finally, you exit the loop and close the event log object with the method Close().

Table 2-5. The Keys of the Event Log Record Hash

KEY	DESCRIPTION
Computer	This is the name of the computer where the event log record is logged.
Source	This is the source that generated the event log record.
EventType	This is one of these constants: EVENTLOG_ERROR_TYPE, EVENTLOG_WARNING_TYPE, EVENTLOG_INFORMATION_TYPE, EVENTLOG_AUDIT_SUCCESS, or EVENTLOG_AUDIT_FAILURE. These constants are exported by the module by default.
EventID	This is the ID of the event.
Category	This could be any string depending on the application that logs the event log records.
TimeGenerated	This is the time when this event log record was generated. It's in epoch seconds and can be directly fed into the Perl functions that expect epoch seconds, such as localtime().
String	This is a string containing the event message.
Message	This key doesn't exist by default. If the variable $Win32::EventLog::GetMessageText is set to 1 or you call the function Win32::EventLog::GetMessageText(), the module will add this key to the hash and the value of this key will have the message text of the current event record.
RecordNumber	This is an internally generated number associated with the event record.

The best way to get a more concrete feel for these hash keys and their values is to use the Data::Dumper module discussed earlier in this chapter. After each Read() to get the hash reference (say, $eventRef) to an event log record, do a print Dumper($eventRef) to dump its contents. You'll know exactly what to expect in an event log record hash after you've tried this method several times on an event log.

Before you take the plunge into the event log scripting with Win32::EventLog, I strongly encourage you to spend some time reviewing the code in EventLog.pm and to pay particular attention to what constants and functions are exported by the module. In this module, only the constants are exported by default. No functions are exported by default or by request. However, through the object-oriented interface, the event log objects can be manipulated via various methods such as Open(), Backup(), and Close(). Studying EventLog.pm will also reveal the hash structures used by the module.

Listing 2-10 connects to a machine whose name is expected on the command line and scans the records logged in the system event log for the past two days.

Listing 2-10. Scanning the System Event Log on a Specified Machine

```
1.  use strict;
2.  use Win32::EventLog;
3.
4.  my $server = shift or die "***Err: $0 expects a server name.";
5.  my $cutoff_days = 2;
6.  my $log = 'system';
7.  $Win32::EventLog::GetMessageText = 1;  # to get the Message hash key
8.
9.  print "\nServer=$server\n";
10.
11. my($logRef, $eventRef);
12.
13. my $cutoff = time() - $cutoff_days * 24 * 3600;
14.
15. $logRef = Win32::EventLog->new($log, $server)
16.         or die "***Err: could not open $log on $server.";
17.
18. while ( $logRef->Read(EVENTLOG_BACKWARDS_READ |
19.                       EVENTLOG_SEQUENTIAL_READ, 0, $eventRef)
20.            && $cutoff < $eventRef->{TimeGenerated} ) {
21.    if ( $eventRef->{EventType} == EVENTLOG_INFORMATION_TYPE ) {
22.        print scalar localtime($eventRef->{TimeGenerated}), ', ';
23.        print $eventRef->{Message}, "\n"
24.    }
25. }
26. $logRef->Close();
```

The heart of this script is the use of the Read(FLAGS, OFFSET, EVENTREF) method on lines 18 and 19. The first parameter, FLAGS, specifies how the read operation is to proceed and can be a combination of the constants described in Table 2-6. The second parameter, OFFSET, is the log event record number from which the read operation will start. This parameter is only effective when the EVENTLOG_SEEK_READ flag is set. These constants are numerical. Therefore, on line 21 the equality operator is == instead of eq. The latter is for comparing strings.

CAUTION *In some languages, the = sign compares values and assigns values. Not so in Perl. The = sign is Perl's assignment operator, not its equality operator. If you use the = sign where you should've used an equality operator, then you'll probably get an unexpected result. For instance,* if ($cnt = 3) *doesn't check whether the variable* $cnt *is equal to 3. Rather, the number 3 is assigned to the variable* $cnt, *and the assignment operator returns the value 3. Therefore, the* if *condition will always be true, regardless of what the value* $cnt *may have been prior to the assignment.*

In Listing 2-10, the OR combination of EVENTLOG_BACKWARDS_READ and EVENTLOG_SEQUENTIAL_READ on line 18 enables the script to read the event log backward—in other words, from the latest to the earliest, one record at a time. Table 2-6 describes the event log read flags.

Table 2-6. Event Log Read Flags

FLAG	DESCRIPTION
EVENTLOG_FORWARDS_READ	The log is read in forward chronological order from the earliest to the latest.
EVENTLOG_BACKWARDS_READ	The log is read in backward chronological order from the latest to the earliest.
EVENTLOG_SEEK_READ	The read operation proceeds directly from the record number specified by the offset parameter of the Read() method.
EVENTLOG_SEQUENTIAL_READ	The read operation proceeds from the last call to the Read() method using the same event log object.

In Table 2-6, it obviously doesn't make any sense to combine the flags EVENTLOG_SEEK_READ and EVENTLOG_SEQUENTIAL_READ. However, you can combine either of these two with EVENTLOG_FORWARDS_READ or EVENTLOG_BACKWARDS_READ, as demonstrated in Listing 2-10.

Checking the Status of the Windows Services

> **SCENARIO**
> *You want to check the status of the Windows services.*

To check the status of the Windows services, use the module Win32::Service, which is bundled with ActivePerl.

To check the status of the Windows services on a machine, you can proceed in three steps:

1. Use the GetServices() function from Win32::Service to enumerate the names of all the services on that machine. This function takes the machine name as the first parameter. The service names will be returned in the second parameter as a reference to a hash whose keys are service names and whose values are the shortened versions of the service names.

2. Apply necessary criteria to filter out the services not relevant to the problem you're trying to solve.

3. For each of the remaining services, apply the function GetStatus() to retrieve the status information for that service. This function accepts three parameters. The first two are the machine name and the service name, respectively, and the third one is a reference to a hash containing the returned service status record.

To use Win32::Service, the key is to understand the data structure returned by the function GetServices() and the service status data structure returned by the function GetStatus(). I present a script first, and then I discuss the data structures used in the script.

Listing 2-11 (saved to the file srvStatus.pl) applies these two Win32::Service functions, GetServices() and GetStatus(), and follows the three steps outlined previously to find the status of all the services whose names start with the string MSSQL on a given server. To help understand the two data structures used by Win32::Service, Listing 2-11 uses Data::Dumper to print them.

Listing 2-11. Checking the Status of MSSQL Services

```
1.   use strict;
2.   use Win32::Service qw( GetServices GetStatus );
3.   use Data::Dumper;
4.
5.   my $serverName = shift or die "***Err: $0 expects a server name.";
6.   my ($key, %services, %status);
7.
```

```
8.    GetServices($serverName,\%services);
9.    print '\\%services: ',Dumper(\%services);
10.
11.   foreach $key (keys %services){
12.       if ($key =~ /^MSSQL/i) {
13.           GetStatus($serverName, $services{$key}, \%status);
14.           print "$key: \\%status: ", Dumper(\%status);
15.       }
16.   }
```

On line 12 in Listing 2-11, the regular expression /^MSSQL/i filters for the services whose names start with the string MSSQL. In a regular expression, the ^ sign matches the beginning of a string, and the /i modifier tells the regular-expression engine to perform case-insensitive pattern matching.

Running this script on my workstation against the server NYSQL01, where several SQL Server instances are installed, I get the following output:

```
cmd>perl srvStatus.pl NYSQL01
\%services: $VAR1 = {
          'Internet Connection Sharing' => 'SharedAccess',
          'SQLServerAgent' => 'SQLServerAgent',
          'MSSQLServer' => 'MSSQLServer',
          'System Event Notification' => 'SENS',
          'Workstation' => 'LanmanWorkstation',
          'SQLAgent$PANTHEON' => 'SQLAgent$PANTHEON',
          'MSSQL$PANTHEON' => 'MSSQL$PANTHEON',
          'MSSQLServerOLAPService' => 'MSSQLServerOLAPService',
          'MSSQLServerADHelper' => 'MSSQLServerADHelper',
          ...
        };
MSSQLServer: \%status: $VAR1 = {
          'CurrentState' => 1,
          'ServiceType' => 0,
          'CheckPoint' => 0,
          'ServiceSpecificExitCode' => 0,
          'WaitHint' => 0,
          'Win32ExitCode' => 0,
          'ControlsAccepted' => 0
        };
MSSQL$PANTHEON: \%status: $VAR1 = {
          'CurrentState' => 1,
          'ServiceType' => 0,
          'CheckPoint' => 0,
          'ServiceSpecificExitCode' => 0,
```

```
        'WaitHint' => 0,
        'Win32ExitCode' => 0,
        'ControlsAccepted' => 0
    };
...
```

If you know the service name, you could use the function GetStatus() directly without calling GetServices() first. You should still consider using the function GetServices() because it gives you precise service names that you can use in the other Win32::Service functions.

For each service, its status is in the value of $status->{CurrentState}. In the previous sample output, this value is 1 for the displayed services, MSSQLServer and MSSQL$PANTHEON. What does this mean? For the value of the CurrentState key, you can consult Table 2-7 to find the corresponding status and its description. In the previous example, both services were stopped.

To understand the other keys in the %status hash, you would have to study the Windows service control architecture and its API, which are beyond the scope of this book. Fortunately, these other keys are rarely, if ever, relevant to solving SQL Server administrative problems.

Win32::Service is a useful module, but it's not one of the greatest modules distributed with Perl. The status constants should have been exported by default or at least documented.

Table 2-7. Windows Service Status Values

SERVICE STATUS	NUMERIC VALUE	DESCRIPTION
SERVICE_STOPPED	0x01	The service has stopped running.
SERVICE_START_PENDING	0x02	The service is starting but isn't yet running.
SERVICE_STOP_PENDING	0x03	The service is stopping but isn't yet stopped.
SERVICE_RUNNING	0x04	The service is running.
SERVICE_CONTINUE_PENDING	0x05	The service is resuming but isn't yet running.
SERVICE_PAUSE_PENDING	0x06	The service is pausing but isn't yet paused.
SERVICE_PAUSED	0x07	The service is paused.

For completeness, I should point out that Win32::Service also provides functions to start, stop, pause, and resume Windows services.

 NOTE *Some books suggest that because the Win32::Service functions aren't exported, you must use the fully qualified names in your scripts. That's not correct. If you read only the documentation, you wouldn't be able to tell whether that's true. But if you take a quick look in the* Service.pm *file, you'll find that all the functions are exported by request; thus, you could import them explicitly as the script in Listing 2-11 does—in other words, by using* use Win32::Service qw(GetServices GetStatus)*. To reiterate, make reviewing the module code part of your learning process.*

Uncovering the Service Status Constants

So, how did I come up with the information in Table 2-7? This sidebar explains how the table was constructed.

The brief documentation of Win32::Service indicates that the third argument of the function GetStatus() must be a hash reference that will be populated with entries corresponding to the SERVICE_STATUS structure of the Win32 API. I then searched the Microsoft Platform SDK documentation for the string SERVICE_STATUS and found the description for the status constants. You can also perform the search at http://msdn.microsoft.com. That's a step forward, but it's still not enough because I needed to know the corresponding numeric values, which I must use in my script if I need to test the status of a service.

Realizing that the constants of this nature are usually defined in an include file, I then searched the SDK's include file folder for the string SERVICE_STOPPED, which is one of the service status constants. *Voilà!* There they are. All the service status constants are defined in header file WinSrv.h, complete with their respective numeric values.

Interacting with a COM Object

SCENARIO

You want to interact with a Component Object Model (COM) object via OLE Automation from your Perl script.

To interact with a COM object via OLE Automation from your Perl script, you use the module Win32::OLE, which is bundled with ActivePerl.

If you're serious about scripting in the Win32 environment, you can't escape accessing and manipulating a COM object from your scripts. COM objects are pervasive in the Win32 environment, and many important applications—including most Microsoft products—expose their features as COM objects.

Not all COM objects can be accessed and manipulated through the Win32::OLE module. Win32::OLE works with those COM objects that are exposed as so-called OLE Automation objects. You need to understand three concepts before working with OLE Automation:

- **OLE Automation server**: This is an application that exposes programmable Automation objects so that other programs—called Automation *controllers* or *clients*—can access and manipulate them in their own code. ADO and SQL-DMO are two examples of OLE Automation servers of close interest to the SQL Server DBA.

- **OLE Automation objects**: These are the COM objects exposed by an OLE Automation server for access by other programs.

- **OLE Automation controller**: This is also known as the OLE Automation *client*. This program uses or drives Automation objects. Visual Basic is one of the most popular languages to program the Automation controller. Through Win32::OLE, Perl is an Automation controller.

NOTE *Lately, it appears that Microsoft has chosen to simply call this technology Automation. But it's difficult to keep up with the rapid speed of terminology changes in this area. By the time you read this book the name may have changed yet again. The best way to stay current is to regularly check the latest Microsoft Platform SDK documentation or browse* http://msdn.microsoft.com.

OLE Automation is a powerful technology from a Perl scripting perspective because it opens up a new world of services of which Perl can take advantage. And the door to that world is the module Win32::OLE.

Listing 2-12 uses SQL-DMO to print the startup account, the service name, the version string, and a count of the databases on a SQL Server instance.

Listing 2-12. Getting the Information on a SQL Server Instance

```
1.  use strict;
2.  use Win32::OLE;
3.
4.  my $serverName = shift or die "***Err: $0 expects a SQL instance name.";
5.
6.  my $server = Win32::OLE->new('SQLDMO.SQLServer2')
7.      or die "**Err: could not create SQLDMO.SQLServer2 object.";
8.  $server->{LoginSecure} = 1;
9.
10. $server->Connect($serverName);
11. ! Win32::OLE->LastError() or
12.    die "***Err: could not connect to $serverName.";
13.
14. print $server->{InstanceName}, "\n";
15. print $server->{StartupAccount}, "\n";
16. print $server->{ServiceName}, "\n";
17. print $server->{VersionString}, "\n";
18. print $server->Databases()->{Count};
19.
20. $server->DisConnect();
```

The script in Listing 2-12 is simple but representative of controlling OLE Automation from Perl. It first calls the new() method to create a Perl object called $server on line 6. It's important to stress that $server is a Perl object, not a SQL-DMO COM object. This request to create a Perl object will be communicated to the SQL-DMO Automation server and cause the latter to create a COM object. The Perl script interacts with this underlying COM object through the $server object. (When the context isn't ambiguous, I refer to $server either as a Win32::OLE object or a SQL-DMO object.)

With the exception of lines 11 and 12 that handle the Win32::OLE errors, the rest of the code is dictated by the SQL-DMO object model. To write the rest of the code, you need to be conversant with the SQL-DMO object hierarchy.

Line 8 sets the LoginSecure property of the SQLServer2 object. This property directs the application—in other words, the script in Listing 2-12—to use the Windows authentication mode when it invokes the Connect() method of the SQLServer2 object to connect to a SQL Server instance. As a direct result, the Connect() method on line 10 doesn't have to specify a login or a password.

> **NOTE** *In SQL Server 2000, there's the* SQLDMO.SQLServer *object and then there's a* SQLDMO.SQLServer2 *object. The* SQLServer2 *object is specific to SQL Server 2000 and inherits the properties and methods of the* SQLServer *object. In Listing 2-12, the object* SQLServer2 *is used on line 6 because the properties* InstanceName *and* StartupAccount *are specific to SQL Server 2000 and hence* SQLServer2.

Translating a COM Object Model to Perl

A COM object model is typically documented in terms of objects, collections, properties, and methods. The following syntactic rules help you translate a COM object model to Perl code.

You specify an object method on the right side of the arrow notation with the object on the left. You typically follow the method with a pair of parentheses enclosing its arguments, if any. If there's no argument, the parentheses can be removed. You can specify optional parameters with the undef placeholder to indicate that the parameter value isn't present. If there's no other parameter to the right, the undef parameters can be completely omitted. Thus, you write $server ->Connect($serverName, undef, undef) as $server->Connect($serverName) on line 10 in Listing 2-12.

You also specify an object property on the right side of the arrow notation. It's customary to enclose the property name in a pair of braces, similar to specifying a hash key. Thus, in $server->{ServerName}, ServerName is a property. These braces aren't mandatory.

You can chain object methods and properties such as $server->Databases() ->{Count} does on line 18 in Listing 2-12.

A *collection* is a special COM object that contains other objects. To get a collection from its parent object, you usually use the collection method that has the same name as the collection itself. For instance, $server->Databases() gives you the Databases collection of the server. The collection methods are often not explicitly listed as methods but simply as collections in the documentation of a COM object model such as SQL-DMO. Syntactically, they are used just like regular methods.

> **TIP** *Even though in some cases you can omit the parentheses following a method or the braces surrounding a property, it's a good programming practice to consistently use parentheses with a method and enclose a property in braces. This avoids ambiguity and makes the code more readable.*

After you've become familiar with the syntactical conventions of Win32::OLE and a few other miscellaneous items such as error handling, your learning curve will no longer be about Win32::OLE. To apply Win32::OLE to a particular area of OLE Automation, your primary challenge is to become comfortable with that COM object model.

Scripting Database Creation via SQL-DMO

Now, let's build on the simple script in Listing 2-12 and do something more useful. Listing 2-13 loops through all the databases except pubs and northwind, and it generates the database creation script for each database.

Listing 2-13. Scripting Database Creation via SQL-DMO

```
1.   use strict;
2.   use Win32::OLE 'in';
3.   use Win32::OLE::Const 'Microsoft SQLDMO';
4.
5.   my $serverName = shift or die "***Err: $0 expects a SQL instance name.";
6.
7.   my $server = Win32::OLE->new('SQLDMO.SQLServer2')
8.       or die "**Err: could not create SQLDMO object.";
9.   $server->{LoginSecure} = 1;
10.
11. $server->Connect($serverName);
12. !Win32::OLE->LastError() or
13.     die "***Err: could not connect to $serverName.";
14.
15. foreach my $db (in($server->Databases())) {
16.     unless ($db->{Name} =~ /^(pubs|northwind|test)$/i) {
17.         print "-- Database: ", $db->{Name}, "\n";
18.         my $sql = $db->Script( SQLDMOScript_Default | SQLDMOScript_Drops |
19.                                SQLDMOScript_IncludeHeaders );
20.         print "$sql\n";
21.     }
22. }
23. $server->DisConnect();
```

In this script, you can see two important features of interfacing Perl with OLE Automation that haven't been discussed before. The first to note is the function in(), which is explicitly imported on line 2. This function makes it more pleasant to work with the OLE Automation collections. On line 15, because of the in()

function, Perl can apply the familiar foreach loop to the SQL-DMO database collection just like it would an ordinary list.

The other feature is the use of a supporting module called Win32::OLE::Const, which imports the constants used by the object model from its type library. In this case, it imports the constants of SQL-DMO, whose type library is Microsoft SQLDMO. With the use declaration on line 3, the constants—for instance, those in the Script() method on lines 18 and 19—are imported and become accessible to the script.

Using Win32::OLE::Const

Win32::OLE::Const is an important module. Because different Automation object models define a different set of constants, they can't all be imported by Win32::OLE. If you can't use the symbolic constants in your script, you have to resort to the actual values, making scripting Automation objects an arduous and unpleasant task. The gruesome thought of having to find these values manually sends a shiver down my spine.

The general syntax for importing the constants is as follows:

```
use Win32::OLE::Const (TYPELIB, MAJOR, MINOR, LANGUAGE);
```

This module searches the registry for a type library name that matches the expression in place of the TYPELIB parameter. Note that the search is case sensitive; thus, the following:

```
use Win32::OLE::Const 'Microsoft sqldmo'
```

will fail to find the SQL-DMO type library. In addition, when the version information isn't supplied with the MAJOR and MINOR parameters, the module will pick the type library with the highest version number.

 TIP *If you're not certain about the exact name of a type library, you can use the Windows utility* regedit.exe *(not* regedt32.exe*) to perform a registry search under* HKEY_CLASSES_ROOT\TypeLib. *For instance, to find the name of the SQL-DMO type library, you can first navigate to this key and then select Find on the right-click menu. Make sure that the Data checkbox is checked and type the string* dmo *or* sqldmo *in the text box to begin the search. Even if your search string is only* SQL, *you'll eventually find the type library for SQL-DMO by repeatedly hitting the F3 key, which looks for the next occurrence of the string.*

There's much more to scripting OLE Automation objects in Perl than I have space to discuss. In addition to the online documentation of Win32::OLE and the related modules, *Win32 Perl Programming: The Standard Extensions, Second Edition* by Dave Roth (New Riders, 2001) extensively covers the topic. Also, refer to *Real-World SQL-DMO for SQL Server* by Allan Mitchell and Mark Allison (Apress, 2002), which is devoted to performing SQL Server DBA tasks with SQL-DMO.

Accessing SQL Server via ODBC

> **SCENARIO**
> *You want to connect to a SQL Server via ODBC and retrieve data from a Transact-SQL (T-SQL) query.*

You can access SQL Server from a Perl script in many ways. Some of the more popular choices are DBI, ODBC, and ActiveX Data Objects (ADO). Because this book is exclusively concerned with the Win32 platform, ODBC and ADO are naturally the chosen database access methods.

NOTE *Tim Bunce created DBI as a database/platform-independent access API for Perl. This is a wildly popular database interface, especially when you need cross-platform database access. You can find the DBI drivers for all the major database management systems at the CPAN site.*

To access SQL Server via ADO, you use the Win32::OLE module, discussed in the previous section, to control the ADO objects. To use ODBC, the module of choice is Win32::ODBC, which is bundled with ActivePerl. This section focuses on Win32::ODBC.

Although functionally Win32::ODBC is a wrapper on the Win32 ODBC API, it's more than a wrapper from a Perl programming perspective; it significantly enhances the usability for the benefit of the Perl programmer.

To run a query on a SQL Server instance using Win32::ODBC, you typically go through five steps:

1. Connect to SQL Server using the new() method. This creates a connection object to be used by the rest of the methods.

2. Submit a query using the Sql() method to be processed by SQL Server.

3. Retrieve the result rows sent back from SQL Server using the FetchRow() method.

4. Process the data using the method `Data()` or the method `DataHash()`. This gets the data in the fetched row from SQL Server into your script for whatever further processing you may fancy.

5. Close the connection using the `Close()` method.

Listing 2-14 (saved to the file `odbcDemo.pl`) demonstrates these steps.

Listing 2-14. Retrieving Data from the `pubs..authors` *Table*

```
1.   use strict;
2.   use Data::Dumper;
3.   use Win32::ODBC;
4.
5.   my $server = shift or die "***Err: $0 expects a server name.";
6.   my $connStr = "Driver={SQL Server};Server=$server;Trusted_Connection=yes";
7.   my $conn = Win32::ODBC->new($connStr) or
8.       die "***Err: " . Win32::ODBC::Error();
9.   my $sql = "SELECT * FROM pubs..authors WHERE phone LIKE '408%'";
10.  if (! $conn->Sql($sql)) {
11.    while ($conn->FetchRow()) {
12.       my %data = $conn->DataHash();
13.       print Dumper(\%data);
14.    }
15. }
16. $conn->Close();
```

The script retrieves data from the `pubs..authors` table. The output from the script looks like the following. Don't be fooled by the look of this printout. The example is to show how to get the data from SQL Server into your own Perl script. Once you have the data, formatting the data for a pretty printout is but one of many things you can do:

```
cmd>perl odbcDemo.pl NYSQLO1\APOLLO
$VAR1 = {
          state => 'CA',
          au_lname => 'White',
          city => 'Menlo Park',
          au_fname => 'Johnson',
          contract => '1',
          zip => '94025',
          address => '10932 Bigge Rd.',
          au_id => '172-32-1176',
          phone => '408 496-7223'
```

```
        };
$VAR1 = {
          state => 'CA',
          au_lname => 'O\'Leary',
          city => 'San Jose',
          au_fname => 'Michael',
          contract => '1',
          address => '22 Cleveland Av. #14',
          zip => '95128',
          au_id => '267-41-2394',
          phone => '408 286-2428'
        };
```

To make an ODBC connection, you need to provide a connection string so that the ODBC driver knows where to connect and how to connect. In Listing 2-14, the connection string is specified on line 6. An ODBC connection string can use a pre-configured Data Source Name (DSN) or can be DSN-less by supplying all the necessary connection information on the fly. For a DSN-less connection, at the minimum, you need to include the driver name, the server name, and the authentication information.

The script in Listing 2-14 makes a DSN-less connection. On line 6, the key word `Trusted_Connection` is set to `yes` to use the Windows authentication. Also, `Driver={SQL Server}` tells the ODBC driver manager to use the Microsoft SQL Server ODBC driver.

> **TIP** *The exact key words and their values permitted in a connection string are specific to the ODBC driver. You need to study the driver documentation to be certain about how to construct a connection string. For the Microsoft SQL Server ODBC driver, the connection string key words are documented in the SQL Server Books Online. They are listed under the section "SQL Server ODBC Driver Programmer's Reference" for the function* `SQLDriverConnect()`.

The SQL query is submitted and executed on line 10. The `Sql()` method is unconventional in its reporting of the error status. It returns a nonzero integer upon failure instead of returning a zero upon failure as all the other Win32::ODBC methods do.

The `while` loop with the `FetchRow()` method on line 11 moves through the rows in the resultset sent back from SQL Server. When no parameter is supplied, the method moves through the resultset one record a time from the first row to the last row. When there aren't any more rows to fetch, it returns an undef, thus false, causing the loop to exit.

You can retrieve the data in the currently fetched row either with the method Data() or with the method DataHash(). The former returns an array with the column values positioned according to their respective column positions in the query, and the latter returns a hash. A column name in the resultset is a key in the hash, and the column value in the resultset is the corresponding hash value. DataHash() is rather convenient when you need to associate the resultset values with their columns. The printout using the Dumper() method on line 13 clearly shows the structure of what's being returned from DataHash().

Finally, note on line 8 in Listing 2-14 the use of the function Win32::ODBC::Error(), which reports the last ODBC error irrespective of which connection may have generated the error. I generally use this function in a scalar context so that it returns a readable error string containing the standard ODBC error message elements.

Win32::ODBC is a rich topic with many more functions, options, features, and performance considerations. They're beyond the scope of this brief introduction. However, with the information in this section, you're well on your way to send queries to SQL Server and use the data returned in your Perl scripts for SQL Server administration.

Walking a Directory Tree

SCENARIO
You want to find all the files larger than 500 kilobytes (KB) in a directory and all its subdirectories.

The most obvious approach is to repeatedly use the Perl functions opendir(), readdir(), and closedir(), starting from the given root directory. Because the function readdir() returns all the entries in a directory, including both the files and subdirectories, you can then filter for the subdirectories and apply opendir(), readdir(), and closedir() to each subdirectory, if any. For each lower-level directory down the directory tree, you'd use these functions in an identical way. This naturally calls for a recursive routine that terminates when there aren't any more subdirectories.

Note that the procedure as outlined is generic in that it remains the same regardless of what you may do with each file in a directory. This sounds like a good action plan. Better still, Perl already comes bundled with a module that performs precisely this recursive procedure. The module is File::Find.

Listing 2-15 shows how to use File::Find. Given a directory name and a size threshold in bytes, the script prints the names of the files that are larger than the size threshold.

Listing 2-15. Finding Files Larger Than a Size Threshold

```perl
use strict;
use File::Find;
use Getopt::Std;

my %opts;

Main: {
    getopts('d:s:', \%opts);
    printUsage() unless (defined $opts{d} and defined $opts{s});

    find(\&wanted, $opts{d});
} # Main


#################
sub wanted {
    if (-f $_ and -s $_ > $opts{s}) {
        print "File: $File::Find::name, Size: ", -s $_, "\n";
    }
}  # wanted


###################
sub printUsage {
    print <<__Usage__;
usage:
    cmd>perl $0 -d <Directory> -s <Size>
__Usage__
    exit;
}
```

The main body of the script—the block labeled with `Main`—includes three lines of code. The function `getopts()` retrieves the command-line arguments, and the function `defined()` checks whether each of the two expected arguments is specified. Recall the discussions in the "Getting Command-Line Arguments" section earlier in this chapter. When the argument for the switch `-s` isn't present or when the switch isn't specified at all, `$opts{s}` is undefined.

The `find(\&wanted, $opts{d})` function does the real work. Before discussing what the `find()` and `wanted()` functions do, let's try the script to get some feel for what it produces.

Save this script to the file `largeFiles.pl` and type the following on the command line to search the directory `d:\dba` and all of its subdirectories for files larger than 500KB:

```
cmd>perl largeFiles.pl -d d:\dba -s 500000
```

On my workstation, the results came back as follows:

```
File: d:\dba/PerfLogs/waste.log,  Size: 1057383
File: d:\dba/Docs/Procs_to_compare_Schemas.rtf, Size: 1189574
File: d:\dba/CheckSQLLogFiles/DBCCLog.txt, Size: 5014871
```

The module File::Find exports the function find(), which expects a reference to a piece of code—often a reference to a function—as its first parameter and a directory path as its second parameter. The directory path is the root of the directory tree that the find() function recursively traverses. For each file or directory found in the directory tree, find() applies the code referenced in the first parameter.

When using File::Find, your job is primarily to provide a function that performs whatever operations you deem important to each file or directory found. This function is customarily named wanted(), as in Listing 2-15, but you can choose any name you fancy. To program wanted(), you should be aware that you have access to the following variables:

- $_: This variable has the current file or directory name. The directory path isn't included.

- $File::Find::dir: This is the current directory name. Note that this is the immediate parent of $_.

- $File::Find::name: This is the current filename with the full path. It's the same as $File::Find::dir\\$_.

- Global variables: The function wanted() has access to the global variables. In Listing 2-15, wanted() uses the global variable %opts.

CAUTION *Since Perl 5, you rarely need to explicitly prefix any function name with the function symbol &. However, you must include the & symbol when taking a reference to a function as in \&wanted in Listing 2-15.*

The wanted() function in Listing 2-15 performs two checks before printing the filename and its size:

- The first is the file test, -f $_, to see whether the current entry is a file.

- The second is the file size test, -s $_ > $opts{s}, to see whether the size of the current file exceeds the threshold. Note that the file test operator, -s, returns the size of the file in bytes, and $opts{s} has the file size specified on the command line.

You'll find it convenient to become familiar with Perl's file test operators; -T, -f, -s, -M, and -d are some of the most commonly used.

Sending SMTP Email Messages

SCENARIO
You want to send email from your Perl scripts.

When it comes to Perl scripting in the Win32 environment, one of the most frequently asked questions is about sending email from a Perl script.

You have many choices. If you're brave and like to get your hands dirty, you can directly speak the SMTP protocol to your mail server over the TCP sockets. Of course, much of that work is already done for you in the form of the CPAN modules, one of which is Net::SMTP. You can save yourself a lot of time by using Net::SMTP to send email. Alternatively, with the knowledge you've just gained about the module Win32::OLE, you can use the Microsoft Collaboration Data Objects (CDO) to send email. Another choice is to wrap your Perl script around a command-line email utility such as sendmail.exe from IndigoSTAR (http://www.indigostar.com).

When you have access to a robust SMTP server in your network environment, the module Net::SMTP, distributed with ActivePerl, is the simplest way to send email from a Perl script and is the focus of this section.

The Net::SMTP module exposes an object-oriented interface that hides some of the details of the SMTP protocol, though not cleanly, as you'll soon see. To send an email, you need to use the methods described in Table 2-8.

Table 2-8. Key Methods of the Module Net::SMTP

METHOD	DESCRIPTION
new()	This creates an object that identifies the SMTP mail server. All the subsequent steps rely on this object to talk to the mail server.
mail()	This method specifies the address of the sender and initiates the sending of the message.
to()	This specifies the recipients. The argument is a Perl list of email addresses.
data()	This method indicates the sending of the email message. Often, no argument is supplied and the email message is to be subsequently specified with the datasend() and dataend() methods.
datasend()	This method sends the message to the mail server. You can apply the method multiple times to send the message in several chunks.
dataend()	This method ends the sending of the message to the mail server.
quit()	This method closes the socket connection to the mail server and completes sending the email. You should always specify this method. Otherwise, your email may not be actually sent.

Listing 2-16 uses the methods in Table 2-8 to send an SMTP email. The steps that are concerned with sending an SMTP email are encapsulated in the function dbaSMTPSend(), defined in the script. All the email addresses used in Listing 2-16 are fictitious.

Listing 2-16. Sending an SMTP Email

```
1.  use strict;
2.  use Net::SMTP;
3.
4.  my $SMTPServer = 'mail.linchi.com';
5.  my $recipientRef = [ 'monica@yourTel.com', ' christine@yourTel.com' ];
6.  my $sender = 'victor@linchi.com';
7.  my $sub = 'Hello, world!';
8.  my ($to, $from) = ( 'sisters@yourTel.com', 'brother@linchi.com' );
9.  my $msg = 'This should be in the message body.';
10.
11. dbaSMTPSend($SMTPServer, $recipientRef, $sender, $msg, $sub, $to, $from);
```

```
12.
13. ############################
14. sub dbaSMTPSend {
15.     my ($smtpServer, $recipRef, $sender, $msg, $sub, $to, $from) = @_;
16.
17.     my $smtp = Net::SMTP->new($smtpServer) or
18.        die "***Err: couldn't create new Net::SMTP object for $smtpServer.";
19.     $smtp->mail($sender);
20.     $smtp->to(@$recipRef);
21.     $smtp->data();
22.     $smtp->datasend("Subject: $sub\n");   # $sub is sent in the subject
23.     $smtp->datasend("To: $to\n");         # will appear in To: header
24.     $smtp->datasend("From: $from\n");     # will appear in From: header
25.     $smtp->datasend("\n");
26.     $smtp->datasend("$msg\n");
27.     $smtp->datasend() or
28.        die "***Err: had problem sending message to the mail server.";
29.     $smtp->quit() or
30.        die "***Err: couldn't close the connection to the mail server.";
31.      return 1;   # if we've gotten this far, we're okay
32. } # dbaSMTPSend
```

Assuming that the SMTP mail server is `mail.linchi.com`, this script sends an email from `victor@linchi.com`, specified with the method `mail()` on line 19, to two recipients, `monica@yourTel.com` and `christine@yourTel.com`. These recipients are the elements of the list specified in the method `to()` on line 20.

Note that at the recipient end, the `Subject`, the `To`, and the `From` fields in the header of the received email message will display those strings specified in the method `datasend()` on lines 22, 23, and 24, respectively. If line 24 specifies that the `From` field is removed from the script, the recipient will then see `victor@linchi.com`, specified in the `mail()` method, in the `From` field instead.

Upon receiving the email message sent from this script, the following is what the recipient may see:

From: brother@linchi.com
To: sister@yourTel.com
Subject: Hello, world!
Message:
        This should be in the message body.

Although the module Net::SMTP only exposes several methods—in other words, the ones in Table 2-8 plus a few more—it's not the most user-friendly module. If you don't know anything about the SMTP protocol, you may find the behavior of the module rather quirky or outright strange at times. You need to be aware of the following issues:

- It's important to end a string for a header field (for example, To and From) with a newline \n; otherwise, the recipient won't see what you think the recipient will see. To see the exact behavior when a newline is dropped, you really have to experiment with different scenarios.

- The single newline that separates the header from the message body on line 25 is required. If it's missing, your message body may not show up at all.

- The quit() method is necessary on line 29 to close the connection and get the email sent. There's no default behavior; the module won't complete the SMTP conversation for you.

The rest of this book, whenever there's a need to send an email from a Perl script, uses the function dbaSMTPSend(), shown in Listing 2-16. In effect, this function hides the quirkiness of the Net::SMTP module so that your script can concentrate on specifying the email elements. In the SQLDBA Toolkit, the function dbaSMTPSend() is exported by the module SQLDBA::Utility.

Parsing Text According to a Grammar

> **SCENARIO**
> *You want to parse the SELECT statement of T-SQL.*

The objective isn't to validate the syntax of a SELECT statement. For that, you can use Query Analyzer or osql.exe with SET PARSEONLY. Rather, you want to parse a SELECT statement to access its individual components so that further actions can be performed on these components such as the FROM clause and the WHERE clause. I use the module Parse::RecDescent to construct a parser for the SELECT statement.

Perl extraordinaire Damian Conway wrote the Parse::RecDescent module, which is available on the CPAN site. Given a formal grammar, you use Parse::RecDescent to generate a recursive descent parser for the grammar (hence the name RecDescent). Once a parser is generated, you can use the parser—which is a Perl object with the names of the grammar rules exposed as its methods—to parse any text. In other words, you can use it to decompose the text into the elements of the grammar if the text is valid per the grammar.

Much of the power of this module comes from the fact that you can specify a piece of Perl code along with any grammar rule to access and manipulate the grammatical elements defined by the grammar rule while the text is being parsed. In addition, the grammar terminals can be any Perl regular expressions.

Introducing the Grammar

Let's define a highly simplified grammar for the SELECT statement. The key assumption is that the expression in the WHERE clause can be only a string, a number, or a column name. For this section, it doesn't serve any useful purpose to accommodate the complexity of arbitrary expressions in a SELECT statement. Listing 2-17 shows the simplified grammar for the SELECT statement.

Listing 2-17. A Simplified Grammar for the SELECT *Statement*

```
select_query :  select_clause from_clause where_clause(?) end_of_str
select_clause : /SELECT/i  select_item(s /,/)
select_item :    /(\*|\w+\.\*)/
                | expression
from_clause :   /FROM/i  from_item(s /,/)
from_item :     '(' select_query ')' alias
              | table alias(?)
table :         ...!key_words /\w+/
alias :         ...!key_words /\w+/
where_clause :   /WHERE/i where_item more_where_item(?)
more_where_item : /AND/i where_item
where_item :     expression '=' expression
expression :     /(\w+\.\w+|\'.*\'|\d+(\.\d+)?)/
               | ...!key_words /\w+/
key_words : /SELECT/i | /FROM/i | /WHERE/i
end_of_str : /\z/
```

This grammar consists of a series of rules, each of which is introduced with the rule name on the left side of a colon, followed by one or more productions separated by vertical bars. Each production consists of zero or more items, separated by spaces. An item can be the name of another rule (referred to as a *subrule* of the current rule) or a *token*, which can be either a regular-expression pattern or a string literal. A token in a grammar is also known as a *terminal*.

For instance, the following is one of the rules from Listing 2-17:

```
from_item :     '(' select_query ')' alias
              | table alias(?)
```

The rule name is from_item. This rule has two productions on the right side of the colon. The first production has four items, two of which are subrules and two of which are string terminals. The second production has two subrules. The second subrule is followed with a repetition quantifier, indicating that it's optional.

(Refer to the upcoming Table 2-9 for more information on the repetition quantifiers.)

A rule matches a string if one of its productions matches the string. A production matches the string if all of the items in the production match the substrings in the same consecutive order. When there are multiple productions for a rule, the productions are tested in the order in which they're specified in the grammar. As soon as the first match is found, the rule is considered successfully matched, and no further match attempt will be made. When all the productions have been tried and no match is found, the string is considered invalid with respect to the grammar.

No Backtracking Across Rules

You should be aware that RecDescent parsers don't backtrack on failure to try a different production of a previously succeeded subrule; they simply fail. For instance, assume you have the following grammar:

```
query :          select_clause from_clause
select_clause :  'SELECT' column alias
select_clause :  'SELECT' column
from_clause :    'FROM' table alias
table :          /\w+/
column :         /\w+/
alias :          /\w+/
```

You may expect the RecDescent parser from this grammar to successfully validate the following query text:

```
SELECT c FROM myTable t
```

Well, it won't. The first production of the rule select_clause matches the substring SELECT c FROM, leaving the rule from_clause unable to match the remaining text. The parser won't backtrack to try the second production of the rule select_clause, which would have succeeded by matching the substring SELECT c.

This behavior may catch you off guard, especially if you're accustomed to the backtracking behavior of Perl regular expressions. You must design your grammar to prevent your parser from running into this type of failure. In this particular grammar, you just have to make sure that the terminals from select_clause don't match anything that is supposed to be part of from_clause. One general solution is to perform a negative *lookahead* to prevent the table or alias rules from matching the key word FROM. The following is the revised grammar that behaves correctly:

```
query :          select_clause from_clause
select_clause :  'SELECT' column alias
select_clause :  'SELECT' column
from_clause :    'FROM' table alias
table :          ...!key_words /\w+/
column :         ...!key_words /\w+/
alias :          ...!key_words /\w+/
key_words :      /SELECT/ | /FROM/
```

In the RecDescent grammar, any item in a production can be prefixed with ... or ...!. The former is the positive lookahead, meaning that the production can succeed only if the item is matched but the match doesn't consume any text. The ...! is the negative lookahead.

In the previous grammar, the alias rule means that an alias matches a word, but the word can't be a key word. Before the parser attempts to use /\w+/ to match the text, it first checks to see if the text matches a T-SQL key word. If it doesn't match any key word, the parser then proceeds to match the same text with /\w+/.

In addition, you can specify a subrule name with a repetition quantifier—in a way similar to Perl's regular-expression quantifiers—indicating how many times the subrule should match. Table 2-9 describes the repetition quantifiers.

Table 2-9. Quantifiers for a Production Item

QUANTIFIER	DESCRIPTION
subrule(?)	Matching the subrule zero or one time
subrule(s)	Matching the subrule one or more times
subrule(s?)	Matching zero or more times
subrule(N)	Matching exactly N times
subrule(N..M)	Matching between N and M times, inclusive
subrule(..M)	Matching between 1 and M times
subrule(N..)	Matching at least N times

Note that just like the regular-expression quantifiers, these grammar repetition quantifiers are greedy. In other words, they'll attempt the maximum number of matches. Finally, you can specify the pattern that separates two consecutive subrules in the same parentheses following the quantifier. For instance, (s /,/) indicates that any two consecutive subrules are to be separated with a comma.

Now, you're ready to interpret the SELECT grammar in Listing 2-17:

- A SELECT statement consists of a select_clause subrule, a from_clause subrule, optionally a where_clause subrule, and an end_of_str subrule.

- A select_clause rule begins with word SELECT, followed by one or more select_item rules, which are separated by commas.

- A select_item can be '*', /\w+\.*/, or an expression.

- An expression can be /(\w+\.\w+|\'.*\'|\d+(\.\d+)?)/ or simply /\w+/ with a negative lookahead. The former consists of three alternatives: two words connected with a dot, a string quoted with single quotation marks, and a number with zero or more decimal places. Note that the latter is a word that must not match any key_words, which can be SELECT, FROM, or WHERE.

- Finally, the end_of_str rule forces the grammar to match the entire string. Note that /\z/ matches the end of a string.

You can interpret the other grammar rules similarly. Now, with the grammar in Listing 2-17, all you have is the ability to check whether a string is a valid SELECT statement. That's useful but not useful enough. You want to extract information from the SELECT statement. To that end, let's turn to the RecDescent actions.

Adding Actions to the Grammar

Earlier, I said that an item of a grammar production is either a subrule or a token. But that's not the full story. It can also be a block of Perl code executed in the namespace of the active parser, which is different from the namespace of your script that generates the parser object and calls its methods. An action item succeeds if its last statement returns a defined value; otherwise, it fails.

NOTE *The code of a RecDescent parser always runs in its own special namespace. Therefore, when you specify the code for the grammar actions, you need to make sure that variables from any other namespace are qualified with their respective package names.*

Before discussing what code to write in an action block, let me point out an important feature: Each item in a successful production returns a value that can be accessed by the code in any action specified after the item in the same production. The following is how a value is associated with an item:

- For a subrule, if its production succeeds, the returned value is either the value of the variable $return if it's assigned a value or the last matched item. When the subrule is specified with a repetition quantifier, the returned value isn't a regular scalar but is a reference to a list of values, each of which is returned from the respective repetition of the successful subrule match.

- For a token, the value is the matched string.

- An action returns the value of its last statement.

There are many ways to access the values returned by the items of a successful production. The most common method is—not surprisingly—to use the array @item, which stores the values returned by each item in the current production. The element $item[0] stores the name of the rule. The element $item[1] stores the value of the first item to the left of the colon, the element $item[2] stores the value of the second item, and so on.

Now, let's add actions to the grammar in Listing 2-17 to give you access to all the elements of the SELECT statement. Listing 2-18 shows the Perl code to retrieve the structural elements of a SELECT statement along with the revised grammar.

Listing 2-18. Parsing the SELECT *Statement*

```
1.   use strict;
2.   use Parse::RecDescent;
3.   use Data::Dumper;
4.
5.   my $parser = Parse::RecDescent->new(q{
6.      query :         select_query end_of_str { $item[1] }
7.      select_query :  select_clause from_clause where_clause(?)
8.                              { { SELECT => $item[1],
9.                                  FROM   => $item[2],
10.                                 WHERE  => $item[3] } }
11.
12.     select_clause : /SELECT/i  select_item(s /,/)  { $item[2] }
13.     select_item :    /(\*|\w+\.\*)/      { $item[1] }
14.                   | expression          { $item[1] }
15.
```

```
16.    from_clause : /FROM/i  from_item(s /,/)      { $item[2] }
17.    from_item :     '(' select_query ')' alias
18.                                    { { subquery => $item[2],
19.                                        alias    =>$item[4]   } }
20.             | table alias(?)  { join(' ', ($item[1], @{$item[2]})) }
21.
22.    table :  ...!key_words /\w+/         { $item[2] }
23.    alias :  ...!key_words /\w+/         { $item[2] }
24.
25.    where_clause :   /WHERE/i where_item more_where_item(?)
26.                                    { [ $item[2], @{$item[3]} ] }
27.    more_where_item : /AND/i where_item   { $item[2] }
28.    where_item : expression '=' expression
29.                                    { $item[1] . '=' . $item[3] }
30.
31.    expression :   /(\w+\.\w+|\'.*\'|\d+(\.\d+)?)/   { $item[1] }
32.               | ...!key_words /\w+/             { $item[2] }
33.    key_words : /SELECT/i | /FROM/i | /WHERE/i
34.    end_of_str : /\z/
35.    }); # end of grammar
36.
37. my $query = q/ SELECT a.au_id, 'xyz', t.*
38.                FROM authors a, (SELECT * FROM titleauthor) t
39.                WHERE a.au_id = t.au_id
40.                 AND t.title_id = 'BU12321' /;
41. my $select = $parser->query($query) or die "***Err: malformed query.";
42. print Dumper($select);
```

The grammar is specified between line 6 and line 34. Note that the entire
grammar is quoted with the q{} operator on line 5, which is equivalent to putting a
pair of single quotation marks around the grammar text. This is important because
the single quotes prevent the embedded variables such as $item[1] from
interpolating. The grammar text is then passed to the new() method of
Parse::RecDescent on line 5 to generate the parser object $parser. Then, on line 41,
the $parser->query() method of the parser is applied to the SELECT statement string
specified between lines 37 and 40. Note that the query() method corresponds to
the name of the rule on line 6. It's not a hard-coded method. If you change the rule
name to, say, myQuery, then the method would now be myQuery().

For the SELECT statement between lines 39 and 40, `$parser->query()` returns the following data structure:

```
$VAR1 = {
        'SELECT' => [ 'a.au_id', '\'xyz\'', 't.*' ],
        'FROM' => [
                  'authors a',
                  { 'subquery' => {
                                    'FROM'   => [ 'titleauthor' ],
                                    'SELECT' => [ '*' ],
                                    'WHERE'  => []
                                  },
                    'alias' => 't'
                  }
                ],
      'WHERE' => [  [ 'a.au_id=t.au_id',
                      't.title_id=\'BU12321\'' ]  ]
    };
```

Clearly, not only has the parser validated the SELECT statement, but it has also decomposed the statement into the elements specified by the grammar. These grammatical elements are obtained by adding the actions to the grammar in Listing 2-17, primarily through passing the @item array back to the next higher-level rule in the grammar. Eventually a reference to the entire hierarchical grammatical structure is returned to the main Perl script.

Let's go through the select_clause rule as an example to see how the SELECT items are captured. At the top level on line 6, the rule is as follows:

```
6.      query :               select_query end_of_str { $item[1] }
```

This means that `$parser->query()` returns whatever `$item[1]` is—in other words, the value of the item select_query. At the next lower level, the production for select_query is as follows:

```
7.      select_query :  select_clause from_clause where_clause(?)
8.                              { { SELECT  => $item[1],
9.                                  FROM    => $item[2],
10.                                 WHERE   => $item[3] } }
```

Recall that a pair of braces, {}, composes a reference to an anonymous hash. This rule returns a reference to a hash whose values are returned from its select_clause, from_clause, and where_clause, respectively. The select_clause is in turn specified as follows:

```
12.     select_clause : /SELECT/i  select_item(s /,/)  { $item[2] }
```

This returns a reference to a list of values, each of which is a value returned by the select_item rule. The select_item rule is as follows:

```
13.     select_item :   /(\*|\w+\.\*)/         { $item[1] }
14.                   | expression            { $item[1] }
```

This has two productions. The first is a regular-expression token or terminal, and the second is an expression subrule. The select_item rule returns whatever matches either of these two. You can continue to follow the expression rule on line 14 to its eventual tokens. Of the two productions, the regular-expression production on line 13 will be tested first. If it succeeds, the production on line 14 will never be tested.

I'll leave it as an exercise for you to study how the values of other rules all bubble up to the top level. The process is much the same as what I just described for the select_clause rule and its subrules.

You may wonder why you go through all this trouble and why you don't simply parse the SELECT statement with a properly written regular expression. Note the recursive nature of the grammar in that the from_clause clause permits a subquery that can be an arbitrary SELECT statement itself. Crafting a regular expression to decompose a SELECT statement with arbitrarily nested subqueries will quickly prove to be difficult and unreliable.

Finally, I strongly encourage you to study the module Parse::RecDescent. After you've gotten used to its behavior and mechanisms, you'll find this module to be extremely powerful. Many Perl scripts in this book, especially those analyzing SQL code, depend on this module. If this module looks intimidating, relax! I've introduced functions in the SQLDBA Toolkit to shield you from the details of the module.

NOTE *The module Parse::RecDescent isn't the fastest parser generator around; however, for analyzing T-SQL code, its performance is adequate. Its author, Damian Conway, planned to introduce a faster version but has since put it on hold because, according to the Perl 6 plan, the new regular-expression engine will incorporate the parsing functionality into the Perl core, thus making a separate RecDescent-like module redundant. This will be an exciting development and will make Perl an even better language for analyzing T-SQL code because the parsing performance will be far better than that with Parse::RecDescent, and it'll be more convenient.*

Summary

No matter what you're working on, one thing you don't want to do is reinvent the wheel. This is particularly true with programming Perl to perform a common task because of the likelihood of finding a piece of code—in the form of a Perl module—that already performs the task and because of the ease with which you can find and use the code through searching the CPAN site and other online facilities.

This chapter gave you a quick tour of some commonly used Perl modules. It's important that you become comfortable with the modules because later chapters use them repeatedly. The focus then will be on solving SQL Server administrative problems instead of explaining how to use these common modules.

However, modules aren't the only things you risk reinventing. The next chapter introduces you to a collection of commonly used routines and scripting techniques. Just like the modules covered in this chapter, these routines and techniques will be used throughout the rest of the book, so it's worth it to become familiar with them now.

CHAPTER 3

Working with Commonly Used Perl Routines

BEFORE YOU FINISH THIS BOOK, you undoubtedly will have noticed that the book's scripts use some Perl programming routines repeatedly. In fact, these routines are used so often that a separate chapter should be dedicated to highlighting them. That's the purpose of this chapter.

Unlike the modules covered in the previous chapter, you won't find all the routines in this chapter in a module bundled with Perl or a module available from the Comprehensive Perl Archive Network (CPAN) at http://www.cpan.org. Some of the routines are well known to any experienced Perl programmer, and others are tailored for the scripts in this book. Moreover, most of them are useful in writing your own scripts beyond this book.

To make it easy for you to use these routines and to simplify the scripts in the book, I've packaged most of them in a module, SQLDBA::Utility, which is an integral part of the SQLDBA Toolkit. This toolkit consists of the scripts discussed in this book.

Table 3-1 describes the functions exported by the module SQLDBA::Utility. As you can see, all of the function names start with dba.

Table 3-1. Functions Exported by SQLDBA::Utility

FUNCTION	DESCRIPTION
dbaReadINI()	Reads a Windows initialization file and returns a reference to the nested data structure that contains the configuration options in the file.
dbaReadConfig()	Reads a configuration file and returns a reference to a nested data structure that contains the configuration options in the file. This function permits duplicate keys.
dbaInSet()	Returns true if the element is in the array.
dbaSetCommon()	Returns the elements common in both arrays.
dbaSetDiff()	Returns the elements that are in the first array but not in the second array.
dbaSetSame()	Returns true if the two arrays have the same elements.
dbaRemoveDuplicates()	Removes duplicates from an array.

Table 3-1. Functions Exported by SQLDBA::Utility (Continued)

FUNCTION	DESCRIPTION
dbaTime2str()	Converts a time in epoch seconds to a readable string.
dbaStr2time()	Converts a date/time string to epoch seconds.
dbaTimeDiff()	Returns the number of seconds between the two time strings.
dbaStringDiff()	Returns the character position and the line number where the two strings start to differ and also returns a string fragment starting from where the strings begin to differ.
dbaSaveRef()	Persists to a file the data structure referenced by the input parameter.
dbaReadSavedRef()	Retrieves from a file the data structure saved by dbaSaveRef() and returns a reference to the data structure.
dbaRunQueryADO()	Executes a SQL query via ActiveX Data Objects (ADO) using Win32::OLE.
dbaRunOsql()	Executes a SQL script via osql.exe.
dbaGetTree()	Builds a dependency tree out of immediate dependencies.

In addition, this chapter covers the four functions described in Table 3-2 that are part of the module SQLDBA::ParseSQL, which is also part of the SQLDBA Toolkit.

Table 3-2. Functions Exported by SQLDBA::ParseSQL

FUNCTION	DESCRIPTION
dbaSplitBatch()	Splits a Transact-SQL (T-SQL) script into an array of individual batches. The batches in a T-SQL script are separated with the word GO on a separate line.
dbaNormalizeSQL()	Converts a T-SQL script into a format in which the comments, quoted strings, and delimited identifiers are replaced with unique token strings. This *normalized* format makes it easy to apply regular-expression pattern matching.
dbaRestoreSQL()	Takes the reference returned by dbaNormalizeSQL() and replaces all the token strings in the code with their originals.
dbaParseQDON()	Decomposes a multiple-part database object name into its individual parts.

NOTE *This chapter introduces you to these functions in the order in which they're listed in Table 3-1 and Table 3-2.*

In addition to the modules SQLDBA::Utility and SQLDBA::ParseSQL, the SQLDBA Toolkit also includes the modules SQLDBA::SQLDMO and SQLDBA::Security. The chapter concludes by introducing the function dbaGetServiceAccount() from SQLDBA::Security and the function dbaScriptSP() from SQLDBA::SQLDMO.

Reading from an Initialization File

SCENARIO
You want to read the configuration options of a Windows initialization file into your script.

The Windows initialization file, or the *INI file* for short, follows a well-defined format. The file is divided into sections, each of which is introduced on a separate line with a unique section heading in square brackets. Each section consists of one or more key/value pairs with the = sign between the key and its value. The keys in the same section must be unique, but they can be the same if they're in different sections.

Because reading from an INI file is such a common task, you probably expect to find the CPAN modules ready for you to use, and you're right. A quick search on the CPAN site for module names containing the string config finds a number of modules that can read an INI file, including Config::iniFiles, Config::iniHash, Config::Tiny, and Config::Simple to name a few. In addition, you can also use two modules specific for the Win32 platform, Win32::AdminMisc::ReadINI and Win32::Tie::Ini.

The scripts in this book read only from INI files, and the function to read from an INI file is rather straightforward, so I've chosen to write the function myself instead of using one from the CPAN site. Although they're excellent, the CPAN modules for working with INI files usually come with many more functions than needed by the scripts in this book.

NOTE   *In addition to reading the configuration options from an INI file, you may be tempted to record simple status information in the file so that the script isn't totally clueless about the history of its previous invocations. However, with its limited flexibility, an INI file isn't the best place to persist the status information of your script. Fortunately, there's a more consistent and convenient way to persist status information in Perl, which is covered in the "Persisting a Data Structure to a File" section. INI files should be dedicated to providing the configuration options for your Perl scripts.*

Listing 3-1 is a simple script that demonstrates the use of the function dbaReadINI() exported by request from SQLDBA::Utility.

NOTE   *In fact, all the functions in SQLDBA::Utility are exported by request only.*

Listing 3-1. Reading from an INI File with dbaReadINI()

```
1. use strict;
2. use SQLDBA::Utility qw( dbaReadINI ); # import function dbaReadINI()
3. use Data::Dumper;
4.
5. my $iniFile = shift or
6.    die "***Err: $0 expects an INI file.";
7.
8. my $ref = dbaReadINI($iniFile);
9. print Dumper($ref);
```

The function dbaReadINI(), shown in Listing 3-2, is imported into Listing 3-1 on line 2. Remember that the function qw() is a shortcut to quote a string of words separated by a space and returns a list with the words being the list elements. The function dbaReadINI() accepts an INI file and returns a reference to a nested hash whose keys are the section headings. The value of each key is a reference to another hash whose keys/values correspond to the keys/values in that section of the INI file.

Listing 3-2. The Function dbaReadINI()

```perl
sub dbaReadINI {
    my $iniFile = shift
        or die "***Err: dbaReadINI() expects an INI file name.";
    my ($ref, $section);

    open(INI, "$iniFile")
        or die "***Err: could not open file $iniFile for read.";
    while (<INI>) {
        next if /^\s*#/;                    # skip a comment line
        s/^((\\\#|\\\\|[^\#])*).*$/$1/;  # remove trailing comments

        if (/^\s*\[(.+)\]\s*$/) {  # read section heading
            $section = uc($1);        # convert to uppercase using uc function
            $section =~ s/^\s*//;   # remove leading whitespace
            $section =~ s/\s*$//;   # remove trailing whitespace

            die "***Err: $section is a duplicate section heading."
                if exists $ref->{$section};
            $ref->{$section} = {};  # initialize the hash for the section
            next;
        }
        # read the key/value pair inside a section
        if ((/^\s*([^=]+)\s*=\s*(.*)\s*$/i) && $section) {
            my ($key, $value) = (uc($1), $2);
            $key =~ s/^\s*//;       # remove leading whitespace
            $key =~ s/\s*$//;       # remove trailing whitespace
            $value =~ s/^\s*//;     # remove leading whitespace
            $value =~ s/\s*$//;     # remove trailing whitespace
            $value = undef if $value =~ /^\s*$/;

            die "***Err: $key has a duplicate in $section."
                if exists $ref->{$section}->{$key};
            $ref->{$section}->{$key} = $value; # record the key/value in the hash
            next;
        }
    } # while

    return $ref;
}  # dbaReadINI
```

Listing 3-3 is a sample INI file, which is artificially constructed to cover various scenarios with which the function dbaReadINI() must deal. The scenarios include cases, comments, missing values, and empty sections.

Listing 3-3. Sample INI File

```
[Control]
DBA=Linchi
Pager=linchi@myTel.com

[ TradeDB ]        # section heading
dataSize = 20MB    # data size
logSize =

# [StockDB]
[EquityDB]
dataSize = 30MB
logSize = 15MB

[ClientDB]
# TBD
```

Save the script in Listing 3-1 to the file readINI.pl and the configuration options in Listing 3-3 to the file config.ini and then execute the script with the INI file from the command line as shown in Listing 3-4.

Listing 3-4. Result of Reading config.ini *to a Hash*

```
cmd>perl readINI.pl config.ini
$VAR1 = {
          EQUITYDB => {
                        DATASIZE => '30MB',
                        LOGSIZE  => '15MB'
                      },
          CLIENTDB => { },
          TRADEDB  => {
                        DATASIZE => '20MB',
                        LOGSIZE  => undef
                      },
          CONTROL => {
                        DBA   => 'Linchi',
                        PAGER => 'linchi@myTel.com'
                      }
        };
```

Examine the output in Listing 3-4 and note the behavior of the function dbaReadINI() with respect to cases, comments, missing values, empty sections, and whitespaces.

The function dbaReadINI() converts all characters in the section headings and in the keys to uppercase characters. This effectively makes the section headings and the keys case insensitive in the INI file. However, the INI values remain unchanged; thus, they're case sensitive.

Any characters after a # sign that isn't escaped with a \ are considered part of a comment and are ignored. You can have comments anywhere in an INI file. The expression to remove a comment in the INI file—actually to keep the part that is not a comment—is as follows:

```
s/^((\\\#|\\\\|[^\#])*).*$/$1/;
```

This expression says that if a string contains \# (in other words, the # sign immediately preceded with a backslash), \\ (in other words, two consecutive backslashes), or anything other than #, it isn't a comment and therefore should be retained. Because # and \ are special symbols, you need escape them with a backslash when you want to use them literally. Note that this expression takes advantage of the fact that a regular expression is evaluated from left to right. Thus, if a string contains \# or \\, then those characters will be matched first before matching "anything other than #."

If a value is missing but its key is specified, the corresponding hash value will be undef, as in the example of $VAR1->{TRADEDB}->{LOGSIZE} in Listing 3-4.

If a section is entirely empty—in other words, only the section heading is specified—a reference to an empty hash is assigned to the corresponding hash key. See the value of $VAR1->{CLIENTDB} in Listing 3-4.

Whitespaces are allowed around a section heading inside the square brackets and around a key or a value. Note that in Listing 3-2, the operators s/^\s*// and s/\s*$// are applied to remove the leading and the trailing whitespaces.

Most important, it's required that the INI file doesn't allow duplicate sections or duplicate keys in a section. The function dbaReadINI() simply terminates the script as soon as it finds a duplicate section heading or a duplicate key. It's better to *crash* a script and fix the INI file that doesn't comply with the format than to continue with an incorrect assumption.

Using INI Configuration Files

In the Windows environment, Microsoft's recommended place for storing the configuration information for your application is the registry, not INI files. This makes sense, especially for applications distributed to end users because the registry is a central repository of configuration information and is much better protected from tampering than INI files.

For most SQL Server administrative tasks, I prefer to use the INI-style configuration files to help configure my Perl scripts. Concerns over the proliferation of INI files and their lack of protection are a nonissue because the scripts are used in environments tightly controlled by the Database Administrator (DBA).

Reading from a Configuration File

SCENARIO
In a configuration file, you want to allow duplicate keys in a section.

When you can specify multiple entries under a section for the same configuration key, you can put all the values for the key in an array and assign the reference to the array to the corresponding hash key.

You only need to make a minor change to the function dbaReadINI() to accommodate this requirement. The result is the function dbaReadConfig(), shown in Listing 3-5. This function is also exported by request from SQLDBA::Utility.

Listing 3-5. The Function for Reading from a Configuration File

```
1.   sub dbaReadConfig {
2.     my ($configFile) = shift or
3.        die "***Err: dbaReadConfig() expects a config file name.";
4.     my ($ref, $section);
5.
6.     open(CONFIG, "$configFile") or
7.        die "***Err: Could not open file $configFile for read.";
8.     while (<CONFIG>) {
9.       next if /^\s*#/;                 # skip a comment line
10.      s/^((\\\#|\\\\|[^\#])*).*$/$1/;  # remove trailing comments
11.
```

```
12.        if (/^\s*\[(.+)\]\s*$/) {    # read section heading
13.            $section = uc($1);        # convert to uppercase
14.            $section =~ s/^\s*//;     # remove leading whitespaces
15.            $section =~ s/\s*$//;     # remove trailing whitespaces
16.
17.            die "***Err: $section is a duplicate section heading."
18.                if exists $ref->{$section};
19.            $ref->{$section} = { };
20.            next;
21.        }
22.
23.        if ((/^\s*([^\s\[\]=]+)\s*=\s*(.+)\s*$/i) and $section) {
24.            my ($key, $value) = (uc($1), $2);
25.            $key =~ s/^\s*//; $key =~ s/\s*$//;
26.            $value =~ s/#.*//;
27.            $value = undef if $value =~ /^\s*$/;
28.            push @{$ref->{$section}->{$key}}, $value;
29.            next;
30.        }
31.    } # while
32.
33.    return $ref;
34. }  # dbaReadConfig
```

The function dbaReadConfig() in Listing 3-5 is nearly identical to the function dbaReadINI() discussed in the previous section. The difference is how the configuration values are recorded in the data structure. Instead of simply assigning the configuration value to a hash key as in Listing 3-2:

```
$ref->{$section}->{$key} = $value;
```

the function dbaReadConfig() adds the value of $value as a new element to the array @{$ref->{$section}->{$key}} on line 28, as follows:

```
push @{$ref->{$section}->{$key}}, $value;
```

This change is necessary to associate multiple values with the same configuration key. Listing 3-6 has the sample configuration options to show how the function dbaReadConfig() works.

Listing 3-6. A Sample Configuration File with Duplicate Keys

```
[TradeDB]
dataFile = d:\sql\data\TradeDB.mdf
logFile = e:\sql\data\TradeDB_log1.ldf
logFile = e:\sql\data\TradeDB_log2.ldf

[EquityDB]
dataFile = d:\sql\data\EquityDB.mdf
dataFile = d:\sql\data\EquityDB_1.ndf
logFile = e:\sql\data\EquityDB_log1.ldf
```

Note the multiple entries for the same key, logFile, in the section TradeDB. Similarly, there are multiple entries for the key dataFile in the section EquityDB. Listing 3-7 shows the script that uses dbaReadConfig().

Listing 3-7. Reading from a Configuration File

```
1.  use strict;
2.  use SQLDBA::Utility qw( dbaReadConfig );
3.  use Data::Dumper;
4.
5.  my $configFile = shift or
6.      die "***Err: $0 expects a configuration file.";
7.
8.  my $ref = dbaReadConfig($configFile);
9.  print Dumper($ref);
```

On line 2, the function dbaReadConfig() is imported from the module SQLDBA::Utility by request. Save the configurations in Listing 3-6 to the file config.txt and save the script in Listing 3-7 to the file readConfig.pl. Then, run the script as follows to see its output:

```
cmd>perl readConfig.pl config.txt
$VAR1 = {
          EQUITYDB => {
                    LOGFILE  => [ 'e:\\sql\\data\\EquityDB_log1.ldf' ],
                    DATAFILE => [ 'd:\\sql\\data\\EquityDB.mdf',
                                  'd:\\sql\\data\\EquityDB_1.ndf' ]
                 },
          TRADEDB => {
```

```
LOGFILE  -> [ 'e:\\sql\\data\\TradeDB_log1.ldf',
              'e:\\sql\\data\\TradeDB_log2.ldf' ],
DATAFILE => [ 'd:\\sql\\data\\TradeDB.mdf'  ]
        }
    };
```

Recall that a pair of square brackets composes a reference to an anonymous array. Thus, the result from Listing 3-7 is a hash of hashes, each of the inner hash values is a reference to an anonymous array of filenames. The format of the configuration file in Listing 3-6 doesn't comply with the Windows INI file format described in the previous section because of the duplicate keys. But the ability to specify repeating values of a key is nevertheless convenient, as you'll see later in the book.

Checking If an Element Is in an Array

SCENARIO
You want to check whether an element is in an array.

To check whether an element is in an array, use the built-in grep() function.

Introducing grep()

Some of you may know that Unix has a special command called *grep* that you can use to find strings in text files. Perl's grep() function is similar but more powerful. The grep() function comes in two flavors:

```
grep BLOCK LIST
grep EXPR, LIST
```

where BLOCK is a block of code and EXPR is an expression. This function evaluates BLOCK or EXPR for each element of LIST (temporarily setting $_ to each element in turn) and returns a list of the elements for which the BLOCK or EXPR is true. Note that a code block returns true if its last statement returns true.

These two syntax examples omit the enclosing parentheses. But you can always use a pair of parentheses around the parameters of any function.

Because the procedure to perform this task is used frequently, it deserves the dedicated function dbaInSet(), which returns true if the first parameter is an element in the array referenced by the second parameter. Listing 3-8 shows the code of dbaInSet().

Listing 3-8. The Function dbaInSet()

```
sub dbaInSet {
    my($element, $setRef) = @_;
    $element = quotemeta($element);
    return scalar grep(/^$element$/, @$setRef);
} # dbaInSet
```

Listing 3-9 shows an example of using this function. Note that the second parameter of dbaInSet() expects a reference to an array instead of an array.

Listing 3-9. Using the Function dbaInSet()

```
use strict;
use SQLDBA::Utility qw( dbaInSet );

my @tables = ('[authors]', 'titles');  # note the square brackets around authors
if (dbaInSet('[authors]', \@tables)) {
  print "It is in the array.\n";
}
```

The built-in Perl function quotemeta() escapes with a backslash each character that's not an alphanumeric or an underline. This prevents these characters from assuming special meaning when used in a regular expression. In Listing 3-9, without the quotemeta() function, the regular expression in the grep() function inside dbaInSet() would be /^[authors]$/, which is completely different from the intended /^\[authors\]$/.

The expression scalar grep(/^$element$/, @$setRef) in Listing 3-8 returns true, even when $element is the string '45' and an element of the array is the integer 45. Perl does the automatic conversion to simplify the scripting task.

Getting the Intersection of Two Arrays

SCENARIO
You want to get the elements that are in both arrays.

The most straightforward solution to getting the elements that are in both arrays is to use two nested loops. For each element in the first array, compare it with every element in the second array and keep it if it matches any element from the second array.

The function dbaSetCommon() in Listing 3-10 is an implementation of this approach. The code in the main body is to demonstrate the function. For the two sample arrays, the script prints out 'master' and 'tempdb'.

Listing 3-10. Getting the Intersection of Two Arrays

```
1.   use strict;
2.
3.   my @set1 = ('master', 'pubs', 'tempdb', 'tempdb');
4.   my @set2 = ('northwind', 'model', 'master', 'tempdb');
5.
6.   my @common = dbaSetCommon(\@set1, \@set2);
7.   foreach my $db (@common) {
8.      print "   $db\n";
9.   }
10.
11. ####################
12. sub dbaSetCommon {
13.    my ($setRef1, $setRef2) = @_;
14.
15.    my @common;
16.    foreach my $e1 (@$setRef1) {
17.       foreach my $e2 (@$setRef2) {
18.          if ($e1 eq $e2) {
19.             push @common, $e1 unless grep($e1 eq $_, @common);
20.          }
21.       }
22.    }
23.    @common;
24. }
```

Because the objective of the function dbaSetCommon() is to retrieve the elements present in both arrays in the sense of the intersection of two sets, no duplicates are allowed in the returned array. The grep() test in the unless condition on line 19 prevents a value that's already an element of the result array from being pushed into the array again. This test is necessary because a Perl array isn't a set, and it allows duplicate elements. A set, on the other hand, can't have any duplicate elements by definition.

CAUTION   *You usually pass two arrays to a function using their references, as shown in Listing 3-10. You could directly pass two arrays to the
function, but then the function wouldn't be able to tell which element is
from which array. Only in rare situations is this what you want.*

You can take advantage of the function dbaInSet() presented in Listing 3-8 to
eliminate the inner loop through the second array—in other words, the loop introduced on line 17 in Listing 3-10. Listing 3-11 shows dbaSetCommon() rewritten using
dbaInSet().

Listing 3-11. Finding the Set Intersection Using dbaInSet()

```
sub dbaSetCommon {
    my ($setRef1, $setRef2) = @_;

    my @common;
    foreach my $e1 (@$setRef1) {
        if (dbaInSet($e1, $setRef2)) {
            push @common, $e1 unless dbaInSet($e1, \@common);
        }
    }
    @common;
}
```

There's also a more idiomatic solution, which uses the following features that
are unique to Perl:

- The keys of a hash are unique.

- The function grep() loops through an array and applies a piece of code to
  each element.

Listing 3-12 shows the idiomatic solution.

Listing 3-12. Getting the Intersection of Two Arrays, an Idiomatic Solution

```
1. sub dbaSetCommon {
2.     my ($setRef1, $setRef2) = @_;
3.     my %temp;
4.     my %common;
5.
6.     grep {$temp{$_}++} @$setRef2;
7.     grep {$temp{$_} and $common{$_}++} @$setRef1;
8.     keys %common;
9. } # dbaSetCommon
```

Because the loops are implicit, this code is slightly more succinct—not necessarily preferred, though—than Listing 3-10. Line 6 exploits the side effect of grep() to assign the elements of one array to the keys of the hash %temp. Line 7 again uses the implicit looping in grep() to check whether an element of the other array is a key in the hash %temp. If it isn't, $temp{$_} returns undef, and $common{$_}++ isn't evaluated because the AND operator short circuits. But if it is, the expression $common{$_}++ is evaluated. This creates a hash key/value pair with the array element as the key if it doesn't already exist in the hash; otherwise, it increments the value of the hash element. On line 8, the keys of the hash %common are returned as an array, whose elements are guaranteed to be unique by virtue of being the keys of a hash.

NOTE *Perl's logical operators (&&, ||, and, or) are also known as short-circuit operators because they stop evaluation as soon as the truth value is determined. For instance, in the expression* x && rest, *as soon as* x *is found to be false, Perl short-circuits the entire expression—in other words, it doesn't even evaluate the rest of the expression.*

I'll leave you with a question: If you run the script in Listing 3-10, what will it print?

NOTE *You may run into some Perl enthusiasts who feel smug about the approach in Listing 3-12. Resist the urge to jump on the bandwagon! The code may not be as succinct, but I actually prefer the straightforward approach in Listing 3-10 or Listing 3-11. It's easy to understand and more efficient. The code in Listing 3-12, however, is a good exercise for acquainting yourself with Perl idioms.*

Getting the Difference Between Two Arrays

| SCENARIO
You want to get the elements that are in the first array but not in the second one.

The solution to this problem is similar to that discussed in the previous section. If you're comfortable with the scripts in Listing 3-11 and Listing 3-12, you should be able to make minor changes to them and have the solutions to the present problem.

See Listing 3-13 for a straightforward solution.

Listing 3-13. Getting the Difference of Two Arrays, a Straightforward Solution

```
1.   sub dbaSetDiff {
2.      my ($setRef1, $setRef2) = @_;
3.
4.      my @diff;
5.      foreach my $e1 (@$setRef1) {
6.          if (!dbaInSet($e1, $setRef2)) {
7.              push @diff, $e1 unless dbaInSet($e1, \@diff);
8.          }
9.      }
10.     @diff;
11.  } # dbaSetDiff
```

The function dbaSetDiff() in Listing 3-13 mirrors the code in Listing 3-11 for the function dbaSetCommon(). On line 6, instead of checking whether an element from the first array is in the second array, it checks whether it isn't in the second array. Notice the negation operator (!) in front of the function dbaInSet().

Listing 3-14 finishes the section by showing the idiomatic solution. Not surprisingly, this function is nearly identical to that in Listing 3-11 except for the addition of the logical negation on line 7.

Listing 3-14. Getting the Difference of Two Arrays, an Idiomatic Solution

```
1.   sub dbaSetDiff {
2.      my($setRef1, $setRef2) = @_;
3.      my %temp = ();
4.      my %diff = ();
5.
6.      grep {$temp{$_}++} @$setRef2;
7.      grep {!$temp{$_} and $diff{$_}++} @$setRef1;
8.      keys %diff;
9.   } # dbaSetDiff
```

The idiomatic solution uses the *hash key lookup* to identify whether an element is already in an array.

Checking If Two Arrays Contain the Same Elements

| **SCENARIO**
| *You want to check whether two arrays contain the same elements.*

To check whether two arrays contain the same elements, use the function dbaSetDiff() discussed in the previous section. The function dbaSetSame(), in Listing 3-15, returns true if the arrays contain the same elements.

Listing 3-15. The Function dbaSetSame()

```
1. sub dbaSetSame {
2.    my($ref1, $ref2) = @_;
3.
4.    return 0 if scalar dbaSetDiff($ref1, $ref2);
5.    return 0 if scalar dbaSetDiff($ref2, $ref1);
6.    return 1;
7. }
```

Line 4 says that if there's an element in array 1 but not in array 2, return false. Similarly, on line 5, if there's an element in array 2, but not in array 1, return false. If the script makes it to line 6, the two arrays must have the same elements; therefore, return true.

Removing Duplicates from an Array

| **SCENARIO**
| *You want to remove duplicate elements from an array.*

To remove duplicate elements from an array, loop through the array. Add the element to the result array if it isn't already there; otherwise, discard it.

The crux of the solution is to check whether an element is already in an array. As shown in the previous two sections, you can approach this either with the grep() function or with the hash key lookup. You can of course also use the function dbaInSet() introduced earlier in this chapter. Listing 3-16 removes the duplicates from an array using grep().

Listing 3-16. Removing Duplicates from an Array Using grep()

```
1.   sub dbaRemoveDuplicates {
2.     my ($setRef) = shift or
3.         die "***Err: dbaRemoveDuplicates() expects a reference.";
4.
5.     my @unique;
6.     foreach my $e (@$setRef) {
7.        push @unique, $e unless grep($e eq $_, @unique);
8.     }
9.     \@unique;
10. } # dbaRemoveDuplicates
```

If you've studied the two previous sections, this function should look familiar. To use dbaInSet(), replace grep($e eq $_, @unique) with dbaInSet($e1, \@unique) on line 7 in Listing 3-16.

Now, turn your attention to the approach using the hash key lookup in Listing 3-17.

Listing 3-17. Removing Duplicates from an Array Using the Hash Key Lookup

```
1.   sub dbaRemoveDuplicates {
2.     my ($setRef) = shift or
3.         die "***Err: dbaRemoveDuplicates() expects a reference.";
4.
5.     my %temp;
6.     map { $temp{$_} = 1 } @$setRef;
7.     return [ keys %temp ];
8.   } # dbaRemoveDuplicates
```

The hash %temp in Listing 3-17 helps extract the distinct elements from the array. For every element of the array, on line 6 the script evaluates $temp{$_} = 1, which creates a new hash element if it doesn't exist and assigns 1 to its value. If the hash element already exists, the evaluation simply reassigns 1 to the value. What the map() function returns or what are assigned to the hash values on line 6 is of no consequence to the problem at hand. The focus is to populate the keys of the hash %temp with the array elements. For that matter, you could have used the function grep() in place of map(), and the result would be the same.

NOTE *When used as an* lvalue *(in other words, a storage location), a Perl construct—for example, an array, a hash, or a reference—will spring into existence upon first use. This is called* autovivification. *You don't need to painstakingly prepare their creation. This feature helps to make Perl code concise. But sometimes it may surprise you if you're not careful.*

Getting the Difference Between Two Time Strings

SCENARIO
You want to get the difference between two time strings.

You can't directly calculate the difference between two time strings. However, recall from the discussions in Chapter 2, "Working with Commonly Used Perl Modules," that you can convert a time string to its equivalent in epoch seconds. Calculating the difference between two epoch seconds is then a matter of doing a simple subtraction.

Listing 3-18 accepts two strings in the YYYY-MM-DD hh:mm:ss format and returns the difference between the two in seconds. The SQLDBA::Utility module exports the function dbaTimeDiff(), which is discussed later in this section.

Listing 3-18. Calculating the Difference Between Two Time Strings

```
use strict;
use SQLDBA::Utility qw( dbaTimeDiff );

my $diff = dbaTimeDiff(shift, shift);
print "Time Diff (seconds): $diff\n";
```

Save this script to the file timeDiff.pl. The following is an example of running the script with two time strings:

```
cmd>perl timeDiff.pl "2003-01-03 10:12:00" "2003-01-03 10:13:02"
Time Diff (seconds): 62
```

Let's look at the function dbaTimeDiff(). I've included dbaStr2time(), also exported from SQLDBA::Utility, in Listing 3-19 because it's called by dbaTimeDiff() to convert a time string to its equivalent epoch seconds. This book uses the function dbaStr2time() frequently.

Listing 3-19. The Functions dbaTimeDiff() *and* dbaStr2time()

```
sub dbaTimeDiff {
   my ($ts1, $ts2) = @_;
   return dbaStr2time($ts2) - dbaStr2time($ts1);
} # dbaTimeDiff

sub dbaStr2time {
#   Accepts time string in these formats:
#       1999/12/23 15:21:35
#       2000-08-03 05:23:12
#
   my($timestr) = @_;
 # search for variations of YYYY-MM-DD hh:mm:ss
   $timestr =~ /^\s*(\d\d\d\d)(\/|-)(\d\d|\d)(\/|-)(\d\d|\d)
                     (\s+(\d\d|\d):(\d\d|\d):(\d\d|\d))?\s*$/x;
   my @timeArray = ($9, $8, $7, $5, $3 - 1, $1 - 1900);

   timelocal(@timeArray);    # timelocal() is exported by Time::Local
} # dbaStr2time
```

The function dbaStr2time() doesn't perform any error checking. It relies on the function timelocal() exported from Time::Local to report any error it may encounter. The most common errors are due to out-of-range values for some time elements. For instance, if you pass in a string '2003-10-14 10:67:00', the function will fail with an error indicating that minute 67 is out of the range 0..59.

Error Checking in Perl Scripts

Extensive error checking is a hallmark of any robust program. It's normal to see the error-checking code longer than the code that implements the problem-solving logic. In fact, in the grand scheme of things, you could very well argue that error checking is part of the problem-solving logic.

Regardless of what programming language you use, it's a constant struggle to decide how much error-checking code to include and where in a program to include error-checking code. In theory, you should check for errors whenever a statement may fail. Although every statement can fail, some statements are unlikely to fail. And if they do fail, you have a much larger problem to worry about than the failure to perform error checking.

I use two rules of thumb in deciding whether to place a piece of error-checking code in my Perl scripts. Be aware that I don't intend to score any comprehensiveness points with these rules:

- If failure to check for errors can cause the subsequent steps to produce misleading information or carry out potentially disastrous actions, error checking is a must.

- If failure to check for errors severely handicaps your debugging effort, error checking is in order. In other words, if you find yourself looking at an error message in great confusion as to where it came from, that's because error checking got a short shrift when the code was written.

The second rule is especially important when you're writing functions and function calls. Rigorous error checking where different components interface with each other will quickly point you to the real source of the problem, saving you much hair pulling.

While still on the topic of dealing with time in Perl, let me sneak in another SQLDBA::Utility function—dbaTime2str()—that converts a time in epoch seconds to a string in the YYYY/MM/DD hh:mm:ss format. The book frequently uses this function, which is shown in Listing 3-20.

Listing 3-20. The Function dbaTime2str()

```
1.   sub dbaTime2str {
2.       my ($time) = shift;
3.       $time = time() if !defined $time;
4.       $time =~ /^\d+$/ or die "***Err: dbaTime2str() expects an integer.";
5.
6.       my($sec, $min, $hour, $mday, $mon, $year, $wday, $yday, $isdst)
7.                             = localtime($time);
8.       sprintf ("%04d\/%02d\/%02d %02d:%02d:%02d ",
9.                     $year+1900, ++$mon, $mday, $hour, $min, $sec);
10. }  # dbaTime2str
```

The error-checking code on line 4 in Listing 3-20 is a perfect case in point for the second rule in the sidebar "Error Checking in Perl Scripts." The Perl built-in function localtime() doesn't carp even when you feed it an illegal alphabetic string; it'll just treat it as if it were zero. Without the error-checking code on line 4, the function call dbaTime2str('xyz') will silently produce the string '1969/12/31 19:00:00' if your computer is set to U.S. eastern standard time (EST). And if the returned string is used elsewhere in a large script, you'd be scratching your head over the weird result spit out of your script.

Line 8 uses `sprintf()` instead of `printf()` because the former returns a string and the latter prints to a file handle.

Finding the Difference in Two T-SQL Scripts

> **SCENARIO**
> *You want to find whether two T-SQL scripts are different and, if they're different, where they start to differ.*

To find whether two T-SQL scripts are different, use the function `dbaStringDiff()` exported by request from the module SQLDBA::Utility.

This function takes two strings and compares them. If there's no difference, it returns `undef`; otherwise, it returns a hash highlighting the difference. Listing 3-21 shows how to compare two T-SQL scripts.

Listing 3-21. Comparing Two T-SQL Scripts

```
use strict;
use SQLDBA::Utility qw( dbaStringDiff );
use Data::Dumper;

my $s1 =<<EofTSQL1;
   USE pubs
   go
   sp_help authors
   go
   SELECT * FROM authors
    WHERE au_id = '172-32-1176'
   go
EofTSQL1

my $s2 =<<EofTSQL2;
   USE pubs
   go
   EXEC sp_help authors
   go
   SELECT * FROM authors
    WHERE au_id = '172-32-1176'
   go
EofTSQL2

my $ref = dbaStringDiff($s1, $s2, 20);
print Dumper($ref);
```

Save the script in Listing 3-21 to the file codeDiff.pl. This is what it produces (for presentation, newlines have been removed from $VAR1->{diff}):

```
cmd>perl codeDiff.pl
$VAR1 = {
          diff => 'EXEC sp_help authors <> sp_help authors  go ',
          line => 3,
          pos => 21
        };
```

The function dbaStringDiff() detects a difference between the two T-SQL scripts and returns a reference to a hash with three values. The value of the diff key shows a fragment of the script where the two scripts start to differ. The third parameter of the function dbaStringDiff() specifies the length of this fragment. It's 20 in this case. The value of the line key indicates on which line the two scripts start to differ. Finally, the value of the pos key indicates at which character position the two scripts start to differ. In this example, the two scripts start to differ on line 3 at character position 21—counting from the beginning of the script.

By default, the comparison is case sensitive. If you want the comparison to be case insensitive, you can set the fourth parameter of dbaStringDiff() to 1.

Listing 3-22 shows the code for the function dbaStringDiff().

Listing 3-22. The Function dbaStringDiff()

```
sub dbaStringDiff {
   my($s1, $s2, $num, $case) = @_;
   $num = 20 unless $num =~ /\d+/;
   $case = 0 unless $case == 1;

   my @a1 = split(//, (length($s1) >= length($s2)) ? $s1: $s2);
   my @a2 = split(//, (length($s1) >= length($s2)) ? $s2: $s1);

   my $ref;
   my $longer = scalar @a1 > scalar @a2 ? scalar @a1 : scalar @a2;
   my $line = 1;
   for(my $i = 0; $i <= $longerer; $i++) {
      ++$line if $a1[$i] eq "\n";
      if ( ($case ? $a1[$i] : lc($a1[$i])) ne
           ($case ? $a2[$i] : lc($a2[$i])) ) {
         $ref = {
                 pos  => $i,
                 line => $line,
                 diff => join ('', @a1[$i..$i+$num], ' <> ', @a2[$i..$i+$num]),
```

```
        };
      last;
    }
  }
  return $ref;
} # dbaStringDiff
```

The comparison is performed by first breaking the strings into arrays of single characters using split(//, …) with a null pattern. In other words, there's nothing between the two consecutive forward slashes. To make it easier to capture the string fragments that start to differ, the array @a1 in Listing 3-22 is always assigned from the longer of the two strings. To find the longer string, the script uses the so-called *conditional* operator in the following statement:

```
my $longer = scalar @a1 > scalar @a2 ? scalar @a1 : scalar @a2;
```

The ternary ?: is the conditional operator. This is similar to the IIF() function in Visual Basic or a CASE expression in T-SQL. Recall that in a scalar context, an array returns the number of elements in the array. The scalar() function in this statement forces the scalar context.

The key part of the function in Listing 3-22 is the for loop that iterates through the arrays one character at a time and compares each character of the two arrays. The line position is determined by counting the number of newlines encountered. As soon as the function finds the first different character, the function populates the hash and returns with a reference to the hash.

This book primarily uses the function dbaStringDiff() to compare T-SQL scripts.

Persisting a Data Structure to a File

| **SCENARIO**
| *You want to persist a data structure to a file for future use.*

Persisting data means to write the data to some nonvolatile media. In the programming context, it invariably means writing a data structure from memory to a file on disk. Files can include plain text files such as Comma-Separated Value (CSV) or Extensible Markup Language (XML) files, internally structured binary files such as NT event log files and registry files, and the more sophisticated database files such as Microsoft Access database files and SQL Server data files.

Because my focus—as it's related to the Perl scripts for assisting SQL Server administration—is primarily to persist the status information used by these administrative scripts, I don't expect to deal with a tremendous amount of data. Consequently, the criteria of uniformity and ease of use are much more important than scalability. In this respect, Perl offers a perfect solution through the Data::Dumper module. Chapter 1, "Introducing Perl Basics," introduced you to this module for debugging complex data structures; now you'll use it to persist arbitrary data structures to text files in a simple and consistent fashion.

Of course, it won't be very useful if you can't read the persisted data from the file. Reading the persisted data is the topic of the next section. This section addresses how to write a data structure to a file. Listing 3-23 is an example of persisting a nested data structure.

Listing 3-23. Persisting a Data Structure

```
use strict;
use SQLDBA::Utility qw( dbaSaveRef );

my $statusFile = 'statusFile.txt';
my $statusVar = 'status';
my $ref = alertLogin();

dbaSaveRef($statusFile, $ref, $statusVar);

##################
sub alertLogin {
   # do some monitoring and alerting here
   # then, return a data structure
   my $statusRef = {
      NYSQL01 => {
         LastAlertedTime => '2003-01-03 20:10:52',
         LastFailedTime  => '2003-01-03 23:20:10',
         FailedConsecutiveTimes => 3
      },
      NJSQL01 => {
         LastAlertedTime => '2003-01-01 04:15:24',
         LastFailedTime  => '2003-01-03 22:25:45',
         FailedConsecutiveTimes => 2
      }
   };
   return $statusRef;
} # alertLogin
```

In Listing 3-23, the dummy function alertLogin() pretends to have performed some monitoring tasks and returns a reference to a data structure that records the status of monitoring in a hash of hashes. Save this script to the file saveRef.pl and run the script as follows:

```
cmd>perl saveRef.pl
```

The content of the text file statusFile.txt, whose name is hard-coded in Listing 3-23 for demonstration purposes, looks like Listing 3-24.

Listing 3-24. Data Structure Written to the File statusFile.txt

```
$status = {
            NJSQL01 => {
                            FailedConsecutiveTimes => 2,
                            LastAlertedTime => '2003-01-01 04:15:24',
                            LastFailedTime  => '2003-01-03 22:25:45'
                       },
            NYSQL01 => {
                            FailedConsecutiveTimes => 3,
                            LastAlertedTime => '2003-01-03 20:10:52',
                            LastFailedTime  => '2003-01-03 23:20:10'
                       }
          };
```

Not only is the data structure preserved in a file, but it should also be apparent that the data structure could be retrieved by evaluating the content of the file, as you'll soon see in the next section. Now, let's find out how the data structure is written to the file in the function dbaSaveRef(), shown in Listing 3-25.

Listing 3-25. The Function dbaSaveRef()

```
1.   sub dbaSaveRef {
2.       my ($file, $ref, $refVar) = @_;
3.
4.       open(DOC, ">$file") or
5.           die "***Err: unable to open $file for write.";
6.       print DOC Data::Dumper->Dump([$ref], [$refVar]);
7.       close(DOC);
8.   }  # dbaSaveRef
```

The function dbaSaveRef() accepts three parameters. The first parameter is the name of the file to which the data structure will be written. The second parameter is a reference to the data structure. The third parameter contains a string that will be the name of the variable. In the file, this variable will be assigned a reference to the data structure specified by the first parameter. This third parameter can be any string you like. Often, it will be intuitive so that if you need to examine the file visually, the name of the variable will help you understand what the data structure may represent.

The previous chapter introduced you to the Data::Dumper module and its exported function Dumper(). The module also has an object-oriented interface. In Listing 3-25, its method Dump() is used instead of the function Dumper(). You must use this method if you want to specify a name for the dumped data structure.

> **NOTE** *When I recommend the module Data::Dumper to persist a Perl data structure, I implicitly assume that the persisted data will later be read by the other Perl scripts. The data structure as written by* Data::Dumper->Dump() *won't be convenient if programs written in a different language need to access the persisted information. To accommodate interoperability, you may consider one of the XML modules such as XML::Simple, which can convert a Perl data structure to an XML document and read an XML document into a Perl data structure.*

Reading from a Persisted Data Structure

SCENARIO
You want to retrieve the data structure saved by the function dbaSaveRef() *from a text file and use the data structure in your script.*

Because what's written by the function dbaSaveRef() in Listing 3-25 is a string of a valid Perl statement, you can evaluate the string to get the data structure using the Perl built-in function eval().

The SQLDBA::Utility module exports the function dbaReadSavedRef() to read the data structure saved by the function dbaSaveRef(); in other words, the former does the reverse of the latter. Let's see how dbaReadSavedRef() is used in a script (see Listing 3-26) before considering how it's implemented.

Listing 3-26. Reading from a Persisted Data Structure

```
1.  use strict;
2.  use Data::Dumper;
3.  use SQLDBA::Utility qw( dbaReadSavedRef );
4.
5.  my $statusFile = 'statusFile.txt';
6.  my $ref = dbaReadSavedRef($statusFile);
7.  print Data::Dumper->Dump([$ref], [ 'status']);
```

Listing 3-26 assumes that the file statusFile.txt shown in Listing 3-24 is in the current directory. Otherwise, you should include the path of the file on line 5. The function dbaReadSavedRef() reads from this file and assigns a reference to the data structure to the $ref variable on line 6. To demonstrate that the data structure is indeed the same as it was written, the Dump() method from Data::Dumper prints the data structure to STDOUT on line 7, which should match the output shown in Listing 3-24.

I bet you can't wait to see how the function dbaReadSavedRef() actually gets the data structure back from the file. Listing 3-27 is a straightforward implementation.

Listing 3-27. The Function dbaReadSavedRef()

```
1.    sub dbaReadSavedRef {
2.        my($file) = shift or die "***Err: readSavedRef() expects a file name.";
3.
4.        my $refStr;
5.        open(DOC, "$file") or
6.            do { warn "***Err: couldn't open $file."; return undef };
7.        read(DOC, $refStr, -s DOC);
8.        close(DOC);
9.
10.    no strict 'vars';
11.    my $ref = eval $refStr;
12.    if ($@) {
13.       warn "***Msg: problem reading file $file. $@";
14.       print Dumper($ref);
15.       return undef;
16.    }
17.
18.    return $ref;
19. }  # dbaReadSavedRef
```

Several points are worth highlighting with regard to Listing 3-27. On line 7, the entire content of the file is read as a single string and is assigned to the variable $refStr using the Perl built-in function read(). This function reads the number of bytes as specified in its third parameter. Recall that the -s file operator returns the file size when applied to a filename or a file handle. Thus, -s DOC on line 7, where DOC is a file handle, causes the read() function to read all the bytes in the file.

Note that all the scripts in this book include the declaration use strict at the beginning of the code so that all variables must be declared before they're used. This function is no exception; you should expect it to be used in a script where use strict is in effect and program accordingly. On line 10, however, the declaration of no strict 'vars' reneges on the restriction. This is necessary because when the string from the file is evaluated on line 11, the script doesn't know what variable is used in the string. Even if you know, you have to explicitly declare the variable in dbaReadSavedRef(), which would severely limit the applicability of the function.

As far as the function dbaReadSavedRef() is concerned, exactly what variable is used in the string from the file is irrelevant; the value is assigned to a local variable $ref.

The data structure becomes accessible to the function—thus to the script that calls this function—through the evaluation on line 11. This is the very heart of the function dbaReadSavedRef(). Line 12 checks the predefined variable $@ for any error that eval() may have encountered.

TIP *If you don't want your script to crash when the string you read from the file turns out to be an invalid Perl statement, you can use the function* eval() *to trap fatal compilation or run-time errors. If* eval() *encountered such an error, the variable* $@ *is set to this error. Otherwise,* $@ *is set to false. The code evaluated by* eval() *may crash, but the code that calls* eval() *continues.*

Finally, note how the different errors are handled differently in the function dbaReadSavedRef(). On line 2, the function terminates the entire script if its expected filename isn't provided. Although it's reasonable to expect that you can't open the file or can't even find the file, it doesn't make sense that a filename isn't provided. On lines 6 and 13, however, an error message is printed to STDERR using the built-in function warn(), and this enables the dbaReadSavedRef() function to return undef instead of crashing the script. The file may be locked or its content may have been mangled. Whatever the cause may be, it's then up to the calling program to decide what to do next. For instance, the program may decide to skip this file and continue with the next one.

Querying Data in SQL Server via ADO

> **SCENARIO**
> *You want to run a T-SQL query and retrieve the results from SQL Server via ADO.*

You saw in Chapter 2, "Working with Commonly Used Perl Modules," that Perl can manipulate COM objects through Automation using the module Win32::OLE. Because ADO objects are exposed as Automation objects, you can use Perl to invoke the ADO objects to communicate with SQL Server.

Also, as mentioned, the primary challenge of controlling Automation objects in Perl lies not in mastering the Win32::OLE module but in understanding the specific object model—in this case, the ADO object model.

Applications using ADO to retrieve data from SQL Server typically go through these steps:

1. Obtaining a connection object, setting the connection properties, and connecting to a data source

2. Sending SQL queries to the data source and retrieving the results returned from the data source

3. Processing the results

4. Handling any errors or messages

5. Closing the connection to the data source

Unless you have special processing requirements, these steps repeat each time you run queries to retrieve data from SQL Server.

NOTE *I'm not suggesting you need to create a new connection for running each query. Because it's relatively expensive to open a connection, it's often more optimal to keep a connection or a pool of connections open.*

To simplify getting data from SQL Server in a DBA script, I've encapsulated these steps in the dbaRunQueryADO() function, which accepts a server name and a query or queries and then returns the results of the query in a Perl data structure. The function is included in the SQLDBA::Utility module. Listing 3-28 shows how you can take advantage of this function in your script.

Listing 3-28. Retrieving Data from SQL Server via ADO

```
1.   use strict;
2.   use Data::Dumper;
3.   use SQLDBA::Utility qw( dbaRunQueryADO );
4.
5.   my $sql = <<__TSQL__;
6.      USE pubs
7.      SET ROWCOUNT 3
8.      SELECT state, 'count' = count(*) FROM pubs..authors
9.      GROUP BY state
10.     SELECT au_id, au_lname, au_fname, phone FROM authors
11. __TSQL__
12.
13. my $ref = dbaRunQueryADO('NYSQL01\APOLLO', $sql, 3);
14. print Dumper($ref);
```

With the function dbaRunQueryADO(), the process of querying data from SQL Server is simplified to a few lines of code. The T-SQL queries are specified on lines 5 through 11 and are assigned to the $sql variable. These queries are then passed to the function dbaRunQueryADO() as a string along with the SQL Server instance name NYSQL01\APOLLO and the connection timeout threshold (3 seconds in this case). The reference to the resultsets returned from SQL Server is assigned to the variable $ref. Now, you can use the data from SQL Server however you want in the Perl script.

To see what result the function dbaRunQueryADO() actually produces, save the script in Listing 3-28 to the file adoQuery.pl. I ran the script on my workstation and received the output shown in Listing 3-29 (trimmed and annotated for presentation).

Listing 3-29. Data Structure of the Resultset from dbaRunQueryADO()

```
cmd>perl adoQuery.pl
$VAR1 = [
          [    # begin first inner array for the first resultset
            { # first record
              state => 'CA',
              count => 15
            },
            { # second record
              state => 'IN',
              count => 1
            },
            { # third record
              state => 'KS',
              count => 1
            }
          ],   # end first inner array for the first resultset
          [    # begin second inner array for the second resultset
            { # first record
              au_id => '172-32-1176',
              au_lname => 'White',
              phone => '408 496-7223',
              au_fname => 'Johnson'
            },
            { # second record
              au_id => '213-46-8915',
              au_lname => 'Green',
              phone => '415 986-7020',
              au_fname => 'Marjorie'
            },
            { # third record
              au_id => '238-95-7766',
              au_lname => 'Carson',
              phone => '415 548-7723',
              au_fname => 'Cheryl'
            }
          ]    # end second inner array for the second resultset
        ];
```

To understand the data structure in Listing 3-29, you should be aware that the function dbaRunQueryADO() supports queries that return multiple resultsets. In Listing 3-28, four T-SQL statements are assigned to the $sql variable. Among them, there are two SELECT statements, each of which returns a resultset.

At the top level of the data structure, the resultsets from SQL Server are represented as an array of arrays. There are as many inner arrays as there are resultsets returned from SQL Server. Each inner array, then, contains an array of hashes, each corresponding to a record of the resultset with the key being the field name. The printout in Listing 3-29 shows this data structure. The array of arrays preserves the order in which the resultsets are returned.

Before studying the implementation of dbaRunQueryADO(), you need to have some familiarity with the ADO object model. Altogether, the ADO object model exposes nine objects and four collections. However, you don't have to use all the objects or collections in an application. The code in the function dbaRunQueryADO() in Listing 3-30, to be presented shortly, uses only the following objects/collections:

Connection object: This object represents a session with SQL Server (or any other data source you may be accessing). This is the most fundamental object of ADO, and other objects are usually obtained through this object. Session properties are set through this object, and queries can be executed with its Execute() method.

Recordset object: This object represents the resultset of the query returned by SQL Server. If there are multiple resultsets, the recordset corresponding to the first resultset is returned first. Your script then needs to go through all the resultsets by enumerating all the Recordset objects.

Fields collection: This collection is obtained from a Recordset object and is made up of Field objects that correspond to the columns of the Recordset object.

Field object: This object represents a column of a record in the corresponding Recordset object. The properties of the column such as its name, type, and value are obtained via this object.

Now let's translate the steps outlined at the beginning of this section into the language of objects, properties, and methods. To query SQL Server via ADO, first you need to obtain a connection object—say $conn—with the new() method: $conn = Win32::OLE->new('ADODB.Connection'). Then, you set the properties—such as ConnectionTimeout—of the connection object and make a connection attempt to SQL Server with the Open() method. You specify the connection string as a parameter of the Open() method.

If you assign a series of SQL queries to a single string and run it in the Execute() method, you end up with multiple Recordset objects. The Execute() method returns the first Recordset object, and you can move to the next Recordset using the method NextRecordset(). For each recordset, you use MoveNext() to enumerate its records. Finally, for each record, you can enumerate the Fields collection to access the value of each column through its associated Field object.

Listing 3-30 shows how these steps are implemented in dbaRunQueryADO().

Listing 3-30. The Function dabRunQueryADO()

```
1.    sub dbaRunQueryADO {
2.        my ($server, $sql, $timeout) = @_;
3.
4.        my @results;
5.
6.        my $conn = Win32::OLE->new('ADODB.Connection') or
7.            do { warn "***Err: Win32::OLE->new() failed."; return undef; };
8.        $conn->{ConnectionTimeout} = $timeout || 4;
9.        $conn->Open("Provider=sqloledb;Server=$server;Trusted_Connection=yes");
10.       ! Win32::OLE->LastError() or
11.           do { warn Win32::OLE->LastError(); return undef; };
12.
13.       my $rs = $conn->Execute($sql) or
14.           do { warn Win32::OLE->LastError(); return undef; };
15.
16.       while ($rs) {
17.           my @resultset = ();
18.           if ( !defined $rs->{EOF} ) {
19.               $rs = $rs->NextRecordSet();
20.               next;
21.           }
22.           while ( !$rs->{EOF} ) {
23.               my $ref;
24.               foreach my $field ( in($rs->Fields()) ) {
25.                   $ref->{$field->{Name}} = $field->{Value};
26.               }
27.               push @resultset, $ref;
28.               $rs->MoveNext;
29.           }
30.           push @results, \@resultset;
31.           $rs = $rs->NextRecordSet();
32.       }
33.       $conn->Close();
34.       return \@results;
35. } # dbaRunQueryADO
```

The attempt to connect to SQL Server using the Windows authentication happens on line 9 with the OLE DB provider SQLOLEDB. Once the connection is established, the Execute() method of the connection object $conn executes on line 13 to send the queries in the $sql variable to SQL Server and to return the Recordset object $rs. The script then works with the resultset object to pull the data out from SQL Server.

It's important to distinguish two types of SQL statements—those that return a resultset and those that don't. Although the Recordset object $rs is always defined for a SQL statement of either type,[1] $rs->{EOF} will be undefined if the SQL statement doesn't return a resultset. Because you want the function dbaRunQueryADO() to work with any arbitrary SQL statement, the code between lines 18 and 21 is required:

```
if ( !defined $rs->{EOF} ) {
    $rs = $rs->NextRecordSet();
    next;
}
```

This code ensures that the script skips to the next resultset (or recordset in terms of the ADO object model) if the corresponding SQL statement doesn't return any resultset. If you remove this code segment, the script in Listing 3-28 will appear to hang.

This is what happens: Upon executing the first statement, which is use pubs, $rs->{EOF} will be undefined and will remain undefined. The while condition on line 22 in Listing 2-30, (!$rs->{EOF}), will therefore always be true, causing the script to never exit the loop. In fact, without the code segment between lines 18 and 21, any INSERT, DELETE, or UPDATE will also send the script to an infinite loop because these statements don't return any resultset either.

When a statement does return a resultset, even if it's empty, the code between lines 22 and 29 retrieves the value from each field in each record and populates a hash—for that record—whose keys are field names and whose values are the corresponding field values. A reference to the hash is then pushed into an array on line 27 when the iteration through the recordset is complete.

When the Fields collection is obtained for each record, the following code segment between lines 24 and 26 in Listing 3-30 populates the hash using the explicitly imported Win32::OLE function in() to enumerate the individual Field objects within the collection:

```
foreach my $field ( in($rs->Fields()) ) {
    $ref->{$field->{Name}} = $field->{Value};
}
```

Recall that from Chapter 2, "Working with Commonly Used Perl Modules," when the function in() is applied to a collection, it returns the objects in the collection in a list.

---

1. You can choose to prevent a Recordset object from being returned by setting additional parameters in the Execute() method. See the ADO documentation at http://msdn.microsoft.com for more details.

In T-SQL parlance, the series of SQL statements you can specify in the Execute() method of a connection object makes up a T-SQL *batch*. In scripting Perl for SQL Server administration, you'll find that it's convenient for dbaRunQueryADO() to allow a batch of queries instead of insisting on a single query. Sometimes, even that's not enough, and you'll want to run multiple batches of queries. The next section addresses this need.

The function dbaRunQueryADO() significantly simplifies the process of running a batch of T-SQL queries. It turns an otherwise involved procedure into a simple function call. With simplification, however, comes limitation. Not available through the interface of the function are many of the powerful features of ADO, such as performance optimization options and support for various cursor types. Once again, the primary purpose of the function dbaRunQueryADO() is to simplify the data retrieval for writing SQL Server administration scripts. In most cases, all you want is to get a tiny volume of data from SQL Server. For this purpose, dbaRunQueryADO() will do just fine without exposing the more advanced ADO features.

Executing a T-SQL Script via osql.exe

SCENARIO
You want to run a script that may contain many batches of T-SQL queries.

With the function dbaRunQueryADO() secured under your belt, you may consider first breaking the T-SQL script into individual batches and running each batch through dbaRunQueryADO(). This approach doesn't always work because each invocation
of dbaRunQueryADO() creates a new session, but the T-SQL script may require all queries to be run in the same session.

For instance, a script may create a temporary table at the beginning and then access this temporary table from a different batch later in the script. The temporary table won't be visible to a different batch if you break the script by batch and run each batch through dbaRunQueryADO().

The easiest way to run a multiple-batch T-SQL script from a Perl script is to invoke osql.exe.

The function dbaRunOsql() in Listing 3-31 accepts a server/instance name, a T-SQL script in a string, and a reference to a hash of osql.exe command-line options; executes the T-SQL script via osql.exe; and returns the result from osql.exe in a string.

Listing 3-31. The Function dbaRunOsql()

```
1.     sub dbaRunOsql {
2.         my ($instance, $sql, $optRef) = @_;
3.         return undef if (!defined $instance or !defined $sql);
4.
5.         my $sqlfile = "sql_tmp_" . time() . "_" . int(rand()*100000) .
6.                             int(rand()*100000) . ".sql";
7.         open(SQL, ">$sqlfile") or
8.             die "***Err: Could not open $sqlfile for write.";
9.         print SQL $sql;
10.        close(SQL);
11.
12.        my $optStr = ' ';
13.        foreach my $opt (keys %$optRef) {
14.            $optStr .= $opt . ' ' . $optRef->{$opt} . ' ';
15.        }
16.
17.        my $osql = "osql -S$instance -i$sqlfile $optStr 2>&1";
18.        my $rs = `$osql`;
19.        unlink($sqlfile);
20.        return $rs;
21.    }  # dbaRunOsql
```

The first two parameters, the server name and T-SQL script, are required because the function checks whether they're present on line 3 and returns undef if either is missing. When you use dbaRunOsql() in your script, you should treat a returned undef as an error condition.

The optional third parameter is a reference to a hash that can include all the other command-line options that you may specify for osql.exe. The keys are the option switches, and the values are the corresponding arguments. For a switch that doesn't accept any argument, an empty string should be assigned to the corresponding hash value if you want to include the switch in the osql.exe command line. For instance, to specify a database name, the Windows authentication, and the width of the output, you can pass the following hash reference to dbaRunOsql():

```
$optRef = {
   '-E' => '',
   '-d' => 'pubs',
   '-w' => '1024'
}
```

Because your Perl script will usually parse the results from osql.exe, you should set the output width to be sufficiently wide so that the lines don't wrap. It becomes nearly impossible to further process the text output if a line wraps around to multiple lines, destroying the expected format.

Before osql.exe can execute your T-SQL script, you need to write the script to a file first. Lines 5 and 6 in Listing 3-31 use a combination of the current time string and two large random numbers to construct a filename that has little chance of colliding with a duplicate. This file is deleted on line 19 immediately after osql.exe uses it. This isn't the perfect solution to generating a filename for a temporary file, but it's good enough for use in the DBA scripts in this book.

The osql.exe command line is prepared on line 17 in Listing 3-31. Although I have not encountered a case where osql.exe writes a message to STDERR, to be safe I've included 2>&1 on the command line to redirect STDERR to STDOUT. The $optStr string includes all the options specified in the hash %$optRef. Lines 13 through 15 concatenate the switches and their respective arguments into this single string. For simplicity, removed from Listing 3-31 is the error-checking code that verifies whether the options in the hash are legal for osql.exe.

The T-SQL script is then executed through osql.exe on line 18, using Perl's backtick operator, which was discussed in Chapter 1, "Introducing Perl Basics."

Listing 3-32 is an example of using dbaRunOsql() in a Perl script. It runs a T-SQL script to create a table, insert a few rows, and retrieve the rows from the table.

Listing 3-32. Using dbaRunOsql()

```perl
use strict;
use SQLDBA::Utility qw( dbaRunOsql );

my $sql =<<__SQL__;
  USE pubs
  go
  SET NOCOUNT on
  SET ROWCOUNT 2
  go
  IF OBJECT_ID('test') IS NOT NULL
      DROP TABLE test
  go
  PRINT 'Creating table test ...'
  CREATE TABLE test(id int, zip char(5))
  go
  PRINT 'Inserting into table test ...'
  INSERT test VALUES(1, '07410')
  INSERT test VALUES(2, '07302')
  INSERT test VALUES(3, '10024')
```

```
  go
  SELECT * FROM test
__SQL__

# specifying the osql command-line options
my $optRef = {
      '-E' =>  undef,
      '-n' =>  undef,
      '-w' => '1024',
      '-d' => 'pubs',
      '-l' => '5'
  };

my $result = dbaRunOsql('.\APOLLO', $sql, $optRef);
if (!defined $result) {
   die "***Err: failed to run osql.exe.";
}
else {
   print $result;
}
```

Save the Perl script in Listing 3-32 to the file runOsql.pl and run it from the command line as follows to see the result produced by the function dbaRunOsql():

cmd>perl runOsql.pl
```
Creating table test ...
Inserting into table test ...
 id      zip
 ------  ---------
      1  07410
      2  07302
```

Producing the Dependency Trees from the Immediate Dependencies

SCENARIO

You have obtained pairs of the immediate dependencies, and now you want to build a dependency tree from these dependency pairs.

In many problem-solving scenarios, obtaining the immediate dependencies of an element is easy. Sometimes, immediate dependencies are already available. For instance, each row of an employee table may identify a relationship between a manager and one of his direct reports. An example close to the SQL Server DBA is the task of finding the dependencies among stored procedures. For a given stored procedure, you can easily determine what procedures are called by it, thus identifying the immediate dependencies.

It gets a little more difficult if you start to ask for the complete chains of stored procedure calls beginning from a given stored procedure.

Perl's data structures make it easy to build the dependency trees. An intuitive way to represent immediate dependencies is a hash of arrays. The hash key represents an element, and its corresponding value is a reference to an array of its direct child elements. The following is an example that represents immediate dependencies among the stored procedures:

```
my $ref = {
        getOrder     => ['getStock', 'getPrice', 'seeCredit'],
        getStock     => ['getInStock', 'getOutStock'],
        getPrice     => ['calcDisc'],
        seeCredit    => ['isBad'],
        getInStock   => [ ],
        getOutStock  => ['getLog'],
        getLog       => [ ],
        calcDisc     => [ ],
        isBad        => [ ]
};
```

In this example, the procedure getOrder calls the procedures getStock, getPrice, and seeCredit. Listing 3-33 prints out the call tree for each stored procedure.

Listing 3-33. Producing Dependency Trees

```
use strict;
use Data::Dumper;

my $ref = {
        getOrder     => ['getStock', 'getPrice', 'seeCredit'],
        getStock     => ['getInStock', 'getOutStock'],
        getPrice     => ['calcDisc'],
        seeCredit    => ['isBad'],
        getInStock   => [ ],
        getOutStock  => ['getLog'],
        getLog       => [ ],
        calcDisc     => [ ],
        isBad        => [ ]
};

my $treeRef = dbaGetTree($ref, [ keys %$ref ], [ ]);
print "getOrder:\n", Dumper($treeRef->{getOrder});
```

```perl
print "seeCredit:\n", Dumper($treeRef->{seeCredit});


#################
sub dbaGetTree {
   my($lookupRef, $ref, $path) = @_;

   my $rc = { };
   foreach my $key (@$ref) {
      if (grep {$key eq $_} @$path) {
         push @$path, $key;
         die "***Err: circular dependency. " . join(', ', @$path);
      }
      my $newPath = [ @$path ];
      push @$newPath, $key;
      $rc->{$key} = dbaGetTree($lookupRef, $lookupRef->{$key}, $newPath);
   }
   return $rc;
}
```

I've included the function dbaGetTree() in Listing 3-33 for illustration purposes. It's bundled with the SQLDBA::Utility module. Save the script to the file getTree.pl. Running this script prints out the complete call tree for the procedure getOrder and the call tree for the procedure seeCredit as follows:

```
cmd>perl getTree.pl
getOrder:
$VAR1 = {
         getPrice => {
                         calcDisc => { }
                     },
         getStock => {
                         getInStock => { },
                         getOutStock => {
                                           getLog => { }
                                        }
                     },
         seeCredit => {
                         isBad => { }
                      }
        };
```

```
seeCredit:
$VAR1 = {
          isBad => { }
        };
```

The critical component in Listing 3-33 is of course the function dbaGetTree(), which recursively calls itself to construct the trees. Note that this function doesn't just produce a tree. It produces a dependency tree for each of the keys in the array referenced by its second parameter.

Disregard the third parameter for now. The strategy is to use the original hash as a constant lookup table so that each call to dbaGetTree() will always have access to the same immediate dependents of each element. Hence, the hash reference is passed as the first parameter in each invocation of dbaGetTree(), and the hash remains intact throughout the entire process.

The reference to an array of elements whose dependency trees you want to construct is passed in as the second parameter. For each element in the array, the function finds all its direct dependents. Now, it's a matter of finding the dependency trees for these direct dependent elements, which is essentially the same problem you begin with; therefore, the function itself is called with the reference to the array of the dependents as the second parameter. The recursion terminates when an element doesn't have any direct dependent.

There's a potential trap, though, in this procedure of constructing the dependency trees. That is, what if there's a circular dependency? In other words, you may have a case—though you really shouldn't—where A depends on B and C, C depends on E, and E in turn depends on A. The recursive procedure described in the previous paragraph will never terminate until it exhausts the computing resources and crashes.

The third parameter of the function dbaGetTree() prevents the function from falling into such a vicious infinite recursion by remembering the elements, which it has seen in its recursive path, in an array. Before the function is called again, it first checks whether the element is already in the path array. The code fragment that detects circular dependency is as follows:

```
if (grep {$key eq $_} @$path) {
    push @$path, $key;
    die "***Err: circular dependency. " . join(', ', @$path);
}
```

If the element is on the path, a circular dependency is detected and there's no point of continuing. The function prints an error message along with the elements in the path array at this moment to aid in debugging.

Splitting a T-SQL Script into Individual Batches

> **SCENARIO**
> *You want to split a T-SQL script into individual batches and preserve the order of the batches.*

You can split the script into T-SQL batches by using the batch terminator GO.

T-SQL batches are terminated with the word GO. However, when trying to split the batches, you need to be careful about the exact pattern you can use. If you check the SQL Server Books Online, it doesn't tell much about the exact syntax of GO.

With Query Analyzer, `osql.exe`, and `isql.exe`, GO should really be the only word on a separate line, and there should be no whitespace before GO. Let's do a small test on the syntactic requirements of the T-SQL batch terminator. Run the following T-SQL script in Query Analyzer, `osql.exe`, or `isql.exe`:

```
select 3
  go  -- comment
Select 4
go -- comment
```

You'll receive this result:

```
go
-----------
3

go
-----------
4
```

This is most likely not what you expected. Apparently, because of the trailing comment, the batch terminator isn't treated as such and is sent to SQL Server as part of the query in a single batch. SQL Server in turn considers the word go as a column alias.

The pattern to split T-SQL batches should therefore be `/\ngo\s*\n/i`; Listing 3-34 is an example of splitting a T-SQL script into individual batches.

Listing 3-34. Splitting T-SQL Batches

```
use strict;
use Data::Dumper;

my $sql =<<END_SQL;
USE pubs
go
sp_help
go
sp_helpdb
go

END_SQL

print Dumper(dbaSplitBatch($sql));

####################
sub dbaSplitBatch {
  my ($sql) = shift or die"***Err: dbaSplitBatch() expects a string.";

  $sql =~ s/^\s*\n//;
  my @batches = split(/\ngo\s*\n/i, $sql);

  \@batches;
} # dbaSplitBatch
```

With the sample T-SQL script embedded in Listing 3-34, the output is as follows:

```
$VAR1 = [
          'use pubs',
          'sp_help',
          'sp_helpdb'
        ];
```

As expected, the three batches are correctly split. The function dbaSplitBatch() is exported by request from the SQLDBA::ParseSQL module.

Normalizing a T-SQL Script

SCENARIO

You want to convert a T-SQL script into a format so that you can apply a regular expression without worrying about it matching a pattern inside a comment, a quoted string, or a delimited identifier in the T-SQL script.

Using regular expressions alone, you can mine T-SQL scripts and find useful information otherwise buried in there. However, comments, quoted strings, and delimited identifiers in a T-SQL script may mislead your regular expression to produce spurious results and sometimes completely derail your pattern matching efforts. Rarely—actually, never in the cases I've ever dealt with—would you care about any pattern in a comment, a quoted string, or a delimited identifier.

The solution is to first convert the T-SQL script to a format in which each of these pesky items—comments, quoted strings, and delimited identifiers—is replaced with a unique token string that's strictly alphanumeric. Each such replacement is recorded in a data structure so that later when you're done with whatever work you need to do on the converted script, you can restore each token string to its corresponding original, if necessary.

More specifically, assuming that the string `ls_token_7634364` has been verified to not be in the T-SQL script file, this string will be used as the token seed. Each time an item—a comment, a quoted string, or a delimited identifier—is found, a sequence number is appended to this token seed to create the unique token string for that item.

> **NOTE** *I just happened to pick* `ls_token` *as the prefix for the unique token strings I'll use to replace comments, quoted strings, and delimited identifiers. You can pick any strings you like as long as they're guaranteed to be unique.*

In addition, the data structure illustrated in Listing 3-35 will be used to record the replacement of the item along with the converted T-SQL script. Because each token string is unique and every replacement is recorded as a key-to-value mapping in a hash inside the data structure, you can use this data structure to restore the converted T-SQL script to its exact original.

Listing 3-35. The Data Structure for Converting and Restoring a T-SQL Script

```
$ref = {   code => '/* ls_token_7634364_1*/ SELECT * from ...',   # converted T-SQL
           comments => {  ls_token_7634364_1 => 'a comment',
                          ls_token_7634364_4 => 'another comment' },
           strings  => { ls_token_7634364_2 => 'a string',
                         ls_token_7634364_3 => 'another string'  },
           double_ids  => { ls_token_7634364_5 => '"Order Detail"' },
           bracket_ids => { ls_token_7634364_6 => '[Trade DB]',
                            ls_token_7634364_7 => '[Stock DB]'  }
       };
```

The converted T-SQL code is in the value of the hash key code. The replacement is performed as follows to guarantee that the original comments, quoted strings, and delimited identifiers can be restored. The replacement strings in the following are arbitrarily chosen for illustration purposes:

- **ANSI comments**: Replace the ANSI comment with the string --ls_token_7634364_1 and record the replacement in the data structure.

- **Quoted comments**: Replace the comment (quoted with /* and */) with the string /*ls_token_7634364_4*/ and record the replacement in the data structure.

- **Quoted strings**: Replace the quoted string with the string 'ls_token_763464_2' and record the replacement in the data structure.

- **Double-quoted delimited identifiers**: Replace the delimited identifier with the string "ls_token_7634364_5" and record the replacement in the data structure.

- **Bracket-quoted delimited identifiers**: Replace the delimited identifier with the string [ls_token_7634364_6] and record the replacement in the data structure.

The code that implements this replacement is in the function dbaNormalizeSQL() exported by request from the SQLDBA::ParseSQL module. Listing 3-36 shows the script of the function dbaNormalizeSQL() along with that of the function dbaGetUniqueToken(), which scans the T-SQL to obtain the token seed and verify its uniqueness.

Although it's not shown, use Parse::RecDescent is already declared in SQLDBA::ParseSQL before these functions. Listing 3-36 heavily depends on the

Parse::RecDescent module. For a brief introduction of this module, refer to
Chapter 2, "Working with Commonly Used Perl Modules."

Listing 3-36. The Functions dbaNormalizeSQL() *and* dbaGetUniqueToken()

```
sub dbaNormalizeSQL {
   my ($script, $option) = @_;
   $script or die "***Err: dbaNormalizeSQL() expects a string.";

# $option == 0   strip off the comments from the code
# $option == 1   normalize but preserve the comments

   my $tokenSeed = dbaGetUniqueToken($script);

   use vars qw( $seed $opt);

   my $grammar=<<'END_SQLGRAMMAR';
      {  my $cnt;
         my $sqlRef = {  code         => '',
                         double_ids   => { },
                         bracket_ids  => { },
                         comments     => { },
                         strings      => { }
                      };
      }
      program : <skip:''> part(s) /\z/ { $sqlRef }

      part    :    comment
                 | string
                 | double_identifier
                 | bracket_identifier
                 | rest_of_SQL_code
      comment :
          ansi_comment
            { ++$cnt;
              if ($SQLDBA::ParseSQL::opt == 1) {
                 $sqlRef->{code} .= '--' . $SQLDBA::ParseSQL::seed . $cnt . "\n";
              }
              else {
                 $sqlRef->{code} .= ' ';
              }
              $sqlRef->{comments}->{$SQLDBA::ParseSQL::seed . $cnt} = $item[1];
            }
          | delimited_comment
```

```
        { ++$cnt;
          if ($SQLDBA::ParseSQL::opt == 1) {
            $sqlRef->{code} .= '/*' . $SQLDBA::ParseSQL::seed . $cnt . "*/";
          }
          else {
            $sqlRef->{code} .= ' ';
          }
          $sqlRef->{comments}->{$SQLDBA::ParseSQL::seed . $cnt} = $item[1];
        }


ansi_comment :        m{ --([^\n]*)\n }x      { $1 }
delimited_comment :   simple_comment    { $item[1] }
                    | nested_comment    { $item[1] }
simple_comment :
          comment_opener pure_comment(s?) comment_closer
                { $item[1] . join('', @{$item[2]}) . $item[3] }
nested_comment :
          comment_opener raw_comment(s) comment_closer
                { $item[1] . join('', @{$item[2]}) . $item[3] }
raw_comment :
          pure_comment(?) delimited_comment pure_comment(?)
             { join('', @{$item[1]}) . $item[2] . join('', @{$item[3]}) }
comment_opener :  m{ /\* }x       { '' }
comment_closer :  m{ \*/ }x       { '' }
pure_comment :
                  m{ (?:   [^*/]+       # no * or /
                       |   \*(?!/)      # if *, then not followed by /
                       |   \/(?!\*)     # if /, then not followed by *
                      )+
                  }x    { $item[1] }

rest_of_SQL_code  :
                  m{( [^\"/'\-\[]+      # one or more non-delimiters
                       (               # then (optionally)...
                           /[^*]       # not an actual comment opener
                         |             # or
                          -[^\-]
                       )?              #
                     )+                # all repeated once or more
                  }x
                  { $sqlRef->{code} .= $item[1] }
string  : m{ \'(((^\'] | (\'\'))*)\'}x
          { ++$cnt;
              $sqlRef->{code}
                  .= "\'" . $SQLDBA::ParseSQL::seed . $cnt . "\'";
```

```
                              $sqlRef->{strings}->{$SQLDBA::ParseSQL::seed . $cnt} = $1;
                      }
            double_identifier :
              m{ \" (([^\"] | (\"\"))+) \" }x
                  { ++$cnt;
                    $sqlRef->{code} .= $SQLDBA::ParseSQL::seed . $cnt;
                    $sqlRef->{double_ids}->{$SQLDBA::ParseSQL::seed . $cnt} = $1;
                  }
            bracket_identifier :
              m{ \[ (([^\]] | \]\])+) \] }x
                  { ++$cnt;
                    $sqlRef->{code} .= $SQLDBA::ParseSQL::seed . $cnt;
                    $sqlRef->{bracket_ids}->{$SQLDBA::ParseSQL::seed . $cnt} = $1;
                  }
END_SQLGRAMMAR

    ($seed, $opt) = ($tokenSeed, $option);
    my $parser = Parse::RecDescent->new($grammar)  or
          die "***Err: invalid TSQL grammar.";
    my $sqlRef = $parser->program($script) or
          print "***Err: malformed TSQL script.\n";
    return $sqlRef;
} # dbaNormalizeSQL


##########################
sub dbaGetUniqueToken {
    my ($script) = shift or
        die "***Err: dbaGetUNiqueToken() expects a string.";

    my $tokenSeed = 'ls_token_123456_';
    while ($script =~ /$tokenSeed/i) {
        $tokenSeed = 'ls_token' . '_' . int(rand(100000)) . '_';
    }
    return $tokenSeed;
} # dbaGetUniqueToken
```

In the function dbaNormalizeSQL(), two variables, $seed and $opt, are declared global variables with use vars qw($seed $opt). This declaration is necessary because the variables are used inside the grammar and in the generated parser, which evaluates in a different namespace.

Using a Simple T-SQL Grammar

Let's first look at the RecDescent grammar used in the function `dbaNormalizeSQL()`.
If you strip off all the actions—in other words, the blocks of Perl code—the T-SQL
grammar is as shown in Listing 3-37.

Listing 3-37. A Simple T-SQL Grammar with No Action Items

```
program : <skip:''> part(s) /\z/
part    :     comment
            | string
            | double_identifier
            | bracket_identifier
            | rest_of_SQL_code
comment :   ansi_comment
          | delimited_comment
ansi_comment : m{ --([^\n]*)\n }x
delimited_comment :   simple_comment
                    | nested_comment
simple_comment :
          comment_opener pure_comment(s?) comment_closer
nested_comment :
          comment_opener raw_comment(s) comment_closer
raw_comment :
          pure_comment(?) delimited_comment pure_comment(?)
comment_opener :  m{ /\* }x
comment_closer :  m{ \*/ }x
pure_comment :
              m{ (?:   [^*/]+       # no * or /
                     | \*(?!/)      # if *, then not followed by /
                     | \/(?!\*)     # if /, then not followed by *
                  )+
              }x
rest_of_SQL_code :
              m{ ( [^\"/'\-\[]+ # one or more non-delimiters
                   (            # then (optionally)...
                      /[^*]     # not an actual comment opener
                    |           # or
                     -[^\-]
                   )?           #
                 )+             # all repeated once or more
              }x
string :            m{ \' (([^\'] | (\'\'))*) \' }x
double_identifier :  m{ \" (([^\"] | (\"\"))+) \" }x
bracket_identifier : m{ \[ (([^\]] | \]\])+) \] }x
```

This grammar views a T-SQL script as consisting of a series of parts, and each part can be any of the following:

- A T-SQL comment

- A string

- A square bracket–quoted identifier

- A double-quoted identifier

- A piece of code that's not a comment, a string, or a delimited identifier

A comment can be an ANSI comment, which is two consecutive dashes (--) followed by any characters up to the next newline, or a comment delimited with /* and */. It takes a few more rules to define the delimited comment because it allows delimited comments to be nested.

Both strings and delimited identifiers are easy to define (see their specifications in the last three rules in Listing 3-37). Note that a single-quoted string must escape any embedded single quote with another single quote. Similarly, any embedded double quote in a double-quoted identifier must be escaped with another double quote. For an identifier quoted with square brackets, it doesn't need to escape any opening bracket, but it must escape any closing bracket with another closing bracket.

The rest of the grammar—specified by the appropriately named rule rest_of_SQL_code—consists of any string that doesn't contain any single quote, double quote, or opening square bracket. It can include a forward slash not followed by an asterisk or a dash not followed by another dash.

Understanding Actions in the Simple T-SQL Parser

The generated parser uses the actions added to Listing 3-37 to accomplish two objectives:

- They identify all the comments, quoted strings, and delimited identifiers in the T-SQL script and replace them with unique token strings.

- They populate the data structure illustrated in Listing 3-35 and return the data structure to the script that calls the parser.

Let's examine the parser actions in the function dbaNormalizeSQL() in Listing 3-36. The first thing to notice is the block of code before the first rule of the grammar. This is a so-called *startup action* that can execute any valid Perl code within the parser's namespace. Typically, though, a startup action declares and initializes variables local to the parser's namespace.

In Listing 3-36, two variables are initialized for the parser: $cnt, which keeps track of the sequence number that will be appended to the token seed, and $sqlRef, which is the reference to the data structure the parser will eventually return to the calling script. During the parsing, every time a comment, a quoted string, or a delimited identifier is found, the variable $cnt is incremented by one, and its replacement is recorded in $sqlRef. Note that the $sqlRef variable is used throughout every step in the parsing. At any point, $sqlRef->{code} always contains the T-SQL code that has been parsed up to that point.

On this first rule of the grammar:

```
program : <skip:''> part(s) /\z/  { $sqlRef }
```

the pattern /\z/ is true only at the end of the string being parsed. Therefore, the rule item part(s) must match all the way to the end of the T-SQL script, and the trailing action returns the reference $sqlRef only if the entire T-SQL script is completely parsed. In Listing 3-36, this reference is returned by the method $parser->program() at the bottom of the function dbaNormalizeSQL().

The special action in angle brackets is a parser directive. By default, Parse::RecDescent automatically skips any whitespace between the grammar terminals. This is convenient in most cases but not in this case where you want to preserve every character in the T-SQL code, including any whitespace, so that you can later restore the code to its exact original. Therefore, <skip: ''> is included to instruct the parser not to skip anything at all.

Let's dissect the actions in the rule comment:

```
comment :
    ansi_comment
      { ++$cnt;
        if ($SQLDBA::ParseSQL::opt == 1) {
           $sqlRef->{code} .= '--' . $SQLDBA::ParseSQL::seed . $cnt . "\n";
        }
        else {
           $sqlRef->{code} .= ' ';
        }
        $sqlRef->{comments}->{$SQLDBA::ParseSQL::seed . $cnt} = $item[1];
      }
```

This says that if the `ansi_comment` subrule is matched, the parser should perform the following:

- Advance the variable `$cnt` by one (in other words, `++$cnt`).

- If the option `$opt` is set to `1` in the second parameter of the function `dbaNormalizeSQL()`, then replace the original comment with a new comment generated by the concatenation of `--`, `$SQLDBA::ParseSQL::seed`, `$cnt`, and `\n` and append the new comment to the code in `$sqlRef->{code}`. Note that both the variable `$opt` and the variable `$seed` are declared outside the parser in the function `dbaNormalizeSQL()`, which is in the SQLDBA::ParseSQL module—a different package and therefore a different namespace—than the parser; thus, you need the package prefix in front of these variables.

- If the option `$opt` isn't set, a single space is appended to `$sqlRef->{code}` in place of the original comment, effectively removing the comment from the converted T-SQL script. Note that if you don't set this option to `1`, you won't be able to restore the converted T-SQL script to its original. In many cases, you simply want to remove the comments and look for information in the script, and you don't care about restoring the code back to the original state.

- Finally, the comment, which is returned in `$item[1]`, is assigned to the hash key `$sqlRef->{comments}->{$SQLDBA::ParseSQL::seed . $cnt}`. Hence, `$sqlRef` remembers the mapping from a token string to the original comment.

The actions for other rules in the grammar are all similar. Once they've found an item (a comment, a quoted string, or a delimited identifier), they advance the sequence counter `$cnt`, perform the replacement, append the item to the T-SQL code in `$sqlRef->{code}`, and record the replacement in the appropriate hash in `$sqlRef`.

Normalizing a T-SQL Script

Now, let's see how you can use the function `dbaNormalizeSQL()` to *normalize* a T-SQL script and see what it actually produces. Listing 3-38 shows a Perl script—in the file `normalizeSQL.pl`—that uses this function to normalize a T-SQL script file whose name is specified on the command line.

Listing 3-38. Normalizing a T-SQL Script

```
use strict;
use SQLDBA::ParseSQL qw( dbaNormalizeSQL dbaRestoreSQL );
use Data::Dumper;

my $file = shift or die "***Err: $0 expects a file name.";

my $sql;
open(SQL, "$file") or die "***Err: couldn't open $file for read.";
read(SQL, $sql, -s SQL);
close(SQL);

my $sqlRef = dbaNormalizeSQL($sql, 1);
print Dumper($sqlRef);

$sqlRef= dbaRestoreSQL($sqlRef);
print $sqlRef->{code};
```

To show what `normalizeSQL.pl` produces, I'll apply it to the following syntactically legal T-SQL script, which has all the pesky pieces you want to avoid in a pattern matching (comments, quoted strings, and delimited identifiers):

```
USE pubs
go
-- create proc
CREATE PROCEDURE [dbo].[place Order]
AS
/* created by: Linchi Shea */

-- EXEC another proce
EXEC @rc = "check Customer" 'Joe Blow',
                           'Executive'
GO
```

Let's save this T-SQL script to the file `testSP.sql` and run the following from the command line. The output from `print Dumper($sqlRef)` appears after the command line (the value of the hash key `'code'` is indented for readability):

```
cmd>perl normalizeSQL.pl testSP.sql
$VAR1 = {
          'double_ids' => {
                            'ls_token_123456_6' => 'check Customer'
                      },
          'comments' => {
                      'ls_token_123456_1' => ' create proc',
                      'ls_token_123456_4' => ' created by: Linchi Shea ',
                      'ls_token_123456_5' => ' EXEC another proce'
                    },
          'strings' => {
                      'ls_token_123456_7' => 'Joe Blow',
                      'ls_token_123456_8' => 'Executive'
                    },
          'bracket_ids' => {
                            'ls_token_123456_2' => 'dbo',
                            'ls_token_123456_3' => 'place Order'
                      }
          'code' => 'use pubs
                      go
                      --ls_token_123456_1
                      CREATE PROCEDURE ls_token_123456_2.ls_token_123456_3
                      AS
                      /*ls_token_123456_4*/

                      --ls_token_123456_5
                      EXEC @rc = ls_token_123456_6 \'ls_token_123456_7\',
                                              \'ls_token_123456_8\'
                      GO',
        };
```

The token seed chosen for normalizing this T-SQL script is 'ls_token_123456_', which doesn't match any character string already in the T-SQL script.

With the T-SQL code normalized and recorded in $sqlRef->{code}, you can now proceed to perform regular-expression pattern matching on the code without worrying about being misled by patterns in a comment, a quoted string, or a delimited identifier.

Restoring the Original T-SQL Code

From the module SQLDBA::ParseSQL, Listing 3-38 also imports the function dbaRestoreSQL(), which takes the reference to the data structure, say $sqlRef, returned by the function dbaNormalizeSQL() and replaces all the token strings in $sqlRef->{code} with their corresponding originals (the comments, the quoted strings, or the delimited identifiers).

In Listing 3-38, print $sqlRef->{code} at the end, immediately after $sqlRef = dbaRestoreSQL($sqlRef), produces this:

```
use pubs
go
-- create proc
CREATE PROCEDURE [dbo].[place Order]
AS
/* created by: Linchi Shea */

-- EXEC another proce
EXEC @rc = "check Customer" 'Joe Blow',
                            'Executive'
GO
```

which is the original T-SQL script.

To reiterate, the function dbaNormalizeSQL() is enormously useful to analyze T-SQL scripts. It permits the analysis to take full advantage of Perl's powerful regular expressions without worrying about matching strings that aren't supposed to be matched.

Implementing the Replace-Match-Restore Strategy

> **SCENARIO**
> *You want to avoid matching a pattern inside a T-SQL comment, a quoted string, or a delimited identifier.*

Let's dwell a little longer on the potential problems you may face when using regular expressions to look for useful information bits and bytes in a T-SQL script.

When Simple Search-and-Replace Doesn't Work

In case you're wondering what the fuss is all about and why you don't just carefully construct your regular expressions to avoid these pesky comments, quoted strings, or delimited identifiers, the answer is that it's not possible to craft clever regular expressions to avoid them in all cases. If you've tried, you probably have already discovered that no sooner than you plug one hole in a regular expression, another surfaces.

To appreciate the difficulty of crafting regular expressions to avoid or find T-SQL comments, quoted strings, and delimited identifiers, consider the following cases of valid T-SQL syntax:

- A comment may include a pattern that appears to be a delimited identifier. This must be ignored.

- A comment delimited with /* and */ may be arbitrarily nested.

- A SQL string may include a pattern that appears to be a delimited identifier. This must be ignored.

- A pair of /* and */ inside a delimited identifier doesn't quote a SQL comment.

What these examples imply is that instead of crafting unrelated regular expressions to deal with various cases, you must handle comments, quoted strings, and delimited identifiers in a T-SQL script simultaneously.

Using the Replace-Match-Restore Strategy

Fortunately, the SQLDBA Toolkit provides a straightforward way to handle these complexities and makes it easy to apply Perl's powerful regular expressions without worrying about T-SQL comments, quoted strings, and delimited identifiers.

The solution is to use the functions dbaNormalizeSQL() and dbaRestoreSQL() exported by the module SQLDBA::ParseSQL. As mentioned in the preceding section, the former transforms a T-SQL script into a normalized form in which the patterns you look for won't be in T-SQL comments, quoted strings, or delimited identifiers without altering anything else in the T-SQL script. You accomplish this by replacing comments, quoted strings, and delimited identifiers with unique token strings. The function dbaRestoreSQL() replaces the meaningless unique token strings with their original comments, quoted strings, and delimited identifiers—hence restoring the T-SQL script.

With the functions `dbaNormalizeSQL()` and `dbaRestoreSQL()` you have a simple generic strategy to deal with the complications caused by T-SQL comments, quoted strings, and delimited identifiers. The strategy works as follows:

1. Before searching a T-SQL script for any useful information, you apply the function `dbaNormalizeSQL()` to convert the script to the normalized format. In this format, each comment, quoted string, or delimited identifier is replaced with a token string that's unique throughout the T-SQL script. The token string is constructed in two steps. First, a string that's unique throughout the script is generated and is used as the seed. Then, as the T-SQL script is being parsed by the function `dbaNormalizeSQL()`, for each new occurrence of comments, quoted strings, or delimited identifiers, a sequence number is appended to the seed token string to make a new token that will replace the current comment, quoted string, or delimited identifier. Note that these token strings are strictly alphanumeric.

2. Apply regular expressions to search for whatever information that's deemed important for solving your problem and perform any actions necessary. This is where you solve your problem.

3. If required, replace the unique token strings with their corresponding originals using the function `dbaRestoreSQL()`. Not all problems require this step.

This generic strategy is extremely useful when you want to fully exploit the power of the Perl regular expressions without having to worry about matching something that shouldn't be matched. You'll see this generic strategy being used repeatedly throughout this book. To make it simple to refer to, I'll call it the *replace-match-restore strategy.*

Parsing Qualified Database Object Names

SCENARIO
You want to parse a qualified database object name to obtain its individual identifiers such as database name, owner name, and object name.

In T-SQL, the name of a database object, such as a table or a stored procedure, may be qualified by its owner, by its database name, or by both. All of the following are acceptable in specifying the `authors` table in the `pubs` database:

```
authors
dbo.authors
pubs..authors
pubs.dbo.authors
```

Life was easy before the delimited identifiers were allowed in SQL Server and has become much more complex ever since. Now, all of the following are legal names:

```
[Order Detail]
"dbo".[Order Detail]
[Order DB].dbo."Order Detail"
[Order ]]DB].dbo."Order ""Detail"
```

Your Perl script that analyzes T-SQL scripts must accommodate all these possibilities. The code that parses a T-SQL multipart database object name is in the function dbaParseQDON(), which is exported by request from the module SQLDBA::ParseSQL. Listing 3-39 is a script that demonstrates using dbaParseQDON(). To simplify exposition, I've included the code of the function in the script.

Listing 3-39. Parsing Qualified Database Object Name

```
1.    use strict;
2.    use Data::Dumper;
3.
4.    my $name = 'pubs."dbo".[qeire[[[ """sd]][]]fda]';
5.    print Dumper(dbaParseQDON($name));
6.
7.    #####################
8.    sub dbaParseQDON {
9.       my $name = shift or die "***Err: dbaParseQDON() expects a string.";
10.      my $obj = q/   [\w@#]+
11.                  |  \" (?: [^\"]|\"\")+ \"
12.                  |  \[ (?: [^\]]|\]\])+ \]
13.             /;
14.      my $re = qr{   ($obj)\.($obj)?\.($obj)
15.               |  (?:($obj)\.)?($obj)
16.            }ix;
17.      my $ref;
18.      if ($name =~ /^\s*$re\s*$/ix) {
19.         $ref = {
20.            db    => $1,
21.            owner => (defined $2 ? $2 : $4),
22.            obj   => (defined $3 ? $3 : $5)
23.         };
24.      }
25.      return $ref;
26.  } # dbaParseQDON
```

The three-part name specified on line 4 is strictly for demonstration purpose. You'd be crazy to use a name like that in your database. Nevertheless, you must prepare your script to deal with such a possibility. Save the script in Listing 3-39 to the file parseQDON.pl and run it at the command line as follows:

```
cmd>perl parseQDON.pl
$VAR1 = {
          'db'    => 'pubs',
          'obj'   => '[qeire[[[ """sd]][[]]fda]',
          'owner' => '"dbo"'
        };
```

Now, let's look at the code in the function dbaParseQDON(), which works with three-part names in the format of database.owner.object. The database and owner are optional. The regular expression string for parsing a qualified database object name is constructed in two steps: a regular expression for an individual name and a regular expression for matching various combinations of the three names.

The string defined between lines 10 and 13 matches an individual T-SQL identifier. Its three alternatives correspond to a regular identifier, a double-quoted identifier, and an identifier quoted with square brackets. Note that in a regular expression, the (?:PATTERN) notation means that the parentheses don't capture a substring that matches the pattern. In other words, Perl doesn't assign the substring that matches PATTERN to any of the $1, ..., $N predefined variables. The q// operator is equivalent to single quotes, keeping whatever inside as is without variable interpolation. To reiterate, $obj isn't a regular expression. Rather, it's a string that represents a regular-expression fragment to be used in a regular expression later on lines 14 and 15.

The regular expression defined between lines 14 and 16 focuses on the various combinations of the three individual identifiers in forming a qualified database object name:

```
14.    my $re = qr{   ($obj)\.($obj)?\.($obj)   # three-part name
15.                  | (?:($obj)\.)?($obj)       # two- or one-part name
16              }ix;
```

Notice how the individual identifiers are captured with the parentheses in the regular expression. It's easy to capture the database name if it's specified because it always comes first. The owner name can come in the second pair of parentheses or in the fourth pair of parentheses, and the object name can be either in the third pair of parentheses or in the fifth pair of parentheses, depending on how the name is qualified.

The qr/STRING/ operator used on line 14 in Listing 3-39 defines and compiles the STRING as a regular expression. Any variable in the STRING—$obj in this case—is interpolated. The regular expression is actually used on line 18 in the =~ operator. Line 21 and line 22 evaluate which pair of parentheses to use for the owner and the object, respectively.

Retrieving the Service Accounts

SCENARIO
You want to find the Windows account used by a service.

Use the QueryServiceConfig() function available from the module Win32::Lanman, which is bundled with ActivePerl.

To shield the details of using QueryServiceConfig(), Listing 3-40 implements the function dbaGetServiceAccount() in the module SQLDBA::Security. The dbaGetServiceAccount() function accepts a server name and a service name, and it returns the Windows account running the service.

Listing 3-40. The Function dbaGetServiceAccount()

```
sub dbaGetServiceAccount {
   my ($server, $service) = @_;

   my %srvConfig;
   if(!Win32::Lanman::QueryServiceConfig("\\\\$server", '',
                                    $service,\%srvConfig)) {
     warn "***Err: Lanman::QueryServiceConfig encountered an error for " .
             "$server and $service. " . Win32::Lanman::GetLastError() ;
     return;
   }
   $srvConfig{'account'} =~ s/\.\\/$server\\/;
   return $srvConfig{'account'};
}
```

Implicit in Listing 3-40 is the assumption that use Win32::Lanman is already declared in the module file where this function resides, which is site\lib\SQLDBA\Security.pm under the Perl root.

When there's no error, the function QueryServiceConfig() populates a hash—%srvConfig in Listing 3-40—whose reference is specified in the fourth parameter. The hash includes a number of useful service configuration options such as the executable of the service, the service startup mode, and of course the service account. Listing 3-40 uses only the 'account' key of the hash to retrieve the name of the service account.

Because a service account that's a local account instead of a domain account may represent the name of the machine with a dot (.), the following statement replaces the dot with the real machine name:

```
$srvConfig{'account'} =~ s/\.\\/$server\\/;
```

Listing 3-41 shows how you can use the function dbaGetServiceAccount() to print out the accounts for a list of services.

Listing 3-41. Finding the Service Accounts for Multiple Machines

```
use strict;
use SQLDBA::Security qw( dbaGetServiceAccount );

my %services = ( NYSQL1 => ['MSSQLServer', 'MSSQL$APOLLO', 'SQLServerAgent'],
                 NYSQL2 => ['MSSQLServer', 'SQLServerAgent'] );

foreach my $server (keys %services) {
   foreach my $service (@{$services{$server}}) {
       my $acct = dbaGetServiceAccount($server, $service);
       print "Server: $server, Service: $service, Account: $acct\n";
   }
}
```

Save the script in Listing 3-41 to the file getServiceAccount.pl and run it on the command line as follows to see the result:

```
cmd>perl getServiceAccount.pl
Server: NYSQL1, Service: MSSQLServer, Account: LocalSystem
Server: NYSQL1, Service: MSSQL$APOLLO, Account: NYDomain\sqldba
Server: NYSQL1, Service: SQLServerAgent, Account: LocalSystem
Server: NYSQL2, Service: MSSQLServer, Account: NYDomain\sqldba
Server: NYSQL2, Service: SQLServerAgent, Account: NYDomain\sqldba
```

In Listing 3-41, I've hard-coded the names of the servers and their services for demonstration purposes. In practice, these names should be read from a configuration file or the registry.

Scripting a Stored Procedure

SCENARIO
You want to obtain the T-SQL script of a stored procedure from SQL Server.

To obtain the T-SQL script of a stored procedure, use the Script() method exposed by the SQL-DMO StoredProcedure object.

Chapter 2, "Working with Commonly Used Perl Modules," introduced the module Win32::OLE and showed you how to use this module as an OLE Automation controller to drive the SQL-DMO objects. Listing 2-13 demonstrates how to generate the CREATE DATABASE scripts for all the databases on a given server.

This section takes this line of approach a step further and focuses on a specific database object—a stored procedure in this case. Listing 3-42 shows the code for the function dbaScriptSP() that accepts a server name, a database name, and a stored procedure name all in a hash and generates the T-SQL script for the stored procedure along with the properties of the stored procedure.

This function is defined in the module SQLDBA::SQLDMO.

Listing 3-42. The Function dbaScriptSP()

```
1.   sub dbaScriptSP {
2.       my $ref = shift or die "***Err: dbaScriptSP() expects a reference.";
3.
4.       my $server = Win32::OLE->new('SQLDMO.SQLServer')
5.         or die "***Err: Could not create SQLDMO object.";
6.       $server->{LoginSecure} = 1;
7.
8.       $server->connect($ref->{srvName}, '', '');
9.       ! Win32::OLE->LastError() or
10.        die "***Err: Could not connect to $ref->{srvName}.";
11.
12.      my $spName = $ref->{spName};
13.      my $sp = $server->Databases($ref->{dbName})->StoredProcedures($spName);
14.      ! Win32::OLE->LastError() or
15.        die "***Err: could not get the table object.";
16.
17.      my $spRef = {
18.         Owner  => $sp->{Owner},
19.         Startup => $sp->{Startup},
20.         AnsiNullsStatus => $sp->{AnsiNullsStatus},
21.         QuotedIdentifierStatus => $sp->{QuotedIdentifierStatus},
22.         Script  => $sp->Script( SQLDMOScript_Default )
23.      };
24.      # remove settings in the code that are already captured in the hash
25.      $spRef->{Script} =~ s/set\s+quoted_identifier\s+(on|off)\s+go\s*//ig;
26.      $spRef->{Script} =~ s/set\s+ansi_nulls\s+(on|off)\s+go\s*//ig;
27.
28.      $server->disconnect();
29.      return $spRef;
30. }
```

The input parameter to the function in Listing 3-42 is a reference to a hash that includes a server name, a database name, and a stored procedure name. The following is an example of the hash that can be fed to the function:

```
$ref = { srvName => 'NYSQL1',
         dbName  => 'pubs',
         spName  => 'dbo.reptq1'
};
```

In Listing 3-42, the function dbaScriptSP() uses the server name to establish a connection to SQL Server on line 8. And on line 13, it uses the database name and the stored procedure name to create the corresponding SQL-DMO stored procedure object. The returned hash is prepared between lines 17 through 23. This hash includes the keys in Table 3-3 for the stored procedure.

Table 3-3. The Stored Procedure Properties Returned by dbaScriptSP()

KEY	DESCRIPTION
Owner	The owner of the stored procedure. Obtained with the Owner property of the SQL-DMO StoredProcedure object.
Startup	When set to 1, the stored procedure will execute automatically when SQL Server starts. Obtained with the Startup property of the SQL-DMO StoredProcedure object.
AnsiNullsStatus	When set to 1, the stored procedure observes the SQL-92 NULL handling behavior. Obtained with the AnsiNullsStatus property of the SQL-DMO StoredProcedure object.
QuotedIdentifierStatus	When set to 1, the stored procedure has been created with a dependency on quoted characters for identifier determination. Obtained with the QuotedIdentifierStatus property of the SQL-DMO StoredProcedure object.
Script	The value of this key is the T-SQL script of the stored procedure. Obtained with the Script() method of the SQL-DMO StoredProcedure object.

Listing 3-43 shows an example of using the function dbaScriptSP() in a Perl script.

Listing 3-43. Scripting a Stored Procedure

```perl
use strict;
use SQLDBA::SQLDMO qw( dbaScriptSP );
use Data::Dumper;

my $ref = {
    srvName => 'NYSQL1',
    dbName  => 'pubs',
    spName  => 'reptq1'
};

my $spRef = dbaScriptSP($ref);
print Dumper($spRef);
```

Save the script in Listing 3-43 to the file scriptSP.pl and execute it as follows on the command line to see the hash returned from dbaScriptSP() (the output script has been slightly edited for readability):

```
cmd>perl scriptSP.pl
$VAR1 = {
        'Script' => 'CREATE PROCEDURE reptq1 AS
                    SELECT pub_id, title_id, price, pubdate
                      FROM titles
                     WHERE price is NOT NULL
                    ORDER BY pub_id
                    COMPUTE avg(price) BY pub_id
                    COMPUTE avg(price)
                    GO',
        'QuotedIdentifierStatus' => 1,
        'Owner' => 'dbo',
        'AnsiNullsStatus' => 1,
        'Startup' => 0
      };
```

Note that the SQL-DMO Script() method will always include setting both ANSI_NULLS and QUOTED_IDENTIFIER as part of the generated T-SQL script. Because the information is already captured with the AnsiNullsStatus key and the QuotedidentifierStatus key, these SET statements don't provide any additional information and therefore are removed from the generated script. Line 25 and line 26 in Listing 3-42 carry out their removal. The /g modifier instructs the s/// operator to replace as many matched string as it can find.

You can easily use the approach in the function `dbaScriptSP()` with little change to script any other database objects in SQL Server.

Summary

This chapter presented the routines that will be frequently used when you write Perl scripts to administer SQL Server. They address tasks that aren't specifically related to administering SQL Server but are generic in nature. The routines include reading options from a configuration file, performing common set operations, manipulating time, persisting data structures, executing T-SQL queries, and parsing T-SQL scripts. They're exported as functions by the modules SQLDBA::Utility, SQLDBA::ParseSQL, SQLDBA::Security, and SQLDBA::SQLDMO, all custom-developed to simplify the Perl scripts for administering SQL Server.

The versions of these modules—which you can obtain from the Downloads area of the Apress Web site (`http://www.apress.com`)—include additional functions that are useful in writing Perl scripts for administering SQL Server. Furthermore, the functions include more complete error-checking code.

With all these functions explained in this chapter, the rest of the book focuses on solving the SQL Server administration problems—what you've all been waiting for, I suspect.

CHAPTER 4

Migrating Data

IN DEVELOPMENT AND PRODUCTION ENVIRONMENTS, Database Administrators (DBAs) often must help migrate data. *Data migration* is the process of moving data from one place to another or transforming data from one format to another. A data migration task can be as simple as moving data from one table to another, or it can be as complex as converting an entire database—perhaps even from a different database platform—to a new schema that requires many intermediate steps and complex data transformation procedures.

The recent advancement in data migration tools, such as Data Transformation Services (DTS), has made these types of tasks much easier in the SQL Server environment. As good as they are, however, built-in and off-the-shelf tools always have their limitations. It simply isn't possible to anticipate all the circumstances and requirements that a data migration job will encounter. When it comes to solving a specific problem, the value of a data migration tool is the amount of work it does for you automatically. If the work done by the tools in your toolset doesn't cover the full spectrum of work you need to perform, you've got gaps in your toolset. A powerful general-purpose tool such as Perl is often your best bet to fill the gaps.

NOTE *You can find many useful SQL Server DTS resources at* http://www.sqldts.com. *SQL Server MVPs Darren Green and Allan Mitchell maintain the site.*

Data migration is a huge topic, and it's not my intention to cover it completely in a single chapter. Instead, this chapter conveys Perl's potential through several specific problem-solving scenarios. It should whet your appetite in the process. This chapter delves into an assortment of data migration issues such as validating the bulk copy program (bcp) process, massaging and validating data for import, importing data rows that are very wide, and dealing with data whose number of columns isn't always fixed.

If you use the bcp utility to move data in a large number of tables manually, validating the bcp process can become laborious. But you must validate the process, especially when compromising the data integrity may result in disaster. In many cases, automating the validation procedure is the only viable solution. Even if you bulk copy only a small number of tables, you may still want to automate the validation. This is especially true if you need to bulk copy the data repeatedly and you don't want to manually perform the same boring data validation routine over and over again. Furthermore, if the bcp task is but one of many steps in a larger job, you may not have a choice but to automate the data validation so you don't cripple the automation of the entire job.

Checking bcp Errors

> **SCENARIO**
> *You use the bcp utility to move data in and out of a large number of tables regularly, and you want to make sure there's no problem in your bulk copy process.*

Even with fancier new tools introduced by Microsoft and third-party vendors, the bcp utility is still the tool of choice for many data migration jobs by many SQL Server DBAs. It's popular because it's simple and minimalist—and it performs well.

Despite its simplicity, if you're dealing with a large number of tables, it can become quite tedious to manually verify that the bcp process is clean and error free. If you're working with the bcp utility regularly, it pays to automate its error checking. If the bulk copy is part of a larger data migration process that's being scripted, it's a must to automate the error checking.

You can apply different levels of rigor to validate the process of bulk copying data. At the minimum, you should check whether the bcp utility has reported any errors. If you direct all the output generated from bulk copying data to the same log file, you can check this single file for any bcp errors.

The Perl script file scanBCPErrors.pl in Listing 4-1 implements the scan for the error messages generated by the bcp utility.

Listing 4-1. Scanning for BCP Error Messages

```
1.   use strict;
2.   my $bcpLog = shift or die "***Err: $0 expects a file name.";
3.
4.   scanBCPError($bcpLog);
5.
6.   ####################
7.   sub scanBCPError {
8.       my $bcpLog = shift or die "***Err: scanBCPError() expects a file name.";
9.
10.      my $dbName  = q/(?:[\w@#]+ | \"(?:[^"]|\\\")+\")/;
```

```perl
11.     my $objName = q/(?:[\w@#]+ | \"(?:[^"]|\\\")+\" | \[(?:[^]]|\]\])+\])/;
12.     my $re = qr{
13.                 (?:         # all in double quotation marks
14.                   \"(?:[^"]|\\\"|\"\")+\"
15.                   |           # one-part name with owner omitted
16.                 $objNameRegEx
17.                   |              # two-part name with owner omitted
18.                 $objNameRegEx\.$objNameRegEx
19.                   |              # three-part name with owner omitted
20.                 $dbNameRegEx\.\.$objNameRegEx
21.                   |            # three-part name
22.                 $dbNameRegEx\.$objNameRegEx\.$objNameRegEx
23.                 )
24.       }ix;
25.
26.     open(BCPLOG, $bcpLog) or die "***Err: couldn't open $bcpLog for read.";
27.     while (<BCPLOG>) {
28.        # parse the bcp command line for table/view/query
29.        if (/\>\s*bcp(\.exe)?\s+($re)\s+(in|out|queryout)/i) {
30.            print "\nBCP $3 $2\n";
31.            next;
32.        }
33.
34.        # check for parameter validation error
35.        if (/(usage:\s+bcp|Unknown argument)/i) {
36.            print "\t***Parameter validation error.\n";
37.            next;
38.        }
39.        # check for SQL Server error
40.        if (/\[Microsoft\]\[ODBC SQL Server Driver\]\[SQL Server\](.+)/i) {
41.            print "\t***$1\n";
42.            next;
43.        }
44.        # check for ODBC driver error
45.        if (/\[Microsoft\]\[ODBC SQL Server Driver\](.+)/i) {
46.            print "\t***$1\n";
47.            next;
48.        }
49.     }
50.     close(BCPLOG);
51. } # scanBCPError
```

To see how this script works, assume that you have a batch file—testBCP.bat—with the following bcp commands:

```
bcp pubs.dbo."authors" in authors.txt      -c -SNYSQL01 -T
bcp pubs.[dbo].sales    in sales.txt        -c -SNYSQL01 -T
bcp pubs..stores         in stores.txt       -c -SNYSQL01 -T
bcp Northwind..[Order Details] out jobs.txt -c -SNYSQL01 -T -q
bcp "select * from pubs..jobs" queryout jobs.txt -c -SNYSQL01 -T
```

This is for illustration purposes only. Usually, you don't mix bcp in and bcp out in the same batch file. Run this batch file and direct the output to the bcp.log file as follows:

```
cmd>testBCP.bat > bcp.log
```

When the batch file finishes executing, the bcp.log file will contain the output that's similar to Listing 4-2 from the bcp utility.

Listing 4-2. Sample bcp Log File Containing a Variety of Errors

```
D:\>bcp pubs.dbo."authors" in authors.txt     -c -SNYSQL01 -T
Starting copy...
SQLState = 22001, NativeError = 0
Error = [Microsoft][ODBC SQL Server Driver]String data, right truncation

21 rows copied.
Network packet size (bytes): 4096
Clock Time (ms.): total      391 Avg        18 (53.71 rows per sec.)


D:\>bcp pubs.[dbo].sales     in sales.txt        -c -SNYSQL01 -T
Starting copy...
SQLState = 23000, NativeError = 2627
Error = [Microsoft][ODBC SQL Server Driver][SQL Server]Violation of PRIMARY KEY
constraint 'PK__authors__77CB91'. Cannot insert duplicate key in object
'authors'. SQLState = 01000, NativeError = 3621
  Warning = [Microsoft][ODBC SQL Server Driver][SQL Server]The statement has
  been terminated.

BCP copy in failed


D:\>bcp pubs..stores              in stores.txt        -c -SNYSQL01 -T
Starting copy...
SQLState = S1000, NativeError = 0
Error = [Microsoft][ODBC SQL Server Driver]Unexpected EOF encountered in BCP ...
```

```
23 rows copied.
Network packet size (bytes): 4096
Clock Time (ms.): total          80 Avg          3 (287.50 rows per sec.)


D:\>bcp Northwind..[Order Details] out jobs.txt  -c -SNYSQL01 -T -q
Copy direction must be either 'in', 'out' or 'format'.
usage: bcp {dbtable | query} {in | out | queryout | format} datafile
  [-m maxerrors]              [-f formatfile]        [-e errfile]
  [-F firstrow]               [-L lastrow]           [-b batchsize]
  [-n native type]            [-c character type]    [-w wide character type]
  [-N keep non-text native]   [-6 6x file format]    [-q quoted identifier]
  [-C code page specifier]    [-t field terminator]  [-r row terminator]
  [-i inputfile]              [-o outfile]           [-a packetsize]
  [-S server name]            [-U username]          [-P password]
  [-T trusted connection]     [-v version]           [-R regional enable]
  [-k keep null values]       [-E keep identity values]
  [-h "load hints"]


D:\>bcp "select * from pubs..jobs" queryout jobs.txt -c -SNYSQL01 -T
Starting copy...


14 rows copied.
Network packet size (bytes): 4096
Clock Time (ms.): total           1 Avg          0 (14000.00 rows per sec.)
```

To glean the error messages from the bcp log file shown in Listing 4-2, run the Perl script in Listing 4-1 as follows:

```
cmd>perl scanBCPErrors.pl bcp.log
```

This produces the following error-checking summary (edited for readability):

```
BCP in pubs.dbo."authors"
   ***String data, right truncation
BCP in pubs.[dbo].sales
   ***Violation of PRIMARY KEY constraint 'PK__authors__77CB91'. Cannot insert
                   duplicate key in object 'authors'.
   ***The statement has been terminated.
BCP in pubs..stores
   ***Unexpected EOF encountered in BCP data-file
BCP out Northwind..[Order Details]
   ***Parameter validation error.
BCP queryout "select * from pubs..jobs"
```

The following sections highlight several salient points about the script in Listing 4-1.

Recording the bcp Command Line

The script assumes that the bcp command line itself is recorded in the log file. You can easily accomplish this as long as you keep the Windows command-echoing feature turned on. Listing 4-2 is an example that contains the bcp command lines. The bcp command line is necessary to identify the source of an error message.

 TIP   *If you put the bcp commands in a batch file, don't place* echo off *or* @echo off *at the beginning of the batch to turn off the command echoing. Otherwise, you'd have a terrible time figuring out which error message is generated by which bcp command.*

Another important point to note is how the bcp command line is parsed (covered in the next section).

Parsing the bcp Command Line

Parsing the bcp command line for the table name, for the view name, or for the query turns out to be more complicated than it appears. The complexity isn't in crafting the correct regular expressions but in understanding the exact syntax that's permitted on the bcp command line. When only simple identifiers are used for the database, owner, table, or view, you can get the table or view name with this straightforward regular expression:

```
/ ( ([\w@#]+\.)?    # optional database name
    [\w@#]*\.       # owner name
  )?                # database.owner can be omitted
  [\w@#]+           # object name is mandatory
/x
```

The situation becomes slightly more complex when an identifier contains an embedded double quotation mark. Note that a double quotation mark has a "double personality": It has special meaning in a Transact-SQL (T-SQL) identifier when SQL Server processes it, and it's treated specially by the Windows command processor on the command line.

You therefore may have to escape an embedded double quotation mark at both the command-line level and the T-SQL level. Unfortunately, the SQL Server Books Online isn't clear on how to escape an embedded double quotation mark on the bcp command line. I've gleaned the following tips largely through trial and error and through repeated experiments:

- You can always escape an embedded double quotation mark on the command line with a backslash.

- If the -q option is specified on the command line, SQL Server will quote all the identifiers with a pair of double quotation marks, and you should double any embedded double quotation mark. Thus, if you want to bcp out a table named a"b in the pubs database, you should specify it on the command line as follows:

```
bcp "pubs..a\"\"b" out ab.txt -c -q ...
```

- If you use the -q option, don't quote any identifier with the square brackets. This most likely won't result in what you intend because the brackets will be put inside the double quotation marks and will thus be treated as part of the identifier.

- Always use the -q option when working with identifiers that have special characters such as spaces and quotation marks. Quoting an identifier with a pair of square brackets—even when you don't use the -q option—doesn't always work with the bcp utility; for example, quoting the database name with square brackets results in an error message from the bcp utility.

These observations led to the construction of the regular expressions in the function scanBCPError() between line 10 and line 24 in Listing 4-1. The final regular expression, as referenced by the variable $re, can parse any table name, view name, or query specified on the bcp command line, and the table name or view name can include the database and/or owner qualifier.

On line 14, the first alternative in the regular expression of the variable $re is an interesting one:

```
\" (?:[^"] | \\\" | \"\" )+ \"
```

You may wonder why the third choice (\"\") is required to match two consecutive double quotation marks inside a pair of delimiting double quotation marks. Note that when the -q option isn't specified, the following example is legal as the source for the queryout option:

```
bcp "select * from pubs..authors where au_id = ""527-72-3246""" queryout ...
```

For the bcp in or bcp out options, the bcp target or source is either a table or a view, which may be qualified with an owner and/or a database name. The regular expression for parsing an object name is the same as that for parsing an owner name. It's specified on line 11 in Listing 4-1 and is reproduced here with additional comments:

```
/(?:  [\w@#]+        # a regular identifier
| \"(?:[^"]|\\\")+\"   # a double-quoted identifier
| \[(?:[^]]|\]\])+\]   # a square-bracket-quoted identifier
)/x
```

The ?: that immediately follows the left parenthesis is to mark that pair of parentheses as noncapturing. This is necessary because on line 11 in Listing 4-1 the "regular expression" is in fact defined as a string that will later be used as part of a more complex regular expression. In Listing 4-1, it's eventually used on line 29 where more parentheses are used to capture various components of a bcp command.

Capturing Three Categories of bcp Errors

All these discussions of parsing the bcp command line have distracted from the real focus of the Perl script in Listing 4-1, which is to capture the errors that the bcp utility may produce. Let's get back to it! The script captures errors from three different sources, each with its distinct pattern:

- **bcp errors**: These are errors generated by the bcp utility itself because a parameter isn't correctly specified. A bcp usage error message identifies such an error.

- **ODBC errors**: These are errors coming from the ODBC driver when it encounters a problem. Such an error is directly prefixed with the string [ODBC SQL Server Driver].

- **SQL Server errors**: These errors are passed to the bcp utility from SQL Server, and they're prefixed with the string [SQL Server].

It's possible that the bcp utility may emit other types of errors. If and when a new one shows up that doesn't fall into any of these three categories, you can modify the script to accommodate it. Not being restricted to what's given is one of the great advantages of scripting a solution yourself.

TIP *I haven't experienced any case where the bcp utility sends error messages to* STDERR *instead of* STDOUT, *at least with respect to the three types of error messages just identified. However, because this isn't clearly documented, you can specify* 2>&1 *on the command line to ensure that all error messages go to* STDOUT.

Dealing with Special Cases

The main objective of writing a script is to get a specific job done. It's also nice to create a script that's generally applicable. But, often, creating such a script is time consuming. If you're working against a tight schedule and are clearly aware of the narrow context in which you're operating, you must make a tradeoff between getting the job done and writing a Perl script that also works outside of this narrow context. It's perfectly acceptable to write a script that works only within that narrow context, especially if it leads to significant savings in scripting time.

For instance, if you already know that in your current database there isn't any delimited identifier and you're not using the queryout option, you can therefore avoid quoting anything on the bcp command line in double quotation marks, thus considerably simplifying the script in Listing 4-1.

NOTE *This may come across as rather self-evident, but there's a lot of wisdom in the saying, "The fact that it's supported doesn't mean you should use it." SQL Server supports delimited identifiers that can have any arbitrary characters including quotation marks and spaces. But as the discussions in this chapter have made it abundantly clear, they can create a lot of headaches. So stick to regular identifiers if you can.*

Streamlining bcp and Error Checking

You can streamline the bcp task and its error checking by putting both the bcp batch file and the execution of the script in Listing 4-1 in another batch file. For instance, you can place the following two lines in the same batch file—for example, bcpWithErrCheck.bat:

```
testBCP.bat > bcp.log    2>&1
perl scanBCPErrors.pl bcp.log
```

Now, you only need to execute `bcpWithErrCheck.bat` to perform the bcp task and scan for any errors in one fell swoop.

Alternatively, you could place everything in a single Perl script as follows:

```
my $bcpLog = 'bcp.log';
`test_bcp.bat 2>&1 > $bcpLog`;

scanBCPError($bcpLog);

###################
sub scanBCPError {
# See Listing 4-1
}
```

You now can run this single Perl script, which performs both the bcp task in the `test_bcp.bat` batch file and the bcp error checking with the function `scanBCPError()`.

Counting bcp Rows

SCENARIO
You use bcp to copy data from one server to another, and you want to know that the number of rows copied out is the same as that copied in.

When the bcp utility produces an error message, you know you've got a problem. The bad news is that you don't know all the error messages that the bcp utility will ever emit. So, checking for error messages alone may not be enough to raise your comfort level.

Fortunately, the bcp utility also logs the number of rows copied in either direction for each table. For the same set of tables, you can direct the output of bulk copying the data out of these tables to a log file and direct the output of bulk copying in the same data to another log file. Then, you can review these two log files to check whether the number of the rows copied out of a table matches the number of the rows copied into the table.

Listing 4-3 shows the script, `bcpRowCount.pl`, to capture and compare the row counts between the bcp in and the bcp out.

Listing 4-3. Comparing bcp Row Counts

```
use strict;
use Getopt::Std;
use Data::Dumper;
```

```perl
my $dbName  = q/(?: [\w@#]+ | \"(?:[^"] | \\\")+\")/;
my $objName = q/(?: [\w@#]+ | \"(?:[^"] | \\\")+\" |
                  \[ (?:[^]] | \]\])+ \] )/;


my %opts;
getopts('i:o:', \%opts);
(defined $opts{i} and defined $opts{o}) or printUsage();


my %inout = ( 'in' => $opts{i}, 'out' => $opts{o} );
my ($ref, $object);


foreach my $io (keys %inout) {
    open(LOG, $inout{$io}) or die "***Err: could not open $inout{$io}.";
    while (<LOG>) {
        if (/\>\s*bcp\s+(\"(?:[^"]|\\\"|\"\")+\")\s+$io/ix) {
            $object = $1;
            next;
        }
        if ( /\>\s*bcp\s+$dbName\. ($objName)?\. ($objName)\s+$io/ix ) {
            $object = $2;
            next;
        }
        if (/(\d+)\s+rows\s+copied/i) {
            if (defined $object) {
                $ref->{$object}->{$io . '_rowcount'}=$1;
            }
            else {
                print "***Err: The regular expressions parsing the bcp command\n";
                print "        line is inadequate. The script should not be here.\n"
            }
            undef $object;
        }
    }
    close(LOG);
}


my $ok = 1;
foreach my $obj (sort keys %$ref) {
    if ($ref->{$obj}->{in_rowcount} != $ref->{$obj}->{out_rowcount}) {
        print "***Msg for $obj: BCP out $ref->{$obj}->{out_rowcount} rows ";
        print "<> BCP in $ref->{$obj}->{in_rowcount} rows.\n";
        $ok = 0;
    }
}
```

```
print "\n*** All table rows match.\n\n" if $ok;
print Data::Dumper->Dump([$ref], ['RowCounts']);

######################
sub printUsage {
    print << '--Usage--';
Usage:
   cmd>perl BCPRowCompare.pl -i <bcp in log> -o <bcp out log>
--Usage--
exit;
} # printUsage
```

Assume that the output of bulk copying out the data from the tables is directed to the file bcpOut.log and the output of bulk copying in the data is logged in bcpIn.log. You can then run the script in Listing 4-3 to compare the row counts, as shown in Listing 4-4.

Listing 4-4. Comparing the Row Counts with bcpRowCompare.pl

```
cmd>perl BCPRowCompare.pl -i bcpIn.log -o bcpOut.log
***Msg for authors: BCP out 23 rows <> BCP in 24 rows.
$RowCounts = {
              discounts => {
                             'out_rowcount' => 3,
                             'in_rowcount'  => 3
                           },
              titles => {
                           'out_rowcount' => 18,
                           'in_rowcount'  => 18
                        },
              jobs => {
                         'out_rowcount' => 14,
                         'in_rowcount'  => 14
                      },
              authors => {
                            'out_rowcount' => 23,
                            'in_rowcount'  => 24
                         }
            };
```

In Listing 4-4, four tables—authors, discounts, jobs, and titles—are bulk copied out and are bulk copied in as well. Of these four tables, the script reports that the row counts for the authors table don't match.

Now, let's see what the script in Listing 4-3 really parses and captures. Note that a typical clean output from the bcp utility for copying a table is similar to this:

```
D:\>bcp pubs..discounts in discounts.txt -c -SNYSQL01 -T

Starting copy...

3 rows copied.
Network packet size (bytes): 4096
Clock Time (ms.): total      20
```

The critical part of the script is to identify for which source or target the rows are copied, which means parsing the bcp command line for the table/view name. In particular, you want to be able to single out the table name without its database or owner qualifier so that this script can still be used even when the database that imports the data is different from the database that exports the data, which is often the case in real-world scenarios. Similar to the issues you had to wrestle with in the preceding section, this task is complicated by the presence of delimited identifiers or double quotation marks.

To deal with all the possible scenarios would result in a rather complex script, especially considering that the same table can be specified on the bcp command line in many different syntactic formats. Fortunately, you usually have total control over the bulk copy process. Thus, it's reasonable to assume that the table names are specified in a consistent format in both directions of the bulk copy. In other words, don't specify the authors table as [authors] on the import, but as "authors" on the export. This difference gives you only trouble with no benefit. Taking this into consideration, the script in Listing 4-3 implements the following approach to capture the table or view name:

- If the entire three-part table name is in double quotation marks, the entire quoted string is captured and isn't further parsed for the table or view name.

- If the entire three-part table name isn't in double quotation marks, it's parsed to find the table name. However, the table or view isn't further parsed to convert it to a consistent naming convention.

The name captured by this approach records the row count of the bulk copy. This means that if you specify the table as authors on bulk copy out but identify it as [authors] on bulk copy in, the script reports a row count mismatch for the table authors and a row count mismatch for the table [authors] because it treats them as two different tables. This clearly isn't desirable. But then why can't you simply be consistent in naming your tables?

Comparing bcp Files

> **SCENARIO**
> *Comparing row counts may not be enough because there may be silent data conversion that alters the data after it has been copied into the target database tables. This may not generate any error message or result in any mismatched row counts. You're paranoid and want to know whether the data has remained the same.*

Bulk copying data out of a database is relatively safe. But you're not alone in being paranoid about the integrity of bulk copying data into a database. I'm paranoid when I'm dealing with critical data that could have a huge negative impact if there's any problem with importing data that isn't caught immediately. What's needed is a tool to help prove the data integrity beyond a shadow of a doubt.

Immediately after the data is copied into the database and before it's further processed by any additional procedures, you can bulk copy the same data out to a set of files in the exact format as the original data files used by the bcp import. Now if nothing has changed, this set of files and the original data files should be the same. Any difference between them would be indicative of a change somewhere along the way.

Comparing the data files used for the import and the data files produced by the export isn't a task to do manually. Even if you could do it, you shouldn't. It would be too boring and unreliable to do it manually. Fortunately, comparing two files to determine whether they're identical is such a common task that a standard Perl module is available to accomplish it. The module is File::Compare, and it performs a byte-by-byte comparison between two files and quits as soon as it finds a difference. This module is bundled with ActivePerl.

The result of these observations is the script bcpFileCompare.pl in Listing 4-5.

Listing 4-5. Comparing bcp Data Files

```
use strict;
use File::Compare;
use SQLDBA::Utility qw( dbaSetDiff dbaSetCommon );
use Getopt::Std;

my %opts;
getopts('i:o:t', \%opts);
my ($indir, $outdir, $textmode) = ($opts{i}, $opts{o}, $opts{t});
(defined $indir && defined $outdir) or printUsage();

# get the list of files in indir
opendir(DIR, "$indir") or die "***Err: can't opendir $indir: $!";
my @infiles = grep {!/^(\.|\.\.)$/} readdir(DIR);
```

```
    closedir DIR;

    # get the list of files in outdir
    opendir(DIR, "$outdir") or die "***Err: can't opendir $outdir";
    my @outfiles = grep {!/^(\.|\.\.)$/} readdir(DIR);
    closedir DIR;

    my @diff = ();
    my $unequal = 0;

    if (@diff = dbaSetDiff(\@infiles, \@outfiles)) {
        print "***Msg: these files in $indir do not exist in $outdir:\n";
        map {print "\t$_\n"} @diff;
        $unequal = 1;
    }

    if (@diff = dbaSetDiff(\@outfiles, \@infiles)) {
        print "***Msg: these files in $outdir do not exist in $indir:\n";
        map {print "\t$_\n"} @diff;
        $unequal = 1;
    }

    print "\nNow we compare files in both directories:\n\n";
    foreach my $file (dbaSetCommon(\@infiles, \@outfiles)) {
        my $f_in = "$indir\\$file";
        my $f_out = "$outdir\\$file";
        print "\tComparing $file ...\n";

        if ($textmode)
            { $unequal = File::Compare::compare_text($f_in, $f_out); }
        else
            { $unequal = compare($f_in, $f_out); }
        push(@diff, $file) if ($unequal);
    }

    if (@diff) {
        print "\n***Msg: these files are different:\n";
        map {print "\t$_\n"} @diff;
    }
    else {
        print "\n*** All the common files are identical.\n";
    }


####################
```

```
sub printUsage {
    print << '--Usage--';
Usage:
    cmd>perl BCPFileCompare.pl -i <bcp in directory> -o <bcp out directory> [-t]
--Usage--
exit;
} # printUsage
```

To use this script, place all the data files to be imported in a directory. After the data files have been bulk copied into the database, bulk copy the same data out to a different directory and name each data file the same as its corresponding original. With these data files in two different directories (for example, d:\bcpin and d:\bcpout), you can run the script as follows to compare the files to see the output:

cmd>perl BCPFileCompare.pl -i d:\bcpin -o d:\bcpout
```
***Msg: these files in .\BCPin do not exist in .\BCPout:
        Territories.txt

Now we compare files in both directories:

        Comparing CustomerCustomerDemo.txt ...
        Comparing Shippers.txt ...
        Comparing Products.txt ...
        Comparing Employees.txt ...
        Comparing Suppliers.txt ...
        Comparing EmployeeTerritories.txt ...
        Comparing Categories.txt ...
        Comparing Customers.txt ...
        Comparing Order_Details.txt ...
        Comparing CustomerDemographics.txt ...
        Comparing Orders.txt ...
        Comparing Region.txt ...

***Msg: these files are different:
        Products.txt
```

In this example, the file Territories.txt is in the folder .\bcpin but not in .\bcpout. Because the two data files for the Products table don't match, you should investigate the bulk copy process to find out what might have caused these two files to differ.

The comparison happens in two steps:

1. The script checks the filenames to see whether a file is present in one directory but not the other.

2. For the files common to both directories, the script compares the content of each file using the Perl standard module File::Compare. If the -t option is specified, the script treats the files as text files and uses the text comparison mode of the File::Compare module. You should specify the -t option if the bulk copy is performed using the character mode—in other words, if -c is used on the bcp command line.

If it's feasible, you should perform bulk copies in the native mode instead of the character mode. The former is much more robust. Although the latter gives you the convenience of inspecting the data files visually, many embedded characters—some are rather common—can easily ruin its integrity and produce strange results.

Before moving on, you should know that this level of scrutiny on the bulk copy process might be a bit excessive for many data import tasks. So, don't get too carried away with the approach described in this section. Use it only when the requirements warrant its use. In particular, if you have a large amount of data, you may not have a big enough maintenance window to validate your data import to such an extent.

That's it for validating the bulk copy process. The next several sections expose you to scenarios where you can use Perl to massage and prepare data before the import.

Splitting Free-Form Text Phone Numbers

SCENARIO

You're converting a legacy system to SQL Server. One of the fields exported by the legacy system contains free-form text phone numbers that were not validated. You want to split the field into two separate columns: area code and local phone number.

SQL Server DBAs routinely run into situations where they need to massage data before it's moved into their final destination. One common method is to perform the massage inside SQL Server with T-SQL. This works well when the data cleanup is conducive to the set-oriented processing that SQL Server performs well.

However, there are plenty of cases where it's easier and more efficient to clean up the data before importing it into the database. Sometimes, you may even want to export the data out, massage it, and then import it back to the tables. Massaging the data outside SQL Server can be efficient when the data volume is large and when you need to make only one pass through the data file. It can also be convenient because you now have all the powerful features of Perl at your disposal.

Parsing telephone numbers is a surprisingly common problem. Do a quick search of the various SQL Server online forums and newsgroups, and you'll find that developers ask questions of this nature frequently. All too often this is cast as a problem looking for a T-SQL solution. Unfortunately, with the exception of a few simple scenarios, T-SQL is the wrong tool for the job.

Now it's time for some examples to help illustrate the nature of the problem. Assume that the legacy system exports the data in the Comma-Separated Value (CSV) format and the second column is supposed to contain the U.S. telephone numbers. Listing 4-6 shows the sample data.

Listing 4-6. Sample Data Containing Phone Numbers in Free Text

```
"1","212-647-5154","Adams","John"
"2","567-3214","Jefferson","Thomas"
"3","(201) 234-9865","Monroe","James"
"4","732.332-2346","Adams","John Q"
"5","604 335-4525","Jackson","Andrew"
"6","2087896537","Truman","Harry"
"7","(704) 5527212","Kennedy","John"
"8","(734) 935  0978","Nixon","Richard"
"9","201.556.3245","Ford","Gerald"
"10","732,336-4245","Carter","Jimmy"
"11","1-204-475-3045","Reagan","Ronald"
```

These telephone numbers present a few examples of many more possible variations. The script `splitPhoneNumber.pl` in Listing 4-7 reads a data file in this format and outputs another data file with the phone numbers split into two columns—area code and local phone number.

Listing 4-7. Splitting a Free-Form Phone Number Field

```
1.  use strict;
2.  use Text::CSV_XS;
3.
4.  my $csv = Text::CSV_XS->new({
5.       'quote_char'   => '"',
6.       'escape_char'  => '"',
```

```
7.        'sep_char'    => ',',
8.        'binary'      => 0,
9.        'always_quote' => 1
10.    });
11.
12. my @columns = ();
13. my @splitNumbers = ();
14. my $string;
15.
16. while (<>) {
17.    if ($csv->parse($_)) {
18.        @columns = $csv->fields();
19.        @splitNumbers = splitPhoneNumber($columns[1]);
20.        splice @columns, 1, 1, @splitNumbers;
21.    }
22.    if ($csv->combine(@columns)) {
23.        $string = $csv->string;
24.        print "$string\n";
25.    }
26. }
27.
28. #######################
29. sub splitPhoneNumber {
30.    my ($phone) = shift;
31.    my ($areaCode, $local);
32.
33.    $phone =~ /^(?: \s*(?:\d\s*[\-\.,\s]?)?  # in case of a prefix like 1-
34.                \s* ( \(\s*\d\d\d\s*\) | \d\d\d )        # area code
35.                \s* [\-\.,\s]? \s* )?    # some optional separator
36.                (\d\d\d) \s* [\-\.,\s]? \s* (\d\d\d\d)\s* # local number
37.            $/x;
39.    ($areaCode, $local) = ($1, "$2\-$3");
40.    $areaCode =~ s/^\s*\(\s*//;
41.    $areaCode =~ s/\s*\)\s*$//;
42.    return ($areaCode, $local);
43. }  # splitPhoneNumber
```

Now, let's see what the script produces. Place the data in Listing 4-6 in the file
legacyData.txt and run this:

```
cmd>perl splitPhoneNumber.pl  legacyData.txt
```

This generates the following output, where the second column contains the area code, which can be empty, and the third column has the local number:

```
"1","212","647-5154","Adams","John"
"2",,"567-3214","Jefferson","Thomas"
"3","201","234-9865","Monroe","James"
"4","732","332-2346","Adams","John Q"
"5","604","335-4525","Jackson","Andrew"
"6","208","789-6537","Truman","Harry"
"7","704","552-7212","Kennedy","John"
"8","734","935-0978","Nixon","Richard"
"9","201","556-3245","Ford","Gerald"
"10","732","336-4245","Carter","Jimmy"
"11","204","475-3045","Reagan","Ronald"
```

Instead of crafting procedures from scratch to construct and deconstruct strings in the CSV format, this script uses the Comprehensive Perl Archive Network (CPAN) module Text::CSV_XS to parse a CSV-formatted string into a list of strings.

On line 17 in Listing 4-7, `$csv->parse($_)` parses the string in the variable `$_` according to the CSV format. Then, on line 18, `$csv->fields()` splits the string into a list, assigning each CSV value to an element in the list. On line 19, the `splitPhoneNumber()` function splits the second element of the list, which corresponds to the free-form phone number in the CSV string, into the area code and the local phone number. On line 20, two elements, the area code and the local number, replace the second element of the list. After that, the list of the elements changes back into a CSV-formatted string using `$csv->combine(@columns)` on line 22. You can then retrieve the combined CSV string through `$csv->string`.

It's interesting to note the use of the Perl function `splice()` on line 20 in Listing 4-7:

```
splice @columns, 1, 1, @splitNumbers;
```

This replaces the second element of the array `@columns` with a list in the array `@splitNumbers`, which includes two values—one for the area code and the other for the local number. In effect, it accomplishes this:

```
@columns = (@columns[0], @splitNumbers, @columns[2..$#columns]);
```

The code for manipulating the CSV strings aside, the essence of the script is none other than the regular expression on lines 33 through 37—reproduced as follows—to parse the free-text phone numbers. With the help of the /x modifier, the regular expression has been split into multiple lines in the function splitPhoneNumber() with extra whitespaces and comments added to improve readability:

```
$phone =~ /^(?: \s*(?:\d\s*[\-\.,\s]?)?    # in case of a prefix like 1-
             \s* ( \(\s*\d\d\d\s*\) | \d\d\d )  # area code
             \s* [\-\.,\s]? \s* )?       # some optional separator
             (\d\d\d) \s* [\-\.,\s]? \s* (\d\d\d\d)\s*  # local number
         $/x;
```

The characters in the square brackets correspond to what one might have used to separate various parts of a phone number in the legacy system. This could include a hyphen, period, comma, or space.

Even though the regular expression has been crafted to parse all the scenarios presented in Listing 4-7, it doesn't cover many other ways in which one may enter a U.S. telephone number. In a real-world case, you need to study the specific data on hand and modify the regular expression accordingly. This is often an iterative process. As you go through the test scenarios with the actual data, you'll keep refining the regular expression—perhaps using several simpler regular expressions instead of an increasingly more complex one—until you cover all the reasonable cases with others logged as exceptions to be dealt with manually.

Working with Data in the CSV Format

The CSV format is commonly used to exchange data between spreadsheets and databases. It appears to be a simple format. In fact, you may think you can quickly split the values in a CSV record on commas and whip up a regular expression to get the individual values. Don't be fooled by what its name may imply, though! Its apparent simplicity can be quite deceiving. Comma-separated values aren't the whole story; the values may also be quoted with double quotation marks, and an embedded double quotation mark must be escaped with another double quotation mark.

As is typically Perl, if it's such a common problem, somebody probably has already solved it and contributed the solution to the CPAN site. Indeed, there are several CPAN modules dealing with composing and decomposing CSV records. Among them, the object-oriented module Text::CSV_XS is one of the best. The two most important methods of this module are parse(), which takes a CSV string and extracts the individual values, and combine(), which takes a list of values and constructs a CSV record out of them—the reverse of the parse() method.

Importing SQL Server Errorlog

SCENARIO

You want to import the SQL Server errorlog into a table with each log entry split into three columns: the log date, the log source, and the message text. If the message text spans multiple lines, you want to make sure it's entered as a single string.

Regardless of whether you really want to import SQL Server errorlogs into a database table, this is representative of a class of data import problems where the row terminator isn't a single newline (\n) or even a string of fixed characters. Rather, the rows are separated by strings with a fixed pattern. In the case of a SQL Server errorlog, the rows—or perhaps more appropriately called the errorlog *entries*—are separated with a newline followed by a date string. To be more precise, each errorlog entry starts with a date string. Assume that the schema of the destination SQL Server table is as follows:

```
CREATE TABLE tbErrorlog (
    EntryID    int Primary Key,
    Date       datetime,
    Source     varchar(128),
    Msg        varchar(5000)
)
```

Obviously, you can't directly bulk copy an errorlog into this table. You need to transform it to a format acceptable to the bcp utility. The transformation must address these two problems:

- The whitespaces separating the three columns in an errorlog aren't unique; they also appear inside the date string and inside the message text. In other words, you can't split an errorlog entry with whitespace.

- The bcp utility doesn't accept a text pattern as a row terminator. In addition, the text pattern doesn't really separate the rows; it indicates the beginning of the rows. Moreover, it's possible to have a newline—followed by a date string—embedded in the message text.

The script importErrorlog.pl in Listing 4-8 overcomes these difficulties. Note that this script doesn't actually import an errorlog; it merely transforms the errorlog to a format ready to be bulk copied into the SQL Server table as described previously.

Listing 4-8. Preparing the SQL Server Errorlog for Bulk Copy

```
use strict;

my $entryCounter = 0;
my $entry = <>;
while(<>) {
   if (!/^ \d\d(\d\d)?\-\d\d\-\d\d\s+        # date
          \d\d\:\d\d\:\d\d\.\d\d\s+          # time
          [^\s]+\s+                          # source
       /x) {
     $entry .= $_;
   }
   else {
      ++$entryCounter;
      if ($entry =~ /^ (\d\d(?:\d\d)?\-\d\d\-\d\d\s+    # date
                        \d\d\:\d\d\:\d\d\.\d\d)\s+      # time
                        ([^\s]+)\s+                     # source
                        (.+)$                           # the rest
                     /xs) {
        my ($datetime, $source, $msg) = ($1, $2, $3);
        print "$entryCounter\|$datetime\|$source\|$msg\@\#\$";
      }
      else {
         print STDERR "***Assert Err: should not reach here.\n";
      }
```

```
            $entry = $_;
      }
   }
++$entryCounter;
if ($entry =~ /^ (\d\d(?:\d\d)?\-\d\d\-\d\d\s+   # date
                  \d\d\:\d\d\:\d\d\.\d\d)\s+      # time
                  ([^\s]+)\s+                     # source
                  (.+)$                           # the rest
             /xs) {
   my ($datetime, $source, $msg) = ($1, $2, $3);
   print "$entryCounter\|$datetime\|$source\|$msg\@\#\$";
}
else {
   print STDERR "***Assert Err: should not reach here.\n";
}
print STDERR "***$entryCounter entrys processed.\n";
```

The strategy implemented in the script in Listing 4-8 is to make a single pass through the errorlog file and use the variable $entry to hold the lines of the current errorlog entry while checking the next line in the $_ variable to see whether another entry starts. If the next line starts with a date string followed by a string with no embedded space or if there's no next line at all, $entry has a complete errorlog entry. Otherwise, the current line is part of the same entry held by $entry and is appended to $entry. See the following if statement:

```
if (! /^ \d\d(\d\d)?\-\d\d\-\d\d\s+       # date
         \d\d\:\d\d\:\d\d\.\d\d\s+          # time
         [^\s]+\s+                          # source
      /x) {
   $entry .= $_;
}
```

When all the lines for the same errorlog entry have been assembled in $entry, the script parses $entry to get the date string, the source, and the message text. You do this with the following if statement and the regular expression in its condition test:

```
if ($entry =~ /^ (\d\d(?:\d\d)?\-\d\d\-\d\d\s+   # date
                  \d\d\:\d\d\:\d\d\.\d\d)\s+      # time
                  ([^\s]+)\s+                     # source
                  (.+)$                           # the rest
             /xs) {
   my ($datetime, $source, $msg) = ($1, $2, $3);
   print "$entryCounter\|$datetime\|$source\|$msg\@\#\$";
}
```

In the output, the script uses the pipe symbol—in other words, the vertical bar (|)—as the column terminator and uses the character string @#$ as the row terminator. Rare as these terminators are, there aren't any guarantees that they don't appear in the message text in the errorlog. To be sure about the choice of the column terminator and the row terminator, you can first scan the errorlog file to ensure that they don't appear in the file. More efficiently, before printing the entry, the script can first check whether $msg contains a pipe symbol or the string @#$:

```
If ($msg !~ /( \| | \@\#\$ )/ix) {
    print "$entryCounter\|$datetime\|$source\|$msg\@\#\$";
}
else {
    print STDERR "$datetime, $msg contains a | or a @#$\n."
}
```

In the script, the transformed errorlog rows are sent to the standard output. Note that STDOUT is the default file handle when no file handle is specified for the print() function. All the other messages including the error messages and a total entry count, which is in the variable $entryCounter, are sent to the standard error output STDERR so that when you redirect the output to a file, you get only the data file ready for the bcp utility.

Validating Data Before Importing

> **SCENARIO**
> *Your bulk copy import fails intermittently. From the logged error messages, it appears that the external data doesn't always comply with the agreed format. You want to single out the bad data before feeding the data to the bcp utility.*

For a data file to be bulk copied into a SQL Server table in the character mode, the file format is rather simple. It has a number of columns, each of which is a string of characters. A field terminator separates two contiguous columns, and a row terminator ends each row.

To validate such a data file, you can perform these checks:

- Check the number of columns as delimited by the expected field terminator and the expected row terminator.

- Check a column for compliance with the expected text patterns.

Listing 4-9 shows the validateImport.pl script that carries out these checks.

Listing 4-9. Validating a Data File Before bcp

```perl
use strict;

# Begin config options
   my $fieldTerminator = '\|';
   my $rowTerminator = "!@#";
   my $columnCount = 9;
   my %columnPatterns = (
           0 => qr/^\d{3}\-\d{2}\-\d{4}$/,
           7 => qr/^\d{5}$/
       );
# End config options

Main: {
   $/ = $rowTerminator;

   my ($total, $errCount) = (0, 0);
   while(<>) {
       s/$rowTerminator$//;
       ++$total;
       my @columns = split /$fieldTerminator/;
       my $OK = 1;

       # Check column count
       unless ($columnCount == scalar @columns) {
          $OK = 0;
          print "***Err: the number of columns is not $columnCount";
          print "        for row $_\n";
          next;
       }
       # Check column patterns
       foreach my $col (sort keys %columnPatterns) {
          unless ($columns[$col] =~ /$columnPatterns{$col}/) {
             $OK = 0;
             print "***Err: column $columns[$col] failed to match pattern";
             print " $columnPatterns{$col}\n";
             print "        for row $_\n";
          }
       }
       ++$errCount unless $OK;
   }
   print "\n$total rows checked in total.\n";
   print "$errCount rows mismatched.\n";
}
```

To use the script in Listing 4-9 for a specific data file, you must modify the lines between #Begin config options and #End config options to meet the requirements of that data file. In Listing 4-9, these specifics are configured as follows:

- The field terminator is the pipe symbol (|).

- The row terminator is the character string !@#.

- The data file is expected to have nine columns for each row.

- The data for the first column should match the regular expression qr/^\d{3}\-\d{2}\-\d{4}$/.

- The data for the eighth column should match the regular expression qr/^\d{5}$/.

In case you didn't guess, Listing 4-9 uses as an example a data file to be bulk copied into the pubs..authors table, and the two regular expressions match the two CHECK constraints declared for the authors table on the corresponding columns:

```
CHECK (au_id like '[0-9][0-9][0-9]-[0-9][0-9]-[0-9][0-9][0-9][0-9]'),
CHECK (zip like '[0-9][0-9][0-9][0-9][0-9]')
```

It's up to you to decide how stringent you want to make the checks on the columns in your data file.

By now, you're probably dying to ask why you should even be bothered with all these validation checks when the bulk copy utility already provides a facility to throw aside the erroneous rows.

It's true that by specifying an error file following the -e option of the bcp utility, rows in the data file that can't be imported will be logged in the file. The problem is that not all the bcp errors are handled by this option. Also, because this option is used while the data is being imported, the behavior may not be to your liking. In some circumstances when you want to have ultimate control of the data import, checking the quality of the data before it's imported is the only viable approach. By conducting validation checks, you can decide exactly what you would like to do with the data, given the various error conditions your checks may discover.

Importing Performance Log into a Database

| **SCENARIO**
| *You have logged performance counter data with the Windows Performance*
| *Logs and Alerts tool. You want to import the data into a SQL Server database*
| *for further analysis.*

Importing Windows performance counter logs into SQL Server is representative of a class of interesting problems that aren't in the format to be directly fed to the bulk copy utility and that aren't particularly convenient to be handled even by DTS.

Windows 2000 introduces the Performance Logs and Alerts feature for logging counter values and event traces and for generating performance-related alerts. This feature is particularly useful if you want to record the counter values for later analysis. Once you set it up, the counter log collects the data in the background. You can also schedule the counter log to start and stop logging at a certain time. Most important, you can include performance counters from a remote computer in the log, thus collecting the performance counter values remotely and storing them in the counter log on your local computer.

You can store the counter values in the log file in one of several formats. If you intend to later import the data into a database, it's convenient to use a text file format such as a comma-separated file (with a `.CSV` file extension).

Importing the data in a performance counter log into a SQL Server database presents a special challenge because the log could be very wide. Worse still, the number of columns in a log can change as new counters are added to the log or existing counters are dropped from the log. This means that you can't simply create a table whose structure mirrors that of the performance counter log file.

Note that it isn't really practical to try to fix the number of counters in a log. For instance, if you decide to include a certain SQL Server database counter in the log for analysis, you'll need to manually add the same counter later for a different database when the new database is created on the server. In other words, the number of counters will change as you add or drop databases.

Let's examine the structure of the Windows performance counter log as created by the Performance Logs and Alerts tool. To keep the discussion brief, assume that you'll log two counters on the server SQL01: `Memory\Pages/sec` and `PhysicalDisk(0 D:)\% Disk Time`. In the counter log, each counter is identified by what is known as the *counter path*, which is a combination of computer name, performance object, performance instance, instance index, and performance counter. A counter path typically follows this format:

```
\\Computer_name\Object_name(Instance_name#Index_Number)\Counter_name
```

Using this notation of the counter path, your two performance counters are identified as follows in the counter log:

```
\\SQL01\Memory\Pages/sec
\\SQL01\PhysicalDisk(0 D:)\% Disk Time
```

The entries of the counter log in the CSV file format should look like Listing 4-10.

Listing 4-10. Sample Counter Log Data

```
"...Time...","\\SQL01\Memory\Pages/sec","\\SQL01\PhysicalDisk(0 D:)\% Disk Time"
"09/08/2002 12:35:45","11.296813511113458","7.0625001143654654e"
"09/08/2002 12:36:00","0.26679653905997197","2.8829087316668804"
"09/08/2002 12:36:15","0.13331924737007395","2.0239260004978679"
```

> **NOTE** *The first column of the header line is actually something such as* (PDH-CSV 4.0) (Eastern Daylight Time)(240); *it has been edited to fit on one line. Additionally, milliseconds have been removed from the date string for the same purpose.*

Now, as the new counters are added, they're added as comma-separated new columns. But note that adding or dropping a counter results in the log data being written to a new log file. For a given log file, the number of columns is fixed and doesn't change. Every time the counter values are recorded in the log, a new line containing all the counter values is appended to the log with the first column providing the time stamp.

Obviously, you don't want to create a table to match the columns of the counter log. If you did, you'd have to change the schema of the table every time you add or remove a counter. What's more devastating with this approach is that you'll eventually run out of the maximum number of columns that a SQL Server table permits. SQL Server has a hard upper limit of 1,024 columns, but it's common to collect many more counters than 1,024.

Several alternative table schemas can adequately handle the performance counter data. Because the focus of this section is the data import instead of the table design, Listing 4-11 shows a straightforward table structure, but it may not be most optimal spacewise.

Listing 4-11. Schema of the Table to Hold the Logged Counter Data

```
CREATE TABLE tbSysperf (
        LogTime       datetime       NOT NULL ,
        Server        varchar (128)  NOT NULL ,
        Object        varchar (128)  NOT NULL ,
        Instance      varchar (128)  NULL ,
        Counter       varchar (128)  NOT NULL ,
        Value         float          NULL
)
```

Now, the job is to import the data illustrated in Listing 4-10 into the table defined in Listing 4-11, and this requires transforming the data in a performance counter log to a format that can be directly bulk copied into the table. Listing 4-12 presents the Perl script `preparePerfLog.pl` to accomplish this.

Listing 4-12. Preparing Performance Counter Log for Bulk Copy Import

```
use strict;

my $log = shift or
    die "***Err: Expects a performance counter log in the CSV format.";

# First get the columns on the first row.
# The columns except the first one are the performance counter paths
open(LOG, "$log") or die "***Err: Could not open performance counter log $log.";
my $header = <LOG>;
my @counterPaths = getCounterPath($header);

# Now move on to process the rest of the rows
my $columnCount = scalar @counterPaths;
my $logRowCount = 0;
my $counterCount = 0;

while (<LOG>) {
    my @columns = map {/"(.+)"/; $1;} split (/,/, $_);
    my $row = undef;

    for (my $i = 0; $i < $columnCount; $i++) {
        print $columns[0] . "\t"
                         . $counterPaths[$i]->[0] . "\t"
                         . $counterPaths[$i]->[1] . "\t"
                         . $counterPaths[$i]->[2] . "\t"
                         . $counterPaths[$i]->[3] . "\t"
```

```perl
                               . $columns[$i+1] . "\n";
         ++$counterCount;
      }
      ++$logRowCount;
   }
   print STDERR "$logRowCount log rows processed in total.\n";
   print STDERR "$counterCount counter values processed in total.\n";


#########################
sub getCounterPath {
   my $header = shift;
   my @counterPaths;
   my @headings = map {/"(.+)"/; $1;} split (/,/, $header);

   shift @headings;    # discard the first column of the header
   foreach my $h (@headings) {
      my ($server, $object, $instance, $counter, $rest);

      if ($h =~ /^\\\\([^\\]+)\\(.+)$/) {        # match for the server name
         $server = $1;
         $rest = $2;
         if ($rest =~ /^(.+)\\([^\\]+)$/) {      # match for counter name
            $object = $1;
            $counter = $2;
            if ($object =~ /^(.+)\((.+)\)$/) { # object followed by instance
               $object = $1;
               $instance = $2;            # object not followed by instance
            }
            else { $instance = ''; }
         }
         else {
            # shouldn't be here
            print STDERR "***Err: counter name format not expected for $h.\n";
         }
      }
      else {
         # shouldn't be here
         print STDERR "***Err: computer name format not expected for $h.\n";
      }
      # record the parsed counter paths for all the columns in an array
      push @counterPaths, [$server, $object, $instance, $counter];
   }
   return @counterPaths;
} # getCounterPath
```

Place the performance counter data in Listing 4-10 in the file perfLog.csv, and run the script in Listing 4-12 as shown in Listing 4-13 to produce the output that's ready to be bulk copied into the table defined in Listing 4-11.

Listing 4-13. Sample Log Data Ready for Bulk Copy

```
cmd>perl preparePerfLog.pl perfLog.csv
09/08/2002 12:35:45 SQL01 Memory             Pages/sec    11.296813511113458
09/08/2002 12:35:45 SQL01 PhysicalDisk  0 D: % Disk Time 7.0625001143654654e
09/08/2002 12:36:00 SQL01 Memory             Pages/sec    0.26679653905997197
09/08/2002 12:36:00 SQL01 PhysicalDisk  0 D: % Disk Time 2.8829087316668804
09/08/2002 12:36:15 SQL01 Memory             Pages/sec    0.13331924737007395
09/08/2002 12:36:15 SQL01 PhysicalDisk  0 D: % Disk Time 2.0239260004978679
```

After examining the table design, any performance-conscious and space-conscious DBA would quickly point out that including the counter paths in the same table as the counter values results in a huge waste of space and consequently impacts the database performance adversely.

A better design is to record the counter paths in a lookup table that identifies each counter path with a unique integer key and then replace the four counter path columns—Server, Object, Instance, and Counter—with this integer key in the counter value table. Spacewise, this replaces 512 bytes (that's 4*128 for the four counter path columns) with 4 bytes for each row. Because the table can easily grow to several million rows, this schema change has the potential of saving significant space and improving performance as well.

 NOTE *I'll leave it as an exercise for you to modify the script in Listing 4-12 so that the prepared data file can be directly bulk copied into the table that identifies the counter path with an integer, as outlined in the preceding paragraph. (A hint—add code to the function* getCounterPath() *to retrieve the integer key from the lookup table if the counter path is already there; otherwise, insert the counter path into the lookup table and return the integer key.)*

You should note that the script in Listing 4-12 uses a rather simplistic method to parse the comma-separated header in the function getCounterPath():

```
my @headings = map {/"(.+)"/; $1;} split (/,/, $header);
```

This assumes that there's no embedded double quotation mark. A more robust approach is to use the CPAN module Text::CSV_XS to do the parsing, as illustrated in the preceding section.

CAUTION   *Unfortunately, the counter log files created by the Windows 2000 Performance Logs and Alerts feature don't escape the embedded double quotation marks properly. I hope this will be fixed in a future release.*

Why Not Use the sysperfinfo Table?

If you have heard about the SQL Server system table sysperfinfo or have played with it briefly, you may wonder why you should go through all that trouble to import Windows performance counter values when you can get them through the sysperfinfo table. The problem is that the sysperfinfo table doesn't always provide the values for the performance counters you want to include. The most severe limitation of the sysperfinfo table is that it gives only SQL Server–specific counters. In addition, it accommodates only the first 99 databases. Together, these two factors render the sysperfinfo table impractical as a tool to collect arbitrary performance counter information.

Exporting Performance Data to a File for Charting

SCENARIO
You have performance counter values already in a SQL Server database. You want to export this data out to a file so that you can use the Windows System Monitor to plot charts.

If you already have the performance counter data in a database, you may not need to export the data to produce pretty charts. Many graphics packages on the market can plot charts directly from data in a database. You can also import data to a program such as Microsoft Excel to plot a variety of charts, which is suited for including the performance charts in your Microsoft Word documents or Microsoft PowerPoint slides.

However, you may still want to use the Windows System Monitor as a tool to graph the performance counter data. Some of its unique features make the System Monitor a terrific tool to look at the performance data.

As mentioned in the previous section, the first row of a performance counter log in the CSV format is the header line, and the rest of the file corresponds to the counter values for all the specified counters collected at a particular time. To generate such a file from a table with a schema similar to that in Listing 4-11 is cumbersome in T-SQL or even with DTS packages. The task is much simpler to accomplish with a combination of T-SQL and Perl scripting.

Assume that you have managed to export the counter values to a file—whose format mirrors the structure of the table defined in Listing 4-12—for a given set of counter paths. In addition, assume that the exported data is sorted by the counter value time stamp. Regardless of the actual table schema, this is easy to do in T-SQL, so I won't belabor the process. Instead, I focus on how a Perl script can take over to produce a file ready to be opened and charted with the System Monitor.

Listing 4-14 presents the script preparePerfLog.pl.

Listing 4-14. Preparing Counter Data in the CSV Format for Charting

```
use strict;
use SQLDBA::Utility qw( dbaSetDiff );

my $timeColumnHeader = '(PDH-CSV 4.0) (Eastern Daylight Time)(240)';
my $sampleDate;
my $sampleCount = 1;
my $rowCount = 0;
my @counters;
my @theCounters;
my @values;

my $file = shift or die "***Err: Expects a tab-separated file.";
open(CNTR, "$file") or die "***Err: Could not open the data file $file.";

while(<CNTR>) {
    ++$rowCount;
    chomp;
    my ($rowDate, $server, $object, $instance, $counter, $value) = split (/\t/);
    my $counterPath = $instance ?
                    "\\\\$server\\$object($instance)\\$counter":
                    "\\\\$server\\$object\\$counter";
```

```perl
    # the very first row is special
    if ($rowCount == 1) {
        $sampleDate  = $rowDate;
        @values      = ($value);
        @counters    = ($counterPath);
        @theCounters = ($counterPath);
    }
    # Now take care of the other rows
    else {
        # the new row is still in the same sample
        if ($sampleDate eq $rowDate) {
            push @values, $value;
            push @counters, $counterPath;
            push @theCounters, $counterPath if $sampleCount == 1;
        }
        # the new row is from a different sample, i.e we are crossing
        # the sample boundary
        else {
            printHeader($timeColumnHeader, @theCounters) if $sampleCount == 1;

            if (dbaSetDiff(\@counters, \@theCounters) or
                dbaSetDiff(\@theCounters, \@counters)) {
                print STDERR "Err: # of counter paths for $sampleDate differs.\n";
            }
            else {
                printValues($sampleDate, @values);
            }
            # now start a new sample
            ++$sampleCount;
            $sampleDate = $rowDate;
            @counters   = ($counterPath);
            @values     = ($value);
        }
    }
}
# if it's still the 1st sample, we have to print the header
printHeader($timeColumnHeader, @counters) if $sampleCount == 1;

# print the last sample
if (dbaSetDiff(\@counters, \@theCounters) or
    dbaSetDiff(\@theCounters, \@counters)) {
    print STDERR "Err: # of counter paths for $sampleDate is different.\n";
}
else {
```

```perl
      printValues($sampleDate, @values);
   }
   exit;


   #################
   sub printHeader {
      my ($timeColumnHeader, @counters) = @_;
      print "\"$timeColumnHeader\"";
      foreach my $col (@counters) {
         print ",\"$col\"";
      }
      print "\n";
   } # printheader


   #################
   sub printValues {
      my ($sampleDate, @values) = @_;
      print "\"$sampleDate\"";
      foreach my $value (@values) {
         print ",\"$value\"";
      }
      print "\n";
   } # printValues
```

Feed the data in Listing 4-13—perfLog.log—to the script in Listing 4-14 as follows:

```
cmd>perl CreatePerfLog.pl perfLog.log
```

This produces the data in Listing 4-10 ready to be plotted with the System Monitor. In effect, this script reverses the process of the script in Listing 4-12; it takes the output of the latter and reconstructs its input.

Several salient points are worth noting about this script. First, let's address the question you may be itching to ask: Why not directly generate the CSV performance counter log file with T-SQL? It's certainly possible to accomplish the task in T-SQL. However, it's going to be rather awkward because the job essentially involves pivoting the relational data similar to that in Listing 4-13, and T-SQL doesn't work well when the columns of the result aren't known in advance and must be handled dynamically. A more seriously limiting factor is that a T-SQL string is inherently constrained to a maximum of 8,000 characters. You must devise kludge workarounds to produce extremely wide output. It's true that the text data types don't suffer such a length limit, but the fact that the text data types aren't valid for T-SQL local variables doesn't help the case.

Second, given the data such as that in Listing 4-13, before you can write a script to "pivot" it, you must first decide on the columns—in other words, what performance counters—to be used in the final CSV output of the performance counter log file. As it passes through the data file, the script in Listing 4-14 picks the first set of performance counters to define the columns of the final output. Because the data file is sorted by the time stamp—in other words, the time at which the performance counter values are collected—procedurally this means all the performance counters before the time stamp value change for the first time. In Listing 4-13, the performance counters are recorded in the array `@theCounters`. From that point, the values for the same set of performance counters will be repeated, representing data sampled at different times. If it turns out that, for a certain time, values for a different set of performance counters are collected, this would be an error condition that's checked with the help of the SQLDBA::Utility function `dbaSetDiff()`.

As mentioned earlier, the script in Listing 4-14 passes through the data file only once. The script itself is fairly straightforward and intuitive if you imagine an invisible mark moving from the top to bottom one row at a time as well as one sample at a time. A *sample* consists of the entire performance counter values collected at a given time.

Finally, in both the function `printHeader()` and the function `printValues()`, the script simply adds a pair of double quotation marks around each header or value and then separates the delimited headers or values with commas. This isn't robust if there are any embedded double quotes. Ideally, you should use the module Text::CSV_XS to combine an array of strings into a CSV string. But unfortunately the System Monitor chokes on a performance counter log with any embedded double quote, so using this CSV module won't gain you much until Microsoft fixes the problem.

Summary

The first several Perl scripts in this chapter help validate the process of the bulk copy process, and the rest of the scripts are all about preparing data for import. Although Perl is a powerful tool for data migration, these scripts don't perform any actual data migration themselves; they work with and complement the existing data migration tools, making them easier and more effective to use. This is consistent with the overall message of this book: Instead of reinventing the wheel, you can write Perl scripts to fill the holes in the existing tools, stop the gaps between the existing tools, or extend the existing tools.

The next chapter further exploits Perl's potential to compare database objects and sort them by dependency.

#### CHAPTER 5

Comparing and Sorting Database Objects

ONE OF THE TASKS DATABASE ADMINISTRATORS (DBAs) OFTEN MUST PERFORM, especially in the context of configuration or change management, is to compare the schemas of database objects. The database objects can be tables, views, stored procedures, triggers, and user-defined functions to name a few. The objects can be in the same database or in two different databases. And the databases could be on the same server or on two different servers.

The other closely related task that DBAs often do is managing object dependencies such as the dependencies among stored procedures because of procedure calls or the dependencies among the tables because of referential integrity constraints.

This chapter presents a set of Perl scripts for comparing database objects and for tracking and sorting their dependencies. Although the primary focus is on stored procedures and tables, the methodology applies to all other database objects.

Comparing Object Schemas

For Perl to compare schemas for different objects, the first step is to get the schema information into a Perl data structure. You can obtain the schema information in two ways: by scanning and parsing a T-SQL script or by using the SQL-DMO interface. The former gives you all the schema information at once in a text file that you need to parse to populate your Perl data structures, and the latter requires you to traverse the SQL-DMO object hierarchy. Most of the Perl scripts in this chapter use SQL-DMO to retrieve the schema information for better control.

NOTE *Parsing an arbitrary Transact SQL (T-SQL) script for the schema information must correctly handle T-SQL comments, quoted strings, and delimited identifiers, as well as resolve the object names. Moreover, if the T-SQL script isn't formatted in a certain pattern, you must resort to a T-SQL parser. Crafting regular expressions isn't sufficient. As a result, if you're looking for specific schema information, it's often more convenient to traverse the SQL-DMO object hierarchy.*

Tracking and Sorting Object Dependencies

How to find all the dependencies of a database object and how to correctly order database objects by dependency are the topics frequently visited and revisited on the SQL Server newsgroups and discussion lists. Tracking object dependencies is an important part of understanding a database and performing the impact analysis of the database objects. Being able to sort database objects by dependency can lead to cleaner SQL scripts.

Comparing the Columns Between Two Tables

> **SCENARIO**
> *You want to compare the schemas of two tables in terms of their columns, data types, and column properties.*

How would you proceed with this scenario? Manual comparison is obviously not an option because the next thing you'll need to do is to compare not two but many tables and perhaps compare them on a regular basis. Three alternatives immediately come to mind: First, you could generate the scripts for the tables and compare the scripts using a file comparison utility to find the differences. Second, you could run sp_help on each table and compare the results of sp_help. Third, you could query the table schema with SQL-DMO, organize the information in a data structure, and perform a comparison.

This section uses the third method for its simplicity and extensibility. The first method often results in too many nuisances because file comparison utilities can't tell that some differences between two table scripts are insignificant and therefore can safely be ignored. The second approach, on the other hand, is subtle because of the potential presence of extended identifiers that may include spaces and other special characters. In addition, the output of sp_help doesn't include all the schema information on the columns, which you need in your comparison. For instance, sp_help simply doesn't report the SQL expression for a computed column.

To be more explicit about what column properties are to be compared, they include the answers to these questions:

- Is the column present?

- Does it allow nulls?

- Is it in the primary key?

- Is it an identity column?

- What's the column collation?

- Does it trim trailing blanks?

These questions form the dimensions on which the script in Listing 5-1 compares two SQL Server tables. As you'll soon see, the beauty of this approach is that you can easily extend the list of the column properties with little change to the Perl script.

Listing 5-1. Comparing the Columns of Two Tables

```perl
use strict;
use SQLDBA::SQLDMO qw( dbaGetTableColumns );
use SQLDBA::Utility qw( dbaSetDiff dbaSetCommon );

Main: {
   # for illustration purposes, I've hard-coded the table names
   # in the next two hashes
   my $tRef1 = { srvName => 'SQL1',
                 dbName  => 'pubs',
                 tabName => 'dbo.authors'};
   my $tRef2 = { srvName => 'SQL1',
                 dbName  => 'pubs',
                 tabName => 'dbo.authors'};
   # get the column information for each table
   my $ref1 = dbaGetTableColumns($tRef1);
   my $ref2 = dbaGetTableColumns($tRef2);
   # compare the columns in $ref1 and $ref2
   compareCol($tRef1, $ref1, $tRef2, $ref2);
} # Main


##################
sub compareCol {
   my ($tRef1, $ref1, $tRef2, $ref2) = @_;

   print "Comparing (1) $tRef1->{tabName} on $tRef1->{srvName}.$tRef1->{dbName}";
   print      " and (2) $tRef2->{tabName} on ",
                      "$tRef2->{serverName}.$tRef2->{dbName}:\n";
   print "   Checking column diff ...\n";
   # determine columns that are in (1) but not in (2)
   if (my @diff = dbaSetDiff([keys %$ref1], [keys %$ref2])) {
      print "\tColumns in (1) $tRef1->{tabName}, ",
                 "not in (2) $tRef2->{tabName}:\n";
      print "\t", join (', ', @diff), "\n";
```

```
    }
    # determine columns that are in (2) but not in (1)
    if (my @diff = dbaSetDiff([keys %$ref2], [keys %$ref1])) {
        print "\tColumns not in (1) $tRef1->{tabName}, ",
                        "but in (2) $tRef2->{tabName}:\n";
        print "\t", join (', ', @diff), "\n";
    }

    # for the common columns, determine whether any properties are different
    print "\n   Checking column property diff ...\n";
    foreach my $col (dbaSetCommon([keys %$ref1], [keys %$ref2])) {
        foreach my $prop (sort keys %{$ref1->{$col}}) {
            my $value1 = $ref1->{$col}->{$prop};
            my $value2 = $ref2->{$col}->{$prop};
            if ($value1 ne $value2) {
                print "\t$col, $prop: (1) = $value1, (2) = $value2\n";
            }
        }
    }
  }
} # compareCol
```

The two tables, along with their database names and SQL Server instance names, are hard-coded in Listing 5-1. This is fine for now because the focus in this section is to highlight the code that retrieves the column information and the code that performs the comparison.

Save the script to the file compareColumns.pl and run the script at the command prompt to see what it reports with regard to the differences between the two authors tables identified in Listing 5-1:

```
cmd>perl compareColumns.pl
Comparing (1) dbo.authors on SQL1.pubs and (2) authors on SQL2.pubs:
    Checking column diff ...
    Columns in (1) dbo.authors, not in (2) dbo.authors:
    contract

    Checking column property diff ...
    zip, AllowNulls: (1) = 0, (2) = 1
    zip, Length: (1) = 9, (2) = 5
    city, Length: (1) = 22, (2) = 20
```

In the output, (1) indicates the first table and (2) the second table. The script reports that the column contact is in the authors table on SQL1, but not in the authors table on SQL2. In addition, it reports the following differences between the columns zip and city:

- The zip column permits nulls on SQL1, but not on SQL2.

- The zip column has a width of nine characters on SQL1, but five characters on SQL2.

- The city column has a width of 22 characters on SQL1, but 20 on SQL2.

The code to retrieve the table columns and their properties is encapsulated in the function dbaGetTableColumns() from the module SQLDBA::SQLDMO, which has a collection of functions that work with SQL-DMO. Listing 5-2 shows the code for the function dbaGetTableColumns().

Listing 5-2. Retrieving Column Information with dbaGetTableColumns()

```
1.    sub dbaGetTableColumns {
2.        my $ref = shift or
3.            die "***Err: dbaGetTableColumns() expects a reference.";
4.        my $server = Win32::OLE->new('SQLDMO.SQLServer')
5.          or die "***Err: Could not create SQLDMO object.";
6.        $server->{LoginSecure} = 1;  # use trusted connection
7.
8.        $server->connect($ref->{srvName}, '', '');
9.        ! Win32::OLE->LastError() or
10.           die "***Err: Could not connect to $ref->{srvName}.";
11.
12.       my $table = $server->Databases($ref->{dbName})->Tables($ref->{tabName});
13.       ! Win32::OLE->LastError() or
14.           die "***Err: could not get the table object.";
15.
16.       my $colRef;
17.       foreach my $col (in($table->Columns())) {  # enumerate the columns
18.           $colRef->{$col->Name()} = {              # record column properties
19.               Position          => $col->ID(),
20.               AllowNulls        => $col->AllowNulls(),
21.               AnsiPaddingStatus => $col->AnsiPaddingStatus(),
22.               Collation         => $col->Collation(),
23.               ComputedText      => $col->ComputedText(),
24.               DataType          => $col->DataType(),
25.               Identity          => $col->Identity(),
26.               InPrimaryKey      => $col->InPrimaryKey(),
27.               Length            => $col->Length(),
```

```
28.           NumericPrecision    => $col->NumericPrecision(),
29.           NumericScale        => $col->NumericScale(),
30.           PhysicalDatatype    => $col->PhysicalDatatype(),
31.       };
32.   }
33.   $server->disconnect();
34.   $server->DESTROY();
35.   return $colRef;
36. } # dbaGetTableColumns
```

Note that the path from the SQLServer object $server to the Columns collection is as follows, using Perl's arrow notation:

```
$server->Databases(<dbName>)->Tables(<tabName>}->Columns()
```

where you should replace <dbName> and <tabName> with the respective database name and table name. Then on line 17 in Listing 5-2, the in() function helps enumerate the Column objects in the foreach loop. The Column object possesses all the properties you would want to compare. From line 19 to 30, the script collects the column properties into a hash with the property name as the key and the property value as the corresponding hash value.

Listing 5-3 is an example of the data structure that dbaGetTableColumns() returns. The data structure is dumped out by the Dumper() function of the Data::Dumper module. This data structure is a hash of hashes. The hash keys at the first level are the column names of the table, and the second-level hash keys are the names of the column properties.

Listing 5-3. Sample Data Structure Returned by dbaGetTableColumns()

```
$ref1 = {
        'contract' => {
                        'Length'           => 1,
                        'AllowNulls'       => 0,
                        'NumericPrecision' => 0,
                        'PhysicalDatatype' => 'bit',
                        'InPrimaryKey'     => 0,

                        ...

                      },
        'zip' => {
                   'Length'           => 9,
                   'Position'         => 8,
                   'AllowNulls'       => 0,
```

```
                   'NumericPrecision'  => 0,
                   'PhysicalDatatype'  => 'char',
                   'AnsiPaddingStatus' => 1,
                   'Collation'         => 'SQL_Latin1_General_CP1_CI_AS',
                   'InPrimaryKey'      => 0,
                   'ComputedText'      => '',
                   'DataType'          => 'char',
                   'Identity'          => 0,
                   'NumericScale'      => 0
              },
    'city' => {
                   'Length' => 22,
                   'AllowNulls' => 1,
                   'Position'          => 6,
                     ...
              },
    ...
};
```

The `compareCol()` function in Listing 5-1 performs the actual comparison of
the column properties. As you can see, the comparison isn't dependent on the specifics of the columns or their properties. The function simply compares the hash
keys and values. Consequently, if you discover you need to include additional
column properties in the comparison—for instance, the property of NOT FOR
REPLICATION—all you need to do is to insert a line of code anywhere between lines
19 and 29 in Listing 5-2 for the function `dbaGetTableColumns()` in order to add the
corresponding hash key/value to the data structure in Listing 5-3. There's no need
to make any other change.

Finally, note that one of the properties of a column in the comparison is the
ordinal position of the column in the table. If the column positions are different
between two tables, the script in Listing 5-1 reports the difference in terms of the
positions of the columns.

Comparing the Indexes Between Two Tables

SCENARIO
You want to compare the indexes of two tables.

Just as with comparing the columns of two tables in the previous section, before
you can compare two indexes you must first obtain the information about the
indexes with respect to all the index properties you want to compare.

Though you can choose to be comprehensive or selective, you should at least include the following index properties in the comparison:

- Which table columns are used in the index? What is their order?

- Is it a clustered index?

- Is it a unique index?

- Is it created as the result of the primary key constraint?

- Is it created as the result of a unique key constraint?

- What's its fillfactor?

- Does it pad the index pages with the fillfactor?

The script in Listing 5-4 compares the indexes between two tables. It populates the nested hash structures with the index information retrieved through SQL-DMO, and it examines the differences between the hash structures to find the indexes present in one table but not the other and to find any differences in their properties between the indexes that are present in both tables.

Listing 5-4. Comparing Indexes Between Two Tables

```
use strict;
use SQLDBA::SQLDMO qw( dbaGetTableIndexes );
use SQLDBA::Utility qw( dbaSetDiff dbaSetCommon );

Main: {
    # for illustration, I've hard-coded the two index names
    my $tRef1 = { srvName => 'SQL1',
                  dbName  => 'pubs',
                  tabName => 'dbo.authors'};
    my $tRef2 = { srvName => 'SQL2',
                  dbName  => 'pubs',
                  tabName => 'authors'};

    # get the index info for each index
    my $ref1 = dbaGetTableIndexes($tRef1);
    my $ref2 = dbaGetTableIndexes($tRef2);
    # compare the two indexes
    compareIdx($tRef1, $ref1, $tRef2, $ref2);
} # Main
```

```
##################
sub compareIdx {
   my ($tRef1, $ref1, $tRef2, $ref2) = @_;
   my ($tbName1, $tbName2) = ($tRef1->{tabName}, $tRef2->{tabName});

   print "Comparing (1) $tbName1 on $tRef1->{srvName}.$tRef1->{dbName}";
   print " and (2) $tbName2 on $tRef2->{srvName}.$tRef2->{dbName}:\n";
   print "   Checking index diff ...\n";
   # determine indexes that are in (1) but not in (2)
   if (my @diff = dbaSetDiff([keys %$ref1], [keys %$ref2])) {
      print "\tIndexes in (1) $tbName1, not in (2) $tbName2:\n";
      print "\t", join (', ', @diff), "\n";
   }
   # determine indexes that are in (2) but not in (1)
   if (my @diff = dbaSetDiff([keys %$ref2], [keys %$ref1])) {
      print "\tIndexes not in (1) $tbName1, but in (2) $tbName2:\n";
      print "\t", join (', ', @diff), "\n";
   }

   # for the common indexes, determine whether their properties are different
   print "\n   Checking index property diff ...\n";
   foreach my $idx (dbaSetCommon([keys %$ref1], [keys %$ref2])) {
      foreach my $prop (sort keys %{$ref1->{$idx}}) {
         my $value1 = $ref1->{$idx}->{$prop};
         my $value2 = $ref2->{$idx}->{$prop};
         if ($value1 ne $value2) {
            print "\t$idx, $prop: (1) = $value1, (2) = $value2\n";
         }
      }
   }
} # compareIdx
```

To see what this script reports, start with a pristine copy of the pubs database on each SQL Server instance and run the following T-SQL script on instance SQL1 to create one index on the authors table:

```
USE pubs
go
CREATE UNIQUE INDEX ix_idphone ON authors(au_id, phone)
go
```

Then, run the following T-SQL script on SQL2 to create two indexes on the authors table and note the index differences between these two authors tables:

```
USE pubs
go
CREATE INDEX ix_idphone ON authors(au_id, phone)
    WITH PAD_INDEX, FILLFACTOR = 60

CREATE INDEX ix_address ON authors(address)
Go
```

Save the script in Listing 5-4 as compareIndexes.pl and execute it from the command line to see the comparison results, as shown in Listing 5-5.

Listing 5-5. Comparing the Indexes on authors *Between Two Servers*

```
cmd>perl compareIndexes.pl
Comparing (1) dbo.authors on SQL1.pubs and (2) authors on SQL2.pubs:
   Checking index diff ...
    Indexes not in (1) dbo.authors, but in (2) authors:
    ix_address

   Checking index property diff ...
    ix_idphone, FillFactor: (1) = 0, (2) = 60
    ix_idphone, PadIndex: (1) = no, (2) = yes
    ix_idphone, Unique: (1) = yes, (2) = no
```

The reported differences correctly reflect the changes introduced by the two previous T-SQL scripts. The key of the script in Listing 5-4 is using the function dbaGetTableIndexes() from the module SQLDBA::SQLDMO to retrieve the index information of a table into a Perl nested data structure—in other words, $ref1. Listing 5-6 is an example of the data structure to represent the indexes of the authors table, which is similar to the data structure illustrated in Listing 5-3.

Listing 5-6. Sample Data Structure for the Indexes of the authors *Table*

```
$ref1 = {
        'aunmind' => {
                        'UniqueKey'     => 'no',
                        'FillFactor'    => 0,
                        'Clustered'     => 'no',
                        'IgnoreDupKey'  => 'no',
                        'NoRecompute'   => 'no',
                        'IndexedColumns' => 'au_lname,au_fname',
```

```
                        'PadIndex'         => 'no',
                        'Unique'           => 'no',
                        'PrimaryKey'       => 'no',
                        'FileGroup'        => 'PRIMARY'
                  },
     'UPKCL_auidind' => {
                          'UniqueKey'      => 'no',
                          'FillFactor'     => 0,
                          'Clustered'      => 'yes',
                          'IgnoreDupKey'   => 'no',
                          'NoRecompute'    => 'no',
                          'IndexedColumns' => 'au_id',
                          'PadIndex'       => 'no',
                          'Unique'         => 'yes',
                          'PrimaryKey'     => 'yes',
                          'FileGroup'      => 'PRIMARY'
                  }
    };
```

Now, you'll see how to obtain this data structure with the function
dbaGetTableIndexes(), which walks the SQL-DMO object hierarchy to retrieve
the information on the index properties. Listing 5-7 shows the code for the
dbaGetTableIndexes() function.

Listing 5-7. Retrieving Table Index Information with dbaGetTableIndexes()

```
1.   sub dbaGetTableIndexes {
2.     my $ref = shift or
3.         die "***Err: dbaGetTableIndexes() expects a reference.";
4.     my $server = Win32::OLE->new('SQLDMO.SQLServer')
5.       or die "***Err: Could not create SQLDMO object.";
6.     $server->{LoginSecure} = 1;  # use trusted connection
7.
8.     $server->connect($ref->{srvName}, '', ''); # connect to the server
9.     ! Win32::OLE->LastError() or
10.       die "***Err: Could not connect to $ref->{srvName}.";
11.
12.    my $table = $server->Databases($ref->{dbName})->Tables($ref->{tabName});
13.    ! Win32::OLE->LastError() or
14.       die "***Err: could not get the table object.";
15.
16.    my $idxRef;
17.    foreach my $idx (in($table->Indexes())) {  # enumerate indexes
18.       next if $idx->Type() & SQLDMOIndex_Hypothetical;
```

```
19.
20.        my @cols;
21.        foreach my $col (in($idx->ListIndexedColumns())) { # enumerate col's
22.            push @cols, $col->Name()
23.        }
24.        $idxRef->{$idx->Name()} = {                 # record index properties
25.            IndexedColumns => join(',', @cols),    # concatenate index keys
26.            FillFactor     => $idx->FillFactor(),
27.            FileGroup      => $idx->FileGroup(),
28.            Clustered =>         # use bit-wise AND to determine the type info
29.                    ($idx->Type() & SQLDMOIndex_Clustered) ? 'yes' : 'no',
30.            IgnoreDupKey =>
31.                    ($idx->Type() & SQLDMOIndex_IgnoreDupKey) ? 'yes' : 'no',
32.            NoRecompute =>
33.                    ($idx->Type() & SQLDMOIndex_NoRecompute) ? 'yes' : 'no',
34.            PadIndex => ($idx->Type() & SQLDMOIndex_PadIndex) ? 'yes' : 'no',
35.            PrimaryKey =>
36.                    ($idx->Type() & SQLDMOIndex_DRIPrimaryKey) ? 'yes' : 'no',
37.            Unique => ($idx->Type() & SQLDMOIndex_Unique) ? 'yes' : 'no',
38.            UniqueKey =>
39.                    ($idx->Type() & SQLDMOIndex_DRIUniqueKey) ? 'yes' : 'no',
40.        };
41.    }
42.
43.    $server->disconnect();
44.    $server->DESTROY();
45.    return $idxRef;
46. } # dbaGetTableIndexes
```

In terms of the structure, this code is similar to that in Listing 5-2 for the function dbaGetTableColumns(). However, you should note several important differences. The first thing to note is how the function dbaGetTableIndexes() obtains the names of the table columns in an index from line 21 to 23. With an index object in the $idx variable on line 21, the function uses the ListIndexedColumns() method to get the index column collection. It then applies a foreach loop to enumerate the column objects in the collection to retrieve the name of each column object. Finally, the column names are recorded in the hash record on line 25 as the value of the key IndexedColumns.

The second salient point about the index object is its Type() property. Many important index properties—such as whether the index is clustered or unique—are not directly listed as the object properties like the Fillfactor property is. Rather, they're encoded in the number returned by the Type() property by setting the appropriate bits of the number, and you can use the & operator (bitwise AND) to retrieve the individual property settings. The symbolic constants you can use to decode these property values are imported at the beginning of the module SQLDBA::SQLDMO, where the `dbaGetTableIndexes()` function is defined, as follows:

```
use Win32::OLE::Const 'Microsoft SQLDMO';
```

Also, note that on line 18, the function checks whether the index is in fact a statistic instead of a conventional index. If a bitwise AND of the constant SQLDMOIndex_Hypothetical and the `Type()` property returns true, it's a statistic.

Finally, the script in Listing 5-4 compares the indexes between two tables, and it addresses the scenario described at the beginning of this section. However, in many cases you want to compare two specific indexes instead of all the indexes between two tables. To meet this requirement, you can use the `dbaGetIndexInfo()` function and the script `compareIndexInfo.pl` that come in the SQLDBA Toolkit, which you can download from the Apress Web site (`http://www.apress.com`) in the Downloads sections (along with the scripts in this chapter).

Comparing the Constraints Between Two Tables

> **SCENARIO**
> *You want to compare the declarative integrity constraints between two tables.*

Constraints help protect data integrity in a table or between tables. You can define the following integrity constraints on SQL Server tables:

- PRIMARY KEY constraints

- UNIQUE KEY constraints

- FOREIGN KEY constraints

- CHECK constraints

- DEFAULT constraints

Broadly speaking, you could also consider column nullability to be a type of constraint. Because Listing 5-1 in the "Comparing Table Columns" section already handled comparing column nullability, this section won't include column nullability in the constraint comparison.

As usual, the critical first step is to retrieve the constraint information into a Perl data structure. Then, you can reduce the problem to comparing the differences between two data structures. Unlike comparing table columns and indexes, you can't simply compare the constraint names because they aren't important in most cases and are often automatically generated.

Comparing DEFAULT Constraints

A DEFAULT constraint is specific to a table column, and a column allows only one default constraint. Thus, you can organize the information of the default constraints by table column. Then, it's a matter of comparing whether the default expressions match for the same column between the two tables.

The data structure for the DEFAULT constraints is simple because it doesn't have any property other than the expression itself. Listing 5-8 is an example of the data structure for all the DEFAULT constraints of the authors table where state and phone are two columns.

Listing 5-8. Sample Data Structure for the DEFAULT Constraints

```
$ref = {
        Defaults => {      # this key identifies DEFAULT constraints
                     state => {   # this key identifies the column
                             Expression => '(\'NY\')'
                         },
                     phone => {   # identifies another column
                             Expression => '(\'UNKNOWN\')'
                         }
             }
};
```

Comparing CHECK Constraints

The difficulty with comparing CHECK constraints is that you can have complete duplicate CHECK constraints on a table as long as you pick a different name for each constraint. However, as far as preserving data integrity is concerned, the CHECK expression uniquely identifies the constraint.

In addition to its expression, the CHECK constraint has two additional properties: Is it NOT FOR REPLICATION? and is it enabled? Listing 5-9 is a sample data structure for recording the CHECK constraints of a table.

Listing 5-9. Sample Data Structure for the CHECK *Constraints*

```
$ref = {
        'Checks' => {     # this key identifies CHECK constraints
                '([zip] like \'[0-9][0-9][0-9][0-9][0-9]\')' => {
                                        'ExcludeReplication' => 0,
                                        'Checked' => 1
                                },
                '([state] like \'[a-zA-Z][a-zA-Z]\')' => {
                                        'ExcludeReplication' => 0,
                                        'Checked' => 1
                                },
        }
};
```

Comparing Key Constraints

The "key" constraints (in other words, primary keys, foreign keys, and unique keys) are more difficult to handle. Like the CHECK constraints, you can have duplicate foreign keys and unique keys on a table as long as their names are distinct. Unlike the CHECK constraints, however, there's no single property to uniquely identify a foreign key or a unique key. For comparison purposes, you can use the concatenation of the following property values to identify a key constraint:

- The names of all the key columns

- The referenced table name (empty for a primary key or a unique key)

- The names of all the referenced key columns (empty if not a foreign key)

- A "yes" or "no" answer to the question, "Is it a unique key?"

This concatenated string will be the hash key to reference the hash for each key constraint of a table. Forward slashes (/) separate the four substrings. Listing 5-10 shows an example of the data structure to record the key constraints of a table.

Lisitng 5-10. Sample Data Structure for the PRIMARY KEY, FOREIGN KEY, *and* UNIQUE *Constraints*

```
$ref = {
        'Keys' => {      # the hash key identifies key constraints
                'title_id/[dbo].[titles]/title_id/yes' => {
                                        'ReferencedTable' => '[dbo].[titles]',
                                        'KeyColumns' => 'title_id',
                                        'ExcludeReplication' => 0,
                                        'Unique' => 'yes',
                                        'ReferencedKeyColumns' => 'title_id',
                                        'Checked' => 1,
                                        'Primary' => 'no',
                                        'Foreign' => 'yes'
                                },
                'au_id,title_id///no' => {
                                        'ReferencedTable' => '',
                                        'KeyColumns' => 'au_id,title_id',
                                        'ExcludeReplication' => 0,
                                        'Unique' => 'no',
                                        'ReferencedKeyColumns' => '',
                                        'Checked' => 1,
                                        'Primary' => 'no',
                                        'Foreign' => 'no'
                                },
        }
};
```

In Listing 5-10, 'title_id/[dbo].[titles]/title_id/yes' is the concatenation of the key column 'title_id', the referenced table '[dbo].[titles]', the referenced key column ' title_id', and a 'yes' to indicate a unique index. Similarly, for the second constraint, 'au_id,title_id///no' is the concatenation of the key columns 'au_id,title_id' and a 'no' to indicate a nonunique index. Because this isn't a foreign key constraint, both the reference key columns and the referenced key columns are empty—hence the empty strings between the forward slashes.

Using a Perl Script to Compare Constraints

Listing 5-11 shows the code for compareConstraints.pl, which compares the integrity constraints between two tables. Again, to focus on the main points, the two table names and their databases and servers are hard-coded in the script.

Listing 5-11. Comparing the Integrity Constraints Between Two Tables

```
1.    use strict;
2.    use SQLDBA::SQLDMO qw( dbaGetTableConstraints );
3.    use SQLDBA::Utility qw( dbaSetDiff dbaSetCommon );
4.
5.    Main: {  # for illustration, I've hard-coded the two table names
6.        my $tRef1 = { srvName => 'SQL1',
7.                      dbName  => 'pubs',
8.                      tbName  => 'authors'};
9.        my $tRef2 = { srvName => 'SQL2',
10.                     dbName  => 'pubs',
11.                     tbName  => 'authors'};
12.       # get table constraints
13.       my $ref1 = dbaGetTableConstraints($tRef1);
14.       my $ref2 = dbaGetTableConstraints($tRef2);
15.       # compare table constraints
16.       compareConstraints($tRef1, $ref1, $tRef2, $ref2);
17. } # Main
18.
19. ###########################
20. sub compareConstraints {
21.     my ($tRef1, $ref1, $tRef2, $ref2) = @_;
22.     my $tbName1 = "$tRef1->{srvName}.$tRef1->{dbName}.$tRef1->{tbName}";
23.     my $tbName2 = "$tRef2->{srvName}.$tRef2->{dbName}.$tRef2->{tbName}";
24.     # Loop thru the constraint types
25.     foreach my $type ('Checks', 'Defaults', 'Keys') {
26.         # check whether a constraint is only on $tbName1
27.         print "\n   Checking $type diff ...\n";
28.         if (my @diff = dbaSetDiff([keys %{$ref1->{$type}}],
29.                                   [keys %{$ref2->{$type}}])) {
30.           print "\t$type in (1) $tbName1, not in (2) $tbName2:\n";
31.           print "\t", join (",\n\t", @diff), "\n";
32.         }
33.         # check whether a constraint is only on $tbName2
34.         if (my @diff = dbaSetDiff([keys %{$ref2->{$type}}],
35.                                   [keys %{$ref1->{$type}}])) {
36.           print "\t$type not in (1) $tbName1, but in (2) $tbName2:\n";
37.           print "\t", join (",\n", @diff), "\n";
38.         }
39.
40.         print "\n   Checking $type property diff ...\n";
41.         # loop thru the common constraints
42.         foreach my $ck (dbaSetCommon([keys %{$ref1->{$type}}],
```

```
43.                                    [keys %{$ref2->{$type}}]])) {
44.          # loop thru the properties to compare their values
45.          foreach my $prop (keys %{$ref1->{$type}->{$ck}}) {
46.              my $value1 = $ref1->{$type}->{$ck}->{$prop};
47.              my $value2 = $ref2->{$type}->{$ck}->{$prop};
48.              if ($value1 ne $value2) {
49.                  print "\t$ck: (1) = $value1, (2) = $value2\n";
50.              }
51.          } # foreach my $prop
52.        } # foreach my $ck
53.      } # foreach my $type
54. } # compareConstraints
```

This script is nearly identical to the one in Listing 5-1 for comparing table columns and the one in Listing 5-4 for comparing table indexes. The reason for this is that they all use nearly identical data structures to store the information captured. In addition, this is because the code to compare these data structures is generic.

Comparing the examples in Listing 5-8 through Listing 5-10 with the examples in Listing 5-5 or Listing 5-6, you may notice an additional layer that doesn't exist in the data structures for storing the table columns and the indexes. With the hash keys such as 'Defaults', 'Checks', and 'Keys', this layer organizes the three types of constraints into their own nested data structures. The function compareConstraints() in Listing 5-11 includes an additional foreach loop over these constraint types between lines 25 and 53.

The following is an example of the script in Listing 5-11 in action:

```
cmd>perl compareConstraints.pl
    Checking Checks diff ...
    Checks in (1) SQL1.pubs..authors, not in (2) SQL2.pubs.dbo.authors:
    ([state] like '[a-zA-Z][a-zA-Z]')


    Checking Checks property diff ...


    Checking Defaults diff ...
    Defaults in (1) SQL1.pubs..authors, not in (2) SQL2.pubs.dbo.authors:
    state


    Checking Defaults property diff ...
    phone: (1) = ('UNKNOWN'), (2) = ('N/A')


    Checking Keys diff ...


    Checking Keys property diff ...
```

This outcome reports three differences in the declarative integrity constraints between the authors table on SQL1 and the authors table on SQL2:

- There's a CHECK constraint—whose expression is ([state] like '[a-zA-Z][a-zA-Z]')—on the authors table on SQL1 only.

- A DEFAULT property is defined for the state column of the authors table on SQL1, but not on SQL2.

- The default value for the phone column is ('UNKNOWN') for SQL1, but the default is ('N/A') on SQL2.

To see how the script may report the differences in the primary keys, foreign keys, or unique keys between two tables, run it against the pubs..titleauthor table between SQL1 and SQL2 to get the following results:

```
cmd>perl compareConstraints.pl
   Checking Checks diff ...

   Checking Checks property diff ...

   Checking Defaults diff ...

   Checking Defaults property diff ...

   Checking Keys diff ...
   Keys in (1) SQL1.pubs..titleauthor, not in (2) SQL2.pubs..titleauthor:
   title_id/[dbo].[titles]/title_id/yes,
   au_id,title_id///no,
   au_id/[dbo].[authors]/au_id/yes

   Checking Keys property diff ...
```

In this report, three key constraints are found on titleauthor on SQL1, but not on SQL2. Two of them are foreign keys (for example, see the string title_id/[dbo].[titles]/title_id/yes, which is a foreign key on the column title_id referencing the same column on the table titles), and the other is a primary key (see the string au_id,title_id///no, which is the primary key on the columns au_id and title_id).

Now, you'll see how the information on the constraints of a table is obtained and stored in the nested data structures shown in Listing 5-8 through Listing 5-10. Listing 5-12 shows the code for the function dbaGetTableConstraints().

Listing 5-12. Retrieving Table Constraints with dbaGetTableConstraints()

```perl
1.    sub dbaGetTableConstraints {
2.        my $ref = shift or    # accept a hash reference
3.            die "***Err: dbaGetTableConstraints() expects a reference.";
4.
5.        my $server = Win32::OLE->new('SQLDMO.SQLServer')
6.            or die "***Err: Could not create SQLDMO object.";
7.        $server->{LoginSecure} = 1;  # use trusted connection
8.        $server->connect($ref->{srvName}, '', '');
9.        ! Win32::OLE->LastError() or
10.           die "***Err: Could not connect to $ref->{srvName}.";
11.
12.       my $table = $server->Databases($ref->{dbName})->Tables($ref->{tbName});
13.       ! Win32::OLE->LastError() or
14.           die "***Err: could not get the table object.";
15.       my $cRef;
16.       # Get info on PKs, FKs, UNIQUEs (key constraints)
17.       foreach my $key (in($table->Keys())) {  # loop thru the key constraints
18.           my @keyCols;  # get columns in a key constraint
19.           for(my $i = 1; $i <= $key->KeyColumns()->Count(); $i++) {
20.               push @keyCols, $key->KeyColumns($i);
21.           }
22.
23.           my @refKeyCols;  # get the referenced columns (FK's only)
24.           for(my $i = 1; $i <= $key->ReferencedColumns()->Count(); $i++) {
25.               push @refKeyCols, $key->ReferencedColumns($i);
26.           }
27.
28.           my $keyID = join(',', @keyCols) . '/' . $key->{ReferencedTable} . '/';
29.           $keyID .= join(',', @refKeyCols) . '/';
30.           $keyID .= $key->Type() & SQLDMOKey_Unique ? 'yes' : 'no';
31.
32.           $cRef->{Keys}->{$keyID} = {
33.               Name => $key->Name(),
34.               KeyColumns => join(',', @keyCols),
35.               ReferencedKeyColumns => join(',', @refKeyCols),
36.               ReferencedTable => $key->{ReferencedTable},
37.               Checked => $key->{Checked},
38.               ExcludeReplication => $key->{ExcludeReplication},
39.               Foreign => $key->Type() == SQLDMOKey_Foreign ? 'yes' : 'no',
40.               Primary => $key->Type() == SQLDMOKey_Primary ? 'yes' : 'no',
41.               Unique => $key->Type() == SQLDMOKey_Unique ? 'yes' : 'no',
42.           };
```

```
43.   }
44.
45.   # Get info on DEFAULT constraints
46.   foreach my $col (in($table->Columns())) {
47.      if ($col->DRIDefault()->Name()) {
48.         $cRef->{Defaults}->{$col->Name()}->{Expression} =
49.                                      $col->DRIDefault()->Text();
50.      }
51.   }
52.
53.   # Get CHECK constraints
54.   foreach my $check (in($table->Checks())) {
55.      $cRef->{Checks}->{$check->Text()} = {
56.         Checked => $check->{Checked},
57.         ExcludeReplication => $check->{ExcludeReplication},
58.      };
59.   }
60.
61.   $server->disconnect();
62.   $server->DESTROY();
63.   return $cRef;
64. } # dbaGetTableConstraints
```

To write this function, all it takes is to study the SQL-DMO object hierarchy from the Table object through the Keys collection to the Key object. Sometimes, you have to be careful in reading the fine print. A case in point is the KeyColumns collection (see lines 19 and 21 in Listing 5-12) or the ReferencedColumns collection (see lines 24 and 26). If you're not careful, you might think these are collections of objects when in fact they're string containers. If you try to apply the in() function to them, you'll get an error—which by the way doesn't explicitly suggest anything wrong with the use of in().

Pay attention to how the identification of a "key" constraint is constructed on lines 28 through 30 by concatenating the names of the key columns, the name of the referenced table, the referenced key columns, and a 'yes' or 'no' depending on whether it's a UNIQUE constraint. Forward slashes (/) separate the substrings to keep the concatenated string more readable. When it's a primary key or a unique key, the reference table name and the referenced key columns are empty.

This identification string is used on lines 32 through 42 as the hash key to reference another hash that records the properties of the "key" constraint.

CAUTION *In the SQL Server 2000 Books Online, the SQL-DMO documentation on the* Keys *collection and the* Key *object only mentions* PRIMARY KEY *constraints or* FOREIGN KEY *constraints as if they didn't apply to* UNIQUE *constraints. For the record, a* UNIQUE *constraint is in the* Keys *collection and is a* Key *object.*

It's important to note that because you can define duplicate foreign keys and duplicate unique keys that are identical with the exception of their names, using the identification string constructed from line 28 to 30 in Listing 5-12 will end up with only one hash record for however many duplicate "key" constraints. For the present purpose—which is to compare constraints—this works fine. Obviously, this won't do if you're trying to flag duplicate constraints to identify poor table design.

 NOTE *SQL-DMO doesn't expose any property with regard to the cascade actions of a* FOREIGN KEY *constraint. If it's important for the constraint comparison to include cascade actions, it makes more sense for the function* dbaGetTableConstraints() *to parse the output of* sp_helpconstraint *than traverse the SQL-DMO object hierarchy.*

Comparing Two Stored Procedures

SCENARIO
You want to compare two stored procedures to see whether they're the same. If they're different, you want to see where they begin to differ.

There's no real difference in approach whether you're comparing two stored procedures, two views, two triggers, two user-defined functions, or even two arbitrary T-SQL scripts—you're simply comparing two T-SQL scripts. This section focuses on comparing two stored procedures, but the method applies to any T-SQL scripts.

The script compareSPs.pl in Listing 5-13 expects the names of the stored procedures, their databases, and their servers, and it retrieves the T-SQL code from their respective databases, compares their code, and reports whether they're different. In addition, the script accepts two options controlling the case sensitivity of the comparison and whether the whitespace should be ignored during the comparison.

Listing 5-13. Comparing Two Stored Procedures

```perl
1.   use strict;
2.   use Getopt::Std;
4.   use SQLDBA::SQLDMO qw( dbaScriptSP );
5.   use SQLDBA::ParseSQL qw( dbaNormalizeSQL dbaRestoreSQL );
6.   use SQLDBA::Utility qw( dbaStringDiff );
7.
8.   my %opts;
9.   getopts('ciS:D:P:s:d:p:', \%opts);     # get command line arguments
10.  my ($case, $ignoreWhitespace) = ($opts{c}, $opts{i});
11.  my $sRef1 = {srvName => $opts{S}, dbName => $opts{D}, spName => $opts{P}};
12.  my $sRef2 = {srvName => $opts{s}, dbName => $opts{d}, spName => $opts{p}};
13.
14.  Main: {
15.     # get the scripts for the SPs
16.     my $ref1 = dbaScriptSP($sRef1);  # script the 1st SP
17.     my $ref2 = dbaScriptSP($sRef2);  # script the 2nd SP
18.
19.     # collapse the whitespaces, if specified
20.     if ($ignoreWhitespace) {
21.        foreach my $ref ($ref1, $ref2) { # work on both SPs
22.           my $sqlRef = dbaNormalizeSQL($ref->{Script}, 1);
23.           $sqlRef->{code} =~ s/\s+/ /g;        # whitespace to single space
24.           $sqlRef = dbaRestoreSQL($sqlRef);
25.           $ref->{Script} = $sqlRef->{code};
26.        }
27.     }
28.     # now compare the SPs
29.     compareSP($sRef1, $ref1, $sRef2, $ref2, $ignoreWhitespace);
30.  } # Main
31.
32.  ##################
33.  sub compareSP {
34.     my ($sRef1, $ref1, $sRef2, $ref2, $ignoreWhitespace, $case) = @_;
35.     my ($spName1, $spName2) = ($sRef1->{spName}, $sRef2->{spName});
36.
37.     print "Comparing (1) $sRef1->{srvName} $sRef1->{dbName} $sRef1->{spName}"
38.        . " (2) $sRef2->{srvName} $sRef2->{dbName} $sRef2->{spName}";
39.     print "\n   Checking SP property diff ...\n";
40.     foreach my $prop (sort keys %$ref1) {
41.        next if $prop eq 'Script';
42.        my ($value1, $value2) = ($ref1->{$prop}, $ref2->{$prop});
43.        if ($value1 ne $value2) {
```

```
44.          print "\t$prop: (1) = $value1, (2) = $value2\n";
45.        }
46.      }
47.      print "\n   Comparing SP code diff ...\n";
48.      my $ref = dbaStringDiff($ref1->{Script}, $ref2->{Script}, 22, $case);
49.      if ($ignoreWhitespace) {
50.        print "\tDiffering position: $ref->{pos}\n";
51.        print "\t        difference: $ref->{diff}\n";
52.      }
53.      else {
54.        print "\tDiffering position: $ref->{pos}\n";
55.        print "\t          line num: $ref->{line}\n";
56.        print "\t        difference: $ref->{diff}\n";
57.      }
58 . } # compareSP
```

The script in Listing 5-13 accepts two sets of command-line arguments. They provide access information for the script to retrieve the two stored procedures that may reside on two different servers. Uppercase letters introduce one set of arguments:

- -S for server name

- -D for database name

- -P for stored procedure name

Lowercase letters introduce the other set:

- -s for server name

- -d for database name

- -p for stored procedure name

In addition, you can specify two command-line switches: the switch -c to change the case sensitivity of the comparison and the switch -i to make the script ignore any whitespace.

The script in Listing 5-13 heavily relies on the functions exported from the SQLDBA modules, including dbaScriptSP() from SQLDBA::SQLDMO, dbaNormalizeSQL() and dbaRestoreSQL() from SQLDBA::ParseSQL, and dbaStringDiff() from SQLDBA::Utility. (Chapter 3, "Working with Commonly Used Perl Routines," covered all these functions.)

Recall that dbaScriptSP() accepts a reference to a hash with three keys: srvName, dbName, and spNam. These correspond to the server name, the database name, and the stored procedure name, respectively. In Listing 5-13, such a hash is populated on line 11 for one stored procedure and on line 12 for the other with the information specified on the command line.

Listing 5-13 generates the T-SQL scripts for the two stored procedures on lines 16 and 17. Note that dbaScriptSP() doesn't return a script in a string. Instead, it returns a reference to a hash; an example of which is as follows:

```
$spRef = {
        'Script' => 'CREATE PROC testSP
                    AS
                    -- a very simple test SP
                      SELECT @@version
                    GO',
        'QuotedIdentifierStatus' => 1,
        'Owner' => 'dbo',
        'AnsiNullsStatus' => 1,
        'Startup' => 0
      };
```

From this example, it should be clear why a hash instead of a simple script string is returned. It's because the settings of QUOTED_IDENTIFIER and ANSI_NULLS are integral to each stored procedure and must be captured to take part in comparing the two stored procedures. In addition, the owner of the stored procedure and whether it's marked as a startup procedure are also captured in the hash. You need the information in addition to the script itself to completely describe a stored procedure.

If the command-line switch -i is specified, the script is instructed to ignore any difference in whitespace in the comparison. The approach in Listing 5-13 is to collapse any consecutive whitespaces into a single space. However, you can't simply apply s/\s+/ /g to replace all the whitespaces with a single space because that will also replace those spaces, tabs, and newlines that are not whitespaces (for instance, the ones inside a string or a delimited identifier).

To protect the significant spaces, tabs, and newlines for each of the two stored procedures, the script in Listing 5-13 uses the function dbaNormalizeSQL() on line 22 to first replace the comments, quoted strings, and delimited identifiers with unique token strings. It then performs s/\s+/ /g on line 23 to collapse the real whitespaces. After that, the dbaRestoreSQL() function replaces the unique token strings with their corresponding originals, thus restoring the scripts to their originals with only the extra whitespaces removed.

Finally, the script calls the compareSPs() function to perform the actual comparison in two steps. First, it compares the properties of the stored procedures, such as their `QUOTED_IDENITIFIER` setting and their `ANSI_NULLS` setting. Second, on line 48, it calls the function `dbaStringDiff()` from SQLDBA::Utility to compare the code of the stored procedures.

For an example, first modify the `pubs..byroyalty` stored procedure on one SQL Server instance, but not the other, and then run the script as follows:

```
cmd>perl compareSPs.pl -SSQL1 -Dpubs -Pdbo.byroyalty
                       -sSQL2 -dpubs -pdbo.byroyalty
Comparing (1) SQL1.pubs.dbo.byroyalty (2) SQL2.pubs.dbo.byroyalty
   Checking SP property diff ...
   AnsiNullsStatus: (1) = 0, (2) = 1

   Comparing SP code diff ...
   Differing position: 46
        difference: (1) /* Here are some commen <> (2) select au_id from title
```

This report shows that the `ANSI_NULLS` setting is different between `pubs..byroyalty` on SQL1 and that on SQL2. Their code starts to become different at character position 46. The report also shows the code fragments where the two stored procedures start to differ. For `pubs..byroyalty` on SQL1, it's `/* Here are some commen`, and for `pubs.byroyalty` on SQL2, it's `select au_id from title`.

You can certainly extend this script in many different ways. One useful extension is to add a command-line switch to exclude all the T-SQL comments from comparison.

Comparing the Schemas of Two Databases

SCENARIO
You want to find the differences between two databases in terms of their schemas.

DBAs often want to know whether there's any difference between the schemas of two databases. The databases may be on the same server or on two different servers.

The schema of a database can mean everything in the database minus the data. For schema comparison, you most likely are interested in the differences between tables, views, stored procedures, triggers, constraints, user-defined functions, and indexes. You may also be interested in comparing filegroups, files, collations, full-text properties, roles and permissions, and other aspects of the databases.

This section focuses on comparing tables and stored procedures in the databases. For tables, you'll compare their columns, indexes, and constraints. Once you know how to compare tables and stored procedures, you can apply the same method to compare any other database objects.

The Perl functions and scripts discussed in the previous sections of this chapter have laid the foundation for comparing database schemas. All that's left is to organize these functions and scripts into a single coherent script. Follow these steps to proceed:

1. Obtain a list of tables and stored procedures from each database.

2. Compare the tables: find tables that are unique in each database, and for the common tables, compare their columns, indexes, and constraints.

3. Compare the stored procedures: find stored procedures that are unique in each database, and for the common stored procedures, compare their properties and code.

Obtaining a List of Tables and Stored Procedures

The function getObjList() in Listing 5-14 accepts a server name and a database name, and it returns a hash that includes a list of table names and a list of stored procedure names.

Listing 5-14. Obtaining a List of Tables and Stored Procedures

```
1.   sub getObjList {
2.       my $optRef = shift or die "***Err: getObjList() expects a reference.";
3.
4.       my $sql =<<END_SQL;
5.          use $optRef->{dbName}
6.          SELECT 'name' = QUOTENAME(user_name(uid)) + '.' + QUOTENAME(name),
7.                 'type' = RTRIM(type)
8.            FROM sysobjects
9.           WHERE type IN ('U', 'P')
10.            AND OBJECTPROPERTY(id, 'IsMSShipped') = 0
11. END_SQL
12.
13.     my $result = dbaRunQueryADO($optRef->{srvName}, $sql, 3); # 3 sec timeout
14.     my $objListRef;
15.     foreach my $tn (@{shift @$result}) {  # comments to follow in the text
16.         push @{$objListRef->{$tn->{type}}}, $tn->{name};
17.     }
18.     return $objListRef;
19. } # getObjList
```

Several points are worth noting about this function. The T-SQL query that retrieves the object names and their types is assigned to the variable $sql on line 4 in Listing 5-14. The query returns the owner-qualified objects, and the T-SQL function QUOTENAME() encloses both the owner name and the object name in square brackets. It facilitates comparison to convert all the T-SQL identifiers into a standard format.

The result of the query is retrieved with the function dbaRunQueryADO() exported from the module SQLDBA::Utility. Because this function supports multiple resultsets and there's only one resultset in this case, shift @$result on line 15 returns the reference to the first and only resultset; therefore, @{shift @$result} is an array of the resultset rows. The foreach loop between lines 15 and 17 goes through each row in the resultset, and populates the data structure $objListRef, whose keys are the object types (for example, 'U' and 'P') and the value of the key is a list of corresponding object names. Listing 5-15 shows an example of what the function getObjList() may produce.

Listing 5-15. Data Structure to Store Tables and Stored Procedures

```
$objListRef = {
                'P' => [
                          '[dbo].[byroyalty]',
                          '[dbo].[reptq1]'
                       ],
                'U' => [
                          '[dbo].[titleauthor]',
                          '[dbo].[authors]',
                          '[dbo].[titles]'
                       ]
              };
```

The function getObjList() can easily accommodate other types of database objects—such as triggers and views—that you may want to include in the comparison. All you need to do is add the appropriate types to the WHERE clause of the T-SQL query in Listing 5-14. The hash in Listing 5-15 will then have additional keys for these types.

Comparing Databases

After you've retrieved the list of tables and stored procedures from each database into the data structure illustrated in Listing 5-15, it's time to present the script, compareDBs.pl, for comparing the schemas of two databases. Listing 5-16 shows the main body of the script.

Listing 5-16. Comparing Two Database Schemas: `compareDBs.pl`

```perl
use strict;
use Getopt::Std;
use SQLDBA::SQLDMO qw( dbaGetTableColumns  dbaGetTableIndexes
                       dbaGetTableConstraints dbaScriptSP );
use SQLDBA::Utility qw( dbaSetDiff  dbaSetCommon  dbaRunQueryADO
                        dbaStringDiff );
use SQLDBA::ParseSQL qw( dbaNormalizeSQL  dbaRestoreSQL );

my %opts;
getopts('ciS:D:s:d:', \%opts); # c -- case sensitive, i -- ignore whitespace
Main: {
   my $optRef = {
                   1 => { srvName => $opts{S},    # server name
                          dbName  => $opts{D} },  # database name
                   2 => { srvName => $opts{s},    # server name
                          dbName  => $opts{d} }   # database name
     };

   my $objListRef = {
                      1 => getObjList($optRef->{1}),  # list of tables and SPs
                      2 => getObjList($optRef->{2})   # list of tables and SPs
     };
   compareTables($optRef, $objListRef);
   compareSPs($optRef, $objListRef, $opts{i}, $opts{c});
} # Main
```

The bulk of the script prepares the command-line arguments, tables, and stored procedures for comparison. All the command-line arguments with the exception of the switches -c and -i are stored in the hash structure $optRef, and all the table names and stored procedure names are retrieved, standardized, and stored in the hash structure $objListRef. The first level of the keys in these two hash structures is either '1' or '2', identifying the two databases, respectively.

The actual comparison is performed with the functions compareTables() and compareSPs().

Note that Listing 5-16 imports 10 functions from the SQLDBA modules. (All of these functions have been individually introduced either in this chapter or in earlier chapters.) None of the functions, imported from the SQLDBA modules, is directly used in the main body of the script in Listing 5-16. They are called in the functions compareTables() and compareSPs().

Comparing Tables

To compare the tables in two databases, you first need to identify the tables in one database, but not in the other. Once you have the list of tables from each database in an array, such as that shown in Listing 5-15, finding the ones that are not in both databases is a simple matter of performing a set difference, which is exactly what the dbaSetDiff() function does. This function is imported from the SQLDBA::Utility module (covered in Chapter 3, "Working with Commonly Used Perl Routines").

For the tables common to both databases, you can proceed to compare each in terms of their columns, indexes, and constraints. The previous sections of this chapter have presented and discussed the functions for comparing table columns, indexes, and constraints. You can reuse these functions with no change.

Listing 5-17 shows the function for comparing the tables in two databases.

Listing 5-17. Comparing Tables with compareTables()

```perl
sub compareTables {
   my ($optRef, $objListRef) = @_;

   my $listRef1 = $objListRef->{1}->{U};
   my $listRef2 = $objListRef->{2}->{U};

   print "\nComparing tables (1) on $optRef->{1}->{srvName}";
   print " and (2) on $optRef->{2}->{srvName}:\n";
   if (my @diff = dbaSetDiff($listRef1, $listRef2)) {
      print "  Tables in (1), not in (2):\n";
      print "\t", join (",\n\t", @diff);
   }
   if (my @diff = dbaSetDiff($listRef2, $listRef1)) {
      print "\n  Tables not in (1), but in (2):\n";
      print "\t", join (",\n\t", @diff);
   }

   print "\n\nComparing common tables on both (1) and (2):\n";
   foreach my $tb (dbaSetCommon($listRef1, $listRef2)) {
      my $tRef1 = { srvName => $optRef->{1}->{srvName},
                    dbName  => $optRef->{1}->{dbName},
                    tbName  => $tb };
      my $tRef2 = { srvName => $optRef->{2}->{srvName},
                    dbName  => $optRef->{2}->{dbName},
                    tbName  => $tb };
```

```
    # Comparing columns
    my $ref1 = dbaGetTableColumns($tRef1);
    my $ref2 = dbaGetTableColumns($tRef2);
    compareCol($tRef1, $ref1, $tRef2, $ref2);  # See Listing 5-1

    # Comparing indexes
    $ref1 = dbaGetTableIndexes($tRef1);
    $ref2 = dbaGetTableIndexes($tRef2);
    compareIdx($tRef1, $ref1, $tRef2, $ref2);  # See Listing 5-4

    # Comparing constraints
    $ref1 = dbaGetTableConstraints($tRef1);
    $ref2 = dbaGetTableConstraints($tRef2);
    compareConstraints($tRef1, $ref1, $tRef2, $ref2); # See Listing 5-11
  }
}
```

The function for comparing the stored procedures in two databases—compareSPs()—is structurally similar to the one in Listing 5-17. You can find the script in the Downloads section of the Apress Web site (http://www.apress.com).

Using compareDBs.pl

This script accepts the following command-line arguments. Note that it needs to access two SQL Servers and two databases:

- -S specifies the name of the first SQL Server.

- -D specifies the name of a database on the first server.

- -s specifies the name of the second SQL Server.

- -d specifies the name of database on the second server.

- -i instructs the comparison to ignore any whitespace.

- -c makes the comparison case insensitive.

For instance, to compare the database pubs on the server SQL1 and database pubs on the server SQL2, you can issue the following at the command line:

```
cmd>perl compareDBs.pl -SSQL1 -Dpubs -sSQL2 -dpubs
```

Let me point out three things about `compareDBs.pl` in Listing 5-17. First, this script isn't complete in terms of what you may want to compare, and there are many more objects and dimensions that may be important in comparing two databases. For instance, `compareDBs.pl` doesn't cover database objects such as triggers, views, user-defined functions, user-defined data types, and so on. Moreover, for tables and stored procedures, object properties such as the filegroup of a table are not included from the comparison.

Second, however, you can easily extend the script `compareDBs.pl` to accommodate these missing pieces. In fact, the code for comparing each type of these missing database objects is nearly a cookie-cutter copy of either that for comparing tables or that for comparing stored procedures.

Finally, given the number of objects in a database and the number of properties these objects may have, the output of `compareDBs.pl` is often voluminous. As such, the presentation of the output is no longer an issue of being pretty but becomes significant in effectively conveying useful information. The version of `compareDBs.pl` you can download from the Apress Web site (`http://www.apress.com`) includes additional command-line switches to control the format of the output.

Producing a Call Tree for a Stored Procedure

SCENARIO
Given the name of a stored procedure, you want to know its complete call tree.

What is the call tree of a stored procedure? The root of the tree is the stored procedure itself. Each node of the tree represents a stored procedure, whose parent is the stored procedure that calls it with the `EXECUTE` statement and whose children are the stored procedures it calls. The leaf node of the tree doesn't call any other stored procedure.

The strategy to construct such a call tree is to first generate the script of the stored procedure and then parse the T-SQL code to find any stored procedures called with the `EXECUTE` statement. This finds all the immediate dependencies of the stored procedure. For each stored procedure it calls, you can go through the same steps to find its immediate dependencies. This process is recursive in nature. When you have found the immediate dependencies for every stored procedure or have determined that a stored procedure doesn't call any other stored procedure, you can apply the `dbaGetTree()` function discussed in Chapter 3, "Working with Commonly Used Perl Routines," to produce the call tree for the original stored procedure.

The first step is to generate the T-SQL script for a stored procedure.

Scripting a Given Stored Procedure

Chapter 3, "Working with Commonly Used Perl Routines," introduced the dbaScriptSP() function to script the T-SQL code of a stored procedure. The compareSPs.pl function also used this function in Listing 5-13.

There's a performance drawback to using dbaScriptSP() when you need to generate the T-SQL scripts for many stored procedures. For each stored procedure, dbaScriptSP() creates a Win32::OLE object that results in a SQLDMO.SQLServer COM object being created, opens a connection to SQL Server, creates more objects, generates the T-SQL script for the procedure, and closes the connection. Repeatedly creating and dropping these objects as well as opening and closing SQL Server connections is expensive and wasteful.

The dbaScriptSP2() function in Listing 5-18 is a variation of dbaScriptSP(). In place of the server name in the parameter hash structure, dbaScriptSP2() accepts a Win32::OLE object for SQLDMO.SQLServer after the connection to SQL Server has already been established. This makes it possible to create a single SQLDMO.SQLServer object and make the connection to SQL Server only once. Then, you can repeatedly call dbaScriptSP2() to script all the stored procedures using the same SQLServer object and the same SQL Server connection.

Listing 5-18. Scripting a Stored Procedure

```
sub dbaScriptSP2 {
   my $ref = shift or die "***Err: dbaScriptSP2() expects a reference.";

   my ($server, $dbName, $spName) =
                     ($ref->{server}, $ref->{dbName}, $ref->{spName});
   my $sp = $server->Databases($ref->{dbName})->StoredProcedures($spName);
   ! Win32::OLE->LastError() or
      do { print "***Err: could not get the proc object for $spName.";
```

```
            return undef;
        };

    my $spRef = {
        Owner   => $sp->Owner(),
        Startup => $sp->Startup(),
        AnsiNullsStatus => $sp->AnsiNullsStatus(),
        QuotedIdentifierStatus => $sp->QuotedIdentifierStatus(),
        Script  => $sp->Script( SQLDMOScript_Default )
    };
    # remove settings in the code that are already captured in the hash
    $spRef->{Script} =~ s/set\s+quoted_identifier\s+(on|off)\s+go\s*//ig;
    $spRef->{Script} =~ s/set\s+ansi_nulls\s+(on|off)\s+go\s*//ig;

    return $spRef;
} # dbaScriptSP2
```

The output of the function in Listing 5-18 is the same as that of `dbaScriptSP()`.

Parsing for Stored Procedure Calls

Now that you have the T-SQL script for a stored procedure, the next step is to find the stored procedures it calls, if any. In other words, you need to find the immediate dependencies of this stored procedure.

> **NOTE** *A stored procedure, say* X, *is an immediate dependency of another stored procedure, say* Y, *if* X *is called in the definition of* Y. X *may in turn call other stored procedures. They're not the immediate dependencies of* Y *as long as* Y *doesn't call them directly in its definition.*

In T-SQL, a stored procedure calls another stored procedure using the EXECUTE or EXEC key word in a syntax similar to the following, where the return variable is optional and there can be zero or more parameters:

```
EXECUTE @rc = dbo.getAuthor '238-95-7766'
```

The job now is to parse the script of the stored procedure for all the EXECUTE statements and identify the name of the stored procedure being called. To rule out the chance of matching a stored procedure mentioned in a T-SQL comment, in a quoted string, or in a delimited identifier, use the function dbaNormalizeSQL() to first replace all the comments, quoted strings, and delimited identifiers with unique token strings. Then, use a regular expression to search for the names of the stored procedures called by this stored procedure.

How can you find all the stored procedure calls? In general, the danger of using a nontrivial regular expression is always two pronged: failing to match a string that should be matched and matching a string that shouldn't be matched. When looking for a pattern in a complex structure such as a T-SQL script, the likelihood of the latter is especially prominent. The following are two examples of perfectly legal T-SQL statements, neither of which is an EXECUTE statement:

```
SELECT * FROM #EXEC t1
DECLARE @EXECUTE int
```

To avoid falling victim to this danger, you can't simply match for the string EXECUTE or EXEC. You must check the context of the matched string EXECUTE or EXEC to verify that it's indeed an EXECUTE statement. The regular expression for matching a stored procedure call in a T-SQL script is as follows:

```
/(?<![\w\@\#\$])        # (?<! ) is negative lookbehind
    EXEC(UTE)?          # match EXECUTE or EXEC
    \s+(\@.+?=\s*)?     # return variable, if any. A dot matches any character.
    ([^(\s]+)           # match proc name that contains no opening paren or space
/igx                    # case insensitive and match all occurrences
```

The first line says that from the current position, if you try to match a character behind (in other words, going backward), this character can't be an alphanumeric, an underline, the @ sign, the # sign, or the $ sign. If any of them immediately precedes the string EXEC, it makes the string EXEC a substring of some other construct instead of a T-SQL keyword. Recall that (?<! PATTERN) is the syntax of Perl's negative lookbehind assertion.

The pattern \s+(\@.+?=\s*)? deserves additional explanation. It matches either of two patterns:

- One or more whitespace (\s+)

- One or more whitespace followed by a @ sign, which is then followed by one or more arbitrary character (.+?). After that, the pattern expects an equal sign followed by zero or more whitespace.

The question mark in the pattern .+? instructs the regular-expression engine to accept the minimum number of characters that match the pattern. By default, the repetition quantifiers in a Perl regular expression are greedy in that they match as many characters as possible. A question mark immediately following the quantifier changes it to accept the minimum number of matched characters.

Listing 5-19 is the code for the findSPCalls() function that returns the names of all the stored procedures called by a given stored procedure:

Listing 5-19. Finding the Immeidate Dependencies with findSPCalls()

```
1.    sub findSPCalls {
2.        my $script = shift or die "***Err: findSPCalls() expects a string.";
3.
4.        my $spRef = dbaNormalizeSQL($script, 0);
5.        my $owner = 'dbo';  # default SP owner to dbo
6.        my @calledSPs;
7.        while ($spRef->{code} =~
8.                        /(?<![\w\@\#\$])       # negative lookbehind
9.                            EXEC(UTE)?         # keywords EXECUTE or EXEC
10.                           \s+(\@.+?=\s*)?    # return variable and whitespaces
11.                           ([^(\s]+)          # proc name
12.                       /igx) {                # case insensitive and match all
13.            my $sp = $3;
14.            # add owner if not specified explicitly
15.            if ($sp =~ /^[^.]+$/) { $sp = $owner . '.' . $sp; }
16.            if ($sp =~ /^([^.]+)\.\.([^.]+)$/) {
17.                $sp = "$1.$owner.$2";
17.            }
19.            # replace tokens with their originals (bracket_id's)
20.            foreach my $token (keys %{$spRef->{bracket_ids}}) {
21.                $sp =~ s/$token/$spRef->{bracket_ids}->{$token}/e;
22.            }
23.            # replace tokens with their originals (double_id's)
24.            foreach my $token (keys %{$spRef->{double_ids}}) {
25.                $sp =~ s/$token/$spRef->{double_ids}->{$token}/e;
26.            }
27.            push @calledSPs, $sp;
28.        }
29.        return @calledSPs;
30. } # findSPCalls
```

Note that the parentheses around the negative lookbehind on line 8 in Listing 5-19 don't capture the substring it matches. Therefore, if you count the opening parenthesis, the name of the called stored procedure is captured by $3, corresponding to the parentheses on line 11.

NOTE *You may be tempted to consider using the system procedure* sp_depends *to find the immediate dependencies of a stored procedure. Unfortunately,* sp_depends *isn't reliable and the best you can do is to stay away from it.*

Because the script may contain delimited identifiers, dbaNormalizeSQL() replaces them with unique token strings. The code between lines 19 and 26 in Listing 5-19 loops through all the token strings for the double-quoted identifiers and for the bracket-enclosed identifiers. If the name of the stored procedure contains any of these token strings, it's replaced with its corresponding original.

Now that for any given stored procedure you've generated its T-SQL script and parsed the code for the names of the stored procedures it calls, it's time to build its call tree.

Constructing the Call Tree

Given a stored procedure, the process to construct its call tree is as follows:

1. Use dbaScriptSP2() to script out the T-SQL code of the stored procedure.

2. Apply findSPCalls() to find all its immediate child procedures.

3. For each of the child stored procedures, construct its call tree.

4. Put all child call trees together in a hash with the names of the child stored procedures as the keys. Return a reference to this hash as the call tree of the stored procedure.

Obviously, this process is recursive in nature. The recursion terminates when a stored procedure doesn't call any other stored procedure. This process is implemented in the function getCallTree() shown in Listing 5-20.

Listing 5-20. Generating a Call Tree with getCallTree()

```
1.   sub getCallTree {
2.      my $ref = shift or die "***Err: getCallTree() expects a reference.";
3.
4.      my %callTree;
5.      my $spRef = dbaScriptSP2($ref) or return \%callTree;
6.      my @SPs = findSPCalls($spRef->{Script});
7.      foreach my $sp (@SPs) {
8.         if ($sp =~ /^\s*([^\s]+)\.([^\s]*\.[^\s]+)/) {
9.            ($ref->{dbName}, $sp) = ($1, $2);
10.        }
11.        # skip the recursion if the SP calls by itself
12.        next if $sp =~ /^$ref->{spName}$/; # assume case sensitive
13.        my $subTree = getCallTree( { srvObj => $ref->{srvObj},
14.                                      dbName => $ref->{dbName},
15.                                      spName => $sp } );
16.        $callTree{$ref->{dbName}. '.' . $sp} = $subTree;  # add to the tree
17.     }
18.     return \%callTree;
19. } # getCallTree
```

The recursive call takes place on line 13 in Listing 5-20, where a reference to a new hash is fed to the same function. However, the spName key now has the name of a child stored procedure, and the dbName key may have a different value, indicating that the child stored procedure belongs to a different database. The srvObj key, however, remains the same, pointing to the same SQLDMO.SQLServer object.

Note that if there's no child stored procedure, the getCallTree() function in Listing 5-20 skips the foreach loop between lines 7 and 17. The %callTree hash will be empty, and getCallTree() returns a reference to an empty hash and terminates the recursion.

NOTE   *In Listing 5-20, a minor bug is deliberately left unfixed. On line 16, either the current database name or the explicitly qualified database name is prefixed to the name of the stored procedure. This isn't correct when a system procedure is called. The system procedure may end up being prefixed with the current database name instead of the* master *database name.*

The %callTree data structure is a hash of hashes, whose levels of nesting are as many as there are levels of stored procedure calls. As an example, let's assume the following dependencies:

- The stored procedure pubs.dbo.spCall executes the procedures pubs..reptq1, pubs..spCall2, and pubs.dbo.reptq3.

- The procedure pubs.dbo.spCall2 in turn executes pubs..spCall3 and pubs..reptq2.

- The procedure pubs.dbo.spCall3 executes Northwind.dbo.reptq4.

- The procedure Northwind.dbo.reptq4 executes Northwind.dbo.reptq5.

The call tree data structure for pubs.dbo.spCall should look like Listing 5-21.

Listing 5-21. Data Structure Representing the Call Tree of pubs.dbo.spCall

```
$callTreeRef = {
            'pubs.dbo.reptq3' => { },
            'pubs.dbo.spCall2' => {
                    'pubs.dbo.reptq2' => { },
                    'pubs.dbo.spCall3' => {
                                    'Northwind.dbo.reptq4' => {
                                        'Northwind.dbo.reptq5' => { }
                                    },
                    },
            'pubs.dbo.reptq1' => { }
    };
```

In Listing 5-21, note that each of the stored procedure names is qualified with its respective database name and owner. When the owner isn't explicitly specified in the EXECUTE statement, owner 'dbo' is assumed.

Putting It All Together

Now that you have the functions dbaScriptSP2(), findSPCalls(), and getCallTree() ready, producing a call tree for a given stored procedure only requires some minor preparation and presentation of the call tree. Listing 5-22 shows the script callTree.pl that accepts a server name, a database name, and a stored procedure name on the command line and prints a call tree for the stored procedure.

Listing 5-22. Producing a Call Tree for a Given Stored Procedure

```perl
use strict;
use Getopt::Std;
use SQLDBA::SQLDMO qw( dbaScriptSP2 );  # See Listing 5-18
use SQLDBA::ParseSQL qw( dbaNormalizeSQL );
use Win32::OLE;

my %opts;
getopts('S:D:P:', \%opts);          # command-line switches
my $ref = { srvName => $opts{S},    # server name
            dbName  => $opts{D},    # database name
            spName  => $opts{P} };  # stored procedure name

my $srvObj = Win32::OLE->new('SQLDMO.SQLServer')
     or die "***Err: Could not create SQLDMO object.";
$srvObj->{LoginSecure} = 1;      # trusted connection
$srvObj->connect($ref->{srvName}, '', '');
! Win32::OLE->LastError() or
     die "***Err: Could not connect to $ref->{srvName}.";

my $srvRef = { srvObj => $srvObj,        # Win32::OLE object
               dbName => $ref->{dbName},
               spName => $ref->{spName} };

my $callTree = getCallTree($srvRef);     # get the call tree recursively
$srvObj->Close();

print "Call tree for: $opts{P}\n";
printCallTree($opts{P}, $callTree, 0);

#####################
sub printCallTree {
   my ($spName, $ref, $level) = @_;
   my $indent = 6;

   foreach my $subSP (keys %$ref) {
      print ' ' x (($level + 1) * $indent), " --> $subSP\n";
      printCallTree($subSP, $ref->{$subSP}, $level + 1);
   }
}
###################
sub findSPCalls {
   # see Listing 5-19
```

```
}
####################
sub getCallTree {
   # see Listing 5-20
}
```

The script in Listing 5-22 accepts three command-line arguments (a server name, a database name, and a stored procedure name) and prints out the call tree for the stored procedure. Applying the script to the stored procedure spCall, discussed in Listing 5-21, produces the following:

```
cmd>perl callTree.pl -S NYSQL1 -D pubs -P dbo.spCall
Call tree for: spCall
        --> pubs.dbo.spCall2
                    --> pubs.dbo.spCall3
                             --> Northwind.dbo.reptq4
                                       --> Northwind.dbo.reptq5
                    --> pubs.dbo.reptq2
        --> pubs.dbo.reptq1
        --> pubs.dbo.reptq3
```

In the printed result, the arrow notation signifies a stored procedure call. All the stored procedures directly called by a stored procedure are listed underneath the latter at the same vertically aligned position as each other. For instance, the stored procedures directly called by pubs.dbo.spCall2 are pubs.dbo.spCall3 and pubs.dbo.reptq2.

As you can see in this result, the script correctly deals with the dependencies across databases.

Finding the Call Trees for All the Stored Procedures

The script callTree.pl in Listing 5-22 produces the complete call tree for a single stored procedure. If you want to generate a call tree for every stored procedure in a database, you can first generate a batch file that runs callTree.pl for each stored procedure in the database. For instance, you can use the output from the following T-SQL query in a Windows 2000/NT batch file:

```
SELECT 'perl callTree.pl -S NYSQL1 -D pubs -P ' + SPECIFIC_NAME
    FROM INFORMATION_SCHEMA.ROUTINES
 WHERE ROUTINE_CATALOG = 'pubs'
       AND ROUTINE_TYPE = 'PROCEDURE'
ORDER BY SPECIFIC_NAME
```

Enhancing callTree.pl

You can enhance this script in many ways. In particular, it's useful for the script to work with the stored procedures defined in T-SQL script files in addition to the stored procedures in a live database. The version of `callTree.pl` available from the Downloads area of the Apress Web site (`http://www.apress.com`) works with both a live SQL Server database and T-SQL script files.

The scripts discussed in Listings 5-19 through 5-22 don't treat the stored procedure identifiers in the most rigorous way. They may not produce the correct result if special characters are used in a stored procedure name. Ideally, you should convert all the identifiers to a common format so that the Perl script can correctly compare them. For a brief discussion on the difficulty in resolving identifier names, see the sidebar "Resolving Identifier Names."

....

Resolving Identifier Names

In SQL Server, you can refer to a database object in many different formats. For instance, the following are five ways you can identify the `reptq1` stored procedure in the `pubs` database in your T-SQL script:

```
pubs.dbo.reptq1
dbo.reptq1
reptq1
dbo.[reptq1]
[dbo]."reptq1"
```

Many more variations are acceptable. As long as they're not ambiguous for a given user connection, SQL Server can resolve these identifiers to the same object internally. However, because a Perl script, such as the one in Listing 5-19, works with character strings, making it understand that the different names all refer to the same database object is a challenge.

An effective strategy is to convert all identifiers to a common canonical format. A format I often use is to quote all identifiers with square brackets and to fully qualify each object name. Thus, the names listed previously will be converted to the following:

```
[pubs].[dbo].[reptq1]
```

Now, when two object names are different, the script knows that they identify different database objects.

One additional twist is the choice of the object owner when an object name isn't owner qualified. Throughout this book, all the scripts assume that the owner is dbo if the ownership is not explicitly specified. Obviously, this assumption is not 100-percent correct, but it works fine for analysis purposes.

Sorting Stored Procedures by Dependency

SCENARIO
You want to sort all the stored procedures in a database by dependency.

To determine the dependencies among the stored procedures, the only reliable approach is to scan the T-SQL scripts of the stored procedures. For each stored procedure, find the stored procedures it calls using the EXECUTE statement. This establishes the immediate dependencies for all the stored procedures and makes it possible to sort the stored procedures by dependency.

Representing the Immediate Dependencies

In the "Producing a Call Tree for a Stored Procedure" section, the findSPCalls() function parses a stored procedure definition and identifies all the immediately dependent stored procedures. Now, let's look at the data structure to store the immediate dependencies of the all the stored procedures you want to sort.

> **NOTE** *A stored procedure may use other database objects in its defini-tion, such as tables, views, and user-defined functions. These objects are therefore also its immediate dependencies. However, in this section, the immediate dependencies of a stored procedure always refer to the stored procedures directly called by the stored procedure.*

The data structure used in this section is a hash of arrays. A key in this hash corresponds to the name of a stored procedure defined in a CREATE PROCEDURE statement, and the value of the key is a reference to an array whose elements are the names of the stored procedures called in this CREATE PROCEDURE statement (in other words, the names of the immediately dependent stored procedures).

Listing 5-23 shows a T-SQL script used to illustrate the data structure for storing the immediate dependencies of the stored procedures.

Listing 5-23. A T-SQL Script Defining Stored Procedures

```
USE pubs
GO

CREATE PROC dbo.spOrder @p  varchar(20)
as
    /* EXEC dbo.reptq1 */ select * from authors
GO

CREATE PROCEDURE/* abc*/spCheck @p1 varchar(20)
as
    EXECUTE pubs.dbo.reptq1
GO
/*** comments ***/
CREATE PROC spCut
as
    -- Comments in spCut
    EXEC dbo.reptq1
    EXEC spCheck 'param one'
    Execute spProc 'adhfklas'
    EXEC dbo.spOrder
GO

CREATE PROC reptq1 AS EXEC [reptq2 - Exec]
GO

CREATE PROCEDURE [reptq2 - Exec] AS
    select au_lname from authors
GO

/* CREATE PROC dba.spTry
    as EXEC reptq1   */
GO

CREATE PROCEDURE dbo.spLoad
as
    declare @rc int
    EXEC pubs.dbo.spCheck 'my login'    -- EXEC reptq2
    EXECUTE spCut 'param one', 'param 2'
    EXEC @rc = spOrder 'abc'
    --      EXECute dbo.spLoad
    EXEC ('master..sp_lock')
    EXECute reptq1
GO
```

Listing 5-24 shows the data structure storing the immediate dependencies of the stored procedures in Listing 5-23.

Listing 5-24. A Hash of Arrays for Immediate Dependencies

```
$ref = {
        '[pubs].[dbo].[spProc]' => [ ],
        '[pubs].[dbo].[reptq1]' => [
                                '[pubs].[dbo].[reptq2 - Exec]'
                        ],
        '[pubs].[dbo].[reptq2 - Exec]' => [ ],
        '[pubs].[dbo].[spCheck]' => [
                                '[pubs].[dbo].[reptq1]'
                        ],
        '[pubs].[dbo].[spCut]' => [
                                '[pubs].[dbo].[reptq1]',
                                '[pubs].[dbo].[spCheck]',
                                '[pubs].[dbo].[spProc]',
                                '[pubs].[dbo].[spOrder]'
                        ],
        '[pubs].[dbo].[spOrder]' => [ ],
        '[pubs].[dbo].[spLoad]' => [
                                '[pubs].[dbo].[spCheck]',
                                '[pubs].[dbo].[spCut]',
                                '[pubs].[dbo].[spOrder]',
                                '[pubs].[dbo].[reptq1]'
                        ]
        };
```

Any stored procedure, either defined or called in the T-SQL script in Listing 5-23, has a key in the hash in Listing 5-24. A stored procedure that doesn't call any other stored procedure has a value referencing an empty array. Otherwise, its value is a reference to an array whose elements are the names of all the stored procedures it calls with the EXECUTE statement. If a stored procedure is only called, but not defined in the T-SQL script, its dependency is set to an empty array. In other words, it's assumed to not depend on any other stored procedure.

For instance, the procedure spOrder in Listing 5-23 doesn't call any other stored procedure; thus, its corresponding key in Listing 5-24 is assigned a value of [ ]—a reference to an empty list. On the other hand, the procedure spCut calls four stored procedures; thus, its corresponding key in Listing 5-24 is assigned a reference to an array whose elements are these four stored procedure names.

Sorting the Stored Procedures

Having captured a hash of arrays like that in Listing 5-24, you can perform the following steps to populate an array with the stored procedures sorted by dependency. Assume that the hash of arrays is %depend, and the sorted stored procedures are in @sorted:

1. Initialize the array @sorted to empty.

2. Push into @sorted those stored procedures of %depend that don't have any dependencies. If you can't find any stored procedure with no dependency and the hash %depend is not empty, there's a circular dependency. That's treated as a fatal error condition.

3. Delete the hash entries of those stored procedures that have been pushed into @sorted and remove the stored procedures from any array referenced in the hash.

4. Repeat step 2 until the hash %depend is empty.

These steps are recursive. Moreover, they're not particular to sorting stored procedures but are generic. As long as the immediate dependencies are captured in a hash of arrays, irrespective of what each element may represent or the nature of the dependencies, the outlined steps will sort the elements by dependency.

The sortObjs() function in Listing 5-25 implements these steps. In the ensuing discussions on sortObjs(),the term *object* means anything you care to sort by dependency. The input parameter to the function is a reference to a hash of arrays as shown in Listing 5-24. The output of the function is a reference to an array whose elements are object names listed in the dependency order. Namely, in this array, an object doesn't depend on any of the objects that come after it in the order of the array elements.

Listing 5-25. Sorting by Dependency with sortObjs()

```
1.   sub sortObjs {
2.       my($dependRef) = shift or die "***Err: sortObjs() expects a reference.";
3.       my @sorted = ();
4.       return \@sorted unless keys %$dependRef > 0;
5.
6.       # move all nondependent objects to @sorted
7.       foreach my $obj (keys %$dependRef) {
8.
9.           # skip it if it depends on other objects
```

```
10.            next if scalar @{$dependRef->{$obj}} > 0;
11.
12.            # Now $obj is nondependent, add it to @sorted
13.            push @sorted, $obj;
14.
15.            # remove the nondependent $obj
16.            foreach my $d (keys %{$dependRef}) {
17.                $dependRef->{$d} = [ grep {$obj ne $_} @{$dependRef->{$d}} ];
18.            }
19.            delete $dependRef->{$obj};
20.        }
21.
22.     # if @sorted is empty at this point, there's circular dependency
23.     if (scalar @sorted == 0) {
24.         print "***Err: circular dependency!\n";
25.         print Dumper($dependRef);
26.         die;
27.     }
28.
29.     # if the tree is not empty, recursively work on what's left
30.     push @sorted, @{ sortObjs($dependRef) } if keys %{$dependRef} > 0;
31.
32.     return \@sorted;
33. }  # sortObjs
```

In Listing 5-25, line 4 is present to force the sortObjs() function to return immediately with an empty array if the input hash is empty. There's no need to waste time when there's nothing to sort.

Between lines 7 and 20, the function deals with the objects that don't have any dependency as indicated by the $dependRef hash at that point in time. It adds these objects to the @sorted array and removes them from the $dependRef hash. Note how they're removed from the arrays referenced in $dependRef:

```
16.            foreach my $d (keys %{$dependRef}) {
17.                $dependRef->{$d} = [ grep {$obj ne $_} @{$dependRef->{$d}} ];
18.            }
```

At this point, the variable $obj has the name of an object that doesn't have any dependency. This code goes through every array referenced in $dependRef, singles out the elements that don't match $obj with grep() to form another array with a pair of square brackets (in other words, [   ]), and assigns the reference of the newly formed array to the same key of the original array, effectively replacing the original array with this new array minus all the nondependent stored procedures.

Remember that grep() implicitly loops through the array in its second parameter and assigns each element to $_, which is used in the code block that's the first parameter of grep(). In list context, which is what grep() is in on line 17, grep() returns a list of elements that the code block evaluates to true.

On line 19, the entry whose key corresponds to this nondependent object is then removed from the hash referenced by $dependRef as follows:

```
19.        delete $dependRef->{$obj};
```

Every time the sortObjs() function is called with a reference to a nonempty hash, it should always find at least one object that has no dependency. If this isn't the case, the input hash contains circular dependency, and the function is aborted on line 26.

The recursive function call takes place on line 30, which essentially tells the function to sort the remaining hash %$dependRef in exactly the same way and append the sorted object that's returned from this call to @sorted.

Finding the Immediate Dependencies

Now you know how to sort stored procedures by dependency. The question that still remains is how to obtain the immediate dependencies and represent them in a hash of arrays. The key steps are similar to those used in the "Producing a Call Tree for a Stored Procedure" section to construct the call tree for a stored procedure:

1. Normalize the script with dbaNormalizeSQL() to remove the complications caused by T-SQL comments, quoted strings, and delimited identifiers.

2. Split the script into batches by the batch terminator GO.

3. For each batch, parse the script of each CREATE PROCEDURE to find the stored procedures called with the EXECUTE statement.

The functions getSPCall() and findSPExec() in Listing 5-26 implement these steps.

Listing 5-26. Finding the Immediate Dependencies of a Stored Procedure

```
sub getSPCall {
    my ($sql, $db) = @_;
    my $spCallRef;
```

```perl
    my $sqlRef = dbaNormalizeSQL($sql, 0);

    foreach my $batch (@{ dbaSplitBatch($sqlRef->{code}) }) {
        if ($batch =~ /^\s*use\s+(\w+)/i) {
            $db = $1;    # remember the most current database
        }
        my ($proc, $dependRef) = findSPExec($batch);
        next unless $proc;    # skip if CREATE PROC(EDURE) not in the batch

        $spCallRef->{$proc} = {
                depends => $dependRef,
                db      => $db    # carry the db name along for name resolution
            };
    }
    return ($spCallRef, $sqlRef);    # carry $sqlRef along to restore originals
}


###################
sub findSPExec {
    my $batch = shift;
    my $proc;
    my @depends;

    if ($batch =~ /\bCREATE\s+(?:PROC|PROCEDURE)\s+(\w+\.\w+|\w+)/i) {
        $proc = $1;
        while ($batch =~ /\b(?:EXEC|EXECUTE)\s+
                         (?:\@\w+\s*=\s*)?                        # SP return variable
                         (\w+\.\w*\.\w+|\w+\.\w+|\w+)  # proc name
                     /igx) {
            push @depends, $1
        }
    }
    ($proc, [@depends]);
}
```

The function getSPCall() accepts two parameters, $sql and $db. The former is the T-SQL script that includes all the stored procedures you want to sort, and the latter is the name of the database that's to be the default in case no database is explicitly identified in the T-SQL script. You need this default database to help resolve the names of the stored procedures used in the T-SQL script.

The getSPCall() function returns two hashes, $spCallRef and $sqlRef. The hash $spCallRef includes all the stored procedures in the T-SQL script as its keys. For each stored procedure, all its dependencies are listed in a nested hash value. In addition, the database in which this stored procedure is created is also listed in the same nested hash value. An example should clarify the nature of the data structure. Listing 5-27 illustrates two stored procedures, spCut and spCheck, for the hash $spCallRef.

Listing 5-27. An Example of $spCallRef *Returned by* getSPCall()

```
$spCallRef = {
        'spCut' => {
                        'db' => 'pubs',
                        'depends' => [
                                        'dbo.reptq1',
                                        'spCheck',
                                        'spProc',
                                        'dbo.spOrder'
                                    ]
        'spCheck' => {
                        'db' => 'pubs',
                        'depends' => [
                                        'pubs.dbo.reptq1'
                                    ]
                    }
        };
```

As mentioned earlier, the reason a database name is carried around for each stored procedure in $spCallRef is for name resolution. Because the same stored procedure may be identified differently in a T-SQL script, before you compare them you should convert all the stored procedure names to a standard naming format. In this book, the standard format consistently used is the three-part database object name with each part delimited with a pair of square brackets. The first part is the database name, the second the owner name, and the third the object name itself.

The other hash returned by getSPCall()—$sqlRef—is actually returned by the function dbaNormalizedSQL(). The $sqlRef hash contains the mappings from the unique tokens to their corresponding original identifiers. You need these mappings later to restore the original stored procedure identifiers. See Chapter 2, "Working with Commonly Used Perl Modules," for more information about the structure of the hash returned by dbaNormalizeSQL().

Normalizing Identifiers

There's still work to be done to bring a data structure like the one in Listing 5-27 to the expected hash of arrays, as illustrated in Listing 5-24, that you can directly feed to the function sortObjs() in Listing 5-25.

The identifiers in $spCallRef don't follow the standard naming format and therefore can't be directly compared. The following steps ensure that the standard naming format is used:

1. Change all the double-quoted identifiers to bracket-quoted identifiers.

2. Change all the identifiers to lowercase if case insensitivity is specified.

3. Change all the stored procedure names to the standard three-part names including the database name and the owner name.

4. Restore the original identifier names that may include special characters such as spaces.

These steps are implemented in the function normalizeID(). The output of this function is a hash of arrays matching the one illustrated in Listing 5-24. Because this function doesn't offer anything conceptually interesting, its code isn't listed in this book. You can obtain the code from the Downloads area of the Apress Web site (http://www.apress.com).

Putting It All Together

Now that all the essential building blocks are ready, you can proceed to assemble them and do something useful. Listing 5-28 shows the script for sorting T-SQL stored procedures.

Listing 5-28. Sorting Stored Procedures by Dependency

```
use strict;
use Getopt::Std;
use SQLDBA::ParseSQL qw( dbaNormalizeSQL dbaSplitBatch );

# get command-line arguments
my $optRef = getCommandLineOpt();
```

```
Main: {
    # read the script into $sql
    my $sql;
    open(SQL, "$optRef->{f}") or
        die "***Err: could not open $optRef->{f} for read.";
    read(SQL, $sql, -s SQL);
    close(SQL);

    # get SPs immediately called
    my ($spCallRef, $sqlRef) = getSPCall($sql, $optRef->{d});

    # normalize IDs
    $spCallRef = normalizeID($spCallRef, $sqlRef, $optRef);

    # fill in the default
    $spCallRef = fillInSP($spCallRef);

    # Sort the procedures by dependency
    my $sortedSPRef = sortObjs($spCallRef);

    print "Stored procedures in dependency order:\n";
    foreach (@$sortedSPRef) { print "\t$_\n"; }
} # Main


###################
sub printUsage {
    print <<__USAGE__;
Usage:
  cmd>perl sortSPs.pl [-c ] [-o <owner>] -d <db> -f <T-SQL file>

   Options:
      -d    set the default database name
      -o    set the default object owner name
      -c    1 = case sensitive, 0 = case insensitive
      -f    name of the T-SQL script file that includes all the SPs
__USAGE__
    exit;
}  # printUsage


############################
sub getCommandLineOpt {
    my %opts;

    getopts('d:o:cf:', \%opts);
```

```
    $opts{f} or printUsage();

    # set default to case insensitive
    $opts{c} = 0 unless defined $opts{c};
    return \%opts;
} # getCommandLineOpt


#################
sub fillInSP {
    my $spCallRef = shift;

    # if a proc is called, but not defined in the script
    # set it to depend on nothing
    foreach my $sp (keys %$spCallRef) {
        foreach my $depend (@{$spCallRef->{$sp}}) {
            unless (exists $spCallRef->{$depend}) {
                $spCallRef->{$depend} = [ ];
            }
        }
    }
    return $spCallRef;
} # fillInSP


#############################
sub getSPCall {
# see Listing 5-26
} # getSPCall


######################
sub findSPExec {
# see Listing 5-26
} # findSPExec


#####################
sub normalizeID {
# download the code from the Apress website
} # normalizeID


##################
sub sortObjs {
# see Listing 5-25
} # sortSObjs
```

Save the script in Listing 5-28 to the file sortSPs.pl and the T-SQL script in Listing 5-23 to the file someSPs.SQL. Now, run sortSPs.pl as follows to see what it produces:

```
cmd>perl sortSPs.pl -d pubs -f someSPs.SQL -c
Stored procedures in dependency order:
    [pubs].[dbo].[myProc]
    [pubs].[dbo].[reptq2 - Exec]
    [pubs].[dbo].[reptq1]
    [pubs].[dbo].[orderSP]
    [pubs].[dbo].[checkSP]
    [pubs].[dbo].[cutSP]
    [pubs].[dbo].[loadSP]
```

This array lists the stored procedures in the correct dependency order. You may have noticed a function named fillSP() in the main body of Listing 5-28. The recursive function sortSPs() requires that every stored procedure must have its immediate dependency identified. In a T-SQL script, it's likely that a stored procedure is called but not defined. Should there be such a stored procedure, it's set to depend on nothing.

The fillSP() function traverses the hash of arrays for the immediate dependencies. For each stored procedure not defined in the T-SQL script, and thus without a corresponding key, it adds a hash entry for the stored procedure and sets its value to reference an empty list.

Before moving on to the next topic, you should know that the requirement that the definitions of all the stored procedures are in a T-SQL script file isn't a limiting one. With the function dbaScriptSP() from SQLDBA::SQLDMO, you can easily generate such a T-SQL script from a live database if you want to sort the stored procedures in a database.

Sorting Stored Procedure Script Files by Dependency

SCENARIO
You want to sort your stored procedure script files by dependency, in other words, in the dependency order of the stored procedures defined in these script files.

You can reduce this problem to the one solved in the "Sorting Stored Procedures by Dependency" section. The following are the steps to reuse the code in the script sortSPs.pl from Listing 5-28:

1. Scan through all the T-SQL scripts to generate a mapping from each stored procedure name to the name of a file, where the stored procedure is defined.

2. Concatenate all the T-SQL scripts into a single string and use the code in Listing 5-28 to generate a hash of arrays, recording the immediate dependencies among the stored procedures.

3. Use the mapping obtained in step 1 to convert the hash of arrays to record the immediate dependencies among the script files.

4. Use the function sortObjs() in Listing 5-25 to sort the script files.

Given the functions and the scripts introduced previously, you only need to make some minor changes to the code in Listing 5-28 to implement these steps. Listing 5-29 first presents the script, sortSPFiles.pl, and then you'll see what these changes are.

Listing 5-29. Sorting Stored Procedure Script Files by Dependency

```
1.   use strict;
2.   use Getopt::Std;
3.   use SQLDBA::ParseSQL qw( dbaNormalizeSQL dbaSplitBatch );
4.
5.   # get command-line arguments
6.   my $optRef = getCommandLineOpt();
7.
8.   Main: {
9.     my $spCallRef;
10.    my $sp2FileRef;
11.
12.    foreach my $file (glob($optRef->{f})) {
13.        # read the script into $sql
14.        my $sql;
15.        open(SQL, "$file") or
16.           die "***Err: could not open $file for read.";
17.        read(SQL, $sql, -s SQL);
18.        close(SQL);
19.
20.        # get SPs immediately called
```

```
21.        my ($spDependRef, $sqlRef) = getSPCall($sql, $optRef->{d});
22.
23.        # normalize IDs
24.        $spDependRef = normalizeID($spDependRef, $sqlRef, $optRef);
25.
26.        # capture SP-to-file mapping
27.        foreach my $proc (keys %$spDependRef) {
28.            $sp2FileRef->{$proc} = $file;
29.        }
30.
31.      # Add the immediate dependencies from this T-SQL file to
32.      # the overall immediate dependency data structure
33.      foreach my $proc (keys %$spDependRef) {
34.          push @{$spCallRef->{$proc}}, @{$spDependRef->{$proc}}
35.      }
36.   } # foreach my $file
37.
38.   # fill in the default
39.   $spCallRef = fillInSP($spCallRef);
40.
41.   # Sort the procedures by dependency
42.   my $sortedSPRef = sortObjs($spCallRef);
43.
44.   foreach my $proc (@$sortedSPRef) {
45.       print "\t$sp2FileRef->{$proc}\n" if $sp2FileRef->{$proc};
46.   }
47. } # Main


###################
sub printUsage {
    print <<__USAGE__;
Usage:
  cmd>perl sortSPFiles.pl [-c ] [-o <owner>] -d <db> -f <T-SQL files>

  Options:
      -d    set the default database name
      -o    set the default object owner name
      -c    1 = case sensitive, 0 = case insensitive
      -f    names of the T-SQL script files, wildcards are OK
```

```
__USAGE__
    exit;
}  # printUsage


#############################
sub getCommandLineOpt {
# see Listing 5-28
}  # getCommandLineOpt


##############################
sub getSPCall {
# see Listing 5-26
}  # getSPCall


######################
sub findSPExec {
# see Listing 5-26
} # findSPExec


######################
sub normalizeID {
# download the code from the Apress Web site
# converts the stored procedure names to the standard three-part names
} # normalizeID


################
sub fillInSP {
# see Listing 5-28
} # fillInSP


##################
sub sortObjs {
# see Listing 5-25
}  # sortObjs
```

Comparing the script in Listing 5-29 with that in Listing 5-28, you should notice that the changes are all in the main body of the code. Let's review some of the key changes.

On the command line for sortSPFiles.pl, the -f switch now accepts a filename that can have embedded wildcards. The built-in Perl glob() function on line 12 expands the -f argument to a list of filenames that don't contain any wildcard.

The foreach loop between line 12 and line 36 performs the following work on each individual script file:

- It opens the file on line 15 and reads in the script as a string to the $sql variable on line 17.

- On line 21 it applies the getSPCall() function from Listing 5-26 to retrieve the immediate dependencies of the stored procedures defined in the script. Note the sortSPFiles.pl file permits multiple stored procedure definitions in a single T-SQL script file.

- On line 24, it calls the function normalizeID() to convert all the stored procedure names to the standard three-part naming format.

- Between lines 27 and 29, it records the mapping from the names of the stored procedures to the name of the T-SQL script file in which they're defined. The mapping is recorded in $sp2FileRef.

- Between lines 33 and 35, it adds the immediate dependencies found in this T-SQL file to the data structure that represents the overall immediate dependencies from all the T-SQL script files. The data structure for the overall immediate dependencies is referenced with $spCallRef.

The following is an example of the data structure to map from the stored procedures to their respective T-SQL script files:

```
$sp2FileRef = {
          '[pubs].[dbo].[reptq2]'          => '.\\test\\reptq2.PRC',
          '[pubs].[dbo].[anSP_0]'          => '.\\test\\anSP_0.PRC',
          '[pubs].[dbo].[ansp]'            => '.\\test\\anSP.PRC',
          '[pubs].[dbo].[reptq1]'          => '.\\test\\reptq1.PRC',
          '[pubs].[dbo].[poorly NamedSP]'  => '.\\test\\poorly_NamedSP.PRC',
          '[pubs].[dbo].[anotherSP]'       => '.\\test\\anotherSP.PRC'
       };
```

After the immediate dependencies of the stored procedures in all the T-SQL script files have been recorded in $spCallRef, the sortSPFiles.pl script calls the fillInSP() function defined in Listing 5-28 to add additional entries to the hash %$spCallRef. These additional entries correspond to the stored procedures that are called, but not defined, in the T-SQL script files. These stored procedures are assumed to have no dependency.

On line 42 in Listing 5-29, the sortObjs() function sorts the stored procedures by dependency. And finally, on lines 44 through 46, the following foreach loop

maps the stored procedure names in the sorted array to their respective T-SQL
script filenames with the help of the hash $sp2FileRef:

```
foreach my $proc (@$sortedSPRef) {
   print "\t$sp2FileRef->{$proc}\n" if $sp2FileRef->{$proc};
}
```

Now, you'll see an example of the script sortSPFiles.pl. You can obtain the following result when you run the sortSPFiles.pl on your workstation with the T-SQL
script files in the test subdirectory under the current directory:

```
cmd>perl sortSPFiles.pl -d pubs -f .\test\*.*
      .\test\reptq2.PRC
      .\test\reptq1.PRC
      .\test\anotherSP.PRC
      .\test\anSP_0.PRC
      .\test\anSP.PRC
      .\test\poorly_NamedSP.PRC
```

Producing a Reference Tree for a Table

> **SCENARIO**
> *You want to find all the tables that depend on a given table through the for-
> eign keys.*

You have several choices in solving this problem. Because the foreign key relationships are explicitly recorded in the SQL Server system tables, you can write a
solution all in T-SQL by querying the system tables or the INFORMATION_SCHEMA
views.

As an alternative, Listing 5-30 presents a simple Perl solution. If you've sur-
vived the previous two sections, you should be able to write the script in
Listing 5-30 without breaking a sweat.

Listing 5-30. Producing a Reference Tree for a Table

```
use strict;
use Getopt::Std;
use SQLDBA::SQLDMO qw( dbaGetReferencedTables );
use SQLDBA::Utility qw( dbaRemoveDuplicates );

my %opts;
getopts('S:D:T:', \%opts);              # command-line switches
my $tabRef = { srvName => $opts{S},     # server name
```

```
                    dbName  => $opts{D},      # database name
                    tbName  => $opts{T} };    # table name

    my $ref = getRefTree($tabRef);

    print "Table reference tree for: $opts{T}\n";
    printTree($opts{T}, $ref, 0);

    ###################
    sub getRefTree {
        my $tabRef = shift;

        my %tabTree;
        my $ref = dbaGetReferencedTables($tabRef);
        $ref = dbaRemoveDuplicates($ref);
        foreach my $childTab (@$ref) {
           my $childTabRef = {
                   srvName => $tabRef->{srvName},
                   dbName  => $tabRef->{dbName},
                   tbName  => $childTab
              };
           my $childTree = getRefTree($childTabRef);
           $tabTree{$childTab} = $childTree;
        }
        return \%tabTree;
    }


    ###################
    sub printTree {
       my ($root, $ref, $level) = @_;
       my $indent = 6;

       foreach my $node (keys %$ref) {
          print ' ' x (($level + 1) * $indent), " --> $node\n";
          printTree($node, $ref->{$node}, $level + 1);
       }
    }
```

The script in Listing 5-30 recursively calls the function getRefTree() to build the reference tree. The script is easy because it's straightforward to obtain the names of the tables referenced through the foreign keys, and, unlike with stored procedures, there's no headache with parsing and resolving a table name.

The dbaGetReferencedTables() function performs the job of retrieving the names of the referenced tables. You can implement the function in many different ways. For instance, you can parse the result of sp_helpconstraint in a text file or process the resultsets similar to those returned from sp_helpconstraint. Listing 5-31 implements dbaGetReferencedTables() using SQL-DMO.

Listing 5-31. Retrieving the Referenced Tables with dbaGetReferencedTables()

```
sub dbaGetReferencedTables {
   my $ref = shift or
      die "***Err: dbaGetReferencedTables() expects a reference.";

   my $server = Win32::OLE->new('SQLDMO.SQLServer')
     or die "***Err: Could not create SQLDMO object.";
   $server->{LoginSecure} = 1;

   $server->connect($ref->{srvName}, '', '');
   ! Win32::OLE->LastError() or
      die "***Err: Could not connect to $ref->{srvName}.";

   my $table = $server->Databases($ref->{dbName})->Tables($ref->{tbName});
   ! Win32::OLE->LastError() or
      die "***Err: could not get the table object.";

   # Get referenced tables
   my @refTables;
   foreach my $key (in($table->Keys())) {
      push @refTables, $key->{ReferencedTable} if $key->{ReferencedTable};
   }

   $server->disconnect();
   return \@refTables;
} # dbaGetReferencedTables
```

There's nothing special about this script. Structurally, it's similar to dbaGetTableColumns() in Listing 5-2 or dbaGetTableIndexes() in Listing 5-7. They're all exported by the module SQLDBA::SQLDMO. As far as SQL-DMO is concerned, the name of the referenced table is a property of a key constraint, which is a member of the Keys collection hanging off the Table object.

Running the script in Listing 5-30 against the table `pubs.dbo.titleauthor` produces the following:

```
cmd>perl tableTree.pl -S .\apollo -D pubs -T dbo.titleauthor
Table reference tree for: dbo.titleauthor
        --> [dbo].[titles]
            --> [dbo].[publishers]
                --> [dbo].[countries]
        --> [dbo].[authors]
```

Summary

This chapter has focused on comparing and sorting database objects. Most DBAs need to perform these tasks from time to time.

Commercial tools on the market can compare database schemas, and to a lesser extent, sort database objects. For database comparison, two packages stand out: SQL Compare from Red Gate Software (`http://www.red-gate.com`) and Embarcadero Change Manager from Embarcadero Technologies (`http://www.embarcadero.com`).

One of the greatest advantages of the commercial tools is their graphical user interface. The point-and-click—as well as drag-and-drop—capabilities make ad-hoc and exploratory work easier. However, if using a graphical user interface isn't among your critical success factors—and for many such tasks, it shouldn't be—the scripts presented in this chapter give you ultimate flexibility to meet your comparison and sorting requirements.

In many environments, acquiring the commercial tools for schema comparison and database object sorting is simply out of the question—cost being one of the prohibiting factors—so rolling out scripts is your only viable resort.

The next chapter shows you how to apply Perl to analyzing databases.

CHAPTER 6

Analyzing Databases

IT SHOULD COME AS NO SURPRISE that the SQL Server Database Administrator (DBA) works with databases. One of the key responsibilities of the DBA is to manage databases and manage them well.

To properly manage SQL Server databases, you need to have an in-depth understanding of how they behave and become aware of the status of your databases before any potential problems turn into real problems.

This chapter covers two tracks of topics related to analyzing SQL Server databases. In the first track, the chapter presents several Perl scripts that help you investigate the SQL Server storage internals and locking behavior in detail. These scripts facilitate the use of tools such as DBCC PAGE and the trace flag 1200. If you're interested in exploring how SQL Server manages its storage and locking, you'll find that these scripts significantly speed up your investigation.

In the second track, the chapter turns to the more practical issues that a DBA is concerned about daily, and it shows how you can write Perl scripts to help scan databases in your environment for potential problems. These scripts flag violations of database best practices.

Converting a Byte-Swapped Hex String to the Page ID

> **SCENARIO**
> *You want to find the file number and the page number from a SQL Server byte-swapped hex string.*

If you're interested in SQL Server storage internals, you've most likely heard the term *byte-swapped format*, which SQL Server uses to store the page IDs. In this format, two hex digits represent each byte; the first byte is placed as the last byte, the second byte is placed as the second last, and so on with the last byte appearing as the first byte. In addition, the last two bytes represent the file number, and the first four bytes represent the page number.

For example, when you retrieve the values of the columns first, root, and firstiam of the sysindexes table using osql.exe or Query Analyzer, you get them in the byte-swapped hex strings.

The problem is that normally a SQL Server page ID is expected to have two decimal numbers separated with a colon: The first number is the file number, and the second number is the page number. For instance, Transact-SQL (T-SQL) commands such as DBCC PAGE—to be discussed shortly in the "Mapping from a Page to the Rows" section—accept the file number and the page number instead of the byte-swapped hex string. If you want to research the SQL Server storage internal issues, you'll constantly run into situations where you must decode these byte-swapped hex strings to find their corresponding page IDs.

You can find published stored procedures that convert a byte-swapped hex string to the page ID. *Microsoft SQL Server 2000 Unleashed, Second Edition* by Ray Rankins, Paul Jensen, and Paul Bertucci (Sams, 2002) includes a stored procedure that displays the page IDs from the byte-swapped hex strings in the sysindexes table. You can also find a similar stored procedure on the CD that accompanies *Inside Microsoft SQL Server 2000* by Kalen Delaney (Microsoft Press, 2000).

These stored procedures save you a few manual steps. However, they fall short if the conversion is but one of the steps in an automated procedure. Similarly, if you have to repeatedly perform the conversion, you still need to manually transcribe the output of such a stored procedure.

An example should clarify how a byte-swapped hex string is structured and how you can decode it. The following SQL query retrieves the location of the first page in the clustered index of the pubs..authors table:

```
USE pubs
SELECT first FROM pubs..sysindexes
 WHERE id = object_id('authors')
   AND indid = 1
```

Running this query in the SQL Server 2000 instance on my notebook computer returns 0xA00000000100. This is the byte-swapped hex string of a page ID, and it has the following structure:

- 0x isn't part of the hex string. It signifies the string that follows to be a hex string.

- Every two hex digits in the string represents a byte.

- The positions of the bytes are reversed in the displayed hex string. The first byte is displayed last, the second byte the second last, and so on. And the last byte is displayed first. After reversing the byte positions of 0xA00000000100, the hex string is 0001000000A0.

- After reversing the byte positions, the first two bytes is the file number, and the last four bytes is the page number. In the example of the original string 0xA00000000100, the file number is 0001 and the page number is 000000A0, both in hex.

Given a byte-swapped hex string, Listing 6-1 shows a Perl function—
getPageID()—that returns the file number and the page number in decimal.

Listing 6-1. Converting a Byte-Swapped Hex String to the Page ID

```
my $root = '0xA00000000100';
print "Page ID = ", getPageID($root), "\n";

sub getPageID {
   my $root = shift or die "***Err: getPageID() expects a string.";

   $root =~ s/^0x//;   # remove 0x hex prefix, if any
   $root =~ /^[A-F\d]{12}$/i or die "***Err: $root is not a hex string.";

   # decompose the string to an array of bytes, and swap the bytes
   my @roots = reverse($root =~ /([A-F\d]{2})/ig);

   # join the bytes and convert to decimal
   return hex(join '', @roots[0, 1]) . ':' . hex(join '', @roots[2..5]);
} # getPageID
```

Save this script to the file getPageID.pl and run it on the command line, and
you should see the following:

cmd>perl getPageID.pl
Page ID = 1:160

The following statement in the function getPageID() from Listing 6-1 validates
that the supplied string is indeed a hex string:

```
$root =~ /^[A-F\d]{12}$/i or die "***Err: $root is not a hex string.";
```

The regular expression matches a string in which there should be exactly 12
characters in the string, and each character can be a number between 0 and 9 or a
letter between A and F. The /i modifier makes the match case insensitive.

Also, note the following statement that decomposes a string to an array of
single-byte hex numbers and then swaps the bytes:

```
my @roots = reverse($root =~ /([A-F\d]{2})/ig);
```

The =~ operator with the /g modifier is evaluated in list context because the reverse() function expects a list. The expression $roots =~ /([A-F\d]{2})/ig therefore returns a list of all the substrings captured by the parentheses. Each of the captured values corresponds to a byte, consisting of two hex letters. The Perl built-in function reverse() effectively swaps the positions of all the bytes in the list.

The function getPageID() in Listing 6-1 by itself isn't interesting except that it can be made much shorter than a similar T-SQL solution. The function becomes useful when you call it from other scripts.

Finding the Row/Page Mapping

> **SCENARIO**
> *You want an automated way to map the rows in a table to the pages and vice versa. This mapping allows you to investigate how an operation affects the rows stored on a page.*

When you study the SQL Server storage internals, you'll often run into situations where you need to map between the rows in a table and the physical pages on which they're stored. In other words, you need to find what rows a given page stores or which page stores a particular row.

Having convenient access to this information enables you to study the impact of various operations on the physical storage. For instance, when you want to study how a page split behaves when you insert a row or multiple rows, a comparison of a snapshot of this mapping before the split and a snapshot of the mapping after the split should tell you exactly how SQL Server moves the rows on the page that would be split.

It's relatively easy to find the rows on a page. If you know the page number, you can use the undocumented but well-known DBCC PAGE command. Unfortunately, there's no simple command to map a row to a page. Let's examine the mapping in these two directions in turn.

Mapping from a Page to the Rows

SQL Server 2000 identifies a page with two numbers—a number identifying the data file on which the page resides, followed by a number identifying the page in the file. These numbers are in the format of file_number:page_number. For instance, 1:123 refers to the page 123 in the file 1.

You can use the DBCC PAGE command to find the rows on a data page. Its syntax is as follows:

```
DBCC PAGE(db_id | db_name, file_no, page_no [, print_option] )
```

If you set print_option to 3, after the hex dump of each row, DBCC PAGE displays the name of each column followed by the value of the column. If you're not crazy about deciphering the hex dumps yourself, you can glean the row information from these column name and value pairs. Listing 6-2 shows a partial output of applying the following DBCC PAGE command to a page of the pubs..authors table:

```
DBCC TRACEON(3604)
DBCC PAGE(5, 1, 160, 3)
```

In this DBCC PAGE command, the database number of pubs is 5 and the page ID of the authors table is 1:160.

Listing 6-2. Sample Output of DBCC PAGE

```
PAGE: (1:160)
-------------


BUFFER:
-------


BUF @0x00D74240
---------------
bpage = 0x19A02000        bhash = 0x00000000        bpageno = (1:160)
bdbid = 5                 breferences = 1           bstat = 0x9
bspin = 0                 bnext = 0x00000000


PAGE HEADER:
------------


Page @0x19A02000
----------------
m_pageId = (1:160)        m_headerVersion = 1       m_type = 1
m_typeFlagBits = 0x0      m_level = 0               m_flagBits = 0x20
m_objId = 1797581442      m_indexId = 0             m_prevPage = (0:0)
m_nextPage = (0:0)        pminlen = 28              m_slotCnt = 23
```

```
m_freeCnt = 5918          m_freeData = 2228          m_reservedCnt = 0
m_lsn = (12:236:194)      m_xactReserved = 0         m_xdesId = (0:1280)
m_ghostRecCnt = 0         m_tornBits = 201341993


Allocation Status
-----------------
GAM (1:2) = ALLOCATED     SGAM (1:3) = NOT ALLOCATED
PFS (1:1) = 0x60 MIXED_EXT ALLOCATED   0_PCT_FULL   DIFF (1:6) = NOT CHANGED
ML (1:7) = NOT MIN_LOGGED


Slot 0 Offset 0x60
------------------
Record Type = PRIMARY_RECORD
Record Attributes =  NULL_BITMAP VARIABLE_COLUMNS
19A02060:  001c0030  20383034  2d363934  33323237 0...408 496-7223

...

19A020A0:  316e6f73  32333930  67694220  52206567 son10932 Bigge R
19A020B0:  654d2e64  206f6c6e  6b726150           d.Menlo Park
au_id                      = 172-32-1176
au_lname                   = White
au_fname                   = Johnson
phone                      = 408 496-7223
address                    = 10932 Bigge Rd.
city                       = Menlo Park
state                      = CA
zip                        = 94025
contract                   = 1


Slot 1 Offset 0xbc
------------------
Record Type = PRIMARY_RECORD
Record Attributes =  NULL_BITMAP VARIABLE_COLUMNS
19A020BC:  001c0030  20353134  2d363839  30323037 0...415 986-7020

...

19A020FC:  6569726f  20393033  64723336  2e745320 orie309 63rd St.
19A0210C:  31342320  6b614f31  646e616c           #411Oakland
au_id                      = 213-46-8915
au_lname                   = Green
au_fname                   = Marjorie
phone                      = 415 986-7020
address                    = 309 63rd St. #411
city                       = Oakland
```

```
state                      = CA
zip                        = 94618
contract                   = 1


... (Slots 2 ~ 21 removed)

Slot 22 Offset 0x855
--------------------
Record Type = PRIMARY_RECORD
Record Attributes =  NULL_BITMAP VARIABLE_COLUMNS
19A02855:   001c0030  20313038  2d363238  32353730 0...801 826-0752
...
19A02895:   36747265  65532037  746e6576  76412068 ert67 Seventh Av
19A028A5:   6c61532e  614c2074  4320656b    797469 .Salt Lake City
au_id                      = 998-72-3567
au_lname                   = Ringer
au_fname                   = Albert
phone                      = 801 826-0752
address                    = 67 Seventh Av.
city                       = Salt Lake City
state                      = UT
zip                        = 84152
contract                   = 1
```

The output of the DBCC PAGE command can be divided into several sections. The important sections include the page header section and the slot sections.

The page header section shows you properties pertinent to the entire page. The properties that will be used in the scripts in this chapter include m_type, m_freeCnt, and m_ghostCnt. The value of m_type indicates what type this page is— data page, index page, and so on. The value of m_freeCnt is the number of free bytes left on the page. The m_ghostCnt tallies the number of ghost records on the page.

For a data page, the DBCC PAGE output may have one or more slot sections, corresponding to the number of rows stored on the page. There are 23 slots on the page shown in Listing 6-2. Each slot begins with a slot number and the offset of the slot on the page.

As you see, you can scan this DBCC PAGE output to find all the rows stored on a given page.

Mapping from a Row to the Page

Given a row in a table, there's no straightforward way to find the page on which it's stored. However, if you scan every page of the table for the rows on that page and record the mapping, you'll be able to find the row and therefore the page on which it's stored.

Now, the question becomes "How do you identify all the data pages used by a table?" You can use the undocumented DBCC TAB command or the undocumented DBCC IND command. The DBCC TAB command displays a complete list of all the pages used by a table.

In both SQL Server 7.0 and SQL Server 2000, the syntax of DBCC TAB is as follows:

```
DBCC TAB(db_id, table_id)
```

Similarly, in both SQL Server 7.0 and SQL Server 2000, if you choose to use the DBCC IND command to retrieve the page IDs of the data pages in a table, you need to specify an index identifier as the third additional parameter. This identifier should be 1 if the table has a clustered index and 0 if it doesn't have a clustered index.

The syntax of DBCC IND is as follows:

```
DBCC IND(db_id, table_id, index_id)
```

Listing 6-3 shows a partial output of the DBCC IND command when it's applied to the Northwind..Customers table. In Listing 6-3, several nonessential columns have been removed from the output to fit the width of the book.

Listing 6-3. Sample Output of DBCC IND

PageFID	PagePID	IndexID	PageType	NextPageFID	NextPagePID	PrevPageFID	PrevPagePID
1	110	1	10	0	0	0	0
1	109	1	2	0	0	0	0
1	111	0	1	1	128	0	0
1	128	0	1	1	129	1	111
1	129	0	1	0	0	1	128

The important points to note about the tabular output in Listing 6-3 are the following:

- PageFID refers to the file number of the page, and PagePID refers to the page number. Thus, PageFID:PagePID forms the page ID.

- PageType identifies the type of the page. For a data page, this value is set to 1. Note a leaf page of a clustered index is considered a data page; thus, its PageType is set to 1. For a data page in a heap table, its PageType is set to 0.

Therefore, in Listing 6-3 the Northwind..Customers table has three data pages in total. They are 1:111, 1:128, and 1:129. Applying DBCC PAGE to each of these three pages gives you complete information on where a row is physically located.

The function getAllPageIDs() in Listing 6-4 executes the DBCC IND command on the table whose name is passed to the function as a parameter, and it retrieves the page IDs of all the data pages in the table into the array @resultset. The variable $conn is an object representing an open ADO connection.

Listing 6-4. Retrieving All the Data Page IDs of a Table

```
sub getAllPageIDs {
   my ($conn, $db, $tb) = @_;

   my $sql ="DECLARE \@db int, \@obj int
             SELECT \@db = db_id(\'$db\'), \@obj = object_id(\'$tb\')
             DBCC IND(\@db, \@obj, 0)";

   my $rs = $conn->Execute($sql) or
      die Win32::OLE->LastError();

   my @resultset = ();
   while ( !$rs->{EOF} ) {
      if ($rs->Fields('PageType')->{Value} != 1) {
         $rs->MoveNext;
         next;
      }
      my $pageID = $rs->Fields('PageFID')->{Value} .':' .
                   $rs->Fields('PagePID')->{Value};
      push @resultset, $pageID;
      $rs->MoveNext;
   }
   return \@resultset;
} # getAllPageIDs
```

Now that you have all the data page IDs for the table, you can apply DBCC PAGE to each page to find its rows.

However, manually applying DBCC PAGE to page numbers is a boring and laborious process and isn't conducive to further process the information extracted from the DBCC PAGE output.

You need a tool to apply the DBCC PAGE command and extract the needed information into a data structure so that other tools can further manipulate the information through accessing the data structure.

That's where Perl comes in. But before you can automate this process, you need to first answer three more questions:

How do you get the output of the DBCC PAGE command into a Perl data structure?

How do you identify each row? To simplify the matter, let's assume that there's a primary key on the table. You can therefore use these primary key columns to identify a row. The question becomes "How do you find the primary key columns of a table?"

How do you search the DBCC PAGE output to locate and store the information on the rows?

The subsequent sections present the answer to each of these three questions in turn.

Reading the DBCC PAGE Output

The DBCC PAGE is nothing more than a T-SQL query. However, it's a special query. Its results aren't returned as a resultset, but they're instead returned as messages through the SQL Server's error handling mechanism that's separate from its resultset processing mechanism. As you probably know, SQL Server has two different types of error handling mechanisms:

- Any error with a severity of 11 or higher is returned as an error. The error either can be SQL Server generated or the result of a T-SQL RAISERROR statement.

- Any error with a severity of 10 or lower is returned as a message. The message either can be SQL Server generated or the result of a T-SQL RAISERROR statement; in addition, the output of the T-SQL PRINT statement or the output of many DBCC commands is also returned as messages.

If you're using ActiveX Data Objects (ADO), you process the errors and messages using the `Error` object of the `Errors` collection in the ADO model. The properties of the `Error` object contain the details about each error or message.

Listing 6-5 is the function `dbccPage()` that accepts an ADO connection object, a database name, a file number, and a page number, and it returns a reference to an array whose elements are the text lines of the DBCC PAGE output.

Listing 6-5. Capturing the DBCC PAGE *Output with an Array*

```
1.   sub dbccPage {
2.       my ($conn, $db, $fileNo, $pageNo) = @_;
3.       my @msgs;
4.
5.       my $sql = "DECLARE \@dbid int
6.                  SET \@dbid = db_id(\'$db\')
7.                  DBCC PAGE(\@dbid,$fileNo,$pageNo,3)";
8.       $conn->Execute($sql) or
9.         die Win32::OLE->LastError();
10.
11.      # note that ADO returns DBCC output in Errors collection
12.      # unless you specify with tableresults
13.      foreach my $err (in($conn->Errors())) {
14.        my $msg = $err->{Description}; # it's in the Description property
15.        $msg =~ s/\s*$//;
16.        push @msgs, $msg;
17.      }
18.      return \@msgs; # contains the DBCC PAGE output
19.   }   # dbccPage
```

In Listing 6-5, the function `dbccPage()` constructs a DBCC PAGE statement on lines 5 through 7, and executes the query on line 8. Because a database name is passed to the function, but the DBCC PAGE command expects a database identifier, the function first gets the corresponding database identifier on lines 5 and 6.

The text messages of the DBCC PAGE command come back in the `Description` property of the `Error` objects in the `Errors` collection. The function hence loops through all the `Error` objects in the `Errors` collection between lines 13 and 17, and for each `Error` it adds the message in the `Description` property to the array `@msg`. Each line of the DBCC PAGE messages becomes an element of the array `@msg`.

Finding the Primary Key Columns

To identify a row, it's sufficient to retrieve the values of its primary key columns from the DBCC PAGE output. But first, you need to determine which columns constitute the primary key of a given table.

One of the convenient methods to find all the columns in a primary key is to query the Information_Schema views. For instance, given the table pubs..authors, the following T-SQL query returns the primary key columns in its resultset in the same order the columns are listed in the primary key—the leftmost column in the primary key is in the first row and the rightmost column is in the last row:

```
USE pubs
SELECT kc.column_name
  FROM information_schema.key_column_usage kc,
       information_schema.table_constraints tc
 WHERE kc.table_name = 'authors'    -- authors table
   AND kc.table_schema = 'dbo'
   AND kc.table_name = tc.table_name
   AND kc.table_schema = tc.table_schema
   AND kc.constraint_name = tc.constraint_name
   AND kc.constraint_schema = tc.constraint_schema
   AND tc.constraint_type = 'PRIMARY KEY'
ORDER BY kc.ordinal_position
```

The function getPKRef() in Listing 6-6 accepts a table name and an open ADO connection, executes this T-SQL query, and places the resulting column names in an array.

Listing 6-6. Retrieving the Primary Key Columns

```
sub getPKRef {
   my ($conn, $tab) = @_;

   my $sql = "SELECT kc.column_name
                FROM information_schema.key_column_usage kc,
                     information_schema.table_constraints tc
               WHERE kc.table_name = \'$tab\'
                 AND kc.table_schema = \'dbo\'
                 AND kc.table_name = tc.table_name
                 AND kc.table_schema = tc.table_schema
                 AND kc.constraint_name = tc.constraint_name
                 AND kc.constraint_schema = tc.constraint_schema
                 AND tc.constraint_type = 'PRIMARY KEY'
            ORDER BY kc.ordinal_position";
```

```
   my $rs = $conn->Execute($sql) or
       die Win32::OLE->LastError();

   my @resultset = ();
   while ( !$rs->{EOF} ) {
       push @resultset, $rs->Fields('column_name')->{Value};
       $rs->MoveNext;
   }
   return \@resultset;
} # getPKRef
```

The script in Listing 6-6 passes the table name into the T-SQL query through the interpolation of the variable $tab. Because the T-SQL query orders the resultset by the ordinal position of the columns in the primary key, the returned array preserves the order of the columns in the primary key.

Retrieving the Rows from DBCC PAGE Output

Now that the information returned by the DBCC PAGE command is captured in an array with the function dbccPage() in Listing 6-5, you can loop through this array to search for the rows by matching the primary key columns and their corresponding values. The function getRows() shown in Listing 6-7 performs this work.

Listing 6-7. Retrieving the Rows from the DBCC PAGE *Results*

```
1.  sub getRows {
2.      my ($pkRef, $msgRef) = @_;  # accept PK columns and DBCC PAGE output
3.
4.      my $rowCnt;          # for validation purpose
5.      my $pageHeader = 0;  # to signal whether the loop is in the header part
6.      my ($page, $slot, $offset);
7.      my $rowRef;
8.      foreach my $msg (@$msgRef) { # each line in DBCC PAGE output
9.          $msg =~ /^\s*PAGE:\s+\((.+)\)/i and $page = $1;  # e.g. PAGE:(1:160)
10.
11.         # if matched, entering the page header
12.         if ($msg =~ /^\s*PAGE\s+HEADER:/i) {
13.             $pageHeader = 1;
14.             next;
15.         }
17.         # if matched, left the page header
18.         if ($msg =~ /^\s*Allocation\s+Status/i) {
```

```
19.        $pageHeader = 0;
20.        next;
21.     }
22.
23.     # get the slot count (i.e. row count) from the header
24.     # the actual row count should match this number if our search works.
25.     # Otherwise, sth went wrong and the result shouldn't be used
26.     if ($pageHeader and $msg =~ /m\_slotCnt\s*=\s*(\d+)/i) {
27.        $rowCnt = $1;
28.        next;
29.     }
30.     # individual slot heading
31.     if ($msg =~ /^\s*Slot\s+(\d+)\s+Offset\s+0x\w+/i) {
32.        $slot = $1;
33.        next;
34.     }
35.     foreach my $key (@$pkRef) {
36.        if ($msg =~ /^\s*$key\s*=\s*(.+?)\s*$/i) {
37.           push @{$rowRef->{$slot}}, $1;
38.        }
39.     }
40.  }
41.  # actual row count should match the slot count in the header
42.  my $actualRowCnt = scalar (keys %$rowRef);
43.  print "Page: $page, Header slot cnt \= $rowCnt, ",
44.        "actual row cnt \= $actualRowCnt\n";
45.  ($rowCnt == $actualRowCnt) or
46.     die "***Err: parsing DBCC PAGE output encountered problem.";
47.
48.  my $r_rowRef;
49.  foreach my $slotNo (keys %$rowRef) {
50.     # concatenate the PK key values if it's composite
51.     my $pk_concat = join('/', @{$rowRef->{$slotNo}});
52.     # reverse key/value
53.     $r_rowRef->{$pk_concat} = $slotNo;
54.  }
55.  return $r_rowRef;  # concatenated PK values is key, slot # is value
56. } # getRows
```

To understand the behavior of the function getRows() in Listing 6-7, it helps to review the sample output of the DBCC PAGE command in Listing 6-2. You may even want to walk through the code in Listing 6-7 with the sample output in Listing 6-2.

The getRows() function uses the variable $pageHeader as a toggle to remember whether the function is currently scanning the page header section of the DBCC PAGE output. The variable $pageHeader is set to 1 when the scan enters the page header, that is, when the output matches the regular expression /^\s*PAGE\s+HEADER:/i on line 12. The variable is set to 0 when the code leaves the page header section, that is, when the output matches the regular expression /^\s*Allocation\s+Status/i on line 18. If you review the sample output of the DBCC PAGE command in Listing 6-2, you should find that Allocation Status is the heading of the next section after the page header.

The variable $pageHeader helps ensure that you're indeed matching the items from the page header section. For instance, on line 26 the function captures the value of m_slotCnt, which is the total count of the slots—in other words, rows—on the data page. Without the variable $pageHeader to restrict the matching to the page header section, you run the risk of matching m_slotCnt somewhere else, for instance, inside the value of a column:

```
26.        if ($pageHeader and $msg =~ /m\_slotCnt\s*=\s*(\d+)/i) {
27.            $rowCnt = $1;
28.            next;
29.        }
```

The value of m_slotCnt captured on line 26 and recorded in the variable $rowCnt on line 27 is for validation purposes. As the function moves through each of the slots that store the rows, the total number of rows actually found should match the value of $rowCnt. Otherwise, the scan for the rows has run into some unexpected problem.

The code fragment between line 31 and line 39 in Listing 6-7 uses a quintessential Perl technique to ensure that the primary key column values for the same slot only—in other words, the same row—are pushed into the same array. This technique depends on the fact that the keys of a Perl hash must be unique. The reproduced code fragment is as follows:

```
31.        if ($msg =~ /^\s*Slot\s+(\d+)\s+Offset\s+0x\w+/i) {
32.            $slot = $1;
33.            next;
34.        }
35.        foreach my $key (@$pkRef) {
36.            if ($msg =~ /^\s*$key\s*=\s*(.+?)\s*$/i) {
37.                push @{$rowRef->{$slot}}, $1;
38.            }
39.        }
```

Let's examine the code fragment between lines 31 and 39 in more detail. As the code enters a slot section, it matches the slot header on line 31 and records the slot number in the variable $slot. As the code continues through the same slot to match the primary key columns and their values, it pushes the matched value into an array referenced by $rowRef->{$slot}. As long as the code still scans the same slot section of the DBCC PAGE output, the variable $slot has the same value, and therefore $rowRef->{$slot} points to the same array.

On line 45 in Listing 6-7, the function getRows() has finished scanning all the lines in the DBCC PAGE output. It compares the actual row count with the row count recorded from the value of m_slotCnt in the page header. If these two values don't match, the function aborts the script on line 46. Something went terribly wrong in scanning the rows, and there's no point continuing.

As the function getRows() scans the output of the DBCC PAGE command, it builds a hash, referenced by $rowRef, to store the collected information. Listing 6-8 is an example of the hash.

Listing 6-8. An Example of the Hash Referenced by $rowRef

```
$rowRef = {
            '29' => [ 'GODOS' ],
            '0'  => [ 'ALFKI' ],
            '1'  => [ 'ANATR' ],
            '2'  => [ 'ANTON' ],
            '3'  => [ 'AROUT' ],
            '4'  => [ 'BERGS' ],
            '10' => [ 'BSBEV' ],
            ...
};
```

To find the mapping from the rows to the pages, it's more convenient to identify the slot number as an attribute of a row.

The code fragment between lines 49 and 54 in Listing 6-7 is to reverse the hash, making the primary key values (actually their concatenation), the hash keys, and the slot numbers the hash values.

Mapping Between Rows and Pages

With the functions dbccPage(), getPKRef(), getAllPageIDs(), and getRows(), you're ready to meet the challenge of producing a mapping between the data page IDs and the rows in a table.

The script mapPageRows.pl in Listing 6-9 puts all these functions together. It accepts a server name, a database name, and a table name on the command line, and it generates a mapping between the data page IDs and the rows—represented with the primary key values—in the format of a hash.

Listing 6-9. Mapping Between the Page IDs and the Rows

```
1.  use strict;
2.  use Win32::OLE 'in';
3.  use Getopt::Std;
4.  use Data::Dumper;
5.
6.  my %opts;
7.  getopts('s:d:t:', \%opts);  # get command line arguments
8.  (defined $opts{s} and defined $opts{d} and defined $opts{t}) or printUsage();
9.
10. MAIN: {
11.    my ($server, $db, $tab) = ($opts{s}, $opts{d}, $opts{t});
12.    print scalar localtime(), "\n";
13.
14.    # open a connection to the server and database
15.    my $conn = getConn($server, $db);
16.
17.    # get the PK column(s)
18.    my $pkRef = getPKRef($conn, $tab);
19.    unless (scalar @$pkRef) {
20.       die "***Err: table $tab doesn't have a primary key.";
21.    }
22.    # get all the page IDs of the table
23.    my $allPageIDsRef = getAllPageIDs($conn, $db, $tab);
24.
25.    # for each page ID, get all the rows on the page
26.    my ($msgRef, $rowRef, $page2Rows);
27.    foreach my $pageID (@$allPageIDsRef) {
28.       my ($fileno, $pageno) = $pageID =~ /(\d+)\:(\d+)/;
29.
30.       #get the result of DBCC PAGE to an array
31.       $msgRef = dbccPage($conn, $db, $fileno, $pageno);
32.
33.       # get the PK values of the rows on a page
34.       $rowRef = getRows($pkRef, $msgRef);
35.
36.       # get mapping from page ID to the PK values on the page
37.       $page2Rows->{$pageID} = [sort keys %$rowRef];
```

271

```
38.     }
39.     $conn->Close();
40.     print Dumper($page2Rows);
41. }


####################
sub printUsage {
   print <<___Usage;
Usage:
   cmd>perl mapPageRows.pl  -s <SQL Server instance>
                            -d <database>
                            -t <table>
___Usage
   exit;
} # printUsage


####################
#  get an ADO connection to be used throughout the script
sub getConn {
   my ($server, $db) = @_;

   my $conn = Win32::OLE->new('ADODB.Connection') or
         die "***Err: Win32::OLE->new() failed.";
   $conn->{ConnectionTimeout} = 4;
   my $connStr = "Provider=sqloledb;Server=$server;" .
                 "database=$db;Trusted_Connection=yes";
   $conn->Open($connStr);
   ! Win32::OLE->LastError() or die Win32::OLE->LastError();

   # 3604 to send trace flag to the client
   $conn->Execute('dbcc traceon(3604)') or
      die Win32::OLE->LastError();
   return $conn;  # this connection will be reused until the script exits
} # getConn


#####################
#  get the DBCC PAGE output to an array
sub dbccPage {
# See Listing 6-5.
} # dbccPage
```

```
#########################
# get the rows, identified by the PKs, for the page from
# the page info dumped by DBCC PAGE
sub getRows {
# See Listing 6-7.
}  # getRows


#############################
#  get all the page IDs of a table
sub getAllPageIDs {
# See Listing 6-4.
}  # getAllPageIDs


#######################
#   get the PK columns
sub getPKRef {
# See Listing 6-6.
}  # getPKRef
```

After verifying that the server name, the database name, and the table name are all specified on the command line, the script mapPageRows.pl in Listing 6-9 opens an ADO connection to the server and the database on line 15. This same ADO connection is used throughout the rest of the script. Then, on line 18 the script applies the function getPKRef() to retrieve the names of the primary key columns of the table into an array and returns its reference to the variable $pkRef. The script retrieves all the data page IDs on line 23 using the getAllPageIDs() function.

Between lines 27 and 38, the script loops through every data page of the table to perform DBCC PAGE with the function dbccPage() and retrieve the primary key values for each row on that page using the function getRows(). Finally, on line 37 the script captures the mapping from the page ID to the rows in a hash referenced by the variable $page2Rows.

The script mapPageRows.pl prints the data structure $page2Rows using the Dump() method of the Data::Dumper module. Listing 6-10 is an example of running the script with the Northwind..Customers table on my notebook computer.

Listing 6-10. A Sample Output of mapPageRows.pl

```
cmd>perl mapPageRows.pl -s .\apollo -d Northwind -t Customers
Sun Apr 27 01:55:12 2003
Page: 1:131, Header slot cnt = 32, actual row cnt = 32
Page: 1:392, Header slot cnt = 29, actual row cnt = 29
Page: 1:393, Header slot cnt = 30, actual row cnt = 30
$mapPage2Rows = {
                '1:131' => [
                            'ALFKI',
                            'ANATR',
                            ...
                            'GREAL'
                        ],
                '1:392' => [
                            'GROSR',
                            'HANAR',
                            ...
                            'QUEDE'
                        ],
                '1:393' => [
                            'QUEEN',
                            'QUICK',
                            ...
                            'WOLZA'
                        ]
            };
```

If you're wondering why you should even bother with such a mapping, consider the following questions:

- If you delete all the rows between HANAR and QUEDE, will the remaining row stay on the page 1:392?

- How do the pages look if you add another 20 rows to the Customers table?

- If you add a row to cause a page split, how does SQL Server redistribute the existing rows for the page split?

You can easily answer these questions by running the script mapPageRows.pl. If you want to study the storage impact of an operation, you can do the following:

1. Run the script and record the result, which is the pre-operation snapshot.

2. Perform the operation.

3. Run the script again and record the new result, which is the post-operation snapshot.

4. Compare the two results to determine what effect, if any, the operation has on the placement of the rows on the pages.

The snapshots have a structure similar to that shown in Listing 6-10.

CAUTION   *Don't apply the* mapPageRows.pl *script to a large table that has numerous data pages. It's time consuming to loop through all these pages to run* DBCC PAGE *and then scan for information. In addition, you'd be overwhelmed by the amount of information it may gather from a large table. Remember that the purpose of* mapPageRows.pl *is to facilitate the study of SQL Server storage internals. You should keep the table as small as possible without losing the characteristics of the problem you want to study.*

Let's examine how SQL Server redistributes the existing rows after a page split to see how the mapPageRows.pl script can expedite your studying of the SQL Server storage internals.

Observing Page Removals and Page Splits

Let's use the output of the script mapPageRows.pl in Listing 6-10 as the baseline to measure the change a SQL query may introduce.

First, save all the rows of the Customers table to the temporary table #tmp with the following query:

```
SELECT * INTO #tmp FROM Customers
```

Then, remove the foreign keys that reference the Customers table and delete all the rows on page 1:392 with the following SQL query:

```
DELETE Customers
 WHERE CustomerID BETWEEN 'GROSR' AND 'QUEDE'
```

Now, you can run the mapPageRows.pl script to check the allocation of the pages and the rows.

As you can see from Listing 6-11, SQL Server deallocated the page 1:392 from the Customers table when all the rows on the page have been deleted.

Listing 6-11. The Page and Row Allocation After Removing the Rows

```
cmd>perl mapPageRows.pl -s .\apollo -d Northwind -t Customers
Sun Apr 27 09:24:54 2003
Page: 1:351, Header slot cnt = 32, actual row cnt = 32
Page: 1:393, Header slot cnt = 30, actual row cnt = 30
$mapPage2Rows = {
                  '1:351' => [
                               'ALFKI',
                               'ANATR',
                               ...
                               'GREAL'
                             ],
                  '1:393' => [
                               'QUEEN',
                               'QUICK',
                               ...
                               'WOLZA'
                             ]
                };
```

Finally, insert one of the deleted rows back into the Customers table with the following query:

```
INSERT Customers
SELECT * FROM #tmp
 WHERE CustomerID = 'GROSR'
```

The result of the mapPageRows.pl script now is as shown in Listing 6-12.

Listing 6-12. The Page and Row Allocation After Inserting the Row

```
cmd>perl mapPageRows.pl -s .\apollo -d Northwind -t Customers
Sun Apr 27 09:26:18 2003
Page: 1:351, Header slot cnt = 17, actual row cnt = 17
Page: 1:392, Header slot cnt = 16, actual row cnt = 16
Page: 1:393, Header slot cnt = 30, actual row cnt = 30
$mapPage2Rows = {
                '1:351' => [
                            'ALFKI',
                            'ANATR',
                            ...
                            'DRACD'
                          ],
                '1:392' => [
                            'DUMON',
                            'EASTC',
                            ...
                            'GREAL',
                            'GROSR'
                          ],
                '1:393' => [
                            'QUEEN',
                            'QUICK',
                            ...
                            'WOLZA'
                          ]
              };
```

Comparing Listing 6-11 and Listing 6-12, you can see clearly that inserting the row of GROSR caused SQL Server to allocate the page 1:392 and split the page 1:351. In this case, the page 1:392 happened to be a page deallocated earlier, but it could be any other page. The page split moved almost half of the original 32 rows on 1:351 to 1:392. More precisely, 17 rows are kept on the page 1:351, and 16 rows including the newly inserted row are on the page 1:392.

The next section shows you how to expand this method to study other aspects of the SQL Server storage internals.

Using the TABLERESULTS Option

Many DBCC commands accept the TABLERESULTS option, which sends the result of a DBCC command back to the client as a resultset instead of a text message. This option isn't always documented. For a DBCC command, if you're not sure whether it takes the TABLERESULTS option, you can always try the TABLERESULTS option in Query Analyzer to see how the results are returned. It helps to turn on the Results in Grid option of Query Analyzer so that the resultset displays in the Grids tab and errors and messages display in the Messages tab.

By testing DBCC PAGE (...) WITH TABLERESULTS, I've confirmed that the DBCC PAGE command does accept the TABLERESULTS option in SQL Server 2000.

This means you can easily insert the result of the DBCC PAGE into a table, and therefore it's possible to perform much of the analysis of the DBCC PAGE results in T-SQL. However, because there's still a lot of text processing, T-SQL is a less convenient approach.

Studying the SQL Server Storage Internals

SCENARIO
You want a tool to help you study the SQL Server storage internals. In particular, you'd like to be able to quickly verify various claims regarding the SQL Server storage internals.

For instance, you're curious about how a deleted row is handled on a page. You may have heard that SQL Server maintains a ghost record for a deleted row, and you want to know how it works. Similarly, you may be interested in the impact of an update on the storage allocation when the updated row doesn't fit on the existing page.

The script mapPageRows.pl in Listing 6-9 retrieves only the primary key values of the rows on a page and thus can't help you answer these questions. You need to capture additional information from the pages. Fortunately, you can easily adapt the script to accommodate any information about the page you may want to retrieve from the output of the DBCC PAGE command.

The first order of business is to determine what information you need to collect from the output of DBCC PAGE. Unless you already know, the best way is to experiment. To study the ghost record for a deleted row and the impact of an updated row that doesn't fit the page, you should include two specific items:

The value of Record Type for each slot. A deleted row may be completely removed from a page, which is the case the mapPageRows.pl script can already help you determine. However, it has been reported that a deleted row in a table with a clustered index may remain on the page as a so-called ghosted record. If such a record exists on a page, the Record Type for the corresponding slot is shown as GHOST_DATA_RECORD in the DBCC PAGE output.

The value of m_freeCnt in each slot. This value is the number of free bytes available on the page.

The second decision you must make is what data structure you should use to store and represent the information from the DBCC PAGE output. It's important to adopt a generic data structure that allows you to accommodate information items that you may need to retrieve in the future. Once again, you can resort to Perl's nested data structure that's built on the basic elements such as arrays and hashes and glued together with references.

Designing the Data Structure

To address the scenario outlined at the beginning of the section, you need to glean information from two sections of the DBCC PAGE output: the page header section and the slot section. The latter may include as many slots as there are rows on the page.

Listing 6-13 illustrates the data structure to capture the information from these two sections.

Listing 6-13. A Sample Data Structure for Capturing the DBCC PAGE *Output*

```
$ref = {
    '1:351' => {
            'PageHeader' => {   # hash for the page header
                        'FreeCnt'     => '3732',
                        'GhostRecCnt' => '0',
                        'SlotCnt'     => '31'
            },
```

```
                'Slots' => {  # hash for the slots
                       'COMMI' => {
                                    'RecordType' => 'PRIMARY_RECORD',
                                    'Offset' => '0xe34',
                                    'Slot' => '14'
                       },
                       'BERGS' => {
                                    'RecordType' => 'PRIMARY_RECORD',
                                    'Offset' => '0x452',
                                    'Slot' => '4'
                       },
                       ...
                       'BLONP' => {
                                    'RecordType' => 'PRIMARY_RECORD',
                                    'Offset' => '0x65e',
                                    'Slot' => '6'
                       }
                }
        },
        '1:392' => {
                'PageHeader' => { # hash for a page
                                'FreeCnt'     => '4142',
                                'GhostRecCnt' => '0'
                },
                'Slots' => {  # hash for the slots
                       'FRANR' => {
                                    'RecordType' => 'PRIMARY_RECORD',
                                    'Offset' => '0x7d0',
                                    'Slot' => '8'
                       },
                       'FOLKO' => {
                                    'RecordType' => 'PRIMARY_RECORD',
                                    'Offset' => '0x61c',
                                    'Slot' => '6'
                       }
                }
        }
    }
};
```

This nested hash data structure has three levels. The keys at the first level are the page IDs such as '1:351' and '1:392'. The keys at the second level are PageHeader and Slots, respectively identifying that the lower-level hash entries record the information from the page header or the information from the slots.

The value of the PageHeader key is a reference to a hash storing FreeCnt, GhostRecCnt, and SlotCnt. The value of the Slots key is a reference to a nested hash whose keys are the concatenated primary key values for the rows on that page. Each concatenated primary key points to a hash storing the values of RecordType, Offset, and Slot. In Listing 6-13, there's only one column in the primary key, thus the concatenation of the primary key values may not be obvious.

If you need to study the behavior of other page header or page slot properties that are reported by the DBCC PAGE command but aren't in the data structure in Listing 6-13, all you need to do is to add the corresponding keys to the innermost hashes either for the page header or for the slots.

Examining the Script for Studying SQL Server Data Pages

You can use the data structure illustrated in Listing 6-13 to record a snapshot of the data pages of a SQL Server table. To expedite your study of the data page behavior in response to a SQL Server operation, you also need a procedure to automatically compare the snapshots from before and after the operation. Manually performing the comparison is too painful a process to be productive.

The following list identifies the major storage changes that happen after you've made a change to a row:

- Any page added or removed.

- Any change to the value in the page header. For now, only the values of FreeCnt and GhostRecCnt are considered.

- Any row added or removed.

- Any change to a value in the slot. For now, only the values of the slot number, the record type, and the offset are considered.

Given the data structure in Listing 6-13, the function reportPageDiff() in Listing 6-14 implements the checking and reporting of these changes to the pages of a table.

Listing 6-14. Reporting the Changes to the Pages of a Table

```
sub reportPageDiff {
   my ($old, $new) = @_;

   foreach my $page (keys %$new) {  # loop through every page in $new
      # report any new page that has been added
```

```perl
    if (!exists $old->{$page}) {
       print "***Page $page has been added.\n";
       next;
    }
  }
  foreach my $page (keys %$old) { # loop through every page in $old
     # report any page that has been removed
     if (!exists $new->{$page}) {
        print "***Page $page has been removed.\n";
        next;
     }

     my $pageChanged = 0;       # to identify whether a page has changed

     # report any changes in the page header
     foreach my $headerEntry (keys %{$old->{$page}->{PageHeader}}) {
        my $oldValue = $old->{$page}->{PageHeader}->{$headerEntry};
        my $newValue = $new->{$page}->{PageHeader}->{$headerEntry};
        if ($oldValue ne $newValue) {
          print "***Page: $page, Header $headerEntry: $oldValue => $newValue\n";
          $pageChanged = 1;
        }
     }

     my $oldRowRef = [keys %{$old->{$page}->{Slots}}];
     my $newRowRef = [keys %{$new->{$page}->{Slots}}];
     # report any row that has been removed from the page
     if (my @removedRows = dbaSetDiff($oldRowRef, $newRowRef)) {
        print "***These rows have been removed from page $page: ",
                join(',', @removedRows), "\n";
        $pageChanged = 1;
        next;
     }

     # report any page with newly added rows
     if (my @addedRows = dbaSetDiff($newRowRef, $oldRowRef)) {
        print "***These rows have been added to page $page: ",
                join(',', @addedRows), "\n";
        $pageChanged = 1;
        next;
     }
```

```
    # for the pages with the same rows, check for any change for each row
    foreach my $row (keys %{$old->{$page}->{Slots}}) {
        my $rowChanged = 0;

        # check the entries for each row
        foreach my $rowEntry (keys %{$old->{$page}->{Slots}->{$row}}) {
            # report any slot change
            my $oldValue = $old->{$page}->{Slots}->{$row}->{$rowEntry};
            my $newValue = $new->{$page}->{Slots}->{$row}->{$rowEntry};

            if ($oldValue ne $newValue) {
                print "***The $rowEntry of row $row: $oldValue => $newValue\n";
                $rowChanged = 1;
                $pageChanged = 1;
            }
        }
        if (! $rowChanged) {    # if the row is not changed
            delete $old->{$page}->{Slots}->{$row};
            delete $new->{$page}->{Slots}->{$row};
        }
    }
    if (! $pageChanged) {   # if the page is not changed
        delete $old->{$page};
        delete $new->{$page};
    }
}
return ($old, $new);
} # reportPageDiff
```

Note that the function `reportPageDiff()` in Listing 6-14 works on the data structure illustrated in Listing 6-13. However, it doesn't hard-code any page header items or slot items. As such, you can add more header items to or remove an existing one from the hash `$ref->{<Page ID>}->{PageHeader}` without making any change to the function `reportPageDiff()`. Similarly, you don't need to make any change to this function if you want to include more items from the slot section of the `DBCC PAGE` output.

Listing 6-15 is the script `checkStoragePages.pl` that you can use to capture a snapshot of the pages for a given table and produce a change report by comparing the current snapshot with a previously captured one.

Listing 6-15. A Script for Studying SQL Server Storage Internals

```perl
1.   use strict;
2.   use Win32::OLE 'in';
3.   use Getopt::Std;
4.   use SQLDBA::Utility qw( dbaReadSavedRef dbaSaveRef dbaSetDiff dbaTime2str );
5.   use Data::Dumper;
6.
7.   my %opts;
8.   getopts('S:d:t:r:s:', \%opts);
9.   (defined $opts{S} and defined $opts{d} and defined $opts{t}) or printUsage();
10.  printUsage() if defined $opts{s} and defined $opts{r};
11.
12.  MAIN: {
13.     my ($server, $db, $tab) = ($opts{S}, $opts{d}, $opts{t});
14.     print dbaTime2str(), "\n";
15.
16.     # open a connection to the server and database
17.     my $conn = getConn($server, $db);
18.
19.     # get the PK column(s) of the table you're studying
20.     my $pkRef = getPKRef($conn, $tab);
21.     unless (scalar @$pkRef) {
22.        die "***Err: table $tab doesn't have a primary key.";
23.     }
24.     # get all the data page IDs of the table
25.     my $allPageIDsRef = getAllPageIDs($conn, $db, $tab);
26.
27.     my $page2Rows;
28.     # for each page ID, get all the rows on the page
29.     foreach my $pageID (@$allPageIDsRef) {
30.        my ($fileno, $pageno) = $pageID =~ /(\d+)\:(\d+)/;
31.
32.        #get the result of DBCC PAGE to an array
33.        my $msgRef = dbccPage($conn, $db, $fileno, $pageno);
34.
35.        # get the PK values of the rows on the page
36.        my $rowRef = getRows($pkRef, $msgRef);
37.
38.        # get mapping from page ID to the PK values
39.        $page2Rows->{$pageID} = $rowRef;
40.     }
41.     if (-e $opts{r}) {
42.        # retrive the saved old pageID to rows mapping
```

```
43.      my $savedPage2Rows = dbaReadSavedRef($opts{r});
44.
45.      # remove the pages that have not changed
46.      my ($oldDiff, $newDiff) =
47.              reportPageDiff($savedPage2Rows, $page2Rows);
48.
49.      # print pages that are removed or changed, and record the diff
50.      print Data::Dumper->Dump([$oldDiff], ['oldPages']);
51.      # print pages that are new or changed
52.      print Data::Dumper->Dump([$newDiff], ['newPages']);
53.   }
54.   if ($opts{s}) {
55.        # record the current page/row mapping
56.        dbaSaveRef($opts{s}, $page2Rows, 'page2Rows');
57.   }
58.   $conn->Close();
59. }
59.
60. #########################
61. # get the row PK values using the info dumped by DBCC PAGE
62. sub getRows {
63.   my ($pkRef, $msgRef) = @_;  # take PK columns and DBCC PAGE output
64.
65.   my $rowCnt;          # for validation purpose
66.   my $pageHeader = 0;  # to signal whether the loop is in the header part
67.   my ($slot, $offset, $pageID);
68.   my $rowRef;
69.   foreach my $msg (@$msgRef) {
70.       $msg =~ /^\s*PAGE:\s+\((.+)\)/i and $pageID = $1;  # e.g. PAGE: (1:160)
71.
72.       # if matched, entering the page header of DBCC PAGE output
73.       if ($msg =~ /^\s*PAGE\s+HEADER:/i) {
74.          $pageHeader = 1;
75.          next;
76.       }
77.
78.       # get the slot count (i.e. row count) from the header
79.       # the actual row count should match this number if our search works.
80.       # Otherwise, sth went wrong and the result shouldn't be used
81.       if ($pageHeader and $msg =~ /m_slotCnt\s*=\s*(\d+)/i) {
82.          $rowCnt = $1;
83.          next;
84.       }
85.
```

```
86.        # get the number of ghost record count
87.        if ($pageHeader and $msg =~ /m\_ghostRecCnt\s*=\s*(\d+)/i) {
88.            $rowRef->{PageHeader}->{GhostRecCnt} = $1;
89.            next;
90.        }
91.
92.        # get the number of free bytes on the page
93.        if ($pageHeader and $msg =~ /m\_freeCnt\s*=\s*(\d+)/i) {
94.            $rowRef->{PageHeader}->{FreeCnt} = $1;
95.            next;
96.        }
97.
98.        # if matched, the script has left the page header
99.        if ($msg =~ /^\s*Allocation\s+Status/i) {
100.           $pageHeader = 0;
101.           next;
102.        }
103.
104.        if ($msg =~ /^\s*Slot\s+(\d+)\s+Offset\s+(0x\w+)/i) {
105.           ($slot, $offset) = ($1, $2);
106.           $rowRef->{Slots}->{$slot}->{Offset} = $offset;
107.           next;
108.        }
109.
110.        # get Record Type
111.        if ($msg =~ /^\s*Record\s*Type\s*=\s*(.+)/i) {
112.           my $recordType = $1;
113.           $recordType =~ s/\s*$//;
114.           $rowRef->{Slots}->{$slot}->{RecordType} = $recordType;
115.           next;
116.        }
117.        # record the PK column values
118.        foreach my $key (@$pkRef) {
119.            if ($msg =~ /^\s*$key\s*=\s*(.+?)\s*$/i) {
120.                push @{$rowRef->{Slots}->{$slot}->{PK}}, $1;
121.            }
122.        }
123.    }
124.    # actual row count should match the slot count in the header
125.    my $actualRowCnt = scalar (keys %{$rowRef->{Slots}});
126.    print "Page: $pid, Header slotCnt = $rowCnt, ",
127.          "actual rowCnt = $actualRowCnt\n";
128.    ($rowCnt == $actualRowCnt) or
129.       die "***Err: parsing DBCC PAGE output encountered problem.";
```

```
130.    $rowRef->{PageHeader}->{SlotCnt} = $actualRowCnt;
131.
132.    my $r_rowRef;
133.    foreach my $slotNo (keys %{$rowRef->{Slots}}) {
134.        # concatenate the PK key values if it's composite to identify a row
135.        my $row_id = join('/', @{$rowRef->{Slots}->{$slotNo}->{PK}});
136.        # reverse key/value for the slots
137.        $r_rowRef->{Slots}->{$row_id} =
138.                        { Slot    => $slotNo,
139.                          Offset => $rowRef->{Slots}->{$slotNo}->{Offset},
140.                          RecordType => $rowRef->{Slots}->{$slotNo}->{RecordType}
141.                        };
142.    }
143.    $r_rowRef->{PageHeader} = $rowRef->{PageHeader};
144.    return $r_rowRef;  # concatenated PK values is key, slot # is value
145.} # getRows


#####################
sub printUsage {
    print <<___Usage;
 Usage:
   cmd>perl checkPages.pl  -S <SQL Server instance>
                           -d <database>
                           -t <table>
                           ( -r <snapshot file> | -s <snapshot file> )
        -S   accepts a SQL Server instance name
        -d   accepts a database name
        -t   accepts a table name
        -r   instructs the script to read from a saved snapshot file
        -s   instructs the script to save a copy of the snapshot
___Usage
   exit;
} # printUsage


#####################
#  get an ADO connection to be used throughout the script
sub getConn {
# See the same function in Listing 6-8.
}  # getConn


######################
#  get the DBCC PAGE output to an array
sub dbccPage {
# See the same function in Listing 6-7.
```

```
}  # dbccPage


##############################
#  get all the page IDs of a table
sub getAllPageIDs {
# See the same function in Listing 6-4.
}  # getAllPageIDs


#########################
#   get the PK columns
sub getPKRef {
# See the same function in Listing 6-6.
}  # getPKRef


#########################
#  report any page difference between what's read from the server and
#  what's saved last time
sub reportPageDiff {
# See the same function in Listing 6-13.
}  # reportPageDiff
```

The script checkStoragePages.pl in Listing 6-15 is similar to the script mapPageRows.pl in Listing 6-9 with the exception of several key differences in the Main code block and in the function getRows().

In the Main block of the script checkStoragePages.pl, the code fragment from line 41 to 53 is new. This code fragment reads the previously saved snapshot of the storage pages from a file and compares it with the current snapshot of the storage pages using the function reportPageDiff() to report page difference, if any. The code from line 54 to 57 is also new. When the -s command-line option is specified with a filename, the code fragment saves the current snapshot to the file.

TIP *To help understand the regular expressions in this script and follow the logic of the script, you may want to have an output of the* DBCC PAGE *command next to you.*

Compared to the version in Listing 6-7, the getRows() function in Listing 6-15 has been expanded to accommodate the new data structure in Listing 6-13. In particular, the script includes the following code to capture the ghost record count in the page header:

```
87.        if ($pageHeader and $msg =~ /m\_ghostRecCnt\s*=\s*(\d+)/i) {
88.            $rowRef->{PageHeader}->{GhostRecCnt} = $1;
89.            next;
90.        }
```

Note the additional level in the nested data structure introduced with the key PageHeader on line 88. The script also includes the following code fragment to scan for the record type for a slot:

```
111.        if ($msg =~ /^\s*Record\s*Type\s*=\s*(.+)/i) {
112.            my $recordType = $1;
113.            $recordType =~ s/\s*$//;
114.            $rowRef->{Slots}->{$slot}->{RecordType} = $recordType;
115.            next;
116.        }
```

Again, note the additional level immediately under $rowRef in the data structure. This time, the key is Slots on line 114.

That's enough about the data structure and the script. It's time to see how all this scripting can actually help you gain insight into SQL Server storage internals.

Studying the Behavior of the SQL Server Storage

To study the behavior of the SQL Server storage, let's again use the Northwind.dbo.Customers table. To ensure you can insert into and delete rows from the table, you need to remove or disable all the foreign keys that reference the Customers table.

It's convenient to study each scenario against the same base line. Let's start with a pristine copy of the Customers table, in other words, the copy created during the SQL Server 2000 installation. Run the script as follows to save a snapshot:

```
cmd>perl checkStoragePages.pl -S SQL1 -d Northwind -t Customers -s snapshot.log
```

When done, the file snapshot.log contains a data structure similar to that illustrated in Listing 6-13. If a previous copy of the file snapshot.log already exists, the script will replace it with an updated snapshot if the -s argument is specified on the command line.

Deleting a Row (Seeing the Ghost)

From Query Analyzer, run the following SQL query:

```
DELETE FROM Customers
 WEHRE CustomerID = 'COMMI'
```

And immediately run the script checkStoragePages.pl as shown in Listing 6-16 to see the changes to the data pages of the Customers table.

Listing 6-16. Seeing the Ghost Record of a Delete

```
cmd>perl checkStoragePages.pl -S SQL1 -d Northwind -t Customers -r snapshot.log
2003/04/27 18:04:31
Page: 1:351, Header slot cnt = 32, actual row cnt = 32
Page: 1:384, Header slot cnt = 29, actual row cnt = 29
Page: 1:385, Header slot cnt = 30, actual row cnt = 30
***Page: 1:351, Header GhostRecCnt: 0 => 1
***The RecordType of row COMMI: PRIMARY_RECORD => GHOST_DATA_RECORD
$oldPages = {
            '1:351' => {
                  'Slots' => {
                        'COMMI' => {
                                'Offset'      => '0xe34',
                                'RecordType' => 'PRIMARY_RECORD',
                                'Slot'        => '14'
                              }
                  },
                  'PageHeader' => {
                                'FreeCnt'     => '40',
                                'GhostRecCnt' => '0',
                                'SlotCnt'     => '32'
                  }
            }
};
```

```
$newPages = {
        '1:351' => {
            'PageHeader' => {
                            'FreeCnt'     => '40',
                            'GhostRecCnt' => '1',
                            'SlotCnt'     => '32'
            },
            'Slots' => {                    .
                    'COMMI' => {
                            'RecordType' => 'GHOST_DATA_RECORD',
                            'Offset' => '0xe34',
                            'Slot' => '14'
                    }
            }
        }
};
```

Overall, the script reports two main changes:

```
***Page: 1:351, Header GhostRecCnt: 0 => 1
***The RecordType of row COMMI: PRIMARY_RECORD => GHOST_DATA_RECORD
```

Listing 6-16 also shows that the deleted row is now marked as a ghost record in the slot allocated to the row on the page 1:351. The ghost record count in the page header has increased to 1. Also, the script prints the variables $oldPages and $newPages. They record only the pages and the rows that have been changed.

Although a record has been deleted from the page, SQL Server didn't update the number of free bytes available on the page when the script was run. It remains to be 40 bytes.

NOTE *The SQL Server housekeeping process that cleans up ghost records is quick and efficient. It may have removed the ghost record before you ran the Perl script. If you don't see any ghost record, you may want to create a batch file to run the delete statement through* osql.exe *and then run* checkStoragePages.pl.

Deleting a Row (Seeing No Ghost)

Let's try it again. From Query Analyzer, run the following SQL query:

```
DELETE FROM Customers
 WEHRE CustomerID = 'COMMI'
```

But let's wait for a few minutes and then run the script checkStoragePages.pl as shown in Listing 6-17 to see the changes it reports.

Listing 6-17. Not Seeing the Ghost Record of a Delete

```
cmd>perl checkStoragePages.pl -S SQL1 -d Northwind -t Customers -r snapshot.log
2003/04/27 18:29:32
Page: 1:351, Header slot cnt = 31, actual row cnt = 31
Page: 1:384, Header slot cnt = 29, actual row cnt = 29
Page: 1:385, Header slot cnt = 30, actual row cnt = 30
***Page: 1:351, Header FreeCnt: 40 => 284
***These rows have been removed from page 1:351: COMMI
$oldPages = {
            '1:351' => {
                    'Slots' => {
                            ...
                            'COMMI' => {
                                    'Offset'     => '0xe34',
                                    'RecordType' => 'PRIMARY_RECORD',
                                    'Slot'       => '14'
                                },
                            'CONSH' => {
                                    'Offset'     => '0xf26',
                                    'RecordType' => 'PRIMARY_RECORD',
                                    'Slot'       => '15'
                                },
                            ...
                        },
                    'PageHeader' => {
                                'FreeCnt'     => '40',
                                'GhostRecCnt' => '0',
                                'SlotCnt'     => '32'
                        }
                }
        }
};
```

```
$newPages = {
          '1:351' => {
                    'PageHeader' => {
                                    'FreeCnt'     => '284',
                                    'GhostRecCnt' => '0',
                                    'SlotCnt'     => '31'
                    },
                    'Slots' => {
                                ...
                          'CONSH' => {
                                      'RecordType' => 'PRIMARY_RECORD',
                                      'Offset'     => '0xf26',
                                      'Slot'       => '14'
                                    },
                          ...
                    }
          }
};
```

In Listing 6-17, the script doesn't report any ghost record. But it does report many more changes to the data page—the page 1:351—where the row was deleted.

- The number of free bytes on the page has increased from 40 bytes to 284 bytes.

- The slot that used to store the deleted row doesn't store the row anymore. Thus, the row isn't shown under $newPages.

- The slot number of the deleted row was 14. Now the row that was in slot 15 is in slot 14. The slot number for each of the rows that comes after the deleted row in the order of the clustered index has been decreased by one.

SQL Server runs a special housekeeping thread to clean up these ghost records asynchronously. Apparently, in this case, waiting for a few minutes after the delete has given this thread the chance to perform its housekeeping.

NOTE *Kalen Delaney described the work of the ghost records and the housekeeping thread that cleans up ghost records during the SQL Server B-tree maintenance. See* Inside Microsoft SQL Server 2000 *by Kalen Delaney (Microsoft Press, 2000).*

Note that the offsets of the remaining rows on the page 1:351 haven't been changed. In other words, SQL Server doesn't physically move any rows on the page. The logical order of the rows is maintained with the slot numbers.

Updating a Row with a Clustered Index

When you update a row that becomes too large to fit on the existing page, how does SQL Server accommodate this row? The behavior depends on whether the table has a clustered index.

If the table has a clustered index, the behavior is the same as a page split. Before you make any change to the Customer table, the page 1:351 has 40 bytes of free space. See $oldPages->{'1:351'}->{PageHeader}->{FreCnt} in Listing 6-18. If you run the following SQL statement, the updated row won't fit on the same page:

```
UPDATE Customers
   SET Address = REPLICATE('A', 60)
 WHERE CustomerID = 'COMMI'
```

Now run the script checkStoragePages.pl to see how SQL Server accommodates this "overflow" row in Listing 6-18.

Listing 6-18. An Update Causing a Page Split

```
cmd>perl checkStoragePages.pl -S SQL1 -d Northwind -t Customers -r snapshot.log
2003/04/27 23:36:45
Page: 1:351, Header slotCnt = 16, actual rowCnt = 16
Page: 1:384, Header slotCnt = 29, actual rowCnt = 29
Page: 1:385, Header slotCnt = 30, actual rowCnt = 30
Page: 1:386, Header slotCnt = 16, actual rowCnt = 16
***Page 1:386 has been added.
***Page: 1:351, Header FreeCnt: 40 => 4148
***These rows have been removed from page 1:351:
BERGS,COMMI,ALFKI,ANTON,BOTTM,CENTC,CACTU,AROUT,ANATR,BLAUS,BSBEV,CHOPS,BOLID,
BONAP,BLONP,CONSH
$oldPages = {
          '1:351' => {
                  'Slots' => {
                        'FOLIG' => {
                                'Offset'     => '0x15fc',
                                'RecordType' => 'PRIMARY_RECORD',
                                'Slot'       => '22'
                        },
                        ...
```

```
                           'BLONP' => {
                                        'Offset'     => '0x65e',
                                        'RecordType' => 'PRIMARY_RECORD',
                                        'Slot'       => '6'
                               }
                       },
                       'PageHeader' => {
                                  'FreeCnt'     => '40',
                                  'GhostRecCnt' => '0',
                                  'SlotCnt'     => '32'
                       }
               }
       }
};
$newPages = {
       '1:351' => {
               'PageHeader' => {
                                  'FreeCnt'     => '4148',
                                  'GhostRecCnt' => '0',
                                  'SlotCnt'     => '16'
               },
               'Slots' => {
                       'FRANR' => {
                                  'RecordType' => 'PRIMARY_RECORD',
                                  'Offset' => '0x18ba',
                                  'Slot' => '9'
                       },
                       ...
                       'FOLKO' => {
                                  'RecordType' => 'PRIMARY_RECORD',
                                  'Offset' => '0x1706',
                                  'Slot' => '7'
                       }
               }
       },
       '1:386' => {
               'PageHeader' => {
                           'FreeCnt' => '3908',
                           'GhostRecCnt' => '0'
                           'SlotCnt'     => '16'
               },
               'Slots' => {
                       'COMMI' => {
                                  'RecordType' => 'PRIMARY_RECORD',
                                  'Offset' => '0x104c',
```

```
                                      'Slot' => '14'
                },
                'BERGS' => {
                                'RecordType' => 'PRIMARY_RECORD',
                                'Offset' => '0x452',
                                'Slot' => '4'
                },
                ...
                'BLONP' => {
                                'RecordType' => 'PRIMARY_RECORD',
                                'Offset' => '0x65e',
                                'Slot' => '6'
                }
            }
        }
    }
};
```

Because the updated row doesn't fit on the page 1:351, SQL Server allocates a new page—the page 1:386—and moves a half of the rows from the page 1:351 to this new page. This is evident if you check the value of SlotCnt for the page 1:351. Before the split, the value is 32. After the split, the value becomes 16, leaving the page 1:351 with 4148 bytes of free space.

Updating a Row Without a Clustered Index

Again, start from a pristine copy of the Customers table in the Northwind database. To see how a similar update affects a heap table, drop the clustered index by removing its primary key and then create a nonclustered primary key on the same column—CustomerID. Proceed to verify that the page 1:351 has only 40 bytes of free space, and run the following update statement to cause the row to become too large to fit on the page:

```
UPDATE Customers
   SET Address = REPLICATE('A', 60)
 WHERE CustomerID = 'COMMI'
```

Listing 6-19 displays the output of the script checkStoragePages.pl, executed after this update statement.

Listing 6-19. An Update Resulting in a Forward Pointer

```
cmd>perl checkStoragePages.pl -S SQL1 -d Northwind -t Customers -r snapshot.log
2003/04/27 22:26:21
```

```
Page: 1:351, Header slot cnt = 32, actual row cnt = 32
Page: 1:384, Header slot cnt = 29, actual row cnt = 29
Page: 1:385, Header slot cnt = 31, actual row cnt = 31
***Header FreeCnt: 40 => 273
***These rows have been removed from page 1:351: COMMI
***Header FreeCnt: 492 => 156
***These rows have been added to page 1:385: COMMI
$oldPages = {
        ...
};
$newPages = {
        '1:351' => {
                'PageHeader' => {
                                'FreeCnt'    => '273',
                                'GhostRecCnt' => '0',
                                'SlotCnt'    => '32'
                },
                'Slots' => {
                        ...
                        'A' => {
                                'RecordType' => 'FORWARDING_STUB',
                                'Offset'     => '0x1f98',
                                'Slot'       => '14'
                        },
                        ...
                }
        },
        '1:385' => {
                'PageHeader' => {
                                'FreeCnt'    => '156',
                                'GhostRecCnt' => '0',
                                'SlotCnt'    => '16'
                },
                'Slots' => {
                        ...
                        'COMMI' => {
                                'RecordType' => 'FORWARDED_RECORD',
                                'Offset'     => '0x1dd8',
                                'Slot'       => '30'
                        },
                        ...
                }
        }
};
```

Listing 6-19 shows that SQL Server moved the updated row from the page 1:351 to the page 1:385. Everything else remained intact. Moreover, if you check the changes recorded under $newPages, a new slot whose record type labeled as FORWARDING_STUB was added to the page 1:351, and a new row marked as FORWARD_RECORD was added to the page 1:385.

The result in Listing 6-19 confirms the statement that when a row in a heap table moves to a new page, SQL Server leaves a forward pointer in the original location.

NOTE *If you're examining changes on a single data page, you can easily do so with the DBCC PAGE command yourself. But if you're not sure which pages may be affected or if you want to repeatedly observe the behavior of a data page, the script checkStoragepages.pl becomes a useful tool.*

Studying Locking Behavior

SCENARIO
You're using the trace flag 1200 to study the locking behavior of SQL Server. The output is voluminous and not readily digestible. You'd like the output to be more intuitive.

A clear understanding of what locks your T-SQL queries will acquire helps you identify, resolve, or even prevent costly concurrency problems. SQL Server provides many tools for you to study the locking behavior of T-SQL queries.

Examining Tools for Monitoring Locking Behavior

The most often used tool is probably the sp_lock system stored procedure, which gives you a snapshot of the locks currently being held or requested. If you don't like what sp_lock presents, you have the option of directly querying the syslockinfo system table in the master database.

In addition, you can open SQL Enterprise Manager and view the locking information under the Current Activity in the Management folder. SQL Enterprise Manager gives you two views: locks grouped by process and locks grouped by object.

SQL Profiler is another useful tool to track the locking activities on a SQL Server instance. You have the convenience of selecting from a collection of lock event classes to decide which events to monitor and what data to collect. Lock:Acquired and Lock:Released are the two common lock event classes.

Windows System Monitor (also known as *Performance Monitor* in Windows NT 4.0) is yet another tool to help gain an understanding of SQL Server locking activities. It exposes a collection of counters—for the SQLServer:Locks object—such as Lock Requests/sec and Lock Waits/sec. Through these counters, you can get an overall statistical view of the locking activities on a given SQL Server instance.

And don't forget the venerable sp_who system stored procedure. Though it's not specifically designed for monitoring locks, it provides the quickest way to reveal whether there's any sustained lock contention.

However, if you really want to study the locking behavior of a given query, the tool to use is the trace flag 1200.

Using the Trace Flag 1200

Because the output of the trace flag 1200 is often voluminous, you should limit it to your connection instead of turning it on for all the connections with TRACEON(-1). In addition, you should turn it on with the trace flag 3604 to send the output to the client as opposed to the errorlog. It's not a good idea to flood your errorlog.

NOTE *The SQL Server 2000 Books Online doesn't document the trace flag 1200. Ray Rankins briefly discussed this trace flag in* Microsoft SQL Server 2000 Unleashed, Second Edition *by Ray Rankins, Paul Jensen, and Paul Bertucci (Sams, 2002). This is an underutilized trace flag.*

The trace flag 1200 can be extremely useful when studying the locking behavior of a specific query. For instance, when you delete a row from a table that's being referenced by a foreign key from another table, you may be curious about exactly what locks the delete will acquire. To find the answer, you can execute the following from Query Analyzer and then study the output:

```
DBCC TRACEON(3604, 1200)
DELETE FROM authors
 WHERE au_id = '111-32-1176'
```

When I ran this query in the SQL Server 2000 instance on my notebook computer, SQL Server printed the output shown in Listing 6-20 (edited to fit the page width).

Listing 6-20. Sample Output of the Trace Flag 1200

```
Process 51 acquiring S lock on KEY: 5:4:1 (c20174aaf259) (class ...) result: OK
Process 51 acquiring S lock on KEY: 5:1:2 (b80175ab6d20) (class ...) result: OK
Process 51 acquiring S lock on KEY: 5:1:1 (820053521616) (class ...) result: OK
Process 51 acquiring Schema lock on TAB: 5:1797581442 [] (class ...) result: OK
Process 51 acquiring S lock on KEY: 5:1:2 (b80175ab6d20) (class ...) result: OK
...
Process 51 acquiring S lock on KEY: 5:14:3 (21014760111f) (class ...) result: OK
Process 51 acquiring S lock on KEY: 5:14:1 (9f00b01a669f) (class ...) result: OK
...
Process 51 acquiring IS lock on TAB: 5:786101841 [] (class ...) result: OK
Process 51 acquiring IX lock on TAB: 5:1797581442 [] (class ...) result: OK
Process 51 acquiring IU lock on PAG: 5:1:87 (class ...) result: OK
Process 51 releasing lock on PAG: 5:1:87
Process 51 releasing lock on TAB: 5:53575229 []
Process 51 releasing lock on TAB: 5:786101841 []
```

The output of the trace flag 1200, shown in Listing 6-20, identifies the lock mode, the lock type, and the resource on which the lock is placed. Useful and comprehensive as it, the output isn't user friendly. It prints only the resource identifiers instead of the more readable object names.

For instance, unless you already know, it's not immediately clear on which object the shared key lock on 5:4:1 (S lock on KEY: 5:4:1 on the first line) is placed. You need to query SQL Server to find which database has the database identifier 5 and which table in that database has the object identifier 4. When the output is large, it takes considerable efforts to wade through the output such as the one in Listing 6-20.

Making the Trace Flag 1200 More User Friendly

You can further process the output of the trace flag 1200 to generate much more useful and succinct information. The script postT1200.pl in Listing 6-21 improves the output of the trace flag 1200 in two respects:

The script translates all the internal identifiers to the names of their corresponding objects. More specifically, a table identifier is translated to a table name qualified with the owner and the database name. In addition, a page lock is no longer identified by its page IDs, but by the corresponding qualified table name. For instance, instead of 5:1:172, the script translates it to [dbo].[sysindexes] for the database pubs.

The script counts the number of times each lock is acquired for each given object resource.

When you just want to get an overview of what locks have been acquired, it's unlikely that you want to count exactly how many times a particular page or key is locked. You're far more likely to inquire how many times such a page or key lock is applied to the table. Listing 6-21 presents the code of the script postT1200.pl.

Listing 6-21. Summarizing the Output of the Trace Flag 1200

```
1.  use strict;
2.  use Win32::OLE 'in';
3.  use Data::Dumper;
4.
5.  my $server = $ARGV[0] or die "***Err: $0 expects a server name.";
6.  my $t1200Log = $ARGV[1] or die "***Err: $0 expects a T1200 log file.";
7.
8.  # open a connection to the server
9.  my $conn = getConn($server);
10.
11. my ($ref, $locking, $mode, $type, $rsc, $objName);
12. open(TLOG, $t1200Log) or die "***Err: failed to open $t1200Log.";
13. while(<TLOG>) {
14.     if (/acquiring\s+(\w+\s+lock\s+on\s+\w+)\:\s*([:\d]+)/i) {
15.         ($locking, $rsc) = ($1, $2);
16.
17.         # working on TAB and KEY locks
18.         if ($locking =~ /(TAB|KEY)$/i) {
19.             if ($rsc =~ /(\d+)\:(\d+)/) {
20.                 my ($dbid, $objid) = ($1, $2);
21.                 if ($dbid !~ /\d+/ or $objid !~ /\d+/) {
22.                     die "***Err: didn't match dbid or objid.";
23.                 }
24.                 $objName = getObjName($conn, $dbid, $objid);
25.             }
26.             else {  # error condition, should never reach here
27.                 die "***Err: lock resource didn't match /(\d+)\:(\d+)/.";
28.             }
29.             $ref->{$objName}->{$locking}++;
30.             next;
31.         }
32.
33.         # working on PAG and RID locks
34.         if ($locking =~ /(PAG|RID)$/i) {
35.             if ($rsc =~ /(\d+)\:(\d+)\:(\d+)/) {
36.                 my ($dbid, $fileNo, $pageNo) = ($1, $2, $3);
37.                 my $objid = dbccPage2objID($conn, $dbid, $fileNo, $pageNo);
38.                 if ($objid !~ /^\d+$/) {
```

```
39.                    die "***Err: dbccPage2objID() didn't return an object no.";
40.                }
41.                $objName = getObjName($conn, $dbid, $objid);
42.            }
43.            else {  # error condition, should never reach here
44.                die "***Err: lock resource didn't match /(\d+)\:(\d+)\:(\d+)/.";
45.            }
46.            $ref->{$objName}->{$locking}++;
47.            next;
48.        }
49.        print;   # print the rows that don't match as is
50.    }
51. }
52. close(TLOG);
53. $conn->Close();
54. print Data::Dumper->Dump([$ref], ['LockSummary']);
55.
56. #####################
57. #  get an ADO connection to be used throughout the script
58. sub getConn {
59.     my $server = shift or die "***Err: getConn() expects a server name.";
60.
61.     my $conn = Win32::OLE->new('ADODB.Connection') or
62.            die "***Err: Win32::OLE->new() failed.";
63.     $conn->{ConnectionTimeout} = 4;
64.     my $connStr = "Provider=sqloledb;Server=$server;Trusted_Connection=yes";
65.     $conn->Open($connStr);
66.     ! Win32::OLE->LastError() or die Win32::OLE->LastError();
67.
68.     $conn->Execute('dbcc traceon(3604)') or  # see trace output to the client
69.         die Win32::OLE->LastError();
70.     return $conn;  # this connection will be used in the rest of the script
71. }  # getConn
72.
73. ######################
74. #  get the objetc name from DBCC PAGE output
75. sub dbccPage2objID {
76.     my ($conn, $dbid, $fileNo, $pageNo) = @_;
77.     my @msgs;
78.     my $objid;
79.
80.     my $sql = "dbcc page($dbid,$fileNo,$pageNo, 0)";
81.     $conn->Execute($sql) or
82.         die Win32::OLE->LastError();
83.
```

```
84.     # note that ADO returns DBCC output in Errors collection
85.     # unless you specify with tableresults
86.     foreach my $err (in($conn->Errors())) {
87.         my $msg = $err->{Description}; # it's in the Description property
88.         if ($msg =~ /m\_objId\s*=\s*(\d+)\b/i) {
89.             return $1;
90.         }
91.     }
92.     return undef;
93. }   # dbccPage2objID
94.
95. ####################
96. sub getObjName {
97.     my ($conn, $dbid, $objid) = @_;
98.
99.     my $sql = "DECLARE \@db varchar(256), \@sql varchar(500)
100.                SET \@db = QUOTENAME(db_name($dbid))
101.                SET \@sql = 'USE ' + \@db +
102.                        'SELECT ''name'' = QUOTENAME(name),
103.                              ''user'' = QUOTENAME(USER_NAME(uid))
104.                         FROM sysobjects
105.                        WHERE id = $objid'
106.                EXEC (\@sql)";
107.     my $rs = $conn->Execute($sql) or
108.         die Win32::OLE->LastError();
109.
110.     while ($rs) {
111.         unless ( $rs->{State} ) {
112.             $rs = $rs->NextRecordSet();
113.             next;
114.         }
115.         while ( !$rs->{EOF} ) {
116.             my $name = $rs->Fields('name')->{Value};
117.             my $user = $rs->Fields('user')->{Value};
118.             $name =~ s/\s*$//;
119.             $user =~ s/\s*$//;
120.
121.             if ($name and $user) {
122.                 return "$user:$name";
123.             }
124.             $rs->MoveNext;
125.         }
126.         $rs = $rs->NextRecordSet();
127.     }
128.     return undef;
129.} # getObjName
```

The script in Listing 6-21 accepts two arguments on the command line. The first argument is a server name, and the second is the name of a file containing the output of the trace flag 1200. The trace flag output must be generated on the server specified in the first parameter. Otherwise, you won't get correct translation from the identifiers to their names. Because the script queries SQL Server to translate the identifiers to their corresponding names, it's imperative that the lock resource identifiers remain unchanged before you run the script postT1200.pl.

The while loop that starts on line 13 goes through each line of the trace flag 1200 output and looks for the lock that's being acquired with the following regular expression:

```
14.     if (/acquiring\s+(\w+\s+lock\s+on\s+\w+)\:\s*([:\d]+)/i) {
```

For each match, the script then determines the lock mode, the lock type, and the resource on which the lock will be placed. The trace flag 1200 identifies the resources differently for different lock types. Table 6-1 describes the four common lock types and how their resources are identified in a trace flag 1200 output.

Table 6-1. Common Lock Types and Resources in the Trace Flag 1200 Output

LOCK TYPE	DESCRIPTION	RESOURCE IDENTIFICATION
TAB	Table lock	The table is identified with a database identifier followed by a table object identifier. For example: 5:53575229, where the database identifier is 5 and the table object identifier is 53575229.
KEY	Row lock on an index entry	The index entry is identified with a database identifier, the table object identifier, followed by the index identifier. For example 5:1634104862:2, where 5 is the database identifier, 1634104862 is the table identifier, and 2 is the index identifier.
PAG	Page lock	The page is identified with a database identifier and a file number, followed by a page number. For example: 5:1:172 where 5 is the database number, 1 is the file number, and 172 is the page number.
RID	Row lock	The row on a page is identified with a database number, a file number, and a page number, followed by a slot number.

The following code fragment captures the database identifier and the object identifier of a TAB or KEY lock:

```
17.        # working on TAB and KEY locks
18.        if ($locking =~ /(TAB|KEY)$/i) {
19.            if ($rsc =~ /(\d+)\:(\d+)/) {
20.                my ($dbid, $objid) = ($1, $2);
21.                if ($dbid !~ /\d+/ or $objid !~ /\d+/) {
22.                    die "***Err: didn't match dbid or objid.";
23.                }
24.                $objName = getObjName($conn, $dbid, $objid);
25.            }
26.            else {  # error condition, should never reach here
27.                die "***Err: lock resource didn't match /(\d+)\:(\d+)/.";
28.            }
29.            $ref->{$objName}->{$locking}++;
30.            next;
31.        }
```

The function getObjName() then translates the identifiers to the object name. The function getObjName() is defined between line 96 and line 129, and it retrieves the object name with the following T-SQL script constructed between lines 99 and 106:

```
DECLARE @db varchar(256), @sql varchar(500)
    SET @db = QUOTENAME(db_name($dbid))
    SET @sql = 'USE ' + @db +
                'SELECT ''name'' = QUOTENAME(name),
                      ''user'' = QUOTENAME(USER_NAME(uid))
                 FROM sysobjects
                WHERE id = $objid'
EXEC (@sql)
```

The variables $dbid and $objid are placeholders that will be replaced with actual identifiers through Perl variable interpolation.

Note that this entire T-SQL script is assigned to the variable $sql in a pair of double quotes. Therefore, you must escape each of the T-SQL local variables with a backslash. Otherwise, the T-SQL local variables will be treated as Perl array variables because of the @ prefix, and Perl will perform variable interpolation, which is clearly not what you want.

The else clause between lines 26 and 28 is for troubleshooting. This basically says that you should never reach this code path. If the resource string doesn't match the regular expression /(\d+)\:(\d+)/, causing the script to enter this else clause, then something has gone terribly wrong. For instance, it may be incorrect for the script to assume that the resource string for a TAB or KEY lock should match the regular expression.

 TIP *It's good programming practice to check all the code paths, including the ones you think are logically impossible. A single line of assertion for an* impossible *code path can save you tons of agony when some of your coding assumptions turn out to be false.*

The code for capturing the information on the PAG and RID locks is similar to that for the TAB or KEY locks.

Also note that the trace flag 3604 is set as soon as the ADO connection is open on line 68. This ensures that all the subsequent DBCC output messages are routed to the client.

You'll now examine two case studies. In each case, the script postT1200.pl is applied to the output of the trace flag 1200 to generate a more user-friendly report.

Examining Locks Acquired by an Insert Statement

Let's run the following T-SQL queries in the pubs database to insert a row into the authors table and save the output to the file t1200_insert.log:

```
DBCC TRACEON(3604, 1200)
INSERT authors
VALUES('111-32-1176', 'Shea', 'Linchi', '408 496-7223', '10932 Bigge Rd.',
       'Menlo Park', 'CA', '94025', 1)
```

Even for this simple query, the output of the trace flag 1200 is voluminous, containing some 253 lines. You can run the script postT1200.pl to produce a summary of the acquired locks as shown in Listing 6-22.

Listing 6-22. A Summary of the Locks Acquired by the Insert Statement

```
cmd>perl postT1200.pl t1200_insert.log
$LockSummary = {
            '[dbo]:[authors]' => {
                                'X lock on KEY'      => '3',
                                'Schema lock on TAB' => '1',
                                'IX lock on TAB'     => '1',
                                'IX lock on PAG'     => '3'
                },
                ...
            '[dbo]:[sysindexes]' => {
                                    'S lock on RID'  => '3',
                                    'S lock on KEY'  => '14',
                                    'IS lock on PAG' => '3'
                    },
                ...
            '[dbo]:[systypes]' => {
                                    'S lock on KEY' => '9'
                    },
            '[dbo]:[syscomments]' => {
                                    'S lock on KEY' => '7'
                      },
            '[dbo]:[sysusers]' => {
                                'S lock on KEY' => '14'
                    },
            '[dbo]:[syscolumns]' => {
                                    'S lock on KEY' => '48'
                    },
            '[dbo]:[sysobjects]' => {
                                    'S lock on KEY' => '57'
                    },
                ...
};
```

The summary result shows that the insert statement placed three exclusive row-level locks (actually they're KEY locks because of the clustered index), three intent exclusive page locks, one intent exclusive table lock, and a schema lock all on the authors table. In addition, the insert statement acquires row-level shared locks on various system tables.

The difference between the original output of the trace flag 1200 and the summary may not appear to be noteworthy in Listing 6-22. For such a simple query, you intuitively know what locks it may acquire. However, the difference becomes significant when you're studying the locks of a more complex query or a stored procedure that may include many queries accessing many tables.

Examining Locks Acquired by an Update Statement

Let's study what locks an update on the authors table acquires. Run the following T-SQL queries in the pubs database to update a single row in the authors table and save the output to the file t1200_update.log:

```
DBCC TRACEON(3604, 1200)
update authors
   set au_id = '111-34-1176'
 where au_id = '111-32-1176'
```

The output of the trace flag 1200 has about 292 lines. Applying the script postT1200.pl to t1200_update.log produces a summary of the acquired locks as shown in Listing 6-23.

Listing 6-23. A Summary of the Locks Acquired by the Update Statement

```
cmd>perl postT1200.pl t1200_update.log
$LockSummary = {
                '[dbo]:[authors]' => {
                                        'X lock on KEY' => '6',
                                        'U lock on KEY' => '2',
                                        'Schema lock on TAB' => '1',
                                        'IX lock on TAB' => '1',
                                        'IX lock on PAG' => '7',
                                        'IU lock on PAG' => '2'
                                      },
                ...
                '[dbo]:[titleauthor]' => {
                                        'IS lock on TAB' => '2',
                                        'Schema lock on TAB' => '1',
                                        'IS lock on PAG' => '1'
                                      },
                ...
              };
```

Because the example in Listing 6-22 has already shown the locks on the system tables, Listing 6-23 doesn't show them so that the locks on the user tables are highlighted. As you can see, the locking behavior of the update statement is more complex than that of the insert statement in the previous case.

In addition to the expected locks on the authors table, the update statement also acquired one intent shared page lock, two intent shared table locks, and one schema lock on the titleauthor table. These locks were the result of a foreign key on the titleauthor table that references the authors table. SQL Server placed these locks on the titleauthor table to protect the referential integrity between these two tables.

If you produce a summary of the locks for a delete from the authors table, you'll see similar locks placed on the titleauthor table to ensure that you aren't deleting any row in the authors table that's referenced by the titleauthor table.

The rest of this chapter turns to more practical topics—scanning databases for potential violations of database best practices.

Identifying Poorly Designed Indexes

SCENARIO

You want to scan all your servers in your environment to identify poorly designed indexes.

For a database of any significant size, its performance depends largely on the design of the indexes. Well-designed indexes can make the queries fly, but a single poorly implemented index has the potential of sinking the performance of the entire database.

You can consider an index poorly designed if it doesn't comply with the following index design best practices:

- Every table should have a clustered index.

- There shouldn't be too many indexes on a table that isn't read only.

- There shouldn't be redundant indexes on a table.

- A clustered index should be as narrow as possible.

- A nonclustered index should be highly selective.

The list of index best practices could go on and on. In a large SQL Server environment, it's not feasible to manually check the conformance to these best practice guidelines on a regular basis. If you've established best practice guidelines but you can't audit your environment regularly for their compliance, you haven't fully realized the value of these guidelines.

> **NOTE** *You may be curious about why every table should have a clustered index. The two primary reasons are more efficient storage management and higher query performance. SQL Server 2000 relies heavily on the clustered index to maintain a table. Many SQL Server storage management utilities are only applicable when the table has a clustered index. Performance-wise, it's well known that the SQL Server query optimizer heavily favors clustered indexes.*

Let's automate the checking of some of these best practices. The script findPoorIndexes.pl, presented in Listing 6-24, checks for any potential violations of the first three guidelines in the previous list.

Listing 6-24. Scanning SQL Server Environment for Poorly Designed Indexes

```
1.  use strict;
2.  use SQLDBA::Utility qw( dbaReadINI dbaRunQueryADO );
3.  use SQLDBA::SQLDMO qw( dbaGetTableIndexes );
4.
5.  my $configFile = shift or die "***Err: $0 expects a config file.";
6.  my $configRef = dbaReadINI($configFile); # read the config file into a hash
6.
7.  foreach my $server (sort keys %$configRef) {  # loop through all the servers
8.      next if $server =~ /^control/i;
9.      print "Checking server $server ...\n";
10.     # get all the tables on the server with more than 1000 pages
11.     my $ref = getTables($server);
12.     foreach my $db (sort keys %$ref) {
13.       foreach my $tb (sort @{$ref->{$db}}) {
14.         my $tRef = { srvName => $server,
15.                      dbName  => $db,
16.                      tbName  => $tb
17.                    };
18.         # get all the indexes of the table
19.         my $idxRef = dbaGetTableIndexes($tRef);
20.
21.         # evaluate the indexes
22.         findPoorIdx($db, $tb, $idxRef);
23.       }
```

```
24.    }
25.  }
26.
27.  ##################
28.  # Check the indexes on the table for best practice violation
29.  sub findPoorIdx {
30.      my ($db, $tb, $ref) = @_;
31.
32.      # Flag it if the table has more than 8 indexes
33.      my $idxNo = scalar keys %$ref;
34.      if ($idxNo > 8) {
35.          print "***$db.$tb has $idxNo indexes.\n";
36.      }
37.
38.      # Flag it if an index includes more than 5 columns
39.      foreach my $idx (sort keys %$ref) {
40.          my $colNo = scalar split(/,/, $ref->{$idx}->{IndexedColumns});
41.          if ($colNo > 5) {
42.              print "***$db.$tb.$idx includes more than 5 columns.\n";
43.          }
44.      }
45.
46.      # Flag it if the table doesn't have a clustered index
47.      my $clustered = 0;
48.      foreach my $idx (sort keys %$ref) {
49.          if ($ref->{$idx}->{Clustered} =~ /yes/i) {
50.              $clustered = 1;
51.              last;
52.          }
53.      }
54.      if ($clustered == 0) {
55.          print "***$db.$tb doesn't have a clustered index.\n";
56.      }
57.
58.      # Flag it if the table has redundant indexes
59.      my @idxCols;
60.      foreach my $idx (sort keys %$ref) {
61.          push @idxCols, $ref->{$idx}->{IndexedColumns};
62.      }
63.      foreach my $cols (@idxCols) {
64.          if (grep(/^$cols,(.+)/, @idxCols)) {
65.              print "***$db.$tb includes indexes redundant on columns $cols.\n";
66.          }
67.          if (grep(/^$cols$/, @idxCols) > 1) {
```

```
68.              print "***$db.$tb includes indexes redundant on columns $cols.\n";
69.          }
70.      }
71. } # findPoorIdx
72.
73. ##################
74. sub getTables {
75.     my $server = shift or die "***Err: getTables() expects a server name.";
76.
77.     my $sql = "sp_MSforeachdb 'USE ?
78.                 SELECT DISTINCT ''table'' = object_name(i.id),
79.                                 ''user'' = user_name(o.uid),
80.                                 ''db'' = db_name()
81.                   FROM sysindexes i JOIN sysobjects o ON i.id = o.id
82.                   WHERE i.indid in (0, 1)
83.                     AND i.dpages > 1000
84.                     AND o.type = ''U''
85.                   ORDER BY object_name(i.id)'";
86.     my $rc = dbaRunQueryADO($server, $sql, 4);
87.     my %results;
88.     foreach my $rset (@$rc) {
89.         next unless $rset;
90.         next unless @$rset;
91.         foreach my $rcd (@$rset) {
92.             push @{$results{$rcd->{db}}}, $rcd->{user} . '.' . $rcd->{table};
93.         }
94.     }
95.     return \%results;
96. } # getTables
```

The main body of the script in Listing 6-24 is rather mundane. It reads the list of servers from a Windows initialization (INI) file and loops through each server to get the names of a list of tables. Then, for each table, it retrieves the information on all its indexes. Finally, the script checks the indexes for compliance to the best practices for index design as outlined at the beginning of this section.

The function getTables() is responsible for retrieving the table names. Its core is the query specified between lines 77 and 85. This query uses an undocumented Microsoft stored procedure sp_MSforeachdb to retrieve the table names from each database. In each database, the query returns the database name, the owner name, and the table name for each table with more than 1,000 data pages. The exact number of 1,000 is an arbitrary one. Even though all indexes should be properly designed, it's more cost effective to focus on large tables for evaluating index design.

The actual check for poor index design is implemented in the function findPoorIdx() between lines 29 and 71. Checking for redundant indexes is an interesting one. Let's review the code that implements this check:

```
58.    # Flag it if the table has redundant indexes
59.    my @idxCols;
60.    foreach my $idx (sort keys %$ref) {
61.        push @idxCols, $ref->{$idx}->{IndexedColumns};
62.    }
63.    foreach my $cols (@idxCols) {
64.        if (grep(/^$cols,(.+)/, @idxCols)) {
65.            print "***$db.$tb includes indexes redundant on columns $cols.\n";
66.        }
67.        if (grep(/^$cols$/, @idxCols) > 1) {
68.            print "***$db.$tb includes indexes redundant on columns $cols.\n";
69.        }
70.    }
```

To understand this fragment of code, it helps to realize that $ref->{$idx}->{IndexColumns} contains a string that has all the columns—separated with comma—of a given index, and the columns are ordered in the same way as they are in the index. To find whether there's any redundancy in the indexes, all you need to do is compare these index strings using the following two rules:

- If the string for one index matches part of the string for another index from left to right with all the columns of the first string matching the corresponding columns of the second string, starting from the first column of both strings, then the former is redundant.

- If the strings for two indexes match exactly, the two indexes are redundant.

The Perl built-in function grep() on line 64 implements the first rule, and the grep() function on line 67 checks for the second rule:

```
64.        if (grep(/^$cols,(.+)/, @idxCols)) {
```

Line 64 says that if the variable $cols, which contains the concatenated column names for an index, matches the beginning of a string in the array @idxCols, the index is redundant.

The ^ sign says that the regular expression must match the beginning of a string. The regular expression fragment ,(.+) on line 64 says that each of the matched columns must be a complete column. A column can't match part of another column.

Line 67 says that if the string in the variable $cols exactly matches at least two elements in @idxCols, two indexes are defined on the identical columns and thus are redundant.

```
67.      if (grep(/^$cols$/, @idxCols) > 1) {
```

In Listing 6-24, I've chosen to implement the check for the first three index design guidelines. Implementing the other two guidelines outlined at the beginning of this section is slightly more complex because you must retrieve additional information to help decide whether the guidelines have been violated.

However, even in its current implementation, the script findPoorIndexes.pl in Listing 6-24 is sufficiently useful. The three best practice guidelines may sound too straightforward for anybody to stray from them. You'll be surprised by what you may find if you run this script in your environment.

Finally, there are good reasons why the best practice guidelines are guidelines, not the law. None of these guidelines are written in stone. You must adjust them to fit your particular environment. In addition, although many guidelines are qualitative in nature, a script has to work with specific numbers—such as, nine columns in a index are considered excessive but seven columns aren't. The moral is that you need to apply reason when interpreting the output of a script such as findPoorIndexes.pl.

Finding Poorly Designed Constraints

> **SCENARIO**
> *You want to scan your SQL Server environment for any poorly designed table constraints.*

The steps of finding poorly designed table constraints is conceptually similar to those of finding poorly designed indexes. Let's first make clear what constitutes a poorly designed constraint. You can consider a constraint poorly designed if it doesn't comply with the following best practice guidelines:

- Every table should have a primary key.

- You shouldn't create a PRIMARY KEY constraint on a column of the type float or real. These are imprecise data types, and creating a primary key on such a column can lead to unexpected results.

- You shouldn't have an excessive number of FOREIGN KEY constraints on a table.

- You shouldn't have any redundant constraints.

The script `findPoorConstraints.pl` in Listing 6-25 automates the check for the violation of these best practices.

Listing 6-25. Scanning SQL Server Environment for Poorly Designed Constraints

```perl
1.  use strict;
2.  use strict;
3.  use SQLDBA::Utility qw( dbaReadINI dbaRunQueryADO );
4.  use SQLDBA::SQLDMO qw( dbaGetKeyConstraints );
5.
6.  my $configFile = shift or die "***Err: $0 expects a config file.";
7.  my $configRef = dbaReadINI($configFile); # read the config file into a hash
8.
9.  # loop through all the servers
10. foreach my $server (sort keys %$configRef) {
11.     print "Checking server $server ...\n";
12.     # get all the tables on the server
13.     my $ref = getTables($server);
14.     foreach my $db (sort keys %$ref) {
15.        # get the data types of all the columns
16.        my $typeRef = getColTypes($server, $db);
17.
18.        foreach my $tb (sort @{$ref->{$db}}) {
19.           my $tRef = { srvName => $server,
20.                        dbName  => $db,
21.                        tbName  => $tb
22.                      };
23.           # get all the constraints of the table
24.           my $keyRef = dbaGetKeyConstraints($tRef);
25.
26.           # evaluate the constraints
27.           findPoorConstraints($tRef, $keyRef, $typeRef);
28.        }
29.     }
30. }
31.
32. ##############################
33. # Check the constraints on the table for best practice violation
34. sub findPoorConstraints {
35.     my ($tRef, $ref, $typeRef) = @_;
36.     my $tb = $tRef->{dbName} . '.' . $tRef->{tbName};
37.
38.     # Flag it if the table has more than 8 FKs
39.     my $fkNo;
```

```perl
40.    foreach my $key (keys %$ref) {
41.        ++$fkNo if $ref->{$key}->{Foreign} =~ /yes/i;
42.    }
43.    if ($fkNo > 8) {
44.        print "\t***$tb has more than 8 FKs\n";
45.    }
46.
47.    # Flag it if the table doesn't have a PK
48.    my $pk = 0;
49.    foreach my $key (keys %$ref) {
50.        if ($ref->{$key}->{Primary} =~ /yes/i) {
51.            $pk = 1;
52.            last;
53.        }
54.    }
55.    if ($pk == 0) {
56.        print "\t***$tb doesn't have a primary key.\n";
57.    }
58.
59.    # Flag it if the primary key is on a float or real column
60.    foreach my $key (keys %$ref) {
61.        if ($ref->{$key}->{Primary} =~ /yes/i) {
62.            foreach my $col (split(/,/, $ref->{$key}->{KeyColumns})) {
63.                if ($typeRef->{$tRef->{tbName}}->{$col} =~ /^(real|float)/i) {
64.                    print "\t***$tb primary key is on a real/float column.\n";
65.                }
66.            }
67.        }
68.    }
69. } # findPoorConstraints
70.
71. ##################
72. sub getTables {
73.    my $server = shift or die "***Err: getTables() expects a server name.";
74.
75.    my $sql = "sp_MSforeachdb 'USE ?
76.      SELECT DISTINCT ''table'' = object_name(id),
77.                      ''user''  = user_name(uid),
78.                      ''db''    = db_name()
79.        FROM sysobjects
80.       WHERE type = ''U''
81.         AND objectproperty(id, ''IsMSShipped'') = 0
82.         AND db_name() not in (''pubs'', ''Northwind'', ''tempdb'', ''model'')
83.       ORDER BY object_name(id)'";
```

```
84.    my $rc = dbaRunQueryADO($server, $sql, 4);
85.    my %results;
86.    foreach my $rset (@$rc) {
87.       next unless $rset;
88.       next unless @$rset;
89.       foreach my $rcd (@$rset) {
90.          push @{$results{$rcd->{db}}}, $rcd->{user} . '.' . $rcd->{table};
91.       }
92.    }
93.    return \%results;
94. } # getTables
95.
96. #################
97. sub getColTypes {
98.    my ($server, $db) = @_;
99.
100.   my $sql = "USE $db
101.             SELECT 'user'  = TABLE_SCHEMA,
102.                    'table' = TABLE_NAME,
103.                    'col'   = COLUMN_NAME,
104.                    'type'  = DATA_TYPE
105.               FROM information_schema.COLUMNS";
106.
107.   my $rc = dbaRunQueryADO($server, $sql, 4);
108.   my %results;
109.   foreach my $rset (@$rc) {
110.      next unless $rset;
111.      next unless @$rset;
112.      foreach my $rcd (@$rset) {
113.         my $tb = $rcd->{user} . '.' . $rcd->{table};
114.         $results{$tb}->{$rcd->{col}} = $rcd->{type};
115.      }
116.   }
117.   return \%results;
118.} # getColTypes
```

Before explaining the code, let's take a look at what the script may produce. Listing 6-26 shows the output of the script findPoorConstraints.pl.

Listing 6-26. Sample Results of Scanning for Poor Constraints

cmd>perl findPoorConstraints.pl config.txt
```
Checking server SQL1\APOLLO ...
    ***Reviews.dbo.History doesn't have a primary key.
    ***TradeDB.dbo.FloatTest primary key is on a real/float column.
    ***TradeDB.dbo.RealTest primary key is on a real/float column.
    ***TradeDB.dbo.test doesn't have a primary key.
    ***TradeDB.dbo.TradeHistory has more than 8 FKs
    ***TradeDB.dbo.TradeHistory doesn't have a primary key.
Checking server SQL1\APOLLO ...

    ...
```

The result reported in Listing 6-26 is self-evident and requires no elaboration. Now, let's make sense of the script findPoorConstraints.pl. The main flow of the script in Listing 6-25 is similar to that of the script in Listing 6-24 with several notable differences.

On line 16, the script calls the function getColTypes() to retrieve the data type for every column of every table in the database. The function getColTypes() is defined between lines 97 and 118, and its core is the following T-SQL query where the value of the variable $db is passed to the function in the second parameter:

```
100.   my $sql = "USE $db
101.          SELECT 'user'  = TABLE_SCHEMA,
102.                 'table' = TABLE_NAME,
103.                 'col'   = COLUMN_NAME,
104.                 'type'  = DATA_TYPE
105.             FROM information_schema.COLUMNS";
```

On line 24, the script findPoorConstraints.pl calls the function dbaGetKeyConstraints() imported from the SQLDBA:SQLDMO module to retrieve the information about the key constraints including PRIMARY KEY constraints, UNIQUE constraints, and FOREIGN KEY constraints. The constraint information is captured in a data structure similar to the example in Listing 6-27, which shows two constraints for the titleauthor table in the pubs database.

Listing 6-27. Sample Data Structure for the Key Constraints

```
$ref = {
    'UPKCL_taind' => {
                        'ReferencedTable' => '',
                        'Primary' => 'yes',
                        'Name' => 'UPKCL_taind',
                        'KeyColumns' => 'au_id,title_id',
                        'ID' => 'au_id,title_id///no',
                        'ExcludeReplication' => 0,
                        'Unique' => 'no',
                        'ReferencedKeyColumns' => '',
                        'Checked' => 1,
                        'Foreign' => 'no'
                    },
    'FK__titleauth__title__7B5B524B' => {
                        'ReferencedTable' => '[dbo].[titles]',
                        'Primary' => 'no',
                        'Name' => 'FK__titleauth__title__7B5B524B',
                        'KeyColumns' => 'title_id',
                        'ID' => 'title_id/[dbo].[titles]/title_id/yes',
                        'ExcludeReplication' => 0,
                        'Unique' => 'no',
                        'ReferencedKeyColumns' => 'title_id',
                        'Checked' => 1,
                        'Foreign' => 'yes'
                    },
};
```

You'll find it convenient to use the data structure in Listing 6-27 as an example when you examine the code in Listing 6-25.

The essence of the script findPoorConstraints.pl is the function findPoorConstraints() defined between lines 34 and 69. This function implements the check for the violation of the best practice guidelines.

Let's examine how it determines whether there are too many FOREIGN KEY constraints and how it checks whether a table doesn't have a primary key.

To find whether a table has too many FOREIGN KEY constraints, the function loops through all the constraints between lines 40 and 42 and counts the ones whose $ref->{$key}->{Foreign} property is yes. The function findPoorConstraints() uses the number eight as the threshold. If the number of FOREIGN KEY constraints on the table is greater than eight, the table has too many FOREIGN KEY constraints.

> **NOTE**   *A threshold number such as the number eight used in Listing 6-25 for checking whether a table has too many* FOREIGN KEY *constraints is necessarily an arbitrary one. Once a table is identified to have more than eight* FOREIGN KEY *constraints, it's up to you to decide whether it really matters.*

To check whether a column in a primary key is defined on the real or float data type, the function first splits the concatenated string of the columns into an array of individual columns on line 62:

```
62.          foreach my $col (split(/,/, $ref->{$key}->{KeyColumns})) {
63.              if ($typeRef->{$tRef->{tbName}}->{$col} =~ /^(real|float)/i) {
64.                  print "\t***$tb primary key is on a real/float column.\n";
65.              }
66.          }
```

Then, for each column, the function uses the data type information returned from the function getColTypes() to determine whether the data type for the column is real or float. This is performed on line 63.

Finding Fragmented Indexes

> **SCENARIO**
> *You want to scan all the databases in your environment to produce a list of tables that have heavily fragmented indexes.*

Because fragmentation can significantly degrade the performance of your database and can waste significant storage space, you should regularly review all your databases for signs of severe fragmentation.

The tool to determine the degree of index fragmentation is DBCC SHOWCONTIG. This DBCC command works on a specific index or on all the indexes of a given table if you specify the ALL_INDEXES option. Listing 6-28 is a sample output of running the DBCC SHOWCONTIG on the Orders table in the Northwind database.

Listing 6-28. Sample Output of DBCC SHOWCONTIG

```
DBCC SHOWCONTIG scanning 'Orders' table...
Table: 'Orders' (21575115); index ID: 1, database ID: 6
TABLE level scan performed.
- Pages Scanned...............................: 20
- Extents Scanned.............................: 3
- Extent Switches.............................: 2
- Avg. Pages per Extent.......................: 6.7
- Scan Density [Best Count:Actual Count].......: 100.00% [3:3]
- Logical Scan Fragmentation ..................: 5.00%
- Extent Scan Fragmentation ...................: 33.33%
- Avg. Bytes Free per Page....................: 146.5
- Avg. Page Density (full)....................: 98.19%
```

To assess the fragmentation level, the important values to watch are Logical Scan Fragmentation, Extent Scan Fragmentation, and Average Page Density. The Logical/Extent Scan Fragmentation shows the degree to which the physical ordering of the index pages doesn't match the logical ordering of these pages. The higher these two values are, the more fragmented the index pages are.

Although there's no hard-and-fast rule, for large indexes, tests show that when Logical Scan Fragmentation is greater than 20 percent, you can significantly improve performance after defragmenting the index.

To highlight the indexes whose defragmentation may yield the most significant performance improvement, the Perl script findIndexFrag.pl in Listing 6-29 implements the following rules:

- In deciding which table to scan, the script selects only large tables. The threshold is set to 1,000 data pages in the script.

- The script checks a table only if it has a clustered index. It doesn't check any heap table.

- The script considers an index only if it has more than 1,000 pages.

- The script highlights an index if its Logical Scan Fragmentation is greater than 20 percent.

- The script highlights an index if its Extent Scan Fragmentation is greater than 40 percent.

- The script highlights an index if its Average Page Density is lower than 60 percent.

Beware that none of the threshold numbers in the preceding list is selected through a scientific process. They are rough numbers that you should adjust to fit your own environment.

Listing 6-29. Scanning for Tables with Fragmented Indexes

```
1.   use strict;
2.   use SQLDBA::Utility qw( dbaReadINI dbaRunOsql dbaRunQueryADO );
3.
4.   my $configFile = shift or die "***Err: $0 expects a config file.";
5.   my $configRef = dbaReadINI($configFile); # read the config file to a hash
6.
7.   foreach my $server (sort keys %$configRef) {  # loop through all the servers
8.       next if $server =~ /^control$/i;
9.       print "Checking server $server ...\n";
10.      # get all the tables on the server with more than 1000 pages
11.      my $ref = getTables($server);
12.      foreach my $db (sort keys %$ref) {
13.          print "  Checking database $db ...\n";
14.          foreach my $tb (sort @{$ref->{$db}}) {
15.              my $tRef = { srvName => $server,
16.                           dbName  => $db,
17.                           tbName  => $tb
18.                         };
19.              # run DBCC SHOWCONTIG on the table
20.              my $fragRef = getIndexFrag($tRef);
21.
22.              # evaluate the fragmentation of the indexes
23.              findIndexFrag($tb, $fragRef);
24.          }
25.      }
26.  }  # foreach my $server
27.
28.  #################
29.  # Check the output of DBCC SHOWCONTIG for severe fragmentation
30.  sub findIndexFrag {
31.      my ($tb, $ref) = @_;
32.
33.      foreach my $indid (keys %$ref) {
34.          # skip an index if it has less than 100 pages
35.          next if $ref->{$indid}->{PagesScanned} < 1000;
36.
37.          #Check Page Density
38.          if ($ref->{$indid}->{PageDensity} < 60) {
```

```perl
39.           print "\t***Msg: $tb: Index $indid, PageDensity = ",
40.                  $ref->{$indid}->{PageDensity},
41.                  "%, PagesScanned: ", $ref->{$indid}->{PagesScanned}, "\n";
42.        }
43.        # Check Logical Scan Fragmentation
44.        if ($ref->{$indid}->{LogicalScanFragmentation} > 20) {
45.           print "\t***Msg: $tb: Index $indid, Logical Scan Frag = ",
46.                  $ref->{$indid}->{LogicalScanFragmentation},
47.                  "%, PagesScanned: ", $ref->{$indid}->{PagesScanned}, "\n";
48.        }
49.        # Check Extent Scan Fragmentation
50.        if ($ref->{$indid}->{ExtentScanFragmentation} > 20) {
51.           print "\t***Msg: $tb: Index $indid, Extent Scan Frag = ",
52.                  $ref->{$indid}->{ExtentScanFragmentation},
53.                  "%, PagesScanned: ", $ref->{$indid}->{PagesScanned}, "\n";
54.        }
55.     }
56. } # findIndexFrag
57.
58. #####################
59. sub getIndexFrag {
60.     my $tRef = shift or die "***Err: getIndexFrag() expects a reference.";
61.     my ($db, $tb) = ($tRef->{dbName}, $tRef->{tbName});
62.
63.     my $sql = "USE $db
64.                DBCC SHOWCONTIG(\'$tb\') WITH ALL_INDEXES";
65.
66.     my $opRef = {'-E' => undef, '-n' => undef, '-h' => '-1', '-w' => 1024};
67.     my $rc = dbaRunOsql($tRef->{srvName}, $sql, $opRef);
68.
69.     my ($indid, $fragRef);
70.     foreach my $msg (split(/\n/, $rc)) {
71.        if ($msg =~ /Table:\s+\'(.+)\'.+Index\s+ID:\s+(\d+)/i) {
72.           $indid = $2;
73.           next;
74.        }
75.        if ($msg =~ /Pages\s+Scanned.+\:\s+(\d+)/i) {
76.           $fragRef->{$indid}->{PagesScanned} = $1;
77.           next;
78.        }
79.        if ($msg =~ /Logical\s+Scan\s+Fragmentation.+\:\s+(.+)\%/i) {
80.           my $frag = $1;
81.           $frag =~ s/\s*$//;
82.           $fragRef->{$indid}->{LogicalScanFragmentation} = $frag;
```

```
83.              next;
84.          }
85.          if ($msg =~ /Extent\s+Scan\s+Fragmentation.+\:\s+(.+)\%/i) {
86.              my $frag = $1;
87.              $frag =~ s/\s*$//;
88.              $fragRef->{$indid}->{ExtentScanFragmentation} = $frag;
89.              next;
90.          }
91.          if ($msg =~ /Page\s+Density.+\:\s+(.+)\%/i) {
92.              my $frag = $1;
93.              $frag =~ s/\s*$//;
94.              $fragRef->{$indid}->{PageDensity} = $frag;
95.              next;
96.          }
97.      }
98.      return $fragRef;
99. } # getIndexFrag
100.
101.#################
102.sub getTables {
103.    my $server = shift or die "***Err: getTables() expects a server name.";
104.
105.    my $sql = "sp_MSforeachdb 'USE ?
106.                  SELECT DISTINCT ''table'' = object_name(i.id),
107.                                  ''user'' = user_name(o.uid),
108.                                  ''db'' = db_name()
109.                    FROM sysindexes i JOIN sysobjects o ON i.id = o.id
110.                   WHERE i.indid = 1
111.                     AND i.dpages > 1000
112.                     AND o.type = ''U''
113.                   ORDER BY object_name(i.id)'";
114.
115.    my $rc = dbaRunQueryADO($server, $sql, 4);
116.    my %results;
117.    foreach my $rset (@$rc) {
118.       next unless $rset;
119.       next unless @$rset;
120.       foreach my $rcd (@$rset) {
121.          push @{$results{$rcd->{db}}}, $rcd->{user} . '.' . $rcd->{table};
122.       }
123.    }
124.    return \%results;
125.} # getTables
```

Let's see the output of the script findIndexFrag.pl in Listing 6-29 by executing it on the command line with a config.txt file that has two SQL Server instances, SQL1\APOLLO and SQL2, listed in the section headings:

```
cmd>perl findIndexFrag.pl config.txt
Checking server SQL1\APOLLO ...
  Checking database TradeDB ...
    ***Msg: dbo.RTCust: Index 1, PageDensity = 59.78%, PagesScanned: 14600
    ***Msg: dbo.RTCust: Index 1, Logical Scan Frag = 41.10%, PagesScanned: 14600
    ***Msg: dbo.RTCust: Index 2, PageDensity = 59.18%, PagesScanned: 6500
    ***Msg: dbo.RTCust: Index 2, Logical Scan Frag = 52.31%, PagesScanned: 6500
Checking server SQL2 ...
  Checking database DealDB ...
    ***Msg: dbo.RTDeal: Index 1, PageDensity = 59.78%, PagesScanned: 2460
    ***Msg: dbo.RTDeal: Index 1, Logical Scan Frag = 41.10%, PagesScanned: 2460
    ***Msg: dbo.RTDeal: Index 2, PageDensity = 59.18%, PagesScanned: 1980
    ***Msg: dbo.RTDeal: Index 2, Logical Scan Frag = 52.31%, PagesScanned: 1980
  Checking database pubDB ...
```

This output highlights the fragmentation. Then, it's up to you to decide whether you want to take any action to further investigate these indexes or to defrag them.

Now let's review the code in Listing 6-29. By now, you're probably bored to see the main body of the script findIndexFrag.pl, which is strikingly similar to the main bodies of the scripts in the previous two sections (see Listing 6-24 and Listing 6-25).

These three scripts share a common flow in the main body. They all start by reading the server names from an INI file. Then, they loop through the servers, for each server they loop through the databases, and for each database they loop through the tables. For each table, they gather information into a data structure and then interrogate the data structure to check for the violation of their respective rules.

These three scripts differ in what information they retrieve and how they retrieve the information as well as the rules they apply to their respective data structures.

The function getTables() in Listing 6-29 retrieves the names of the tables that are larger than 1,000 pages and that have clustered indexes (see line 110 and line 111).

The function getIndexFrag() between lines 59 and 99 retrieves the fragmentation information of all the indexes of a given table by running the DBCC SHOWCONTIG command through the dbaRunOsql() function imported from the SQLDBA::Utility module. The output of the dbaRunOsql() function is passed to the variable $rc on line 67. This output should be similar to the output in Listing 6-28. As soon as it has received the output of the DBCC SHOWCOINTIG procedure, the function getIndexFrag() proceeds to match the text output for the values of Page Scanned, Logical Scan Fragmentation, Physical Scan Fragmentation.

For instance, the following code fragment captures the value for Logical Scan Fragmentation:

```
79.      if ($msg =~ /Logical\s+Scan\s+Fragmentation.+\:\s+(.+)\%/i) {
80.          my $frag = $1;
81.          $frag =~ s/\s*$//;
82.          $fragRef->{$indid}->{LogicalScanFragmentation} = $frag;
83.          next;
84.      }
```

The function that actually decides what to report with regard to the DBCC SHOWCONTIG output is findIndexFrag(). In this function, the code to check whether the Logical Scan Fragmentation has exceeded the threshold is as follows:

```
43.      # Check Logical Scan Fragmentation
44.      if ($ref->{$indid}->{LogicalScanFragmentation} > 20) {
45.          print "\t***Msg: $tb: Index $indid, Logical Scan Frag = ",
46.              $ref->{$indid}->{LogicalScanFragmentation},
47.              "%, PagesScanned: ", $ref->{$indid}->{PagesScanned}, "\n";
48.      }
```

Line 44 says that if the Logical Scan Fragmentation is greater than the threshold of 20, there's significant logical scan fragmentation, and a message should be printed.

Summary

Gaining a clear understanding of the SQL Server database behavior is an integral part of a DBA's education. Curious DBAs often want to go beyond what's generally documented in SQL Server Books Online to explore SQL Server technical details such as its storage internals and locking behavior. This chapter showed how you can use Perl to make the process of studying the SQL Server storage internals and locking behavior less painful by automating highly repetitive steps and by eliminating high volume but nonessential data to expose the key information.

This chapter also showed you how you can go beyond paying lip service to database best practices and actually automate the checks for violations of these best practice guidelines. It covered three examples of using Perl to help scan all the databases in your environment for violations of best practices with regard to indexes, constraints, and table fragmentation.

The next chapter shows how you can apply Perl to analyze T-SQL scripts and query execution plans.

CHAPTER 7

Analyzing SQL Code

BY NOW, YOU MAY HAVE grown tired of my incessant praise of Perl as a powerful tool for text processing. But I hope you haven't because you've seen only the beginning of it. This chapter continues to exploit Perl's text processing features to help analyze SQL code. Any Database Administrator (DBA) who spends a significant amount of time working with SQL scripts will find Perl's text processing power a real boon.

NOTE *This chapter uses SQL and Transact-SQL (T-SQL) interchangeably.*

If you work in a development environment, "analyzing" SQL code is no doubt one of the most important tasks in your DBA work. However, it's a time-consuming endeavor that's often done manually. In addition, SQL code analysis frequently requires deep knowledge of SQL Server, T-SQL, and the application itself, making it seemingly an unlikely candidate for automation. Indeed, any attempt to fully automate it would be a misguided effort. This, however, doesn't mean you can't automate some of the specific tasks of SQL code analysis. In fact, if you carefully examine many of the recommended procedures, techniques, or best practices—available from numerous public Web sites, books, and magazine articles—for analyzing SQL code, you'll discover that you can automate them if there's an easy way to extract the necessary information out of SQL code.

What Does Analyzing SQL Code Mean?

SQL code analysis is the study of SQL queries or scripts to find useful information primarily by examining the SQL elements and their relationships. The SQL code elements include everything defined and illustrated in the "Transaction-SQL Reference" section of the SQL Server Books Online. Data types, operators, functions, statements, control flows, and database objects are some examples of SQL elements.

What constitutes useful information depends on your objective. In most cases, it's to identify potential problems or poor coding practices in such areas as naming conventions, performance guidelines, and scripting standards.

Although you can find an abundance of information in terms of rules, guidelines, and best practices for coding SQL, there's little available in terms of automated tools for SQL code analysis in the public domain.

Source code analysis fares better in other programming languages and frameworks. There has been a long tradition in automating source code analysis for languages such as C or COBOL. There also has been some interesting recent progress in automating code analysis for the .NET Framework. For a great example, visit `http://www.gotdotnet.com/team/libraries` for the work on FxCop, which is a code analysis tool that checks .NET assemblies for compliance with the Microsoft .NET Framework design guideline.

The objective of this chapter isn't to construct a tool for comprehensive SQL code analysis. Instead, it focuses on writing short and mostly throwaway Perl scripts to perform specific and targeted analysis. All of these scripts came out of real-world scenarios of analyzing SQL code, and they're useful for their intended purposes. No doubt you'll run into situations that are radically different from what's documented in this chapter, and it would be no surprise that none of the scripts in this chapter apply. But the scripts in this chapter provide you with enough basics to effectively write your own. Better yet, these scripts may help trigger more ideas that lead to other useful scripts for performing SQL code analysis.

The scripts presented in this chapter roughly fall into two categories. First, the chapter presents a collection of scripts that analyze SQL code indirectly. These Perl scripts don't directly work with SQL scripts; they help study the execution plans of the SQL scripts. Second, the rest of the scripts examine SQL script files directly to extract useful information for analysis.

Cleaning Up Query Execution Plans for Analysis

> **SCENARIO**
> *You use SQL Profiler to trace the execution plans of the queries sent from an application. But the amount of trace data is huge. You want to reduce the amount of data before analyzing the plans.*

One of the difficulties of working with SQL Profiler is information overload. Just from tracing the execution plans alone, the trace data can easily grow into tens or hundreds of megabytes (MB) on a modestly busy database.

For one of my applications, I turned on the trace of the Execution Plan event class in the Performance event category and captured the trace data to a SQL Server table named TraceData. Then, I saved the output of the following query, effectively exporting the execution plans to a text file:

```
SELECT TextData FROM TraceData WHERE EventClass = 68
```

 TIP *The event number for the Execution Plan event class is 68. In the documentation for the system stored procedure* sp_trace_setevent *in the SQL Server 2000 Books Online, you can find a comprehensive list of event numbers for the event classes that you can add to or remove from a trace.*

I traced the application for two hours, and at the close of the trace, the size of the resulting text data for the execution plans exported with the previous SQL query was more than 50MB. You can easily end up with an even larger file when tracing a busier database. Opening and browsing a file of 50MB or larger isn't something you would enjoy doing with Notepad or any of your favorite text editors.

I therefore set out to remove extraneous bits and bytes from the text file, wanting to pare down the file to a more manageable size without adversely impacting the analysis. What may be considered extraneous is highly situation dependent. In my case, I found three useless items taking up a lot of space:

- Trailing whitespaces

- An entire query execution plan consisting of a single entry (Constant Scan), which is largely irrelevant for my analysis

- Multiple consecutive blank lines

Listing 7-1 removes these items from the execution plan text file.

Listing 7-1. Filtering Out Useless Items from a Query Execution Plan File

```
1.  use strict;
2.
3.  my $empty = 0;
4.  my $plan = shift or die "***Err: $0 expects a file.";
5.  open(PLAN, $plan) or die "***Err: could not open file $plan.";
6.
```

```
7.   while(<PLAN>) {
8.       s/\s*\n$/\n/;   # 1. remove trailing spaces
9.       if (/^\s*Execution\s+Tree\s*$/i) {     # indicates the start of the plan
10.         my $line = $_;
11.         if ($_ = <PLAN>, /^\s*\-+\s*$/) {    # a line of nothing but -'s
12.             $line .= $_;                     # keep the header
13.             # 2. skip the query plan if its root is Constant Scan
14.             next if ($_ = <PLAN>, /^\s*Constant\s+Scan\s*$/i);
15.         }
16.         print $line;
17.     }
18.     # 3. collapse multiple blank lines into one
19.     if (/^\s*$/) {
20.         next if ++$empty > 1;
21.     }
22.     else {
23.         $empty = 0;
24.     }
25.     print;  # otherwise, print as is
26. }
27. close(PLAN);
```

The script in Listing 7-1, saved as `filterQueryPlans.pl`, accepts a filename on the command line. I then ran this script against the previously mentioned 50MB execution plan file as follows:

```
cmd>perl filterQueryPlans.pl TraceData.txt > reducedTraceData.txt
```

where `TraceData.txt` is the 50MB file that contained the query plans. This reduced the trace data to a file slightly more than 4MB—manageable even with Notepad.

You may wonder why you don't simply filter out things considered extraneous when the execution plans are being selected out of the database table. That's an excellent observation! However, handling the execution plans in a text file allows the Perl script to also work with execution plans captured by other means. For instance, it can work with those plans captured as the result of setting STATISTICS PROFILE or SHOWPLAN_TEXT, which most likely won't end up storing the execution plans in a table.

The script in Listing 7-1 uses mostly basic Perl programming constructs. However, line 14 requires some explanation:

```
14.             next if ($_ = <PLAN>, /^\s*Constant\s+Scan\s*$/i);
```

In the if condition, there are two expressions separated with a comma. In this case, the comma is an operator that accepts the two expressions as its arguments. The comma operator evaluates the first expression and throws away its return value, and it then evaluates the second expression and returns its value. The first expression assigns a line from the file handle PLAN to the predefined special variable $_, and the second expression matches $_ against the pattern /^\s*Constant\s+Scan\s*$/i. If the match is successful, it returns true, and the next command executes to start the next iteration of the while loop, effectively preventing Constant Scan from appearing in the output.

Working with Large Text Files

Opening and browsing a large text file is always a hassle. Unfortunately, it's common for a DBA to run into text files that are too large to be effectively handled by any text editor. The SQL Server errorlog file and the SQL Profiler trace files routinely grow to a significant size.

On the Windows platform, one common technique to page through a large text file is to control the output of the type command with the more command using a pipe (|), as illustrated in the following example:

```
cmd>type SQLTrace.log | more
```

Alternatively, you could use the following simple Perl script (page.pl), which allows you to jump directly to any line in a text file and then view a specific range of lines from there onward:

```
my ($file, $start, $end) = @ARGV;
open(FL, $file) or die "***Err: could not open $file.";
while(<FL>) {
   next if $. < $start;
   exit if $. > $end;
   print;
}
close(FL);
```

For instance, the following displays the lines between line 1000 and line 1250 in the TraceData.txt file:

```
cmd>perl page.pl TraceData.txt 1000 1250
```

Finding Excessive Joins

SCENARIO
While reviewing the queries sent to SQL Server from an application, you found JOIN *clauses that included six or more tables. You now want to find all such outrageous joins.*

To find all the JOIN clauses in a large T-SQL script file, you need a comprehensive T-SQL parser; it's too complex a job for pattern matching with regular expressions.

Fortunately, if you can trace these queries with SQL Profiler, you don't need a T-SQL parser to help find the JOIN clauses. Instead of parsing an arbitrary SQL script file, you can take advantage of the well-formatted execution plans. By counting the number of logical join operators in the query plan for a SQL statement, you'll be able to determine the number of JOIN clauses used in that query.

The following are five examples of the JOIN operators, taken out of actual execution plans:

```
1. Nested Loops(Inner Join)
2. |--Hash Match(Inner Join, HASH:([b].[Name])=([p].[Name]), RESIDUAL: ...
3. |    |         |--Nested Loops(Inner Join, OUTER REFERENCES:([g].[Name]))
4. |--Nested Loops(Left Semi Join, DEFINE:([Expr1004] = [PROBE VALUE]))
5. |--Merge Join(Inner Join, MANY-TO-MANY MERGE:([a].[Code])=([b].[Code]), ...
```

As you can see, the text patterns to search for the JOIN operators are quite simple and unique.

Assume that you've traced the queries with the Execution Plan event class and exported the execution plans to a text file using the same method described in the previous section. Running the Perl script excessiveJoins.pl in Listing 7-2 against the text file prints those query plans that include a JOIN clause with six or more tables.

Listing 7-2. Finding Queries with Excessive Joins

```
1.    use strict;
2.
3.    my $joinNum = 6;
4.    # define a new line separator
5.    $/ = "\n Execution Tree\n";
6.    while (<>) {              # get a new query plan
7.       s{$/}{};              # remove the line separator itself
```

```
8.       s/^\s*//; s/\s*$//;      # remove leading and trailing spaces
9.       s/^\s*\-+\s*\n//;        # remove the line of dashes
10.
11.    my @joins = /\n[\s\-\|]*?([\s\w]+?\s*\([\s\w]+?\s+join)/ig;
12.    if (scalar @joins > $joinNum) {  # number of join operators
13.        print "$_\n";
14.    }
15. }
```

Note that each individual query execution plan in the exported text file starts with the same header line Execution Tree followed by a line of dashes:

```
Execution Tree
--------------
Sort(ORDER BY:([tbTempName].[fieldOrder] ASC))
  |--Table Scan(OBJECT:([RMDB].[dbo].[tbTempName]))

Execution Tree
--------------
Index Delete(OBJECT:([trades].[dbo].[ClientOrders].[pkey]))
  |--Clustered Index Delete(OBJECT:([trades].[dbo].[ClientOrders].[PK_...]))
  |--Top(ROWCOUNT est 0)
      --Index Seek(OBJECT:([trades].[dbo].[ClientOrders].[pkey]), SEEK: ... )
```

On line 5 in Listing 7-2, the input record separator—designated with the special Perl variable $/—is set to the string "\n Execution Tree\n", which allows the angle input operator (<>) to read in one complete query plan at a time (instead of the default of one line at a time). Depending on how you actually export the traced execution plans to the text file, there may not be any leading space in front of the string Execution Tree. You need to study the file to be certain about the exact string you can use to separate the query plans.

NOTE   *You can set the Perl input record separator (represented with the predefined special variable $/) to a string only. You can't set it to a pattern (in other words, a regular expression). Enabling $/ to accept a regular expression would be a powerful addition to Perl and is at the top of my Perl wish list.*

Because the strategy is to find excessive joins by counting the number of logical join operators in a query plan, you need to be certain about what these operators are. The following are the logical join operators from the SQL Server 2000 Books Online:

- Inner join

- Left outer join

- Left semi join

- Left anti semi join

- Right outer join

- Right semi join

- Right anti semi join

The regular expression that matches the join operators is in the following statement, reproduced from Listing 7-2:

```
11. my @joins = /\n[\s\-\|]*?([\s\w]+?\s*\([\s\w]+?\s+join)/ig;
```

It uses the /g modifier to get all the matched strings into the array @joins. Then, it's a matter of counting the number of elements in the array.

This regular expression needs some further clarification. The following is the same regular expression rewritten using the /x modifier:

```
my @joins = /\n [\s\-\|]*?     # a newline followed by zero or more -'s,
                               # |'s, or spaces. Nongreedy
            (  [\s\w]+?         # match spaces or words. Nongreedy
                               # This is a physical operator, for
                               # instance, Hash Match
               \s*\(            # zero or more spaces, then a left paren
               [\s\w]+?         # first part of a logical operator, e.g. Inner
               \s+join          # some spaces followed by string join
            )/igx;
```

If you happen to use the T-SQL union operator to combine the results of two or more queries into a single resultset, you'll quickly discover a drawback of the Perl script in Listing 7-2. Consider the case where a UNION statement consists of two queries and each query has a three-way join. Because it counts the number of logical join operators for the entire UNION statement, the Perl script reports a six-way join, which isn't exactly what you want. What you need to do is further split the execution plan for the UNION statement into execution plans for each constituent query.

Although this script can find the excessive joins, it reports only the query plans—not the actual queries—that use these joins. Reporting the actual queries with outrageous joins would be more useful to a DBA. That's what the next section accomplishes.

Finding Queries with Excessive Joins

SCENARIO
You want to identify the queries whose joins involve six or more tables.

Like in the preceding section, this section continues to rely on analyzing the execution plans captured with SQL Profiler to tell you whether a join is excessive (has too many tables). But there needs to be a way to correlate an execution plan with its original SQL statement. The solution is to trace the event class SQL:Batch-Starting and the event class SQL:BatchCompleted, in addition to tracing the Execution Plan event class.

The event classes SQL:BatchStarting and SQL:BatchCompleted capture the same batch of SQL queries at different points in time. The former captures the queries at the beginning of the batch, and the latter captures the queries when the batch has completed. For a given connection, the execution plans captured by the event class Execution Plan appear chronologically between SQL:BatchStarting and SQL:BatchCompleted. This allows you to relate execution plans to their SQL statements.

With the trace data for these three event classes saved to a database table, you can use the Perl script in Listing 7-3—queriesWithExcessiveJoins.pl—to find the queries whose joins involve six or more tables.

Listing 7-3. Finding Queries with Excessive Joins

```
use strict;
use Getopt::Std;
use Win32::OLE;

my %opts;
getopts('S:d:t:', \%opts);
# store the command-line arguments into more meaningful variables
my ($server, $db, $threshold) = ($opts{S}, $opts{d}, $opts{t});
# check whether the mandatory arguments are missing
(defined $server and defined $db and defined $threshold) or printUsage();
```

```perl
Main: {
    my $cn = Win32::OLE->new('ADODB.Connection') or
        die "***Err: unable to create the ADODB.Connection object.";
    $cn->{ConnectionTimeout} = 2;   # set the connection timeout to 2 seconds
    # make a trusted connection attempt
    $cn->Open("Driver={SQL Server};Server=$server;Trusted_Connection=yes");


    # prepare the SQL query string. $db interpolates in qq//
    my $sql = qq/SELECT SPID, RowNumber, EventClass, TextData
                   FROM $db..TraceData
                  WHERE EventClass in (12,13,68)
               ORDER BY SPID, RowNumber/;
    my $rs = $cn->Execute($sql);   # execute the query


    my $planRef;
    if ($rs) {
        while ( !$rs->{EOF} ) {
            $planRef = findExcessiveJoins($rs, $planRef, $threshold);
            $rs->MoveNext();
        }
    }
    else {
        print '***Err: ' . Win32::OLE->LastError() . "\n";
    }
    $cn->Close;
} # Main


##################
sub findExcessiveJoins {
    my($rs, $planRef, $threshold) = @_;

    $planRef->{spid} = $rs->Fields('SPID')->value unless $planRef->{spid};
    if ($rs->Fields('EventClass')->value == 13) {   # BatchStarting
        $planRef->{BatchStart} = $rs->Fields('TextData')->value;
        $planRef->{BatchStart} =~ s/\s*$//;
        $planRef->{BatchStart} =~ s/^\s*//;
    }
    if ($rs->Fields('EventClass')->value == 68) {  # Execution Plan
        my $plan = $rs->Fields('TextData')->value;
        if (hasExcessiveJoins($plan, $threshold)) {
            $plan =~ s/\s*$//;
            $planRef->{Plan} .= $plan;
        }
```

```
        }
        if ($rs->Fields('EventClass')->value == 12) {   # BatchCompleted
            $planRef->{BatchComplete} = $rs->Fields('TextData')->value;
            $planRef->{BatchComplete} =~ s/\s*$//;
            $planRef->{BatchComplete} =~ s/^\s*//;
            if ($planRef->{spid} == $rs->Fields('SPID')->value) {
                if ($planRef->{BatchStart} eq $planRef->{BatchComplete}) {
                    if (defined $planRef->{Plan}) {
                        print "\nTSQL: \n$planRef->{BatchStart}";
                        $planRef->{Plan} =~ s/\n/\n\t/g;
                        print "\n\n\t", $planRef->{Plan};
                    }
                    undef $planRef;
                }
                else {
                    print "***Err: the SQL statement for BatchStart didn't match";
                    print " that for BatchComplete. This is not expected.\n";
                }
            }
            else {
                print "***Err: it has crossed the spid boundary. ";
                print "This is not expected.\n";
            }
        }
    }
    return $planRef;
}   # findExcessiveJoins


########################
sub hasExcessiveJoins {
    my ($plan, $threshod) = @_;

    my @joins = $plan =~ /\n[\s\-\|]*?([\s\w]+?\s*\([\s\w]+?\s+join)/ig;
    if (scalar @joins > $threshold) {   # number of joins > the threshold
        return 1;
    }
    else {
        return 0;
    }
}  # hasExcessiveJoins


##################
sub printUsage {
    print << '--Usage--';
Usage:
```

```
cmd>perl queriesWithExcessiveJoins.pl -S <SQL server or instance>
                                      -d <database name>
                                      -t <join threshold>
--Usage--
exit;
} # printUsage
```

Assume that you've saved the trace data in the table TraceData in the pubs database on server SQL01\APOLLO. Run the script as follows to find and print the queries with six-way or more complex joins:

```
cmd>perl queriesWithExcessiveJoins.pl -S SQL01\APOLLO -d pubs -t 6
```

Unlike in the preceding section where the Perl script needs to split the query plans in a text file into individual plans—one for each SQL statement—the script in Listing 7-3 retrieves individual plans and their associated SQL statements from the database table where the SQL Profiler trace data is saved. You retrieve the query plans with this SQL statement:

```
SELECT SPID, RowNumber, EventClass, TextData
  FROM $db..TraceData
 WHERE EventClass in (12,13,68)
ORDER BY SPID, RowNumber
```

Through Perl's variable interpolation, the $db variable in this query will be replaced with the database name, specified on the command line with the -d parameter, before the query is sent to SQL Server. Also note that in this SQL query, the event number 13 is for the event class SQL:BatchStarting, the event number 12 is for the event class SQL:BatchCompleted, and the event number 68 is for the event class Performance:Execution Plan. The result of the query guarantees that for each SQL batch, the trace data for the event class SQL:BatchStarting comes first, followed by one or more execution plans and then the trace data for the event class SQL:BatchCompleted.

In the main body of the Perl script in Listing 7-3, as it moves through the records in the ADO recordset generated with the previous SQL query, the script applies the function findExcessiveJoins() to each record to update a hash structure—referenced with the variable $planRef. This hash structure remembers the SQL statements captured by SQL:BatchStarting and the matching SQL statements captured by the event SQL:BatchCompleted for the same connection. The hash structure also remembers any execution plan between SQL:BatchStarting and its matching event SQL:BatchCompleted that has a join with the number of the logical join operators exceeding the threshold. You specify the threshold on the command line with the parameter -t.

Summarizing Index Usage

> **SCENARIO**
>
> *You want to get an overview of how the indexes in a database are being used.*

The best place to find comprehensive information on the index usage is in the query plans, especially if you obtain the query plans by tracing a representative workload. However, even on a modestly busy server, tracing the query plans often produces a massive amount of data. Manually searching for the index usage information in a large volume of query plans is an arduous and inefficient undertaking. Fortunately, this is where Perl comes in handy.

First, a query plan consists of a series of operators such as Index Seek, Bookmark Lookup, and Table Scan. Second, an index is used by one of these operators in query plans:

- Clustered Index Seek

- Clustered Index Scan

- Clustered Index Delete

- Clustered Index Update

- Clustered Index Insert

- Index Seek

- Index Scan

- Index Delete

- Index Update

- Index Insert

Finally, each operator identifies an index in a query plan with a consistent four-part name, fully qualifying the index with the database name, the owner name, and the table name. For instance, the query plan operator Index Seek may specify OBJECT: ([pubs].[dbo].[authors].[authors_idx1]) as its argument, where [authors_idx1] is the index.

The Perl script indexSummary.pl presented later in Listing 7-5 takes advantage of these observations. It scans the SQL Server query plans and counts the number of times the different query plan operators use an index. In addition, it scans for the Table Scan operator and counts how many times a table is scanned. You can run this Perl script from the command line as follows:

```
cmd>perl indexSummary.pl  -S SQL01 -d pubs  -q QueryPlan.log
```

In this example, the script `IndexSummary.pl` scans the query plans saved in the text file `QueryPlan.log` for the indexes used in the `pubs` database on the server SQL01.

To clarify what this script does, refer to the sample index usage summary shown in Listing 7-4.

Listing 7-4. A Sample Index Usage Summary

```
Index summary for database pubs...


Index/Table           Total   Cnt     Operator
--------------------- ------- ------- -----------------------
authors               3
                      3       Table Scan
authors.PK_auidind    9
                      1       Clustered Index Scan
                      6       Clustered Index Seek
                      1       Clustered Index Update
                      1       Clustered Index Delete
authors.aunmind       5
                      1       Index Seek
                      4       Index Scan
publishers.PK_pub     3
                      3       Clustered Index Seek
roysched              2
                      2       Table Scan
sales.titleidind      4
                      3       Index Seek
                      1       Index Scan
titles.PK_idind       13
                      7       Clustered Index Scan
                      4       Clustered Index Seek
                      2       Clustered Index Update


Unused indexes in database pubs...

employee.PK_emp_id
jobs.PK__jobs__22AA2996
pub_info.UPKCL_pubinfo
```

```
roysched.titleidind
stores.UPK_storeid
titleauthor.UPKCL_taind
titles.titleind
```

Among other things, the index summary reported in Listing 7-4 tells you that the authors table is table scanned three times, the clustered index authors.PK_auidind is used nine times, and the nonclustered index authors.aunmind is used five times. In addition, out of the five times the authors.aunmind index is used, the script counts Index Seek once and Index Scan four times. More than that, toward the end of Listing 7-4, the report also highlights the indexes that aren't used with respect to the captured execution plans of the workload. For instance, the index employee.PK_emp_id isn't used by the workload.

Now, Listing 7-5 presents the code.

Listing 7-5. Summarizing the Index Usage

```perl
use strict;
use Getopt::Std;
use SQLDBA::Utility qw( dbaSetDiff );

# get command-line parameters
my %opts;
getopts('S:d:q:', \%opts);
my ($server, $db, $query_plan) = ($opts{S}, $opts{d}, $opts{q});
printUsage() unless (-e $query_plan);

Main: {
    # get the indexes and operators from query plans
    my $idxRef = getIdxOperators($query_plan);

    # print a summary of the indexes/operators
    printIdxOperators($db, $idxRef);

    # get and print unused indexes
    if ($server && $db) {
        my $unIdxRef = getUnusedIdx($server, $db, $idxRef);
        printUnusedIdx($db, $unIdxRef);
    }
} # Main

######################
sub getIdxOperators {
    my ($query_plan) = shift or
```

```perl
    die "***Err: getIdxOperators() expects a file name.";
  my $idxRef;

  open(LOG, "$query_plan")
    or die "***Err: could not open $query_plan.";
  while(<LOG>) {
    # e.g. look for Index Scan(OBJECT:([pubs].[dbo].[jobs].[jobs_ix])
    if (m{^[\s | \d | \|]*\|\-\-
        ( Clustered\s+Index\s+Seek  | Clustered\s+Index\s+Scan |
          Clustered\s+Index\s+Delete | Clustered\s+Index\s+Update |
          Clustered\s+Index\s+Insert | Index\s+Seek | Index\s+Scan |
          Index\s+Delete | Index\s+Update | Index\s+Insert | Table\s+Scan
        )
        \(OBJECT\:\(
         (
           ( \[ ([^\]] | \]\])+ \] )        # database name
            \.\[ ([^\]] | \]\])+ \]         # owner
            \.\[ ([^\]] | \]\])+ \]         # object
           ( \.\[ ([^\]] | \]\])+ \] )?     # index
         )
        \)
    }ix) {
      # count the index and operator usage
      my ($ops, $obj, $db) = ($1, $2, $3);
      if ($db =~ /tempdb/i) {
        $obj =~ s/\_{4,}\w+//; # remove the appendix of a temp table
      }
      $idxRef->{$db}->{$obj}->{count}++;
      $idxRef->{$db}->{$obj}->{ops}->{$ops}->{count}++;
    }
  }
  close(LOG);

  return $idxRef;
} # getIdxOperators


####################
sub printIdxOperators {
  my ($database, $idxRef) = @_;

  # exclusde system tables from summary
  my @systables = qw( sysobjects syscolumns syscomments sysindexes
                      sysdepends sysreferences sysfiles sysfilegroups
                      syspermissions sysprotects sysindexkeys
```

```
                          sysforeignkeys sysallocations sysusers systypes);

        print "\nIndex summary for database $database...\n\n";
        printf " %-75s %-5s %-7s %-25s\n", 'Index/Table', 'Total',
                        'Op Cnt', 'Operator';
        printf " %-75s %-5s %-7s %-25s\n", '-' x 75, '-' x 5,
                        '-' x 7, '-' x 25;
        foreach my $db (keys %{$idxRef}) {
          next if defined $db and $db ne "[$database]";

          foreach my $idx (sort keys %{$idxRef->{$db}}) {
              # skip system table indexes
              next if grep {$idx =~ /\[dbo\]\.\[$_\]/i} @systables;

              printf " %-75s %s\n", $idx, $idxRef->{$db}->{$idx}->{count};
              foreach my $op (sort keys %{$idxRef->{$db}->{$idx}->{ops}}) {
                 printf " %-75s %-5s %-7s %-25s\n", ' ' x 75, ' ' x 5,
                        $idxRef->{$db}->{$idx}->{ops}->{$op}->{count}, $op;
              }
          }
        }
    }
} # printIdxOperators


#####################
sub getUnusedIdx {
    my ($server, $database, $idxRef) = @_;
    unless (defined $server and defined $database) {
        die "***Err: getUnusedIdx() expects both server and database.";
    }

    # get indexes from the database
    my $sql = "use $database " .
            q/SET NOCOUNT ON
                SELECT QUOTENAME(db_name()) + '.' +
                        QUOTENAME(user_name(o.uid)) + '.' +
                        QUOTENAME(o.name) + '.' + QUOTENAME(i.name)
                    FROM sysindexes i, sysobjects o
                WHERE i.indid > 0 AND i.indid < 255 AND (i.status & 64) = 0
                        AND o.id = i.id
                        AND OBJECTPROPERTY(o.id, 'IsMSShipped') <> 1/;

    my @result = `osql -S$server -E -Q\"$sql\" -n -h-1 -w2048 -l2`;
    my @allIndexes;
    foreach (@result) {
```

```perl
        s/\s+$//; s/^\s+//;
        next if /^\s*$/;
        push @allIndexes, $_;
    }

    # get the list of indexes used in the query plan
    my @usedIndexes = ();
    foreach my $db (keys %$idxRef) {
        next unless ($db eq $database) or ($db =~ /\[$database\]/);
        @usedIndexes = keys %{$idxRef->{$db}};
    }

    # compare the two lists to get a list of unused indexes
    dbaSetDiff(\@allIndexes, \@usedIndexes);
} # getUnusedIdx


#####################
sub printUnusedIdx {
    my ($database, $unusedIdxRef) = @_;

    if (scalar @$unusedIdxRef) {
        print "\nUnused indexes in database $database...\n\n";
        foreach (sort @$unusedIdxRef) {
            print " $_\n";
        }
    }
    else {
        print "\nNo unused indexes in database $database.\n";
    }
} # printUnusedIdx


#####################
sub printUsage {
    print << '--Usage--';
Usage:
    cmd>perl IndexSummary.pl [ -S <SQL server or instance> ]
                             [ -d <database name> ]
                              -q <Query plan log>
--Usage--
    exit;
} # printUsage
```

The script in Listing 7-5 consists of four major functions. The function getIdxOperators() extracts indexes and their operators from the query plan and stores the information in a hash structure referenced by $idxRef; the function printIdxOperators() prints a summary of the indexes in terms of how often each is used, and by what query plan operator, using the information captured in the hash structure $idxRef.

To produce a list of indexes that aren't used, the function getUnusedIdx() retrieves the complete list of indexes from the database and compares it with the list of indexes obtained from the query plans. Finally and logically, printUnusedIdx() prints the indexes unused in the database.

To reiterate, an index is considered unused only with respect to the query plans and therefore to the workload. For the result to be useful, it's important to make sure the workload is comprehensive—ideally capturing all the queries.

NOTE   *SQL Server comes with a great tool: the Index Tuning Wizard. This wizard accepts a workload in the form of a T-SQL script, evaluates the performance implications of various indexes—real or hypothetical—by using the query optimizer to analyze the queries in the workload, and recommends an optimal set of indexes to create. On the other hand, the Perl script in Listing 7-5 summarizes how the indexes are actually being used in a collection of query plans. You can use its index usage summaries to complement the Index Tuning Wizard.*

The heart of the script is the regular expression in the getIdxOperators() function (see Listing 7-6).

Listing 7-6. The Regular Expression Capturing the Index Operators

```
m{^[\s | \d | \|]*\|\-\-
    ( Clustered\s+Index\s+Seek | Clustered\s+Index\s+Scan |
      Clustered\s+Index\s+Delete | Clustered\s+Index\s+Update |
      Clustered\s+Index\s+Insert | Index\s+Seek | Index\s+Scan |
      Index\s+Delete | Index\s+Update | Index\s+Insert | Table\s+Scan
    )
    \(OBJECT\:\(
      (
        ( \[ ([^\]] | \]\])+ \] )         # database name
          \.\[ ([^\]] | \]\])+ \]         # owner
          \.\[ ([^\]] | \]\])+ \]         # object
        ( \.\[ ([^\]] | \]\])+ \] )?      # index
      )
    \)
}ix
```

This regular expression matches a query plan index operator and its object argument, which follow a pattern similar to these three examples:

```
1. |--Index Seek(OBJECT:([pubs].[dbo].[authors].[nmind])
2. |   |   |--Index Seek(OBJECT:([pubs].[dbo].[authors].[nmind])
3. 0   1   |--Index Seek(OBJECT:([pubs].[dbo].[authors].[nmind])
```

Note that the fourth part of the object name corresponds to the index name. The postfixed question mark makes it optional. This captures operators such as Table Scan whose object is the table instead of the index.

In the previous three examples, the regular expression in Listing 7-6 captures both the index operator and the index name—Index Seek and [pubs].[dbo].[authors].[nmind], respectively. The script also keeps a total count of the times the index is used as well as a count of the times a query plan operator is applied to the index.

To get a list of all the indexes created for the user tables in a database, the script in Listing 7-5 runs this SQL query through osql.exe in the function getUnusedIdx():

```
SELECT QUOTENAME(db_name()) + '.' +
       QUOTENAME(user_name(o.uid)) + '.' +
       QUOTENAME(o.name) + '.' + QUOTENAME(i.name)
  FROM sysindexes i, sysobjects o
 WHERE i.indid > 0 AND i.indid < 255 AND (i.status & 64) = 0
   AND o.id = i.id
   AND OBJECTPROPERTY(o.id, 'IsMSShipped') <> 1
```

The indexes listed by this SQL query will all have the standard four-part names; also, a pair of square brackets delimits each part of the name in exactly the same format as the names of the indexes extracted from the query plans. This makes it easy to compare the indexes from the database to the indexes from the query plans. It's through this comparison that the function getUnusedIdx() finds the unused indexes in the database.

TIP *The T-SQL function* QUOTENAME() *is one of the most underutilized functions. Without using this function, you have to escape any embedded square brackets yourself, making the code ugly and much less readable. One of the best places to become educated on functions such as* QUOTENAME() *is the source code of the system procedures that come with SQL Server. Simply browsing the code of the system procedures reveals many T-SQL programming techniques that you'll find useful.*

If you already have a database workload in the form of a T-SQL script, you can obtain its query plans in one of three ways. Recall that you can set SHOWPLAN_TEXT to ON to cause SQL Server to return the estimated execution plans for the workload queries. Alternatively, you can set STATISTICS PROFILE before executing the queries in the workload, which will capture the actual execution plans. In addition, you can use SQL Profiler to trace the Execution Plan event class. The script in Listing 7-5 doesn't care how you obtain the query plans; it works with execution plans produced with any of these three alternatives.

I generally prefer using SQL Profiler because it gets the actual query plans as opposed to the estimated ones, and the query plans aren't buried deep in the resultsets, as in the case of setting STATISTICS PROFILE.

Creating a Chart of Query Operators

SCENARIO
You want to get an overview of how your tables are being accessed.

A while ago, one of my mainframe friends showed me a technique called *CRUD charting* that lists table columns against critical transactions. For each transaction, the chart highlights which operations—in terms of Create, Retrieve, Update, and Delete (or insert, select, update, and delete in SQL Server parlance)—will be applied to which table columns. At a glance, this type of chart gives useful information on how applications access the tables and their columns. Useful as it is, CRUD charting isn't regularly practiced in the SQL Server environment. It's too tedious and time consuming to create and maintain for any nontrivial application.

With the execution plans of the critical transactions captured by SQL Profiler, you can proceed to create similar charts for each table. But instead of identifying inserts, selects, updates, and deletes, you can go a step further to summarize the access patterns in terms of how specific query plan operators—such as Index Seek, Table Insert, Table Scan, and Clustered Index Seek—are applied to the tables. In a complex SQL Server database environment or in an environment that's new to the DBA, such a summary can help the DBA quickly identify the trouble spots and focus on areas with higher impact.

Without any further ado, let's plunge right into the Perl script opChart.pl in Listing 7-7 that scans the execution plans to create a chart of the query plan operators as applied to the tables.

Listing 7-7. Charting Query Plan Operators

```perl
use strict;
use Getopt::Std;
use Data::Dumper;

# get command-line parameters
my %opts;
getopts('tq:', \%opts);
my ($include_tempdb, $query_plan) = ($opts{t}, $opts{q});
printUsage() unless (-e $query_plan);

# exclude system tables from the chart. We are primarily interested in
# the user tables
my @systables = qw(
                sysprocesses sysjobservers sysxlogins
                sysobjects syscolumns syscomments
                sysindexes sysdepends sysreferences
                sysfiles sysfilegroups syspermissions
                sysprotects sysindexkeys sysforeignkeys
                sysallocations sysusers systypes
                sysservers sysdatabases sysjobhistory
                sysjobschedules sysjobsteps sysjobs
                syslanguages syslockinfo sysmembers
                backupfile backupmediaset
                backupmediafamily
                sysdbmaintplan_databases
                sysdbmaintplan_history );

my $objRef;
open(PLAN, "$query_plan") or
```

```perl
        die "***Err: couldn't open file $query_plan.";
while(<PLAN>) {
    if (m{^[\s|\d|\||]*(?:\|\-\-)?
              (\w[\s\w]+\w) \s* \(OBJECT:\((.+?)\)
          }ix) {
        my ($op, $obj) = ($1, $2);
        # remove the trailing appendix of a temp table name
        $obj =~ s/\[(\#\w+?)\_{4,}\w+\]/\[$1\]/g;
        # remove as [...]
        $obj =~ s/\s+AS\s+\[.+\]$//;
        # add [tempdb].[dbo] prefix, if not present
        if ($obj =~ /^\[\#.+\]$/) {
            $obj = '[tempdb].[dbo].' . $obj;
        }
        # skip system tables
        next if grep {$obj =~ /^\[.+\]\.\[.+\]\.\[$_\]/i} @systables;

        # decide whether to skip tempdb objects
        unless ($include_tempdb) {
            next if $obj =~ /^\[.+\]\.\[.+\]\.\[\#.+\]/;
        }
        if ($obj =~ /^(\[.+\]\.\[.+\]\.\[.+\])\.(\[.+\])$/) {
            $objRef->{$1}->{$2}->{$op}++;
        }
        else {
            $objRef->{$obj}->{$op}++;
        }
    }
}
close(PLAN);
print Dumper($objRef);


#################
sub printUsage {
    print << '--Usage--';
Usage:
    cmd>perl opChart.pl [ -t ] -q <Query plan log>
--Usage--
    exit;
} # printUsage
```

In addition to the parameter -q, the script also accepts the command-line switch -t, which instructs the script to include the temporary tables in the output.

Save the captured execution plans of the SQL workload from the application to a text file, queryPlans.log. Running the Perl script in Listing 7-7 as follows produces a chart of the query plan operators:

```
cmd>perl opChart.pl -q queryPlans.log
```

Listing 7-8 is a sample report from the script, printed using the Dumper() function from the Data::Dumper module. (The output has been slightly edited for readability.)

Listing 7-8. A Sample Chart of Query Plan Operators

```
$objRef = {
        '[Trade].[dbo].[Client]' => {
                'Table Scan'        => '9',
                '[Client_Index1]' => { 'Index Seek' => '170' },
                '[Client_Index2]' => { 'Index Seek' => '18' }
            },
        '[Trade].[dbo].[Portfolios]' => {
                'Table Update' => '33',
                'Table Scan'   => '667',
                'Table Insert' => '10',
                '[PKey]'       => { 'Index Seek' => '343' }
            },
        '[Trade].[dbo].[Account]' => {
                'Table Delete' => '1',
                'Table Update' => '2',
                'Table Scan'   => '2',
                'Table Insert' => '11'
                '[Account_Index1]' => { 'Index Scan' => '104' },
                '[Account_Index2]' => { 'Index Seek' => '114' },
                '[Account_Index3]' => { 'Index Seek' => '139' },
                '[Account_Index4]' => { 'Index Seek' => '284' },
            },
        '[Trade].[dbo].[ClientTrades]' => {
                'Table Delete' => '8',
                'Table Update' => '43',
                'Table Insert' => '20',
                '[tradeRef]'   => { 'Index Seek' => '9',
                                    'Index Scan' => '93'  },
                '[PKey]' => { 'Index Seek' => '273' }
            },
        '[Trade].[dbo].[CDC]' => { 'Table Update' => '66',
                                   'Table Scan'   => '330' }
};
```

Use the table `Trade.dbo.ClientTrades` as an example. For the given workload, the report in Listing 7-8 shows that the `UPDATE` statement is applied to the table 43 times, and the `DELETE` and `INSERT` statements are applied eight and 20 times, respectively. Of the two indexes used by the workload, the index `tradeRef` is used in Index Seek nine times and in Index Scan 93 times, and the index `PKey` is used 273 times exclusively to perform Index Seek.

This chart helps you focus on the potential problem areas. For instance, if the table `ClientTrades` is large, you may want to investigate whether the scan on the index `tradeRef`, which SQL Server performs 93 times in the workload, has any significant performance implication.

TIP *It's important to consider the table size—primarily the number of rows in each table—when analyzing the performance implications of a chart similar to that in Listing 7-8. For instance, you can see that the table [Trade].[dbo].[Portfolios] is table scanned 667 times, which appears to be a lot relative to the numbers in this particular workload. But if this turns out to be a small table, there's no reason to panic.*

The script in Listing 7-7 explicitly excludes the system tables from appearing in the final chart. For performance analysis, knowing how the system tables are being accessed doesn't really help you gain insight into your application. Hence, including the system tables serves no useful purpose other than cluttering the chart. You can remove the system tables with the following line of code:

```
next if grep {$obj =~ /^\[.+\]\.\[.+\]\.\[$_\]/i} @systables;
```

The array `@systables` is populated with the SQL Server system tables. The script makes no effort to add all the system tables to the array. If you find one that you want to prevent from showing up in the chart but that isn't already in the array, you can always add it to the array. Alternatively, to prevent any system from showing up in the chart, you can run the following T-SQL query in all the databases on your server and populate the `@systables` array with the union of their results:

```
SELECT name
  FROM sysobjects
 WHERE xtype = 'S'          -- system table
    OR (   OBJECTPROPERTY(id, 'IsMSShipped') = 1
       AND xtype = 'U')  -- Microsoft supplied user table
```

Temporary tables can also help muddy your analysis. But instead of choosing to exclude temporary tables altogether, you may find it useful in some cases to study how they're accessed. The script in Listing 7-7 accepts a -t switch on the command line. When this switch is present, temporary tables are included in the chart of the query plan operators.

> **NOTE** *I'll leave it to the reader as an exercise to modify the script so that the number of rows for each table is included in the chart. This would be a useful addition.*

Another improvement you may want to make is better presentation. The script in its current form uses the Dumper() function from the Data::Dumper module to print the final result. If you want to see the result in a real matrix format, you could export the data structure displayed in Listing 7-1 to a Comma-Separated Value (CSV) file and then import the CSV file into Excel.

As you can see, when scripting yourself, flexibility is one of the inherent advantages you have over using shrink-wrapped software.

Finding Updates on the Clustered Index Keys

SCENARIO
As part of a performance tuning exercise, you want to find out whether the columns in your clustered indexes are updated frequently.

When it comes to picking a column or columns for a clustered index, important advice to heed is to avoid columns whose values frequently change. Unlike other performance tuning advice, this isn't ambiguous; it's universally recommended.

Modifying the values of a column used by a clustered index forces SQL Server to move the rows so that the physical order is maintained. In addition, every time you modify the value of a column in the clustered index, all the non-clustered indexes on that table must also be modified, resulting in additional Input/Output (I/O).

So how do you find the updates on the key columns of your clustered indexes? And more important, how do you find how often a column in a clustered index is updated? If you have a SQL workload script, you can parse the script to find all the UPDATE statements and check whether a clustered index column happens to be modified in their SET clauses. But there's an easier way. You can again exploit the query execution plans from SQL Profiler, taking advantage of its well-formatted output to simplify your search.

The solution is to find, from the execution plans of a workload, all the columns that have been updated. Then you count how many times the columns have been updated and compare them with the columns used in the clustered indexes (which you can find in the database). This gives you the number of updates applied to each column of every clustered index in the database.

Listing 7-9 shows the Perl script updatedClusteredCol.pl to find all those insidious updates on the columns of the clustered indexes in a given database.

Listing 7-9. Finding the Updates on the Columns Used in the Clustered Indexes

```perl
use strict;
use Getopt::Std;
use Win32::ODBC;
use SQLDBA::Utility qw( dbaInSet );
use Data::Dumper;

# get command line parameters
my %opts;
getopts('S:d:q:', \%opts);
my ($server, $db, $queryPlan) = ($opts{S}, $opts{d}, $opts{q});
printUsage() unless (defined $server and defined $db and defined $queryPlan);

Main: {
   my $colUpdateRef = getUpdateInfo($db, $queryPlan);
   my $clusteredColRef = getClusteredColumns($server, $db);
   my $colRef = findUpdatedClusteredCol($colUpdateRef, $clusteredColRef);
   print Data::Dumper->Dump([$colRef], ['updatedClusteredCol']);
} # Main

#########################
sub findUpdatedClusteredCol {
   my ($colUpdateRef, $clusteredColRef) = @_;
   die "***Err: keepClusteredCol() expects two references."
        if !ref($colUpdateRef) || !ref($clusteredColRef);

   my $ref;
   foreach my $tb (keys %$colUpdateRef) {
      foreach my $col (keys %{$colUpdateRef->{$tb}}) {
         if (dbaInSet($col, $clusteredColRef->{$tb})) {
            $ref->{$tb}->{$col} = $colUpdateRef->{$tb}->{$col};
         }
      }
   }
   return $ref;
```

```perl
    } # findUpdatedClusteredCol


##############################
sub getUpdateInfo {
    my ($db, $queryPlan) = @_;
    die "***Err: getUpdateInfo() expects a database name and a file name."
        if !defined $db || !defined $queryPlan;

    $db = '[' . $db if $db !~ /^\[/;
    $db = $db . ']' if $db !~ /^\]/;
    $db = quotemeta($db);
    my $updateRef;
    open(PLAN, "$queryPlan") or die "***Err: could not open $queryPlan.";
    while(<PLAN>) {
        s/\s*\n$/\n/;
        if (/^[\s\|\-]* ([\w\s]+\s+Update)      # Update operator
                      \(OBJECT:\((.+?)\),     # Table name in (.+?)
                      \s*SET:\((.+)\)\)        # Updated column(s) in (.+)
           \s*$/ix) {
            my ($op, $table, $columns) = ($1, $2, $3);
            $columns =~ s/DEFINE:.+$//;
            $columns =~ s/WHERE:.+$//;
            my @columns = map {/(.+)=/; $1;} split /,\s*/, $columns;
            foreach my $col (@columns) {
                $col =~ s/^\[.+?\]\.//;
                if ($table =~ /^(\[.+?\])\.(\[.+?\]\.\[.+?\])/) {
                    my ($database, $tb) = ($1, $2);
                    next if $database !~ /^$db$/i;
                    $updateRef->{$tb}->{$col}->{$op}++;
                }
                else {
                    print "***Err: $table is not properly formed.\n";
                }
            }
        }
    }
    close(PLAN);
    return $updateRef;
} #getUpdateInfo


#########################
sub getClusteredColumns {
    my ($server, $db) = @_;
```

```perl
   my $updateRef;
   my $connStr = "Driver={SQL Server};Server=$server;" .
                          "Database=$db;Trusted_Connection=yes";
   my $conn = new Win32::ODBC($connStr) or
                  die "***Err: " . Win32::ODBC::Error();


  my $sql =<< "__SQL__";
   SELECT QUOTENAME(USER_NAME(OBJECTPROPERTY(id, 'OwnerId'))) + '.' +
          QUOTENAME(OBJECT_NAME(id)) as 'tb_name',
          QUOTENAME(COL_NAME(id, colid)) as 'column_name'
      FROM sysindexkeys
     WHERE indid = 1
       AND ObjectProperty(id, 'IsUserTable') = 1
       AND ObjectProperty(id, 'TableHasClustIndex') = 1
   ORDER BY object_name(id), col_name(id, colid)
__SQL__

   if (! $conn->Sql($sql) ) {
      while ($conn->FetchRow()) {
          my %data = $conn->DataHash();
          push @{$updateRef->{$data{'tb_name'}}}, $data{'column_name'};
      }
   }
   else {
      die Win32::ODBC::Error();
   }
   $conn->Close();
   return $updateRef;
} # getClusteredColumns


####################
sub printUsage {
   print << '--Usage--';
Usage:
   cmd>perl updatedClusteredCol.pl -S <SQL Server instance>
                                   -d <database name>
                                   -q <Query plan log>
--Usage--
   exit;
} # printUsage
```

The updatedClusteredCol.pl script in Listing 7-9 accepts three command-line arguments: a SQL Server name following -S, a database name after -d, and a filename after -q. The file is expected to contain the query execution plans for the workload.

To find the updated columns, you need to look for these operators in an execution plan:

- Table Update

- Index Update

- Clustered Index Update

Once you find an update operator, you'll find the columns in its SET clause. A typical update operator in an execution plan looks like the following on one line (the following has been edited for readability):

```
|--Clustered Index Update(OBJECT:([pubs].[dbo].[authors].[UPKCL_auidind]),
                    SET:([authors].[au_id]=RaiseIfNull([Expr04])),
                    DEFINE:([Expr04]=Convert([@1])),
                    WHERE:([authors].[au_id]=[@2]))
```

There could be multiple entries in the SET clause for updating multiple columns. The Perl code fragment to capture the updated columns is as follows:

```
if (/^[\s\|\-]* ([\w\s]+\s+Update)      # Update operator
                \(OBJECT:\((.+?)\),     # Table name in (.+?)
                \s*SET:\((.+)\)\)\)     # Updated column(s) in (.+)
    \s*$/ix) {
  my ($op, $table, $columns) = ($1, $2, $3);
  $columns =~ s/DEFINE:.+$//;
  $columns =~ s/WHERE:.+$//;
  my @columns = map {/(.+)=/; $1;} split /,\s*/, $columns;
```

The regular expression in the test expression of the if statement is at the heart of the function getUpdateInfo(), which reads the execution plan and returns a reference to a hash record that has the number of updates for each updated column. The third pair of parentheses captures the names of the columns in the SET clause of an UPDATE statement. Note how the column names are singled out using a split() followed by a map().

The `getClusteredColumns()` function retrieves the columns of the clustered indexes for all the user tables in the database. The following SQL query retrieves the columns of the clustered indexes:

```
SELECT QUOTENAME(USER_NAME(OBJECTPROPERTY(id, 'OwnerId'))) + '.' +
       QUOTENAME(OBJECT_NAME(id)) as 'tb_name',
       QUOTENAME(COL_NAME(id, colid)) as 'column_name'
  FROM sysindexkeys
 WHERE indid = 1
   AND OBJECTPROPERTY(id, 'IsUserTable') = 1
   AND OBJECTPROPERTY(id, 'TableHasClustIndex') = 1
ORDER BY OBJECT_NAME(id), COL_NAME(id, colid)
```

With the information on both the updated columns and the columns used in the clustered indexes, the script is ready to check whether a clustered index column is updated and how many times it's updated. The function `findUpdatedClusteredCol()` in Listing 7-9 accomplished this.

Assuming that you already have the query execution plans for a workload on the `pubs` database in the file `queryPlans.log`, you can run the script as follows to produce a report highlighting the updated columns of the clustered indexes in the database:

```
cmd>perl updatedClusteredCol.pl -S NYSQL01 -d pubs -q queryPlans.log
$updatedClusteredCol = {
            '[dbo].[publishers]' => {
                    '[pub_id]' => { 'Clustered Index Update' => '54' }
                },
            '[dbo].[authors]' => {
                    '[au_id]' => { 'Clustered Index Update' => '31' }
                }
};
```

The report shows that for the given workload, the `pub_id` column in the `publishers` table is updated 54 times, and the `au_id` column in the `authors` table is updated 31 times. Each of these two columns is part of the key of their respective clustered indexes. It's then up to the DBA to assess the performance impact of these updates.

Checking Stored Procedures for Violations of Coding Best Practices

> **SCENARIO**
> *Reviewing stored procedure scripts for violations of coding best practices is a repetitive and tedious task. You want to automate this task as much as possible.*

Although each locale may have its own T-SQL coding standards, there's a solid consensus on a common set of best practices, some of which follow:

Explicitly identify the database at the beginning of each script file: There should be a USE <database> statement at the beginning of a stored procedure script to identify in which database this stored procedure is created.

Use only ANSI outer join syntax: Don't use the old style of outer joins that's either =* or *= in the WHERE clause. Instead, use LEFT OUTER JOIN or RIGHT OUTER JOIN in the FROM clause.

Don't use SELECT * to return a resultset that will be either inserted into another table or returned to the client: Not explicitly specifying the columns can easily lead to a broken application when the table schema changes.

Owner-qualify a stored procedure when executing it: This helps SQL Server resolve the procedure name and find a cached execution plan quickly, thus improving performance.

Don't prefix a user stored procedure name with sp_: This prefix leads SQL Server to try to resolve the name with the special rules for the system procedures, resulting in wasted effort.

Don't interleave DDL and DML: Mixing the DML statements (SELECT, DELETE, INSERT, and UPDATE) with the DDL statements (CREATE TABLE, ALTER TABLE, DROP TABLE, CREATE INDEX, and so on) forces the SQL Server query optimizer to recompile the stored procedure at runtime, thus degrading performance.

Create one stored procedure per file: Storing multiple stored procedures in one script file makes code management a nightmare.

Use dynamic SQL sparingly: Dynamic SQL queries in a production environment introduce a host of security and performance issues.

This isn't an exhaustive list of the best practices for coding SQL Server stored procedures. Instead of trying to be comprehensive on the coding best practices, this section uses the best practices previously mentioned as a starting point for creating a Perl script that you can use as a generic framework to accommodate other coding best practices.

Beware that although the script in Listing 7-10 may look lengthy, its structure is rather straightforward. The bulk of the code is in the function reviewTSQL(), which contains regular expressions corresponding to the best practices listed previously.

Listing 7-10. Checking Stored Procedures for Coding Best Practice Violations

```
use strict;
use SQLDBA::ParseSQL qw( dbaNormalizeSQL dbaSplitBatch );

Main: {
    my $dir = shift or die "***Err: $0 expects a directory name.";
    (-d $dir) or die "***Err: directory $dir does not exist.";

    # read the filenames in the directory
    opendir(DIR, $dir) or die "could not open $dir.\n";
    my @fileNames = map { "$dir\\$_" } grep {!/^\.\.?/} readdir(DIR);
    closedir(DIR);

    my $counterRef;
    # now work on each file
    print "\nPerforming T-SQL stored procedure review ...\n";
    foreach my $sqlFile (sort @fileNames) {
        # read T-SQL script into a string
        my $sql;
        open(SQL, "$sqlFile") or die "***Err: couldn't open $sqlFile for read.";
        read(SQL, $sql, -s SQL);
        close(SQL);

        # replace comments, strings, and delimited identifiers
        # with unique string tokens
        my $sqlRef = dbaNormalizeSQL($sql, 1);
        next unless $sqlRef;

        # split the SQL code into batches by batch separator GO
        $sqlRef->{code} = dbaSplitBatch($sqlRef->{code});

        # review the batches
        my $reviewRef = reviewTSQL($sqlRef);

        # print the review for this T-SQL script file
        printReview($reviewRef, $sqlRef, $sqlFile);
```

```
        # update global counters
        $counterRef = updateGlobalCounters($reviewRef, $counterRef);
    }
    # print out the global counters
    printGlobalCounters($counterRef);
} # Main


##################
sub reviewTSQL {
    my ($sqlRef) = shift;
    my $reviewRef = { DynamicSQL => 0 }; # initialize dynamic SQL counter to 0

    # Standard: Use <db>
    foreach my $batch (@{$sqlRef->{code}}) { # loop through all the batches
        next if $batch =~ /^\s*\-\-.+$/;       # skip comments-only batch
        if ($batch !~ /^\s*use\s+\w+/is) {     # gripe if the next batch is not USE
            push @{$reviewRef->{comments}}, 'No explicit USE <DB>';
        }
        last;
    }


    # Standard: Use ANSI OUTER JOIN
    foreach my $batch (@{$sqlRef->{code}}) {  # loop through all the batches
        if ($batch =~ /(=\*|\*=)/) {           # found an older outer join
            push @{$reviewRef->{comments}},
                'Old style non-ANSI outer join syntax used';
            last;
        }
    }


    # Standard: Do not use SELECT * to generate rowset
    foreach my $batch (@{$sqlRef->{code}}) { # loop through every batch to check
        while ($batch =~ /SELECT\s*\*/ig) {   # only interested in SELECT *
            if ($` !~ /EXISTS\s*\(\s*$/i) {    # not in an EXISTS ( )
                push @{$reviewRef->{comments}}, # found the bad SELECT *
                    'SELECT * to generate rowset';
                last;
            }
        }
    }


    # Standard: Use dynamic SQL sparingly
    foreach my $batch (@{$sqlRef->{code}}) {           # loop thru all the batches
```

```
        if ($batch =~ /(?<![\w\@\#\$])               # negative lookbehind
                       ( EXEC(UTE)?\s+\(     |  # three ways to dynamic SQL
                         sp\_executesql\s+   |
                         sp\_sqlexec\s+
                       )
                /ix) {
    push @{$reviewRef->{comments}}, 'Dynamic SQL used';
    my $sql = $batch;
    ++$reviewRef->{DynamicSQL}                    # update dynamic SQL counter
        while $sql =~ / (?<![\w\@\#\$])            # the same pattern
                       ( EXEC(UTE)?\s+\(    |
                         sp\_executesql\s+  |
                         sp\_sqlexec\s+
                       )
                /ixg;    # /g for as many times as it matches
    }
}


# Standard: Owner-qualify a stored procedure when executing it
foreach my $batch (@{$sqlRef->{code}}) {  # loop through all the batches
    if ($batch =~ /(?<![\w\@\#\$])         # negative lookbehind
                    EXEC(UTE)?\s+          # EXEC(UTE)
                    (\@.+?=\s*)?           # optional return variable
                    ([^(\s]+)              # SP name
                /ix) {
    my $proc = $3;
    unless ($proc =~ /([^.]+\.)?
                       [^.]+\.[^.]+  # unless it's owner qualified
                    /x) {
        push @{$reviewRef->{comments}},
             "Stored proc $3 called without explicit owner";
        next;
    }
  }
}


# Standard: Do not prefix the stored procedure name with sp_
foreach my $batch (@{$sqlRef->{code}}) {
    if ($batch =~ /CREATE\s+PROC(EDURE)?\s+(\w+\.sp\_|sp\_)/i) {
    push @{$reviewRef->{comments}},
         'Stored proc name prefixed with sp_';
    last;
  }
}
```

```
# Standard: Do not interleave DDL and DML
foreach my $batch (@{$sqlRef->{code}}) {
    if ($batch =~ /(?<![\w\@\#\$])   # only interested in CREATE PRC batch
                       CREATE\s+PROC(EDURE)?\s+([^\s]+)
                     /ix) {
        my $proc = $2;
        while ($batch =~ /(?<![\w\@\#\$])                 # found a DDL
                          (  CREATE\s+TABLE   |
                             ALTER\s+TABLE    |
                             CREATE\s+INDEX   |
                             DROP\s+TABLE     |
                             DROP\s+INDEX     |
                             UPDATE\s+STATISTICS )
                       /ixg) {
            my $pre = $`;                       # string before the DDL
            my $post = $';                      # string after the DDL
            if (($pre =~ /(?<![\w\@\#\$])        # found a DML in the before
                         ( SELECT\s+(?!\@) |
                           INSERT\s        |
                           DELETE\s        |
                           UPDATE\s )
                       /ix) and
               ($post =~ /(?<![\w\@\#\$])            # found a DML in the after
                         ( SELECT\s+(?!\@) |
                           INSERT\s        |
                           DELETE\s        |
                           UPDATE\s )
                       /ix)) {
                push @{$reviewRef->{comments}},
                    "DDL interleaved with DML in $proc";
            }
        }
    }
}

# Standard: Create one stored procedure per file
my $procFile = 0;
foreach my $batch (@{$sqlRef->{code}}) {
    if ($batch =~ /(?<![\w\@\#\$])
                      CREATE\s+PROC(EDURE)?
                /ix and $procFile++) { # $procFile is 1 the second time
        push @{$reviewRef->{comments}},
            "Multiple stored proc created in this file";
```

```perl
            last;
        }
    }
    return $reviewRef;
} # reviewTSQL


###################
sub printReview {
    my ($reviewRef, $sqlRef, $sqlFile) = @_;

    print "\nScript: $sqlFile\n";
    my $i = 0;
    my %seen;
    foreach my $commentWithToken (@{$reviewRef->{comments}}) {
        my $comment = restoreIdentifier($commentWithToken, $sqlRef);
        print "\t ", ++$i, ". $comment\n" unless $seen{$comment};
        $seen{$comment}++;
    }
} # printReview


#########################
sub updateGlobalCounters {
    my ($reviewRef, $counterRef) = @_;

    $counterRef->{DynamicSQL} += $reviewRef->{DynamicSQL};
    ++$counterRef->{FilesReviewed};
    return $counterRef;
} # updateGlobalCounters


######################
sub printGlobalCounters {
    my $counterRef = shift;

    printf "\n%s\n", "Overall stats in all scripts:";
    printf "\t%-21s %s\n", "# of script files reviewed:",
                                  $counterRef->{FilesReviewed};
    printf "\t%-21s %s\n", "# of Dynamic SQL:", $counterRef->{DynamicSQL};
} # printGlobalCounters


#####################
sub restoreIdentifier {
    my ($comment, $sqlRef) = @_;

    foreach my $id (keys %{$sqlRef->{double_ids}}) {
```

365

```
        $comment =~ s/$id/\"$sqlRef->{double_ids}->{$id}\"/i;
    }
    foreach my $id (keys %{$sqlRef->{bracket_ids}}) {
        $comment =~ s/$id/\[$sqlRef->{bracket_ids}->{$id}\]/i;
    }
    return $comment;
} # restoreIdentifier
```

Before examining the code in Listing 7-10, let's apply it to two simple T-SQL scripts to get a better feel for what the Perl script may find. Listing 7-11 and Listing 7-12 show the two T-SQL scripts (which are poorly coded on purpose).

Listing 7-11. Poorly Coded T-SQL Script in getAuthorInfo.SQL

```
USE pubs
GO
CREATE PROC dbo.[getAuthorInfo]
    @id  varchar(20)
AS
  SET NOCOUNT ON

  EXEC updateID @id

  SELECT * FROM "authors" WITH (HOLDLOCK)
   WHERE au_id = @id
  OPTION (MAXDOP 3)
GO
```

Listing 7-12. Poorly Coded T-SQL Script in Proc1and2.SQL

```
IF EXISTS (SELECT * FROM dbo.sysobjects
            WHERE id = object_id('dbo.sp_proc1'))
    DROP PROCEDURE dbo.sp_reptq1
GO

CREATE PROC sp_proc1
AS
  INSERT employees
  SELECT t1.lname, t2.salary
    FROM fte t1 HASH JOIN salary t2
        on t1.eid=t2.eid
  OPTION (fast 3)

  CREATE TABLE #tmp (a int)
```

```
   IF EXISTS (SELECT * FROM abc)
      INSERT #tmp(a) EXECUTE ('select 1')

   SELECT c1
      FROM authors t1, (SELECT * FROM titleauthor
                          WHERE au_id like '010%') t2
     WHERE t1.au_id = t2.au_id
GO


CREATE PROC proc2
AS
   SET NOCOUNT ON
   SELECT @@version
GO
```

Place these two T-SQL script files in a subdirectory named appSP under the current directory, and run the Perl script in Listing 7-10 as follows:

```
cmd>perl reviewSP.pl .\appSP
Performing T-SQL stored procedure review ...

Script: .\appSP\Proc1and2.PRC
      1. No explicit USE <DB>
      2. SELECT * to generate rowset
      3. Dynamic SQL used
      4. Stored proc name prefixed with sp_
      5. NOCOUNT not set at the beginning of sp_proc1
      6. DDL interleaved with DML in sp_proc1
      7. Multiple stored proc created in this file

Script: .\appSP\getAuthorInfo.SQL
      1. SELECT * to generate rowset
      2. Stored proc updateID called without explicit owner

Overall stats in all scripts:
      # of script files reviewed: 2
      # of Dynamic SQL:       1
```

This example is almost trivial. But as you can see, if you have a large number of stored procedures to review or if you have to review stored procedures on a regular basis, this Perl script can quickly highlight the areas where the coding best practices are violated. You can then focus your attention on areas that require more in-depth analysis, on areas that require more knowledge and experience, and on areas where improvement can have a much higher impact.

For instance, instead of checking for these best practice violations, you could better spend your time on studying the design of the queries and indexes and on evaluating whether using a cursor is warranted.

Now, turn to the Perl script in Listing 7-10 itself. At the top level—the code within the Main: { … } block, the script loops through each T-SQL script file in the directory identified on the command line. For each T-SQL file, the Perl script first applies the function dbaNormalizeSQL() from the module SQLDBA::ParseSQL to replace the comments, the quoted strings, and the delimited identifiers in the T-SQL script with the unique token strings. This is necessary because you'll apply regular expressions to find T-SQL code patterns that aren't consistent with the best practices, and the T-SQL comments, the quoted strings, and the delimited identifiers may confuse the regular expressions. Consider the case where a pattern you're looking for happens to be inside a comment. For more information on dbaNormalizeSQL(), see Chapter 3, "Working with Commonly Used Perl Routines."

The next step is to split the T-SQL file into batches by the batch separator GO. You do this with the function dbaSplitBatch(), which is also from the module SQLDBA::ParseSQL. Note that the individual batches that have been split are stored in an array to preserve the order of the batches. This is important because some best practices are concerned with the ordering of the batches. For instance, you typically want to see the USE <DB> statement at the beginning of a T-SQL script that defines a stored procedure.

The reviewTSQL() function performs the actual check for the best practice violations. The function consists of a collection of code fragments, each checking a particular best practice standard. Let's look at three examples: checking for the use of SELECT *, checking for the use of dynamic SQL, and checking for the interleaving of DDL and DML statements.

Checking for SELECT *

Finding a poor use of SELECT * requires slightly more effort than looking for the string SELECT * in a T-SQL script because it's perfectly fine to use it in an existence test such as EXISTS (SELECT * FROM myTable). The code fragment from Listing 7-10 for checking this standard is as follows:

```
# Standard: Do not use SELECT * to generate rowset
foreach my $batch (@{$sqlRef->{code}}) {   # loop through every batch to check
    while ($batch =~ /SELECT\s*\*/ig) {     # only interested in SELECT *
        if ($` !~ /EXISTS\s*\(\s*$/i) {     # not in an EXISTS ( )
            push @{$reviewRef->{comments}},  # found the bad SELECT *
                'SELECT * to generate rowset';
```

```
        last;
    }
  }
}
```

Note that `$sqlRef->{code}` is a reference to an array of strings, each of which corresponds to a batch in the T-SQL script file currently being reviewed. To make sure that `SELECT *` isn't used inside a T-SQL `EXISTS` test, the string that immediately precedes `SELECT *` is checked as follows:

```
$` !~ /EXISTS\s*\(\s*$/I
```

Recall that the predefined special variable `$`` captures the string immediately preceding what's matched by the most recently completed regular expression evaluation.

If a coding standard is violated, a comment string is pushed as a new element into the array referenced by `$reviewRef->{comments}`. Upon completion, the script produces the final report by dumping out these comment strings.

Checking for Dynamic SQL

The coding best practices call for sparing use of dynamic SQL queries. But you can't really script what *sparing* might mean. Instead of trying to be smart, the Perl script in Listing 7-10 simply counts the number of times a dynamic SQL query is used in the T-SQL scripts and leaves the interpretation to the DBA. Again, as shown in the following code fragment reproduced from Listing 7-10, finding a dynamic SQL query in a T-SQL script is more than searching for the string `EXECUTE`:

```
# Standard: Use dynamic SQL sparingly
foreach my $batch (@{$sqlRef->{code}}) {       # loop through all the batches
    if ($batch =~ /(?<![\w\@\#\$])            # negative lookbehind
                    ( EXEC(UTE)?\s+\(    | # three ways to run dynamic SQL
                      sp\_executesql\s+ |
                      sp\_sqlexec\s+
                    )
                 /ix) {
        push @{$reviewRef->{comments}}, 'Dynamic SQL used';
        my $sql = $batch;
        ++$reviewRef->{DynamicSQL}              # update dynamic SQL counter
            while $sql =~ / (?<![\w\@\#\$])             # the same pattern
                            ( EXEC(UTE)?\s+\(   |
                              sp\_executesql\s+ |
```

```
                                    sp\_sqlexec\s+
                        )
              /ixg;      # /g for as many times as it matches
      }
}
```

Note the use of so-called negative lookbehind in the somewhat odd-looking syntax form of (?<!PATTERN). This helps ensure that EXECUTE is really the T-SQL reserved word and not part of another identifier. Without the negative lookbehind, the regular expression would have matched the string EXECUTE in INSERT #EXECUTE (elname) or INSERT #sp_execute (elname), both of which are harmless albeit not good naming practice.

Checking for Interleaved DDL and DML Statements

This is trickier than the previous two standards. First, you need to be more precise about what it means to interleave DDL and DML statements. This section covers the case where there exists a DDL statement, before which you can find a DML and after which you can find another DML. This means you must check all the DDL statements in the stored procedure.

Second, because regular expressions will be the tool to identify the DDL and DML statements, you must avoid mistaking a partial word for a T-SQL reserved word. For instance, DECLARE @SELECT int shouldn't lead your search patterns to conclude that you've found a SELECT statement. This may sound silly, but this is one of the professional hazards of working with Perl regular expressions. Even the experienced sometimes trip over these little things and end up with something entirely unexpected.

The following is the code fragment, from Listing 7-10, that checks for interleaved DDL and DML statements:

```
# Standard: Do not interleave DDL and DML
foreach my $batch (@{$sqlRef->{code}}) {
   if ($batch =~ /(?<![\w\@\#\$])     # only interested in CREATE PRC batch
                   # make sure we are in an SP batch
                   CREATE\s+PROC(EDURE)?\s+([^\s]+)
                /ix) {
      my $proc = $2;
      # first find DDL
```

```
      while ($batch =~ /(?<![\w\@\#\$])          # found a DDL
                        (  CREATE\s+TABLE  |
                           ALTER\s+TABLE   |
                           CREATE\s+INDEX  |
                           DROP\s+TABLE    |
                           DROP\s+INDEX    |
                           UPDATE\s+STATISTICS )
                  /ixg) {
        my $pre = $`;        # string before the DDL
        my $post = $';       # string after the DDL
        # now find DML that comes before
        if (($pre =~ /(?<![\w\@\#\$])          # found a DML in the before
                      ( SELECT\s+(?!\@) |
                        INSERT\s        |
                        DELETE\s        |
                        UPDATE\s )
                /ix) and
          # and find DML that comes afterwards
          ($post =~ /(?<![\w\@\#\$])          # found a DML in the after
                      ( SELECT\s+(?!\@) |
                        INSERT\s        |
                        DELETE\s        |
                        UPDATE\s )
                /ix)) {
          push @{$reviewRef->{comments}},
              "DDL interleaved with DML in $proc";
    }
   }
  }
}
```

Note how the script takes advantage of the /g modifier in scalar context to find all the matches of a DDL statement and iterate through each of them in a while loop. For each matched DDL, the script checks the code before it and the code after it for any DML statement. If there's a DML statement both before and after the DDL statement, it's found a case of interleaving DDL and DML statements.

The next section details how you can check for other coding standard violations by adding Perl code fragments to the reviewTSQL() function in Listing 7-10.

Checking for More Coding Standard Violations

> **SCENARIO**
> *You want to check the coding standards that aren't included in the Perl script discussed in the previous section.*

As mentioned in the "Checking Stored Procedures for Violations of Coding Best Practices" section, you don't want to create a Perl script just for a fixed set of T-SQL coding standards. The return may not be enough to justify the investment in the programming effort. Rather, the goal is to create a Perl script that also serves as a generic framework that can be easily adapted to check for the violation of other coding standards.

Using the following two coding standards as the examples, this section illustrates how you can adapt the script in Listing 7-10 to accommodate more coding standards.

Include SET NOCOUNT ON at the beginning of a stored procedure: This cuts down on the unnecessary traffic communicating each affected row count to the client.

Create each stored procedure with ANSI_NULLS and QUOTED_IDENTIFIER set to ON: These options are sticky; they stay with the stored procedure. In other words, they are saved and used for subsequent invocations of the stored procedure.

With the Perl script in Listing 7-10, you can check each best practice violation by adding a code fragment in the function reviewTSQL() to scan for its corresponding text pattern. If the code finds a violation, the code fragment adds an appropriate review comment to the comment array referenced by $reviewRef->{comments}.

In terms of text patterns, the T-SQL coding standards you've seen so far fall into two categories: ones that can be verified with regular expressions applying to a T-SQL batch and ones that are about the relationships among the batches. You'll now see examples from each category.

Checking for SET NOCOUNT ON

Finding SET NOCOUNT ON, or the lack of it, is easy. Checking whether it's specified at the beginning of the stored procedure takes a bit more effort. To programmatically perform the checking, you must be precise about what it means for SET NOCOUNT ON to be at the beginning of a stored procedure.

Because you want to prevent SQL Server from sending the client application messages indicating the number of rows affected by a T-SQL statement as part of the results, SET NOCOUNT ON needs to come before any T-SQL statement that may return results. SELECT, INSERT, UPDATE, and DELETE are such T-SQL statements. Other T-SQL statements may also return row counts, but these are the most common ones.

The following code fragment first checks whether SET NOCOUNT ON isn't set at all in the stored procedure. If it's there, the code then checks whether any SELECT, INSERT, DELETE, and UPDATE statement exists in the preceding T-SQL code:

```
# Standard: SET NOCOUNT ON at the beginning of a proc
foreach my $batch (@{$sqlRef->{code}}) {
    if ($batch =~ /CREATE\s+PROC(EDURE)?\s+([^\s]+)/i) {
        my $proc = $2;
        if ($batch !~ /CREATE\s+PROC(EDURE)?\s+[^\s]+
                        (.+)?
                        AS\s+
                        (.+)
                        SET\s+NOCOUNT\s+ON/isx) {  # if not found at all
            push @{$reviewRef->{comments}},
                "NOCOUNT not set at the beginning of $proc";
        }
        else {   # if found, check what comes before it
            my $code = $3;
            if ($code =~ /(?<![\w\@\#\$])  # if any of these comes before, gripe
                        ( SELECT\s+(?!\@) |
                          INSERT\s        |
                          DELETE\s        |
                          UPDATE\s
                        )
                       /ix) {
                push @{$reviewRef->{comments}},
                    "NOCOUNT not set at the beginning of $proc";
            }
        }
    }
}
```

Plug this code fragment into the reviewTSQL() function, and the Perl script in Listing 7-10 is ready to flag any stored procedure that doesn't have this important T-SQL setting turned on before any data is retrieved or manipulated.

Checking for ANSI_NULLS and QUOTED_IDENTIFIER Settings

This best practice requires you to look at the settings of these two options when the stored procedure is created. The fact that the order of the batches is preserved when they're split with the function dbaSplitBatch() makes it simple to find these settings preceding the creation of a stored procedure.

   If they're not set at all, you can consider them to be off. With that as the default, you start with the first batch and move through all the batches sequentially. Recall that the script in Listing 7-10 records these batches in an array. For each batch, look for SET ANSI_NULLS and SET QUOTED_IDENTIFIER and remember only the latest setting for each option. Well, you can just keep writing to the same variables, $ansi_nulls and $quoted_identifier. This ensures that only the latest setting is kept. When you reach CREATE PROCEDURE, you then check whether both options are set to ON. The following is the code fragment implementing this method:

```
# Standard: Create SP with ANSI_NULLS and QUOTED_IDENTIFIER set ON
my $ansi_nulls = 'off';          # default to off
my $quoted_identifier = 'off';   # default to off
foreach my $batch (@{$sqlRef->{code}}) {
   if ($batch =~ /SET\s+ANSI\_NULLS\s+ON/i) {
      $ansi_nulls = 'on';          # set to on
   }
   if ($batch =~ /SET\s+QUOTED\_IDENTIFIER\s+ON/i) {
      $quoted_identifier = 'on';   # set to on
   }

   if ($batch =~ /(?<![\w\@\#\$])   # it's a CREATE PRC batch
                    CREATE\s+PROC(EDURE)?\s+([^\s]+)
               /ix) {
      my $proc = $2;
      if ($ansi_nulls ne 'on') {     # ansi_nulls shouldn't be off by now
           push @{$reviewRef->{comments}},
              "ANSI_NULLS not set before $proc";
      }
      if ($quoted_identifier ne 'on') {  # quoted_id shouldn't be off by now
           push @{$reviewRef->{comments}},
              "QUOTED_IDENTIFIER not set before $proc";
      }
   }
}
```

Again, all that's left is to plug this code fragment into the function reviewTSQL() in Listing 7-10 and start checking stored procedures for not setting these options properly.

These two examples plus the coding standards discussed in the "Checking Stored Procedures for Violations of Coding Best Practices" section should make you comfortable with adding code fragments to check for the violation of any coding standards as long as they can be searched with regular expressions. Your imagination is the only limit on what you can check!

Summary

If you have copious SQL code to analyze, you need good tools to help you out—beyond what Query Analyzer, the Index Tuning Wizard, and SQL Profiler may already provide. Unfortunately, good tools for SQL code analysis are hard to come by.

This chapter exploited Perl's awesome text processing power and its flexible data structures to facilitate SQL code analysis. The Perl scripts presented in this chapter take either query execution plans or SQL scripts as input and extract useful information from them to help performance tuning or compliance with the coding best practices.

Like most other chapters in this book, it has only touched the tip of the iceberg that is SQL code analysis. But the techniques illustrated in the Perl scripts should go a long way toward analyzing SQL code in a variety of scenarios.

The next chapter explores how Perl can help you generate useful T-SQL code.

Generating SQL Code

IF YOU AREN'T STRICTLY A point-and-click SQL Server Database Administrator (DBA), then you've probably practiced the art of generating SQL code. You've probably tried to do something such as this from within Query Analyzer:

```
SELECT -'KILL ' + CONVERT(varchar(10), spid)
  FROM  master..sysprocesses
 WHERE dbid = DB_ID('pubs')
```

This SELECT statement produces zero or more Transact-SQL (T-SQL) KILL statements to terminate any user process that has pubs as its current database. And you've probably run the following query numerous times to generate GRANT statements that give EXECUTE permission on all the stored procedures in the current database to the app_users role:

```
SELECT 'GRANT EXECUTE on ' + name + ' to app_users'
  FROM sysobjects
 WHERE type = 'P'
```

Some DBAs have mastered SQL code generation and can produce complex SQL code using only T-SQL. To some extent, the ability to generate effective SQL code is a strong indicator of the sophistication of a DBA because it requires a solid understanding of both SQL Server and T-SQL and, even more important, a firm grasp of the SQL Server system tables and views.

Nevertheless, as you begin to explore SQL code generation, you'll soon realize that although you can use SQL to generate many interesting and useful SQL scripts out of data already stored in SQL Server tables and views (including the system tables), SQL can be limiting at times. Generating SQL code goes far beyond what you can accomplish with the data in relational tables.

SQL Server 2000 offers several Graphic User Interface (GUI) tools for generating SQL scripts. Two important scripting tools are the Generate SQL Scripts task from the Enterprise Manager and the scripting features of the Object Browser tool in SQL Query Analyzer. These tools allow you to script various objects and their properties in a database via simple point and click. When you have an ad-hoc scripting requirement, these GUI tools can be your best friends. However, GUI tools aren't the right choice if you need to perform a scripting task repeatedly or in an unattended manner. Furthermore, for many scripting requirements, you simply can't find a GUI tool.

Sometimes, you may need to generate SQL code using the information specified in a configuration file or a SQL template. Other times, given some SQL scripts, you may want to generate additional SQL code. This can be as simple as adding a piece of code to a SQL script, merging multiple SQL scripts into a single file, or splitting a SQL script into many smaller scripts. And it can be more complex and require parsing and transforming the existing SQL scripts.

This chapter is about using Perl to help generate SQL code. You'll get a taste of a diverse array of code generation scenarios. It begins with a simple case of generating a database creation script with the information read from a configuration file, and it then proceeds to generate SQL code for data conversion. Next, it covers Perl scripts that modify existing T-SQL scripts to emit new T-SQL scripts. The chapter ends with several examples of generating SQL scripts using SQL Distributed Management Objects (SQL-DMO).

Generating SQL from Configuration Options

SCENARIO
Your application needs to create a database. But you don't want to hard-code any of the key parameters such as the database name and data files. You want to read them from a configuration file and then generate the code accordingly.

This scenario is slightly more involved than preparing a CREATE DATABASE statement. You want to make sure that if the database already exists, it's first dropped. After you've created the database, you need to set the appropriate database options.

Examine several database creation scripts, and you'll discover that although the database name, the filenames, and the file locations may change, the bulk of the SQL code doesn't change. Therefore, you can put it in a SQL *template*—a block of SQL code that may contain placeholders.

But how do you deal with the components that do change? Although a straightforward search-and-replace approach may be sufficient to plug in the database name, it falls short when there's a need to accommodate a varying number of data files or log files in the CREATE DATABASE statement.

The Perl script in Listing 8-1 (generateDB.pl) reads the database name, the complete data file paths, and the complete log file paths from a configuration file. The script then constructs a CREATE DATABASE statement and plugs it into a SQL template that includes additional code for preparation and cleanup.

Listing 8-1. Generating a Database Creation Script from Options in a Configuration File

```perl
use strict;
use SQLDBA::Utility qw( dbaReadINI );

my $configFile = shift or
    die "***Err: generateDB.pl expects a config file.";
Main: {
   my $configRef = dbaReadINI($configFile);  # read the INI file
   # DB options are specified in the CONTROL section
   generateCreateDB($configRef->{CONTROL});
} # Main


#######################
sub generateCreateDB {
   my $cRef = shift or
      die "***Err: generateCreateDB() expects a reference.";

   # get the database and filenames
   my $db = $cRef->{DB};
   # data/log files are comma/semi-colon separated
   my @dataFiles = split /\s*[,;]\s*/, $cRef->{DATAFILE};
   my @logFiles = split /\s*[,;]\s*/, $cRef->{LOGFILE};
   # get the file sizes by evenly dividing the size among the files
   my ($dataFileSize, $logFileSize) =
                  ( int($cRef->{DATASIZE}/scalar(@dataFiles)),
                    int($cRef->{LOGSIZE}/scalar(@logFiles)));

   my $createDB = "CREATE DATABASE $db\n   ON PRIMARY";
   my $i = 0;
   # generate the data file specs
   foreach my $dataFile (@dataFiles) {
      $createDB .= ( (++$i-1) ? ',' : ' ' ) . "
           ( NAME=\'$db\_dat$i\',
             FILENAME=\'$dataFile\',
             SIZE=$dataFileSize,
             FILEGROWTH=0)";  # you may set it to a different value
   }
   $createDB .= "\n   LOG ON";
   $i = 0;
   # generate the log file specs
   foreach my $logFile (@logFiles) {
      $createDB .= ( (++$i-1) ? ',' : ' ' ) . "
```

```perl
            ( NAME = \'$db\_log$i\',
              FILENAME = \'$logFile\',
              SIZE = $logFileSize,
              FILEGROWTH=0)";  # you may set it to a different value
    }
    my $sql = useCreateDBTemplate($db, $createDB);
    print $sql, "\n";
} # generateCreateDB


############################
sub useCreateDBTemplate {
    my ($db, $createDB) = @_;

    # use here document to assign a T-SQL script to $sql
    # note that each local variable symbol @ is escaped with a \
    # to prevent Perl from interpolate it as an array variable
    my $sql = <<"__CREATEDB_TEMPLATE";
    USE master
    GO
    DECLARE \@spid smallint, \@sql varchar(255)

    DECLARE c_spid CURSOR FOR
     SELECT req_spid FROM master..syslockinfo
      WHERE rsc_dbid = db_id(\'$db\')
     ORDER BY req_spid
     FOR READ ONLY

    OPEN c_spid
    FETCH c_spid INTO \@spid
    WHILE (\@\@FETCH_STATUS <> -1)
    BEGIN
       IF (\@\@FETCH_STATUS <> -2)
       BEGIN
          SELECT \@sql = 'KILL ' + CONVERT(varchar(3), \@spid)
          # terminate the processes that are accessing the database
          EXECUTE(\@sql)
       END
       FETCH c_spid INTO \@spid
    END
    CLOSE c_spid
    DEALLOCATE c_spid
    GO
    -- Drop the database if it already exists
```

```
      IF db_id(\'$db\') IS NOT NULL
          DROP DATABASE $db
      GO
      -- plug in the database creation here
      $createDB
      GO
      ALTER DATABASE $db SET RECOVERY SIMPLE
      GO
__CREATEDB_TEMPLATE
   $sql =~ s/(^|\n)        /\n/g;  # remove the indented spaces in $sql
   return $sql;
} # useCreateDBTemplate
```

You'll now see this script in action with the following example. Assume that the options in the configuration file are as follows:

```
[Control]
Server=SQL01\APOLLO
DB=Orders
DataFile=E:\mssql\data\Orders_dat1.mdf,E:\mssql\data\Orders_dat2.ndf
LogFile=F:\mssql\data\Orders_log1.ldf,F:\mssql\data\Orders_log2.ldf
DataSize=200  # in MB
LogSize=100   # in MB
```

In this configuration file, the name of the database is Orders specified with the option DB. The data files (including their complete paths) are listed in a comma-separated format for the option DataFile, and the transaction log files are specified with the option LogFile in a similar fashion. The size of the database is 200MB for data and 100MB for log. To keep it simple, the script distributes the data size across all the data files evenly and likewise distributes the log size evenly across all the log files. The script calculates the size of each data file and the size of each log file as follows:

```
# get the file sizes
my ($dataFileSize, $logFileSize) =
            ( int($cRef->{DATASIZE} / (scalar @dataFiles)),
              int($cRef->{LOGSIZE} / (scalar @logFiles)) );
```

The hash reference $cRef is returned by the function dbaReadINI()—available in the module SQLDBA::Utility—that reads the specifications in a configuration file into the hash. The Perl function scalar() forces the array @dataFiles (or @logFiles) to be evaluated in the scalar context and thus returns the number of elements in the array.

Save the configuration options to the file config.txt and then run the Perl script in Listing 8-1 with this configuration file to produce the T-SQL code shown in Listing 8-2.

Listing 8-2. Generating a CREATE DATABASE *Statement*

```
cmd>perl generateDB.pl config.txt
USE master
GO
DECLARE @spid smallint,
        @sql varchar(255)

DECLARE c_spid CURSOR FOR
 SELECT req_spid FROM master..syslockinfo
  WHERE rsc_dbid = db_id('Orders')
 ORDER BY req_spid
 FOR READ ONLY

OPEN c_spid
FETCH c_spid INTO @spid
WHILE (@@FETCH_STATUS <> -1)
BEGIN
   IF (@@FETCH_STATUS <> -2)
   BEGIN
       SELECT @sql = 'KILL ' + CONVERT(varchar(3), @spid)
       EXECUTE(@sql)
   END
   FETCH c_spid INTO @spid
END
CLOSE c_spid
DEALLOCATE c_spid
GO
-- Drop the database if it already exists
IF db_id('Orders') IS NOT NULL
   DROP DATABASE Orders
GO
-- plug in the database creation here
CREATE DATABASE Orders
   ON PRIMARY
      ( NAME='Orders_dat1',
        FILENAME='E:\mssql\data\Orders_dat1.mdf',
        SIZE=100, FILEGROWTH=0),
      ( NAME='Orders_dat2',
        FILENAME='E:\mssql\data\Orders_dat2.ndf',
```

```
        SIZE=100, FILEGROWTH=0)
    LOG ON
       ( NAME = 'Orders_log1',
         FILENAME = 'F:\mssql\data\Orders_log1.ldf',
         SIZE = 50, FILEGROWTH=0),
       ( NAME = 'Orders_log2',
         FILENAME = 'F:\mssql\data\Orders_log2.ldf',
         SIZE = 50, FILEGROWTH=0)
GO
ALTER DATABASE Orders SET RECOVERY SIMPLE
GO
```

The bulk of the code is in the function `generateCreateDB()`, which generates the SQL Server `CREATE DATABASE` statement using the information read from the options in the configuration file. The complete `CREATE DATABASE` statement is stored as a string in the $createDB variable. Toward the end of the function, it calls another function, `useCreateDBTemplate()`, and passes it the database name in $db and the `CREATE DATABASE` statement in $createDB.

The function `useCreateDBTemplate()` contains a template—in a *here* document[1]—for creating a database. The here document is introduced with a pair of double quotation marks, and therefore it'll interpolate its embedded variables, $db and $createDB. These variables serve as placeholders for the template. Note that in the here document, every T-SQL local variable is escaped with a backslash; otherwise, the T-SQL local variable—prefixed with the @ character—will be treated by Perl as an array variable and the variable interpolation will kick in, which isn't the behavior you want to see.

In Listing 8-1, the function `generateCreateDB()` is also like a template because it freely mixes Perl code with blocks of strings that represent SQL statement fragments. The function uses Perl code to control the repeating elements—data file and log file specifications—and relies on Perl's handy variable interpolation to handle the changing database and filenames. For instance, the data file specifications are controlled by this loop in the function:

```
my $i = 0;
foreach my $dataFile (@dataFiles) {
    $createDB .= ( (++$i-1) ? ',' : ' ' ) . "
        ( NAME=\'$db\_dat$i\',
          FILENAME=\'$dataFile\',
          SIZE=$dataSize,
          FILEGROWTH=0)";   # you may set it to a different value
}
```

---

1. Refer to the section "Using the Here Document" in Chapter 1 for more information about here documents.

Finally, toward the end of the function `useCreateDBTemplate()`, note the global substitutions performed on the SQL script in the variable `$sql`:

```
$sql =~ s/(^|\n)      /\n/g;
```

This removes six leading spaces from each line. In the template, all the lines are indented by six positions to keep the embedded T-SQL code more readable in the Perl script. You need to remove these leading spaces to move the batch separator `GO` back to column 1.

Generating SQL for Data Conversion

> **SCENARIO**
> *Given a populated database table whose structure needs to be modified, you want to generate a SQL script that you can apply to convert the table along with its data from its current version to the new structure.*

In a SQL Server environment, when you make changes to a table schema, you can choose from many methods to implement the transformation from the current table to the new one. Although the Data Transformation Services (DTS) come to mind immediately, the most common and straightforward approach is still to write conversion scripts in T-SQL, especially when the data doesn't need to travel out of the SQL Server instance and the transformation is relatively simple for T-SQL to handle.

If you've had the experience of dealing with data conversions, you no doubt have discovered that irrespective of how many different methods you have or want to try in transforming a table, it's important you organize your data conversion scripts consistently and follow a common structure to simplify maintenance. This call for consistency leads naturally to code generation. What could be better to enforce scripting consistency than to have the data conversion script generated automatically?

As an illustration, this section deals with a simple case of generating SQL code for data conversion. You can apply the method to work on other, more complex data conversion scenarios.

The Perl script in Listing 8-3 reads both the current table structure and the new table structure, identifies the changes in the table structures, generates a data conversion script that creates the new table, and copies the data in the current table into the new table.

Writing T-SQL Data Conversion Scripts

In the old days, writing a T-SQL script was about the only way to convert your SQL Server data. The introduction of DTS in SQL Server 7.0 changed the landscape of data conversion, giving users a powerful choice.

A frequently asked question is "If I have DTS, why do I need to write any T-SQL conversion scripts?"

The question implicitly assumes that the two are competing methods when in fact they should complement each other. In particular, DTS in no way renders T-SQL conversion scripts unnecessary. When your data conversion is entirely within a SQL Server instance and the conversion logic is conducive to set processing, T-SQL conversion scripts give you simplicity and performance.

DTS excels when you need to work with multiple data sources or destinations and when you need to implement more complex workflow logic during the data transformation.

For performance, your DTS package can incorporate a T-SQL data conversion script as one of the steps in the package workflow.

Make no mistake, I'm not suggesting that data conversion can be fully automated! And I'm not trying to put all the ETL vendors out of business.[2] Because specific business logic often has to be applied before the current data can be copied into the new table structure, and the information about the structural difference between the two tables is obviously not sufficient to reveal all the business logic that must be applied during the conversion, full automation isn't possible. However, you can at least generate a data conversion template that captures the common elements and the basic flow of the conversion. With such a template, the DBA or the developer doesn't have to start from scratch every time and can immediately proceed to add the business logic to the generated conversion script.

Listing 8-3 shows the script SQLDataConversion.pl.

---

2. The process of extracting the data from the data sources, transforming it, and loading it into the warehouse servers is often called the *ETL process*. ETL stands for *Extracting, Transforming, and Loading*.

Listing 8-3. Generating a Data Conversion Script

```perl
1.   use strict;
2.   use Getopt::Std;
3.   use SQLDBA::Utility qw( dbaRunOsql dbaGetTableStruct_sp_help );
4.   use SQLDBA::ScriptSQL qw( dbaScriptCreateTable dbaScriptConversion );
5.
6.   my %opts;
7.   getopts('S:d:n:o:', \%opts);  # get the command-line arguments
8.   my ($server, $db, $new, $old) = ($opts{S}, $opts{d}, $opts{n}, $opts{o});
9.   (defined $server and defined $db and defined $new and defined $old)
10.    or printUsage();
11.
12. Main: {
13.    my ($spHelp, $oldRef, $newRef, $sql);
14.    my $optRef = {              # specify the osql command-line options
15.            '-E' => undef;      # use trusted connection
16.            '-n' => undef,      # remove numbering and the prompt symbol (>)
17.            '-w' => '5000',     # set the output wide to prevent text wrapping
18.            '-d' => 'pubs' }; # set the default database for the connection
19.    # run sp_help to get table info for the old table
20.    $spHelp = dbaRunOsql($server, "sp_help \'$old\'", $optRef);
21.    # parse the result of sp_help to get table structure
22.    $oldRef = dbaGetTableStruct_sp_help($spHelp);
23.    # run sp_help to get table info for the new table
24.    $spHelp = dbaRunOsql($server, "sp_help \'$new\'", $optRef);
25.    # parse the result of sp_help to get table structure
26.    $newRef = dbaGetTableStruct_sp_help($spHelp);
27.    # compare the structures to generate the conversion script
28.    $sql = dbaScriptConversion($newRef, $oldRef);
29.    print "USE $db\nGO\n";
30.    print $sql;
31. } # Main
32.
33. ###################
34. sub printUsage {
35.    print << '--Usage--';
36. Usage:
37.    cmd>perl SQLDataConversion.pl -S <SQL server or instance>
38.                                  -d <database name>
39.                                  -n <new table name>
40.                                  -o <old table name>
41. --Usage--
42. exit;
43. } # printUsage
```

The Perl script in Listing 8-3 relies heavily on the functions imported from the modules SQLDBA::Utility and SQLDBA::ScriptSQL.

To find the schema information of a table, the script calls dbaRunOsql() to execute sp_help for the table on the server and returns the result of sp_help in a single string to $spHelp on line 20 for the old table and on line 24 for the new table. Then, the function dbaGetTableStruct_sp_help() scans and parses $spHelp to store the table schema information in a hash, thus making the table schema information readily accessible to the Perl script. When this is done for both the current table and the new table, the script calls the function dbaScriptConversion on line 28 to compare the two hashes of the table schemas and generates a bare minimum data conversion script in T-SQL for the two tables based on the differences found during the schema comparison.

Listing 8-4 shows an example of the hash for the columns of the pubs..authors table, as produced on line 22 of Listing 8-3 (with many columns omitted).

Listing 8-4. The Hash Record for a Table Structure

```
$oldRef = {
        Columns => {
                    ...       # more columns omitted
                au_id   => {
                            nullable => 'no',
                            prec     => '',
                            computed => 'no',
                            length   => '11',
                            scale    => '',
                            colid    => 1,
                            type     => 'id'
                },
                au_lname => {
                            nullable => 'no',
                            prec     => '',
                            computed => 'no',
                            length   => '40',
                            scale    => '',
                            colid    => 2,
                            type     => 'varchar'
                }
        }
};
```

Each innermost hash in Listing 8-4 captures the properties of a column listed in the result of sp_help. Of course, you don't have to run sp_help to get the table schema information into the hash. You can obtain the same information by parsing the CREATE TABLE statement for the table. Alternatively, you can write a simple SQL query to get the same schema information from the INFORMATION_SCHEMA views. You can also retrieve the table schema via SQL-DMO using the function dbaGetTableColumns(), discussed in Chapter 5, "Comparing and Sorting Database Objects."

Clearly, there's more than one way to do it! To the function dbaScriptConversion(), it doesn't matter how the hash in Listing 8-4 is populated as long as it's populated. In general, I prefer to retrieve the column information using SQL-DMO. This is more versatile and robust than parsing the result of sp_help. When there's a nonregular identifier, parsing the result of sp_help can be cumbersome and error prone.

If you've followed the discussions of Listing 8-3 to this point, you should have noticed that all the script has done so far is to prepare for the real work of comparing the schema differences and generating SQL code, which is performed on line 28 with the function dbaScriptConversion() imported from the module SQLDBA::ScriptSQL. This function is central to the script and to the current discussion. Listing 8-5 shows its script.

Listing 8-5. The Function dbaScriptConversion()

```
sub dbaScriptConversion {
   my ($newRef, $oldRef) = @_;
   unless (ref($newRef) && ref($oldRef)) {
      die "***Err: dbaScriptConversion() expects two references.";
   }
   my $newTB = $newRef->{TableName};
   my $oldTB = $oldRef->{TableName};

   my $sql = dbaScriptCreateTable($newRef);
   $sql .= "GO\n";

   if (exists $newRef->{Identity}) {
      $sql .= "SET IDENTITY_INSERT $newTB ON\nGO\n";
   }
   $sql .= "IF EXISTS (SELECT * FROM $oldTB)\n";
   $sql .= "   INSERT INTO $newTB (\n";
   # order the columns by colid
```

```
     my @newColumns = (sort { $newRef->{Columns}->{$a}->{colid}
                             <=>
                             $newRef->{Columns}->{$b}->{colid}
                           } keys %{$newRef->{Columns}});
     # construct the column list for INSERT
     $sql .= "\t" . join(", ", @newColumns) . "\n";
     $sql .= "     )\n";
     # now for each column in the new table, decide how to include
     # the column on the SELECT list
     my $column = shift @newColumns;
     $sql .= "     SELECT \n\t" . (exists($oldRef->{Columns}->{$column}) ?
                              $column : '?');
     foreach $column (@newColumns) {
        $sql .= ", " . (exists($oldRef->{Columns}->{$column}) ? $column : '?');
     }
     $sql .= "\n     FROM $oldTB\nGO\n";
     if (exists $newRef->{Identity}) {
        $sql .= "SET IDENTITY_INSERT $newTB OFF\nGO\n";
     }
     $sql .= "DROP TABLE $oldTB\nGO\n";
     return $sql;
} # dbaScriptConversion
```

In Listing 8-5, the dbaScriptConversion() function intermingles the Perl code with the SQL code, but the structure of the SQL code is clearly visible. First, it calls the function dbaScriptCreateTable() from the module SQLDBA::ScriptSQL to read the table schema hash for the new table and produce the corresponding CREATE TABLE statement. Then, the function checks whether there's an identity column in the new table. If there is, it adds a SET IDENTITY_INSERT ON statement before it generates the INSERT … SELECT … statement to get the data from the old table into the new table. Finally, it inserts a SET IDENTITY_INSERT OFF statement to turn off the identity insert setting, if necessary, and generates a DROP TABLE statement for the old table.

Two simple rules are used to construct the INSERT … SELECT … statement: First, if there's an identical column in both tables, then no change is made, and the column is included on both the INSERT list and the SELECT list. Second, if a column is only in the new table, a question mark is placed on the SELECT list. The idea is to generate a data conversion template that the DBA can further customize with the knowledge of business logic for transforming the current table to the new one.

An example should help make things abundantly clear. Assume you have the following table in the pubs database on the server SQL01:

```
CREATE TABLE authors (
    au_id       char(11) NOT NULL PRIMARY KEY,
    au_lname    varchar (40) NOT NULL ,
    au_fname    varchar (30) NOT NULL ,
    address     varchar (40) NULL ,
    zip         char (5) NULL,
    contract    bit NOT NULL
)
```

as well as the following table in the same pubs database on the server SQL01. Pay attention to the structural differences between these two tables:

```
CREATE TABLE authors_new (
    id          int IDENTITY (1, 1) NOT NULL ,
    au_id       char(11) NOT NULL PRIMARY KEY,
    au_lname    varchar (40) NOT NULL ,
    au_fname    varchar (30) NOT NULL ,
    address     varchar (40) NULL ,
    zip         char (5) NULL
)
```

To produce a SQL script template that converts data from the authors table to the authors_new table, run the Perl script in Listing 8-3 as shown in Listing 8-6.

Listing 8-6. Producing a Sample T-SQL Conversion Script

```
cmd> perl SQLDataConversion.pl -S SQL01 -d pubs -o authors -n authors_new
USE pubs
GO
CREATE TABLE dbo.authors_new (
    id int NOT NULL IDENTITY (1, 1) ,
    au_id char(11) NOT NULL,
    au_lname varchar ( 40 )  NOT NULL,
    au_fname varchar ( 30 )  NOT NULL,
    address varchar ( 40 )   NULL,
    zip char ( 5 )  NULL
)
GO
SET IDENTITY_INSERT dbo.authors_new ON
GO
IF EXISTS (SELECT * FROM dbo.authors)
```

```
    INSERT INTO dbo.authors_new (
    id, au_id, au_lname, au_fname, address, zip
    )
    SELECT
        ?, au_id, au_lname, au_fname, address, zip
      FROM dbo.authors
GO
SET IDENTITY_INSERT dbo.authors_new OFF
GO
DROP TABLE dbo.authors
GO
```

Obviously, what Listing 8-6 shows is the most basic data conversion template script in T-SQL. In your particular environment, you often have additional knowledge of generic transformations that you may want to include in the script template, and you can customize the function dbaScriptConversion() to include that knowledge.

> **NOTE** *You may want to take advantage of the schema comparison scripts presented in Chapter 5, "Comparing and Sorting Database Objects." In addition to column changes, these scripts identify changes in indexes and constraints. You can therefore generate data conversion scripts to accommodate not only column changes but also changes in indexes and constraints.*

Consider, for instance, the situation where the timestamp data type is used by one of the columns. You could easily modify the function dbaScriptConversion() in Listing 8-5 so that it works with the timestamp data type.

Adding a DROP PROC Before Each CREATE PROC

SCENARIO
You often receive T-SQL scripts that have the definitions of many stored procedures in a single file. You want to add a DROP PROC *immediately prior to each* CREATE PROC.

There are many advantages of having a DROP PROC immediately preceding each CREATE PROC, one of which is that you can easily re-execute a block of code in the script without running into reams of errors.

Unfortunately, it's all too common to see a script of CREATE PROC statements with no accompanying DROP PROCEDURE statements or with the DROP PROCEDURE statements all lumped together as is the case when you use the SQL Server Enterprise Manager to generate the stored procedure scripts to a single file.

Manually adding a DROP PROC for every CREATE PROC is only feasible when there are few stored procedures. The Perl solution presented in this section makes the number of stored procedures a nonfactor.

As you'll soon see, the task is relatively simple with Perl. Briefly, Perl needs to first find the right CREATE PROC string, record the procedure name, and insert a DROP PROCEDURE statement with the procedure name in a separate batch immediately preceding the CREATE PROCEDURE statement.

There is, however, a minor complication, which is that the procedure name can come in a variety of patterns. But pattern matching is what Perl is good at doing. Listing 8-7 shows the code to add a DROP PROCEDURE statement before the CREATE PROCEDURE statement.

Listing 8-7. Adding a DROP PROC *Before Each* CREATE PROC

```
use strict;
my ($infile, $outfile) = @ARGV;
die "***Err: need an input file $infile." unless (-e $infile);

# define and compile a regular expression to parse the proc name
# the name can be a regular identifier or a delimited identifier
my $name = q/(?:
                     [\w\$@#]+                # regular identifer
                 | \" (?: [^"] | \"\" )+ \"  # double-quoted id
                 | \[ (?: [^]] | \]\] )+ \]  # bracket-quoted id
            )/;
# the proc name may be prefixed with owner
my $re = qr{  (?:   $name          # one-part name w no owner
                 | $name\.$name   # two-part name w owner
              )
          }ix;

my $spName;
unless (open(OUT, ">$outfile")) {
   warn "***Msg: couldn't open $outfile for write." if $outfile;
   open(OUT, ">&STDOUT");
}
open(IN, "<$infile") or die "***Err: could not open $infile for read.";
while(<IN>) {
   if (/^\s*create\s+proc(edure)?\s+(.*)$/i) {
```

```
    my $proc = $2;
    my $sql = $_;
    if ($proc =~ /^($re)(\s+.*)?$/) { $spName = $1; }
    else {
        while (<IN>) {
            $sql .= $_;
            if (/^\s*($re)(\s+.*)?$/) { $spName = $1; last; }
        }
    }
    if ($spName =~ /$re/) { # by now $spName should have the proc name
        $sql = getSPDrop($spName) . $sql; # add a DROP PROC clause
    }
    else { die "***Err: failed to grab the proc name."; }
    print OUT $sql;
  }
  else { print OUT; } # just pass it along
} # while
close(IN); close(OUT);


###############
sub getSPDrop {
    my $sp = shift or die "***Err: getSPDrop() expects a proc name.";
    my $sql = "if exists (select * from dbo.sysobjects where id = ";
    $sql .= "object_id(N'" . $sp . "') and OBJECTPROPERTY(id, ";
    $sql .= "N'IsProcedure') = 1)\n    drop procedure $sp\nGO\n\n";
    return $sql;
} # getSPDrop
```

At the beginning of the script in Listing 8-7, the regular expression for parsing the name of a stored procedure is defined and compiled:

```
# define and compile a regular expression to parse the proc name
# the name can be a simple identifier and a delimited identifier
my $name = q/(?:
                [\w\$@#]+                # regular identifer
            | \" (?: [^"] | \"\" )+ \"  # double-quoted id
            | \[ (?: [^]] | \]\] )+ \]  # bracket-quoted id
          )/;
# the proc name may be prefixed with owner
my $re = qr{  (?:   $name           # one-part name w no owner
                | $name\.$name   # two-part name w owner
              )
          }ix;
```

You specify the string $name separately to make the regular expression $re more readable. Because the /x modifier modifies the regular expression, you can have whitespaces and even Perl comments inside the regular expression. There are three possibilities for a procedure name or an owner name:

- **A regular identifier**: This will be matched with the pattern [\w\$@#]+. Note that this pattern actually matches more than what's allowed for a T-SQL regular identifier. But given the context, it's safe to be less precise.

- **An identifier delimited with double quotation marks**: The pattern to match is \" (?: [^"] | \"\")+ \".

- **An identifier delimited with square brackets**: The pattern to match is \[(?: [^]] | \]\])+ \].

The compiled regular expression $re can handle either the regular identifier or the delimited identifier with or without being owner qualified.

The Perl script in Listing 8-7 searches the SQL script for each CREATE PROCEDURE statement and uses the compiled regular expression $re to capture the name of the procedure in the variable $spName. When it finds a CREATE PROCEDURE statement, it passes the procedure name to the function getSPDrop(), which returns a DROP PROCEDURE batch with the correct procedure name. The Perl script then writes this batch to the output before it writes the corresponding CREATE PROCEDURE statement. Any other line in the SQL script is passed to the output as is.

You should be able to easily modify the script in Listing 8-7 to handle tables, indexes, views, triggers, and other SQL Server database objects.

It's important to note that the script in Listing 8-7 produces correct T-SQL scripts in most cases and is sufficiently useful. But it isn't 100-percent robust. The script has two obvious flaws. The first flaw lies in the assumption that there are only whitespaces between CREATE and PROCEDURE or between PROCEDURE and the name of the procedure. The syntax of T-SQL allows delimited T-SQL comments wherever whitespace is permitted. For instance, the following T-SQL statement would confuse the Perl script in Listing 8-7:

```
CREATE PROC/* valid comments */dbo.spGetNextID
```

The second flaw is that not every CREATE PROC string is a real CREATE PROCEDURE statement; it could be inside a comment, a quoted string, or even a delimited identifier.

It turns out that these problems are a special case of a more general problem—a problem caused by the presence of T-SQL comments, quoted strings, and delimited identifiers. Because these elements can have embedded string patterns that may otherwise be considered as valid SQL constructs, simply using a regular expression to match a string pattern in a SQL script isn't safe. Instead, you must make sure any string pattern inside these elements is taken out of the consideration.

The "Implementing the Replace-Match-Restore Strategy" section in Chapter 3 introduced a generic method to handle the presence of T-SQL comments, quoted strings, and delimited identifiers. The next several sections show you the application of this useful strategy.

Stripping off Identifier Delimiters

> **SCENARIO**
> *You want to remove the delimiters around any T-SQL identifier whenever it's safe to do so.*

SQL Server allows you to quote an identifier with a pair of delimiters. The delimiters can be square brackets or double quotation marks if QUOTED_IDENTIFIER is set to ON. When an identifier is quoted, it can contain any character, including spaces and the delimiters themselves. Unfortunately, not all the tools are created to correctly handle delimited identifiers, so using them in your SQL scripts has a potential to come back and bite you.

TIP *I generally advise against using delimited identifiers in SQL scripts. In fact, when I conduct a SQL code review, I look for any use of delimited identifiers in the submitted SQL scripts, in particular the ones whose delimiters can't be safely removed.*

To strip off the identifier delimiters, you can apply the replace-match-restore strategy introduced in the section "Implementing the Replace-Match-Restore Strategy" in Chapter 3. You can proceed as follows:

1. Call the function dbaNormalizeSQL() to identify the comments, the quoted strings, and the delimited identifiers and then replace them with their respective unique token strings.

2. Evaluate each delimited identifier to see whether it conforms to the T-SQL regular identifier naming rules, convert it to a regular identifier if it does, and replace its token string in the script with the regular identifier.

3. Restore the other unique tokens to their originals.

Now, it's time to present the code to safely strip off identifier delimiters in a T-SQL script. Pay particular attention to how the replace-match-restore strategy is used in the script stripDelimiters.pl in Listing 8-8.

Listing 8-8. Script to Safely Strip Off T-SQL Identifier Delimiters

```
1.   use strict;
2.   use SQLDBA::ParseSQL qw( dbaNormalizeSQL dbaRestoreSQL
3.                            $TSQLReservedWords );
4.   my $sqlFile = shift or die "***Err: $0 expects a SQL script file.";
5.
6.   Main: {
7.     # read the T-SQL script into a variable first
8.     my $sql;
9.     open(FL, $sqlFile) or die "***Err: could not open $sqlFile for read.";
10.    read(FL, $sql, -s FL);
11.    close(FL);
12.
13.    # replace comments, strings, and delimited identifiers
14.    # with unique string tokens
15.    my $sqlRef = dbaNormalizeSQL($sql, 1);
16.    $sqlRef = removeDelimiters($sqlRef); # remove the delimiters if safe
17.    $sqlRef = dbaRestoreSQL($sqlRef);    # restore the other identifiers
18.    print $sqlRef->{code};
19. }  # Main
20.
21. #####################
22. sub removeDelimiters {
23.    my $sqlRef = shift or
24.       die "***Err: removeDelimiters() expects a reference.";
25.
26.    # remove double quotes, if safe
27.    foreach my $id (keys %{$sqlRef->{double_ids}}) {
28.       if ($sqlRef->{double_ids}->{$id} =~ /^[a-zA-Z\@\#\_]
29.                                    [\w\@\#\$\.]*$/ix) {
30.          if ($sqlRef->{double_ids}->{$id} !~ /$TSQLReservedWords/i) {
31.             $sqlRef->{code} =~ s/$id/$sqlRef->{double_ids}->{$id}/;
32.          }
33.       }
34.    }
35.    # remove square brackets
36.    foreach my $id (keys %{$sqlRef->{bracket_ids}}) {
37.       if ($sqlRef->{bracket_ids}->{$id} =~ /^[a-zA-Z\@\#\_]
38.                                    [\w\@\#\$\.]*$/ix) {
```

```
39.          if ($sqlRef->{bracket_ids}->{$id} !~ /$TSQLReservedWords/i) {
40.              $sqlRef->{code} =~ s/$id/$sqlRef->{bracket_ids}->{$id}/;
41.          }
42.      }
43.    }
44.    return $sqlRef;
45. } # removeDelimiters
```

After `stripDelimiter.pl` reads the T-SQL script into the variable `$sql` from line 8 through 11, the main body of this script consists of three function calls. It first calls the function `dbaNormalizeSQL()`, imported from SQLDBA::ParseSQL on line 2, to replace comments, quoted strings, and delimited identifiers with unique token strings. Then, the function `removeDelimiters()`, defined from line 22 through 45, examines each delimited identifier to find those whose delimiters can be removed without altering the semantics of the SQL script and removes these delimiters from `$sqlRef->{code}`. Note that the function removes both double quotes and square brackets. Finally, the function `dbaRestoreSQL()` is called to put the original comments, quoted strings, and identifiers back in `$sqlRef->{code}`.

To be able to safely strip off a pair of T-SQL identifier delimiters, you must ensure that the identifier minus the delimiters conforms to the rules of T-SQL regular identifiers (in other words, identifiers that are not delimited with either double quotation marks or square brackets). Let's review the rules for the format of the regular identifier on SQL Server 2000. These rules are documented in the SQL Server 2000 Books Online in the "Rules for Regular Identifiers" section:

- The first character must be a letter, an underscore (_), the at (@) sign, or the number sign (#).

- Subsequent characters can be letters, decimal numbers, the at (@) sign, the underscore (_), the number sign (#), or the dollar sign ($).

- The identifier must not be a T-SQL reserved word.

- Embedded spaces or special characters aren't allowed.

The function `removeDelimiters()` checks each identifier, either delimited by square brackets or by double quotation marks, against these rules and strips the delimiters off those conforming to the rules. Of particular interest is the variable `$TSQLReservedWords` used on line 30 and line 39. The variable is imported by request from the module SQLDBA::ParseSQL on line 3 and is a reference to a compiled regular expression that matches any of the SQL Server reserved words. (The SQL Server 2000 Books Online documents the reserved words.)

Handling the T-SQL Whitespace

SCENARIO
You normally use the Perl whitespace \s+ to match the whitespace that separates two T-SQL reserved words. But this isn't always correct because they can also be legitimately separated with a T-SQL comment. You want your Perl scripts to correctly match the T-SQL whitespaces.

The previous section "Adding a DROP PROC Before Each CREATE PROC" used the following regular expression to match a CREATE PROCEDURE statement:

```
/^\s*create\s+proc(edure)?\s+(.*)$/i
```

This works in most cases, but it isn't totally robust. Recall that the Perl whitespace \s can match a space, a tab, or a new line, and now consider the following legal SQL syntax:

```
CREATE/* This may not be common, but is still correct */PROCEDURE dbo.getAuthor
    @au_id varchar(11)
AS
    SELECT au_id, au_lname, au_fname FROM authors
    WHERE au_id = @au_id
```

The previous regular expression will fail to match this CREATE PROCEDURE statement.

Dealing with the T-SQL whitespace that separates the T-SQL reserved words, object identifiers, strings, operators, and numbers is a general problem. To show a general solution, this section defines a regular expression to match the T-SQL whitespace.

Assume that you've already normalized a SQL script with the SQLDBA::ParseSQL function dbaNormalizeSQL(); you can then match the whitespaces in the script with this regular expression:

```
$SQLws = qr{ (?:  \s        # space, tab, carriage return, form feed, or newline
             | /\*\w+\*/      # /* and */ delimited comment
             | \-\-\w+\n )+  # -- prefixed ANSI comment
        }ix;
```

With this regular expression, you can now properly parse the CREATE PROCEDURE statement as follows:

```
m{^
     (?: $SQLws)? CREATE $SQLws PROC(EDURE)? $SQLws (.+)
   }ix
```

I can't stress enough how important the function dbaNormalizeSQL() is. Without applying this function first, it wouldn't be possible to craft such a simple regular expression to deal with the SQL whitespace. The SQL whitespace regular expression is only correct when the SQL script has been normalized with this function.

Recall that the function dbaNormalizeDBA() accepts a second parameter, and setting the parameter to 0 results in a comment being replaced with a space. If all the comments are replaced with spaces, \s+ would be enough to match T-SQL whitespaces.

NOTE   *In most places throughout this book, for simplicity I use the Perl whitespace to match a SQL whitespace—with the implicit understanding that you should replace the Perl whitespace with the SQL whitespace regular expression if you need the scripts to be more robust.*

Capitalizing the T-SQL Reserved Words

SCENARIO
You want to reformat your script so that all the T-SQL reserved words are in uppercase.

This may sound like a trivial problem. Why not just search for all the T-SQL reserved words in the script and capitalize them? Think again! Here's a hint: An otherwise reserved word may be embedded in a comment, a quoted string, or a delimited identifier.

Again, you can enlist the replace-match-restore strategy discussed in Chapter 3, "Working with Commonly Used Perl Routines," to help. Listing 8-9 shows the script.

Listing 8-9. Capitalizing All the T-SQL Reserved Words

```perl
use strict;
use SQLDBA::ParseSQL qw( dbaNormalizeSQL dbaRestoreSQL $TSQLReservedWords );

my $sqlFile = shift or die "***Err: $0 expects a SQL script.";

Main: {
   # read the T-SQL script into a variable first
   my $sql;
   open(FL, $sqlFile) or die "***Err: could not open $sqlFile for read.";
   read(FL, $sql, -s FL);
   close(FL);

   # replace comments, strings, and delimited identifiers
   # with unique string tokens
   my $sqlRef = dbaNormalizeSQL($sql, 1);
   # search and uppercase all the reserved words
   $sqlRef = upperCaseReserved($sqlRef);
   # restore T-SQL comments, quoted strings, and/or delimited identifiers
   $sqlRef = dbaRestoreSQL($sqlRef);
   print $sqlRef->{code};
} # Main


#######################
sub upperCaseReserved {
   my ($sqlRcf) = shift or
      die "***Err: upperCaseReserved() expects a reference.";

   # replace any reserved word with its uppercase
   $sqlRef->{code} =~ s/($TSQLReservedWords)/uc($1)/eg;
   return $sqlRef;
} # upperCaseReserved
```

Indeed, after you've normalized the T-SQL code, the problem of capitalizing the reserved words becomes trivial. All you need to do now is search all the T-SQL reserved words in the script and replace them with their respective uppercase letters, which is the work performed by the function upperCaseReserved() in Listing 8-9. In fact, it's primarily this single statement:

```perl
$sqlRef->{code} =~ s/($TSQLReservedWords)/uc($1)/eg;
```

Note the use of the /e modifier, which causes the replacement part of the s///
operator to be evaluated as a Perl expression before the replacement takes place.
In this statement, the regular-expression engine evaluates uc($1), which changes
to uppercase every character in the substring captured by the first pair of parentheses—actually, the only pair of parentheses—in the match part of the s///
operator. The substring in this case matches a T-SQL reserved word. The /g modifier ensures that all occurrences of the T-SQL reserved words are converted to
uppercase.

This script is another good demonstration of the replace-match-restore
strategy in action. The next section gives you one more example of applying
this strategy to modify COLLATE clauses in a T-SQL script.

Changing Collations in a T-SQL Script

SCENARIO
*You need to replace the collation in a script with a different one or remove all
the COLLATE clauses.*

The naïve solution to remove all the COLLATE clauses from a T-SQL script is to use
the following Perl one liner:

```
while (<>) {s/COLLATE\s*\w+/ /ig; print;}
```

If you know your SQL code, this is probably all you need. Recall that when no
file handle is specified in the input operator <>, the loop while (<>) goes through
each line of each file on the command line and assigns the line to the predefined
variable $_. Therefore, to replace every occurrence of COLLATE <Collation Name>
with a space, place the one liner in a file, say rmCollate.pl, and run the following at
the command line:

```
cmd>perl rmCollate.pl pubs.SQL
```

where pubs.SQL is a T-SQL script with the COLLATE clauses you want to remove. This
prints the T-SQL script from pubs.SQL minus the COLLATE clauses to STDOUT—usually
your computer screen.

This one liner works fine when no COLLATE clause appears in a comment, a
quoted string, or a delimited identifier. However, it falls flat as a general solution to
the problem of removing all the COLLATE clauses. After all, it wouldn't be outlandish
to see a SQL comment like this:

```
/** changed from collate SQL_Latin1_General_CP850_CS_AS
       to collate SQL_Latin1_General_CP1_CI_AS
**/
```

It's unlikely you would want to change this comment to the following:

```
/** changed from
        to
**/
```

Again, the replace-match-restore strategy comes to rescue. Listing 8-10 is a Perl script, replaceCollate.pl, that correctly replaces the collation specified in the COLLATE clauses in a SQL script with a new collation.

Listing 8-10. Replacing the Collation with a Different One

```
1.  use strict;
2.  use Getopt::Std;
3.  use SQLDBA::ParseSQL qw( dbaNormalizeSQL dbaRestoreSQL );
4.
5.  my %opts;
6.  getopts('s:o:n:', \%opts);  # get command-line arguments
7.  my ($sqlFile, $old, $new) = ($opts{s}, $opts{o}, $opts{n});
8.  (defined $sqlFile && defined $old) or printUsage();
9.
10. Main: {
11.     # read the T-SQL script into a variable first
12.     my $sql;
13.     open(FL, $sqlFile) or die "***Err: could not open $sqlFile for read.";
14.     read(FL, $sql, -s FL);
15.     close(FL);
16.
17.     # replace comments, strings, and delimited identifiers
18.     # with unique string tokens
19.     my $sqlRef = dbaNormalizeSQL($sql, 1);
20.
21.     $new = "COLLATE $new" if $new =~ /\w+/; # replace the collation
22.     $sqlRef->{code} =~ s/\bCOLLATE\s+$old\b/$new/ig;
23.
24.     # restore the original comments, strings, and delimited identifiers
25.     $sqlRef = dbaRestoreSQL($sqlRef);
26.     print $sqlRef->{code};
27. }  # Main
28.
29. ###############
30. sub printUsage {
31.     print << '--Usage--';
32. Usage:
```

```
33.    cmd>perl replaceCollate.pl  -s <script file>
34.                                 -o <old collation>
35.                                 -n [<new collation> ]
36. --Usage--
37. exit;
38. } # printUsage
```

With the help of the functions dbaNormalizeSQL() and dbaRestoreSQL(), the script in Listing 8-10 overcomes the complication caused by comments, quoted strings, and delimited identifiers. It reduces the problem to a simple search-and-replace problem that's solved with the following two lines of code in Listing 8-10:

```
21. $new = "COLLATE $new" if $new =~ /\w+/;
22. $sqlRef->{code} =~ s/\bCOLLATE\s+$old\b/$new/ige;
```

On line 22, the /e modifier causes the replacement part of the s/// operator to be evaluated as a Perl expression before the replacement takes place. The string matched by the first part—in other words, /\bCOLLATE\s+$old\b/—is replaced with the value of the $new variable—the new COLLATE clause. The /g modifier ensures that the s/// operator replaces all the matched COLLATE clauses, and the /i modifier tells the operator to ignore the case.

Note that when the new collation isn't specified with the command-line parameter -n, each COLLATE clause will be replaced with an empty string—in other words, the COLLATE clause is removed. If you run the following on the command line, you change the COLLATE clauses in the T-SQL script tradeRelease.SQL from Latin1_General_CI_AS to Latin1_General_BIN:

```
cmd>perl replaceCollate.pl -s tradeRelease.SQL
                           -o Latin1_General_CI_AS
                           -n Latin1_General_BIN
```

After all, you weren't too far off with the naïve one liner if only you had normalized the T-SQL code!

Generating Audit Tables

> **SCENARIO**
> *You want to create an audit table to shadow every table in your database. The audit table will be used to log every change made to the table, including* INSERT, DELETE, *and* UPDATE.

Depending on the details of the requirement, the structure of the audit table for a given user table varies. The following example is a simplified case where the audit table includes only the primary key columns from the base table plus three audit columns:

- modifyType: A column to identify the type of change—whether it is INSERT, UPDATE, or DELETE

- modifyBy: A column to identify the login that executes the change

- modifyDate: A column to record the date and time when the change is made to the base table

To construct a definition for such an audit table, the main task is to find the columns in the primary key of the corresponding base table. Once these columns are found for a base table, defining the audit table is no more than adding a boiler-plate of the additional audit columns—in other words, the three columns listed previously. There are many different ways to find the primary key columns. This section uses the function dbaGetTableStruct_sp_help() from the module SQLDBA::Utility to parse the output of running sp_help against the base table. This function makes the information of the primary key columns readily accessible.

Listing 8-11 shows the Perl script scriptAuditTable.pl to generate the definition of the audit table when a base table is given or the definitions of multiple audit tables, one for every user table in the database, when no base table is given.

Listing 8-11. Generating the Definition of an Audit Table

```perl
use strict;
use Getopt::Std;
use SQLDBA::Utility qw( dbaRunOsql dbaGetTableStruct_sp_help );

Main : {
   my %opts;
   getopts('S:d:t:', \%opts);  # get command-line arguments
   my ($server, $dbName, $tbName) = ($opts{S}, $opts{d}, $opts{t});
   # check if the required arguments are present
   (defined $server && defined $dbName) or printUsage();

   my @tbNames = getTableNames($server, $dbName, $tbName);
   foreach my $tb (@tbNames) {
      scriptAuditTable($server, $dbName, $tb);
   }
} # Main


####################
```

```perl
sub getTableNames {
   my ($server, $dbName, $tbName) = @_;


   my @tbNames;
   if ( defined $tbName ) {
      @tbNames = ($tbName);
   }
   else {
      # prepare osql command-line options
      my $optRef = { '-E' => undef,      # use trusted connection
                     '-n' => undef,      # remove numbering and prompt symbol
                     '-w' => '5000',     # prevent text wrapping
                     '-d' => $dbName };  # set default database for the connection
      my $tbList = dbaRunOsql($server,
                          "SET NOCOUNT ON
                           SELECT name
                              FROM $dbName\.dbo\.sysobjects
                             WHERE type=\'U\'
                               AND OBJECTPROPERTY(id, \'IsMSShipped\') = 0",
                           $optRef);
      @tbNames = split /\n/, $tbList;
   }
   foreach my $tb (@tbNames) {
      # remove leading and trailing spaces
      $tb =~ s/^\s*//; $tb =~ s/\s*$//;
   }
   return @tbNames;
} # getTableNames


####################
sub scriptAuditTable {
   my ($server, $dbName, $tbName) = @_;

   # prepare osql command-line options
   my $optRef = { '-E' => undef,      # use trusted connection
                  '-n' => undef,      # remove numbering and prompt symbol
                  '-w' => '5000',     # prevent text wrapping
                  '-d' => $dbName };  # set default database for the connection
   my $spHelp = dbaRunOsql($server, "sp_help \'$tbName\'", $optRef);
   my $tbRef = dbaGetTableStruct_sp_help($spHelp);
   unless ($tbRef) {
      print "\n***Err: dbaGetTableStruct_sp_help() failed to get ";
      print "structure info for table $tbName.\n";
      return;
```

```perl
    }

    my $sql = "CREATE TABLE $tbName\_audit (\n";
    my @columns = split /\s*,\s*/,
                    $tbRef->{Constraints}->{PrimaryKey}->{Constraint};
    unless (@columns) {
        print "\n***Err: table $tbName doesn't have the primary key.";
        return;
    }
    foreach my $column (@columns) {
        $column =~ s/\s*//; $column =~ s/\s*$//;
        $sql .= "   $column " . $tbRef->{Columns}->{$column}->{type};
        # the following columns require length
        if ($tbRef->{Columns}->{$column}->{type} =~
                    /^( char|varchar|binary|varbinary
                        |nchar|nvarchar)/ix) {
            $sql .= " ( $tbRef->{Columns}->{$column}->{length} ) ";
        }
        # the following columns require precision and scale
        if ($tbRef->{Columns}->{$column}->{type} =~
                                    /^( decimal|numeric)/ix) {
            $sql .= " (" . $tbRef->{Columns}->{$column}->{prec} . ", "
                    . $tbRef->{Columns}->{$column}->{scale} . ")";
        }
        # specify column nullability
        $sql .= $tbRef->{Columns}->{$column}->{nullable} =~ /yes/i ?
                    " NULL\n" : " NOT NULL,\n";
    }
    # now, add the three audit columns
    $sql .= "   modifyType char(1) NOT NULL ";
    $sql .=          "CHECK (modifyType in ('U', 'I', 'D')),\n";
    $sql .= "   modifyBy varchar(128) NOT NULL ";
    $sql .=          "DEFAULT (suser_sname()),\n";
    $sql .= "   modifyDate datetime NOT NULL DEFAULT (getdate())\n";
    $sql .= ")\nGO\n";
    print "-- Audit table for $tbName \n";
    print $sql;
} # scriptAuditTable


###############
sub printUsage {
    print << '--Usage--';
Usage:
    cmd>perl scriptAuditTable.pl    -S <SQL server or instance>
```

```
                              -d <database name>
                            [ -t <table name> ]
--Usage--
exit;
} # printUsage
```

You can run the script as follows to generate the audit table for the
pubs..authors table on the SQL Server instance SQL01\APOLLO:

```
cmd>perl scriptAuditTable.pl -S SQL01\APOLLO -d pubs -t authors
CREATE TABLE authors_audit (
   au_id id NOT NULL,
   modifyType char(1) NOT NULL CHECK (modifyType in ('U', 'I', 'D')),
   modifyBy varchar(128) NOT NULL DEFAULT (suser_sname()),
   modifyDate datetime NOT NULL DEFAULT (getdate())
)
GO
```

Note that there's nothing inherent about this problem to make it particularly
amenable to Perl. In fact, because the information needed to construct the audit
table is already well structured in SQL Server and is immediately accessible to
T-SQL queries, it's just as easy to give an exclusively T-SQL solution. A T-SQL
solution can use the following query to obtain the information of the columns in
the primary key of every table in a database:

```
SELECT c.*
   FROM information_schema.table_constraints tc JOIN
              information_schema.constraint_column_usage ccu
        ON  tc.constraint_name = ccu.constraint_name JOIN
              information_schema.columns c
        ON  ccu.table_name = c.table_name AND
              ccu.column_name = c.column_name
 WHERE constraint_type = 'PRIMARY KEY'
ORDER BY c.table_name, c.ordinal_position
```

Better still, you could change the Perl code in Listing 8-11 to take advantage of
this query instead of relying on parsing the output of sp_help.

In Listing 8-11, the function dbaGetTableStruct_sp_help() is imported from
SQLDBA::Utility to retrieve the schema of a table. This function parses the text
output of the system procedure sp_help and stores the table structure in a Perl
nested data structure. The function handles only regular identifiers. If there are
identifiers that don't comply with all the rules of a regular identifier, you should
instead use the function dbaGetTableColumns() exported from the module

SQLDBA::SQLDMO. To learn more about the function `dbaGetTableColumns()`, see the section "Comparing the Columns Between Two Tables" in Chapter 5 and Listing 5-2.

Generating Audit Triggers

> **SCENARIO**
> *Now that you have the audit table, you need triggers to log changes made to the user table. You can log the changes in the audit table created in the preceding section.*

Why do you want to log changes to your data? Sometimes, you have no choice because it's a regulatory requirement. Other times, you want to preserve an audit trail for security reasons so that you can go back and investigate who made what changes and when. You may also want to log the changes for troubleshooting purposes, for instance, when you suspect an application is making unexpected changes to your data. This is often more useful during the development than during the production.

Generally speaking, there are many ways you can log changes to a table. To use the audit tables discussed in the preceding section, your best choice is to use triggers. The following example clarifies what triggers you should generate for these audit tables. The following are three audit triggers for the `pubs..authors` table for `INSERT`, `DELETE`, and `UPDATE`, respectively:

```
/**** insert trigger ****/
CREATE TRIGGER tri_authors
ON authors FOR INSERT
AS
    INSERT authors_audit(au_id, ModifyType)
    SELECT au_id, 'I' FROM inserted
GO
/**** delete trigger ****/
CREATE TRIGGER trd_authors
ON authors FOR DELETE
AS
    INSERT authors_audit(au_id, ModifyType)
    SELECT au_id, 'D'  FROM deleted
GO
/**** update trigger ****/
CREATE TRIGGER tru_authors
ON authors FOR UPDATE
AS
    INSERT authors_audit(au_id, ModifyType)
```

```
    SELECT au_id, 'U' FROM deleted
    UNION
    SELECT au_id, 'U' FROM inserted
GO
```

As you can see, the T-SQL code of these audit triggers has a lot in common regardless of for which user table they're defined. Similar to the case of generating the audit tables (discussed in the previous section), once the name of a user table is given, the task of generating these triggers is reduced to finding the primary key columns of the user table, and the rest of the code is boilerplate. Listing 8-12 shows the Perl script for generating the audit triggers.

Listing 8-12. Generating Audit Triggers

```
use strict;
use Getopt::Std;
use SQLDBA::Utility qw( dbaRunOsql dbaGetTableStruct_sp_help );

Main : {
   my %opts;
   getopts('S:d:t:', \%opts);  # get command-line arguments
   my ($server, $dbName, $tbName) = ($opts{S}, $opts{d}, $opts{t});
   (defined $server && defined $dbName) or printUsage();

   my @tbNames = getTableNames($server, $dbName, $tbName);
   foreach my $tb (@tbNames) {
      generateAuditTrigger($server, $dbName, $tb);
   }
} # Main


####################
sub getTableNames {
   my ($server, $dbName, $tbName) = @_;

   my @tbNames;
   if ( defined $tbName ) {
      @tbNames = ($tbName);
   }
   else {
      # prepare osql command-line options
      my $optRef = { '-E' => undef,     # use trusted connection
                     '-n' => undef,     # remove numbering and prompt symbol
                     '-w' => '5000',    # set width to prevent text wrapping
                     '-d' => $dbName }; # set default database for the connection
```

```perl
    my $tbList = dbaRunOsql($server,
                            "SET NOCOUNT ON
                             SELECT name
                               FROM $dbName\.dbo\.sysobjects
                              WHERE type=\'U\'
                                AND OBJECTPROPERTY(id, \'IsMSShipped\') = 0",
                            $optRef);
    @tbNames = split /\n/, $tbList;
  }
  foreach my $tb (@tbNames) {
    $tb =~ s/^\s*//; $tb =~ s/\s*$//;
  }
  return @tbNames;
} # getTableNames


########################
sub generateAuditTrigger {
  my ($server, $dbName, $tbName) = @_;

  # prepare osql command-line options
  my $optRef = { '-E' => undef,      # use trusted connection
                 '-n' => undef,      # remove numbering and prompt symbol
                 '-w' => '5000',     # set width to prevent text wrapping
                 '-d' => $dbName };  # set default database for the connection
  my $spHelp = dbaRunOsql($server, "sp_help \'$tbName\'", $optRef);
  my $tbRef = dbaGetTableStruct_sp_help($spHelp);
  unless ($tbRef) {
    print "\n***Err: dbaGetTableStruct_sp_help() failed to get ";
    print "structure info for table $tbName.\n";
    return;
  }
  my @columns = split /\s*,\s*/,
                $tbRef->{Constraints}->{PrimaryKey}->{Constraint};
  unless (@columns) {
    print "\n***Err: table $tbName doesn't have the primary key.\n";
    return;
  }
  my $pkColStr = shift @columns;
  foreach my $column (@columns) {
    $column =~ s/\s*//; $column =~ s/\s*$//; $pkColStr .= ", $column";
  }
  # now that we have found the PK columns
  print scriptTriggerSQL($tbName, 'insert', $pkColStr);
  print scriptTriggerSQL($tbName, 'delete', $pkColStr);
```

```
      print scriptTriggerSQL($tbName, 'update', $pkColStr);
} # generateAuditTriggers


#####################
sub scriptTriggerSQL {
   my ($tbName, $type, $pkColStr) = @_;
   unless ($type =~ /^( insert | delete | update )$/ix) {
      die "***Err: the type paramter of function scriptTriggerSQL " .
            "expects one of insert, delete, and insert.";
   }

   my $sql;
   if (lc($type) eq 'insert') {  # if it's insert
      $sql  =<<"__INSERT_TRIGGER__";
      CREATE TRIGGER tri_$tbName
      ON $tbName FOR INSERT
      AS
         INSERT ${tbName}_audit($pkColStr, ModifyType)
         SELECT $pkColStr, 'I' FROM inserted
      GO
__INSERT_TRIGGER__
   }
   elsif (lc($type) eq 'delete') {  # if it's delete
      $sql  =<<"__DELETE_TRIGGER__";
      CREATE TRIGGER trd_$tbName
      ON $tbName FOR DELETE
      AS
         INSERT ${tbName}_audit($pkColStr, ModifyType)
         SELECT $pkColStr, 'D' FROM deleted
      GO
__DELETE_TRIGGER__
   }
   elsif (lc($type) eq 'update') {  # if it's update
      $sql  =<<"__UPDATE_TRIGGER__";
      CREATE TRIGGER tru_$tbName
      ON $tbName FOR UPDATE
      AS
         INSERT ${tbName}_audit($pkColStr, ModifyType)
         SELECT $pkColStr, 'U' FROM deleted
         UNION
         SELECT $pkColStr, 'U' FROM inserted
      GO
__UPDATE_TRIGGER__
   }
```

411

```
    $sql =~ s/(^|\n)\s{6}/$1/g;
    return $sql;
} # scriptTriggerSQL


################
sub printUsage {
    print << '--Usage--';
Usage:
    cmd>perl GenerateAuditTriggers.pl  -S <SQL server or instance>
                                       -d <database name>
                                       [ -t <table name> ]
--Usage--
exit;
} # printUsage
```

The overall structure of the script in Listing 8-12 isn't significantly different from that of the script for generating audit tables in Listing 8-11. The main body of the script first gets the names of the tables for which the triggers will be generated. This could be a single table specified on the command line with the parameter -t, or it could be all the user tables in the database when the -t parameter isn't specified. Then, for each table, it calls the function generateAuditTrigger() to perform the real task—generating the SQL code for the insert trigger, the delete trigger, and the update trigger.

As mentioned, the crux of the task is to find the columns in the primary key of the user table. Similar to the previous section, this section uses the function dbaGetTableStruct_sp_help() from the module SQLDBA::Utility to parse the output of sp_help. Note that if the table has a primary key, the list of the columns in the primary key is recorded in the following hash where $tbRef is the reference returned by the function dbaGetTableStruct_sp_help():

```
$tbRef->{Constraints}->{PrimaryKey}->{Constraint}
```

With the primary key columns in hand, you're ready to generate the code for the audit triggers on the user table. You do this with the function scriptTriggerSQL(), which takes the table name, the trigger type (in other words, DELETE, INSERT, or UPDATE), and the comma-separated list of the primary key columns. For each trigger type, a here document is the template for the trigger code. For instance, Listing 8-13 shows the here document for the insert trigger.

Listing 8-13. The Template for the Insert Trigger

```
$sql =<<"__INSERT_TRIGGER__";
CREATE TRIGGER tri_$tbName
ON $tbName FOR INSERT
AS
    INSERT ${tbName}_audit($pkColStr, ModifyType)
    SELECT $pkColStr, 'I' FROM inserted
GO
__INSERT_TRIGGER__
```

To complete the code generation, the placeholders—in the form of Perl variables—for the table name, the trigger type, and the primary key columns are interpolated.

Generating Data INSERT Statements

SCENARIO
You want to generate a series of INSERT *statements using the data from a table so that you can repopulate the table by running these* INSERT *statements.*

Generating a series of INSERT statements using the data in a table allows you to preserve a table entirely in a SQL script. Putting both the table schema and the table data in a single SQL script can be convenient when working with a small table, especially in a development environment. For instance, you can then simply send the SQL script to another site for restore with little need for instructions. You can also generate a script to capture a snapshot of your test database and then execute the script to restore the test environment to a known state.

Given a table, the Perl script in Listing 8-14 generates an INSERT statement for each row in the table. It first reads the table definition, then reads every row from the table, applies necessary transformation to each column per its definition, and constructs the INSERT statement. A column may require transformation so that it can be correctly represented in a character string in the INSERT statement. You'll learn more about this after the code.

Listing 8-14. Generating INSERT *Statements*

```
use strict;
use Win32::ODBC;
use Getopt::Std;
```

```perl
my %opts;
getopts('S:d:t:', \%opts);  # get command-line arguments
my ($server, $dbName, $tbName) = ($opts{S}, $opts{d}, $opts{t});
(defined $server && defined $dbName && defined $tbName) or printUsage();

Main: {
   # construct the connection string
   my $connStr = "Driver={SQL Server};Server=$server;" .
             "Database=$dbName;Trusted_Connection=yes";
   my $conn = new Win32::ODBC($connStr) or
       die "***Err: " . Win32::ODBC::Error();

   my ($columnRef, $attribRef) = getColumnProperties($tbName, $conn);
   my $sql = constructINSERT($columnRef, $attribRef, $conn);
   print $sql;

   $conn->Close();
} # Main

############################
sub getColumnProperties {
   my($tbName, $conn) = @_;

   my @columns;
   my %attrib;
   if (! $conn->Sql("select * from $tbName where 1=2") ) {
      1 while $conn->FetchRow();

      # first get the data type for each column
      my @fields = $conn->FieldNames();
      %attrib - $conn->ColAttributes($conn->SQL_COLUMN_TYPE_NAME, @fields);

      # in case the data type is user defined, we need
      # the real data type to help us decide how to handle
      # the retrieved data in an INSERT statement
      foreach my $field (@fields) {
         if (! $conn->Sql("sp_help \'$attrib{$field}\'") ) {
            while($conn->FetchRow()) {
               my ($type) = $conn->Data("Storage_type");
               $attrib{$field} = $type;
            }
         }
         if ($attrib{$field} =~ /^(image|sql_variant)$/i) {
            die "***Err: data type $attrib{$field} not supported.";
```

```
         }
         push @columns, $field if lc($attrib{$field}) ne 'timestamp';
      }
   }
   else {
      die "***Err: failed to run select * from $tbName where 1=2.";
   }
   return (\@columns, \%attrib);
} # getColumnProperties


#########################
sub constructINSERT {
   my($columnRef, $attribRef, $conn) = @_;

   (scalar @$columnRef && scalar %$attribRef) or
      die "***Err: \$columnRef or \$attribRef is empty.";


   my $sql;
   if (! $conn->Sql("select * from $tbName") ) {
      # now get the data values for each row
      while ($conn->FetchRow()) {
         $sql .= "INSERT $tbName (" . join(',', @$columnRef) . ")\n";
         my @values = ();
         my %data = $conn->DataHash();
         # decide how to handle the VALUE clause of the INSERT
         foreach my $column (@$columnRef) {
            # the values of these data types can be used as is
            if ($attribRef->{$column} =~
                                   / int | smallint | bigint | tinyint
                                   | bit | decimal | numeric | money
                                   | smallmoney | float|real
                                   /ix) {
               if (defined $data{$column}) {
                  push @values, $data{$column};
               }
               else {
                  push @values, 'NULL';
               }
            }
            # the values of these types must be quoted with a pair of
            # single quotation marks
            elsif ($attribRef->{$column} =~
                                      / datetime|smalldatetime | char
                                      | varchar | nchar | nvarchar
```

```
                                         | text |ntext | uniqueidentifier
                                  /ix) {
                if (defined $data{$column}) {
                    $data{$column} =~ s/\'/\'\'/g;
                    push @values, "\'$data{$column}\'";
                }
                else {
                    push @values, 'NULL';
                }
            }
            # the binary data must be converted to a HEX string format
            elsif ($attribRef->{$column} =~ /binary|varbinary
                                      /ix) {
                if (defined $data{$column}) {
                    push @values, '0x' . unpack("H*", $data{$column});
                }
                else {
                    push @values, 'NULL';
                }
            }
            else {
                print "***Assert: invalid code path. Skip this row.\n";
                next;
            }
        }
    }
    $sql .= "VALUES (" . join(',', @values) . ")\n";
        }
    }
    return $sql;
} # constructINSERT


###################
sub printUsage {
    print << '--Usage--';
Usage:
    cmd>perl GeneratedataInserts.pl  -S <SQL server or instance>
                                     -d <database name>
                                     [ -t <table name> ]
--Usage--
exit;
} # printUsage
```

The script in Listing 8-14 relies heavily on the metadata information exposed by Open Database Connectivity (ODBC). In the function getColumnProperties(), the script uses the FieldNames() method and the ColAttributes() method—both from the module Win32::ODBC—to obtain the columns of the table and the data types of these columns, respectively.

However, there's one twist: A data type retrieved with the ColAttributes() method may be a user-defined data type, which doesn't directly tell how to handle the data in the VALUES clause of the INSERT statement. What you need is the corresponding SQL Server built-in data type. To accomplish that, the function getColumnProperties() loops through each column returned by the FieldName() method and executes a T-SQL sp_help on its data type. The storage_type column in the resultset of sp_help shows the SQL Server data type.

NOTE *A simpler approach to retrieving the system-supplied data types of all the columns in a user table is to query the INFORMATION_SCHEMA.COLUMNS view. The DATA_TYPE column of this view shows the system-supplied data type for each column in each user table.*

The function getColumnProperties() in Listing 8-14 returns two references, $columnRef and $attribRef. The former references an array of columns, and the latter a hash whose keys are columns and whose values are corresponding SQL Server data types. This may appear to be redundant because the columns names are already in the keys of the hash. However, recall that the hash keys aren't ordered, and you need the array to help remember the ordering of the columns.

These two data structures guide the construction of each INSERT statement in the function constructINSERT().

Constructing an INSERT statement is straightforward. But still you need to format data differently in the VALUES clause depending on its data type. When it comes to formatting, the SQL Server data types fall into three categories:

- **Data that can be used as is:** The data types in this category include the integer types, the number types, the money types, and the bit type.

- **Data that must be quoted**: A data value of type datetime, char, text, uniqueidentifier, and the like needs to be in single quotation marks.

- **Data that requires conversion**: A data value of the binary data type must be converted to a hexadecimal string.

In case a data value has embedded single quotation marks, you need to escape them when dealing with the data types in the second category. The following code fragment takes care of adding the quotation marks:

```
if (defined $data{$column}) {
      $data{$column} =~ s/\'/\'\'/g;
      push @values, "\'$data{$column}\'";
}
else {
      push @values, 'NULL';
}
```

The array `@values` will eventually include all the required data values in their proper formats ready to be concatenated into the string inside the `VALUES` clause of the `INSERT` statement.

A data value that's of the binary or varbinary type requires additional effort before you can add it to the `VALUES` clause. Note that the syntax for inserting a binary value into a table is similar to this example:

```
INSERT binTable(binCol) VALUES(0x782374)
```

In Query Analyzer, you may have noted that when you select from a table that has a column of the binary data type, the result is displayed as a hexadecimal string because Query Analyzer performs the conversion for you automatically. The script in Listing 8-14 gets the binary data through ODBC, which does no such conversion automatically. Fortunately, Perl has the rather versatile built-in function `unpack()` for this sort of conversion. The `unpack()` function takes a string (a binary string in this case) and expands it out into a list of values (hexadecimal values in this case). The following code from Listing 8-14 shows how you do the conversion for a binary value in the function `constructINSERT()`:

```
if (defined $data{$column}) {
      push @values, '0x' . unpack("H*", $data{$column});
}
else {
      push @values, 'NULL';
}
```

Merging Multiple SQL Scripts into a Single File

SCENARIO
You want to merge all the SQL scripts in a folder into a single script file.

The first question that jumps into to your mind may be "Why not just copy all the files to a single file using the Windows copy command?" For instance, the following command merges all the files in the current folder to a new file named merged.SQL:

```
cmd>copy *.* merged.SQL
```

This works fine except that often you want to add a header to introduce the script from each file so that each original script is clearly identified in the merged script file. In this case, you'd probably be thankful that you have such a header when the merged script runs into trouble and you're trying to find out which of the original scripts is the culprit.

The Perl script in Listing 8-15 adds a header in the format of a SQL comment that includes the original filename and the date/time when the files are merged.

Listing 8-15. Merging Scripts into a Single File

```perl
use strict;

my $dir = shift or die "***Err: $0 expects a folder name.";
(-d $dir) or die "***Err: Folder $dir does not exist.";

my $time = localtime();   # current local time

# read the filenames in the directory
my @fileNames = glob("$dir\\*.*");

# read each line from each of the files and writes
# the line to the merged file
foreach my $sqlFile (sort @fileNames) {
   open(SQL, "$sqlFile") or die "***Err: couldn't open $sqlFile.";

   # add the header first
   print "/**** Script from file $sqlFile on $time ****/\n";
   # write the rest of the lines unchanged
   print while(<SQL>);
   close(SQL);
   print "\n\n";
}
```

The script in Listing 8-15 accepts a directory name on the command line. It uses Perl's glob() function to list all the files in the directory. For each file, it first prints a header:

```
print "/**** Script from file $sqlFile on $time ****/\n";
```

and then it prints every line in the file as is:

```
print while(<SQL>);
```

This simple script uses only the most basic Perl features for manipulating files. It becomes more interesting when you consider the reverse of this problem—to split a script file that contains the definitions of multiple SQL Server database objects such as tables and stored procedures. This is the topic of the next section.

Splitting a SQL Script File into Multiple Files

SCENARIO
You often receive SQL script files that have the definitions of multiple stored procedures in a single file. You want to split such a file into multiple script files, each of which defines a single stored procedure.

My recommended best practices for SQL scripting call for one stored procedure per script file. This helps simplify source code management on such issues as version control and the consistent organization of source code files, and it's particularly important in a large development project.

However, in reality this best practice isn't often followed. I wouldn't be surprised that you routinely receive SQL scripts that include the definitions of multiple stored procedures in a single script file. You need to split the script into multiple files, each of which contains the definition of a single stored procedure so that the stored procedures can be individually version controlled.

Before discussing the code, consider how you can split such a SQL script. Intuitively, you can split a T-SQL script of stored procedures using this regular-expression pattern:

```
/\n\s*CREATE\s+PROC(EDURE)?\s+($spNameRE)/i
```

Note that the variable $spNameRE is itself a regular expression matching the name of a stored procedure. The exact nature of this regular expression isn't relevant for the current discussion. However, this approach is flawed in three respects:

- The Perl whitespace (in other words, \s) isn't sufficient to separate the T-SQL syntax elements.

- T-SQL comments, quoted strings, and delimited identifiers can confuse this regular expression, resulting in an incorrect split.

- Splitting a script by this pattern won't keep the settings of QUOTED_IDENTIFIER and ANSI_NULLS together with the definition of the stored procedure, thus altering the meaning of the stored procedure.

You can easily fix the first problem by replacing the Perl whitespace with the regular expression for the SQL whitespace, as discussed earlier in this chapter.

You can handle the second problem with the replace-match-restore strategy demonstrated in the previous sections. The section "Implementing the Replace-Match-Restore Strategy" in Chapter 3 introduced this strategy.

The third problem is more insidious. To handle the problem with the settings of QUOTED_IDENTIFIER and ANSI_NULLS, you can first break the script into an array of batches by the batch separator GO. Then, for each array element—in other words, a batch—that contains a CREATE PROCEDURE statement, you then search the array backwards to find the two settings immediately preceding the statement. Similarly, you search the array forward to find the next two settings immediately following the statement but before the next CREATE PROCEDURE statement. Joining these array elements together produces the script for the stored procedure.

The Perl script splitSPScript.pl in Listing 8-16 implements this strategy for splitting a T-SQL script of stored procedures.

Listing 8-16. Splitting a Script into One File per Stored Procedure

```perl
use strict;
use SQLDBA::ParseSQL qw( dbaNormalizeSQL dbaRestoreSQL
                         dbaSplitBatch );

my $infile = shift or
   die "***Err: $0 expects a file on the command line.";

# the object name can be a simple identifier and a delimited one
my $name = q/(?:
                [\w@\#]+              |
                \"(?:[^"] | \\\")+\" |
                \[(?:[^]]|\]\])+\])
           /;
# the proc name may be prefixed with the owner
my $SPNameRE = qr{ (?:
                    $name         # one-part name
                  | $name\.$name  # two-part name w owner
                 )
```

```
                        }ix;
        # T-SQL whitespace
        my $SQLws = qr{ (?: \s           |    # Perl whitespace
                            /\*\w+\*/     |    # Delimited comment
                            \-\-\w+\n          # ANSI comment
                    )+
                }ix;


Main : {
    # read the T-SQL script into a variable first
    my $sql;
    open(FL, $infile) or die "***Err: could not open $infile for read.";
    read(FL, $sql, -s FL);
    close(FL);

    # replace comments, strings, and delimited identifiers
    # with unique string tokens
    my $sqlRef = dbaNormalizeSQL($sql, 1);

    # split the SQL code into batches by batch separator GO
    my $batchRef = dbaSplitBatch($sqlRef->{code});

    # combine batches of an SP into a script
    my $spRef= combineBatches($batchRef);

    # restore the original comments, strings, delimited id's
    foreach my $spName (keys %{$spRef}) {
        $sqlRef->{code} = $spRef->{$spName};
        # restore the original strings, delimited id's, and comments
        $sqlRef = dbaRestoreSQL($sqlRef);
        # write the SP script to a file
        writeSQLFile($sqlRef->{code}, $spName);
    }
} # Main


######################
sub combineBatches {
    my $batchRef = shift or
        die "***Err: combineBatches() expects a reference.";

    # Find the array elements that are CREATE PROCEDURE statements
    # Use hash %index2Names to record the mapping from the array index
    # to the SP name
    my @sps;
```

```perl
my %index2Names;
for(my $i = 0; $i <= $#{$batchRef}; $i++) {
    if ( $batchRef->[$i] =~
            m{^ (?: $SQLws)? create $SQLws proc(edure)?
                $SQLws ($SPNameRE) }ix
        ) {
        push @sps, $i;
        $index2Names{$i} = $2;
    }
}


# now verify that each CREATE PROCEDURE is preceded with
# settings ANSI_NULLS and QUOTED_IDENTIFIER
foreach my $i (@sps) {
    # verify that the two batches preceding the CREATE PROCEUDRE are
    # for ANSI_NULLS and QUOTED_IDENTIFIER settings
    if (     ($batchRef->[$i-1] . ' ' . $batchRef->[$i-2])
              !~ /set $SQLws quoted_identifier $SQLws \w+/ix
        or ($batchRef->[$i-1] . ' ' . $batchRef->[$i-2])
              !~ /set $SQLws ansi_nulls $SQLws \w+/ix
        ) {
        die "***Err: ANSI_NULLS or QUOTED_IDENTIFIER setting is missing.";
    }
}


my ($spRef, $line, $finish);

# find the first and the last batch for each SP, and combine the batches
# for the SP into a single script. Use the array index of the first batch
# and the array index of the last batch to find the SP name from hash
# %index2Names
my $start = 0;
shift @sps;     # toss off the first index
foreach my $i (@sps) {
    $finish = $i-3;
    ($line) = grep {$_ >= $start and $_ < $finish} keys %index2Names;
    $spRef->{$index2Names{$line}} =
            join("\nGO\n", @{$batchRef}[$start..$finish]) . "\nGO\n";
    $start = $i-2;
}
# For the very last SP, $finish must be handled differently
$finish = $#{$batchRef};
($line) = grep {$_ >= $start and $_ < $finish} keys %index2Names;
$spRef->{$index2Names{$line}} =
```

```
                        join("\nGO\n", @{$batchRef}[$start..$finish]) . "\nGO\n";
      return $spRef;
} # combineBatches


#######################
sub writeSQLFile {
   my ($sql, $spName) = @_;

   # convert all non-alphanumeric to underline for filename
   $spName =~ s/\W/\_/g;
   my $fileName = $spName . ".SQL";
   open(SQL, ">$fileName") or
      die "***Err: couln't open $fileName.";
   print SQL $sql;
   close(SQL);
} # writeSQLFile
```

Take another look at the main body of the script in Listing 8-16. The script is first normalized with the now all-too-familiar function dbaNormalizeSQL(), and then it's split into an array of batches with dbaSplitBatch(). The main work happens in the function combineBatches(), which combines the batches of a stored procedure to make the script for that stored procedure and does so for every stored procedure. Finally, the function dbaRestoreSQL() restores the original strings, delimited identifiers, and comments in each stored procedure.

Let's see how combineBatches() finds the name of a stored procedure. The for loop in the function, shown in Listing 8-17, does the trick.

Listing 8-17. The for *Loop in* combineBatches()

```
for(my $i = 0; $i <= $#{$batchRef}; $i++) {
   if ( $batchRef->[$i] =~
           m{^ (?: $SQLws)? create $SQLws proc(edure)?
                    $SQLws ($SPNameRE) }ix
      ) {
         push @sps, $i;
         $index2Names{$i} = $2;
   }
}
```

The whitespace in the CREATE PROCEDURE <SP name> statement is matched with the regular expression $SQLws, which is defined to be as follows:

```
# T-SQL whitespace
my $SQLws = qr{ (?: \s           |     # Perl whitespace
                    /\*\w+\*/     |     # Delimited comment
                    \-\-\w+\n           # ANSI comment
                )+
              }ix;
```

Recall that after the T-SQL script is normalized, the entire comment is reduced to an alphanumeric string, thus permitting $SQLws to be as simple as it is. For more information on the T-SQL whitespaces, refer to the section "Handling the T-SQL Whitespace" earlier in this chapter.

Note that in the for loop in Listing 8-17, the hash %index2Names remembers which batch has the definition of a stored procedure. Knowing where the stored procedures are defined in the array of batches tells the Perl script, for each stored procedure, where to start search backward and forward for the settings of ANSI_NULLS and QUOTED_IDENTIFIER. In addition, this allows the Perl script to find the first and the last batch for each stored procedure and therefore combine all the batches for that stored procedure into a single T-SQL script.

Scripting the Database Objects with SQL-DMO

SCENARIO
For a given database, you want to periodically script out the database creation, all the tables, all the stored procedures, all the triggers, and all the constraints.

As a DBA, if you haven't been asked the following questions, you will be:

- What has changed in this stored procedure since last week? Or has anything changed?

- This stored procedure doesn't work as expected. Could you restore the one from the last week?

- Why did that index disappear? I could swear it was there last week.

One of the approaches for making sure you have answers for these questions is to regularly script out all the database objects and then archive these scripts. Ideally, you should schedule a job to generate the scripts every night and check the scripts into a source control program such as Microsoft Visual SourceSafe. Checking your scripts into a source control program reduces storage space consumption and facilitates ad-hoc comparison between different versions.

The best way to generate T-SQL scripts for all the database objects is to take advantage of the object-oriented interface provided by SQL-DMO, which includes a `Script()` method for an extensive list of objects covering almost every aspect of SQL Server.

In theory, you could query the SQL Server system tables yourself to produce SQL scripts for re-creating these objects. But that would be quite tedious and error prone. More important, Microsoft strongly discourages such a direct reliance on the internals of the system tables. And most undesirably, this amounts to reinventing the wheel when comprehensive scripting methods are already available in SQL-DMO.

The key to programming SQL-DMO is to become familiar with its object model. This means familiarity with the objects, the collections, the properties, and the methods. You especially should become comfortable with traversing the SQL-DMO object hierarchy, which is a tree-like structure relating one SQL-DMO object to another, often via their exposed collection methods.

NOTE *The section "Interacting with a COM Object" in Chapter 2 has a brief introduction to the* `Script()` *method of SQL-DMO. Then, the section "Scripting a Stored Procedure" in Chapter 3 discusses scripting a stored procedure in detail.*

Of particular importance is a special type of object, namely collections. A *collection* is an object containing other objects of the same type. When you traverse the SQL-DMO object hierarchy, you can't avoid running into object collections. For instance, to travel from a `Database` object to a `Table` object in the database, you must go through the `Tables` collection under the `Database` object.

To script out database objects such as tables and stored procedures, you follow the same basic logical flow that all SQL-DMO applications share, which is as follows:

1. First, you create a `SQLDMO.SQLServer` object or `SQLDMO.SQLServer2` object in your script.

2. Then, you use its `Connect()` method to establish a session with a particular SQL Server instance.

3. Now, you're ready to follow the object hierarchy from the `SQLServer` or `SQLServer2` object to any desired object within that instance of SQL Server.

NOTE *In SQL Server 2000,* SQLServer2 *is recommended. It inherits all the properties and methods from* SQL *Server, plus several new ones unique to SQL Server 2000.*

Listing 8-18 is a Perl script to generate the T-SQL script for re-creating all the tables, stored procedures, views, triggers, and Declarative Referential Integrity (DRI) constraints in a database.

Listing 8-18. Scripting SQL Server Objects with SQL-DMO

```perl
use strict;
use Getopt::Std;
use Win32::OLE 'in';
use Win32::OLE::Const 'Microsoft SQLDMO';

my %opts;
getopts('S:d:o:u:p:', \%opts);  # get command-line arguments
my ($serverName, $dbName, , $user, $password, $output)
      = ($opts{S}, $opts{d}, $opts{u}, $opts{p}, $opts{o});
# check if the required command-line arguments are present
(defined $serverName && defined $dbName && defined $output)
      or printUsage();

my $server = Win32::OLE->new('SQLDMO.SQLServer') or
    die "***Err: could not create SQLDMO object.";
if (defined $user) {
   $server->{LoginSecure} = 0;   # SQL connection
}
else {
   $server->{LoginSecure} = 1;   # trusted connection
}
# make connection to the server
$server->connect($serverName, $opts{u}, $opts{p});
! Win32::OLE->LastError() or
    die "***Err: SQLDMO could not connect to $serverName.";

my $db = $server->Databases($dbName);
# script the database creation
$db->Script(SQLDMOScript_Default | SQLDMOScript_AppendToFile |
          SQLDMOScript_IncludeHeaders | SQLDMOScript_Drops |
          SQLDMOScript_ToFileOnly, $output);
```

```perl
my $tables = $server->Databases($dbName)->Tables();
! Win32::OLE->LastError() or
    die "***Err: could not get the tables in $dbName.";

# Script tables including triggers and DRI constraints
foreach my $obj (in($tables)) {
    if (($obj->TypeOf()) == SQLDMOObj_UserTable) {
        $obj->Script(SQLDMOScript_Default | SQLDMOScript_AppendToFile |
                     SQLDMOScript_OwnerQualify | SQLDMOScript_Triggers |
                     SQLDMOScript_IncludeHeaders | SQLDMOScript_Drops |
                     SQLDMOScript_DRI_All | SQLDMOScript_ToFileOnly,
                     $output);
    }
}

# Script stored procedures
foreach my $obj (in($server->Databases($dbName)->StoredProcedures())) {
    $obj->Script(SQLDMOScript_Default | SQLDMOScript_AppendToFile |
                 SQLDMOScript_IncludeHeaders | SQLDMOScript_Drops |
                 SQLDMOScript_ToFileOnly,
                 $output);
}

# Script views
foreach my $obj (in($server->Databases($dbName)->Views())) {
    if ($obj->{Owner} ne 'INFORMATION_SCHEMA') {
        $obj->Script(SQLDMOScript_Default | SQLDMOScript_AppendToFile |
                     SQLDMOScript_IncludeHeaders | SQLDMOScript_Drops |
                     SQLDMOScript_ToFileOnly,
                     $output);
    }
}
$server->disconnect();
$server->DESTROY();

sub printUsage {
    print << '--Usage--';
Usage:
    cmd>perl scriptSQLDMO.pl -S <SQL server or instance>
                             -d <database name>
                             -o <output file>
                             -u <SQL login>
                             -p <password>
```

```
--Usage--
exit;
} # printUsage
```

As briefly mentioned in Chapter 2, "Working with Commonly Used Perl Modules," SQL-DMO defines a large number of constant names—such as SQLDMOScript_Default—that you can use to modify the behavior of a method. You make the SQL-DMO constants available to the Perl script by using the following module at the beginning of Listing 8-18:

```
use Win32::OLE::Const 'Microsoft SQLDMO';
```

> **NOTE** *For more information on the module Win32::OLE::Const, refer to the section "Interacting with a COM Object" in Chapter 2. For a more detailed description of the constants exported by SQL-DMO, see* Real-World SQL-DMO for SQL Server *by Allan Mitchell and Mark Allison (Apress, 2002) or SQL Server Books Online.*

The other point to note is that the Perl script in Listing 8-18 only enumerates the objects in the Tables collection, the StoredProcedures collection, and the Views collection and applies the Script() method to each object in these collections. So how are the scripts for the triggers and the DRI constraints generated? They're generated because the ScriptType argument of the Script() method—applied to the Table object—includes SQLDMOScript_Triggers and SQLDMOScript_DRI_All.

If you prefer to script the triggers separately so that you can include separate headers or individual DROP TRIGGER statements for each trigger, you can include the following code fragment, where $tables is the SQL-DMO Tables collection in the database:

```
foreach my $obj (in($tables)) {
    if (($obj->TypeOf()) == SQLDMOObj_UserTable) {
       my $triggers = $obj->Triggers();
       foreach my $tr (in($triggers)) {
         $tr->Script(SQLDMOScript_Default | SQLDMOScript_AppendToFile |
                   SQLDMOScript_OwnerQualify | SQLDMOScript_IncludeHeaders |
                   SQLDMOScript_Drops | SQLDMOScript_ToFileOnly,
                   $output);  # script file
       }
    }
}
```

Unfortunately, it's not so easy to separately script all the constraints. SQL-DMO doesn't expose a single collection to contain all the constraints of a table, and there's no generic constraint object either; instead, you must deal with each type of constraint individually. For instance, to script all the check constraints in a database, you can apply the Script() method to each check constraint in the Checks collection of each table, as follows:

```
foreach my $obj (in($tables)) {
    if (($obj->TypeOf()) == SQLDMOObj_UserTable) {
        my $checks = $obj->Checks();
        foreach my $check (in($checks)) {
          $check->Script(SQLDMOScript_Default | SQLDMOScript_AppendToFile |
                         SQLDMOScript_OwnerQualify | SQLDMOScript_Drops |
                         SQLDMOScript_ToFileOnly,
                         $output);    # script file
        }
    }
}
```

Similarly, you can go through the Keys collection to script the primary key and the foreign keys of a table. To script the default constraints of a table, you must traverse through the Columns collection of the table, through the Column object, and to the DRIDefault object. As you can see, life would be much simpler if a generic constraint collection were provided for each table in SQL-DMO.

Finally, the T-SQL scripts generated by the Script() method in SQL-DMO conform to a consistent format. You can take full advantage of this consistent format to simplify pattern matching.

Summary

Generating SQL code is far more than concatenating strings selected from a SQL Server table. Although you can generate wonderful T-SQL code with T-SQL queries, T-SQL as a code generation language is rather limiting because it practically confines you to the universe of the relational database. Beyond the relational database, there's a much larger world that you must deal with when working with SQL Server, and Perl gives you the power to generate SQL code from a wide diversity of sources.

This chapter demonstrated Perl scripts that generate T-SQL code from a configuration file, from database schemas, from the data in a table, from existing T-SQL scripts, and from the SQL-DMO objects.

The next chapter shows you how to use Perl to help reduce information overload caused by rampant log files—not the database transaction log files—that are constantly being generated or updated in SQL Server environments. It also shows you how to tap into these files to extract useful information.

CHAPTER 9

Analyzing Log Files

EVEN IN A SMALL **SQL SERVER ENVIRONMENT** with half a dozen machines, a Database Administrator (DBA) has to deal with numerous log files. There are Windows event logs, SQL Server errorlogs, SQL Server Agent log files, DBCC CHECKDB output files, and the log files generated by various scheduled jobs including backups and other maintenance tasks.

Understanding Log Files

If you pay close attention to the various log files in a SQL Server environment, you'll observe the following:

- There can be numerous log files.

- They can be large.

- They contain valuable information for SQL Server administration.

- You need tools to make better use of these log files.

Log Files Can Be Numerous

In one of the SQL Server environments I worked in, there were several dozens of production SQL Servers and a similar number of servers used for Quality Assurance (QA) or development purposes. Altogether, I had about 100 SQL Server machines. A rough count identified the number of the log files updated or generated every day to be substantially more than 1,000. This came as a surprise initially.

But upon a closer examination, I found that for each SQL Server, there was an errorlog, a SQL Server Agent output file, a system event log, an application event log, and one or more output files for DBCC CHECKDB. That amounted to more than 500 files for 100 SQL Servers. In addition, every SQL Server had several scheduled tasks, each generating at least one log file. As you can see, it isn't difficult to end up with an impressive number of log files. I didn't even count the log files generated by the Microsoft cluster servers on which some of the SQL Server instances were running. Furthermore, I didn't count the ones generated by the replication agents.

Log Files in a SQL Server DBA's Work

What log files do you have to deal with in your job as a SQL Server DBA? The following is a list of the log files that require a DBA's attention. The files you're most likely to work with are at the top of the list:

- SQL Server errorlogs

- Windows event logs

- DBCC output files

- Log files from the scheduled jobs

- SQL Sever Agent log files

- Replication error logs and agent output files

- Windows cluster log files

- Third-party and in-house application log files

- Various trace files including the Open Database Connectivity (ODBC) trace logs

Log Files Can Be Large

The number of files is only one dimension of the problem. Another dimension is the file size. Some log files can grow to be massive, especially when there are problems or when certain trace flags are set.

This is a lot of information to cope with on a daily basis. Without adequate tools to help reduce the information overload, many DBAs simply give up checking the log files, hoping that the monitoring facility catches any serious errors. Others only do spot checks on a few log files that are deemed more important such as the errorlog files. Other DBAs don't want to be bothered by these files at all until a problem is brought to their attention.

If you remember one tip from this chapter, remember this: You must manage your log files.

Dealing with the log files ineffectively carries a huge risk of missing important SQL Server behavior or, worse, missing misbehavior until it is too late or too costly. These log files often contain telltale signs of potential problems or unintended changes. They also may contain critical messages that the monitoring facility isn't configured or designed to capture. Scanning the log files provides you with a safety net to prevent noteworthy error conditions from slipping through unnoticed.

Log Files Are a Goldmine

These log files contain a wealth of information that's much more than mere error conditions. You can conduct detailed and focused analysis to reveal useful patterns or uncover bits and bytes that can help diagnose SQL Server problems. For instance, in SQL Server errorlogs, valuable informational messages may include the database or transaction log backup history. A summary of the backup history shows you the pattern of the backups and may alert you to missing backups or unintended changes to the backup configuration.

Using Tools for Analyzing Log Files

Given the number of files and the amount of information, manually reviewing the log files daily is clearly out of the question. Even if it could be done, it would not be a good use of the DBA's time and would not be effective anyway. It isn't hard to imagine what will happen when the DBA gets bored and starts to scroll through the files at a speed reserved only for an android.

What about using utilities such as the Windows built-in command findstr.exe or the POSIX command grep.exe? Indeed, there have been published recommendations on using tools such as these to single out, from the log files, those lines that contain error text strings or string patterns. These tools allow you to search for strings or regular-expression patterns in text files. But they're not designed to do anything beyond that. In addition, their support for regular expressions is limited, and they're totally unaware of the context of those lines. Consequently, they tend to produce too many "false positives," including repetitive log lines that contain the same information or lines that are innocuous. Also note that these tools work only with text files. The log files a DBA has to work with, on the other hand, aren't limited to the text format.

 NOTE *If you want to use the Unix text search commands such as* grep, egrep, *and* fgrep *in Windows 2000/NT, you can find them in the Windows Services for UNIX product from Microsoft. The Windows 2000/NT Resource Kit also ships a collection of POSIX utilities, including* grep.exe.

You may decide to look or wait for an off-the-shelf tool that performs log file analysis. Even if you could find such a tool, most likely it will not meet all your needs. If you limit yourself to using only the off-the-shelf tools to perform log analysis, I can guarantee that you'll be in for a long wait. In the meantime, you have all these log files with which to cope.

If you're overwhelmed by the log files or are concerned with how to effectively handle them, you're reading the right chapter. Perl is a perfect tool for analyzing log files. You can use Perl to scan the log files for potentially useful information, store the data extracted from the scan, and then make decisions based on the collected data.

This chapter is about reducing information overload and minimizing boredom. It starts with two scripts for extracting information out of the event logs and out of the ODBC trace logs. Then, the chapter focuses on Windows event logs, first discussing a general script to summarize the event logs and then focusing on two specific threads of events—one to identify the ports used by SQL Server instances and the other to help highlight the machine reboot history.

Finally, the chapter discusses using Perl to extract valuable information from SQL Server errorlogs. Similarly, the chapter presents a script to produce a condensed general summary report out of SQL Server errorlogs and then moves on to two more focused case studies: detecting broken transaction log backup chains and summarizing deadlock information from the trace flag 1204 output.

Extracting Information from Windows Event Logs

SCENARIO
You want to extract specific information that matches certain criteria out of the Windows event logs.

In a Unix environment, system administrators often use a powerful utility called grep to look for information in files. A file isn't limited to the conventional disk files. It can be any of a diverse array of input/output devices such as the output redirected from a program, a pipe, and a network socket. The grep utility applies a pattern to each line in the file and outputs those lines that evaluate the pattern to true.

In fact, the grep utility proves to be so useful that a class of grep-like utilities is available. Some of the examples are egrep, fgrep, ngrep, and grepmail. The ngrep utility is an interesting one. It applies regular-expression patterns to the network packets to sniff out the packets that match the patterns. Even though it has little direct relevance to the SQL Server DBA in the tasks it's designed to perform, the ngrep utility epitomizes a general approach to greping information—extracting information with regular expressions—out of special data structures such as network packets and emails.[1]

---

1. See the January 2003 article, "Searching in Unusual Ways and Places," by Æleen Frisch in *Sys Admin* (http://www.samag.com/documents/s=7762/sam0301a/0301a.htm) for an interesting discussion on searching with utilities such as grep, ngrep, and grepmail.

That is, you first use an interface mechanism to expose the data elements in the data structure and then apply regular expressions to the data elements to find the information in which you're interested.

This section follows the same approach to build a Windows event log greping utility—grepEventlog.pl. The utility uses the Win32::EventLog module to access and expose the records and fields of the Windows event logs to regular-expression pattern matching.

 NOTE *If you're a fan of the Unix* grep-*related utilities, you'll love Perl. Because it blends regular expressions with other language features such as looping through a file, a list, or a hash, Perl is really a highly flexible toolkit for building greping utilities. In addition, Perl has a built-in function* grep() *that's far more powerful than the Unix* grep *or the Windows* findstr.exe.

Listing 9-1 shows the script grepEventlog.pl for extracting information out of the Windows event logs. You can specify a variety of criteria on the command line including the full-featured Perl regular expressions for filtering event source and event message text.

Listing 9-1. Greping Information from the Windows Event Logs

```
1.  use strict;
2.  use Getopt::Std;
3.  use SQLDBA::Utility qw ( dbaTime2str dbaSetDiff dbaStr2time
4.                           dbaSetCommon dbaInSet);
5.  use Win32::EventLog;
6.
7.  # The global data structures %types, @types, @logs, @fields
8.  # are all used to help validate command-line arguments
9.  my %types = ( EVENTLOG_ERROR_TYPE       , 'ERROR',
10.               EVENTLOG_INFORMATION_TYPE , 'INFORMATION',
11.               EVENTLOG_WARNING_TYPE     , 'WARNING',
12.             );
13. my @types = values(%types);
14. my @logs =('SYSTEM', 'APPLICATION');
15. my @fields = ('TYPE', 'SOURCE', 'EVENTID', 'MESSAGE');
16.
17. Main: {
18.     my %opts;
19.     getopts('M:L:e:t:s:d:m:', \%opts); # get command-line arguments
```

```
20.
21.    # check and normalize command-line arguments
22.    my $argsRef = checkArgs(\%opts);
23.
24.    # scan the eventlog entries for matches
25.    grepEventLog($argsRef);
26. } # Main
27.
28. ####################
29. sub checkArgs {
30. ####################
31.    my $argsRef = shift or
32.        die "***Err: checkArgs() expects a reference.";
33.
34. # This function validates the command-line arguments and sets
35. # the default values.
36. # The output of this function is explained in the text.
37. # The code is omitted. See the code from the Apress Downloads area.
38.    return $argsRef;
39. } # checkArgs
40.
41. #########################
42. sub grepEventLog {
43.    my $argsRef = shift or
44.        die "***Err: grepEventLog() expects a reference.";
45.    my($handle, $eventRef);
46.
47.    $Win32::EventLog::GetMessageText = 1;
48.    foreach my $log (@{$argsRef->{L}}) {    # APPLICATION and/or SYSTEM
49.        $handle = Win32::EventLog->new($log, $argsRef->{M})
50.                or die "***Err: could not open $log on $argsRef->{M}";
51.        # loop through the eventlog records backwards
52.        while (    $handle->Read( EVENTLOG_BACKWARDS_READ |
53.                                 EVENTLOG_SEQUENTIAL_READ, 0, $eventRef)
54.                && $argsRef->{d1} < $eventRef->{TimeGenerated}
55.                && $argsRef->{d2} > $eventRef->{TimeGenerated} ) {
56.            # for each record, check if it meets the criteria
57.            my $rc = matchLogEntry($argsRef, $eventRef);
58.            if ( $rc == 1 ) {
59.                # for each record that meets the criteria, print a single
60.                # string including date/time, type, source, ID, and msg text
```

```
61.              my $msg = dbaTime2str($eventRef->{TimeGenerated});
62.              $msg .= ', ' . $types{$eventRef->{EventType}};
63.              $msg .= ', ' . $eventRef->{Source};
64.              $msg .= ', ' . ($eventRef->{EventID} & 0xffff);
65.              my $text = $eventRef->{Message};
66.              $text =~ s/[\n\r]/ /g;
67.              $msg .= ', ' . $text;
68.              print "$msg\n";
69.          }
70.        }
71.        Win32::EventLog::CloseEventLog($handle);
72.    }
73. } #grepEventLog
74.
75. #######################
76. # this function is to keep the if condition in grepEventLog() readable
77. sub matchLogEntry {
78.    my ($argsRef, $eventRef) = @_;
79.    my $return = 0;
80.
81.    # check event Type. Return -1 if not expected
82.    if (exists $argsRef->{t}) {
83.        return -1 if (!dbaInSet(uc($types{$eventRef->{EventType}}),
84.                            $argsRef->{t}));
85.    }
86.    # now check event Source. Return -2 if not expected
87.    if (exists $argsRef->{s}) {
88.        return -2 unless eval { $eventRef->{Source} =~ /$argsRef->{s}/ }
89.    }
90.    # check event IDs. Return -3 if not expected
91.    if (exists $argsRef->{e}) {
92.        return -3 if (!dbaInSet($eventRef->{EventID} & 0xffff,
93.                            $argsRef->{e}));
94.    }
95.
96.    # now check message body. Return -4 if not expected
97.    if (exists $argsRef->{m}) {
98.        return -4 unless eval { $eventRef->{Message} =~ /$argsRef->{m}/ }
99.    }
100.   return 1;
101.} # matchLogEntry
```

The `grepEventlog.pl` script in Listing 9-1 accepts the command-line arguments described in Table 9-1.

Table 9-1. Command-Line Arguments for the Script `grepEventlog.pl`

ARGUMENT	DESCRIPTION
`-M <computer name>`	This mandatory argument specifies the computer name.
`-L <event log>`	This mandatory argument specifies which event log to scan. It must be either SYSTEM or APPLICATION.
`-e <event IDs>`	This optional argument accepts a list of comma-separated event IDs. If not specified, the script scans all the event IDs.
`-t <event type>`	This mandatory argument specifies the type of the event. It can be information, warning, or error, or a comma-separated string of any of these three.
`-s <event source pattern>`	This optional argument accepts a regular expression to include the event sources in the scan. The regular expression can be any valid Perl regular expression.
`-d <beginning date/time>-<end date/time>`	This optional argument specifies a date/time range. The script scans only the event log entries in this range. If not specified, the script scans all the event log entries. The `<beginning date/time>` and `<end date/time>` arguments are in the format of YYYY/MM/DD hh:mm:ss. The time portion is optional.
`-m <event message pattern>`	This mandatory argument specifies a regular expression to match the strings in the message text of the event log entries. The regular expression can be any valid Perl regular expression.

The following two examples show how you can use the script in Listing 9-1 to extract useful information out of the Windows event logs.

Using *grepEventlog.pl*

The first example uses `grepEventlog.pl` to find the recent entries indicating that the event log service was started. The later section "Summarizing Reboot History" shows how to take advantage of the event log service entries to obtain a summary of the Windows reboot history.

I ran the following command line on a machine named SQL1 and obtained the event log entries since 2003/03/02 15:23:32. The entire command line should be on the same line (I've split it into three lines for readability):

```
cmd>perl eventlogGrep.pl -M SQL1 -L system -t information
                    -d"2003/03/02 15:23:32-"
                    -m"/event log service was started/i"
2003/03/09 01:54:18, INFORMATION, EventLog, 6005, The Event log ... was started.
2003/03/08 21:38:15, INFORMATION, EventLog, 6005, The Event log ... was started.
2003/03/07 21:11:41, INFORMATION, EventLog, 6005, The Event log ... was started.
2003/03/04 17:20:23, INFORMATION, EventLog, 6005, The Event log ... was started.
2003/03/03 19:00:53, INFORMATION, EventLog, 6005, The Event log ... was started.
2003/03/03 00:09:15, INFORMATION, EventLog, 6005, The Event log ... was started.
2003/03/02 17:54:33, INFORMATION, EventLog, 6005, The Event log ... was started.
```

Note that because the -d and -m arguments include spaces and special characters, you must enclose both in double quotes.

The second example is to get the Windows process IDs for all the SQL Server instances on the computer SQL1. The following shows the command line and the results:

```
cmd>perl eventlogGrep.pl -M SQL1 -L application -t information
                    -s "/^MSSQL/i"
                    -d "2003/03/08 15:23:32-"
                    -m "/SQL Server .+ using a process id of \d+/i"
2003/03/09 15:51:21, INFORMATION, MSSQL$SQL1, 17176 ... a process id of 1164
2003/03/09 15:07:02, INFORMATION, MSSQL$SQL2, 17176 ... a process id of 564
2003/03/09 01:54:47, INFORMATION, MSSQL$SQL2, 17176 ... a process id of 596
2003/03/09 00:00:05, INFORMATION, MSSQL$SQL2, 17177 ... a process id of 596
```

To fit the line width, I've replaced much of the event log message text with ellipses (...). The results show that the latest process ID used by the SQL Server named instance, SQL1, is 1164, and the latest process ID used by SQL2 is 564.

Examining *grepEventlog.pl*

Because Chapter 2 already covered the basics of working with the Windows event logs, this chapter focuses on the salient points in the script grepEventlog.pl in Listing 9-1.

Using Global Data Structures for Validation

The constants EVENTLOG_ERROR_TYPE, EVENTLOG_WARNING_TYPE, and
EVENTLOG_INFORMATION_TYPE are imported from the module Win32::EventLog.
Because these constants are numeric values, the script defines the following global
hash on line 9 in Listing 9-1 to translate them into the readable strings:

```
my %types = ( EVENTLOG_ERROR_TYPE,         'ERROR',
              EVENTLOG_INFORMATION_TYPE,   'INFORMATION',
              EVENTLOG_WARNING_TYPE,        'WARNING' );
```

The other three global arrays (@types, @logs, and @fields, defined on lines 13
through 15) help validate the command-line arguments. For instance, @logs
ensures that the only acceptable values for the -L argument are SYSTEM and
APPLICATION.

Examining the Hash Structure Returned by checkArgs()

The code of the function checkArgs() isn't shown in Listing 9-1 because it consists
of repetitive code fragments of a similar nature. However, it's important to understand its output, which is best explained with an example.

Given the following command line:

```
cmd>perl eventlogGrep.pl -M SQL1 -L system.application
                         -t information,warning,error -s "/^MSSQL/i"
                         -d "2003/03/01-2003/03/09"
                         -m "/SQL Server .+ using a process id/i"
```

the hash reference returned by the function checkArgs() is as shown in Listing 9-2.

Listing 9-2. A Sample $argsRef *Returned by* checkArgs()

```
1.  $argsRef = {
2.          'm' => qr/(?i-xsm:SQL Serer .+ using a process id)/,
3.          'd1' => '1046494800',
4.          'd2' => '1047186000',
5.          's' => qr/(?i-xsm:^MSSQL)/,
6.          'L' => [
7.                   'APPLICATION',
8.                   'SYSTEM'
9.                 ],
10.         't' => [
11.                  'ERROR',
```

```
12.                      'WARNING',
13.                      'INFORMATION'
14.                   ],
15.           'M' => 'SQL1'
16.        };
```

The function checkArgs() transforms the command-line arguments into the hash reference in Listing 9-2 in a format that can be directly applied to the various event log fields. The hash keys correspond to the letters of the command-line argument switches with the exception of the hash keys d1 and d2. The date/time range of the -d argument is split into two separate values corresponding to the beginning date/time and the end date/time, as explained in Table 9-1. The value for the key d1 is the beginning date/time in epoch seconds; similarly, the value for d2 is the end date/time in epoch seconds.

The two regular expressions for -m and -s, respectively, are compiled with the qr// operator before checkArgs() assigns them to the hash keys in Listing 9-2, thus the specially formatted regular expressions on lines 2 and 5.

The code fragment for compiling the regular expression for -m is as follows:

```
1.   # check -m for message regular expression
2.   # -m is mandatory, and must be a valid regular expression.
3.   defined $argsRef->{m} or
4.      die "***Err: option -m must be specified.";
5.   my $re = 'qr' . $argsRef->{m} unless $argsRef->{m} =~ /^\s*qr/;
6.   my $regex = eval $re;  # compile the regex to check its validity
7.   if ($@) {
8.      die "***Err: $argsRef->{m} is not a valid regex.";
9.   }
10.  $argsRef->{m} = $regex;  # convert to compiled regex
```

Line 5 prefixes the string 'qr' to the expression in $argsRef->{m} if it isn't already present. Line 6 then evaluates the qr// expression in the variable $re in the eval() function so that even if $re isn't a valid regular expression, the script can trap the error and won't crash. When the expression is valid, the output of the eval() function is a compiled regular expression and is assigned to the m key in the hash referenced by $argsRef.

Finally, the function checkArgs() converts the comma-separated values for the arguments -L and -t into arrays, and it assigns the array references to the respective hash keys in Listing 9-2.

Extracting Information from ODBC Trace Logs

> **SCENARIO**
> *You want to retrieve the SQL queries recorded in an ODBC trace log.*

An ODBC trace is an important troubleshooting tool when you work with ODBC client applications. When enabled, it provides detailed tracing of all the ODBC function calls.

The problem with ODBC trace is that its log file quickly grows. A single SQL query from an application can result in hundreds or thousands of lines in the ODBC trace log. On my workstation, I ran several simple SQL queries through Query Analyzer and recorded the number of lines logged in the ODBC trace log for each query as follows:

- 324 lines for USE pubs

- 576 lines for SELECT au_id FROM authors WHERE au_id = '172-32-1176'

- 1382 lines for sp_who

Apparently, the amount of logging is application dependent because different applications may interact with ODBC differently even for the same SQL query. For instance, I also ran sp_who through osql.exe, and that added 16,868 lines to the trace log. Regardless, if you trace an ODBC application for some time, the trace log will become large, and manually searching for information may not be viable.

To extract the SQL queries out of an ODBC trace log, the first order of business is to study the trace log and find the text patterns associated with the SQL queries that Perl can use. This type of exercise is often an iterative process. Because the documentation about the text patterns either doesn't exist or is insufficient, you can rarely gain complete knowledge with regard to the patterns even after repeated experiments.

The advantage of using Perl is that your scripts quickly become useful as soon as you gain some knowledge about the text patterns, and they can continue to improve as you gain more knowledge.

Text Patterns Containing SQL Queries

Rather than writing a script that may be generally applicable, this section focuses on extracting from the ODBC trace log the SQL queries sent from Query Analyzer or osql.exe.

Listing 9-3 shows three examples of the SQL queries captured in ODBC trace logs. The first two examples include the queries sp_who and SELECT "abc", both from Query Analyzer, and the third example includes the query from osql.exe.

Listing 9-3. Examples of SQL Queries in an ODBC Trace Log

```
isqlw       2d0-5e8   ENTER SQLExecDirectW
            HSTMT             00C11738
            WCHAR *           0x00157028 [    -3] "sp_who\ d\ a\ d\ a\ 0"
            SDWORD            -3


isqlw       438-59c   ENTER SQLExecDirectW
            HSTMT             00C11738
            WCHAR *           0x00146C60 [    -3] "select '"abc"'\ d\ a\ 0"
            SDWORD            -3


osql -Dtest -E 4b8-454 ENTER SQLExecDirectW
            HSTMT             007B16C0
            WCHAR *           0x00797744 [    10] "use pubs\ d\ a"
            SDWORD            10
```

You can draw the following conclusions from studying the ODBC trace logs:

- An ODBC trace records SQL queries when it logs the ODBC functions SQLExecDirect and SQLPrepare. The second parameter of these two functions includes a SQL query.

- An ODBC trace records each ODBC function twice, once when the function begins and once when the function exits.

- An ODBC trace records each embedded carriage return/linefeed combination as \ d \ a, which is the ASCII value 13 followed by the ASCII value 10.

- An ODBC trace encloses a SQL query with a pair of double quotation marks. However, it doesn't escape any embedded double quotes.

Extracting SQL Queries from ODBC Trace Logs

The script getODBCSQL.pl in Listing 9-4 implements these conclusions to scan an ODBC trace log and extract the SQL queries.

Listing 9-4. Extracting SQL Queries from an ODBC Trace Log

```
use strict;

my $traceLog = shift or
    die "***Err: $0 expects an ODBC trace log file.";

my $sql;
open(TRACE, $traceLog) or die "***Err: failed to open $traceLog for read.";
while(<TRACE>) {
    # look for SQLExecDirect or SQLPrepare
    if (/ENTER\s+(SQLExecDirect|SQLPrepare)/i) {
        <TRACE>;                          # skip the first parameter
        $_ = <TRACE>;                     # this should be the 2nd parameter
        if (/WCHAR\s+\*\[^\"]+\"(.+)\"/) { # the 2nd paramter has this pattern
            $sql = $1;
            $sql =~ s/\\ d\\ a/\n/g;       # replace \d \ a with \n
            $sql =~ s/\\ 0//g;             # remove the terminating null charatcer
            $sql .= "\n" unless $sql =~ /\n$/; # append a newline if not present
            print $sql;
        }
        else {  # if the 2nd parameter doesn't, the problem isn't handled
            print "***Err: incorrect code path. Should never be here.\n";
        }
    }
}
close(TRACE);
```

On my workstation, I enabled the ODBC trace to the log file SQL.log, ran the following SQL queries, and then turned off the ODBC trace:

```
SELECT au_id FROM "authors"
 WHERE au_id = '123-43-4523'
go
EXEC sp_who
go
```

Next, I ran the following to extract the SQL queries from the ODBC trace log SQL.log:

```
cmd>perl getODBCSQL.pl SQL.log
SELECT au_id FROM "authors"
 WHERE au_id = '123-43-4523'
SELECT au_id FROM "authors"
 WHERE au_id = '123-43-4523'
SELECT au_id FROM "authors"
 WHERE au_id = '123-43-4523'
SELECT au_id FROM "authors"
 WHERE au_id = '123-43-4523'
EXEC sp_who
EXEC sp_who
EXEC sp_who
EXEC sp_who
```

In this example, each SQL query was logged four times in the trace log SQL.log because the SQLExecDirect function was entered four times. The number of times a query is logged in the ODBC trace log may be different if you run the same query using a different application such as osql.exe. Unfortunately, it's not clear how you can remove the extraneous copies of the SQL queries recorded in an ODBC trace log.

Listing 9-4 demonstrates that you can first study the text patterns in a file and then apply Perl's powerful text processing features to find and extract information from the file. You can do much more with ODBC trace logs than extracting the SQL queries. For instance, if you're troubleshooting an ODBC application, you may be more interested in extracting the SQL queries that are logged when the execution exits the SQLExecDirect function and an error code is recorded in the trace log.

Note that there's no need to compile a comprehensive list of information bits and bytes you may ever need to extract before you start writing a script to extract them. When the need arises, you can study the requirements and write the script on demand to meet the requirements.

Summarizing Windows Event Logs

SCENARIO

Lately, you've noticed that the Windows administrators haven't been paying enough attention to the errors in the Windows event logs. This increases your exposure to potential server problems; you want to keep an eye on the event logs yourself.

A Windows event log can be voluminous. To regularly review a single event log is time consuming enough, not to mention monitoring multiple event logs on different servers. If you've ever tried to keep up with the log entries generated on a moderately busy server, you wouldn't dispute my claim that manually checking the Windows event logs every day on a large number of servers is out of the question. Well, it's not completely impossible to do so manually. But it would be error prone, boring, and at the expense of doing other more useful work.

An automated daily summary report of the event log records generated in the last few days should give you a good overall picture.

If you've been looking into the event logs regularly in your own environment, as any diligent DBA would, you probably have developed preferences in how you want to summarize your event logs. For instance, you may find out that you need to pay more attention to errors and warnings from some event sources while safely ignoring those from certain other sources. Instead of tailoring the script to meet specific requirements, you want a script that you can configure and customize to suit your specific needs. The script eventLogSummary.pl in Listing 9-5 is the result of this effort.

Listing 9-5. Summarizing Event Logs

```
use strict;
use SQLDBA::Utility qw ( dbaTime2str dbaSetDiff dbaSetCommon dbaInSet
                         dbaReadINI dbaReadEventLog dbaFilterLogEntry );
Main: {
   my $configFile = shift or
        die "***Err: config file must be specified on the command line.";
   (-e $configFile) or die "Config file $configFile does not exist.";

   # get config options
   my $configRef - getConfig($configFile);

   # read and summarize the eventlog entries for each server
   foreach my $server (sort keys %$configRef) {
     my $summaryRef = dbaReadEventLog($server, \&dbaFilterLogEntry, $configRef);
     printEventLog($server, $summaryRef, $configRef);
   }
} # Main


##################
sub getConfig {
   my $configFile = shift or die "***Err: getConfig() expects a file name.";

   my $ref = dbaReadINI($configFile);
```

```perl
    foreach my $server (keys %$ref) {
        foreach my $key (keys %{$ref->{$server}}) {
            if (! defined $ref->{$server}->{$key}) {
                delete $ref->{$server}->{$key}; # remove config key with no value
                next;
            }
            if ($key !~ /(includeMessage|ExcludeMessage)/i) {
                # split the comma-separated values into an array
                $ref->{$server}->{$key} =
                    [ split /\s*,\s*/, uc($ref->{$server}->{$key}) ];
            }
            else {
                # for IncludeMessage or ExcludeMessage keys,
                # split the comma-separated values, evaluate each value
                # as a regex, and put the regex into an array
                my @res;
                foreach my $re (split /\s*,\s*/, $ref->{$server}->{$key}) {
                    $re = 'qr' . $re unless $re =~ /^\s*qr/;
                    my $regex = eval $re;  # evaluate the qr// expression in eval()
                    if ($@) {              # trap the error if not a valid regex
                        print "***Err: $re is not a valid regex.";
                        next;
                    }
                    push @res, $regex;  # add the compiled regex to the array
                }
                # now the key has a reference to an array of compiled regex'es
                $ref->{$server}->{$key} = \@res;
            }
        }
    }
    return $ref;
} # getConfig


##########################
sub printEventLog {
    my ($server, $summaryRef, $configRef) = @_;
    my (@keys);

    foreach my $log (@{$configRef->{$server}->{LOG}}) {
        @keys = sort {     $summaryRef->{$log}->{$b}->{Source}
                       cmp $summaryRef->{$log}->{$a}->{Source} }
                  (keys %{$summaryRef->{$log}});

        if (@keys) {
```

```
        print "\n", "*" x 50, "\n";
        print "***  Server = $server -- ", $log, " log ***\n";
        print "*" x 50, "\n";
    }

    foreach my $header (@keys) {
    printf " %-20s %-6s %-5s %s\n",
           $summaryRef->{$log}->{$header}->{TimeGeneratedStr},
           "Total:", $summaryRef->{$log}->{$header}->{No}, $header;
    }
  }
} # printEventLog
```

Before getting into the details of the script, let's discuss what you may want to
see in an event log summary.

Deciding What to Summarize

Listing 9-5 produces the simplest form of summary reports. For each server, it
scans the system event log or the application log and produces a count of log
records by a selected grouping of event log fields. These log fields identify how the
record count should be grouped, much as the rows are counted in a SELECT
statement by the columns in the GROUP BY clause. Depending on the kind of
summary you want to produce, it's up to you to decide how you would like to select
and group the event log fields.

Perhaps you want to have a report that shows the number of times errors from
each distinct source is logged on a computer; in that case, you count by event
source. Or maybe you only want to know how many errors, warnings, and informational messages were logged; you count the records by event type—the values
can be error, warning, or information for both the system event log and the
application event log.

You have to decide what event log fields to use to summarize your event log. In
general, the event user and event category, by themselves, aren't useful for summarizing the system event log or the application event log, though these two fields
play a more useful role in the security log. Similarly, the event ID is of dubious
value by itself. It's often the case that the same event ID is assigned to two different
messages, each of which is individually significant to a DBA and thus should be
reported separately. My experience is that in most cases you'll likely summarize
the log records by a combination of event type, event source, event ID, and event
description.

Deciding What to Configure

For flexibility, I've pulled into a configuration file the options concerning, among other things, what to count, how to count, what to include, and what to exclude from the summary report. These are the options you can specify with respect to the fields of an event log record, including the event time, event type, event source, and event ID. I've intentionally omitted the event category and event user because, as mentioned earlier, they're of little value when working with the system or the application event log. You provide the configuration file to the Perl script on the command line as follows:

```
cmd>perl eventLogSummary.pl config.txt
```

where `config.txt` is the name of the configuration file. Listing 9-6 shows a sample configuration file for the script `eventLogSummary.pl`.

Listing 9-6. A Sample Configuration File for `eventLogSummary.pl`

```
[SQL1]
Log = system,application
LogElement = Type,Source,EventID,Message
IncludeDays = 6
IncludeType = Error,Warning
ExcludeType =
IncludeSource =
ExcludeSource = MSSQLServer,SQLServerAgent,SQLExecutive
IncludeEventID =
ExcludeEventID =
IncludeMessage =
ExcludeMessage = /Import\s+Error/i

[SQL2]
Log = system
LogElement = Type,Source,EventID
IncludeDays = 7
IncludeType = Error,Warning,Information
ExcludeEventID = 6006,6009
```

You specify the computer name in the section heading between a pair of square brackets. If you need to add another computer to the summary report, all you need to do is add another section in the configuration file for that computer. In Listing 9-6, for the computer SQL1, the `Log` option instructs `eventLogSummary.pl` to scan both the system log events and the application log events, and the

`LogElement` option specifies that the event type, event source, event ID, and event message will uniquely identify each unit for counting in the summary report. The `IncludeDays` option tells the script how many days to go back when scanning the event log. For the computer SQL1, the script in Listing 9-5 counts only the entries generated over the past six days for the summary report.

> **NOTE** `LogElement` *isn't a term used in the Windows event log documen-tation. It's a term used by the script* `eventLogSummary.pl` *in Listing 9-5 to refer to a group of event log fields.*

For illustration purposes, under the section heading [`SQL1`] I've listed all the options explicitly. When no value is specified for an option, the option doesn't need to be present in the configuration file.

For the computer SQL2, however, the script counts for each unique grouping of event type, event source, and event ID only in the system event log. Because the `IncludeDays` option is set to 7, the script counts the number of times each dis-tinctive event ID was logged over the past seven days.

For each of the event log fields—type, source, ID, and message—you can use an include option (for instance, `IncludeType` for the event type field) to instruct what the script should include in the summary report, and you can use an exclude option (for instance, `ExcludeType` for the event type field) to specify what to exclude from the summary report. If you don't specify an include option explicitly for a field, the script includes everything for that field. On the other hand, if you don't specify an exclude option, the script doesn't exclude anything.

In Listing 9-6, the summary for SQL1 will include both errors and warnings but exclude all the log records from the source `MSSQLServer`, `SQLServerAgent`, and `SQLExecutive`. The events from these sources are excluded from the summary because it's better to handle the SQL Server messages with a dedicated script. For SQL2, the summary will include records of all three types but without counting any log records with the event IDs 6006 and 6009.

> **NOTE** *For those who are curious about the event IDs 6006 and 6009, they're both logged by the event log service. The former is logged when the event log service is stopped, and the latter records the Windows version at the event log service startup. I didn't just exclude them randomly. They always go together with the event ID 6005 from the event log service, and therefore they're redundant for summary reporting purposes.*

Looking More Closely at the Script eventLogSummary.pl

Examining the main body of the script in Listing 9-5, you'll see two key data structures, the configuration hash structure ($configRef) and the summary hash structure ($summaryRef). The former is created from reading the configuration file with the function getConfig(), and the latter is produced by the function dbaReadEventLog(), which is imported from the module SQLDBA::Utility.

The function getConfig() first calls dbaReadINI() from SQLDBA::Utility to read the options from the configuration file into the variable $configRef; it then traverses the data structure referenced by $configRef to perform the following for each option:

- It removes the entry from $configRef if no value is specified for the option.

- If the value is a comma-separated string, it splits the string by comma into an array of strings and assigns a reference of the array to the configuration option.

- However, for the option IncludeMessage or ExcludeMessage, the option value is expected to consist of comma-separated regular expressions. The function getConfig() compiles each regular expression with the qr// operator in eval(). All the valid regular expressions are placed in an array, whose reference is assigned to the option. Invalid regular expressions are discarded.

For the sample configurations in Listing 9-6, when the function getConfig() finishes, the hash structure $configRef contains the structure shown in Listing 9-7.

Listing 9-7. A Sample Data Structure for the Configuration Options

```
$configRef = {
        SQL1 => {
                LOG => ['SYSTEM', 'APPLICATION'],
                LOGELEMENT    => ['TYPE', 'SOURCE', 'eventid', 'MESSAGE'],
                INCLUDEDAYS   => ['6'],
                INCLUDETYPE   => ['ERROR', 'WARNING'],
                EXCLUDESOURCE =>
                            ['MSSQLSERVER','SQLSERVERAGENT','SQLEXECUTIVE'],
                EXCLUDEMESSAGE => [ qr/(?i-xsm:Import\s+Error)/ ]
        }
        SQL2 => {
                LOG => ['SYSTEM'],
                LOGELEMENT   =>   ['TYPE', 'SOURCE', 'EVENTID'],
```

```
                INCLUDEDAYS  =>    ['7'],
                INCLUDETYPE  =>    ['ERROR', 'WARNING', 'INFORMATION'],
                EXCLUDEEVENTID => ['6006', '6009']
        }

}
```

Briefly, $configRef is a reference to a hash of hashes of arrays. If you aren't sure
about what this all means, review the section "Using References and Nested Data
Structures" in Chapter 1 and consult one of the Perl tutorial books listed in
Appendix A, "Perl Resources."

In Listing 9-7, the value of $configRef->{SQL1}->{EXCLUDEMESSAGE} is a reference
to an anonymous array whose only element is the following expression:

```
qr/(?i-xsm:Import\s+Error)/
```

This expression returns a compiled regular expression. The Dumper() function
of Data::Dumper reconstructs this qr// expression using the internal represen-
tation of the compiled regular expression.

With $configRef, the script in Listing 9-5 loops through each server specified
in the configuration file. For each server, it calls the function dbaReadEventLog() to
populate the hash structure $summaryRef that records the log summary information
and then prints the summary for that server with the function printEventLog().

The function dbaReadEventLog() is the heart of the script eventLogSummary.pl in
Listing 9-5 and is based on the same core engine in Listing 2-10 that iterates
through the event log records on a given server. Listing 9-8 shows the code of the
function dbaReadEventLog().

Listing 9-8. The Function dbaReadEventLog()

```
1.   sub dbaReadEventLog {
2.     my($server, $filterRef, $configRef) = @_;
3.     my($summaryRef, $element);
4.
5.   # this hash is used to map numeric constants to meaningful strings
6.     my %types = ( EVENTLOG_ERROR_TYPE,        'ERROR',
7.                   EVENTLOG_INFORMATION_TYPE,  'INFORMATION',
8.                   EVENTLOG_WARNING_TYPE,      'WARNING' );
9.
10.    $Win32::EventLog::GetMessageText = 1; # add Message key to $eventRef hash
11.    foreach my $log (@{$configRef->{$server}->{LOG}}) {
12.      my $cutoff = time() -
13.                   ${$configRef->{$server}->{INCLUDEDAYS}}[0] * 24 * 3600;
14.      # get the handle to the event log
```

```perl
15.     my $handle = Win32::EventLog->new($log, $server)
16.             or die "Could not open $log on $server: $!\n";
17.     my $eventRef;
18.     # loop through the log backwards, one record a time
19.     while (    $handle->Read( EVENTLOG_BACKWARDS_READ |
20.                             EVENTLOG_SEQUENTIAL_READ, 0, $eventRef)
21.             && $cutoff < $eventRef->{TimeGenerated} ) {
22.         # only process a record if it meets the criteria
23.         if ( &$filterRef($server, $configRef, $eventRef) == 1 )
24.         {   # concat the event fields specified in the LogElement option
25.             foreach my $field (@{$configRef->{$server}->{LOGELEMENT}}) {
26.                 if ($field eq 'TYPE') {
27.                     $element .= $types{$eventRef->{EventType}} . ', ';
28.                 }
29.                 elsif ($field eq 'SOURCE') {
30.                     $element .= 'Source: ' . $eventRef->{Source} . ', ';
31.                 }
32.                 elsif ($field eq 'EVENTID') {
33.                     $element .=
34.                         'EventID: ' .($eventRef->{EventID} & 0xffff). ', ';
35.                 }
36.                 elsif ($field eq 'MESSAGE') {
37.                     my $msg = substr($eventRef->{Message}, 0, 100);
38.                     $msg =~ s/\s*$//;
39.                     $msg =~ s/[\n\r]/ /g;
40.                     $element .= 'Message: ' . $msg . ', ';
41.                 }
42.             } # foreach my $field
43.             # record the event fields in the summary hash if not there
44.             if (!exists $summaryRef->{$log}->{$element}) {
45.                 $summaryRef->{$log}->{$element}->{Type}
46.                                 = $types{$eventRef->{EventType}};
47.                 $summaryRef->{$log}->{$element}->{Source}
48.                                 = $eventRef->{Source};
49.                 $summaryRef->{$log}->{$element}->{EventID}
50.                                 = $eventRef->{EventID} & 0xffff;
51.                 $summaryRef->{$log}->{$element}->{TimeGeneratedStr}
52.                                 = dbaTime2str($eventRef->{TimeGenerated});
53.                 $summaryRef->{$log}->{$element}->{TimeGenerated}
54.                                 = $eventRef->{TimeGenerated};
55.             }
56.             $summaryRef->{$log}->{$element}->{No}++; # increment the tally
57.         } # if (&$filterRef(...) == 1)
58.         $element = '';
```

```
59.      } # while
60.      Win32::EventLog::CloseEventLog($handle);
61.    } # foreach my $log
62.    return $summaryRef;
63. } # dbaReadEventLog
```

Because the section "Reading the Windows Event Logs" in Chapter 2 has already covered the basics of reading an event log, this section highlights several salient points in Listing 9-8. The first point to note is that in the while loop between lines 19 and 59, dbaReadEventLog() calls another function on line 23 to determine whether the log entry should be skipped:

```
23.    if (&$filterRef($server, $configRef, $eventRef) == 1)
```

The function &$filterRef(), however, isn't hard-coded in dbaReadEventLog(). Instead, its reference is passed in as the second parameter. This gives the function dbaReadEventLog() flexibility. In Listing 9-5, the function passed to dbaReadEventLog() is dbaFilterLogEntry(), also imported from SQLDBA::Utility. If this function doesn't do what you want, you can choose to write your own function for filtering event log entries and pass its reference to dbaReadEventLog().

Because the function dbaReadEventLog() scans the event log entries backwards from the latest to the oldest, the following code segment from line 44 through 57 ensures that only the information from the latest log record is kept for each log element. All the other repeating records of the same log element only increment the final total tally:

```
if (!exists $summaryRef->{$log}->{$element}) {
    $summaryRef->{$log}->{$element}->{Type}
                      = $types{$eventRef->{EventType}};
    $summaryRef->{$log}->{$element}->{Source}
                      = $eventRef->{Source};
    $summaryRef->{$log}->{$element}->{EventID}
                      = $eventRef->{EventID} & 0xffff;
    $summaryRef->{$log}->{$element}->{TimeGeneratedStr}
                      = dbaTime2str($eventRef->{TimeGenerated});
    $summaryRef->{$log}->{$element}->{TimeGenerated}
                      = $eventRef->{TimeGenerated};
}
$summaryRef->{$log}->{$element}->{No}++; # increment the tally
```

This is by design. By grouping certain event fields as the log element in the configuration file, you're saying that as long as the event records are the same in these fields, any other differences among them are immaterial for the summary report.

 CAUTION *In addition to using the number of days to control the* while *loop in Listing 9-8, you may consider adding a variable to count the number of event log records the function has already scanned and setting an upper limit, such as 2000, to force the loop to exit. When your machine is experiencing problems recurring at a high frequency, the records from a single day can easily fill up a large event log. If you rely on the* TimeGenerated *event log field alone, the* while *loop may never exit until it has exhausted all the records, which can take a long time.*

Once you have the summary hash structure returned from the function dbaReadEventlog(), your work is nearly done. Of course, you still need to print the summary in a readable format, which is the job of the function printEventlog().

Finally, let's look at an example of $summaryRef. Only the entries from the system event log are reproduced in Listing 9-9.

Listing 9-9. An Example of the Data Structure $summaryRef

```
$summaryRef = {
   'SYSTEM' => {
      'WARNING, Source: w32time, EventID: 11, Message: The NTP ... respond,'
                  => {
                        'No' => '17',
                        'TimeGenerated' => 1019844121,
                        'Source' => 'w32time',
                        'Type' => 'WARNING',
                        'EventID' => 11,
                        'TimeGeneratedStr' => '2002/04/26 14:02:01'
                  },
      'ERROR, Source: NETLOGON, EventID: 5719, Message: No Windows NT ... ,'
                  => {
                        'No' => '2',
                        'TimeGenerated' => 1019775571,
                        'Source' => ' NETLOGON ',
                        'Type' => 'ERROR',
                        'EventID' => 5719,
                        'TimeGeneratedStr' => '2002/04/25 18:59:31'
                  },
```

```
'WARNING, Source: Srv, EventID: 2013, Message: The F: disk is at or ... ,'
                => {
                        'No' => '5',
                        'TimeGenerated' => 1019700308,
                        'Source' => 'Srv',
                        'Type' => 'WARNING',
                        'EventID' => 2013,
                        'TimeGeneratedStr' => '2002/04/24 22:05:08'
                    }
    };
```

The $summaryRef hash structure is specific to each server that dbaReadEventLog() is working on at the time. In Listing 9-9, the keys of $summaryRef->{SYSTEM} are distinct values of the log elements in the system log. For each log element, the hash structure records the latest value of each event log field and the total number of occurrences of the distinct values of the log element. You can then write a function to print $summaryRef in a format you like. The function printEventLog() in Listing 9-5 is an example.

Examining a Sample Event Log Summary

Now, it's time to see an output of running the script in Listing 9-5. Save the configuration options in Listing 9-6 to the file config.txt and run the script as shown in Listing 9-10 (which shows only the result for the server SQL1).

Listing 9-10. Generating an Event Log Summary

```
cmd>perl perl eventLogSummary.pl config.txt
***********************************************************
*** SQL Server = SQL1 -- APPLICATION log ***
***********************************************************
2002/04/26 14:02:01 #: 4124 INFORMATION, Source: Network, EventID: 1, Message:
                          om:boostrap succeeded
2002/04/25 18:16:26 #: 5 INFORMATION, Source: SysmonLog, EventID: 2023, Message:
                          Log SQL3 has been started or restarted and,
2002/04/21 17:45:56 #: 6 ERROR, Source: SysmonLog, EventID: 2003, Message:
                          Unable to open the Performance Logs and Alerts,
```

```
****************************************************
*** SQL Server = SQL1 -- SYSTEM log ***
****************************************************
2002/04/26 01:06:01 #: 17 WARNING, Source: w32time, EventID: 11, Message:
                           The NTP server didn't respond,
2002/04/25 18:59:31 #: 2  ERROR, Source: NETLOGON, EventID: 5719, Message:
                           No Windows NT or Windows 2000 Domain Controller is,
2002/04/24 22:05:08 #: 5  WARNING, Source: Srv, EventID: 2013, Message:
                           The F: disk is at or near capacity. You may need,
```

For readability, I've generously sanitized this listing by removing or truncating many entries. On a real-world server, you may need to filter out many more event sources to obtain a short summary that's pertinent to your job.

The summary in Listing 9-10 shows that the application log has 4,124 entries from a source named Network, which happened to be issued by a backup facility. If the log entries from this source have no impact on the SQL Server operations, you can include Network in the ExcludeSource list to further reduce the summary and let the owner of the backup facility worry about whether these 4,124 messages are of any concern. The numerous application log entries generated by SQL Server aren't shown in the summary because in the configuration file their sources (MSSQLServer and SQLServerAgent) are excluded. The SQL Server entries should be handled separately, which is the topic of the next section.

In the summary in Listing 9-10, of all the warning messages found in the system log, seven are about the F drive being near capacity. Ideally, you should have already been alerted by these warnings through a server monitoring facility, and this summary can serve as a reminder in case you didn't act on the alert.

After you've been running the event log summary report for a while, you'll no doubt begin to notice what you may consider as noise in your report. However, if you try to get rid of it by configuring the exclude options of the event type, event source, or event ID, you may find that you'll be filtering out more than the noise—in other words, throwing out the baby with the bath water, so to speak.

This is where the configuration option ExcludeMessage (and IncludeMessage) becomes useful. Because an event message can contain arbitrary text, being able to exclude a few words wouldn't be sufficient. Instead, the option accepts any valid Perl regular expression. This is a powerful feature.

Filtering Out Noise with Regular Expressions

I remember working with an application that ran as a service to scrub and import external data into SQL Server. During the process, it would write various error messages to the application event log. Most of them were of no interest to the DBA except those with the message string `Import Error`. To include only these import error entries in the summary, all I needed to do was add `IncludeMessage = /Import\s+Error/i` to the configuration file.

Improving eventLogSummary.pl

If you want to deploy a solution similar to the script in Listing 9-5, you need to improve its robustness. To highlight the key points, I've stripped the validation code off the script. At the minimum, you need to validate the options specified in the configuration file.

> **NOTE** *On a different note, I'd like to stress that a daily event log summary isn't meant to be a substitute for server monitoring. Rather, it's best used as a complement to the monitoring infrastructure that should already be in place to immediately alert the administrators of any critical server errors.*

Scanning for TCP Ports Used by SQL Server

SCENARIO
You want to scan your SQL Server 2000 machines to find the Internet Protocol (IP) addresses and ports used by the SQL Server instances.

You can scan the application event log on each machine for messages similar to the following:

```
SQL server listening on 170.242.93.87: 2433.
```

Each SQL Server instance records a message like this in the application event log during its startup. It also records the same message in its errorlog.

The downside of scanning the errorlog for the IP and port information is that the errorlog may have been recycled and that message is no longer there. Although the event logs can also be recycled, their content is often kept much longer. In addition, for each server there's only one application event log to scan, even when the server runs multiple SQL Server instances.

The event log fields of this message have the following characteristics:

- The event type is information.

- The event ID is 17055.

- The event source is MSSQLServer or MSSQL$ followed by the SQL Server instance name.

Obviously, you can't rely on the previous three fields to identify the event log records that contain the SQL Server listening IP addresses and ports. The solution is to use a regular expression to match the message text. Listing 9-11 is the script scanIPPorts.pl to scan for the IP addresses and the ports on which a list of SQL Server instances are listening.

Listing 9-11. Scanning for SQL Server Listening IP Addresses and Ports

```
use strict;
use SQLDBA::Utility qw ( dbaTime2str dbaSetDiff dbaSetCommon dbaInSet
                         dbaReadINI dbaReadEventLog dbaFilterLogEntry );
Main: {
   my $configFile = shift or
        die "***Err: config file must be specified on the command line.";
   (-e $configFile) or die "Config file $configFile does not exist.";

   # get config options
   my $configRef = getConfig($configFile);

   # read and summarize the eventlog entries for each server
   foreach my $server (sort keys %$configRef) {
     my $summaryRef = dbaReadEventLog($server, \&dbaFilterLogEntry, $configRef);
     printIPPorts($server, $summaryRef, $configRef);
   }
} # Main


##################
sub getConfig {
# see the same function in Listing 9-5
```

```
} # getConfig


#########################
sub printIPPorts {
   my ($server, $summaryRef, $configRef) = @_;
   my (@keys);

   foreach my $log (@{$configRef->{$server}->{LOG}}) {
      # sort the summary log keys by Source
      @keys = sort {  $summaryRef->{$log}->{$b}->{Source} cmp
                      $summaryRef->{$log}->{$a}->{Source} }
                 (keys %{$summaryRef->{$log}});

      if (@keys) {
         print "\n", "*" x 50, "\n";
         print "***  Server = $server ***\n";
         print "*" x 50, "\n";
      }

      foreach my $header (@keys) {
         my ($source, $msg) =
              $header =~ /Source: (.+?,) EventId.+SQL server (listening.*)/i;
         printf " %-20s %2s %-3s %s\n",
             $summaryRef->{$log}->{$header}->{TimeGeneratedStr},
             "#:", $summaryRef->{$log}->{$header}->{No}, "$source $msg";
      }
   }
} # printEventLog
```

The script in Listing 9-11 expects a configuration file that contains the options similar to those in Listing 9-12.

Listing 9-12. Sample Configuration Options for a Single Machine

```
[SQL1]
log = application
LogElement = Type, Source, EventID, Message
IncludeDays = 10
IncludeType = Information
IncludeEventID = 17055
IncludeMessage = /SQL server listening on/i
```

The options in this example are for the server SQL1 only. You can specify the options for multiple machines in the configuration file. Save the options in Listing 9-12 to the file config.txt, and run scanIPPorts.pl on the command line as follows to report the IP addresses and ports used by the SQL Server instances running on the machine SQL1:

```
cmd>perl scanIPPorts.pl config.txt
*************************************************
***   Server = SQL1 ***
*************************************************
 2003/01/31 10:17:09  #: 5    MSSQL$APOLLO, listening on 170.242.93.97: 2433.,
 2003/02/02 10:33:05  #: 17   MSSQL$APOLLO, listening on 127.0.0.1: 2433.,
 2003/02/02 10:33:05  #: 17   MSSQL$APOLLO, listening on TCP, Named Pipes.,
 2003/02/02 14:59:34  #: 5    MSSQL$PANTHEON, listening on 127.0.0.1: 1057.,
 2003/01/28 13:47:50  #: 1    MSSQL$PANTHEON, listening on 170.242.93.97: 1057.
 2003/02/02 14:59:38  #: 5    MSSQL$PANTHEON, listening on TCP, Shared Memory.,
```

This report shows how many times various IP addresses and ports were used during the 10 days prior to the time when the script was run. By the way, this report was obtained on a notebook computer.

The script in Listing 9-11 is nearly identical to that in Listing 9-5 with the exception of the function printIPPorts().

If you're looking for the IP addresses and the ports currently in use by the SQL Server instances on a given computer, there's a simpler method. You can use the script grepEventlog.pl in Listing 9-1 to extract the event log entries whose message text contains the SQL Server listening IP address and the port.

For instance, to find the SQL Server listening IP addresses and the ports on the computer SQL1, you can run the script grepEventlog.pl as follows (all the options should be on the same command line):

```
cmd>perl grepEventlog.pl -M SQL1 -L application -t information
                   -d "2003/03/04-"
                   -m "/SQL\s+server\s+listening\s+on\s+[\d.]+/i"
2003/03/11 17:32:38, INFORMATION, MSSQL$SQL1, 17055, ... on 170.25.60.1: 2433.
2003/03/10 03:10:14, INFORMATION, MSSQL$SQL1, 17055, ... on 170.25.60.1: 2433.
2003/03/09 15:51:28, INFORMATION, MSSQL$SQL2, 17055, ... on 170.25.60.1: 1057.
2003/03/07 21:12:51, INFORMATION, MSSQL$SQL1, 17055, ... on 170.25.60.1: 2433.
```

Summarizing Reboot History

SCENARIO
You want to get a summary of how frequently Windows 2000/NT on your SQL Server machines were rebooted in the past few days or weeks.

A summary report of the reboot history across all the machines managed by the DBA group is helpful to highlight the frequency of the machine reboots.

How do you generate a reboot history for Windows 2000/NT? There are several options. You can ask your network administrators. But that wouldn't be effective, not to mention that you may need the information on a regular basis. You can also manually review the system event log for any reboot clues. If you examine the system log carefully, you'll notice that whenever Windows 2000/NT starts, the event log service logs a message with the event ID 6005 and the description "The Event log service was started."

I have not yet encountered a case in which the event log service was shut down without the machine also being down. For your purposes, it's reliable enough to use this event as the indicator of an operating system reboot.

Of course, counting the event 6005 in all the system event logs manually is too boring to do regularly. So let's get Perl to help out. You could configure the Perl script in Listing 9-1 to filter for the event ID 6005. That gives you a report on how many times a machine was rebooted and the last time it was rebooted.

This section uses Win32::EventLog directly so that you can count how many times a machine is rebooted each day. The result is the script rebootSummary.pl in Listing 9-13. To highlight the code that deals with the operating system reboots, I've hard-coded the machine names in the script. You can easily modify the code to read a list of computer names from a configuration file. See Listing 9-5 for an example.

Listing 9-13. Summarizing the Reboot History for SQL1 and SQL2

```perl
use strict;
use SQLDBA::Utility qw( dbaTime2str dbaTime2dateStr );
use Win32::EventLog;

Main: {
    my @servers = qw( SQL1 SQL2 );
    my $cutoff_days = 14;
    my $eventID = 6005;    # event log service started

    foreach my $server (sort @servers) {
        print "\nServer=$server\n";
        my $rebootRef = readEventLog($server, "system", $eventID, $cutoff_days);
```

```perl
            printReboot($rebootRef);
      }
} # Main


#######################
sub readEventLog {
    my($server, $log, $eventID, $days) = @_;
    my($logRef, $eventRef, $rebootRef);

    my $cutoff = time() - $days * 24 * 3600;

    $logRef = Win32::EventLog->new($log, $server)
            or die "***Err: could not open $log on $server.\n";

    while ( $logRef->Read(EVENTLOG_BACKWARDS_READ |
                        EVENTLOG_SEQUENTIAL_READ, 0, $eventRef) and
        $cutoff < $eventRef->{TimeGenerated}) {
      if ( $eventRef->{EventType} == EVENTLOG_INFORMATION_TYPE and
              ($eventRef->{EventID} & 0xffff) == $eventID ) {
         $rebootRef->{dbaTime2dateStr($eventRef->{TimeGenerated})}->{count}++;
         $rebootRef->{dbaTime2dateStr($eventRef->{TimeGenerated})}->{lastReboot}
                            = dbaTime2str($eventRef->{TimeGenerated});
      }
    }
    Win32::EventLog::CloseEventLog($logRef);
    return $rebootRef;
} # readEventLog


###################
sub printReboot {
    my ($rebootRef) = shift or die "***Err: printReboot() expects reference.";

    my($date, $rebootCount, $lastReboot);
    if (scalar keys %$rebootRef) {
      print ' Date         Reboot # Last Rebooted', "\n";
      print ' ============= ========= =======================', "\n";
      foreach $date (sort keys %$rebootRef) {
         $rebootCount = $rebootRef->{$date}->{count};
         $lastReboot = $rebootRef->{$date}->{lastReboot};
         write;
      }
    }
    else {
      print "    None\n";
```

```
    }

format STDOUT =
  @<<<<<<<<<<<< @>>>>>>> @<<<<<<<<<<<<<<<<<<<<<<
  $date,        $rebootCount,  $lastReboot
.
} # printReboot
```

For the sake of brevity and to keep the discussion focused, the script in Listing 9-13 is as bare bones as possible. At the beginning of the main body of the script, I've hard-coded the two machine names in the array `@servers` and set the cutoff days to 14 in the variable `$cutoff_days`. The script will ignore any event entries older than the cutoff days.

Note the following code fragment reproduced from the function `readEventlog()`:

```
$rebootRef->{dbaTime2dateStr($eventRef->{TimeGenerated})}->{count}++;
$rebootRef->{dbaTime2dateStr($eventRef->{TimeGenerated})}->{lastReboot}
                    = dbaTime2str($eventRef->{TimeGenerated});
```

I use the function `dbaTime2dateStr()` imported from SQLDBA::Utility to convert epoch seconds into a date string without the time portion. This allows the script to count the number of reboots on the same day.

The following is a sample reboot history report for the two servers, SQL1 and SQL2:

```
Server=SQL1
  Date           Reboot #  Last Rebooted
  ============= =========  =====================
  2002/03/31    2          2002/03/31 13:50:24
  2002/04/12    1          2002/04/12 11:50:41
  2002/04/13    3          2002/04/13 15:24:51
  2002/04/14    1          2002/04/14 11:38:39

Server=SQL2
  Date           Reboot #  Last Rebooted
  ===========   ========   =====================
```

The script was run on April 14, 2002. The report shows that within the 14 days prior to April 14, 2002, the server SQL1 was rebooted seven times, and the reboots were particularly frequent in the last three days. The server SQL2, on the other hand, wasn't rebooted during these same 14 days.

Now let's turn to a topic that's near and dear the heart of every SQL Server DBA—the SQL Server errorlog.

Summarizing SQL Server Errorlogs

SCENARIO

You want to summarize the SQL Server errorlogs from all your servers, keeping only the most important information.

Of all the log files, the SQL Server errorlog is the most important to the SQL Server DBA. It contains a wealth of information that's critical to administering SQL Server. For the SQL Server DBA, to emphasize the importance of the errorlog is to belabor the obvious.

What's not obvious, though, is that the value of the errorlog is often not fully realized. Most DBAs know to check the errorlog when there's a problem, and they're aware that regularly reviewing the errorlogs is the recommended best practice. However, when things get hectic, as they often do in a DBA's world, reviewing the errorlogs may get pushed down the priority list and become less than regular.

There's often a good reason when people genuinely believe in one thing but end up doing another. In this case, it's information overload on the part of the DBA. Manually scanning the errorlogs on many servers is an arduous and monotonous process. Also, when there's a problem, the errorlog often becomes bulky, burying critical information in a jungle of text data and making it difficult to see the trees through the forest. In the face of other more pressing deliverables, the DBA tends to take the calculated risk that on a regular day he or she just may not miss anything of consequence if the errorlogs aren't reviewed.

The bad news is that it just may not be a regular day. The good news is that it doesn't have to be a choice between working on the deliverables or putting out fires and reviewing the errorlogs. Furthermore, it doesn't even have to be boring.

If you look at the errorlogs carefully, you should find that the following is true:

- They are text files.

- They contain a significant amount of "noise" that's not totally useless but doesn't need to be reviewed by a DBA every day.

- There's a lot of repetitions of the same or essentially the same messages.

- The bulk of the errorlog is old and obsolete.

- The errorlog entries exhibit recognizable text patterns that aren't always consistent, especially between SQL Server versions.

These characteristics make Perl a good tool to help out with errorlog analysis. You can write a Perl script to scan all the SQL Server errorlogs; find the information you deem important; ignore nonessential, repetitive, or old messages; and produce a succinct summary report. This gives you a huge "conceptual compression ratio" without losing any critical information.

If you've studied the event log script in Listing 9-1, you may wonder why you can't just use that script because SQL Server also writes to the application log. That's an excellent observation! But, unfortunately, not all that's written to the errorlog is also written to the Windows application log. In fact, too many critical messages can be found only in the errorlog. For instance, the trace flag output typically doesn't appear in the application log.

Let's study the SQL Server errorlog in more detail. This will help you decide what information you should include in the summary report.

Dissecting the SQL Server Errorlog

My acid test of what should or shouldn't be in the summary report is simple: I'll include whatever may cause me to look closer at SQL Server in the summary but with repetition removed. The following items are potential candidates to be included in an errorlog summary:

Errorlog header: When not recycled, the first part of the errorlog contains important information on server startup and database startup. I want to include any abnormal or nonstandard startup behavior. An example is when SQL Server complains about not being able to obtain the allocated memory or not being able to listen on a port.

Size of the errorlog file: If the errorlog becomes large, it's often indicative of trouble somewhere. If it becomes extraordinarily large, you want to skip scanning the file altogether. It's good enough to just note in the summary that it's too large, and you can later take care of it manually.

Database startups: If a database starts up too many times within a short time span, it could be caused by the autoclose database option being set to true; in an enterprise environment, that generally isn't best practice.

Regular SQL Server errors: These are regularly formatted SQL Server error messages with error numbers and severity levels—for instance, Error: 14421, Severity: 16.

SQL Server warnings: It turns out that some warning messages can be more important than many error messages. For instance, you wouldn't want to miss the warnings on memory shortage.

Deadlocks: Setting trace flags 1204 and 3605 directs SQL Server to write deadlock information to the errorlog. A few deadlocks are normal, but you want to be informed when there are too many deadlocks.

Stack dumps and Access Violations (AV): Prior to SQL Server 7.0, AV errors are not well formatted when written to the errorlog. Since SQL Server 7.0, scanning for regular SQL Server errors with error numbers and severity levels will catch most of them, if not all.

DBCC CHECKDB entries: Every time that a DBCC CHECKDB is performed, it's noted with an entry in the errorlog along with the total number of errors found for each database.

Backups: Whenever a database or transaction log is backed up, it's noted in the errorlog. Both the successful backups and the failed backup attempts are recorded.

Process killed: It's probably difficult to find a DBA who hasn't had the pleasure to terminate a user connection. In some environments, this has become routine. In a well-run environment, this is really an extraordinary event and should be noted as such.

Most of the items listed previously have multiple entries in the errorlog, some of them recurring frequently. That's where the bulk of the repetition lies. By condensing the repetitions of an item to a statistical count, you significantly reduce the amount of the information you have to absorb.

NOTE *You need to decide for your own environment what to include in the summary of your SQL Server errorlogs. For instance, if you already have in place a robust backup process that comes with reliable monitoring, you may want to exclude the backup information from the summary to further reduce the size of the summary.*

Examining the Anatomy of an Errorlog Entry

An errorlog entry typically consists of three parts from left to right and may span multiple text lines:

- **Date/time string**: The string patterns have changed slightly between the versions and service packs. But it typically resembles 2002-02-05 12:57:01.43.

- **Message source**: This can be `server`, `kernel`, `ods`, or `backup`, among others. This can also be the string `spid`, postfixed with a spid number.

- **Message body**: In the majority of cases, this is a single line of text. In some cases, though, this may span multiple lines because the message body contains embedded newlines.

Each of the items in this list can be identified with a text pattern. In some cases, the message source can help narrow down the pattern matching in the message body.

Creating a Script for Summarizing Errorlogs

Listing 9-14 shows the script `errorlogSummary.pl` to summarize the errorlog files from multiple SQL Servers. This script accepts a configuration file as its parameter.

Listing 9-14. Summarizing SQL Server Errorlogs

```
use strict;
use Win32;
use SQLDBA::Utility qw( dbaReadINI dbaTime2str dbaStr2time );

Main: {
   my $configFile = shift;
   # if the config file is not found, abort
   (-e $configFile) or
      die "***Err: config file $configFile doesn't exist.";

   # Read config file into $configRef and validate it
   my $configRef = dbaReadINI($configFile);
   $configRef = validateConfig($configRef);

   # Now scan and summarize each errorlog
   foreach my $server (sort keys %$configRef) {
     # scan and summarize SQL Server errorlog
     my $logRef = scanErrorlog($server, $configRef->{$server});

     # Now print out the errorlog summary
     printLogSummary($logRef, $server, $configRef->{$server});
   }
} # Main


###########################
```

```perl
sub validateConfig {
    my $configRef = shift or
        die "***Err: validateConfig() expects a reference.";
    my $server;

    # set the default if an option is not specified
    foreach my $server (keys %$configRef) {
        # default LogWarningSize to 5000KB
        $configRef->{$server}->{LOGWARNINGSIZE} =~ /^\d+/ or
            $configRef->{$server}->{LOGWARNINGSIZE} = 5000;

        # default LogStopSize to 10000KB
        $configRef->{$server}->{LOGSTOPSIZE} =~ /^\d+/ or
            $configRef->{$server}->{LOGSTOPSIZE} = 10000;

        # default ScanErrorlogLastDays to 5 days
        $configRef->{$server}->{SCANERRORLOGLASTDAYS} =~ /^\d+/ or
            $configRef->{$server}->{SCANERRORLOGLASTDAYS} = 5;

        # default WarnMissingBackupLastDays to 2 days
        $configRef->{$server}->{WARNMISSINGBACKUPLASTDAYS} =~ /^\d+/ or
            $configRef->{$server}->{WARNMISSINGBACKUPLASTDAYS} = 2;

        # default ExcludeBackupHistory to no
        $configRef->{$server}->{EXCLUDEBACKUPHISTORY} =~ /^(y|n)/ or
            $configRef->{$server}->{EXCLUDEBACKUPHISTORY} = 'no';

        # default ExcludeDBCCHistory to no
        $configRef->{$server}->{EXCLUDEDBCCHISTORY} =~ /^(y|n)/ or
            $configRef->{$server}->{EXCLUDEDBCCHISTORY} = 'no';
    }

    # check whether errorlog files are specified
    foreach my $server (sort keys %$configRef) {
        unless ( exists $configRef->{$server}->{SQLERRORLOG} ) {
            print "***Err: SQLErrorlog not specified for $server.\n";
            print "    Server $server errorlog will not be scanned.\n";

            # if its errorlog is not specified,
            # remove the server from the scan list
            delete $configRef->{$server};
        }
    }
    return $configRef;
```

```perl
   }   # validateConfig


#########################
sub scanErrorlog {
   my($server, $serverRef) = @_;
   die "***Err: scanErrorlog() expects a server name and a reference."
         unless (defined $server && defined $serverRef);

   my $ref;
   my $sqlErrorlog = $serverRef->{SQLERRORLOG};

   # Check whether the errorlog file exists
   unless (-e $sqlErrorlog) {
      $ref->{notExist} = "***Errorlog $sqlErrorlog doesn't exist.";
      return $ref;
   }

   # Get errorlog actual size in KB
   $ref->{actualLogsize} = int((stat($sqlErrorlog))[7]/1024);

   # Check errorlog size
   if ($ref->{actualLogsize} >= $serverRef->{LOGSTOPSIZE}) {
      $ref->{logsizeError} =
            "***Errorlog over $serverRef->{LOGSTOPSIZE} KB.";
      return $ref;          # too big to bother openning it
   }
   elsif ($ref->{actualLogsize} >= $serverRef->{LOGWARNINGSIZE}) {
      $ref->{logsizeWarning} =
            "***Errorlog over $serverRef->{LOGWARNINGSIZE} KB.";
   }
   # now open the errorlog file for scan
   unless (open(LOG, "$sqlErrorlog")) {
      $ref->{logOpenError} = "***Could not open $sqlErrorlog for read. ";
      $ref->{logOpenError} .= Win32::FormatMessage(Win32::GetLastError);
      return $ref;
   }

   # from the very first errorlog line, get the SQL version and
   # the date/time of the first entry
   $_ = <LOG>;
   if (/^\s*([\d\/\-]+\s+[\d:\.]+)\s+[^\s]+\s+(Microsoft\s+SQL .+)/i) {
      ($ref->{firstRecordedDate}, $ref->{sqlVersion}) = ($1, $2);
   }
```

```
# skip old errorlog entries
my $prevLine;
while ($prevLine = $_, <LOG>) {
   if (/^\s*([\d\/\-]+\s+[\d\.\:]+)\s+/) {
      next if ( (time() - dbaStr2time($1)) >
                      $serverRef->{SCANERRORLOGLASTDAYS} * 24*3600 );
      $ref->{startCheckDatetime} = $1;
      last;
   }
}


# now start scan and summarize the errorlog entries
while (<LOG>) {
  # SQL7,2000: for regular SQL errors , capture the error # and severity
  if (m{^\s*([\d\/\-]+\s+[\d\.\:]+)\s+[^\s]+\s+
          Error\s*\:\s*(\d+)\s*\,\s*Severity\s*\:\s*(\d+)}ix) {
     # identify the error with error # and severity
     my $error = "$2\_$3";

     $ref->{$error}->{time} = $1;         # record the latest date/time
     $ref->{$error}->{type} = 'error';
     $ref->{$error}->{error} = $2;       # error #
     $ref->{$error}->{severity} = $3;    # severity
     $ref->{$error}->{no}++;             # increase the tally
     # the message text is on the next line
     $_ = <LOG>;
     /^\s*[^\s]+\s+[^\s]+\s+[^\s]+\s+(.+)\s*$/ and
           ($ref->{$error}->{msg} = substr($1, 0, 80));
     next;
  }


  # SQL7,2000: record and count failed db/log backups
  if (m{^\s*([\d\/\-]+\s+[\d\.\:]+)\s+
          backup+\s+(BACKUP\s+failed)\s+to\s+complete.+
          (database|log)\s+([^\s]+)}ix) {
     # identify the entry with 'BACKUP failed' + 'database' + <DB name>
     #                     or 'BACKUP failed' + 'log' + <DB name>
     my $error = "$2\_$3\_$4";
     $ref->{failedBackup}->{$error}->{time} = $1;
     $ref->{failedBackup}->{$error}->{type} = 'failedBackup';
     $ref->{failedBackup}->{$error}->{msg} = "$2 $3 $4";
     $ref->{failedBackup}->{$error}->{no}++;
     next;
```

```
    }

    # SQL7,2000: record SQL warnings
    if (/^\s*([\d\/\-]+\s+[\d\.\:]+)\s.+(Warning.+)$/i) {
        my $warning = lc($2);

        $ref->{warning}->{$warning}->{time} = $1;
        $ref->{warning}->{$warning}->{type} = 'warning';
        $ref->{warning}->{$warning}->{msg} = $warning;
        $ref->{warning}->{$warning}->{no}++;
        next;
    }


    # SQL7: count the # of deadlocks
    if (m{^\s*([\d\/\-]+\s+[\d\.\:]+)\s+[^\s]+\s+
              (\*\*\*\s*Deadlock\s+Detected)}ix) {
        $ref->{deadlock}->{time} = $1;
        $ref->{deadlock}->{type} = 'deadlock';
        $ref->{deadlock}->{msg} = $2;
        $ref->{deadlock}->{no}++;
        next;
    }


    # SQL2000: count the # of deadlocks
    if (m{^\s*Deadlock\s+encountered}ix) {
        $prevLine =~ /^\s*([\d\/\-]+\s+[\d\.\:]+)\s+/;
        $ref->{deadlock}->{time} = $1;
        $ref->{deadlock}->{type} = 'deadlock';
        $ref->{deadlock}->{msg} = '*** Deadlock encountered';
        $ref->{deadlock}->{no}++;
        next;
    }


    # SQL7,2000: record and count process killed
    if (m{^\s*([\d\/\-]+\s+[\d\.\:]+)\s+[^\s]+\s+
              (Process\s+id\s+\d+\s+killed\s+.+)$}ix) {
        $ref->{kill}->{time} = $1;
        $ref->{kill}->{type} = 'kill';
        $ref->{kill}->{msg} = $2;
        $ref->{kill}->{no}++;
        next;
    }


    # SQL7,2000: record and count stack dumps
```

```perl
if (m{^\s*([\d\/\-]+\s+[\d\.\:]+)\s+[^\s]+\s+
        (SqlDumpExceptionHandler:)}ix) {
    $ref->{stackDump}->{time} = $1;
    $ref->{stackDump}->{type} = 'stackDump';
    $ref->{stackDump}->{msg} = $2;
    $ref->{stackDump}->{no}++;
    next;
}


# SQL7,2000: record and count database starting up
if (m{^\s*([\d\/\-]+\s+[\d\.\:]+)\s+[^\s]+\s+
        (Starting\s+up\s+database\s+\'([^\']+)\')}ix) {
    my $db = "startingDatabase_" . $3;
    $ref->{$db}->{time} = $1;
    $ref->{$db}->{type} = 'startingDatabase';
    $ref->{$db}->{msg} = $2;
    $ref->{$db}->{no}++;
    next;
}


# SQL7,2000: record and count successful DB backups
if (m{^\s*([\d\/\-]+\s+[\d\.\:]+)\s+[^\s]+\s+
        Database\s+backed\s+up.+Database:\s+([^,]+)\,}ix) {
    my $error = $2 . "_dbBackup";
    $ref->{$error}->{time} = $1;
    $ref->{$error}->{type} = 'dbBackup';
    $ref->{$error}->{database} = $2;
    $ref->{$error}->{msg} = "DB $2 last backed up at $1";
    $ref->{$error}->{no}++;
    next;
}


# SQL7,2000: record and count successful log backups
if (m{^\s*([\d\/\-]+\s+[\d\.\:]+)\s+[^\s]+\s+
        Log\s+backed\s+up.+Database:\s+([^,]+)\,}ix) {
    my $error = $2 . "_logBackup";
    $ref->{$error}->{time} = $1;
    $ref->{$error}->{type} = 'logBackup';
    $ref->{$error}->{database} = $2;
    $ref->{$error}->{msg} = "Log for DB $2 last backed up at $1";
    $ref->{$error}->{no}++;
    next;
}
```

```
          # SQL7,2000: record and count DBCC CHECKDB's
          if (m{^\s*([\d\/\-]+\s+[\d\.\:]+)\s+[^\s]+\s+DBCC\s+CHECKDB\s+
                  \(([^)]+)\).+found\s+(\d+)\s+.+repaired\s+(\d+)}ix) {
             my $error = $2 . "_checkdb";
             $ref->{$error}->{time} = $1;
             $ref->{$error}->{type} = 'checkdb';
             $ref->{$error}->{database} = $2;
             $ref->{$error}->{msg} = "DBCC last CHECKDB $2";
             $ref->{$error}->{no}++;
             $ref->{$error}->{FoundErrors} = $3;
             $ref->{$error}->{RepairedErrors} = $4;
             next;
          }
       }
       close(LOG);
       return $ref;
    } # scanErrorlog


    ##############################
    sub printLogSummary {
       my($ref, $server, $serverRef) = @_;

       print "\n***Server: $server\n";
       print "Checking errorlog $serverRef->{SQLERRORLOG}\n";
       if (exists $ref->{notExist}) {
          print "  $ref->{notExist}\n";
          return;
       }

       if (exists $ref->{logsizeError}) {
          print "  $ref->{logsizeError}\n";
       }
       elsif(exists $ref->{logOpenError}) {
          print "  $ref->{logOpenError}\n";
       }
       else {
          print "  SQL Server restarted or errorlog recycled at: ";
          print "$ref->{firstRecordedDate}\n";
          print "  $ref->{sqlVersion}\n";
          if ($ref->{logsizeWarning}) {
             print "  $ref->{logsizeWarning}\n";
          }
          else {
             print "  Errorlog size = $ref->{actualLogsize} KB\n";
```

```
   }
   if ($ref->{startCheckDatetime}) {
      print "  Checking entries newer than $ref->{startCheckDatetime}\n";
   }
   else {
      print "  ***Errorlog does not have any entries less ";
      print "than $serverRef->{SCANERRORLOGLASTDAYS} days old.\n";
   }


   # print backup history summary
   my @backups = grep {/_(db|log)Backup$/i} (keys %$ref);
   if ($serverRef->{EXCLUDEDATABASES}) {
      @backups = grep !/^$serverRef->{EXCLUDEDATABASES}/i, @backups;
   }


   unless ($serverRef->{EXCLUDEBACKUPHISTORY} =~ /y/i) {
      if (@backups) {
         printf "\n  %-11s %-25s %-20s %5s\n", 'Type', 'Database',
                                     'Last Backup Time', 'Total';
         printf "  %-11s %-25s %-20s %5s\n", '-' x 11, '-' x 25,
                                     '-' x 20, '-' x 5;
         foreach my $backup (sort @backups)  {
            printf "  %-11s %-25s %-20s %5d\n",
                    $ref->{$backup}->{type},
                    substr($ref->{$backup}->{database}, 0, 25),
                    substr($ref->{$backup}->{time}, 0, 19),
                    $ref->{$backup}->{no};
         }
      }
   }


   # print a warning if no backup is found for a database
   # when errorlog has more than two-day history
   if ( time() - dbaStr2time($ref->{firstRecordedDate})
            > 3600*24*$serverRef->{WARNMISSINGBACKUPLASTDAYS}) {
      my %backupTime;
      foreach my $backup (@backups) {
         if ($backupTime{$ref->{$backup}->{database}}) {
            if ( dbaStr2time($backupTime{$ref->{$backup}->{database}})
                       < dbaStr2time($ref->{$backup}->{time})  ) {
               $backupTime{$ref->{$backup}->{database}} =
                                     $ref->{$backup}->{time};
            }
         }
```

```
        else {
           $backupTime{$ref->{$backup}->{database}} =
                                    $ref->{$backup}->{time};
        }
     }
     # use grep() to find the keys whose values evaluate the code to true
     my @dbs = grep { time() - dbaStr2time($backupTime{$_})
                      > 3600*24*$serverRef->{WARNMISSINGBACKUPLASTDAYS} }
                   keys %backupTime;
     print "\n" if scalar @dbs;
     foreach my $db (@dbs) {
        my $msg = "   ***Warning: $db was not backed up within last ";
        $msg .= "$serverRef->{WARNMISSINGBACKUPLASTDAYS} days\n";
        print $msg;
     }
  }


  # print DBCC history
  unless ($serverRef->{EXCLUDEDBCCHISTORY} =~ /y/i) {
     my @checkdbs = grep {/_checkdb$/i} (keys %$ref);

     if (@checkdbs) {
        printf "\n  %-28s %-8s\n", ' ' x 29, "Found";
        printf "  %-8s %-20s %-8s %-20s %5s\n",
              'Type', 'Database', 'Errors', 'Last DBCC Time', 'Total';
        printf "  %-8s %-20s %-8s %-20s %5s\n",
                  '-' x 8, '-' x 20, '-' x 8, '-' x 20, '-' x 5;
        foreach my $dbcc (sort @checkdbs)  {
           printf "  %-8s %-20s %-8d %-20s %5d\n",
                       $ref->{$dbcc}->{type},
                       substr($ref->{$dbcc}->{database}, 0, 25),
                       $ref->{$dbcc}->{FoundErrors},
                       substr($ref->{$dbcc}->{time}, 0, 19),
                       $ref->{$dbcc}->{no};
        }
     }
  }


  # print deadlock summary
  if (ref $ref->{deadlock}) {
     print "\n  $ref->{deadlock}->{msg}, Last occurred: ";
     print "$ref->{deadlock}->{time},";
     print " Total #: $ref->{deadlock}->{no}\n";
  }
```

```perl
# print process killed summary
if (ref $ref->{kill}) {
   print "\n  Process killed. Total #: $ref->{kill}->{no}, ";
   print "Last occurred: $ref->{kill}->{time}\n";
   print   "\t\t$ref->{kill}->{msg},\n";
}


# print stackDump summary
if (ref $ref->{stackDump}) {
   print "\n  $ref->{stack_dump}->{msg}, ";
   print "Last occurred: $ref->{stackDump}->{time},";
   print " Total #: $ref->{stackDump}->{no}\n";
}


# print warning summary
if (ref $ref->{'warning'}) {
   foreach my $warning (keys %{$ref->{'warning'}}) {
       print "\n  $ref->{'warning'}->{$warning}->{msg},";
       print " Last occurred: $ref->{'warning'}->{$warning}->{time},";
       print " Total #: $ref->{'warning'}->{$warning}->{no}\n";
   }
}


# print failedBackup summary
if (ref $ref->{failedBackup}) {
   print "\n";
   foreach my $failedBackup (keys %{$ref->{failedBackup}}) {
     print "  $ref->{failedBackup}->{$failedBackup}->{msg},";
     print " Last occurred: ",
             "$ref->{failedBackup}->{$failedBackup}->{time},";
     print " Total #: $ref->{failedBackup}->{$failedBackup}->{no}\n";
   }
}


# print avError summary
if (ref $ref->{avError}) {
   print "\n  $ref->{avError}->{msg}, Total #: $ref->{avError}->{no}\n";
}


# print database startup summary
my @errors = grep {/startingDatabase/i} keys %$ref;
print "\n" if @errors;
foreach my $error (@errors) {
```

```
        next if $ref->{$error}->{NO} <= 3;
        my ($database) = $error =~ /startingDatabase_(.+)/;
        print "  $ref->{$error}->{msg}, Total #: $ref->{$error}->{no},";
        print "  Last occurred: $ref->{$error}->{time}\n";
    }

    # print Error_Severity summary
    my @errors = grep {/^\d+_\d+$/} keys %$ref;
    print "\n" if @errors;
    foreach my $error (@errors) {
        if (ref $ref->{$error}) {
            print "  Err: $ref->{$error}->{error}, ";
            print "Severity: $ref->{$error}->{severity}, ";
            print " Total #: $ref->{$error}->{no}, Last occurred: ";
            print "$ref->{$error}->{time}\n";
            print "\t\t$ref->{$error}->{msg}\n";
        }
    }
  }
}  # printLogSummary
```

Assuming that the configuration file is config.txt in the current directory, you can run the script in Listing 9-14 as follows:

```
cmd>perl errorlogSummary.pl config.txt
```

The following sections examine various aspects of the script in Listing 9-14 in more detail.

Setting Configuration Options

The configuration file, accepted by the script in Listing 9-14, follows the standard Windows INI file format and specifies a variety of options for summarizing SQL Server errorlogs. In each section heading is a SQL Server instance name. Listing 9-15 is a sample configuration file for two SQL Server instances.

Listing 9-15. Sample Configuraions for errorlogSummary.pl

```
[SQL1]
 SQLErrorlog=\\SQL1\H$\MSSQL\LOG\Errorlog
 LogWarningSize=3000      # in KB
 LogStopSize=10000        # in KB
 ScanErrorlogLastDays = 3
```

```
ExcludeBackupHistory = no
ExcludeDBCCHistory = no
ExcludeDatabases = NorthWind,pubs
WarnMissingBackupLastDays=1

[SQL2\APOLLO]
SQLErrorlog=\\SQL2\H$\MSSQL\APOLLO\log\Errorlog
LogWarningSize=3000    # in KB
LogStopSize=10000      # in KB
ScanErrorlogLastDays = 3
ExcludeBackupHistory = yes
ExcludeDBCCHistory = yes
ExcludeDatabases = NorthWind,pubs,ComDB
WarnMissingBackupLastDays=2
```

Table 9-2 describes each configuration option that you can specify in the configuration file expected by the script in Listing 9-14.

Table 9-2. Configuration Options for the Script errorlogSummary.pl

OPTION	DESCRIPTION
SQLErrorlog	This option specifies the full path to the errorlog. The script uses this path to open the errorlog file. The path should use the Uniform Naming Convention (UNC) so that you can run the script from any machine.
LogWarningSize	If the size of the errorlog is greater than this kilobyte (KB) value, a warning message will be included in the summary report, but the script will proceed to scan the errorlog. If not specified, it defaults to 5,000KB.
LogStopSize	If the script detects that the size of the errorlog exceeds this threshold (in KB), it will not open the file. Instead, only a note is made in the summary. It defaults to 10,000KB.
ScanErrorlogLastDays	This option specifies how many days the script should go back during its scan of the errorlog. Any entry with an older time stamp will be skipped. The default is five days if the option isn't specified.
ExcludeBackupHistory	When this option is set to no or isn't specified at all, a table will be included in the summary to show the number of database backups and log backups performed.

Table 9-2. Configuration Options for the Script `errorlogSummary.pl` *(Continued)*

OPTION	DESCRIPTION
ExcludeDBCCHistory	This is similar to the previous option. When it's set to no or not specified at all, the table shows the history of DBCC_CHECKDB instead. The table also includes the number of errors found by DBCC.
ExcludeDatabases	There may be databases whose backups are of no concerns to you, and you don't want to see these databases in the backup summary. This option specifies a comma-separated list of databases that are excluded from the backup history table that the script may otherwise print. In Listing 9-15, the backup summary for the server SQL2\APOLLO won't include the databases Northwind, pubs, and ComDB.
WarnMissingBackupLastDays	If the script finds a database with no database backup for this many days and the database isn't excluded with the ExcludeDatabases option, the script issues a warning in the summary.

Examining the Structure of errorlogSummary.pl

The script in Listing 9-14 may appear to be lengthy. Its structure, however, is straightforward. The main body of the script follows a familiar coding pattern. It first uses the SQLDBA::Utility function dbaReadINI() to read the configuration options into a hash structure—referenced by $configRef—and then calls the function validateConfig() to validate the options and set the default values for some of the options.

Next, for each server the script scans the errorlog to extract the summary information and stores it in another hash structure—referenced by $logRef. Finally, the function printLogSummary() prints the summary with minimal formatting.

The heart of the script in Listing 9-14 is the function scanErrorlog(), which takes up the bulk of the script. For each entry in the errorlog, the function tries regular-expression pattern matching for each of many possible scenarios, including the following: Is it a regular SQL Server error? Is it a deadlock entry? Is it an entry for a database backup? Is it an entry for starting up a database?

All the regular expressions used by scanErrorlog() to match the errorlog entries and capture the key information are similar. Let's examine one of them. The following code fragment, reproduced from the script in Listing 9-14, captures the database startup entries in the errorlog (I've reformatted the regular expression for readability and added comments to each line):

```
if (m{^\s*                          # match the beginning of the entry
        ([\d\/\-]+\s+[\d\.\:]+)\s+   # match date string
        [^\s]+\s+                    # match the source of errorlog entry
        (Starting\s+up\s+database\s+ # match "Starting up database"
        \'([^\']+)\')                # match database name in single quotes
    }ix) {
  my $db = $3 . "_startingDatabase";   # create a string for the hash key
  $ref->{$db}->{time} = $1;            # record the database startup time
  $ref->{$db}->{type} = 'startingDatabase';
  $ref->{$db}->{msg} = $2;             # record the start up message
  $ref->{$db}->{no}++;                 # increment the count
  next;                                # move on to the next errorlog entry
}
```

Assuming that the script in Listing 9-14 found several startup entries in the errorlog for the databases ComDB and NetDB, the summary hash structure would be similar to Listing 9-16 for the database startup entries.

Listing 9-16. A Sample Errorlog Summary Hash

```
$ref = { ComDB_startingDatabase => {
                    time => '2002-04-22 05:05:01.15',
                    type => 'startingDatabase',
                    msg  => 'Starting up database \'ComDB\'',
                    no   => '12'
        },
        NetDB_startingDatabase => {
                    time => '2002-04-21 05:05:03.24',
                    type => 'startingDatabase',
                    msg  => 'Starting up database \'NetDB\'',
                    no   => '2'
        },
        # other summary entries in this hash structure
        deadlock => { ... },
        ComDB_dbBackup => { ... },
        NetDB_dbBackup => { ... },
        Warning  => { ... },
        50000_18 => { ... },
        14421_16 => { ... },
        ComDB_checkdb => { ... },
        NetDB_checkdb => { ... }
}
```

In addition to the database startup entries, the hash structure in Listing 9-16 includes an entry for deadlocks, two entries for the backups of the databases ComDB and NetDB, and two entries for DBCC CHECKDB of the two databases ComDB and NetDB. It also includes one entry for warnings and two entries for SQL Server error messages (error number 50000 with severity 18 and error number 14421 with severity 16). (To avoid cluttering the discussion, Listing 9-16 doesn't show the details of these entries.)

Examining a Sample Errorlog Summary Report

Now it's time to see what the script in Listing 9-14 actually produces. Listing 9-17 is a trimmed sample output of running the script with the configuration options in Listing 9-15. In the following report, the message body is deliberately truncated to fit on a single line.

Listing 9-17. A Sample Errorlog Summary Report

```
***Server: SQL1
Checking SQL errorlog \\SQL1\H$\MSSQL\LOG\Errorlog
  SQL Server restarted or errorlog recycled at: 2002-04-12 04:38:55.50
  Microsoft SQL Server 2000 - 8.00.384 (Intel X86)
  Errorlog size = 254 KB
  Checking errorlog entries younger than 2002-04-22 07:05:01.15


  Type              Database          Last Backup Time        Total
  ---------------   ---------------   ---------------------   --------

  db_backup         ComDB             2002-04-24 17:38:31     6
  log_backup        ComDB             2002-04-25 06:45:01     124
  db_backup         NetDB             2002-04-22 17:38:31     3
  db_backup         master            2002-04-25 16:10:41     3
  db_backup         msdb              2002-04-25 16:10:47     3


  ***Warning: NetDB was not backed up within last 1 days


                             Found
  Type            Database   Errors     Last DBCC Time          Total
  -------------   ---------- ---------- ---------------------   -----

  checkdb         ComDB      0          2002-04-24 20:16:11     3
  checkdb         NetDB      0          2002-04-24 19:10:06     3
  checkdb         master     0          2002-04-24 19:00:03     3
  checkdb         model      0          2002-04-24 19:00:04     3
  checkdb         msdb       0          2002-04-24 19:00:05     3
```

```
    Err: 50000, Severity: 19, Total #: 3, Last occurred: 2002-04-24 10:00:06.90
              B drive on SQL1 is below 200MB.
    Err: 14421, Severity: 16, Total #: 4319, Last occurred: 2002-04-25 06:49:00.64
              The log shipping destination SQL1.NetDB is out of sync by 16890


    warning: unable to allocate 'min server memory' of 450mb.,
              Last occurred: 2002-04-23 19:24:02.75, Total #: 1
    Err: 1204, Severity: 19, Total #: 18, Last occurred: 2002-04-23 18:13:46.67
              The SQL Server cannot obtain a LOCK resource at this time.
    Process killed. Total #: 6, Last occurred: 2002-04-22 16:15:42.26
              Process ID 72 killed by hostname WSW060, host process ID 498.

***Server: SQL2\APOLLO
Checking SQL errorlog \\SQL2\H$\MSSQL\APOLLO\LOG\Errorlog
  SQL Server restarted or errorlog recycled at: 2002-04-17 17:37:28.34
  Microsoft SQL Server 7.00 - 7.00.842 (Intel X86)
  Errorlog size = 530 KB
  Checking errorlog entries younger than 2002-04-22 07:02:02.57

  Starting up database 'RecDB', Total #: 10, Last occurred: 2002-04-24 22:05:29
```

The first thing to notice in the output in Listing 9-17 is that it's a significantly condensed report compared with the two actual SQL Server errorlogs. The errorlogSummary.pl script is able to achieve this reduction with no loss of useful information, primarily by removing the old errorlog entries and by collapsing the repetitive messages. For instance, for the server SQL1, 4,319 entries of the log shipping error message are replaced with the following single entry:

```
Err: 14421, Severity: 16, Total #: 4319, Last occurred: 2002-04-25 06:49:00.64
          The log shipping destination SQL1. NetDB is out of sync by 16890
```

This entry in the summary report represents the latest recording of the error, along with the total count of the error in the errorlog.

In the report, also notice that there's a backup summary table and a DBCC CHECKDB summary table. They make it visually convenient to spot any inconsistencies. The backup summary has helped me several times in my own environments to catch database backups that failed to get performed. Of course, in an ideal environment, your SQL Server monitoring system should have caught any missing database backups. However, everyone knows that most environments are not ideal and will never be. Things do fall through the cracks in any monitoring infrastructure. Therefore, a summary report such as this one gives you an additional means to rescue you from blissful ignorance.

For the server SQL2\APOLLO, the script reports that the database RecDB was
started 10 times during the past three days. This may or may not be a problem, but
it needs to be investigated. If the report brings a potential issue to the attention of
the DBA, it has added value to your SQL Server support service.

Beyond Summarizing Errorlogs

As mentioned, the SQL Server errorlog is but one of many log files a DBA has to
cope with on a daily basis. Another important group of log files are DBCC CHECKDB
output files. Because you already get a count of errors encountered in checking
each database from the errorlog, what you may be interested in with a DBCC CHECKDB
output file is a summary of the actual error messages. You can take comfort in
knowing that the error messages in a DBCC CHECKDB output file follow a simple and
consistent format, similar to the following:

```
Server: Msg 8905, Level 16, State 1, Line 0
Extent (1:2704) in database ID 2 is marked allocated in the GAM, but no SGAM ...
```

It would be a breeze to expand the script in Listing 9-14 to include a summary
of DBCC CHECKDB output files. In fact, you can reuse the following code fragment in
the function scanErrorlog() with only minor modifications. This code fragment
scans for regularly formatted SQL Server errors:

```
# SQL7,2000: Regular SQL errors
if (m{^\s*([\d\/\-]+\s+[\d\.\:]+)\s+[^\s]+\s+
              Error\s*\:\s*(\d+)\s*\,\s*Severity\s*\:\s*(\d+)}ix) {
    my $error = "$2\_$3";  # identify errors with the err number and severity

    $ref->{$error}->{time} = $1; # record the date/time of the latest error
    $ref->{$error}->{type} = 'error';
    $ref->{$error}->{error} = $2;      # error number
    $ref->{$error}->{severity} = $3;   # severity
    $ref->{$error}->{no}++;            # increment the tally
    $_ = <LOG>;       # the error message text is on the next line
    /^\s*[^\s]+\s+[^\s]+\s+[^\s]+\s+(.+)\s*$/ and
          ($ref->{$error}->{msg} = substr($1, 0, 80));
    next;
}
```

To work with the DBCC CHECKDB output, you need to change the regular expression in this code fragment. The pattern to match a typical DBCC CHECKDB error message is simply as follows:

```
/Msg\s+\d+,\d+Level\s+\d+/i
```

Another group of log files you may want to summarize are the log files generated by various scheduled jobs. In any SQL Server environment, there are usually a large number of these files because there are many scheduled jobs. Unlike the SQL Server errorlog and the DBCC CHECKDB output, these files could contain arbitrary error messages. In addition, the nature of an error message could vary dramatically between different environments; you must study your environments to determine what to capture and how to capture them. Regardless of what else you may want to capture, the following error conditions appear to be common and therefore should always be included:

- SQL Server error messages

- Error messages from the database access Application Programming Interface (API), such as those generated by DB-Library, ODBC, or OLEDB

- Login failures

- Connection failures

I can't predict what other log files you may want to include in the summary. As for the task embarked upon in this section, an effective route to the log file nirvana, where the log files are kept nicely under control, is through constantly modifying a totally open script such as those just discussed.

Checking Transaction Log Backup Chains

SCENARIO
You want to check whether a transaction log backup chain might have been broken.

In SQL Server 7 and 2000, when a log backup chain is already broken, subsequent log backups will continue to succeed, giving a false impression that the log backups are all hunky-dory. What further aggravates the problem is that only an informational message is sent to the client that performs the first log backup after the log backup chain has been invalidated. There's no good way to get alerted at the time when the chain is broken. This can be disastrous if the broken chain is discovered when you're trying to do the restore from the backup files.

If you can't be alerted when a log backup chain breaks, is there a way to check it after it has been broken? Well, to be absolutely certain, you need to actually restore from the log backups in the chain. This of course isn't always possible unless you maintain a warm standby server. The situation could at least be alleviated somewhat if you know that the chain is obviously broken.

One such obvious case is when the transaction log is truncated between two consecutive log backups of the same database or when the database recovery model is switched from full to simple and back to full. When this happens, the first Log Sequence Number (LSN) of the second transaction log backup will not match the last LSN of the first transaction backup. Conversely, when the LSNs of two consecutive log backups don't match, observations suggest that the log backup chain is broken.

NOTE *The correlation between an LSN mismatch and a broken log backup chain doesn't appear in the official SQL Server documentation. This is based on empirical observations from numerous experiments and the daily examination of the log backup entries in my SQL Server environments.*

Having been burned a few times by the broken log backup chains, I prefer to be informed of any LSN mismatch between consecutive log backups, rather than be ignorant about it. With the knowledge of a mismatched LSN, I can then decide whether to pursue the issue further. At the worst, it's a minor inconvenience if it turns out you can still restore from a log backup even with a mismatched LSN, albeit I have not yet seen such a case.

Now that I've warned you of the potential pitfalls of using LSNs to find a broken log backup chain, let's work out a procedure to check for mismatched LSNs.

You can find the log backup LSNs in three places: the log backup files, the system table `msdb.dbo.backupset`, and the log backup entries recorded in the SQL Server errorlog. The Perl script presented in Listing 9-18 works with the SQL Server errorlog.

When examining the backup entries in the errorlog, bear in mind the possibility that the errorlog might have been recycled recently, leaving you only the tail of the chain with which to work. To keep the script short, I check only the current errorlog.

For each log backup entry in the errorlog, you need to deal with three situations:

- If the entry is a database backup, simply take note that this is a database backup.

- If the entry is the first log backup in the errorlog for the database, or is the first log backup after a full database backup, you can assume the log chain is good at this point.

- The third situation is when the entry isn't the first log backup in the errorlog, and there's an immediate preceding log backup with no database backup in between. In this case, if the first LSN of this log backup matches the last LSN of the previous log backup, the log backup chain remains good. Otherwise, it's broken.

Listing 9-18 shows the code to detect any LSN mismatch between two consecutive transaction log backups.

Listing 9-18. Finding Mismatched LSNs Between Two Consecutive Log Backups

```
use strict;

Main: {
   my $logFile = shift or die "***Err: $0 expects an errorlog file.";
   my $ref = readLogChain($logFile);
   printBrokenLogChain($ref);
} # Main


#######################
sub readLogChain {
   my ($logFile) = shift or "***Err: readLogChain() expects a file name.";
   open(LOG, "$logFile") or die "***Err: could not open $logFile for read.";

   my ($ref, $time, $type, $dbName, $first, $last);
   while (<LOG>) {
      # match only the backup entries and ignore others
      if (m{^\s*([\d\/\-]+\s+[\d\.\:]+)\s+       # date/time
             [^\s]+\s+                            # source
             (Database|log)\s+backed\s+up.+Database:\s+
             ([^,]+)\,                            # database name
             .+                                   # more text
            first\s+LSN:\s+([\d:]+)\,\s+ # first LSN
            last\s+LSN:\s+([\d:]+)\,     # last LSN
```

```perl
        }ix) {
      ($time, $type, $dbName, $first, $last) = ($1, $2, $3, $4, $5);
   }
   else {
      next;   # skip if not a backup entry
   }


   # work on database backup entry
   # a full database backup starts a good log backup chain
   if ($type =~ /database/i) {
      $ref->{$dbName}->{wasDBBackup}    = 1;
      $ref->{$dbName}->{logChainBroken} = 0;  # restart a good log chain
      next;
   }


   # SQL7,2000: log backup
   if ($type =~ /log/i) {
      # skip it if log chain already broken. All subsequent log entries
      # are ignored until next full backup
      next if $ref->{$dbName}->{logChainBroken};
      $ref->{$dbName}->{logTime} = $time;
      if (!exists $ref->{$dbName}->{firstLSN} ||   # first log backup or
          $ref->{$dbName}->{wasDBBackup} ) {       # first after a full backup
            $ref->{$dbName}->{logChainBroken} = 0; # assume a good start
            $ref->{$dbName}->{firstLSN} = $first;
            $ref->{$dbName}->{lastLSN} = $last;
      }
      else {
         # if immediate preceding backup is a log backup,
         # compare the current first LSN with the previous last LSN
         if ($first eq $ref->{$dbName}->{lastLSN}) {
            $ref->{$dbName}->{logChainBroken} = 0;
            $ref->{$dbName}->{firstLSN} = $first;
            $ref->{$dbName}->{lastLSN} = $last;
         }
         else {
            $ref->{$dbName}->{logChainBroken} = 1;
            $ref->{$dbName}->{firstLSN} = $first;
            $ref->{$dbName}->{lastLSN} = $last;
         }
      }
```

```perl
        # remember this is not a full backup to help interpret
        # the next backup entry
        $ref->{$dbName}->{wasDBBackup} = 0;
        next;
      }
    }
    close(LOG);
    return $ref;
} # readLogChain


###########################
sub printBrokenLogChain {
    my ($ref) = shift or
      die "***Err: printBrokenLogChain() expects a reference.";

    foreach my $dbName (sort keys %$ref) {
      next if !$ref->{$dbName}->{logChainBroken};
      printf "%s %s log backup chain broken, first/last LSN: %s/%s\n",
             $ref->{$dbName}->{logTime},
             $dbName,
             $ref->{$dbName}->{firstLSN},
             $ref->{$dbName}->{lastLSN};
    }
} # printBrokenLogChain
```

The following are two typical backup entries you may find in a SQL Server errorlog. The first one is for a database backup, and the second is for a transaction log backup. In the errorlog, each of these entries is on a single line (for readability, I've broken them into multiple lines and rearranged the alignment):

```
2002-04-22 15:07:09 backup Database backed up: Database: RecDB,
                    creation date(time): 2002/04/17(13:38:14), pages dumped: 147,
                    first LSN: 10:502:1, last LSN: 10:506:1,
                    number of dump devices: 1, device information:
                    (FILE=1, TYPE=DISK:{'e:\mssql\mssql\backup\RecDB.bak'})
2002-04-22 15:07:29 backup Log backed up: Database: RecDB,
                    creation date(time): 2002/04/17(13:38:14),
                    first LSN: 10:502:1, last LSN: 10:509:1,
                    number of dump devices: 1, device information:
                    (FILE=1, TYPE=DISK: {'e:\mssql\mssql\backup\RecDBLog1.bak'})
```

The information in the database/log backup entry is captured with the following pattern in the function readLogChain() in Listing 9-18:

```
m{^\s*(?:[\d\/\-]+\s+[\d\.\:]+)\s+      # date/time string
    [^\s]+\s+                           # source
    (Database|log)\s+backed\s+up.+      # type of backup
    Database:\s+([^,]+)\,               # database name
    .+                                  # some more text
    first\s+LSN:\s+([\d:]+)\,\s+        # first LSN
    last\s+LSN:\s+([\d:]+)\,            # last LSN
}ix
```

Let's work through an example to get a better feel for what the script produces. For the databases pubs and myDB, the Transact-SQL (T-SQL) code in Listing 9-19 first sets the database recovery model to full, performs a full database backup, and then backs up the transaction logs. Note that the SQL statement BACKUP LOG pubs WITH NO_LOG breaks the log backup log chain of the pubs database, and the SQL statement that sets the recovery model of the myDB database to simple breaks its log backup chain.

Listing 9-19. T-SQL Script to Break Log Backup Chains

```
use pubs
go
create table tbTest (i int)
go
alter database pubs set recovery full
backup database pubs to pubsDBback
insert tbTest values(123)
backup log pubs to pubsLogBack1
insert tbTest values(123)
/* break the log backup chain */
backup log pubs with no_log
backup log pubs to pubsLogBack2
insert tbTest values(123)
backup log pubs to pubsLogBack3
go

use myDB
go
create table tbTest (i int)
go
alter database myDB set recovery full
backup database myDB to myDBback
```

```
insert tbTest values(123)
backup log myDB to myDBLogBack1
insert tbTest values(123)
go
/* break the log backup chain */
alter database myDB set recovery simple
checkpoint
alter database myDB set recovery full
go
backup log myDB to myDBLogBack2
insert tbTest values(123)
backup log myDB to myDBLogBack3
go
```

After executing the preceding T-SQL script on a SQL Server 2000 instance, if you run the Perl script in Listing 9-18 against the errorlog of the SQL Server instance, the output from the script will look like the following:

```
2002-05-01 16:13 pubs log backup chain broken,first/last LSN: 6:375:1/6:389:1
2002-05-01 16:13 myDB log backup chain broken,first/last LSN: 29:482:1/29:489:1
```

With the information reported here, you should investigate the log backups of the databases pubs and myDB at around 4:13 P.M., May 1, 2002. It's most likely that both log backup chains were broken there, and your database backup and recovery is in jeopardy.

Analyzing Deadlock Traces

> **SCENARIO**
> *When your SQL Server is experiencing massive deadlocks, you need a method to help analyze the deadlock information in the errorlog.*

By default, SQL Server doesn't record any deadlock information. If you want to investigate the deadlocks on your system, you need to explicitly set the trace flag 1204 to make SQL Server write out information when a deadlock is detected. You should also set the trace flag 3605 to direct the trace output to the errorlog.

Another method to get deadlock information is to use SQL Profiler to trace the deadlock events in the Locks event category. SQL Profiler provides information for basic deadlock detection, and you can find more comprehensive information in the errorlog with the trace flag 1204. I prefer to see the deadlock information in plain text in the errorlog, and the Perl script introduced in this section is written to work with the errorlog.

Running into a few deadlocks occasionally is normal in the relational database world and is no reason to panic. Instead of trying to eliminate the deadlock altogether, it's often more effective to simply let the client code gracefully handle it. However, if you're running into hundreds of deadlocks a day, you should look into them. You may still decide to leave them to the client code because they are still relatively inexpensive, especially if for instance the deadlock victims aren't experiencing massive rollbacks.

When your database is running into a significant number of deadlocks, you need to examine the nature of these deadlocks. How and where do they take place? What database resources are involved? They could be concentrated on a small number of SQL statements and resources, or they could be all over the place in the database involving many different database objects. You need to identify the database resources and the SQL statements that are the cause of the deadlocks.

Dealing with Large Deadlock Trace Results

When you encounter massive deadlocks, your trace flag 1204 output can become very large.

Once, I was called to help with a large database that was running into thousands of deadlocks per hour. After turning on the trace flag 1204, the next day I found that the errorlog had ballooned into a file of more than 100 megabytes. Manually performing a comprehensive analysis of the trace flag output became practically impossible.

I ended up writing a Perl script to scan for the key deadlock information, which helped reveal that the deadlocks were concentrated on a few tables and were all caused by the same data import procedures that were being executed concurrently from multiple threads to pump data into the database throughout the day.

This discovery steered the troubleshooting effort toward the design of the data import procedures and the design of the tables, and it enabled me to safely ignore tens of thousands of individual deadlock chains logged in the errorlog.

Dissecting Deadlock Trace Records

Listing 9-20 is a typical example of the output produced by the trace flag 1204 on
SQL Server 2000 (I've edited the output to present only the essential information):

Listing 9-20. Deadlock Information from Trace Flag 1204

```
1. Deadlock encountered... Printing deadlock information
2.    Node:1
3.    TAB: 6:21575115 [ ]                CleanCnt:1 Mode: X
4.      Grant List::
5.        Owner:0x19051360 Mode: X  SPID:52
6.        Input Buf: Language Event: select * from employees (holdlock tablockx)
7.      Requested By:
8.        ResType:LockOwner Stype:'OR' Mode: X SPID:51
9.
10. Node:2
11. TAB: 6:1977058079 [ ]              CleanCnt:1 Mode: X
12.    Grant List::
13.      Owner:0x190513a0 Mode: X  SPID:51
14.      Input Buf: Language Event: select * from orders (holdlock tablockx)
15.    Requested By:
16.      ResType:LockOwner Stype:'OR' Mode: X SPID:52
17.
18. Victim Resource Owner:
19.      ResType:LockOwner Stype:'OR' Mode: X SPID:52
```

This deadlock chain has two entries (or *nodes* in the trace flag 1204 parlance):
Node:1 and Node:2. Let's investigate what's reported in Listing 9-20 with respect to
these two nodes:

- At Node:1, SPID 52 has an exclusive lock (Mode: X on line 5) on the table
  Northwind..employees (TAB: 6:21575115 on line 3, where the database ID is 6
  and the object ID is 21575115). A new request is now being made from SPID
  51 to exclusively lock the same table (Mode: X SPID:51 on line 8).

- Similarly, at Node:2, SPID 51 already has an exclusive lock (Mode: X on line 13)
  on the table Northwind..orders (TAB: 6:1977058079 on line 11, where the
  database ID is 6 and the object ID is 1977058079). A new request is being
  made from SPID 52 to exclusively lock the same table (Mode: X SPID:52 on
  line 16).

In addition to TAB (for table) in the previous output, other common resources that may be reported in a deadlock include KEY (for index key or key range), PAG (for data page or index page), EXT (for extent), and so on. The lock modes in this example are all exclusive (X), but they can be almost any lock mode such as shared (S) and update (U).

Note that each version of SQL Server writes the trace flag output differently. Future versions of SQL Server may again change the trace flag output. The difference is primarily in the format of the output, however. Regardless of the SQL Server versions, for each deadlock chain, the trace flag output contains the information on the same basic elements. For troubleshooting purposes, you can consider a deadlock to consist of the following essential elements:

- How many nodes are there in the chain?

- For each node, what resource is involved? What's the granted lock mode? What's the requested lock mode? And what SQL statement is requesting the lock in the input buffer?

Analyzing Deadlock Chains

To simplify exposition, let me introduce the new term *node signature*, which is the concatenation of the resource name, the granted lock mode, the requested lock mode, and the input buffer. The node signature identifies a deadlock node. If two deadlock nodes have the same signature, they're considered to be the same node. Now you can identify a deadlock chain by the signatures of all its nodes.

For the purposes of this section, the order of the nodes and which node is chosen as the victim isn't important. Therefore, if two deadlock chains have the same set of node signatures, you can consider them to be the different occurrences of the same unique deadlock. The first step in analyzing a large number of deadlocks then becomes an effort to single out these unique deadlocks by comparing the node signatures of each deadlock chain.

It's important to note that when a large number of deadlocks are reported, they're often recurrences of a small number of unique deadlocks. If you can write a script to help find these unique deadlocks automatically, your analysis of deadlocks can then focus on these unique deadlocks and, therefore, will be significantly expedited.

The script deadlockSummary.pl in Listing 9-21 scans and parses the output from the trace flag 1204, gleans the key information from each reported deadlock, records its node signatures, identifies the deadlock chains with their node signatures, counts their occurrences, and finally reports only the unique deadlocks.

This script works with SQL Server 2000 only. Once you've studied this script and become familiar with the output of the trace flag 1204 on the other versions of SQL Server, you should be able to easily adapt the script in Listing 9-21 to work with the other versions of SQL Server.

Listing 9-21. Summarizing Deadlock Information in a SQL Server Errorlog

```
use strict;
use SQLDBA::Utility qw( dbaSetDiff dbaSetSame );

Main:{
   my $logFile = shift or die "***Err: $0 expects an errorlog file.";
   my $logFile2 = $logFile . "_v2";

   # scan the errorlog to extract and format the deadlock entries
   # into file $logFile2
   getDeadlockEntries($logFile, $logFile2);
   # summarize the deadlock entries in $logFile2
   my $deadlockRef = getDeadlockSummary($logFile2);
   printDeadlockSummary($deadlockRef);
} # Main


################################
sub getDeadlockEntries {
   my ($logFile, $logFile2) =@_;

   open(LOG, "$logFile") or die "***Err: cannot open $logFile for read.";
   open(LOG1, ">$logFile2") or die "***Err: cannot open $logFile2 for write.";

   $_ = <LOG>;
   m{^\s*[\d\/\-]+\s+[\d\:\.]+\s+[\w\d]+\s+
         Microsoft\s+SQL\s+Server\s+2000\s+}ix
      or die "***Err: this is not a SQL 2000 errorlog.";

   my $deadlockON = 0;
   while (<LOG>) {
      if (/Deadlock\s+encountered\s+/i) {  # entering the deadlock info block
         print LOG1 "Deadlock encountered\n";
         $deadlockON = 1;     # indicating entrance into the deadlock info block
         next;
      }
      if (m{^\s*[\d\/\-]+\s+[\d\:\.]+\s+[\w\d]+\s+
               Node:\d+}ix && $deadlockON) {  # entering a node
         my $line = $_;
```

```
            while(<LOG>) {
                if (/^\s*[\d\/\-]+\s+[\d\:\.]+\s+[\w\d]+(\s+.+)/) {
                    $line .= $1;  # a new errorlog entry
                }
                else {
                    $line .= $_;  # continuation of a line
                }
                # leaving the node
                last if /^\s*[\d\/\-]+\s+[\d\:\.]+\s+[\w\d]+\s+ResType:LockOwner/;
            }
            $line =~ s/\n/ /g;         # remove all the embedded newlines
            print LOG1 "$line\n";     # print a line per node
            next;
        }
        if (m{^\s*[\d\/\-]+\s+[\d\:\.]+\s+[\w\d]+\s+
                Victim\s+Resource\s+Owner}ix && $deadlockON) {
            # leaving the deadlock info block
            my $line = $_;
            $_ = <LOG>;
            /^\s*[\d\/\-]+\s+[\d\:\.]+\s+[\w\d]+\s+(.+)/ && ($line .= $1);
            $line .= $1;             # record the last line for this deadlock
            $line =~ s/\n/ /g;      # remove the embedded newlines
            print LOG1 "$line\n";
            $deadlockON = 0;         # indicating exit of the deadlock info block
            next;
        }
    }
    close(LOG);
    close(LOG1);
} # getDeadlockEntries


#########################
sub getDeadlockSummary {
    my ($logFile2) =shift or
            die "***Err: getDeadlockSummary() expects a log file.";

    my $deadlockRef = { };
    my $i;
    $/ = "Deadlock encountered\n";   # set the new input record separator
    open(LOG, "$logFile2")
            or die "Cannot open $logFile2 for read.";
    while(<LOG>) {                        # read one deadlock a time
        s/\s*Deadlock encountered\s*//;
        next if /^\s*$/;
```

```perl
        my $ref = { };
        for (split /\n/) { # split by \n, i.e. a list of node info items
            /^\s*([\d\/\-]+\s+[\d\:\.]+)\s+[\w\d]+\s+/
                                 and $ref->{time} = $1;

            if (m{ (Node:\d+)\s+                          # node #
                     (\w+:\s+[\w\d\:]+)\s+.+?             # node resource
                     Grant\s+List::.+?(Mode:\s+[^\s]+)\s+.+ # granted mode
                     Input\s+Buf:\s+(.+)                    # input buffer content
                     Requested\s+by:.+?(Mode:\s+[^\s]+)\s+  # requested mode
                   }ix) {
                $ref->{$1}->{resource} = $2;
                $ref->{$1}->{grantedLockMode} = $3;
                $ref->{$1}->{inputBuffer} = $4;
                $ref->{$1}->{requestedLockMode} = $5;
                push @{$ref->{signatures}}, "$2//$3//$4//$5";
            }
        }
        # check whether a deadlock with that signature is already recorded
        my $found = 0;
        foreach my $d (keys %$deadlockRef) {
            if (dbaSetSame($deadlockRef->{$d}->{signatures}, $ref->{signatures})) {
                $deadlockRef->{$d}->{count}++;
                $deadlockRef->{$d}->{time} = $ref->{time};
                $found = 1;
                last;
            }
        }
        unless ($found) {
            ++$i;
            $deadlockRef->{$i} = $ref;
            $deadlockRef->{$i}->{count} = 1;
        }
    }
    close(LOG);
    return $deadlockRef;
} # getDeadlockSummary


#############################
sub printDeadlockSummary {
    my ($deadlockRef) = shift or
            die "***Err: printDeadlockSummary() expects a reference.";
```

```
    foreach my $dl (sort keys %$deadlockRef) {
      print "*** Deadlock $dl\n";
      print "\tLast Occurred Time:  $deadlockRef->{$dl}->{time}\n";
      print "\tCount: $deadlockRef->{$dl}->{count}\n";
      foreach my $node (sort keys %{$deadlockRef->{$dl}}) {
        next if $node !~ /node:\d+/i;
        print "\t$node info:\n";
        print "\t\tResource:    ",
                   "$deadlockRef->{$dl}->{$node}->{resource}\n";
        print "\t\tGranted Lock: ",
                   "$deadlockRef->{$dl}->{$node}->{grantedLockMode}\n";
        print "\t\tRequest Lock: ",
                   "$deadlockRef->{$dl}->{$node}->{requestedLockMode}\n";
        print "\t\tInput Buffer: ",
              substr($deadlockRef->{$dl}->{$node}->{inputBuffer}, 0, 50), "\n";
      }
    }
} # printDeadlockSummary
```

The script in Listing 9-21 expects the filename of a SQL Server 2000 errorlog on the command line. You can run the script as follows:

```
cmd>perl deadlockSummary.pl d:\mssql\log\errorlog.txt
```

Before discussing the key features of the script, it helps to see an example of what the script in Listing 9-21 produces. Listing 9-22 shows a trimmed deadlock summary report.

Listing 9-22. A Sample Deadlock Summary

```
*** Deadlock 1
    Last Occurred Time:  2002-04-12 00:55:19.32
    Count: 2
    Node:1 info:
        Resource:    KEY: 6:1977058079:1
        Granted Lock: Mode: U
        Request Lock: Mode: U
        Input Buffer: select * from employees (holdlock
    Node:2 info:
        Resource:    KEY: 6:1977058079:1
        Granted Lock: Mode: U
        Request Lock: Mode: U
        Input Buffer: begin tran select * from employees
*** Deadlock 2
```

```
    Last Occurred Time:   2002-04-16 00:58:37.10
    Count: 150
    Node:1 info:
        Resource:      KEY: 6:1977058079:1
        Granted Lock: Mode: U
        Request Lock: Mode: U
        Input Buffer: begin tran select * from employees
    Node:2 info:
        Resource:      KEY: 6:1977058079:1
        Granted Lock: Mode: U
        Request Lock: Mode: U
        Input Buffer: select * from employees (holdlock
*** Deadlock 3
    Last Occurred Time:   2002-04-18 09:50:46.27
    Count: 23
    Node:1 info:
        Resource:      TAB: 6:21575115
        Granted Lock: Mode: X
        Request Lock: Mode: X
        Input Buffer: select * from employees (holdlock tablockx)
    Node:2 info:
        Resource:      TAB: 6:1977058079
        Granted Lock: Mode: X
        Request Lock: Mode: X
        Input Buffer: select * from orders (holdlock
```

In the report in Listing 9-22, the script `deadlockSummary.pl` identifies three unique deadlocks. For each unique deadlock, it also reports the date and the time of its last occurrence and the total number of occurrences. In addition, the report includes the basic elements for each deadlock node.

For instance, deadlock 3 in Listing 9-22 was last logged at 9:50:46.27 on April 18, 2002, and was found 23 times in the errorlog file. In each of these 23 occurrences, this deadlock had two nodes. On node 1, a process has been granted an exclusive lock on the table orders (object ID 21575115) while another process is requesting an exclusive lock on the same table and is being blocked. On node 2, the second process has been granted an exclusive lock on the table employees (object ID 1977058079) while the first process is trying to obtain another exclusive lock on the same table, thus causing a deadlock. Moreover, in each of the 23 occurrences, the input buffer of the corresponding node had the same SQL statement: `select * from orders (holdlock tablockx)` for node 1 and `select * from employees (holdlock tablockx)` for node 2.

More on the Script deadlockSummary.pl

Now let's discuss several key features of the script in Listing 9-21.

This script first makes one pass through the errorlog file to pick out the entries related to the trace flag 1204, skipping all the other entries. This is the job of the function `getDeadlockEntries()`. This pass produces an intermediate file consisting of the better-formatted lines for the deadlock chains. For each deadlock chain, the entries in this intermediate file are similar to the following:

```
Deadlock encountered
2002-04-16 00:55:19 spid4 Node:1 KEY... Grant List... Input Buf... Requested By:
2002-04-16 00:55:19 spid4 Node:2 KEY... Grant List... Input Buf... Requested By:
2002-04-16 00:55:19 spid4 Victim Resource Owner: ... Mode: U ...
```

Recall that each element of a node may occupy multiple lines in the original trace flag output, and the input buffer often has embedded newlines. Also recall that when the script reads from the errorlog file, it reads in one line at a time. To mix inputting errorlog lines with searching for deadlock information in the same function would render the code unwieldy and not readable. Therefore, I added this preprocessing pass through the errorlog to extract the deadlock lines and format each deadlock chain as follows:

- The output starts a deadlock chain with the string `Deadlock encountered`.

- Then, there are two or more lines, each for a single node.

- The output ends the deadlock chain with a line containing the string `Victim Resource Owner`.

With the trace flag output cleanly formatted as such, it becomes straightforward for the function `getDeadlockSummary()` to apply pattern matching to capture the basic elements of each node and construct the node signature. At the beginning of the function `getDeadlockSummary()`, the input record separator `$/` is set to the string `Deadlock encountered\n`, causing the angle operator (`<>`) in the `while` statement to slurp in one deadlock chain at a time, as opposed to one line at a time.

When the deadlock chain is completely read into the predefined Perl variable `$_`, the script splits the chain into separate strings, one for each node. Then, the following code segment in `getDeadlockSummary()` matches each node string for the node elements—including node resource, granted lock mode, input buffer, and requested lock mode—and records the node elements in a hash structure:

```
if (m{ (Node:\d+)\s+                         # node number
         (\w+:\s+[\w\d\:]+)\s+.+?              # node resource
         Grant\s+List::.+?(Mode:\s+[^\s]+)\s+.+ # granted mode
         Input\s+Buf:\s+(.+)                   # input buffer content
         Requested\s+by:.+?(Mode:\s+[^\s]+)\s+ # requested mode
    }ix) {
  $ref->{$1}->{resource} = $2;
  $ref->{$1}->{grantedLockMode} = $3;
  $ref->{$1}->{inputBuffer} = $4;
  $ref->{$1}->{requestedLockMode} = $5;
  push @{$ref->{signatures}}, "$2//$3//$4//$5";
}
```

Listing 9-23 shows an example of the hash structure for a two-node deadlock chain (edited for readability).

Listing 9-23. Hash Structure for a Single Two-Node Deadlock Chain

```
$ref = {
        'Node:1' => {
                'requestedLockMode' => 'Mode: X',
                'resource' => 'TAB: 6:21575115',
                'inputBuffer' => 'select * from employees (holdlock tablockx)',
                'grantedLockMode' => 'Mode: X'
        },
        'Node:2' => {
                'requestedLockMode' => 'Mode: X',
                'resource' => 'TAB: 6:1977058079',
                'inputBuffer' => 'select * from orders (holdlock tablockx)',
                'grantedLockMode' => 'Mode: X'
        },
        'signatures' => [
                'TAB: 6:21575115//Mode: X//select ... //Mode: X',
                'TAB: 6:1977058079//Mode: X//select ... //Mode: X'
        ],
        'time' => '2002-04-18 09:50:46.27'
}
```

Note that Listing 9-23 has two separate node signatures, one for each node. The signature is the concatenation of the values of the node elements (node resource, granted lock mode, input buffer, and requested lock mode), separated by forward slashes. This hash structure records the information about a single occurrence of a deadlock. To keep the example short, the SQL statements in the input buffers aren't printed in full for the node signatures.

The data structure for the overall deadlock summary is similar but of course includes additional information (see Listing 9-24).

Listing 9-24. A Sample Hash Structure for the Deadlock Summary

```
$deadlockRef = {
    1 => {
        'count' => 24,
        'Node:1' => {
            'requestedLockMode' => 'Mode: U',
            'resource' => 'KEY: 6:1977058079:1',
            'inputBuffer' => 'select * from employees (holdlock rowlock updlock)',
            'grantedLockMode' => 'Mode: U'
        },
        'Node:2' => {
            'requestedLockMode' => 'Mode: U',
            'resource' => 'KEY: 6:1977058079:1',
            'inputBuffer' => 'select * from employees (holdlock rowlock updlock)',
            'grantedLockMode' => 'Mode: U'
        },
        'signatures' => [
            'KEY: 6:1977058079:1//Mode: U//select ... //Mode: U',
            'KEY: 6:1977058079:1//Mode: U//select ... //Mode: U'
        ],
        'time' => '2002-04-16 00:56:46.94'
    },
    2 => {
        'count' => 78,
        'Node:1' => {
            'requestedLockMode' => 'Mode: U',
            'resource' => 'KEY: 6:1977058079:1',
            'inputBuffer' => 'select * from employees (holdlock rowlock updlock)',
            'grantedLockMode' => 'Mode: U'
        },
        'Node:2' => {
            'requestedLockMode' => 'Mode: U',
            'resource' => 'KEY: 6:1977058079:1',
            'inputBuffer' => 'select * from employees (holdlock rowlock updlock)',
            'grantedLockMode' => 'Mode: U'
        },
        'Node:3' => {
            'requestedLockMode' => 'Mode: U',
            'resource' => 'KEY: 6:1977058079:1',
            'inputBuffer' => 'select * from employees (holdlock rowlock updlock)',
```

```
        'grantedLockMode' => 'Mode: U'
      },
      'signatures' => [
         'KEY: 6:1977058079:1//Mode: U//select * ...//Mode: U',
         'KEY: 6:1977058079:1//Mode: U//select * ...//Mode: U',
         'KEY: 6:1977058079:1//Mode: U//select * ...//Mode: U'
      ],
      'time' => '2002-04-16 01:07:00.38'
  },
}
```

In the hash structure in Listing 9-24, there are two unique deadlocks. A number identifies each deadlock, and this number is used as the key in the hash. At the time this structure is printed, the script deadlockSummary.pl has found, in the trace flag 1204 output, 24 instances of deadlock 1 and 78 instances of deadlock 2.

In the following code fragment from the function getDeadlockSummary(), note that the script does a set comparison, using dbaSetSame(), to compare the node signatures of the deadlock chain that's currently being scanned with those of the unique deadlocks already recorded in the summary hash structure. This comparison determines whether this is a new deadlock:

```
# check whether a deadlock with that signature is already recorded
my $found = 0;
foreach my $d (keys %$deadlockRef) {
   if (dbaSetSame($deadlockRef->{$d}->{signatures}, $ref->{signatures})) {
      $deadlockRef->{$d}->{count}++;
      $deadlockRef->{$d}->{time} = $ref->{time};
      $found = 1;
      last;
   }
}
```

If it's a new deadlock, the hash structure of the current deadlock chain is added to the summary hash structure. If it isn't new, the script updates the deadlock occurrence counter $deadlockRef->{$d}->{count} and refreshes the latest deadlock time in $deadlockRef->{$d}->{time}.

Before concluding the discussion of deadlocks, I'd be remiss if I didn't point out that the script in Listing 9-21 was written to deal with the most common type of deadlocks. The trace flag 1204 also reports in different formats on other types of deadlocks such as those involving parallelism. Once you become familiar with the trace flag output for those deadlocks, it's not difficult to modify the script in Listing 9-8 to include the other deadlock types in the summary.

Summary

This chapter discussed using Perl to analyze Windows event logs, ODBC trace logs, and SQL Server errorlog files, especially to condense these files to manageable summary reports.

If you study the scripts in this chapter, you'll no doubt notice a common thread of programming technique that's prominent in all the scripts. The technique is to use regular-expression patterns to search for useful tidbits followed by storing the captured information in hash structures, possibly nested. The combination of regular expressions and hash structures is elegant and powerful.

One good side effect of writing Perl scripts to get information out of a log file is that it forces you to become intimately familiar with that log file. You'd be surprised by what you can learn about the Windows event logs, ODBC trace logs, and SQL Server errorlog files when you pay such a close attention to them.

The next chapter shows how you can use Perl to help manage SQL Server security.

CHAPTER 10

Managing SQL Server Security

SQL SERVER IS TIGHTLY INTEGRATED with the Windows operating system. One of the areas where this tight integration is particularly evident is SQL Server security. It's not possible to effectively administer SQL Server security without a solid grasp of Windows security concepts such as domains, authentication, users and groups, permissions, privileges, service accounts, and security auditing. Inadequate understanding of the Windows security model rapidly leads a SQL Server Database Administrator (DBA) to confusion.

Consider this frequently asked question from novice DBAs: "How come this SQL script works in Query Analyzer but fails when run from a scheduled job?" This can almost invariably be attributed to the failure of the DBA to grasp the concept of the Windows security context.

Another notable characteristic of SQL Server security is that it's a concern throughout the entire life cycle of any SQL Server project. During the initial installation of SQL Server, the DBA has to worry about such security issues as the service accounts, security mode, and security lockdown of the server. As databases are being deployed, migrated, or decommissioned, the DBA needs to assign security roles, grant permissions, resolve orphaned users, and clean up obsolete logins, users, and permissions. During the regular operations, the DBA should perform regular reviews and audits for any breach of the established security policies.

SQL Server environments differ significantly in their approaches to managing security. Some environments have well-formulated, rigorous security policies that incorporate the industry best practices. Others follow general and informal guidelines. Still other environments may not have any explicitly formulated security policies at all, leaving the management of security to the discretion of the DBA.

Regardless of how the management chooses to address the SQL Server security policies, managing security requires constant patience and attention to detail from the DBA. Indeed, security is no trivial matter in a SQL Server environment. The DBA should always be proactive in keeping the SQL Server environment under control. It takes only a single incident for the management to be all over the DBA like a hound on a hare.

Before you start enforcing security policies or tackling any security issues at all, you must first become aware of what's currently going on with security in your SQL Server environment. This chapter discusses several cases in which Perl helps keep track of SQL Server security. More specifically, this chapter presents Perl scripts to list all the accounts that have sysadmin privileges, scan the network for machines with SQL Server installed, scan for SQL Server instances with null sa passwords, track SQL Server service accounts, report significant changes to SQL Server security configurations, summarize security audit logs, and identify wide-open shares on SQL Servers.

Listing Sysadmin Accounts and Logins

SCENARIO
You want to find all the Windows user and group accounts and SQL Server logins that have been granted a SQL Server sysadmin role directly or indirectly via Windows group memberships.

SQL Server provides several fixed server roles, one of which is the almighty sysadmin role. A sysadmin member can do anything in SQL Server; there's no restriction imposed and no permission required. Obviously, a DBA must be extremely careful in granting the sysadmin membership to a Windows account or a SQL Server login. The sysadmin membership must be kept to the bare minimum, and the DBA must regularly track the membership.

How do you track the membership of the sysadmin role? Because you can gain the sysadmin membership by virtue of being a member of a Windows group that has already been added to the sysadmin role, tracking the sysadmin membership is more complicated than it first appears. To find the complete list of the user accounts that have sysadmin privileges, you must first get all the Windows groups in the sysadmin role. Then, for each of the groups, you need to discover all its member accounts.

There's one small twist, though. Because a Windows local group can contain one or more Windows global groups, you must get the user accounts of all the global groups within each local group that's a member of the sysadmin role. Fortunately, because a Windows global group can't contain any other group account, there's no need to search for individual user accounts recursively.

The following is a summary of the steps to find all the Windows user accounts and SQL Server logins that have SQL Server sysadmin privileges:

1. Start with three empty sets: the resultset, the group set, and the user set.

2. Add all the Windows user accounts and the SQL Server logins in the sysadmin role to the resultset.

3. Add all the Windows group accounts in the sysadmin role to the group set.

4. Now, the group set may include both local and global groups. For each group in the group set, do the following: First, if it's a local group, add all

its members to the user set, and second, if it's not a local group, then it must be a global group. Add it to the user set.

5. Now, the user set may include both user accounts and global group accounts. For each member in the user set, do the following: First, if it's a global group, add its members to the resultset, and second, if it's not a global group, then it must be a user account. Add it to the resultset.

6. The resultset now has all the Windows user accounts and SQL Server logins that have sysadmin privileges.

The Perl script ListSysadmin.pl in Listing 10-1 implements this procedure. As you'll see, the resultset, the group set, and the user set used in the procedure are implemented with respective Perl arrays.

Listing 10-1. Listing Individual Users and Logins in the Sysadmin Role

```perl
use strict;
use Win32::ODBC;
use SQLDBA::Utility qw( dbaRemoveDuplicates );
use Win32::NetAdmin qw( GetDomainController GroupGetMembers
                        LocalGroupGetMembersWithDomain UsersExist );

Main: {
   my $serverConn = shift or
       die "***Err: a server is expected on the command line.";

   # get all the accounts/logins with sysadmin role from SQL Server
   my $loginRef = getSQLSysadmins($serverConn);
   # in case the server name is followed by an instance name
   my ($server) = $serverConn =~ /([^\\]+)(\\.+)?/;

   # replace BUILTIN with the server name
   foreach (@{$loginRef->{groupSet}}) {
      s/BUILTIN\\/uc($server) . "\\"/e; # evaluate the right side before replace
   }

   # remove all local groups and get their members
   $loginRef = removeLocalGroups($loginRef);

   # get global group members
   $loginRef = getGlobalGroupMembers($loginRef);

   # now print out all the NT/SQL logins that are SQL sysadmin
```

```perl
      print "Listing all NT/SQL logins with the sysadmin rights ...\n";
      foreach (sort @{$loginRef->{resultSet}}) { print "\t$_\n"; }
} # Main


########################
sub getSQLSysadmins {
    my $serverConn = shift or
        die "***Err: getSQLSysadmins() expects a server.";

    # construct the connection string
    my $connStr = "Driver={SQL Server};Server=$serverConn;"  .
                             "Trusted_Connection=Yes;Database=master";
    # make the connection
    my $conn = new Win32::ODBC ($connStr) or
        die "***Err: can't connect to $serverConn. " . Win32::ODBC::Error();

    # get sysadmin logins (NT and SQL)
    my @logins = ();
    my $sql = q/SELECT loginname FROM master.dbo.syslogins
                WHERE sysadmin = 1
                   AND isntgroup = 0/;

    unless ($conn->Sql( $sql )) {
        while ($conn->FetchRow()) {
          @logins = (@logins, $conn->Data);
        }
    } else {
        print "***Err: executing $sql. ", Win32::ODBC::Error(), "\n";
    }


    # get sysadmin nt groups
    my @groups = ();
    my $sql =  q/SELECT loginname FROM master.dbo.syslogins
                WHERE sysadmin = 1
                   AND isntgroup = 1/;

    unless ($conn->Sql( $sql )) {
        while ($conn->FetchRow()) {
          @groups = (@groups, $conn->Data);
        }
    } else {
        print "***Err: executing $sql. ", Win32::ODBC::Error(), "\n";
    }
    $conn->Close();
```

```perl
    # return a reference to a hash. This hash is used throughout the script
    return { resultSet  => \@logins,
             groupSet   => \@groups,
             userSet    => undef };
} # getSQLSysadmins


#########################
sub removeLocalGroups {
    my $loginRef = shift or
        die "***Err: removeLocalGroups() expects a reference.";

    foreach my $group (@{$loginRef->{groupSet}}) {
        if (my $rc = getLocalGroupMembers($group)) {  # if it's a local group
            # push the local group members into the userset
            push @{$loginRef->{userSet}}, @{$rc};
        }
        else {   # it's not a local group. It's either a global group or a user
            # push the group into userset
            push @{$loginRef->{userSet}}, $group;
        }
    }
    delete $loginRef->{groupSet};  # done with the local group
    return $loginRef;
} # removeLocalGroups


#########################
sub getGlobalGroupMembers {
    my $loginRef = shift or
        die "***Err: getGlobalGroupMembers() expects a reference.";
    my @logins = ();

    # examine every member in the userset
    foreach my $user (@{$loginRef->{userSet}}) {
        if ($user =~ /^NT\s+AUTHORITY\\/) {
            push @logins, $user;
            next;
        }

        my ($domain, $name) = $user =~ /^(.+?)\\(.+)$/;
        if ( UsersExist($domain, $name ) ) { # a user account
            push @logins, $user;
        }
        else {
            my $pdc;
            my @users;
```

```
                    if (GetDomainController(undef, $domain, $pdc)) {
                        $pdc =~ s/\\//g;

                        if ( UsersExist($pdc, $name ) ) { # a user account
                            push @logins, $user;
                        }
                        else {   # $name is a global group account
                            # get users in the global group
                            if (GroupGetMembers($pdc, $name, \@users)) {
                                # prefix the users with the domain name
                                push @logins, map { "$domain\\$_"; } @users;
                            }
                            else {   # you shouldn't reach here
                                print "***Err: can't get users for $domain\\$name.\n";
                                next;
                            }
                        }
                    }
                    else {
                        print "***Err: can't find domain controller for $domain.\n";
                        next;
                    }
                }
            }
        }

        push @logins, @{$loginRef->{resultSet}};
        $loginRef->{resultSet} = dbaRemoveDuplicates(\@logins);
        return $loginRef;
    } # getGlobalGroupMembers


    #########################
    sub getLocalGroupMembers {
        my $group = shift or
            die "***Err: getLocalGroupMember() expects a group name.";

        my ($domain, $group_name) = $group =~ /^(.+?)\\(.+)$/    or
            die "***Err: $group must be qualified with a domain/machine name.";

        my @users = ();
        if (LocalGroupGetMembersWithDomain($domain, $group_name, \@users)) {
            return \@users;
        }
        else { return undef; }
    }  # getLocalGroupMembers
```

This script takes a SQL Server name on the command line. To print all the Windows user accounts and SQL Server logins that have sysadmin privileges on the SQL Server instance SQL1\APOLLO, log on to the domain with a Windows account that has been granted access to the instance and run the script as follows on the command line:

```
cmd>perl ListSysadmin.pl SQL1\APOLLO
```

Now, let's dissect the script in Listing 10-1.

NOTE *To successfully run this script, you should be a member of the local administrators group on the machine against which you're running the script. You don't need any special membership at the domain level other than being a domain user.*

The script begins with a call to the function getSQLSysadmin(), which queries the SQL Server system view syslogins in the master database to get the logins—both the Windows user accounts and the SQL Server logins—as well as the Windows groups that are sysadmin members. The function getSQLSysadmin() first runs the following SQL query via the module Win32::ODBC to get the sysadmin members that are *not* Windows groups:

```
SELECT login
  FROM master.dbo.syslogins
 WHERE issysadmin = 1 AND isntgroup = 0
```

The getSQLSysadmin() function then runs the following SQL query to get the sysadmin members that are Windows groups:

```
SELECT login
  FROM master.dbo.syslogins
 WHERE issysadmin = 1 AND isntgroup = 1
```

The script in Listing 10-1 captures the results of these two queries separately because it needs to further work on the Windows groups. The function getSQLSysadmin() returns the query results in a hash data structure referenced by $loginRef. The following is a sample of this hash data structure:

```
$loginRef = {
   groupSet   => [ 'BUILTIN\\Administrators', 'NYDomain\\SQLDBAs' ],
   resultSet  => [ 'distributor_admin', 'SQL1\\lshea', 'sa' ],
   userSet    => undef
}
```

Subsequent steps in the script all work on this data structure to get the user accounts from each group in the array referenced by the hash key groupSet and to add the user accounts to the array referenced by the hash key resultSet. To simplify the exposition, I'll refer to these arrays as the groupSet array and the resultSet array, respectively.

It's not clear why Microsoft chose to represent the local administrators group as BUILTIN\Administrators in SQL Server. But to work with the Windows groups, you need to replace the string BUILTIN with the corresponding server name before feeding the group name to the functions imported from the module Win32::NetAdmin. You accomplish this with the following code fragment:

```
# replace BUILTIN with the server name
foreach (@{$loginRef->{groupSet}}) {
   s/BUILTIN\\/uc($server) . "\\"/e;
}
```

Note the use of the /e modifier in the s/// operator. Recall that, normally, the right side—the replacement part—of the s/// operator is an interpolated string. The /e modifier evaluates the right side as a piece of Perl code before the s/// operator uses the result as the replacement. In this example, the script first converts the server name in the variable $server to all uppercase letters and appends a backslash (\) to the server name. The s/// operator then replaces the string BUILTIN\ with the result.

Next, the function removeLocalGroup() goes through the groups in the groupSet array and adds all the global groups and all the members of each local group to the array referenced by the hash key userSet–referred to as the userSet array in the ensuing discussions. You obtain the members of a local group using the function getLocalGroupMembers() from the module Win32::NetAdmin. At this point, the data structure should look like the following:

```
$loginRef = {
   resultSet => [ 'distributor_admin', 'SQL1\\lshea', 'sa'  ],
   userSet   => [ 'NYDomain\\SQLDBAs', 'NYDomain\\DomainAdmins',
                  'NYDomain\\vshea' ]
}
```

By now, the script has deleted the groupSet array from $loginRef because it's no longer useful and has populated the userSet array. The latter doesn't have any local groups but has either Windows global groups or individual user accounts. Once again, you see the ease with which you can dynamically expand and reduce the nested data structures that are built on Perl's arrays, hashes, and references.

Let's return to the main body of the script in Listing 10-1, where the script calls the function getGlobalGroupMembers() to add the user accounts or the members of the global groups in the userSet array to the resultSet array. This function again relies on the functions available from the Win32::NetAdmin module to determine whether an element in the userSet array is a user account or a global group. If it's a global group, getGlobalGroupMembers() calls the GroupGetMembers() function imported from Win32::NetAdmin to retrieve the members of the group as follows:

```
if ( UsersExist($pdc, $name ) ) { # a user account
    push @logins, $user;
}
else {  # $name is a global group account
    # get users in the global group
    if (GroupGetMembers($pdc, $name, \@users)) {
        # prefix the users with the domain name
        push @logins, map { "$domain\\$_"; } @users;
    }
    else {  # you shouldn't reach here
        print "***Err: can't get users for $domain\\$name.\n";
        next;
    }
}
```

Now, when the function getGlobalGroupMembers() returns, the resultSet array has all the SQL Server logins and the Windows user accounts that have been granted membership in the sysadmin role, and it's ready to be printed.

It's nice to find what user accounts or SQL Server logins have the sysadmin privileges in a SQL Server instance. It's even nicer to be able to keep track of any changes to the sysadmin membership across your servers. In some security-conscious environments, you may even want to run such a script regularly to take snapshots of the sysadmin membership. If you persist these snapshots, you can compare them or compare the snapshots with a canonical version—one of the snapshots you designate as representing what should be the membership of the sysadmin role for each of the SQL Server instances. You can then schedule this comparison to alert you of any noteworthy changes to the sysadmin membership.

Finding SQL Server Machines

> **SCENARIO**
> *You want to find all the machines on the network that have SQL Server installed.*

Perhaps because SQL Server is easy to install and use, it's common to find more installed SQL Server instances than the DBA knows are there. For many valid reasons (licensing and security, for example), management may want to track down all the machines with SQL Server installed, and you just might be the one called upon to perform the task.

> **NOTE** *The SQL Slammer attack that wreaked havoc around the world in January 2003 clearly highlights the need to keep track of your SQL Server instances.*

If you're not careful, you may walk away from the SQL Server documentation with the impression that a tool is already provided to get a list of SQL Servers on your network. Among the many switches of the osql command-line utility, -L is documented to list the locally configured servers and the names of the servers broadcasting on the network. Similarly, SQL Distributed Management Objects (SQL-DMO) expose a method called ListAvailableSQLServers—for the Application object—that enumerates network-visible instances of SQL Server.

Unfortunately, this is a false impression. These documented mechanisms for listing SQL Server instances rely on broadcasting packets that are usually blocked by network routers. Unless you have a small network, you'll find that broadcasting packets can reach only a tiny fraction of your network. If you happen to work in a larger network environment, you can easily confirm this by testing out osql -L at a Windows command prompt; many of your SQL Server instances won't be on the displayed list.

Finding all or most SQL Server machines on a network—especially on a large network—isn't trivial. The script scanForSQLServer.pl, presented in Listing 10-2, provides a method to sweep through all the machines in your Windows domains and tests each for the presence of an installed SQL Server.

Listing 10-2. Scanning for SQL Servers

```perl
use strict;
use Win32::NetAdmin;
use Win32::OLE;
use Win32::Service;
use Getopt::Std;

my %opts;
getopts('lhmd:s:', \%opts);          # get the command-line arguments
printUsage() if $opts{h};            # print the usage info and exit if -h
select((select(STDOUT), $| = 1)[0]); # flush STDOUT after each output

Main: {
   my @domains;
   my @servers;
   my ($user, $password) = ('sa', undef);

   # enumerate domains
   Win32::NetAdmin::GetServers('', '', SV_TYPE_DOMAIN_ENUM, \@domains);

   foreach my $domain (sort @domains) {  # loop through the domains
      print scalar localtime(), "   *** Domain: $domain";

      # if there are any arguments
      if( $opts{d} ) {   # work on a particular domain introduced by -d
         if ( $opts{d} ne $domain) {
            # skip to next domain
            print " skipped\n";
            next;
         }
      }
      else {
         if( $opts{s} ) {  # work on the domains starting from the one by -s
            # if the specified domain hasn't been reached yet
            if( $opts{s} gt $domain) {
               # skip to next domain
               print " skipped\n";
               next;
            }
         }
      }
      print "\n";
```

```perl
        # now enumerate machines in the domain
        Win32::NetAdmin::GetServers('', $domain, SV_TYPE_NT, \@servers);
        print "\t\t Found ", scalar @servers, " NT machines in this domain\n";

        foreach my $server (sort @servers) {      # loop through the servers
            if ($opts{m}) {
                print "\t\t Scanning machine $server\n";
            }
            next if $opts{l};
            # check the server to see if it has a SQL instance
            my $whatisit = isSQLServer($server, $user, $password);
            print "\t\t$whatisit\n";
        }
    }
} # Main


######################
sub isSQLServer {
    my ($server, $user, $password) = @_;
    my $whatisit;

    my $conn = Win32::OLE->new('ADODB.Connection');
    $conn->{CoonectionTimeout} = 2;  # set a shorter timeout
    # try to open an ADO connection
    $conn->Open("Driver={SQL Server};Server=$server;UID=$user;PWD=$password");
    my $err = Win32::OLE->LastError();
    if (!$err) {
        $whatisit = "Null sa password> $server";
        $conn->Close;
    }
    else {
        if ($err =~ /Login\s+failed/i) {  # only SQL can respond with this msg
            $whatisit = "Failed Login> $server";
        }
        else {  # if that's inconclusive, check the installed services
            my %Services;
            Win32::Service::GetServices($server, \%Services);
            if (grep(/^\s*(MSSQLServer|MSSQL\$\w+)\s*$/i,
                        keys %Services)) {
                $whatisit = "Win32::Service> $server";
            }
        }
    }
```

```
    return $whatisit;
} # isSQLServer


######################
sub printUsage {
    print << '--Usage--';
Usage:
 cmd>perl scanForSQLServer.pl [-h] [-m] [-l] [-d <domain> | -s <domain>]

    When no arguments are specified, scan all domains and all NT machines.

    -h              print this usage info
    -m              list all the machines as they are being scanned
    -l              list the machines only. Do not scan for SQL Server
    -d<domain>      scan machines in this domain only
    -s<domain>      skip to this domain and start scanning in this domain
                          and all the subsequent domains
--Usage--
  exit;
} # printUsage
```

The script uses the module Win32::NetAdmin to enumerate the domains and the servers in a domain. See the following lines at the beginning of the Main code block:

```
# now enumerate domains
Win32::NetAdmin::GetServers('', '', SV_TYPE_DOMAIN_ENUM, \@domains);
```

The domains that are found will be returned in the array @domains. Then, for each domain in @domains, the script again uses the function GetServers to retrieve a list of machine accounts that are running Windows 2000/NT:

```
# now enumerate machines in the domain
Win32::NetAdmin::GetServers('', $domain, SV_TYPE_NT, \@servers);
```

The machine names are in the array @servers. Finally, for each machine in the array, the script calls the function isSQLServer() to test whether SQL Server is running or installed on the machine.

Several tests are implemented in the function `isSQLServer()`. First, it tries to log in to the SQL Server using ActiveX Data Objects (ADO) as if a SQL Server default instance was running. The function then checks for the following two conditions:

- If the login attempt succeeds, it's indicative of a running SQL Server default instance.

- If the login attempt receives a login failure error, it's again indicative of a running SQL Server default instance.

Any other return status from the login attempt doesn't provide sufficient information for a positive identification. The function therefore performs one more test with the help of the module Win32::Service. It calls the function `Win32::Service::GetServices()` to enumerate the Win32 services—both active and inactive—on the machine, and it looks for these string patterns in the service names: `MSSQLServer` and `MSSQL\$\w+`. The presence of any of these string patterns is enough to conclude that a SQL Server instance is installed on that machine.

TIP *If you want to significantly speed up the scan for SQL Servers, you can do away with trying to log into SQL Server and scan for the presence of `MSSQLServer` or `MSSQL$\w+` in the service names.*

I've made several observations from running this script in large network environments. First, it takes time to test whether SQL Server is installed on a machine. Even if it only spends a few seconds per machine, the script may take as long as several days to complete in a large domain or a group of domains. When I was running this script on a group of trusted domains for the first time, I didn't set the login timeout. The script just kept running until I realized that by default each login attempt needed eight seconds to time out and that it would take more than a week to finish scanning the 70,000+ machines in the enumerated domains. Of course, I aborted the script as soon as I did the math and reduced the ADO connection timeout used by the script. I added `$conn->{ConnectionTimeout} = 2` to the function `isSQLServer()` in Listing 10-2 to set the connection timeout to two seconds.

Second, you often don't need or even want to scan all the domains that can be enumerated. To this end, the script accepts the command-line argument `-d` to specify a domain name. When this argument is used, only the machines in this specific domain are scanned for SQL Server installations.

Third, when scanning a large network, you should avoid starting from the beginning after an aborted run. The command-line argument -s specifies a domain name, which tells the script to skip directly to this domain and scan only the machines in this and subsequent domains. Note that the script sorts the enumerated domains in alphabetical order.

Fourth, it's worth stressing that this script doesn't guarantee to enumerate all the machines in a domain or even all the domains. This is by design—not of the Perl script but of the underlying Windows networking Application Programming Interface (API). The Win32::NetAdmin module is built on top of the Windows networking API. In a large, complex network environment, it's common for the function Win32::NetAdmin::GetServers() to return a slightly different list of machines in two consecutive calls.

NOTE *As long as you're a domain user, you don't need any special rights to run this script. In particular, you don't need to be the member of the local administrators group.*

Finally, you've probably noticed the repeated mention of the SQL Server default instance. As implemented, the script in Listing 10-2 tries the login attempt only on the default instance. If a machine has a named instance but doesn't have the default instance, the script can still conclude that the machine has SQL Server installed. The login attempt will fail, but the script will attempt to match service names with the pattern MSSQL\$\w+, which in turn will succeed because the service name of a named SQL Server instance always starts with the string MSSQL\$.

This final point takes you right back to the problem you're trying to solve, which is to find all the machines with SQL Server installed instead of finding all the installed SQL Server instances. The next section discusses the latter.

Scanning for Null sa Passwords

SCENARIO
You want to find SQL Server instances with null sa passwords on your network.

Hackers have exploited SQL Server not only as a primary target of attack but also as a conduit or a port of entry for invading other targets in a computing environment. There has been virus software specifically designed to take advantage of SQL Server instances whose sa logins aren't protected with passwords. Because most SQL Server instances run in the security context of a highly privileged

Windows user account—usually a member of the local administrators group, a compromised sa login not only can wreak havoc to that computer at the minimum, it may also easily lead the attacker to penetrate many other computers.

Like the task of finding machines with SQL Server installed, locating the SQL Server instances with null sa passwords isn't trivial in a large network environment. If you already have a list of all the SQL Server instances in your environment, verifying whether there's a null sa password is a simple matter of actually trying to log in each instance using the sa login with a null password.

 NOTE *In fact, you don't need to explicitly log in each instance on the list. Chapter 12, "Managing SQL Servers in the Enterprise," gives you the script* msql.pl, *which you can use to run a Transact-TSQL (T-SQL) query on multiple SQL Server instances as if you were executing the query with* osql.exe *on a single SQL Server instance.*

Unfortunately, such a comprehensive list may be hard to come by in an environment where no single individual or group has exclusive authority over all the installed SQL Servers or over installing SQL Server.

The good news is that you already have a solution—well, almost—to find these dangerous null sa passwords. Recall that in the course of finding SQL Server machines, the script in Listing 10-2 attempts to log in to SQL Server using the sa login with a null password. The script returns a list of machines with null sa passwords. However, it tests only the default SQL Server instance on each machine, and it doesn't report the null sa passwords for any named instances.

You can adapt the script in Listing 10-2 to sweep the network for any SQL Server instance whose sa password is null.

Most of the script can remain unchanged with the exception of the function isSQLServer(). Instead of testing whether a machine has an installed SQL Server, you need to first find all the installed SQL Server instances on that machine and then test each for a null sa password. The script scanNullSAPasswords.pl in Listing 10-3 closely resembles that in Listing 10-2, but the function findNullSAInstances() replaces the function isSQLServer().

Listing 10-3. Finding SQL Server Instances with Null sa Passwords

```
1.  use strict;
2.  use Win32::NetAdmin;
3.  use Win32::OLE;
4.  use Win32::Service;
5.  use Getopt::Std;
```

```
6.
7.   my %opts;
8.   getopts('lhmd:s:', \%opts);           # get command-line arguments
9.   printUsage() if $opts{h};             # if -h, print usgae and exit
10.  select((select(STDOUT), $| = 1)[0]);  # flush STDOUT after each output
11.
12. Main: {
13.     my @domains;
14.     my @servers;
15.     my ($user, $pwd) = ('sa', undef);
16.
17.     # now enumerate domains
18.     Win32::NetAdmin::GetServers( '', '', SV_TYPE_DOMAIN_ENUM, \@domains);
19.
20.     foreach my $domain (sort @domains) {
21.         print scalar localtime(), "   *** Domain: $domain";
22.
23.         # if there are any arguments
24.         if( $opts{d} ) {  # only work on the machines in this domain
25.           if( $opts{d} ne $domain) {
26.               print " skipped\n";
27.               next;  # skip to the next domain
28.           }
29.         }
30.         else {
31.           if ( $opts{s} ) {
32.               # if the specified domain hasn't been reached yet
33.               if( $opts{s} gt $domain) {
34.                   print " skipped\n";
35.                   next;  # skip to the next domain
36.               }
37.           }
38.         }
39.         print "\n";
40.
41.         # now enumerate machines in the domain
42.         Win32::NetAdmin::GetServers( '', $domain, SV_TYPE_NT, \@servers);
43.         print "\t\t Found ", scalar @servers, " NT machines in this domain\n";
44.
45.         foreach my $server (sort @servers) {
46.           if ($opts{m} or $opts{l}) {  # if -m or -l, print machine names
47.               print "\t\t Scanning machine $server\n";
48.           }
49.           if (!$opts{l}) {  # if not -l
```

```
50.              my @nullSAInstances = findNullSAInstances($server, 'sa', $pwd);
51.
52.              # print the instance names, if any
53.              foreach my $instance (@nullSAInstances) {
54.                  print "\t\t\t$instance\n";
55.              }
56.          }
57.      } # foreach my $server
58.   } # foreach my $domain
59. } # Main
60.
61. ###########################
62. sub findNullSAInstances {
63.    my ($server, $user, $pwd) = @_;
64.    my @sqlServices;
65.    my @nullSAInstances;
66.
67.    # first get all the SQL Server services for the server
68.    my %Services;
69.    Win32::Service::GetServices($server, \%Services);
70.    @sqlServices = grep(/^\s*(MSSQLServer|MSSQL\$\w+)\s*$/i, keys %Services));
71.
72.    # now test each instance with null sa password
73.    foreach my $service (@sqlServices) {
74.       # work with only the active service
75.       my %status;
76.       Win32::Service::GetStatus($server, $service, \%status);
77.       next if $status{'CurrentState'} != 4; # if not running
78.
79.       # construct the server name on the connection string
80.       my $instance;
81.       if ($service =~ /^MSSQLServer$/i) {
82.           $instance = $server;
83.       }
84.       else {
85.           $service =~ /^MSSQL\$(.+)$/i;
86.           $instance = "$server\\$1";
87.       }
88.
89.       # connect to the instance
90.       my $db = Win32::OLE->new('ADODB.Connection');
91.       $db->{CoonectionTimeout} = 2;
92.       $db->Open("Driver={SQL Server};Server=$instance;UID=$user;PWD=$pwd");
93.       my $err = Win32::OLE->LastError();
```

```
94.      if (!$err) {
95.           push @nullSAInstances, $instance;
96.           $db->Close;
97.      }
98.   }
99.   return @nullSAInstances;
100. } # findNullSAInstances
101.
102. #####################
103. sub printUsage {
104.     print << '--Usage--';
105. Usage:
106.   cmd>perl ScanNullSAPasswords.pl [-h] [-m] [-l] [-d <domain> | -s <domain>]
107.
108.     When no arguments specified, scan all domains and all NT/Win2K machines
109.
110.     -h              print this usage info
111.     -m              list all the machines as they are being scanned
113.     -l              list the machines only. Do not scan for SQL Server
114.     -d<domain>      scan machines in this domain only
115.     -s<domain>      skip to this domain and start scanning in this domain
116.                             and all the subsequent domains
117. --Usage--
118.    exit;
119. } # printUsage
```

Because the Main block of the script in Listing 10-3 is similar to that in Listing 10-2, the rest of this section focuses on the function findNullSAPasswords().

For each server found in a domain, the function findNullSAPasswords() calls GetServices() of the module Win32::Service on line 69 to get a list of all the services installed on the server. Then, on line 70, it filters for the service names that match the string MSSQLServer for the default SQL Server instance or the pattern MSSQL\$\w+ for the named SQL Server instances:

```
67. # first get all the SQL Server services for the server
68. my %Services;
69. Win32::Service::GetServices($server, \%Services);
70. @sqlServices = grep(/^\s*(MSSQLServer|MSSQL\$\w+)\s*$/i, keys %Services));
```

This code fragment finds all the SQL Server instances on that server. For each SQL Server instance, the script then calls the function Win32::Service::GetStatus() on line 76 to retrieve the current status of the instance:

```
76. Win32::Service::GetStatus($server, $service, \%status);
77. next if $status{'CurrentState'} != 4; # if not running
```

Because you need to actually log in a SQL Server instance to check whether its sa password is null, it's no use working with an offline SQL Server instance. Thus, on line 77 the script skips any SQL Server instance whose service status isn't running. Note that the current state of a service is identified with a numeric value. The number 4 in the `if` condition means that the service is currently running. The current state of a service can be running, stopped, paused, and so on. The most authoritative place to look up the meaning of a current state numeric value returned by `Win32::Service::GetStatus()` is the Windows Platform Software Development Kit (SDK) at `http://msdn.microsoft.com`.

NOTE *For more information on how to find the numbers that represent the service status, refer to the section "Checking the Status of the Windows Services" in Chapter 2.*

Between lines 80 and 87, for each service the function `findNullSAPasswords()` constructs the correct instance name to be used on the ADO connection string. The service `MSSQLServer` is the default instance, and you use the server name in the connection string. For the service `MSSQL$<InstanceName>`, you use `<ServerName>\<InstanceName>` in the connection string. The function makes an ADO connection on line 92 via the module Win32::OLE to the SQL Server instance using the sa login with a null password. If this succeeds, the instance is recorded as having the null sa password.

Tracking SQL Server Service Accounts

SCENARIO
You have a large number of SQL Server instances to manage. You want to keep track of the Windows user accounts that run all the SQL Server services.

SQL Server runs as a group of Windows services. The two most important services are `MSSQLServer` and `SQLServerAgent`, which will be the focus of this discussion. The former is the SQL Server engine, and the latter is the SQL Server job scheduler. Both services run as Windows user processes. In the Microsoft Windows world, a user process always operates in the security context of a user account, and the security context dictates what resources the process is permitted to access. Choosing a user account for a SQL Server service is therefore an important security configuration decision that has far-reaching impact on the operational behavior of a SQL Server instance.

Once configured, the service accounts remain relatively stable. Any change to the service account configuration should be considered as a significant event and therefore should be carefully managed. When the SQL Server instances are managed by a group of DBAs, it's also important to communicate service account changes within the group so that the following happens:

- The entire DBA group has the correct information of the service accounts used by the SQL Server instances.

- Any unintentional change to a service account is caught.

The Perl script trackSQLAccounts.pl in Listing 10-4 keeps track of the SQL Server service accounts and any changes made to them. More specifically, the script allows a DBA to perform the following tasks on a group of SQL Server instances:

- Produce a list of the service accounts

- Report whether a SQL Server service has been changed to run under a different user account

The script retrieves the service account for a service using the function dbaGetServiceAccount() imported from SQLDBA::Security, which in turn relies on the QueryServiceConfig() function of the Win32::Lanman module. For change tracking, the script saves a snapshot of the service account configurations consisting of the service accounts and their corresponding services, instances, and servers. It then compares the current snapshot of the SQL Server service account configurations with the saved configurations to identify whether any change has been introduced.

Listing 10-4. Tracking SQL Server Service Account Changes

```perl
use strict;
use SQLDBA::Utility qw( dbaReadINI dbaReadSavedRef dbaSaveRef );
use SQLDBA::Security qw( dbaGetServiceAccount );
use Getopt::Std;

Main: {
   my $diffRef;

   my %opts;
```

```perl
    getopts('sdc:', \%opts);

    # config file must be specified on the command line
    my $file = $opts{c} or die "***Err: $0 expects a config file name.\n";
    my $configRef = dbaReadINI($file);

    # remove the disabled servers from the hash
    foreach my $server (keys %$configRef) { # skip the disabled server
        delete $configRef->{$server} if $configRef->{$server}->{DISABLED} =~ /y/i;
    }
    # read the current service accounts
    my $currentRef = readCurrentAccounts($configRef);

    if ($opts{d}) { # check for any difference from the canonical
        # read the saved service accounts
        my $savedRef = dbaReadSavedRef($configRef->{CONTROL}->{SERVICEACCOUNTLOG});
        if ($savedRef) {  # if there are saved service accounts,
            # compare the current with the saved
            $diffRef = compareAccounts($currentRef, $savedRef);
        }
        if ($diffRef) {  # report the difference, if any
            printAccountDiff($diffRef);
        }
        else { print "***Found no change to SQL Server service accounts.\n";  }
    }
    else {  # if -d is not specified, no comparison is performed
        printCurrentAccounts($currentRef);  # just print the current accounts
    }

    # if -s, the save the current as the canonical
    if ($opts{s}) { # save the current configuration as canonical
        dbaSaveRef($configRef->{CONTROL}->{SERVICEACCOUNTLOG}, $currentRef, 'ref');
    }
} # Main


############################
sub readCurrentAccounts {
    my $configRef = shift;
    ref($configRef) or die "***Err: readCurrentAccounts() expects a reference.";
    my $ref;

    foreach my $server (sort keys %$configRef) {
        next if uc($server) eq 'CONTROL';
        foreach my $instance (sort split /\s*,\s*/,
```

```
                                    $configRef->{$server}->{INSTANCES}) {
      my @services;
      if (uc($instance) eq uc('MSSQLServer')) { # default instance
         push @services, uc('MSSQLServer');
         push @services, uc('SQLServerAgent');
      }
      else {    # named instance
         push @services, 'MSSQL$' . uc($instance);
         push @services, uc('SQLAgent$') . uc($instance);
      }

      foreach my $service (sort @services) {
         #get the current service accounts
         $ref->{$server}->{uc($instance)}->{$service}
                 = dbaGetServiceAccount($server, $service);
      }
    }
  }
  return $ref;
} #readCurrentAccounts


#############################
sub compareAccounts {
   my($currentRef, $savedRef) = @_;
   my $diffRef;

   foreach my $server (keys %$currentRef) {
      next if !exists $savedRef->{$server};
      foreach my $instance (keys %{$currentRef->{$server}}) {
         next if !exists $savedRef->{$server}->{$instance};
         foreach my $service (keys %{$currentRef->{$server}->{$instance}}) {
            next if !exists $savedRef->{$server}->{$instance}->{$service};
            if ( uc($currentRef->{$server}->{$instance}->{$service}) ne
                 uc($savedRef->{$server}->{$instance}->{$service})) {
               $diffRef->{$server}->{$instance}->{$service} =
                   $savedRef->{$server}->{$instance}->{$service} . ' => ' .
                   $currentRef->{$server}->{$instance}->{$service};
            }
         }
      }
   }
   return $diffRef;
} # compareAccounts
```

```
########################
sub printAccountDiff {
   my ($diffRef) = shift;
   ref($diffRef) or die "***Err: printAccountDiff expects a reference.";

   foreach my $server (sort keys %$diffRef) {
      print "Server $server:\n";
      foreach my $instance (sort keys %{$diffRef->{$server}}) {
         print "  Instance $instance:\n";
         foreach my $service (sort keys %{$diffRef->{$server}->{$instance}}) {
            print "    Service account change ($service): ",
                      $diffRef->{$server}->{$instance}->{$service}, "\n";
         }
      }
   }
} # printAccountDiff


########################
sub printCurrentAccounts {
   my ($currentRef) = shift;
   ref($currentRef) or die "***Err: printCurrentAccounts expects a reference.";

   foreach my $server (sort keys %$currentRef) {
      print "Server $server:\n";
      foreach my $instance (sort keys %{$currentRef->{$server}}) {
         print "  Instance $instance:\n";
         foreach my $service (sort keys %{$currentRef->{$server}->{$instance}}) {
            print "    ($service): ",
                      $currentRef->{$server}->{$instance}->{$service}, "\n";
         }
      }
   }
} # printServiceAccounts
```

You can invoke the script in Listing 10-4 from the command line as follows to compare the current SQL Server service account configurations with a previously saved snapshot of the service account configurations:

```
cmd>perl trackSQLAccounts.pl -d -c d:\dba\config.txt
```

The SQL Server instances for which the service accounts are tracked are listed in the configuration file specified by the parameter -c. When the optional parameter -d is specified, the script prints the difference between the service accounts currently used by the SQL Server instances and the accounts used when the script is last executed with the optional -s command-line parameter. The -s parameter instructs the script to save the snapshot of the service account configurations to a text file whose path is specified in the configuration file. When you don't include -d on the command line, the script simply reports all the user accounts used by the SQL Server services.

As with many other Perl scripts discussed in this book, using a configuration file to list the SQL Server instances whose service accounts you want to track is particularly useful in a large environment. Listing 10-5 shows a sample configuration file that trackSQLAccounts.pl accepts.

Listing 10-5. A Sample Configuration File

```
[Control]
ServiceAccountLog=D:\DBA\SavedAccounts.txt

[SQL1]
Instances=MSSQLServer, APOLLO, PANTHEON
Disabled=no

[SQL2]
Instances=MSSQLServer, JUPITER
Disabled=no
```

The Control section of the configuration file instructs trackSQLAccounts.pl to read the previously saved snapshot of the service accounts from the file D:\DBA\SavedAccounts.txt. The current snapshot, created by retrieving the configuration information directly from the servers, is saved to this same file if you specify the -s command-line parameter.

With the exception of the Control section, server names are listed in the section headings. As specified in Listing 10-5, the script in Listing 10-4 tracks changes to the service accounts of the default SQL Server instance, the named instance APOLLO, and the named instance PANTHEON on the server SQL1. Similarly, the script also tracks the service accounts of the named instance JUPITER and the default instance on the server SQL2.

To use the script in Listing 10-4, I typically list all my SQL Server instances in a configuration file, schedule to run the script with the -d parameter once daily to produce an account difference report, and have another utility email me the report. The report should be extremely short or contain no entry at all because the SQL Server service accounts rarely need to be changed en masse.

Let's take a closer look at the data structures used by the script. Three different data structures are used throughout the script:

- The data structure for the configuration options

- The data structure for the service accounts

- The data structure for the difference between service accounts

The following sections discuss these data structures.

Introducing the Hash $configRef for the Configuration Options

Populated with the SQLDBA::Utility function dbaReadINI() at the beginning of the script, this data structure has the complete information of the options in the configuration file. For the sample configuration file in Listing 10-5, the script generates the data structure as follows:

```
$configRef = {
    'CONTROL' => {
        'SERVICEACCOUNTLOG' => 'D:\\DBA\\\\SavedAccounts.txt'
    },
    'SQL1' => {
        'DISABLED'  => 'no',
        'INSTANCES' => 'MSSQLServer,Apollo,Pantheon'
    }
    'SQL2' => {
        'DISABLED'  => 'no',
        'INSTANCES' => 'MSSQLServer,Jupiter'
    }
};
```

The section "Reading from an Initialization File" in Chapter 3 covered the dbaReadINI() function in detail.

Introducing the Hashes $currentRef and $savedRef for the Service Accounts

The $currentRef and $savedRef hashes are the same in terms of their structures. The former records the current service accounts retrieved from the servers, and the latter contains the information read from the saved service accounts in the file identified by the ServiceAccountLog option in the configuration file. In other words, the data structure $currentRef captures the current snapshot of the service accounts, and $savedRef represents the snapshot of the service accounts saved the last time when you ran the script trackSQLAccounts.pl with the -s command-line switch. For the configuration file in Listing 10-5, $currentRef looks like the following:

```
$currentRef = {
     'SQL1' => {                                        # server
         'PANTHEON' => {                                # instance
                 'SQLAGENT$PANTHEON' => 'LocalSystem',  # SQLAgent service
                 'MSSQL$PANTHEON'    => 'SQL1\\lshea'    # SQL Server service
         },
         'APOLLO' => {
                 'SQLAGENT$APOLLO' => 'SQL1\\lshea',
                 'MSSQL$APOLLO'    => 'SQL1\\lshea'
         },
         'Mssqlserver' => {
                 'SQLSERVERAGENT' => 'SQL1\\lshea',
                 'MSSQLSERVER'    => 'LocalSystem'
         }
     }
     'SQL2' => {
         'JUPITER' => {
                 'SQLAGENT$PANTHEON' => 'LocalSystem',
                 'MSSQL$JUPITER'     => 'NJDOMAIN\\lshea'
         },
         'MSSQLSERVER' => {
                 'SQLSERVERAGENT' => 'NJDOMAIN\\lshea',
                 'MSSQLSERVER'    => 'NJDOMAIN\\lshea'
         }
     }
};
```

The data structure $currentRef is populated with the function readCurrentAccounts(). The bulk of the work in this function is to get all the services for each server into the array @services. Then, for each service, the function dbaGetServiceAccount() from the module SQLDBA::Security retrieves the user account that runs the service. Chapter 3's "Retrieving the Service Accounts" section discussed the code of this function.

The data structure $savedRef is populated with the function dbaReadSavedRef() imported from the module SQLDBA::Utility, which opens the file specified with the configuration option ServiceAccountLog and evaluates the content to a reference. The reference is then assigned to $savedRef in the main body of the script. If the -s command-line switch is specified, the file is overwritten with the current snapshot in $currentRef using the function dbaSavedRef() from the module SQLDBA::Utility, thus persisting the current snapshot as the canonical configurations for later comparison.

Introducing the Hash $diffRef for the Service Accounts Difference

The data structure $diffRef is populated by traversing $currentRef and $savedRef through each server, instance, and service and by comparing the service account of the corresponding service. Continuing with the example, if the service account of MSSQL$PANTHEON on the server SQL1 changes from SQL1\lshea to LocalSystem and everything else is the same, the script in Listing 10-4 records $diffRef as follows:

```
$diffRef = {
    SQL1 => {
        PANTHEON => {
            'MSSQL$PANTHEON' => 'SQL1\\lshea => LocalSystem'
        }
    }
};
```

These three data structures comprise the core of the script trackSQLAccounts.pl in Listing 10-4. The functions in the script populate, update, or print these data structures. As such, you're free to implement some of these functions differently as long as the data structures are maintained appropriately. The subsequent section shows a different method of retrieving the service account.

There's More Than One Way to Retrieve Service Accounts

Of particular interest is the function dbaGetServiceAccount(), which retrieves the user account name for a service on a server. In the SQLDBA::Security module, this function is implemented using the QueryServiceConfig() function imported from the Win32::Lanman module. Listing 10-6 shows a different implementation of the function dbaGetServiceAccount() using the command-line utility sc.exe available from the Windows NT/2000 Resource Kit.

Listing 10-6. Reading Service Account via sc.exe

```
1.  ########################
2.  sub readSrvAccount {
3.     my ($server, $service) = @_;
4.
5.     my $srvConfig = `sc \\\\$server qc $service`;
6.     my ($account) = $srvConfig =~ /SERVICE_START_NAME\s*:\s*(.+)$/i;
7.     $account =~ s/\s+$//;
8.     $account =~ s/\.\\/$server\\/;
9.     return $account;
10. } # readSrvAccount
```

On line 5 in Listing 10-6, the service configuration information is returned by executing sc.exe within a pair of backticks and is assigned to the variable $srvConfig. On line 6 the account name is then picked out from $srvConfig. On line 8, the script replaces the dot in an account name with the local server name. Therefore, instead of .\lshea, for instance, you get SQL1\lshea if SQL1 happens to be the local server.

Readers with a knack for T-SQL will be quick to point out that an exclusive T-SQL solution isn't difficult to devise for tracking SQL Server service accounts. That's true. With a list of SQL Server instances, you can first configure linked servers to access them from a central SQL Server instance. Then, you can loop through these linked servers to retrieve service account information for each linked server and store the retrieved information in a database on the central SQL Server instance. Once you have the current service account information and the previously saved service account information for these linked servers, it's straightforward to write a T-SQL script to compare them. To obtain the service account information on a SQL Server instance (say, APOLLO), you can execute the following query:

```
EXEC master.. xp_instance_regread N'HKEY_LOCAL_MACHINE',
                   N'SYSTEM\CurrentControlSet\Services\MSSQL$APOLLO',
                   N'ObjectName'
```

One of the advantages of the Perl script in Listing 10-4 is the flexibility of its high-level dynamic data structures. You can expand these data structures to cover new requirements with little effort. This advantage will become much clearer in the "Alerting Security Changes" section when you move beyond mere service accounts alerting on changes to a broader of range SQL Server security configurations.

Before moving on to the next topic, you'll get some insight on managing SQL Server service accounts in a large enterprise environment.

Managing Service Accounts in a Large Enterprise

When there are many SQL Server instances to administer, choosing what service accounts to use becomes a concern. At one extreme, you can run all the SQL Server services under a single domain user account. The obvious advantage of this approach is simplicity. Of course, your Information Technology (IT) security folks may object to sharing a user account because if one instance is compromised, all instances are compromised. In addition, simplicity may be deceiving. If you need to change the password of the account for one of many good reasons, the change will have a widespread impact on all the SQL Server instances and thus can actually complicate your work.

At the other extreme, you can assign a different user account for each individual SQL Server instance. If you implement this approach, you would have as many SQL Server service accounts as there are SQL Server instances, and there could be many SQL Server instances in a large environment. This will inevitably become cumbersome and unwieldy in practice. The fact that people hate to deal with too many passwords is often the cause for poor password practices.

Not surprisingly, something in the middle is the best. For service account management, the middle of the road is to divide SQL Server instances by some natural grouping and let each group of SQL Server instances share a service account but don't let a service account be shared across different groups. The exact nature of the grouping may differ from environment to environment. For one environment, it could be by application so that SQL Server instances owned by the same application share a common user account. For another environment, it could be by user community so that instances serving the same business user group or division run under the same account.

Finally, I have some anecdotes to share: In one case, with a report generated by this script, I was able to confront a cowboy DBA and ask for an explanation of an apparently unauthorized change to a SQL Server service account. In another case, the service account of an SQLServerAgent service was inadvertently changed to the LocalSystem account when a DBA was browsing the security tab of the Enterprise Manager. The report caught the change, and I was able to correct the situation before the scheduled jobs started to trigger a flood of alerts.

SQL Slammer and Service Accounts

Bad as it was, the SQL Slammer attack in January 2003 helped highlight many security issues, one of which was the need to track the service accounts of the SQL Server instances.

To prevent SQL Slammer from spreading, network security folks quickly shut down the network, thus rendering the domain controllers unreachable. In the frenzy of patching the SQL Server instances and getting them up and running, the administrators changed the service accounts of most SQL Server instances to LocalSystem. When the network connectivity was eventually restored, a script such as that in Listing 10-4 was useful in identifying all the changes to the SQL Server service accounts.

Alerting Security Changes

SCENARIO
You want to be alerted when a significant change is made to your SQL Server security configurations.

You can build on the work in the previous section and expand the script in Listing 10-4 to track changes beyond the SQL Server service accounts.

Let's first consider what security configurations you may want to track in a SQL Server environment. Depending on your security policies and your experience with security breaches, the types of changes you want to capture vary. Regardless, the following is a reasonable list with which to start:

Changes to the SQL Server service accounts: This has been discussed at length in the previous "Tracking SQL Server Service Accounts" section.

Changes to the SQL Server authentication mode (also known as *security mode*): SQL Server authentication can be changed from Windows authentication to allow both Windows and SQL Server authentication and vice versa.

Changes to the security audit level: You can configure SQL Server to audit logins at several levels including None for no auditing, Success for auditing only successful login attempts, Failure for auditing failed login attempts, and All for auditing both successful and failed login attempts.

Changes to the sysadmin membership: The first section of this chapter, "Listing Sysadmin Accounts and Logins," discussed the importance and the issues of tracking the membership of the sysadmin role.

Changes to the network shares on a SQL Server machine: In general, it isn't advisable to create ad-hoc network shares on a SQL Server machine. It's particularly not advisable to share the SQL Server directories. When there are good reasons to do so, you should be aware that SQL Server directories and files have been made accessible through such a share.

Changes to SQL Server registry permissions: Critical SQL Server configuration information is stored in the Windows registry. Permissions to SQL Server registry keys are usually set at the setup time and shouldn't be altered. If they change, you should know.

Listing 10-7 presents the script `trackSecurityConfig.pl` to track changes to these security configurations.

Listing 10-7. Tracking Changes to SQL Server Security Configurations

```perl
use strict;
use SQLDBA::Utility qw( dbaReadConfig2 dbaReadSavedRef dbaSaveRef
                        dbaSetDiff dbaSetCommon );
use SQLDBA::Security qw( dbaGetServiceAccount dbaGetLoginConfig
                         dbaGetSysadminMembers dbaGetShares
                         dbaGetSQLRegistryPerms );
use Getopt::Std;

Main: {
   my $diffRef;

   my %opts;
   getopts('hdc:', \%opts);
   printUsage() if $opts{h} or $opts{c};

   my $file = $opts{c};
   # read configurations from the config file
   # and split the comma-separated value into an array
   my $configRef = dbaReadConfig2($file);

   # remove the entries that are disabled in the config file
   foreach my $server (keys %$configRef) {
     delete $configRef->{$server}
             if $configRef->{$server}->{DISABLED} =~ /^y/i;
   }
```

```
    # read the current security configurations
    my $currentRef = readCurrentSecurityConfig($configRef)
        or die "***Err: unable to read the current security configurations.";

    # compare security config differences
    if ($opts{d}) {
       my $savedRef
            = dbaReadSavedRef($configRef->{CONTROL}->{SECURITYCONFIGLOG});

       if ($savedRef) {
          # find the difference betwene current and saved security config
          $diffRef = compareSecurityConfig($currentRef, $savedRef);
       }

       if ($diffRef) {
          # print the security config differences
          printSecurityConfigDiff($diffRef);
       }
       else {
          print "***Msg: No change to SQL Server security configurations.\n";
       }
    }
    else { # if -d not specified
       # print the current security configurations
       printCurrentSecurityConfig($currentRef);
    }

    if ($opts{s}) {
       # save the current security configurations
       dbaSaveRef($configRef->{CONTROL}->{SECURITYCONFIGLOG},
                  $currentRef, 'ref');
    }
} # Main


#####################
sub printUsage {
    print << '--Usage--';
Usage:
 perl trackSecurityConfig.pl [-h] [-s] [-d] -c <configuration file>

    -h     print this usage info
    -s     save the current service accounts as the canonical config
    -d     report changes to the SQL Server security configurations
```

```
          -c      specify a configuration file
      --Usage--
        exit;
      } # printUsage


      ################################
      sub readCurrentSecurityConfig {
         my $configRef = shift;
         ref($configRef) or
              die "***Err: readCurrentSecurityConfig() expects a reference.";

         my $ref;
         foreach my $server (sort keys %$configRef) {
            next if uc($server) eq 'CONTROL';
            foreach my $instance (sort split /\s*,\s*/,
                                        $configRef->{$server}->{INSTANCES}) {
               my @services;
               my $instanceStr;
               if (uc($instance) eq uc('MSSQLServer')) {
                  push @services, uc('MSSQLServer');
                  push @services, uc('SQLServerAgent');
                  $instanceStr = $server;
               }
               else {
                  push @services, 'MSSQL$' . uc($instance);
                  push @services, uc('SQLAgent$') . uc($instance);
                  $instanceStr = "$server\\" . $instance;
               }

               #get current service accounts
               foreach my $service (sort @services) {
                  $ref->{$server}->{uc($instance)}->{ServiceAccounts}->{$service}
                          = dbaGetServiceAccount($server, $service);
               }

               # get current authentication mode
               $ref->{$server}->{uc($instance)}->{AuthenticationMode}
                       = dbaGetLoginConfig($instanceStr, 'login mode');

               # get current audit level
               $ref->{$server}->{uc($instance)}->{AuditLevel}
                       = dbaGetLoginConfig($instanceStr, 'audit level');
```

```
          # get current sysadmin members
          $ref->{$server}->{uc($instance)}->{SysadminMembers}
                  = dbaGetSysadminMembers($instanceStr);

          # get shares
          $ref->{$server}->{uc($instance)}->{Shares}
                  = dbaGetShares($server);

          # get current registry key permissions
          $ref->{$server}->{uc($instance)}->{RegistryPermissions}
                  = dbaGetSQLRegistryPerms($server, $instance);
      }
    }
    return $ref;
} # readCurrentSecurityConfig

##############################
sub compareSecurityConfig {
    my($currentRef, $savedRef) = @_;

    my $diffRef;
    foreach my $server (keys %$currentRef) {
        next unless exists $savedRef->{$server};
        foreach my $instance (keys %{$currentRef->{$server}}) {
            next unless exists $savedRef->{$server}->{$instance};

            my $currentInstanceRef = $currentRef->{$server}->{$instance};
            my $savedInstanceRef = $savedRef->{$server}->{$instance};

            my $typeDiffRef;
            foreach my $configType (keys %$currentInstanceRef) {
                next unless exists $savedInstanceRef->{$configType};

                # these two variables are used to contain the cod ewidth
                # Note they may references or simple scalar values
                my $currentConfigType = $currentInstanceRef->{$configType};
                my $savedConfigType = $savedInstanceRef->{$configType};

                # record any service account difference
                if (uc($configType) eq uc('ServiceAccounts')) {
                    foreach my $service (keys %$currentConfigType) {
                        next unless exists $savedConfigType->{$service};
                        if ( uc($savedConfigType->{$service}) ne
                            uc($currentConfigType->{$service}) ) {
```

```perl
                    $typeDiffRef->{$configType}->{$service} =
                        $savedConfigType->{$service} . " => " .
                        $currentConfigType->{$service};
        }
    }
}

# record any difference between sysadmin memberships
if (uc($configType) eq uc('SysadminMembers')) {
    if (my @diff = dbaSetDiff($savedConfigType,
                              $currentConfigType)) {
        $typeDiffRef->{$configType}->{Removed} = [ @diff ];
    }
    if (my @diff = dbaSetDiff($currentConfigType,
                              $savedConfigType)) {
        $typeDiffRef->{$configType}->{Added} = [ @diff ];
    }
}

# record any difference between shares
if (uc($configType) eq uc('Shares')) {
    if (my @diff = dbaSetDiff($savedConfigType,
                              $currentConfigType)) {
        $typeDiffRef->{$configType}->{Removed} = [ @diff ];
    }
    if (my @diff = dbaSetDiff($currentConfigType,
                              $savedConfigType)) {
        $typeDiffRef->{$configType}->{Added} = [ @diff ];
    }
}

# record audit level or authentication mode change
if ( (uc($configType) eq uc('AuditLevel')) or
     (uc($configType) eq uc('AuthenticationMode')) ) {
    if ( uc($savedConfigType) ne
         uc($currentConfigType) ) {
        $typeDiffRef->{$configType} =
            $savedConfigType . " => " . $currentConfigType;
    }
}

# record changes to SQL registry permissions
if (uc($configType) eq uc('RegistryPermissions')) {
    # if a user account is removed
```

```
                if (my @diff = dbaSetDiff([ keys %$savedConfigType ],
                                          [ keys %$currentConfigType ])) {
                    $typeDiffRef->{$configType}->{AccountRemoved} =
                                [ @diff ];
                }
                # if a new user account is granted access
                if (my @diff = dbaSetDiff([ keys %$currentConfigType ],
                                          [ keys %$savedConfigType ])) {
                    $typeDiffRef->{$configType}->{AccountAdded} =
                                [ @diff ];
                }
                # if access rights are changed for an account
                if (my @common = dbaSetCommon([ keys %$currentConfigType ],
                                              [ keys %$savedConfigType ])) {
                  foreach my $acct (@common) {
                    # record added rights
                    if (my @added = dbaSetDiff($currentConfigType->{$acct},
                                               $savedConfigType->{$acct})) {
                        $typeDiffRef->{$configType}->{$acct}->{PermsAdded}
                                = [ @added ];
                    }
                    # record removed rights
                    if (my @removed =
                                dbaSetDiff($savedConfigType->{$acct},
                                           $currentConfigType->{$acct})) {
                        $typeDiffRef->{$configType}->{$acct}->{PermsRemoved}
                                = [ @removed ];
                    }
                  }
                }
             }
          }
          $diffRef->{$server}->{$instance} = $typeDiffRef if $typeDiffRef;
       }
    }
    return $diffRef;
} # compareSecurityConfig

###############################
sub printSecurityConfigDiff {
   my ($diffRef) = shift;
   ref($diffRef) or die "***Err: printSecurityConfigDiff expects a reference.";

   foreach my $server (sort keys %$diffRef) {
```

```perl
            print "Server $server:\n";
            foreach my $instance (sort keys %{$diffRef->{$server}}) {
                print "\n\tInstance $instance:\n";
                my $instanceRef = $diffRef->{$server}->{$instance};
                foreach my $configType (sort keys %$instanceRef) {
                    print "\t\t$configType: \n";
                        my $configRef = $instanceRef->{$configType};

                        # print service account diff
                        if (uc($configType) eq uc('ServiceAccounts')) {
                            foreach my $service (sort keys %$configRef) {
                                print "\t\t\t$service : $configRef->{$service} \n";
                            }
                        }

                        # print sysadmin membership diff
                        if (uc($configType) eq uc('SysadminMembers')) {
                            foreach my $delta (sort keys %$configRef) {
                                foreach my $login (@{$configRef->{$delta}}) {
                                    print "\t\t\t$delta: $login \n";
                                }
                            }
                        }

                        # print share diff
                        if (uc($configType) eq uc('Shares')) {
                            foreach my $delta (sort keys %$configRef) {
                                foreach my $share (@{$configRef->{$delta}}) {
                                    print "\t\t\t$delta: $share \n";
                                }
                            }
                        }

                        if ((uc($configType) eq uc('AuditLevel')) or
                            (uc($configType) eq uc('AuthenticationMode')) )   {
                            print "\t\t\t$instanceRef->{$configType} \n";
                        }

                        if (uc($configType) eq uc('RegistryPermissions')) {
                            foreach my $delta (sort keys %$configRef) {
                                if (uc($delta) eq uc('AccountAdded') or
                                    uc($delta) eq uc('AccountRemoved')) {
                                    print "\t\t\t$delta :  [ ";
                                    foreach my $acct (sort @{$configRef->{$delta}}) {
```

```perl
                                print " $acct, ";
                            }
                            print " ]\n";
                        }
                        else {
                            print "\t\t\t$delta: \n";
                            foreach my $permDelta (sort
                                            keys %{$configRef->{$delta}}) {
                                print "\t\t\t\t$permDelta : ";
                                foreach my $right (sort
                                        @{$configRef->{$delta}->{$permDelta}}) {
                                    print " $right ";
                                }
                                print "\n";
                            }
                        }
                    }
                }
            }
        }
    }
} # printSecurityConfigDiff


#####################################
sub printCurrentSecurityConfig {
    my ($currentRef) = shift;
    ref($currentRef) or
        die "***Err: printCurrentSecurityConfig() expects a reference.";

    foreach my $server (sort keys %$currentRef) {
        print "Server $server:\n";
        foreach my $instance (sort keys %{$currentRef->{$server}}) {
            print "\n\tInstance $instance:\n";
            my $instanceRef = $currentRef->{$server}->{$instance};
            foreach my $configType (sort keys %$instanceRef) {
                print "\t\t$configType: \n";
                    my $configRef = $instanceRef->{$configType};

                    # print service accounts
                    if (uc($configType) eq uc('ServiceAccounts')) {
                        foreach my $service (sort keys %$configRef) {
                            print "\t\t\t$service => $configRef->{$service} \n";
                        }
                    }
```

```
                    # print sysadmin members
                    if (uc($configType) eq uc('SysadminMembers')) {
                        foreach my $login (sort @$configRef) {
                          print "\t\t\t$login \n";
                        }
                    }

                    # print shares
                    if (uc($configType) eq uc('Shares')) {
                        foreach my $share (sort @$configRef) {
                          print "\t\t\t$share \n";
                        }
                    }

                    # print audit level or authentication mode
                    if ((uc($configType) eq uc('AuditLevel')) or
                        (uc($configType) eq uc('AuthenticationMode')) ) {
                        print "\t\t\t$instanceRef->{$configType} \n";
                    }

                    # print registry permissions
                    if (uc($configType) eq uc('RegistryPermissions')) {
                        foreach my $login (sort keys %$configRef) {
                            print "\t\t\t$login :  [ ";
                            foreach my $perm (@{$configRef->{$login}}) {
                                print " $perm,";
                            }
                            print " ]\n";
                        }
                    }
                }
            }
        }
} # printCurrentSecurityConfig
```

The overall structure of this script is similar to that of the script in Listing 10-4. In the main body of the script, it first reads the configuration options from a configuration file specified on the command line with the -c parameter. Then, for each SQL Server instance listed in the configuration file, the script reads in the current security configurations of the instance. After that, it reads the saved security configurations from a file, performs the comparison, and reports the difference, if any.

The configuration file is almost exactly the same as the one for the service account tracking script in Listing 10-5. A sample configuration file is as follows:

```
[Control]
SecurityConfigLog=D:\DBA\SavedSecurityConfig.txt

[SQL1]
Instances=MSSQLServer, Apollo, Pantheon
Disabled=no

[SQL2]
Instances=MSSQLServer, Jupiter
Disabled=no
```

The option SecurityConfigLog under the Control section identifies the file that has the security configurations saved when the script was last run with the -c parameter.

Because it deals with more than service accounts, the script in Listing 10-7 is necessarily longer and slightly more complicated than the script in Listing 10-4, which tracks only the SQL Server service accounts.

To understand how the script in Listing 10-7 works, you need to first become familiar with its key data structure—the one representing the security configurations—because the entire script is built around this data structure. Now you'll see an example of the data structure. For the SQL Server default instance on the server SQL1, its security configurations, as referenced by $ref in the function readCurrentSecurityConfig(), may look like that shown in Listing 10-8.

Listing 10-8. A Sample Data Structure for Security Configurations

```
$ref->{NYSQL01}->{MSSQLServer} = {
        ServiceAccounts => { MSSQLServer => 'SQL1\Lshea',
                             SQLServerAgent => 'LocalSystem'
                           },
        AuthenticationMode => 'Windows and SQL Server',
        AuditLevel => 'Failure',
        SysadminMembers => ['BUILTIN\Administrators',
                            'SQL1\Lshea', 'NYDOMAIN\DBAs'],
        Shares => ['C$', 'D$', 'E$', 'ADMIN$', 'IPC$', 'Public'],
        RegistryPermissions => {
                    'HKEY_LOCAL_MACHINE\Microsoft\MSSQLServer' => {
                        Users => [ 'KEY_READ' ],
                        Administrators => [ 'KEY_READ', 'KEY_WRITE' ],
```

```
                              SYSTEM => [ 'KEY_READ', 'KEY_WRITE' ],
                              lshea  => [ 'KEY_READ' ],
                              'Power Users' => [ 'KEY_READ', 'KEY_WRITE' ]
                      }
              }
     };
```

Each top-level key of this data structure—such as `ServiceAccounts` or `AuditLevel`—corresponds to an area of the SQL Server security configurations you want to track. The rationale and meaning of this data structure should become clearer after a brief explanation on how it's populated:

Service accounts: They are retrieved with the function `dbaGetServiceAccount()` imported from the SQLDBA::Security module. The section "Retrieving the Service Accounts" in Chapter 3 introduced this function.

Authentication mode: Running the T-SQL query `EXEC master..xp_loginconfig 'login mode'` returns the SQL Server authentication mode. The function `dbaGetLoginConfig()`, also imported from the module SQLDBA::Security, runs `xp_loginconfig` to retrieve the login mode.

Audit level: The function `dbaGetLoginConfig()` also returns the audit level of the SQL Server instance.

Sysadmin members: The first section of this chapter, "Listing Sysadmin Accounts and Logins," presented a script in Listing 10-1 to obtain all the individual user accounts that have sysadmin privileges. To keep it manageable, the script `trackSecurityConfig.pl` in Listing 10-7 tracks only changes to the direct membership of the sysadmin role.

Directory shares: Although you can use the Windows 2000/NT built-in command `net share` to enumerate shares locally and use `net view` to enumerate the shares remotely, they don't give you the complete list of shares on a remote machine. The function `dbaGetShares()` calls `NetShareEnum()` from Win32::Lanman to enumerate all the shares on a remote machine.

Registry permissions: The script in Listing 10-7 tracks only the permissions on the root registry key for a SQL Server instance. For the default SQL Server instance, the root registry key is `HKEY_LOCAL_MACHINE\Microsoft\MSSQLServer`, and for a named instance (for example, APOLLO), the root registry key is `HKEY_LOCAL_MACHINE\Microsoft\Microsoft SQL Server\APOLLO`. The function `dbaGetSQLRegistryPerms()` uses the module Win32::Perms. This is a versatile module that can, among other things, report the Access Control List (ACL) of many common Windows objects. You can download Win32::Perms from `http://www.roth.com`.

TIP *A handy tool to manipulate shares remotely is* RMTShare.exe, *available from the Windows 2000/NT Resource Kit. This command-line tool allows you to list remote shares, create remote shares, delete remote shares, and grant permissions to remote shares, all from the comfort of your own workstation.*

For aesthetically minded readers, it may appear odd that the data structure shown in Listing 10-8 places the list of the shared directories under a SQL Server instance. Unlike the other security configurations, the list of the shares is unique to a server instead of a SQL Server instance. Therefore, it's redundant to list the shares under each SQL Server instance. This is done on purpose to keep the script in Listing 10-7 simple and compact.

PPM and Win32::Perms

As briefly mentioned in the section "Using a Perl Module" in Chapter 2, ActivePerl comes with a wonderful tool that significantly simplifies the installation of Perl modules. The tool is the Programmer's Package Manager (PPM), formerly known as the *Perl Package Manager*.

For instance, to install Win32::Perms on my workstation that's running Perl 5.6, all I need to do is the following:

1. At the Windows command prompt, execute ppm3 to launch PPM.

2. At the PPM prompt, execute the PPM3 command repository add Roth http://www.roth.net/perl/packages. This adds the Uniform Resource Locator (URL) to the list of Perl module repositories.

3. At the PPM prompt, execute repository to find the number for the Roth repository.

4. At the PPM prompt, execute repository set <number> to set the Roth repository active, where <number> is the number found in the previous step for the Roth repository.

5. At the PPM prompt, execute install Win32-Perms -force -follow. This installs the Win32::Perms module on my workstation.

For more information about the PPM commands, see the PPM documentation that comes with the Hypertext Markup Language (HTML)–formatted ActivePerl User Guide.

As mentioned at the beginning of this chapter, different SQL Server environments may adopt different approaches for managing SQL Server security. Similarly, there are naturally different opinions on what constitutes a significant change to SQL Server security configurations. As is the case with most of the solutions discussed in this book, I'll leave it for you to decide what's important in your own environment and focus instead on providing the script as a starting point that you can customize to accommodate your particular requirements.

Summarizing SQL Server Login Audits

SCENARIO
You're auditing user access to SQL Server and would like to produce a short daily summary from your recorded login audits.

SQL Server provides several levels of login audit; it can track successful login attempts, failed login attempts, or both, regardless of whether these login attempts are authenticated by Windows or by SQL Server. Login audits in SQL Server are recorded in both the SQL Server errorlog and the Windows application event log. Lest you wonder, the Windows login audits are recorded in the Security event log.

You can use the SQL Server Enterprise Manager to enable login audits for SQL Server. Right-click the SQL Server instance, and select the Properties menu item. Under the Security tab, you can then pick the audit level at which the user accesses to SQL Server are recorded.

It isn't clear why there isn't a supported T-SQL procedure to change the audit level, but you can certainly achieve the same result by directly altering a registry value with an unsupported but well-known extended stored procedure: xp_regwrite or xp_instance_regwrite. For example, to enable an audit of failed user accesses to a SQL Server 2000 instance, you can connect to that instance and execute the following T-SQL extended stored procedure in Query Analyzer:

```
EXEC master..xp_instance_regwrite N'HKEY_LOCAL_MACHINE',
            N'SOFTWARE\Microsoft\MSSQLServer\MSSQLServer',N'AuditLevel',
            REG_DWORD,2
```

 TIP   *SQL Server MVP Mark Allison brought to my attention that in addition to using the unsupported* xp_regwrite, *you could change the SQL Server login audit level through the supported* AuditLevel *property of the* IntegratedSecurity *object in SQL-DMO.*

One way to get value out of the recorded SQL Server login audits is to produce summary reports from them. Manually reviewing these audits is out of the question, especially in an enterprise environment where many SQL Server instances may have been enabled for login audit.

Recorded login audits aren't limited to help spot suspicious login attempts for potential security breaches. They are also useful in identifying SQL Server login patterns. For example, it may be useful to know during what time of the day most of the new connections are made.

The script loginAuditSummary.pl in Listing 10-9 produces a simple summary by tallying the number of successful logins and the number of failed logins for a given time period. For the successful logins, the number is further divided into the number of Windows authenticated logins and the number of SQL Server authenticated logins. You can configure the script to further break down these numbers by each user account or SQL Server login.

Listing 10-9. Summary of SQL Server Login Audits

```perl
use strict;
use SQLDBA::Utility qw( dbaReadINI dbaTime2str dbaStr2time );

Main: {
   my $configFile = shift;
   unless (-e $configFile) {   # the config file must exist
      print "***Err: Config file $configFile doesn't exist.";
      printUsage();
   }

   # Read config file into $configRef and validate it
   my $configRef = dbaReadINI($configFile);

   # Now scan errorlog and summarize login audit info
   foreach my $instance (sort keys %$configRef) {
     # scan errorlog and summarize login audit info
     my $auditRef = auditSummary($instance, $configRef);

     # Now print out the errorlog summary
     printAuditSummary($auditRef, $instance, $configRef);
   }
} # Main


####################
sub auditSummary {
   my($instance, $configRef) = @_;
```

```perl
    die "***Err: auditSummary() expects an instance and a reference."
          unless ($instance && $configRef);


    my $ref;
    my $instConfigRef = $configRef->{$instance};

    # Check whether the file exists
    unless (-e $instConfigRef->{SQLERRORLOG}) {
       print "***Err: Errorlog $instConfigRef->{SQLERRORLOG} doesn't exist.";
       return;
    }

    # now open the errorlog file for scan
    unless (open(LOG, $instConfigRef->{SQLERRORLOG})) {
       print "***Err: Could not open $instConfigRef->{SQLERRORLOG} for read. ";
       return;
    }

    # skip old errorlog entries
    while (<LOG>) {
       if (/^\s*([\d\/\-]+\s+[\d\.\:]+)\s+/) {
          next if ( (time() - dbaStr2time($1)) >
                          $instConfigRef->{SCANERRORLOGLASTDAYS} * 24*3600 );
          $ref->{startCheckDatetime} = $1;
          last;
       }
    }

    # now start scan and summarize login audit entries
    while (<LOG>) {
      if (m{^\s*([\d\/\-]+\s+[\d\.\:]+)\s+logon\s+
               Login\s+(succeeded|failed)\s+for\s+user\s+
               \'([^']+?)\'\'\.(.*)}ix) {
         my ($time, $status, $user, $trusted) = ($1, $2, $3, $4);
         my $conn = ($trusted =~ /trusted/i) ? 'trusted' : 'non-trusted';

         if ($instConfigRef->{INCLUDEUSER} =~ /^y/i) {
            # count audit entries for each user
            if ($status =~ /^succeeded/i) {
              $ref->{auditAccounts}->{$user}->{$status}->{$conn}->{time} = $time;
              $ref->{auditAccounts}->{$user}->{$status}->{$conn}->{count}++;
            }
            else {
              $ref->{auditAccounts}->{$user}->{$status}->{time} = $time;
```

```
                        $ref->{auditAccounts}->{$user}->{$status}->{count}++;
                }
        }
        else {
            # Otherwise, do not count them for each user
            if ($status =~ /^succeeded/i) {
                $ref->{auditAccounts}->{$status}->{$conn}->{time} = $time;
                $ref->{auditAccounts}->{$status}->{$conn}->{count}++;
            }
            else {
                $ref->{auditAccounts}->{$status}->{time} = $time;
                $ref->{auditAccounts}->{$status}->{count}++;
            }
        }
        next;
      }
    }
    close(LOG);
    return $ref;
} # auditSummary


########################
sub printAuditSummary {
    my($ref, $instance, $configRef) = @_;

    print "\nInstance $instance since $ref->{startCheckDatetime}\n";
    my $auditRef = $ref->{auditAccounts};

    if ($configRef->{$instance}->{INCLUDEUSER} =~ /y/i) {
        foreach my $acct (sort keys %$auditRef) {
            print "    $acct\n";
            foreach my $status (sort keys %{$auditRef->{$acct}}) {
                my $statusRef = $auditRef->{$acct}->{$status};
                if ($status =~ /succeeded/i) {
                    # succeeded logins may be trusted or non-trusted
                    foreach my $conn (sort keys %{$statusRef}) {
                        print "\t$conn connection $status \n";
                        print "\t\tCount: $statusRef->{$conn}->{count}\n";
                        print "\t\tLast attempt time: $statusRef->{$conn}->{time}\n";
                    }
                }
                else {
                    # The security mode of a failed login is not identified
                    print "\tconnection $status \n";
```

```
                    print "\t\tCount: $statusRef->{count}\n";
                    print "\t\tLast attempt time: $statusRef->{time}\n";
                }
            }
        }
    }
    else {
        foreach my $status (sort keys %$auditRef) {
            if ($status =~ /succeeded/i) {
                # succeeded logins may be trusted or non-trusted
                foreach my $conn (sort keys %{$auditRef->{$status}}) {
                    print "\t$conn connection $status \n";
                    print "\t\tCount: $auditRef->{$status}->{$conn}->{count}\n";
                    print "\t\tLast attempt time: ",
                          "    $auditRef->{$status}->{$conn}->{time}\n";
                }
            }
            else {
                # The security mode of a failed login is not identified
                print "\tconnection $status \n";
                print "\t\tCount: $auditRef->{$status}->{count}\n";
                print "\t\tLast attempt time: $auditRef->{$status}->{time}\n";
            }
        }
    }
} # printAuditSummary


#####################
sub printUsage {
    print << '--Usage--';
Usage:
 perl loginAuditSummary.pl <configuration file>

--Usage--
  exit;
} # printUsage
```

This script accepts a configuration file that specifies a list of SQL Server instances whose login audits you want to summarize. For each SQL Server instance, the configuration file identifies the complete path to the SQL Server errorlog, the number of days going back from today in which login audits should be included in the summary, and whether the summary should include counts for each user account or SQL Server login. Listing 10-10

is a sample configuration file for two SQL Server instances, SQL1 and
SQL2\APOLLO.

Listing 10-10. A Sample Configuration File

```
[SQL1]
SQLErrorlog=\\SQL1\d$:\MSSQL\LOG\Errorlog
ScanErrorlogLastDays = 10
IncludeUser=no

[SQL2\APOLLO]
SQLErrorlog=\\SQL2\E$:\MSSQL\MSSQL$APOLLO\log\Errorlog
ScanErrorlogLastDays = 10
IncludeUser=yes
```

With this configuration file, the script in Listing 10-9 scans the SQL
Server login audit entries recorded in the last 10 days (specified with
ScanErrorlogLastDays = 10) in the errorlogs of the two SQL Server instances,
SQL1 and SQL2\APOLLO, both of which are listed in the section headings of the
configuration file. In addition, for the SQL1 default instance, because the option
IncludeUser is set to no, the configuration file instructs the script not to tally the
login attempts for either the Windows user account or SQL Server login.

Run the script in Listing 10-11 on the command line as follows with the
configuration options in Listing 10-10:

```
cmd>perl loginAuditSummary.pl config.txt
```

You'll receive a summary report that looks like Listing 10-11.

Listing 10-11. A Sample Login Audit Summary Report

```
Instance SQL1 since 2002-07-04 22:44:46.90
    connection failed
        Count: 2
        Last attempt time: 2002-07-04 22:51:00.01
    trusted connection succeeded
        Count: 12
        Last attempt time: 2002-07-04 23:02:40.34

Instance SQL2\APOLLO since 2002-07-04 21:41:47.14
    SQL2\mshea
        connection failed
            Count: 1
            Last attempt time: 2002-07-04 22:46:53.62
```

```
NJRES\vshea
    trusted connection succeeded
            Count: 10
            Last attempt time: 2002-07-04 22:26:55.61
sa
    connection failed
            Count: 102
            Last attempt time: 2002-07-04 22:47:17.20
```

The heart of the script in Listing 10-9 is the function auditSummary(), which scans the errorlog of a given SQL Server instance for login audit entries and records the login counts in a nested hash structure. An example of the hash structure for the instance SQL1 may look like Listing 10-12.

Listing 10-12. Data Structure for the Instance SQL1

```
$ref = {
    startCheckDatetime => '2002-07-04 22:44:46.90',
    auditAccounts => {
            failed => {
                        count => 2,
                        time => '2002-07-04 22:51:00.01'
            },
            succeeded => {
                        trusted => {
                                count => 12,
                                time => '2002-07-04 23:02:40.34'
                        }
            }
    }
};
```

Similarly, Listing 10-13 shows the data structure for SQL2\APOLLO. Note that for this instance the option IncludeUser is set to yes; therefore, the presence of the Windows user accounts or SQL Server logins add one more layer to the hash structure.

Listing 10-13. Data Structure for the Instance SQL1\APOLLO

```
$ref = {
    startCheckDatetime => '2002-07-04 21:41:47.14',
    auditAccounts => {
            'NJRES\\vshea' => {
                        succeeded => {
```

```
                                    trusted => {
                                            count => 10,
                                            time => '2002-07-04 22:26:55.61'
                                    }
                            }
                    },
                    'SQL2\\mshea' => {
                            failed => {
                                    count => 1,
                                    time => '2002-07-04 22:46:53.62'
                            }
                    },
                    sa => {
                            failed => {
                                    count => 102,
                                    time => '2002-07-04 22:47:17.20'
                            },
                            succeeded => {
                                    trusted => {
                                            count => 1,
                                            time => '2002-07-04 22:47:11.44'
                                    }
                            }
                    }
            }
    }
};
```

This section closes with several remarks about summarizing the SQL Server login audits. First, in a real-world scenario, you may want to integrate this script into the script errorlogSummary.pl in Listing 9-14. The latter scans SQL Server errorlogs to create a succinct summary. It's convenient to deal with only one report.

Second, reviewing the NT security log is generally the responsibility of the network administration, not that of a DBA. But it often makes sense to include the NT login audits recorded in the security event log in the DBA login audit summary, especially on a machine dedicated to SQL Server.

Finally, some DBAs may still find reading login audit summaries such as the one in Listing 10-11 a boring chore and prefer strictly exception-based reporting. For instance, you may establish a rule that 50 or more failed logins per day is a significant security exception and should be reported. If the script in Listing 10-9 supported this rule, the 102 failed login attempts shown in Listing 10-11 would have been reported as a security exception. With the data structure in Listing 10-12 or Listing 10-13, checking the number of failed login attempts requires little additional effort, and the change to the script in Listing 10-9 would be minor.

Identifying Wide-Open Shares

> **SCENARIO**
> *You suspect that the permissions on some file shares of your SQL Server machines may not be set properly. You want to get a report of the shares that are widely accessible.*

You can query each server to get all its shares and then check the permissions on each share.

To enumerate the shares on a remote server, you can use the module Win32::Lanman that comes with ActivePerl. The SQLDBA::Security function dbaGetShares() discussed in Listing 2-7 is an example of using Win32::Lanman. To discover the permissions on a share, you can use the module Win32::Perms, available from http://www.roth.net.

This section takes a shortcut and relies on the Windows 2000/NT Resource Kit utility srvcheck.exe to enumerate the shares, local or remote, and retrieve the permissions on the shares. The following is an example of using srvcheck.exe to find the shares and their access permissions on the server SQL1:

```
cmd>srvcheck \\SQL1
\\SQL1\Backup
                NYDomain\SQLDBAS        Read
                NYDomain\lshea          Read
                Everyone                Read

\\SQL1\Remote
                BUILTIN\Administrators   Full Control

\\SQL1\sqlbackup
                Everyone                 Full Control
```

For some groups such as the local administrators, having full control over a share is expected. What should be of concern are the shares that have been granted Change or Full Control to Everyone. On a sensitive server, you may want to question whether Everyone should indeed be granted Read access.

The script findOpenShares.pl in Listing 10-14 loops through a list of servers, applying srvcheck.exe to each server, grabbing the results, and parsing for shares that allow everyone to make changes, or worse, that have been granted Full Control to Everyone.

Listing 10-14. Identifying Wide-Open Directory Shares

```perl
1.   use strict;
2.   use SQLDBA::Utility qw( dbaReadINI );
3.
4.   my @servers = getServers();   # retrieve server names
5.   my $shareRef;
6.   foreach my $server (sort @servers) {   # loop through the servers
7.       # use the backtick operator to retrieve shares
8.       my @srvcheck = `srvcheck.exe \\\\$server 2>&1`;
9.       my $share;
10.       foreach (@srvcheck) {   # loop through the shares
11.           if ($_ =~ /^\s*(\\\\.+)/) {   # match for the share \\server\share
12.               $share = $1;
13.               $share =~ s/\s*$//;   # remove trailing blanks, if any
14.           }
15.           # look for Everyone with Full control or Change
16.           if ($_ =~ /^\s*(Everyone).+(Full\s+control|Change)/i) {
17.               push @{$shareRef->{$server}->{$share}}, "$1 : $2";
18.           }
19.       }
20. }
21.
22. # print the open shares
23. foreach my $server (sort keys %$shareRef) {
24.     print "Server: $server\n";
25.     foreach my $share (sort keys %{$shareRef->{$server}}) {
26.         print "\tShare: $share\n";
27.         foreach my $perm (sort @{$shareRef->{$server}->{$share}}) {
28.             print "\t\t$perm\n";
29.         }
30.     }
31. }
32.
33. ################
34. sub getServers {
35.
36.     my $configFile = $ARGV[0] or die "***Err: $0 expects a file.";
37.     my $configRef = dbaReadINI($configFile);  # read in the INI file
38.     my @servers;
39.
40.     foreach my $instance (keys %$configRef) {
41.         next if $instance =~ /^CONTROL$/i;
```

```
42.        $instance =~ s/\\.+//;
43.        push @servers, $instance if !grep(/^$instance$/, @servers);
44.    }
45.    return @servers;
46. } # getServers
```

This script loops through a list of servers to check permissions on their shares. How the server names are obtained isn't central to the script. In Listing 10-14, the code for getting the server names is wrapped up inside the function getServers() defined from line 34 to 46, which expects an INI file that has the server names in its section headings.

On line 8 in Listing 10-14, the script uses Perl's backtick operator to run the Windows 2000/NT Resource Kit utility srvcheck.exe with the server that's currently being worked on in the foreach loop, and then it assigns the results to the array @srvcheck. Because this forces the backtick operator to be evaluated in list context, the results are split by newline, and each line becomes an element of the array @srvcheck.

From line 8 to 17, the script goes through each element in @srvcheck and looks for share names, user accounts, and access permissions. In particular, for each share, the script searches for user Everyone and permissions Change or Full Control. The script records the share name, the user account, and the access permissions that match the search pattern in a data structure referenced by $shareRef.

Listing 10-15 shows an example of running the script findOpenShares.pl with a configuration file in which the server names are in the section headings. The other options in the configuration file aren't relevant.

Listing 10-15. Identifying Wide-Open Shares

```
cmd>perl findOpenShares.pl config.txt
Server: SQL1
      Share: \\SQL1\sqlbackup
            Everyone : Full Control
Server: SQL2
      Share: \\SQL2\temp$
            Everyone : Change
      Share: \\SQL2\datatemp$
            Everyone : Full Control
Server: SQL2
      Share: \\SQL2\FtpTemp
            Everyone : Full Control
```

In this example, the script findOpenShares.pl found three servers—among all the servers listed in the file config.txt—that have shares giving everyone full control or allowing everyone to make changes. You should investigate whether these shares should be there and whether the permissions are warranted.

Summary

SQL Server security requires a lot of attention to detail from the DBA. In the scenarios discussed in this chapter, the Perl scripts help reduce the amount of routines the DBA has to perform to become acquainted with and stay abreast of the security configurations or changes to the security configurations in a SQL Server environment, especially one with many SQL Server installations.

Perl scripting can be useful in many more SQL Server security scenarios. For instance, checking the SQL Server security lockdown would be a good job for a Perl script. This chapter is just a start, and you have much more territory to explore.

To a certain degree, you can view some of the scripts in this chapter as the scripts that help monitor SQL Server security.

In the next chapter, you'll be immersed in the issues of monitoring SQL Server.

CHAPTER 11

Monitoring SQL Servers

ONE OF THE CARDINAL RULES every SQL Server Database Administrator (DBA) will inevitably learn is "Never let your users tell you there's a SQL Server problem." If you want to run a smooth SQL Server operation and always want to be able to tell your users that you have the situation under control when they call, you need to monitor your SQL Servers closely and effectively.

This chapter discusses the Perl solutions to some common SQL Server monitoring problems and presents a suite of Perl scripts that together form a comprehensive toolset for detecting SQL Server problems and alerting you of them.

Let's pause to consider the nature of SQL Server monitoring. Broadly speaking, you need two types of monitoring in place. One is proactive monitoring, which is to identify system states or behavior patterns that could result in the disrupted database service, unhappy users, or even lost business if you don't take any corrective action.

Proactive monitoring may include, for instance, monitoring disk space usage so that you don't run out of space unexpectedly when the database is being used during the business hours and so that you can effectively conduct disk capacity planning. Proactive monitoring may also include checking the SQL Server configurations for best-practice compliance. In general, any aspect of SQL Server that has a potential to degrade the quality of the database service you provide to your user community should be monitored proactively.

The other type of monitoring is exception monitoring, which means to alert the DBA of any critical event or error condition—in other words, an *exception*—that has already taken place in the SQL Server environment. The following are the most common SQL Server exceptions:

- A significant message is recorded in the SQL Server errorlog.

- The server becomes unreachable.

- The SQL Server instance becomes unavailable.

- A database becomes unusable.

- The SQL Server Agent becomes unresponsive.

- The SQL Server cluster experiences a significant state change.

Other events or error conditions that you could consider exceptions include an excessively large errorlog, a failed SQL Server Agent job, a failed replication agent, and unusable SQL Mail.

The focus of this chapter is on monitoring SQL Server exceptions, particularly the ones identified in the previous list.

Proactive monitoring, although extremely important, is too broad a topic for a single chapter because you should proactively monitor every aspect of SQL Server. However, as you read this book, you'll notice that proactive monitoring is in fact promoted throughout the entire book.

It should be noted that the exceptions identified in the previous list are the exceptions to the normal SQL Server database service you provide to the users, which ultimately is to allow them to submit queries and receive results within an acceptable response time. An exception may be caused by a variety of root problems such as hardware failure, excessive resource consumption, fatal software bugs, and so on. When it comes to SQL Server monitoring, you're not so much concerned with immediately identifying the root cause of an exception as getting notified promptly and accurately. Only after you've been notified of an exception can you then start to troubleshoot its root cause.

Using Perl Scripts vs. Third-Party Tools

Numerous third-party monitoring tools are on the market ranging from ones that work exclusively with the Windows event logs to comprehensive enterprise-scale packages that support plug-in modules for monitoring various systems or applications including SQL Server. Until you've tested them carefully or have tried them in production environments, the sales brochures may lead you to believe that any of them could satisfy your entire SQL Server monitoring needs.

Don't believe that! Your local requirements will sooner or later outgrow the limited configuration options in any third-party tool, making it necessary to request additional customization either from the vendor or the in-house specialists of that tool. Such requests are often painful and time consuming to get fulfilled. It's also common that a tool may be right for your requirements, but it turns out to be much too expensive for your organization.

Fortunately, writing robust Perl scripts to monitor SQL Server and notify the DBA of exceptions isn't a monumental task and is in fact quite doable even for a busy DBA. When designed properly, the scripts can be highly configurable and can be conveniently modified to accommodate almost any monitoring requirements you may fancy. You can write a suite of monitoring scripts at a fraction of the cost for purchasing an equivalent third-party solution.

I should note that this is all dependent on your comfort level with Perl and the attitude of your management toward a tool such as Perl or toward scripting in general. However, even in an environment hostile toward Perl and friendly toward purchasing off-the-shelf tools, Perl scripts for monitoring servers can be effectively used to complement the officially sponsored monitoring solution, filling the inevitable cracks that will develop between these tools and your requirements.

This chapter focuses on exception detection—finding what exceptions have occurred and making decisions on notification. It won't dwell on the actual delivery of notifications. For exception monitoring, the most common way to deliver an urgent notification is to send a message to a pager or a similar device. Different environments may have different automated paging infrastructures. It can be the low-level socket interface to a paging server or a higher-level email-to-paging gateway. You may also find command-line utilities for sending messages to a pager. For this chapter, all notifications will be delivered via Simple Mail Transfer Protocol (SMTP) emails to their intended pagers. Sending email messages to a pager has worked well in practice.

 NOTE *Beware of the inherent delay in an email system. If you find that too many of your alerts take too long to reach their destinations, you should consider an alternative mechanism to deliver your alerts.*

This chapter builds three major monitoring tools in multiple steps. These three tools are for monitoring SQL Server errorlogs, SQL Server availability, and SQL Server cluster status.

First, the chapter starts by building a bare-bones script for monitoring errors recorded in a SQL Server errorlog. Then, it adds more features to the script to improve its robustness and usability and to make it a comprehensive tool for monitoring errorlogs in an enterprise.

Then, the chapter presents a basic script to check whether a server is available and whether the script can connect to the SQL Server instance. The chapter adds more availability checks including querying the databases and checking the SQL Server support services, such as SQL Server Agents, as well as improving the usability of the script.

Finally, the third tool monitors whether a SQL Server cluster has experienced a significant state change. Again, this chapter develops a basic version first and then a more robust and comprehensive version.

These three scripts lay the foundation for a comprehensive SQL Server monitoring infrastructure. This chapter uses a simple script for monitoring critically low free drive space to illustrate how other monitoring tasks can take advantage of this infrastructure.

Monitoring SQL Server Errorlogs: The Basic Version

SCENARIO
You want to be alerted when your SQL Server errorlog records a critical error.

For now, let's assume a critical SQL Server error in the errorlog is an error with severity level 17 or higher. In a SQL Server 7.0 or 2000 errorlog, the message text of a SQL Server error normally adheres to a common format similar to this one:

```
2002-07-12 23:39:59.58 spid51 Error: 15430, Severity: 19, State: 1 ...
```

You can therefore write a script to scan the errorlog at regular intervals for any new entries matching this format. If there's a match and the severity level is 17 or higher, you've found a critical error. Then, you need to decide whether to send a notification.

You obviously don't want to send a notification for every error of severity level 17 or higher in the errorlog. This will flood the pager when errors are generated repeatedly at a high frequency on the SQL Server instance, and it's not at all uncommon to see the errorlog filled with the entries of the same error (in other words, entries with the same error number and severity level). For instance, when the database space is used up and can't be automatically expanded, in the errorlog of a busy server you may see a barrage of SQL Server error 1105 or 9002, complaining about data files or log files being full.

On the other hand, you don't want to insist on sending the next alert only when it's a different error. If the same error is still being logged to the errorlog half an hour or one hour after the first notification is sent, either the DBA hasn't received or responded to the first alert or the problem is still being worked on and hasn't yet been solved. Because there's no way to automatically tell which is the case from a script, another notification of the same error is in order.

You can avoid flooding the DBA with repetitive alerts on the same error with a combination of the following mechanisms:

- Only recording the last entry for the same error during a scan

- Controlling the frequency of scanning the errorlog

- Controlling the frequency of alerting on the same error after it has been detected

The issue of how you implement these mechanisms will become clear momentarily when you see the script alertErrorlog.pl (in Listing 11-1). First, let's use an example to see how you can run this bare-bones script to monitor a SQL Server errorlog for critical errors.

Monitoring an Errorlog

To monitor the errorlog of SQL Server instance SQL1\APOLLO, you can schedule to run the script alertErrorlog.pl as follows (with the command and all the parameters on a single line) at a regular interval:

```
cmd>perl alertErrorlog.pl   -e \\SQL1\e$\mssql\mssql$apollo\log\errorlog
                            -a sql@linchi.com
                            -i 20
                            -s d:\dba\log\status.log
                            -S SQL1
                            -r 4321557@myTel.com
                            -m mail.linchi.com
                            -q 22-7
```

The script alertErrorlog.pl accepts the command-line arguments described in Table 11-1.

Table 11-1. The Command-Line Arguments Accepted by `alertErrorlog.pl`

COMMAND-LINE ARGUMENT	DESCRIPTION
-a <SMTP account>	Specifies the account of the SMTP email sender.
-e <Errorlog>	Specifies the SQL Server errorlog in Uniform Naming Convention (UNC).
-i <Min alert interval>	Specifies the minimum amount of time in minutes between two consecutive alerts for the same error.
-s <Status log file>	Specifies the file to which the data structure representing the errorlog monitoring status will be saved. The saved information gives the script memory of what has taken place and helps it make better notification decisions.
-S <SQL Server name>	Specifies the name of the SQL Server instance to be identified in the notification message.
-r <Recipient>	The email address of the alert recipient. Often, this is the email address of a pager.
-m <SMTP server>	The SMTP mail server, typically in the format of `mail.linchi.com`.
-q <Quiet time>	Specifies a period of time in the format of hh-hh where hh is hours between 0 and 24, inclusive. No alerts will be sent between these two hours.
-h	When specified, the script only prints the usage information.

For example, you could schedule to run this script once every five minutes. In this example, whenever the script `alertErrorlog.pl` runs, it scans the errorlog file in the folder \\SQL1\e$\mssql\mssql$apollo\log. If it finds a critical error in the errorlog and it's between 7 A.M. and 10 P.M., the script notifies the alert recipient, which is a pager at 4321557@myTel.com specified with argument -r.

The script sends the alert message in an email using the SMTP server `mail.linchi.com` specified with the argument -m. To the recipient, the message appears to be sent by sql@linchi.com, which is introduced with the argument -a.

The script `alertErrorlog.pl` reads the previously saved status from the file d:\dba\log\status.log, which is specified with the argument -s. The script then updates the status with the current information from the errorlog and saves the status to be used next time around.

Now it's time to discuss the code.

Examining the alertErrorlog.pl Script

The script `alertErrorlog.pl` in Listing 11-1 scans a single errorlog for errors of severity level 17 or higher.

Listing 11-1. Monitoring SQL Server Errorlog: The Basic Version

```
1.   use strict;
2.   use SQLDBA::Utility qw( dbaTimeDiff dbaSMTPSend dbaTime2str dbaStr2time
3.                           dbaSaveRef dbaReadSavedRef dbaIsBetweenTime );
4.   use Getopt::Std;
5.
6.   Main: {
7.      my %opts;
8.      getopts('S:a:e:r:i:s:m:q:h', \%opts);
9.
10.     # check mandatory switches
11.     if ( $opts{'h'} or
12.          !defined $opts{e} or !defined $opts{r} or !defined $opts{s} or
13.          !defined $opts{a} or !defined $opts{m} or !defined $opts{S} ) {
14.          printUsage();
15.     }
16.     my $configRef = {  # put the command-line arg's in a more readable hash
17.          QuietTime          => $opts{q},
18.          Errorlog           => $opts{e},
19.          SenderAccount      => $opts{a},
20.          StatusFile         => $opts{s},
21.          SMTPServer         => $opts{m},
22.          SQLErrAlertInterval => $opts{i},
23.          DBAPager           => $opts{r},
24.          SQLInstance        => $opts{S}
25.     };
26.
27.     # read saved status from the status file, if any
28.     my $statusRef = (-T $configRef->{StatusFile}) ?
29.                         dbaReadSavedRef($configRef->{StatusFile}) : {};
30.
31.     my $ref = { Config => $configRef,
32.                 Status => $statusRef };
33.
34.     # Check the errorlog for critical errors
35.     $ref = scanErrorlog($ref);
36.
37.     #  Decide whether to send alert on critical errors
```

```
38.    $ref = alertErrorlog($ref);
39.
40.    # Save status to the status file
41.    dbaSaveRef($configRef->{StatusFile}, $ref->{Status}, 'ref');
42. } # Main
43.
44. ##################
45. sub scanErrorlog {
46.    my($ref) = shift or die "***Err: scanErrorlogs() expects a reference.";
47.
48.    my $statusRef = $ref->{Status};
49.
50.    # Remove old entries recorded in the status data structure
51.    # For now, if the entry is more than 24 hours old, it is old.
52.    foreach my $errType (keys %{$statusRef->{SQLErr}}) {
53.       if ((time() - $statusRef->{SQLErr}->{$errType}->{Time})
54.             > 3600*24) {
55.          delete $statusRef->{SQLErr}->{$errType};   # remove from the hash
56.          next;
57.       }
58.       # if the entry is not that old, reset its status to good
59.       $statusRef->{SQLErr}->{$errType}->{OK} = 1;
60.    }
61.    # these two variables help shorten the expressions
62.    my $errorlog = $ref->{Config}->{Errorlog};
63.    my $server = $ref->{Config}->{SQLInstance};
64.
65.    # Now open the errorlog file and check for errors
66.    unless (open(LOG, "$errorlog")) {
67.       my $msg = "Msg: could not open $errorlog on $server.";
68.       $statusRef->{SQLErr}->{FileOpen} = {
69.                    OK       => 0,     # FileOpen is no good
70.                    ErrMsg   => $msg,
71.                    Time     => time(),
72.                    TimeStr  => dbaTime2str()
73.                };
74.       return $ref;
75.    }
76.
77.    # Now we scan the errorlog file for regular SQL Server errors in
78.    #   the format of Error <#>, Severity <#>
79.    my ($logTime, $logTimeStr);
80.
81.    while (<LOG>) {
```

```
82.        # to match yyyy-mm-dd hh:mm:ss.mmm or yyyy/mm/dd hh:mm:ss.mmm
83.        ($logTimeStr) = /^\s*([\d\/\-]+\s+[\d\.\:]+)\s+/;
84.        # skip it if can't match the date/time string of the following formats
85.        next if ($logTimeStr !~ /\d\d(\/|-)\d\d(\/|-)\d\d\s+\d\d:\d\d:\d\d/);
86.        # covert to epoch seconds
87.        $logTime = dbaStr2time($logTimeStr);
88.
89.        # skip the log entries already read by a previous run of the script
90.        #   as remembered in the status file
91.        next if ($logTime <= $statusRef->{ErrorlogLastReadTime});
92.
93.        # if it's a regular SQL error, read in the next line
94.        if (/Error\s*\:\s*(\d+)\s*\,\s*Severity\s*\:\s*(\d+)/i) {
95.            my ($error, $severity) = ($1, $2);
96.            my $msg;
97.
98.            # get the next line since it contains the actual error message text
99.            $_ = <LOG>;
100.           /^\s*[^\s]+\s+[^\s]+\s+(.+)$/ and ($msg = $1);
101.
102.           $msg = "Err $error, $severity on $server at $logTimeStr. $msg";
103.           if ($severity >= 17) { # handle the error if severity >= 17
104.               $statusRef->{SQLErr}->{"$error\_$severity"} = {
105.                                 OK      => 0,          # not OK
106.                                 ErrMsg  => $msg,
107.                                 Time    => $logTime,   # epoch seconds
108.                                 TimeStr => $logTimeStr # date/time string
109.                            };
110.           }
111.       }
112.   }
113.   close(LOG);
114.   # record the date/time of the last entry so that next time any entry older
115.   # than this date/time is skipped.
116.   $statusRef->{ErrorlogLastReadTime} = $logTime;
117.   $statusRef->{ErrorlogLastReadTimeStr} = $logTimeStr;
118.
119.   return $ref;
120. } # readErrorlog
121.
122. ################
123. sub alertErrorlog {
124.   my($ref) = shift or die "***Err: alertErrorlog() expects a reference.";
125.   my ($now, $nowHour, $nowStr) = (time, (localtime)[2],dbaTime2str(time));
```

```
126.    my $msg;
127.    # for now, only one recipient. But can add more
128.    my @recipients = ($ref->{Config}->{DBAPager});
129.
130.    # Rule for alerting SQL Errors
131.    #    if 1. there is a critical SQL error
132.    #       2. SQL error was last alerted SQLErrAlertInterval minutes ago
133.    #       3. it's not in the SQLErr quiet time
134.    #    then send alert
135.
136.    foreach my $errType (keys %{$ref->{Status}->{SQLErr}}) {
137.       next if $ref->{Status}->{SQLErr}->{$errType}->{OK};    # no problem
138.       my $errRef = $ref->{Status}->{SQLErr}->{$errType};
139.
140.       # check alert time interval threshold
141.       if ( ($now - $errRef->{LastAlertedTime})
142.                    > 60*$ref->{Config}->{SQLErrAlertInterval} and
143.            !dbaIsBetweenTime($ref->{Config}->{QuietTime}) ) {
144.
145.            # send alert for this error
146.            $errRef->{SendAlertOK} = 0;  # default to bad unless proven good
147.            if ( dbaSMTPSend($ref->{Config}->{SMTPServer},
148.                             \@recipients,
149.                             $ref->{Config}->{SenderAccount},
150.                             undef,
151.                             $errRef->{ErrMsg} )) {  # send alert in header
152.                # record alert date/time in epoch seconds and date string
153.                $errRef->{LastAlertedTime} = time();
154.                $errRef->{LastAlertedTimeStr} = dbaTime2str(time);
155.                $errRef->{SendAlertOK} = 1; # alert sent successfully
156.
157.                printf " ***%s Sent to %s; %s\n", dbaTime2str(),
158.                       $ref->{Config}->{DBAPager}, $errRef>{ErrMsg};
159.            }
160.       }
161.       $ref->{Status}->{SQLErr}->{$errType} = $errRef;
162.    }
163.    return $ref;
164. } # alertErrorlog
165.
166. ##################
167. sub printUsage {
168.    print << '--Usage--';
169. Usage:
```

```
170.  perl alertErrorlog1.pl  [-h] -a <sender account> -e <errorlog>
171.                              -i <interval> -r <pager address>
172.                              -s <status log> -q <quiet time>
173.                              -m <SMTP server> -S <SQL Server instance>
174.        -h  print this usage info
175.        -a  Sender account
176.        -e  path to the SQL Server errorlog
177.        -i  the minimum time interval between two alerts on the same error
178.        -r  alert recipient
179.        -s  status log file to save the current status of the errorlog scan
180.        -q  quiet time in hh-hh format where hh is from 0 to 24
181.        -m  SMTP mail server
182.        -S  SQL Server instance
183. --Usage--
184.    exit;
185. } # printUsage
```

This section now highlights the overall structure of the script in Listing 11-1 because you'll see it repeatedly in this chapter.

The main body of the script is structured as follows:

1. The script first organizes the command-line arguments with a more readable hash record referenced by $configRef on line 16. It would be cumbersome to refer to each command-line argument with a separate variable.

2. On line 28, the script reads the previously saved status information, if any, into the data structure $statusRef with the SQLDBA::Utility function dbaReadSavedRef().

3. On line 31, the script merges the two data structures—$configRef and $statusRef—into a single hash structure under the reference $ref.

4. On line 35, the data structure $ref is passed to the function scanErrorlog(), which scans the errorlog with the help of the configuration options in $ref->{Config} and updates the status hash values in $ref->{Status}.

5. On line 38, the function alertErrorlog() examines the data structure $ref with the updated status information and decides whether to send an alert. If an alert is deemed necessary, the function sends the alert with a call to the function dbaSMTPSend() on line 147.

6. Finally, the SQLDBA::Utility function `dbaSaveRef()` saves the data structure `$ref->{Status}` to the text file, specified with the command-line option `-s`.

Using a single reference to the configuration data structure and the status data structure makes clear the logic of the script. Because a reference-based Perl data structure can arbitrarily and dynamically grow and shrink, a reference can point to any Perl data structure. As a result, the monitoring scripts in this chapter all use such a single-reference approach at the top level of the scripts to keep their overall flow consistent, nearly identical, and succinct.

Introducing the Status Data Structure

The script needs to know what has already taken place so that it can make intelligent decisions on where in the errorlog to start a new scan and whether to send a notification. More specifically, the following information should be persisted before the script exits to help guide the next invocation of the script:

- The date/time string of the last scanned entry in the errorlog

- The date/time when the last alert was sent successfully for each error

Instead of persisting only these values, it's easier and more useful to persist the entire data structure used by the script `alertErrorlog.pl` in Listing 11-1 to record the current status of the errorlog monitoring. This is possible because of the two SQLDBA::Utility functions, `dbaSaveRef()` and `dbaReadSavedRef()`. The former saves an arbitrary Perl data structure to a text file, and the latter reads from the text file the saved data structure and assigns it to a reference. If you're not familiar with these two functions, you may want to review the sections "Persisting a Data Structure to a File" and "Reading from a Persisted Data Structure" in Chapter 3.

Listing 11-2 is an example of the data structure that stores the status of monitoring a SQL Server errorlog (slightly edited for to fit the page width for readability).

Listing 11-2. The Status Data Structure Used by alertErrorlog.pl

```
$ref->{Status} = {
    ErrorlogLastReadTime => '1028950362',
    ErrorlogLastReadTimeStr => '2002-08-09 23:32:42.45'
    SQLErr => {
        '50000_17' => {
            OK => '0',
            ErrMsg => 'Err 50000, 17 on SQL1 at 2002-08-09 23:32. Test message.',
            Time    => '1028950362'
            TimeStr => '2002-08-09 23:32:42.45',
            SendAlertOK => 1,
            LastAlertedTime    => '1028950366',
            LastAlertedTimeStr => '2002/08/09 23:32:46 ',
        },
        '1105_17' => {
            OK => '0',
            ErrMsg => 'Err 1105, 17 on SQL1 at 2002-08-09 23:32. Could not ...',
            Time    => '1028950362'
            TimeStr => '2002-08-09 23:32:42.45',
            SendAlertOK => 1,
            LastAlertedTime    => '1028950366',
            LastAlertedTimeStr => '2002/08/09 23:32:46 ',
        },
        '50000_19' => {
            OK => '0',
            ErrMsg => 'Err 50000, 19 on SQL1 at 2002-08-09 23:32. Test message.',
            Time    => '1028950362'
            TimeStr => '2002-08-09 23:32:42.45',
            SendAlertOK => 1,
            LastAlertedTime    => '1028950366',
            LastAlertedTimeStr => '2002/08/09 23:32:46 ',
        },
    },
};
```

There are three keys underneath $ref->{Status}. Besides the time of the last entry in the errorlog (ErrorlogLastReadtime and ErrorlogLastReadtimeStr), SQLErr references the data structure that records the necessary details of each error found in the errorlog.

The script relies on ErrorlogLastReadTime to avoid repeatedly considering the log entries that have already been scanned when the script was previously invoked. The logic is implemented on line 91 in Listing 11-1:

```
91.        next if ($logTime <= $statusRef->{ErrorlogLastReadTime});
```

One level deeper in the nested data structure underneath $ref->{Status}->{SQLErr} is a hash key for each SQL Server error encountered during the errorlog scan. The code between lines 103 and 110 in Listing 11-1 populates the data structure at this level. As you can see, the concatenation of the error number and the severity level is used as the hash key to uniquely identify the error. In the example shown in Listing 11-2, there are three errors. For each error, a hash with the keys described in Table 11-2 are recorded or updated.

Table 11-2. The Keys of the Hash That Records the SQL Server Errors

ATTRIBUTE	DESCRIPTION
OK	A value of 0 indicates that an entry for the error is found during the current scan. A value of 1 indicates that no critical error is found during the current scan and that the hash record for the error, if any, is carried over from a previous run of the script, and it's not updated during the current scan.
ErrMsg	The message to be sent in the alert. The message includes the error number, the severity level, the SQL Server instance name, the date/time of the error, and the error message text.
Time	Date/time of the error as recorded in the errorlog. The format is epoch seconds—the number of non-leap seconds since 00:00:00 on January 1, 1970 GMT.
TimeStr	Date/time of the error as recorded in the errorlog in the readable format of YYYY-MM-DD hh:mi:ss.mm.
SendAlertOK	Value 1 indicates that the alert for this error is sent successfully, and 0 indicates otherwise.
LastAlertTime	Date/time when the alert is sent in the epoch seconds.
LastAlertTimeStr	Date/time when the alert is sent in the format of YYYY-MM-DD hh:mi:ss.mm.

NOTE *Each of the date/time related values in the status data structure is recorded in two formats: the epoch seconds—the number of non-leap seconds since 00:00:00 on Jan. 1, 1970 Greenwich mean time (GMT)— and a readable string in the format of YYYY-MM-DD hh:mi:ss.mm. This is a practice I use in most of my scripts to avoid constantly having to convert back and forth between the two formats. I sacrifice a little extra space for a gain in programming convenience and readability—a worthwhile tradeoff.*

As mentioned, the hash key for an error (for instance, error 1105) is the concatenation of its error number and its severity level (1105_17 in this case), and the hash record for this error (referenced by $ref->{Status}->{SQLErr}->{1105_17} in this case) is updated whenever such an error is found during the scan of the errorlog. Because the script scans the errorlog in the chronological order, only the information from the last occurrence of the error is kept. This is precisely desirable because it guarantees that the DBA is notified of this particular error at most once during each scan.

Note that as more errors are found in the errorlog, the number of hash records under $ref->{Status}->{SQLErr} will increase. For troubleshooting and review purposes, you don't want to immediately remove all the information for an error from the hash even if no new occurrence of this error is found during the next scan of the errorlog. However, you don't want to keep the information forever either. In this script, the entry for an error is removed if it was last logged more than 24 hours ago. The following code segment in the function scanErrorlog() implements this logic:

```
50.     # Remove old entries recorded in the status data structure
51.     # For now, if the entry is more than 24 hours old, it is old.
52.     foreach my $errType (keys %{$statusRef->{SQLErr}}) {
53.         if ((time() - $statusRef->{SQLErr}->{$errType}->{Time})
54.                 > 3600*24) {
55.             delete $statusRef->{SQLErr}->{$errType};  # remove from the hash
56.             next;
57.         }
58.         # if the entry is not that old, reset its status to good
59.         $statusRef->{SQLErr}->{$errType}->{OK} = 1;
60.     }
```

Meeting the Monitoring Requirements

The script `alertErrorlog.pl` in Listing 11-1 implements the following notification rule between lines 141 and 143:

```
If    (1) there's a new SQL Server error matching the configured criticality
          criteria (any error with severity level 17 or higher)
      (2) SQL error was last alerted SQLErrAlertInterval minutes ago
      (3) it's not in the quiet time period
Then  send an alert
```

The quiet time period is the time in which you don't want to be alerted no matter what error is logged in the errorlog. This is useful for a SQL Server instance that's not being supported on a 24/7 basis. For such a system, you may not appreciate being paged at 3 A.M.

The script `alertErrorlog.pl` in Listing 11-1 monitors a single errorlog and thus a single SQL Server instance. To monitor multiple instances, you can create a Windows batch file to run the Perl script in a series, each for an individual errorlog, and then schedule to run the batch file at a regular interval. It's most convenient to run such a batch file on a DBA utility server that has good network connectivity to all the monitored SQL Server machines.

The Perl script `alertErrorlog.pl` gives you a fully functional and reasonably useful tool for monitoring a SQL Server instance for any critical errors in its errorlog. That's not bad for fewer than 200 lines of code—not counting the functions imported from the utility module SQLDBA::Utility. But there's no reason to count the lines of code in that module. Just like using any other Perl modules, the work is already done for you.

"But wait! You can't be serious about monitoring SQL Server errorlogs with such a simple script," you may object. Well, you're right. But then this chapter hasn't claimed that this script is robust and comprehensive. It's a mere start to familiarize you with the basic issues of monitoring the SQL Server errorlog. The next section builds on this script and presents a robust and comprehensive script for monitoring multiple SQL Server errorlogs in a coherent manner.

Monitoring SQL Server Errorlogs: The Robust Version

> **SCENARIO**
> *You want to monitor multiple SQL Server errorlogs not only for SQL Server errors with high severity level but also for any messages deemed critical. In addition, you want to be able to accommodate future changes in monitoring requirements with little or no need to alter the script itself.*

Let's first examine where the script in Listing 11-1 may have failed to adequately address the SQL Server errorlog monitoring requirements in a typical SQL Server enterprise environment.

Investigating the Drawbacks of the Script alertErrorlog.pl

The following are the key drawbacks of the script alertErrorlog.pl in Listing 11-1.

There needs to be more configurations, less hard coding. What's considered a critical exception is hard-coded in the script alertErrorlog.pl to be any error with severity level of 17 or higher. This isn't always desirable. Not all errors with severity 17 or higher are worth knowing at 3 A.M. In addition, as you gain more experience monitoring your SQL Server installations, you'll become more specific about the errors about which you want to be notified. You definitely don't want to modify the script every time you have gained new insight into your monitoring requirements.

There's a need to monitor the size of an SQL Server errorlog. An excessively large errorlog is itself a critical exception. It makes more sense to alert the DBA of the large errorlog size than open the errorlog and scan for logged errors.

There *is* a need to notify multiple alert recipients. The script alertErrorlog.pl in Listing 11-1 supports only a single recipient. In an enterprise environment, a group of DBAs often manage the SQL Server installations. For a given SQL Server, there may be a need to alert both its primary DBA and its backup DBA and/or send the notification to a duty pager or even an email alias for the DBA group. Another common requirement is to alert an application support person—not the DBA— when an application process fails its database job and writes an error to the errorlog.

577

There *is* a need to monitor multiple errorlogs. To monitor multiple SQL Server errorlogs, you can call the script multiple times from a batch file, each with different parameters for a different SQL Server errorlog. Furthermore, note that some configuration options specified on the command line aren't specific to individual errorlogs, but common to the errorlog monitoring as a whole. For instance, it would be repetitive to specify the same SMTP server for each SQL Server errorlog. Another drawback of running the script multiple times in a batch file is that there will be as many files to persist the errorlog monitoring status as there are monitored SQL Server errorlogs.

There *is* a need to alert based on pattern-matched strings. You may want to get alerted when an errorlog entry matches a specified text pattern. This is extremely useful as a catchall mechanism because it isn't realistic to expect that everything that is or isn't worth notifying is already known at the time when the script is written.

Finally, there *is* a need to use a configuration file. It becomes unwieldy to include too many parameters all on the command line.

Building a More Versatile and Robust Script for Monitoring Errorlogs

The script `monitorErrorlogs.pl` in Listing 11-3 is built on the script in Listing 11-1 and is specifically written to overcome the drawbacks identified previously.

Listing 11-3. Monitoring SQL Server Errorlogs: The Robust Version

```
use strict;
use SQLDBA::Utility qw( dbaReadINI dbaSMTPSend dbaTime2str dbaStr2time
                        dbaSaveRef dbaReadSavedRef dbaIsBetweenTime );
use Win32::ODBC;

Main: {
    my $configFile = shift or printUsage();
    (-T $configFile) or
        die "***Err: specified config file $configFile does not exist.";

    # Read config file into $configRef
    my $configRef = dbaReadINI($configFile);

    # validate config options and set defaults
    $configRef = validateConfig($configRef);

    # read from the status file, if exists
```

```perl
    my $statusRef = (-T $configRef->{CONTROL}->{STATUSFILE})
                  ? dbaReadSavedRef($configRef->{CONTROL}->{STATUSFILE}) : {};
    # merge into a single hash
    my $ref = { Config => $configRef, Status => $statusRef };

    # initialize the status data structure, if necessary
    $ref = initializeStatus($ref);

    # Check the errorlog files for critical errors
    $ref = scanErrorlogs($ref);

    #  Send alert on critical errors
    $ref = alertErrorlogs($ref);

    # Save status to the status file
    dbaSaveRef($configRef->{CONTROL}->{STATUSFILE}, $ref->{Status}, 'ref');
} # Main


####################
sub printUsage {
    print << '--Usage--';
Usage:
  cmd>perl monitorErrorlogs.pl <Config File>
       <Config File>   file to specify config options for alerting errorlogs
--Usage--
    exit;
}


##################
sub validateConfig {
    my $ref = shift or die "***Err: validateConfigRef() expects a reference.";

    # make sure that status file is specified
    defined $ref->{CONTROL}->{STATUSFILE}
       or die "***Err: StatusFile option is not specified.";

    #  Make sure that intervals and thresholds are set
    foreach my $server (keys %$ref) {
       next if ($server =~ /^CONTROL$/i);   # skip the CONTROL section
       # Make sure that SQL errorlog is identified for each server
       $server =~ /^server\s*:/i or
          die "***Err: $server in the heading must be prefixed with Server:";
       defined $ref->{$server}->{SQLERRORLOG} or
          die "***Err: SQLErrorlog is not specified for \[$server\].";
```

```perl
        # intervals are all in minutes. If they are not set explicitly
        # in the config file, their default values are set here.
        $ref->{$server}->{CONFIGERRALERTINTERVAL} ||= 60;      # in minutes
        $ref->{$server}->{ERRORLOGSIZEALERTINTERVAL} ||= 120; # in minutes
        $ref->{$server}->{SQLERRALERTINTERVAL} ||= 10;         # in minutes
        $ref->{$server}->{ONPATTERNALERTINTERVAL} ||= 20;      # in minutes
        $ref->{$server}->{ERRORLOGSIZETHRESHOLD} ||= 4000;     # in KB

        # strip off KB postfix, if any. The threshold is always
        # in KB regardless of the postfix.
        $ref->{$server}->{ERRORLOGSIZETHRESHOLD} =~ s/\s*(K|KB)\s*$//i;

        # validate OnPattern regular expressions
        foreach my $op (grep /^\s*OnPattern\d*\s*$/i, keys %{$ref->{$server}}) {
            $ref->{$server}->{$op} =~ /^(.+)\s*,\s*\[([^\[]+)\]$/;
            my ($exp, $email) = ($1, $2);
            $exp = "qr$exp" if $exp =~ /^\s*\//; # if not qr// aready, add it
            eval $exp;      # evaluate the regex
            if ($@) {       # if it's not a valid regex, skip it
                print "***$exp is not a valid regular expression.\n";
                next;
            }
            else { # for a valid regex, put associated email addresses in an array
                my %addresses;  # use its keys to get unique email addresses
                map { $addresses{$_} = 1; } split /[,;\s]+/, $email;
                $ref->{$server}->{$op} = { 'REGEX' => $exp,
                                           'EMAIL' => [ keys %addresses ]
                                         }
            }
        }
    }
    return $ref;
} # validateConfig


###################
sub initializeStatus {
    my $ref = shift or die "***Err: initializeStatus() expects a reference.";

    foreach my $server (sort keys %{$ref->{Config}}) {
        next if $server =~ /^CONTROL$/i;
        # skip the server if its monitoring is disabled
        next if $ref->{Config}->{$server}->{DISABLED} =~ /y/i;
        my ($serverName) = $server =~ /^server\s*:\s*(.+)$/i;
```

```perl
# reset and/or initialize the status indicators
# (assuming eveything is fine to begin with)
# This will also initialize the hash elements, if do not exist already
$ref->{Status}->{$server}->{ErrorlogOK} = 1;
$ref->{Status}->{$server}->{Exception}->{ConfigErr}->{OK} = 1;
$ref->{Status}->{$server}->{Exception}->{ErrorlogSize}->{OK} = 1;
$ref->{Status}->{$server}->{Exception}->{SQLErr}->{OK} = 1;
$ref->{Status}->{$server}->{Exception}->{OnPattern}->{OK} = 1;

# these two intermediate variables are used to shorten expressions
# in the rest of this function
my $exceptionRef = $ref->{Status}->{$server}->{Exception};
my $configRef    = $ref->{Config}->{$server};

# Remove old entries from the status data structure
# for each exception category.

# Exception category: ConfigErr
if ((time() - $exceptionRef->{ConfigErr}->{Time})
            > 3600*24*$configRef->{REMOVESAVEDSTATUSOLDERTHAN}) {
   $exceptionRef->{ConfigErr} = { OK => 1 };
}
# Exception category: ErrorlogSize
if ((time() - $exceptionRef->{ErrorlogSize}->{Time})
            > 3600*24*$configRef->{REMOVESAVEDSTATUSOLDERTHAN}) {
   $exceptionRef->{ErrorlogSize} = { OK => 1 };
}
# Exception category: SQLErr
foreach my $err (keys %{$exceptionRef->{SQLErr}}) {
   next if $err eq 'OK';
   if ((time() - $exceptionRef->{SQLErr}->{$err}->{Time})
            > 3600*24*$configRef->{REMOVESAVEDSTATUSOLDERTHAN}) {
      delete $exceptionRef->{SQLErr}->{$err};
      next;
   }
   $exceptionRef->{SQLErr}->{$err}->{OK} = 1;
}
# Exception category: OnPattern
foreach my $err (keys %{$exceptionRef->{OnPattern}}) {
   next if $err eq 'OK';
   if ((time() - $exceptionRef->{OnPattern}->{$err}->{Time})
            > 3600*24*$configRef->{REMOVESAVEDSTATUSOLDERTHAN}) {
      delete $exceptionRef->{OnPattern}->{$err};
```

```perl
                next;
            }
            $exceptionRef->{OnPattern}->{$err}->{OK} = 1;
        }
    }
    return $ref;
} # initializeStatus


####################
sub scanErrorlogs {
    my $ref = shift or die "***Err: scanErrorlogs() expects a reference.";

    SERVER_LOOP:
    foreach my $server (sort keys %{$ref->{Config}}) {
        next if $server =~ /^CONTROL$/i;
        next if $ref->{Config}->{$server}->{DISABLED} =~ /y/i;
        my ($serverName) = $server =~ /^server\s*:\s*(.+)$/i;
        print "Scanning $serverName errorlog ...\n";

        # these intermediate variables are used to shorten expressions. They
        # are specific to this server
        my $statusRef    = $ref->{Status}->{$server};
        my $exceptionRef = $ref->{Status}->{$server}->{Exception};
        my $configRef    = $ref->{Config}->{$server};
        my $errorlog     = $configRef->{SQLERRORLOG};

        # Errorlog size check, if the threshold is specified.
        $exceptionRef->{ErrorlogSize}->{ActualErrorlogSize}
                     = int((stat($errorlog))[7] /1024);  # in KB
        # if the actual errorlog size is greater than the errorlog size threshold,
        # record an errorlog size exception.
        if ($exceptionRef->{ErrorlogSize}->{ActualErrorlogSize}
                  > $configRef->{ERRORLOGSIZETHRESHOLD}) {
            my $msg = "$errorlog on $server too big. Scan not performed.";
            $statusRef->{ErrorlogOK} = 0;             # not OK overall
            $exceptionRef->{ErrorlogSize}->{OK} = 0;  # not OK with errorlog size
            $exceptionRef->{ErrorlogSize}->{ErrMsg} = $msg; # record the msg
            $exceptionRef->{ErrorlogSize}->{Time} = time(); # in epoch seconds
            $exceptionRef->{ErrorlogSize}->{TimeStr} = dbaTime2str(); # date string
            print "  ***$msg\n";
            # if AutoCycleErrorlog not set, don't even open the errorlog
            next SERVER_LOOP if $configRef->{AUTOCYCLEERRORLOG} !~ /y/i;
        }
```

```perl
# Now open the errorlog file and check for errors
my $Tries = 0;
# try three times. If still can't open the errorlog, then give up.
while (!open(LOG, "$errorlog")) {
   if (++$Tries < 3) { sleep(2); next; } # sleep for 2 seconds, and retry
   else {
      my $msg = "$Tries tries. Couldn't open $errorlog on $server.";
      $statusRef->{ErrorlogOK} = 0;
      $exceptionRef->{ConfigErr}->{OK} = 0;
      $exceptionRef->{ConfigErr}->{ErrMsg} = $msg;
      $exceptionRef->{ConfigErr}->{Time} = time();
      $exceptionRef->{ConfigErr}->{TimeStr} = dbaTime2str();
      print "   ***$msg\n";
      next SERVER_LOOP;  # can't open, then quit trying this errorlog
   }
}


# Now we scan the errorlog file
my ($time, $timeStr, $error, $severity, $msg);
while (<LOG>) {
   $statusRef->{MajorVersion}=6 if (/Microsoft\s+SQL\s+Server\s+6/i);
   ($timeStr) = /^\s*([\d\/\-]+\s+[\d\.\:]+)\s+/;
   # skip the line it if it cannot match the leading datetime string
   next if ($timeStr !~ /\d\d(\/|-)\d\d(\/|-)\d\d\s+\d\d:\d\d:\d\d/);
   $time = dbaStr2time($timeStr);

   # skip the log entries already read by a previous run
   next if $time <= $statusRef->{ErrorlogLastReadTime};
   # skip the entries older than IgnoreEntryOlderThan minutes
   next if (time() - $time) > 60*$configRef->{IGNOREENTRYOLDERTHAN};

   # if it's a regular SQL error, we need to read in the next line
   if (/Error\s*\:\s*(\d+)\s*\,\s*Severity\s*\:\s*(\d+)/i) {
      ($error, $severity)  = ($1, $2);
      # get the next line since it contains the actual error message
      $_ = <LOG>;
      /^\s*[^\s]+\s+[^\s]+[^\s]+\s+(.+)$/ and ($msg = $1);
      $_ = "Error: $error, Severity: $severity, $msg";
   }

   # checking OnPattern exceptions with matchOnPattern()
   if (my $emailAddressRef = matchOnPattern($server, $ref, $_)) {
      chomp($_);
      my $errMsg = "$timeStr OnPattern on $serverName " . $_;
```

```
                  $statusRef->{ErrorlogOK} = 0;
                  $exceptionRef->{OnPattern}->{OK} = 0;
                  $exceptionRef->{OnPattern}->{$msg}->{Time} = $time;
                  $exceptionRef->{OnPattern}->{$msg}->{TimeStr} = $timeStr;
                  $exceptionRef->{OnPattern}->{$msg}->{ErrMsg} = $errMsg;
                  $exceptionRef->{OnPattern}->{$msg}->{EmailAddress}
                                                    = $emailAddressRef;
              print "   ***$errMsg\n";
              next;  # perform no more check on this log entry
          }

          # checking SQLErr exceptions
          if (/Error\s*\:\s*(\d+)\s*\,\s*Severity\s*\:\s*(\d+)/i) {
              my ($error, $severity) = ($1, $2);
              my $errMsg = "$timeStr Err: $error, Severity: $severity " .
                           "on $server. $msg";
              # skip it if this error # is on the exclude list
              next if ($configRef->{EXCLUDESQLERRORS} =~ /\b$error\b/i);

              #  skip it if it's on the severity include list
              if ($configRef->{INCLUDESQLSEVERITIES} =~ /\b$severity\b/i) {
                  $statusRef->{ErrorlogOK} = 0;
                  $exceptionRef->{SQLErr}->{OK} = 0;
                  my $sqlErr = "$error\_$severity";
                  $exceptionRef->{SQLErr}->{$sqlErr}->{Time} = $time;
                  $exceptionRef->{SQLErr}->{$sqlErr}->{TimeStr} = $timeStr;
                  $exceptionRef->{SQLErr}->{$sqlErr}->{ErrMsg} = $errMsg;
                  print "   ***$errMsg\n";
              }
          }
      } # while
      close(LOG);
      $statusRef->{ErrorlogLastReadTime} = $time;
      $statusRef->{ErrorlogLastReadTimeStr} = $timeStr;
   }
   return $ref;
} # scanErrorlogs


#######################
sub matchOnPattern {
   my ($server, $ref, $msg) = @_;
   ($server && $ref && $msg) or
        die "***Err: matchOnPattern() expects a server, a reference," .
                   " and the message body.";
```

```perl
    my %addresses;
    my $configRef = $ref->{Config}->{$server};

    foreach my $op (grep /^\s*OnPattern\d*\s*$/i, keys %$configRef) {
        my $re = eval $configRef->{$op}->{REGEX}; # already validated
        if ($msg =~ /$re/) {
            map {$addresses{$_} = 1;} @{$configRef->{$op}->{EMAIL}};
        }
    }
    my @emails = keys %addresses;
    scalar @emails ? return [ @emails ] : return undef;
} # matchOnPattern


####################
sub alertErrorlogs {
    my $ref = shift or die "***Err: alertrrorlogs() expects a reference.";
    my ($server, $msg);
    my ($nowHour, $nowStr) = ((localtime)[2], dbaTime2str());

    foreach $server (sort keys %{$ref->{Status}}) {
        # these two intermediate variables are used to shorten
        # expressions in the rest of this chapter
        my $statusRef = $ref->{Status}->{$server};
        my $configRef = $ref->{Config}->{$server};

        next if ($configRef->{DISABLED} =~ /y/i);
        next if $statusRef->{ErrorlogOK};    # if there is no problem

    # Rule for alerting a config error
    # if 1. config error alert is enabled,
    #    2. there is a config error,
    #    3. it's not ConfigErr quiet time, and
    #    4. Last config error alerted ConfigErrorAlertInterval minutes ago
    # then  send ConfigErr alert
        my $configErrRef = $statusRef->{Exception}->{ConfigErr};
        if ( $configRef->{ALERTCONFIGERR} =~ /y/i and
             $configErrRef->{OK} == 0 and
             !dbaIsBetweenTime($configRef->{CONFIGERRQUIETTIME} ) and
             ((time() - $configErrRef->{LastAlertedTime})
                        > ($configRef->{CONFIGERRALERTINTERVAL})*60 ) ) {
            $ref = sendAlert($server, $ref, 'ConfigErr');
            next;
        }
```

```
# Rule for alerting an Errorlog Size error
# if   1. ErrorlogSize alert is enabled
#      2. Actual errorlog size > errorlog size therhold
#      3. ActualErrorlogSize > Errorlog Size Threshold
#      4. Last ErrorlogSize alerted ErrorlogSizeAlertInterval minutes old
#      5. it is not ErrorlogSize quiet time
# then  send Errorlog Size Alert
   my $errorlogSizeRef = $statusRef->{Exception}->{ErrorlogSize};
   if ($configRef->{ALERTERRORLOGSIZE} =~ /y/i and
       $errorlogSizeRef->{OK} == 0 and
       $errorlogSizeRef->{ActualErrorlogSize}
               > $configRef->{ERRORLOGSIZETHRESHOLD}  and
       (time() - $errorlogSizeRef->{LastAlertedTime})
               > 60*$configRef->{ERRORLOGSIZEALERTINTERVAL} and
      !dbaIsBetweenTime($configRef->{ERRORLOGSIZEQUIETTIME}) ) {
          $ref = sendAlert($server, $ref, 'ErrorlogSize');
   }


# Rule for alerting on text patterns
# if    1. OnPatternAlert is enabled,
#       2. there is a error message matching a pattern
#       3. it's not OnPatternQuietTime
#       4. This error was last alerted OnPatternInterval minutes ago
# then  send alert
   my $onPatternRef = $statusRef->{Exception}->{OnPattern};
   if ($configRef->{ALERTONPATTERN} =~ /y/i and
      !$onPatternRef->{OK} and
      !dbaIsBetweenTime($configRef->{ONPATTERNQUIETTIME})) {
     foreach my $err (keys %{$onPatternRef}) {
       next if $err =~ /^OK$/i;
       next if $onPatternRef->{$err}->{OK};

       if ((time() - $onPatternRef->{$err}->{LastAlertedTime})
               > 60*$configRef->{ONPATTERNALERTINTERVAL}) {
          $ref = sendAlert($server, $ref, 'OnPattern', $err);
       }
     }
   }


# Rule for alerting SQL Errors
# if    1. SQLErr alert is enabled
#       2. there is a critical SQL error
#       3. it's not SQLErr quiet time
#       4. This error was last alerted SQLErrAlterInterval minutes ago
```

```perl
      # then  send alert
        my $SQLErrRef = $statusRef->{Exception}->{SQLErr};
        if ($configRef->{ALERTSQLERROR} =~ /y/i and
             !$SQLErrRef->{OK} and
             !dbaIsBetweenTime($configRef->{SQLERRQUIETTIME})) {
           # There might be multiple critical errors. Loop through them
           # all to check.
           foreach my $err (keys %{$SQLErrRef}) {
              next if $err =~ /^OK$/i;
              next if $SQLErrRef->{$err}->{OK};

              if ( (time() - $SQLErrRef->{$err}->{LastAlertedTime})
                          > 60*$configRef->{SQLERRALERTINTERVAL} ) {
                 $ref = sendAlert($server, $ref, 'SQLErr', $err);
              }
           }
        }

   # Rule for cycling errorlog
   # if    1. AutoCycleErrorlog is enabled
   #       2. ActualErrorlogSize > Errorlog Size Threshold
   #       3. It's not SQL6.5
   # then  cycle the errorlog
      if ( ($configRef->{AUTOCYCLEERRORLOG} =~ /y/i) &&
           ($statusRef->{Exception}->{ErrorlogSize}->{ActualErrorlogSize}
                    > $configRef->{ERRORLOGSIZETHRESHOLD}) &&
           $statusRef->{MajorVersion} != 6 ) {
              $ref = cycleErrorlog($server, $ref);
      }
   }
   return $ref;
} # alertErrorlogs


###############
sub sendAlert {
   my($server, $ref, $type, $err) = @_;

   # $type must one of ConfigErr, ErrorlogSize, SQLErr, OnPattern
   unless ($type =~ /^(ConfigErr|ErrorlogSize|SQLErr|OnPattern)$/i) {
      print "***Err: $type not among ConfigErr,ErrorlogSize,SQLErr,OnPattern\n";
      return $ref;
   }

   my $configRef = $ref->{Config};
```

```
my $statusRef = $ref->{Status}->{$server}->{Exception}->{$type};
my @recipients;
if ($type eq 'OnPattern') {
   @recipients = @{$statusRef->{$err}->{EmailAddress}};
}
else { # add DBAPAGER for this server to the list
   @recipients = split (/[;,\s]+/, $configRef->{$server}->{DBAPAGER});
   # if there is no recipient, use the DUTYPAGER in the Control section
   @recipients = ($configRef->{CONTROL}->{DUTYPAGER}) if !@recipients;
}


# send alerts for OnPattern or SQLErr messages
if ($type =~ /^(OnPattern|SQLErr)$/i ) {
   my $errRef = $statusRef->{$err};
   $errRef->{SendAlertOK} = 0;
   if (dbaSMTPSend($configRef->{CONTROL}->{SMTPSERVER},
                  \@recipients,
                  $configRef->{CONTROL}->{SMTPSENDER},
                  undef,                      # msg body
                  $errRef->{ErrMsg})) {       # msg header
      $errRef->{LastAlertedTime} = time(); # record alert sent time
      $errRef->{LastAlertedTimeStr} = dbaTime2str();
      $errRef->{SendAlertOK} = 1;            # record a successful send

      # record the sent alert in the alert log file for posterity
      my $logFile = $configRef->{CONTROL}->{ALERTLOGFILE};
      if (open (LOG, ">>$logFile")) {
         printf LOG "%s  %s  %s Sent to %s\n", dbaTime2str(),
                    $type, $errRef->{ErrMsg}, join(',', @recipients);
         close(LOG);
      }
      else { print "***Failed to open $logFile\n"; }
   }
   $ref->{Status}->{$server}->{Exception}->{$type}->{$err} = $errRef;
}


# Send alerts for ConfigErr or ErrorlogSize messages
if ($type =~ /^(ConfigErr|ErrorlogSize)$/i ) {
   my $typeRef = $ref->{Status}->{$server}->{Exception}->{$type};
   $typeRef->{SendAlertOK} = 0;
   if (dbaSMTPSend($configRef->{CONTROL}->{SMTPSERVER},
                  \@recipients,
                  $configRef->{CONTROL}->{SMTPSENDER},
                  undef,                            # msg body
```

```
                      $typeRef->{ErrMsg})) {          # msg header
           $typeRef->{LastAlertedTime} = time();     # record alert sent time
           $typeRef->{LastAlertedTimeStr} = dbaTime2str();
           $typeRef->{SendAlertOK} = 1;               # record a successful send

           # record in the alert log file for posterity
           my $logFile = $configRef->{CONTROL}->{ALERTLOGFILE};
           if (open (LOG, ">>$logFile")) {
              printf LOG "%s  %s  %s Sent to %s\n", dbaTime2str(),
                         $type, $typeRef->{ErrMsg}, join(',', @recipients);
              close(LOG);
           }
           else { print "***Failed to open $logFile\n"; }
        }
        $ref->{Status}->{$server}->{Exception}->{$type} = $typeRef;
    }
    return $ref;
}  # sendAlert


###################
sub cycleErrorlog {
    my($server, $ref) = @_;
    ($server && $ref) or
       die "***Err: cycleErrorlog() expects server and reference.";

    my $conn;
    my $cycleRef = $ref->{Status}->{$server}->{Exception}->{CycleErrorlog};
    my ($serverName) = $server =~ /^server\s*:\s*(.+)$/i;
    my $connStr = "Driver={SQL Server};Server=$serverName;" .
                  "Trusted_Connection=Yes;database=master";

    # connect to the server to execute DBCC errorlog
    unless($conn = new Win32::ODBC ($connStr)) {
      $cycleRef->{OK} = 0;
      $cycleRef->{ErrMsg} =
            "ODBC failed to connect to $server. " . Win32::ODBC::Error();
      $cycleRef->{CycleErrorlogTimeStr} = dbaTime2str();
      $cycleRef->{CycleErrorlogTime} = time();
      $ref->{Status}->{$server}->{Exception}->{CycleErrorlog} = $cycleRef;
      return $ref;
    }

    # execute DBCC errorlog to recycle the errorlog
    if ($conn->Sql( 'DBCC errorlog' )) {
```

```
    $cycleRef->{OK} = 0;
    $cycleRef->{ErrMsg} =
          "ODBC couldn't execute DBCC ERRORLOG. " . Win32::ODBC::Error();
    $cycleRef->{CycleErrorlogTimeStr} = dbaTime2str();
    $cycleRef->{CycleErrorlogTime} = time();
  }
  else {
    1 while $conn->FetchRow();
    $cycleRef->{OK} = 1;
    $cycleRef->{ErrMsg} = "Errorlog on $server cycled";
    $cycleRef->{CycleErrorlogTimeStr} = dbaTime2str();
    $cycleRef->{CycleErrorlogTime} = time();

    if (open (LOG, ">>$ref->{Config}->{CONTROL}->{ALERTLOGFILE}")) {
      printf LOG "%s  %s\n", dbaTime2str(), $cycleRef->{ErrMsg};
      close(LOG);
    }
    else {
      print "***Err: cnnot open $ref->{Config}->{CONTROL}->{ALERTLOGFILE}\n";
    }
  }
  $ref->{Status}->{$server}->{Exception}->{CycleErrorlog} = $cycleRef;
  return $ref;
} # cycleErrorlog
```

Wow! The script in Listing 11-3 is considerably longer than any other scripts you've seen so far in this book. However, given what it accomplishes, it isn't as complex as its length might otherwise suggest. Let's dissect the script from several perspectives: what it monitors, the configuration options it permits, its main control flow, and its key data structures.

Later, the "Setting the Options for Pattern-Matched Exceptions" section looks at the pattern-matched exceptions in more detail and gives an example to show how you can further customize the script.

Choosing What to Monitor

You can group the SQL Server exceptions monitored by this script into four categories:

- Exceptions caused by inappropriate configurations of the monitoring script itself.

- Exceptions caused by excessively large errorlog size.

- Exceptions caused by SQL Server errors.

- Exceptions as the result of matching string patterns in the errorlog. The exceptions in the same category are detected and notified with the same logic.

Understanding the Configuration Exceptions

These aren't really SQL Server error conditions. Instead, they're incorrect configurations in the configuration file passed to the script. For the script in Listing 11-3, the only configuration exception that may result in an alert to the DBA is when the errorlog path is incorrectly specified—for example, if the path points to a nonexistent directory. Whenever the script can't open an errorlog after three consecutively failed attempts, it records a configuration exception. The following code fragment from the function scanErrorlogs() shows how this is done:

```
my $Tries = 0;
while (!open(LOG, "$errorlog")) {
    if (++$Tries < 3) { sleep(2); next; } # sleep for 2 seconds and re-try
    else {
        my $msg = "$Tries tries. Couldn't open $errorlog on $server.";
        $statusRef->{ErrorlogOK} = 0;
        $exceptionRef->{ConfigErr}->{OK} = 0;
        $exceptionRef->{ConfigErr}->{ErrMsg} = $msg;
        $exceptionRef->{ConfigErr}->{Time} = time();
        $exceptionRef->{ConfigErr}->{TimeStr} = dbaTime2str();
        print "   ***$msg\n";
        next SERVER_LOOP;  # can't open, then quit trying this errorlog
    }
}
```

Note that the script can't tell whether an errorlog is specified correctly except that it can't open the file,[1] and failure to open the errorlog file may not necessarily be caused by an incorrectly specified errorlog path. Any one of numerous networking problems can prevent an errorlog from being opened from where the script is running.

---

1. This is a bit of a fib because the script could try to verify the errorlog path by checking the corresponding registry entry remotely on SQL Server. However, this introduces dependency on accessing the remote registry.

Understanding the Errorlog Size Exception

If an errorlog becomes larger than a specified size threshold, the script records an errorlog size exception. The following code fragment from the function scanErrorlogs() checks the errorlog size and records an errorlog size exception, if necessary:

```
# Errorlog size check, if the threshold is specified.
$exceptionRef->{ErrorlogSize}->{ActualErrorlogSize}
            = int((stat($errorlog))[7] /1024);  # actual size in KB
# compare with the size threshold
if ($exceptionRef->{ErrorlogSize}->{ActualErrorlogSize}
        > $configRef->{ERRORLOGSIZETHRESHOLD}) {
  my $msg = "$errorlog on $server too big. Scan not performed.";
  $statusRef->{ErrorlogOK} = 0;
  $exceptionRef->{ErrorlogSize}->{OK} = 0;
  $exceptionRef->{ErrorlogSize}->{ErrMsg} = $msg;
  $exceptionRef->{ErrorlogSize}->{Time} = time();
  $exceptionRef->{ErrorlogSize}->{TimeStr} = dbaTime2str();
  print "  ***$msg\n";
  # if AutoCycleErrorlog not set, don't even open the errorlog
  next SERVER_LOOP if $configRef->{AUTOCYCLEERRORLOG} !~ /y/i;
}
```

In addition to notifying the DBA of the excessive errorlog size, you can configure the script to automatically recycle the errorlog when it reaches the threshold size.

Understanding the SQL Server Error Exceptions

These are the regular SQL Server errors, each of which is identified with an error number and a severity level. The code fragment from the function scanErrorlog() that scans for regular SQL Server errors is as follows:

```
# if it's a regular SQL error, we need to read in the next line
if (/Error\s*\:\s*(\d+)\s*\,\s*Severity\s*\:\s*(\d+)/i) {
    ($error, $severity)  = ($1, $2);
    # get the next line since it contains the actual error message
    $_ = <LOG>;
    /^\s*[^\s]+\s+[^\s]+[^\s]+\s+(.+)$/ and ($msg = $1);
    $_ = "Error: $error, Severity: $severity, $msg";
}
```

Understanding the Pattern-Matched Exceptions

This feature allows the script to monitor the errorlog for entries that match any valid regular expression you may specify in the configuration file. Note that the errorlog entries matching a regular expression aren't necessarily exceptions in the sense that they're indicative of some sort of undesirable problems. Rather, this feature gives you ability to alert on any event, as long as an entry with an identifiable text pattern is logged in the errorlog for that event—without making any change to the script code. You'll learn more about pattern-matched exceptions in the "Setting the Options for Pattern-Matched Exceptions" section.

Setting the Configuration Options

The script in Listing 11-3 accepts a single command-line parameter—the name of a configuration file where, not surprisingly, you specify all the configuration options. Assuming the configuration file is config.txt in the current directory, you can run the script as follows:

```
cmd>perl monitorErrorlogs.pl config.txt
```

What the script in Listing 11-3 accomplishes will become much clearer once you've looked at the options you can specify in a configuration file. Listing 11-4 is a sample configuration file for the errorlogs of SQL Server instances, SQL1 and SQL1\APOLLO.

Listing 11-4. Sample Configuration Options for Two Errorlogs

```
[Control]
DutyPager=74321@myTel.com
SMTPServer=mail.linchi.com
SMTPSender=sql@linchi.com
AlertLogFile=e:\dba\alertErrorlog\Alert.log
StatusFile=e:\dba\alertErrorlog\Status.log


[Server:SQL1]
SQLErrorlog=\\SQL1\D$\MSSQL\LOG\Errorlog
Disabled=no
DBAPager=75114@myTel.com
IgnoreEntryOlderThan=300
RemoveSavedStatusOlderThan=2
```

```
AlertConfigErr=yes
ConfigErrAlertInterval=50
ConfigErrQuietTime=23-7

AlertErrorlogSize=yes
ErrorlogSizeThreshold=3000
ErrorlogSizeAlertInterval=120
ErrorlogSizeQuietTime=18-8

AlertSQLErr=yes
IncludeSQLSeverities=17,18,19,20,21,22,23,24,25
ExcludeSQLErrors=1608,17832,17824
SQLErrAlertInterval=5
SQLErrQuietTime=22-7

OnPattern01=/BACKUP failed.+database (SMD|RMD)\s/i, [75114@myTel.com]
OnPattern02=/Fatal error in database (?!(pubs|NorthWind)\b)/i,[73056@myTel.com]
OnPatternQuietTime = 22-7
OnPatternAlertInterval = 2
```

[Server:SQL1\APOLLO]
```
SQLErrorlog=\\SQL1\E$\MSSQL\MSSQL$APOLLO\LOG\Errorlog
Disabled=no
DBAPager=74321@myTel.com
IgnoreEntryOlderThan=300
RemoveSavedStatusOlderThan=2

AlertConfigErr=yes
ConfigErrAlertInterval=60
ConfigErrQuietTime=12-7

AlertErrorlogSize=yes
ErrorlogSizeThreshold=3000
ErrorlogSizeAlertInterval=120
ErrorlogSizeQuietTime=18-8

AlertSQLErr=yes
IncludeSQLErrors=
IncludeSQLSeverities=17,18,19,20,21,22,23,24,25
ExcludeSQLErrors=1608,17832,17824
SQLErrAlertInterval=5
SQLErrQuietTime=22-7
```

Understanding the Overall Configuration Options

The `Control` section includes the options that aren't particular to any individual SQL Server errorlog. Rather, they apply to the overall working of the script. Alerts for a SQL Server errorlog will be sent to the address of `DutyPager` if no pager address is specified with the option `DBAPager` under the section for that specific SQL Server errorlog. In other words, `DutyPager` in the `Control` section is used as a convenient fallback or default pager. The following two lines of code from the function `sendAlert()` show how the alert recipients are compiled from these options:

```
@recipients = split (/[;,\s]+/, $configRef->{$server}->{DBAPAGER});
@recipients = ($configRef->{CONTROL}->{DUTYPAGER}) if !@recipients;
```

The option `SMTPServer` specifies the address of the SMTP server that handles all the outgoing notification emails. `SMTPSender` identifies the sender of all the SMTP emails. `AlertLogFile` specifies the location of the file in which the script will record an entry after it has successfully sent an alert. This log file gives the DBA a history of the alerts sent by the script and is useful for troubleshooting purposes.

Finally, the script persists the errorlog monitoring status to the file specified by the option `StatusFile`. The information in the status file helps the script `monitorErrorlogs.pl` make better decisions when it runs again. You'll see the status data structure for the errorlog monitoring later in the "Exploring the Status Data Structure" section.

Understanding the General Errorlog Options

Underneath the section heading for a SQL Server instance such as [`Server:SQL1`],[2] the configuration options fall into five categories. The first category of options isn't related to any particular type of exceptions. Five options are in this category:

SQLErrorlog: This option informs the script which SQL Server errorlog to open and scan. A filename using Uniform Naming Convention (UNC) is expected for this option so that the script can always find the errorlog no matter where it may be running. Because given a SQL Server instance you can easily find the location of its errorlog, you may be wondering why the script `monitorErrorlogs.pl` even requires this option. I have chosen to explicitly specify the errorlog file so that there's no dependency on having access to the remote registry where the location of the SQL Server errorlog is stored.

---

2. Note that the `Server:` prefix is required before each SQL Server instance name in the section heading so that the [`Control`] section heading can be reserved for the overall configurations without clashing with a server that happens to be named Control.

Disabled: This is an option to enhance the usability of the script. By setting this option to yes, you can conveniently exclude an errorlog from being monitored while keeping its configuration values intact in case you need to later turn on the monitoring again. If this option is set to yes for an errorlog, the scanErrorlogs() function skips the errorlog with this regular expression matching:

```
next if $ref->{Config}->{$server}->{DISABLED} =~ /^y/i;
```

DBAPager: This identifies the email address to which the script sends notifications for this particular SQL Server errorlog. This can be any email address—not necessarily that of a pager. If a list of comma-separated email addresses is specified, the notification is sent to each address on the list.

IgnoreEntryOlderThan=300: This tells the script to ignore any errorlog entries recorded more than 300 minutes ago. This essentially says that as far as monitoring errorlogs is concerned, you don't care about any entries if they are that old. The option is useful when there's no previously saved status information to tell the script where to start scanning in the errorlog, such as when the script is run for the first time.

RemoveSavedStatusOlderThan=2: This tells the script to remove from the saved status file any exception entries that are older than two days. The function initializeStatus() uses this option to help initialize the status hash structure—which will be discussed shortly—when the script monitorErrorlogs.pl starts.

Each of the other four configuration categories specifies options for a particular type of exception.

Setting the Options for Configuration Exceptions

For configuration exceptions, you can set three options:

- AlertConfigErr=yes enables the script to monitor configuration exceptions. If this is set to no, the script ignores configuration exceptions.

- ConfigErrAlertInterval=50 instructs the script to send an alert on a configuration exception only when the previous alert for a configuration exception was sent more than 50 minutes ago.

- ConfigErrQuietTime=23-7 says that between 23:00 and 07:00, the script should suppress any alert caused by a configuration exception.

The script `monitorErrorlogs.pl` also uses these three options in the notification rule for alerting a configuration exception. The following code fragment in the function `alertErrorlogs()` implements this configuration rule:

```
# Rule for alerting a config error
# if 1. config error alert is enabled,
#    2. there is a config error,
#    3. it's not ConfigErr quiet time, and
#    4. Last config error alerted ConfigErrorAlertInterval minutes ago
# then  send ConfigErr alert
   my $configErrRef = $statusRef->{Exception}->{ConfigErr};
   if ( $configRef->{ALERTCONFIGERR} =~ /y/i and
       $configErrRef->{OK} == 0 and
       !dbaIsBetweenTime($configRef->{CONFIGERRQUIETTIME}) and
      (time() - $configErrRef->{LastAlertedTime})
                     > ($configRef->{CONFIGERRALERTINTERVAL})*60 ) {
          $ref = sendAlert($server, $ref, 'ConfigErr');
          next;
   }
```

The other three categories have similar options, and they're used similarly to implement their respective notification rules in the function `alertErrorlogs()`. Instead of belaboring what are essentially the same options for each category, the subsequent sections only highlight the unique options.

Setting the Options for the Errorlog Size Exception

For the errorlog size exceptions, you can set a size threshold. For instance, with `ErrorlogSizeThreshold=3000`, the script doesn't record any exception unless the errorlog is larger than 3,000 kilobytes.

Setting the Options for the SQL Server Error Exception

For the regular SQL Server errors with error numbers and severity levels, the script `monitorErrorlogs.pl` accepts two options to explicitly include or exclude certain groups of errors:

- `ExcludeSQLErrors=1608,17832,17824` tells the script to ignore the errors with these error numbers regardless of their severity levels.

- `IncludeSQLSeverities=17,18,19,20,21,22,23,24,25` instructs the script to alert only on the errors whose severity levels are on the list.

Both these options help reduce the number of nuisance alerts that may be caused by harmless SQL Server errors. The script implements these options in the function scanErrorlogs() as follows:

```
1.   # skip it if this error is on the exclusion list
2.   next if ($configRef->{EXCLUDESQLERRORS} =~ /\b$error\b/i);
3.
4.   #  if it's on the severity list
5.   if ($configRef->{INCLUDESQLSEVERITIES} =~ /\b$severity\b/i) {
6.       $statusRef->{ErrorlogOK} = 0;
7.       $exceptionRef->{SQLErr}->{OK} = 0;
8.       my $sqlErr = "$error\_$severity";
9.       $exceptionRef->{SQLErr}->{$sqlErr}->{Time} = $time;
10.      $exceptionRef->{SQLErr}->{$sqlErr}->{TimeStr} = $timeStr;
11.      $exceptionRef->{SQLErr}->{$sqlErr}->{ErrMsg} = $errMsg;
12.      print "   ***$errMsg\n";
13. }
```

Note that on line 2 and line 5 in this code fragment, the Perl regular expression symbol \b matches at the word boundary. This ensures that an error number such as 1702 captured from the errorlog doesn't match 702.

Why isn't there an option to exclude a SQL Server severity level or an option to include a SQL Server error? Bear in mind that there are a limited number of severity levels in total, so there's no need to have both an exclusion option and an inclusion option. For the error numbers, experience shows that for severity levels greater than 16, only a few error numbers should be explicitly ignored.

Setting the Options for Pattern-Matched Exceptions

Finally, for pattern-matched exceptions, you can set a list of OnPattern options. These options are distinguished from one another by postfixing each with a sequence number. The script monitorErrorlogs.pl doesn't care what these sequence numbers are as long as they're unique. Furthermore, you can specify as many of these OnPattern options as you want. Let's examine the two OnPattern options in Listing 11-4:

```
OnPattern01=/BACKUP failed.+database (SMD|RMD)\s/i, [75114@myTel.com]
OnPattern02=/Fatal error in database (?!(pubs|Northwind)\b)/i,[73056@myTel.com]
```

An OnPattern option has two parts—a Perl regular expression and a list of comma-separated email addresses enclosed in a pair of square brackets. Any errorlog entry matching the pattern causes an alert to be sent to each of the email addresses listed immediately after the regular expression. If an errorlog entry matches more than one OnPattern regular expression, an alert goes to all the email addresses associated with the matched patterns. If multiple errorlog entries match an OnPattern regular expression, only the last one is included in the alert.

In the preceding example, a backup failure message for the database SMD or the database RMD—and only for these two databases—would trigger an alert to be sent to the address 75114@myTel.com. Similarly, if a message containing the string Fatal error in database is written to the errorlog and pubs or Northwind doesn't immediately follow the string, the regular expression in OnPattern02 matches and consequently will trigger an alert to 73056@myTel.com.

Examining the Flow of the Script

The main body of the script monitorErrorlogs.pl in Listing 11-3 consists of the following steps.

The script first reads the configurations from the file into a data structure referenced by $configRef, and then it validates with the function validateConfig() that the key configuration options are properly specified.

If the status file exists, the script reads the previously saved errorlog monitoring status from the status file into the data structure $statusRef. This happens with the SQLDBA::Utility function dbaReadSavedRef() in the following code fragment from the main body of the script:

```
# read from the status file
my $statusRef = (-T $configRef->{CONTROL}->{STATUSFILE})
            ? dbaReadSavedRef($configRef->{CONTROL}->{STATUSFILE}) : {};
```

After both the configuration data structure and the status data structure are merged under a single reference $ref, the script calls the function initializeStatus() to initialize the status data structure for each exception category under each enabled SQL Server instance and removes status entries that are older than the threshold specified with the option RemoveSavedStatusOlderThan in the configuration file.

Next, the function scanErrorlogs() loops through all the errorlogs listed in the configuration file to scan for the specified exceptions and update the data structure $ref->{Status} accordingly along the way. The function scanErrorlogs() is where the bulk of the work happens.

When all the errorlogs have been scanned, the script now has the updated status data structure with the information on the exceptions found in the errorlogs. The script then calls the function `alertErrorlogs()` to examine the status data structure to do the following:

1. Decide whether any alerts should be sent

2. Actually send the alerts, if any

3. Update the status data structure to record the status of sending the alerts

Finally, the script saves the updated status data structure back to the status file by calling the SQLDBA::Utility function `dbaSaveRef()`, overwriting any content already in the file. The status file is now ready to be read when the script runs the next time.

Understanding the Two Key Data Structures

The key to understanding the script `monitorErrorlogs.pl` in Listing 11-3 is understanding these two data structures:

- The configuration data structure

- The status data structure

The former stores the configuration values read from the configuration file. Once populated, this data structure doesn't change and is carried throughout the script as `$ref->{Config}`. The latter—referenced as `$ref->{Status}`—is updated with the information read from the errorlogs. It's also updated to reflect the current notification status.

Exploring the Configuration Data Structure

Listing 11-5 is a sample of the configuration data structure for the configuration options in Listing 11-4. It shows only the `Control` section and the section for the SQL Server SQL1.

Listing 11-5. A Sample Configuration Data Structure

```
$ref->{Config} = {
    CONTROL => {
        DUTYPAGER    => '74321@myTel.com',
        SMTPSERVER   => 'mail.linchi.com',
        SMTPSENDER   => 'sql@linchi.com',
        ALERTLOGFILE => 'e:\\dba\\alertErrorlog\\Alert.log',
        STATUSFILE   => 'e:\\dba\\alertErrorlog\\Status.log'
    },
    'SERVER:SQL1' => {
        SQLERRORLOG => '\\\\SQL1\\e$\\mssql\\mssql\\log\\errorlog',
        DISABLED    => 'no',
        DBAPAGER    => '75114@myTel.com',
        IGNOREENTRYOLDERTHAN       => 600,
        REMOVESAVEDSTATUSOLDERTHAN => 2,

        ALERTCONFIGERR       => 'yes',
        CONFIGERRALERTINTERVAL => 60,
        CONFIGERRQUIETTIME   => '12-7',

        ALERTERRORLOGSIZE        => 'yes',
        ERRORLOGSIZETHRESHOLD    => 3000,
        ERRORLOGSIZEALERTINTERVAL => 120,
        ERRORLOGSIZEQUIETTIME    => '18-8',

        ALERTSQLERR          => 'yes',
        INCLUDESQLSEVERITIES => '17,18,19,20,21,22,23,24,25',
        EXCLUDESQLERRORS     => '1608,17832,17824',
        SQLERRALERTINTERVAL  => 5,
        SQLERRQUIETTIME      => '22-7',

        ONPATTERN01 => '/BACKUP failed.+database (SMD|RMD)\s/i,
                                        [75114@myTel.com]',
        ONPATTERN02 => '/Fatal error in database (?!(pubs|NorthWind)\b)/i,
                                        [73056@myTel.com]',
        ONPATTERNALERTINTERVAL => 2,
        ONPATTERNQUIETTIME     => '22-7'
    }
};
```

This data structure almost mirrors the options in Listing 11-4. If you've read other chapters of this book, you should already be familiar with this data structure, produced with the SQLDBA::Utility function dbaReadINI(). The configuration data structure is generic across scripts. The status data structure is more interesting—and better characterizes the script monitorErrorlogs.pl.

Exploring the Status Data Structure

Listing 11-6 is a sample of the status data structure for the SQL Server SQL1 at the time when the script finishes executing the function alertErrorlogs().

NOTE *This listing has been edited slightly for formatting purposes. Long strings, referred to by* ErrMsg, *are wrapped around to fit the page width. Also, the ellipse (...) is used in place of the real message text to keep the string short.*

Listing 11-6. A Sample Status Data Structure for SQL1

```
$ref->{Status}->{'SERVER:SQL1'} = {
    ErrorlogOK => '0',
    ErrorlogLastReadTime    => '1029178730',
    ErrorlogLastReadTimeStr => '2002-08-12 14:58:50.51',
    Exception => {
        SQLErr => {
            OK => '0',
            '15430_19' => {
                ErrMsg => '2002-08-12 14:58:50 Err: 15430, Severity: 19 on
                            SQL1. Limit exceeded for number of servers.',
                Time    => '1029178730'
                TimeStr => '2002-08-12 14:58:50.51',
                SendAlertOK => 1,
                LastAlertedTime    => '1029178738',
                LastAlertedTimeStr => '2002/08/12 14:58:58',
            },
            '1105_17' => {
                ErrMsg => '2002-08-12 14:58:50 Err: 1105, Severity: 17 on
                            SQL1. Could not allocate space for ...',
                Time    => '1029178790'
                TimeStr => '2002-08-12 14:59:50.32',
                SendAlertOK => 1,
```

```
                    LastAlertedTime    => '1029178791',
                    LastAlertedTimeStr => '2002/08/12 14:59:51',
                }
            },
        OnPattern => {
            OK => '1',
        },
        ErrorlogSize => {
            OK => 1
            ActualErrorlogSize => 10,
        },
        ConfigErr => {
            OK => 1
        }
    }
};
```

Let's examine this data structure in more detail. The hash record for each
server—for example, $ref->{Status}->{'SERVER:SQL1'} for SQL1—has four keys:

ErrorlogOK => '0' indicates that the script has detected one or more
exceptions during the scan. This is an overall status indicator. When the
script loops through the servers to decide whether to send an alert in
the function alertErrorlogs(), this indicator makes it easy to skip those
servers where the script didn't find any exception, in other words, with the
setting ErrorlogOK => '1'.

ErrorlogLastReadTime records the date/time—in epoch seconds—of the
last scanned entry in the errorlog. Next time, when the script runs, it skips
all the entries in the errorlog that are older than this date/time. For
instance, in Listing 11-6, only entries with a date/time later than
2002-08-12 14:58:50.51—which is the value of ErrorlogLastReadTime—are
considered new.

ErrorlogLastReadTimeStr contains the same information as
ErrorlogLastReadTime does but in a readable string format.

Exception references yet another hash record representing the exceptions
found. In this hash, the script stores information necessary for alerting
these exceptions.

Underneath the Exception hash key (for example, $ref->{Status}->
{'SERVER:SQL1'}->{Exception} in Listing 11-6) are four keys representing the
four exception categories:

- ConfigErr

- ErrorlogSize

- SQLErr

- OnPattern

When the script detects an exception in any of these four categories—
configurations, errorlog size, SQL Server errors, and pattern-matched exceptions,
the value of the OK hash key for that category is set to 0 along with the recorded
error message and the time stamp. In Listing 11-6, the script has detected
an error 15430 with severity level 19 and an error 1105 with severity 17 in the
errorlog on SQL1. It therefore records the two SQL Server error exceptions shown
in Listing 11-7.

Listing 11-7. A Sample Data Structure for SQL Server Error Exceptions

```
$ref->{Status}->{SQL1}->{Exception}->{SQLErr} = {
        OK => '0',
        '15430_19' => {
            ErrMsg => '2002-08-12 14:58:50 Err: 15430, Severity: 19 on
                         SQL1. Limit exceeded for number of servers.',
            Time    => '1029178730'
            TimeStr => '2002-08-12 14:58:50.51',
            SendAlertOK => 1,
            LastAlertedTime    => '1029178738',
            LastAlertedTimeStr => '2002/08/12 14:58:58',
        }
        1105_17 => {
            ErrMsg => '2002-08-12 14:58:50 Err: 1105, Severity: 17 on
                         SQL1. Could not allocate space for ...',
            Time    => '1029178790'
            TimeStr => '2002-08-12 14:59:50.32',
            SendAlertOK => 1,
            LastAlertedTime    => '1029178791',
            LastAlertedTimeStr => '2002/08/12 14:59:51',
        }
    };
```

The value of the hash key OK in Listing 11-7 is set to 0 to flag that a SQL Server exception is detected. This flag makes it easy to loop through the exception categories because the script needs only check the value of this key for each category without having to examine any more details. In this case, there's no exception detected for any of the other three categories, thus the value of their respective hash key OK is set to 1 by default.

When the function alertErrorlogs() applies the notification rule for SQL Server error exceptions and an alert is sent, the status data structure for SQL1 is updated to include the status of sending the alert (SendAlertOK) and the date/time when the alert is sent (LastAlertedTime and LastAlertedTimeStr).

Understanding Pattern-Matched Exceptions

Among the four exception categories monitored by the script monitorErrorlogs.pl in Listing 11-3, the pattern-matched exceptions are particularly interesting. This is a powerful feature because it allows a DBA to be notified of any errorlog entry that matches an arbitrary regular expression. Now, let's find out how the script monitorErrorlogs.pl implements this feature.

Note that there's always a danger that the specified pattern might not be a valid regular expression. You absolutely do *not* want an invalid regular expression to cause a run-time error that crashes your script. Furthermore, you don't want to repeatedly contend with an invalid pattern when matching every errorlog entry.

To this end, the function validateConfig() in Listing 11-3 includes code to verify whether an OnPattern option includes a valid regular expression and removes from the configuration data structure any OnPattern option that's not valid. The validateConfig() function also updates the configuration data structure so that the regular expression and the corresponding email address for a valid OnPattern are stored explicitly as separate hash values instead of being embedded in a string, as they are originally specified in the configuration file. For example, the data structure for the OnPattern options in Listing 11-4 now looks like the following—in this case, both patterns are valid regular expressions:[3]

```
$ref->{'Config'}->{'SERVER:SQL1'}->{'ONPATTERNO1'} = {
                REGEX => 'qr/BACKUP failed.+database (SMD|RMD)\s/i',
                EMAIL => [ 75114@myTel.com ]
    };
```

---

3. It would have been more optimal to store the compiled regular expressions under the hash key REGEX in the example. Unfortunately, the module Data::Dumper doesn't support the special reference returned by the quote regex operator qr//. Even though these scripts don't use Data::Dumper directly, I prefer to keep Data::Dumper available because it's such a useful tool for troubleshooting nested data structures and thus a good choice for storing the uncompiled regular expression strings.

```
$ref->{'Config'}->{'SERVER:SQL1'}->{'ONPATTERN02'} = {
           REGEX => 'qr/Fatal error in database (?!(pubs|NorthWind)\b)/i',
           EMAIL => [ 73056@myTel.com ]
};
```

In the function `validateConfig()`, the script first normalizes each of the specified patterns with Perl's quote regex operator `qr//` and then evaluates the string with the Perl's built-in `eval()` function. If there's no error, then the pattern is a valid regular expression. Otherwise, it's not a valid regular expression, and the pattern is removed from the configuration data structure.

 NOTE *Using the* `eval()` *function is a standard Perl technique for trapping errors that may otherwise be fatal.*

Then, in the function `scanErrorlogs()`, before it checks each errorlog entry to determine whether it's a critical SQL Server error, the script first calls the function `matchOnPattern()` to see whether the entry matches any of the specified regular expressions. If there's a match, the script sets the value of the `OK` key to 0 under `OnPattern`, for instance, `$ref->{Status}->{'SERVER:SQL1'}->{Exception}->{OnPattern}`. Listing 11-8 illustrates a sample of the data structure for recording a pattern-matched exception.

Listing 11-8. A Sample Data Structure for `OnPattern` *Exceptions*

```
$ref->{'Status'}->{'SERVER:SQL1'}->{Exception}->{'OnPattern'} = {
     'OK' => '0',
     'Backup failed for database RDM.' => {
          'ErrMsg' => '2002-08-13 00:01:08.30 OnPattern on SQL1
                        Error: 50000, Severity: 17, Backup failed for RDM.',
          'Time'    => '1029211268',
          'TimeStr' => '2002-08-13 00:01:08.30',
          'SendAlertOK' => 1,
          'LastAlertedTime'    => '1029211393',
          'LastAlertedTimeStr' => '2002/08/13 00:03:13 ',
          'EmailAddress' => [
                              '75114@myTel.com'
                            ]
     },
     'Fatal error in database RDM.' => {
```

```
    'ErrMsg' => '2002-08-13 00:01:21.39 OnPattern on SQL1
                Error: 50000, Severity: 19, Fatal error in database RDM.',
    'Time'    => '1029211281',
    'TimeStr' => '2002-08-13 00:01:21.39',
    'SendAlertOK' => 1,
    'LastAlertedTime'    => '1029211393',
    'LastAlertedTimeStr' => '2002/08/13 00:03:13 ',
    'EmailAddress' => [ '73056@myTel.com ' ]
  }
};
```

This data structure is similar to that for SQL Server error exceptions, illustrated in Listing 11-7. But instead of using the number and the severity level of an error in the hash key, an OnPattern exception is identified with the message text itself. In Listing 11-8, the error messages Backup failed for database RDM and Fatal error in database RDM are the two hash keys under $ref->{Status}-> {'SERVER:SQL1'}->{Exception}->{OnPattern}. The information recorded under these keys is similar to that recorded for a SQL Server error exception in Listing 11-7. The main difference is the presence of a list of email addresses referenced by the key EmailAddress. Later, the function alertErrorlogs() sends the OnPattern message—the value of the key ErrMsg in the same hash record—to each address on this list.

Because the message text is used as the hash key, by its very nature when the same messages are found in a scan, only the last one is recorded. Different messages in the errorlog may match the same regular expression. However, because they're different, their information will be recorded separately under different hash keys and therefore will result in different alerts.

Customizing the Script monitorErrorlogs.pl

Comprehensive as it may be in monitoring SQL Server errorlogs, the script monitorErrorlogs.pl in Listing 11-3 is far from complete. You can further improve the script in numerous ways. Experience has convinced me that I'll never be able to anticipate all the details of the monitoring requirements in my SQL Server environment, let alone anticipate those of your environments.

Customizing the script in Listing 11-3 most likely means adding another exception category. Let's see with an example what it takes to make the script monitor a new category of exceptions.

Assume that you'd like to be alerted when a SQL Server instance is restarted. How do you accomplish that? Not surprisingly, you can turn to the errorlog to tell when the instance is restarted. Numerous entries at the beginning of the SQL

Server errorlog are indicative of a freshly started SQL Server instance. The following is an example:

```
2002-08-18 20:53:26.74 server SQL Server is starting at priority ...
```

If the script is scheduled to run once every five minutes, you can look for this entry and check whether its time is within the last seven minutes or any number of minutes greater than five and smaller than 10. This is to guarantee that you receive at least one alert and at most two about the fact that the SQL Server instance was restarted.

To support alerting on a SQL Server restart, you can introduce a new exception category. Let's call it the *restart* category. You must make the following modifications to the script in Listing 11-3 to monitor exceptions in the restart category:

At the minimum, the configuration file should include the following options for the restart exception: `AlertRestart`, `RestartThreshold`, and `RestartQuietTime`. Only when `AlertRestart` is yes will the script check for any restart exception. A restart exception is detected if the SQL Server instance was restarted less than `RestartThreshold` minutes ago. The option `RestartQuietTime` specifies the time during which no alerts of the restart exception should be sent.

In the function `initializeStatus()`, you need to add code mimicking the initialization of the data structures for the `ConfigErr` and `ErrorlogSize` exceptions.

In the function `scanErrorlogs()`, you also need to add code to scan for restart exceptions and populate the data structure `$exceptionRef->{Restart}` if the instance was restarted more recently than `RestartThreshold` minutes ago.

In the function `alertErrorlogs()`, you again need to add code to implement the rule for alerting the restart exception. This code segment should mimic that for alerting a `ConfigErr` exception or an `ErrorlogSize` exception.

This chapter won't present the complete script that supports the monitoring of restart exceptions. Instead, this chapter leaves that as an exercise for you.

 NOTE *If you don't care about the ability to specify special notification requirements such as* `RestartQuietTime`, *you can simply use an* `OnPattern` *regular expression to capture the errorlog string that indicates the server is starting. That way, you don't need to modify any code.*

Monitoring Drive Space Shortage

SCENARIO

You want to be alerted when the free space on a disk drive on any of your SQL Servers drops below a critical threshold—say 200MB—so that you can take immediate measures to prevent the server from actually running out of disk space or misbehaving because of a disk space shortage.

A disk drive running low on free space isn't on the list of exceptions outlined at the beginning of this chapter. So why is it being discussed here?

It's true that monitoring disk drives for low free space is probably considered as proactive monitoring because you're monitoring something that's not yet a problem but is likely to be a problem if the trend continues. The primary motivation for discussing it in this section is to demonstrate the advantage of reusing the infrastructure for monitoring SQL Server errorlogs.

Alternatively, you can of course write a self-contained script to scan the servers and check the free space of each disk drive on every server. If the free space of a drive is smaller than the threshold, the script sends a notification to the DBA.

However, because you've already put in place the errorlog monitoring script `monitorErrorlogs.pl` in Listing 11-3, why not take advantage of it? You can translate many monitoring problems into a problem of writing appropriate messages to the SQL Server errorlog and then let the errorlog monitoring tool pick up the errors and send the alerts.

Monitoring disk drives that are running critically low on space is one such problem.

The script `alertDriveSpace.pl` in Listing 11-9 loops through a list of SQL Servers. For each, it executes the SQL Server extended stored procedure `xp_fixeddrives`, via Open Database Connectivity (ODBC), to list the local hard drives with their respective free space. If the free space of a drive is below a threshold value, the script raises a SQL Server error of severity level 18. The error is written to the errorlog and will then be caught by the script `monitorErrorlogs.pl` when it scans that errorlog or for that matter by any tool you may be using to monitor the SQL Server errorlog.

Listing 11-9. Alerting on the Critically Low Free Drive Space

```perl
use strict;
use SQLDBA::Utility qw( dbaReadINI dbaTime2str dbaStr2time );
use Win32::ODBC;

Main: {
   my $configFile = shift or printUsage();

   (-T $configFile) or
      die "***Err: specified config file $configFile does not exist.";

   # Read config file into $configRef
   my $ref = dbaReadINI($configFile);

   # check free drive space for each drive and alert accordingly
   $ref = checkFreeSpace($ref);
} # Main


####################
sub checkFreeSpace {
   my $ref = shift or die "***Err: checkFreeSpace() expects a reference.";

   foreach my $server (sort keys %$ref) { # loop through each server
      next if $server =~ /^control$/i;    # skip Control section
      next if $ref->{$server}->{DISABLED} =~ /^y/i; # skip disabled server
      # skip the server if its disk free space threshold is not properly set
      next unless $ref->{$server}->{FREESPACETHRESHOLD} =~ /^\d+/;

      # strip off the Server: prefix if any
      my ($instance) = $server =~ /^server\s*:\s*(.+)/i;
      $instance ||= $server;

      my $sql;
      my $connStr = "Driver={SQL Server};Server=$instance;" .
                         "Trusted_Connection=Yes;Database=master";
      my $db = new Win32::ODBC ($connStr);
      unless ($db) {
         print "***could not connect to server $instance.\n";
         next;
      };

      $sql = 'EXEC master..xp_fixeddrives';
      unless ($db->Sql($sql)) {
```

```perl
        while ($db->FetchRow()) {
          my ($d, $s) = $db->Data;
          $ref->{$server}->{FREEDRIVESPACE}->{$d} = $s;
        }
      }
      else {
        print "***executing $sql. ", Win32::ODBC::Error(), "\n";
      }

      # loop through the drives to decide whether to alert
      foreach my $drive (sort keys %{$ref->{$server}->{FREEDRIVESPACE}}) {
        if ($ref->{$server}->{FREEDRIVESPACE}->{$drive} <
                   $ref->{$server}->{FREESPACETHRESHOLD}) {
          $sql = "raiserror('$drive drive on $instance is below " .
                        $ref->{$server}->{FREESPACETHRESHOLD} .
                        "MB',18, -1) with log";
          unless ($db->Sql($sql)) {   # raise the error
            1 while $db->FetchRow();
          }
          else {
            print "***executing $sql.\n";
          }
        }
      }

      $db->Close();
      return $ref;
  }
} # checkFreeSpace


################
sub printUsage {
   print << '--Usage--';
Usage:
  cmd>perl alertDriveSpace.pl <Config File>

      <Config File>   Config file that specifies what servers to check
--Usage--
   exit;
} # printUsage
```

This script accepts a configuration file on the command line. The expected configuration file looks like Listing 11-10.

Listing 11-10. Configuration Options for Alerting on Low Drive Space

```
[Server:SQL1]
Disabled=no
FreeSpaceThreshold=500    # in MB

[Server:SQL2\APOLLO]
Disabled=no
FreeSpaceThreshold=200    # in MB
```

For each server identified with a section heading in the file illustrated in Listing 11-10, you can specify two options for this script: Disabled and FreeSpaceThreshold. If Disabled is set to yes, the script doesn't check the drive space on that server. FreeSpaceThreshold, not surprisingly, specifies the free space threshold in megabytes (MB) below which an alert will be sent. For instance, FreeSpaceThreshold=500 under [Server:SQL1] indicates that the free drive space threshold is 500MB for the server SQL1. You can schedule to run the script once every few minutes as follows:

```
cmd>perl alertDriveSpace.pl config.txt
```

With the configuration file in Listing 11-10, if a drive—for example, the E drive—is found to have less than 500MB of free space on SQL1, the script alertDriveSpace.pl logs the following error in its SQL Server errorlog:

```
2002-08-06 21:37:56.84 spid52 Error: 50000, Severity: 18, State: 1
2002-08-06 21:37:56.84 spid52 E drive on SQL1 is below 500MB.
```

In practice, there's no need to use a separate configuration file just for this script. It's better to share a configuration file used by some other SQL Server monitoring script, such as monitorErrorlogs.pl in Listing 11-3. As long as the option FreeSpaceThreshold is specified for a server, the script alertDriveSpace.pl will check the free space for each drive on that server and log an error in the SQL Server errorlog if the free space is below the threshold. The script will ignore any other options in the configuration file, which may be specified and used by other scripts.

Again, this script does *not* make any decision on whether an alert should be sent or actually send any alert. That's the job of the errorlog monitoring facility. The strategy of taking advantage of the available SQL Server errorlog monitoring infrastructure helps prevent you from reinventing the wheel and therefore keeps the script short and compact. It also helps curtail the proliferation of ad-hoc monitoring setups.

NOTE *As long as you carefully control what's being written to it, the SQL Server errorlog can conveniently serve as a central repository for all the DBA-related messages. For instance, instead of having each scheduled job include a specially customized mechanism for sending alerts, they can all simply raise appropriate SQL Server errors and leave the rest of the notification work to the errorlog monitoring infrastructure. This also makes it convenient to review the job-related error messages in a single place.*

Monitoring Availability: The Basic Version

SCENARIO
You want to be notified when your SQL Server machine becomes unreachable or when the connection attempt to a SQL Server instance fails.

Listing 11-3 presented a robust and comprehensive script for monitoring errors recorded in SQL Server errorlogs. The script is only concerned with what's in the errorlog, and it's completely oblivious of whether the SQL Server instance and its various components are functioning properly or functioning at all. The fact that you don't see any error in an errorlog doesn't mean that the state of the SQL Server instance is good. Perhaps nothing is written to the errorlog because SQL Server is hung.

In addition to monitoring the errorlog, you must also check that SQL Server is available along with various services it offers.

For now, let's assume that SQL Server availability means that a client can log into the SQL Server instance. SQL Server becomes unavailable either when the machine isn't reachable over the network or when the SQL Server instance isn't accepting any connection attempt for whatever reason.

To verify that the machine is reachable, you can ping its Internet Protocol (IP) address. However, because most of the application clients connect to the SQL Server instance name instead of its IP address, it's better to ping the server name. This helps test the network name resolution in the process. To verify that SQL Server is accepting client connections, you can try to actually log into the instance. As is often said, the proof of the pudding is in the eating.

In summary, you need to perform two availability checks: a reachability check and a SQL Server connectivity check. The next section explores alerting on more problems that may cause SQL Server to become less than completely available and expands the script to perform additional availability checks.

The key design objectives for the script to monitor SQL Server availability are twofold:

- To accurately and promptly detect that SQL Server isn't available

- To sufficiently notify the DBA of the unavailability with minimal redundancy in notification

To accomplish these two objectives, the script alertAvailability.pl in Listing 11-11 monitors SQL Server availability as follows:

1. The script runs from a job scheduler at a regular interval—about once every five minutes.

2. The script performs two availability checks on the SQL Server instance: First, it pings the machine using the Net::Ping module, and second, if the ping is successful, it attempts to connect to the SQL Server instance via ActiveX Data Objects (ADO).

3. If one of the availability checks fails, the availability status is set to bad, and a bad status counter is incremented to record the consecutive number of times the bad status is reported.

4. If both availability checks are successful, the availability status is set to good, and the bad status counter is reset to zero.

5. If the value of the bad status counter reaches three, the script sends a notification to the DBA.

6. The script saves the data structure representing the status of the availability monitoring to a text file to be used when the script runs the next time.

Listing 11-11 shows the script alertAvailability.pl to monitor the availability of a SQL Server instance.

Listing 11-11. Monitoring SQL Server Availability: The Basic Version

```perl
use strict;
use Getopt::Std;
use Win32::OLE;
use SQLDBA::Utility qw( dbaTimeDiff dbaSMTPSend dbaTime2str dbaStr2time
                        dbaSaveRef dbaReadSavedRef dbaIsBetweenTime );
use Net::Ping;

Main: {
   my %opts;
   getopts('S:a:s:m:r:q:h', \%opts);  # get the command-line arguments

   # check mandatory switches
   if (   $opts{'h'}
       or !defined $opts{S} or !defined $opts{a} or !defined $opts{s}
       or !defined $opts{m} or !defined $opts{r} ) {
       printUsage();
   }
   # put the command-line options in a more readable hash
   my $configRef = {
         SQLInstance   => $opts{S},
         SenderAccount => $opts{a},
         StatusFile    => $opts{s},
         SMTPServer    => $opts{m},
         DBAPager      => $opts{r},
         QuietTime     => $opts{q}
   };

   # read saved status from the status file, if any
   my $statusRef = (-T $configRef->{StatusFile}) ?
                     dbaReadSavedRef($configRef->{StatusFile}) : {};

   # merge the config hash and the status hash so that later steps only
   # need to pass a single reference
   my $ref = { Config => $configRef,
               Status => $statusRef };
```

```
        # Check availability
        $ref = checkAvailability($ref);

        # Decide whether to send an alert, and send the alert if necessary
        $ref = alertAvailability($ref);

        # Save status to the status file
        dbaSaveRef($configRef->{StatusFile}, $ref->{Status}, 'ref');
    } # Main

###########################
sub checkAvailability {
    my $ref = shift or
        die "***Err: checkAvailability() expects a reference.";
    my $server = $ref->{Config}->{SQLInstance};

    CheckHeartbeat: {
        if (isPingOK($server)) {                  # first ping the server
            $ref->{Status}->{Ping}->{OK} = 1;      # ping is good
        }
        else {
            $ref->{Status}->{Ping}->{OK} = 0;        # ping is not good
            $ref->{Status}->{Ping}->{LastFailed} = dbaTime2str();
            $ref->{Status}->{BadStatusCounter}++;  # increment bad status counter
            $ref->{Status}->{ErrMsg} = 'Failed to ping ' . $server;
            last CheckHeartbeat;
        }

        if (isSQLConnectOK($server)) {              # then test SQL connection
            $ref->{Status}->{SQLConnect}->{OK} = 1; # SQL connect is good
        }
        else {
            $ref->{Status}->{SQLConnect}->{OK} = 0; # SQL connect is bad
            $ref->{Status}->{SQLConnect}->{LastFailed} = dbaTime2str();
            $ref->{Status}->{BadStatusCounter}++;   # increment bad status counter
            $ref->{Status}->{ErrMsg} = 'Failed to connect to ' . $server;
            last CheckHeartbeat;
        }
    } # CheckHeartbeat
```

```
    if ($ref->{Status}->{Ping}->{OK} and
        $ref->{Status}->{SQLConnect}->{OK}) {  # both ping and SQL connect is good
        $ref->{Status}->{OK} = 1;                # availability check is good
        $ref->{Status}->{BadStatusCounter} = 0; # reset the bad status counter to 0
    }
    else {                                       # availability check is not good
        $ref->{Status}->{OK} = 0;
    }
    return $ref;
} # checkAvailability


####################
sub isPingOK {
    my $server = shift or
        die "***Err: IsPingOK() expects a server name.";

    $server =~ s/\\.+$//;   # remove the instance name, if any

    my $p = Net::Ping->new("icmp");    # ICMP ping
    my $r = $p->ping($server, 2);      # 2 second timeout
    $p->close();
    return $r;
} # IsPingOK


######################
sub isSQLConnectOK {
    my $server = shift or
        die "***Err: IsSQLConnectOK() expects a server name.";

    my $conn = Win32::OLE->new('ADODB.Connection');  # use ADO
    $conn->{ConnectionTimeout} = 2;                  # 2 second timeout
    $conn->Open("Driver={SQL Server};Server=$server;Trusted_Connection=yes");
    my $err = Win32::OLE->LastError();
    $conn->Close();
    $err ? return 0 : return 1;    # if there is no error, it's good
} # isSQLConnectOK


#########################
sub alertAvailability {
    my $ref = shift or die "***Err: alertAvailability() expects a reference.";

    my @recipients = ($ref->{Config}->{DBAPager});  # set recipient to DBAPager
    $ref->{Status}->{AlertSent} = 0; # assume nothing is sent
```

```perl
        # if there is an availability problem and is not quiet time
        # send an alert
        if ($ref->{Status}->{OK} == 0 and              # availability is not good
            $ref->{Status}->{BadStatusCounter} > 2 and   # not good for > 2 times
            !dbaIsBetweenTime($ref->{Config}->{QuietTime})) { # not in quiet time
            if (dbaSMTPSend($ref->{Config}->{SMTPServer},   # send it via SMTP mail
                         \@recipients,
                         $ref->{Config}->{SenderAccount},
                         undef,
                         $ref->{Status}->{ErrMsg})) {        # send msg in the header
                $ref->{Status}->{AlertSent} = 1;            # successfully sent
                $ref->{Status}->{LastAlertSent} = dbaTime2str();
                $ref->{Status}->{BadStatusCounter} = 0;     # reset to 0

                printf "%s  %s Sent to %s\n", dbaTime2str(),
                          $ref->{Status}->{ErrMsg}, $ref->{Config}->{DBAPager};
            }
        }
    return $ref;
} # alertAvailability


##################
sub printUsage {
    print << '--Usage--';
Usage:
    cmd>perl alertAvailability.pl [-h] -S <instance>
                                       -a <sender account>
                                       -s <status file>
                                       -m <SMTP server>
                                       -r <recipient>
                                       -q <quiet time>

        -h    print this usage info
        -S    SQL Server instance
        -a    Sender account
        -s    status log file to save the current availability status
        -m    SMTP mail server
        -r    alert recipient
        -q    quiet time
--Usage--
    exit;
} # printUsage
```

If you want to monitor the SQL Server instance SQL1 and send alerts to dba@myTel.com, you can schedule to run the script alertAvailability.pl in Listing 11-11 as follows (all should be on a single command line):

```
cmd>perl alertAvailability.pl -S NJSQL01 -a sql@linchi.com -s status.log
                       -m smtp.linchi.com -r dba@myTel.com -q 22-7
```

Table 11-3 describes all the command-line arguments accepted by the script alertAvailability.pl.

Table 11-3. Command-Line Parameters for the Script in Listing 11-11

PARAMETER	DESCRIPTION
-S <SQL Server name>	Specifies the name of the SQL Server instance to be checked for availability.
-s <Status file>	The file to which the availability monitoring status will be saved.
-r <Recipient>	The email address of the alert recipient.
-m <SMTP server>	The SMTP mail server.
-a <SMTP account>	Specifies the account of the SMTP email sender.
-q <Quiet time>	Specifies a period of time—in the format of hh-hh—in which no alerts will be sent, where hh is between 1 and 24, inclusive.
-h	When specified, the script only prints out the usage information.

The data structure used throughout the script is referenced by the variable $ref. The command-line arguments are kept in the hash record referenced by $ref->{Config}. This hash record is intuitive because its keys mirror the command-line options.

The data structure referenced by $ref->{Status} is more interesting. The script alertAvailability.pl in Listing 11-11 updates this data structure in the functions checkAvailability() and alertAvailability(). The data structure represents the status of availability monitoring. Listing 11-12 illustrates a sample of this data structure.

Listing 11-12. A Sample Status Data Structure `$ref->{Status}`

```
$ref = {Status} = {
        OK => '0',
        ErrMsg => 'Failed to connect to SQL1',
        BadStatusCounter => '2',
        AlertSent => '0',
        LastAlertSent => '2002/08/18 00:52:07 ',
        SQLConnect => {
                        OK => '0'
                        LastFailed => '2002/08/19 00:52:36 ',
        },
        Ping => {
                OK => 1
        }
};
```

Table 11-4 describes the keys used to record the availability status of a SQL Server instance:

Table 11-4. The Keys of the Hash Record `$ref->{Status}`

KEY	DESCRIPTION
OK	A value of 0 indicates that one of the availability checks failed, whereas a value of 1 shows that both availability checks succeeded.
ErrMsg	The value is updated with the message from the latest failed availability check. This message will be sent if an alert is deemed necessary.
BadStatusCounter	Number of consecutive times an availability check has failed. It's reset to 0 if an availability check finds no problem.
AlertSent	A value of 1 indicates that an alert is sent successfully during the current run of the script, and 0 indicates no alert is sent during this run.
LastAlertSent	Time when the last alert is sent.
SQLConnect	A reference to a hash recording the status of the SQL Server connectivity check.
Ping	A reference to a hash recording the status of the reachability check.

Before the script exits its main body, it calls the SQLDBA::Utility function dbaSaveRef() to write the data structure $ref->{Status} to the status file—specified on the command line with parameter -s—for the script alertAvailability.pl to read when the script runs the next time.

In the status data structure $ref->{Status}, the only information that's required is $ref->{Status}->{BadStatusCounter}, which records the number of consecutive times the availability check has failed. When this fails three times, the alertAvailability() function sends an alert if the other alert conditions are also met. As is the case in the other scripts in this chapter, it's convenient to save and read the entire status data structure.

The function isPingOK() and the function isSQLConnectOK() perform two availability checks. The former uses the Perl module Net::Ping to test for reachability by sending an Internet Control Message Protocol (ICMP) echo message to the remote host. The following code fragment reproduced from Listing 11-11 implements the function isPingOK():

```
###############
sub isPingOK {
    my $server = shift or
      die "***Err: IsPingOK() expects a server name.";

    $server =~ s/\\.+$//;   # remove the instance name, if any

    my $p = Net::Ping->new("icmp");   # ICMP ping
    my $r = $p->ping($server, 2);      # 2 second timeout
    $p->close();
    return $r;
} # IsPingOK
```

The function isSQLConnectOK() tries to establish a trusted connection to the SQL Server instance through ADO using the SQL Server ODBC driver.

The function alertAvailability() implements the following notification rule:

```
If    (1) one of the availability checks fails,
      (2) the availability checks have failed for more than two consecutive
          times, and it is not in the quiet time period
Then  send an alert.
```

It's no accident to insist that the availability check must have failed three consecutive times before an alert is sent. This number came out of using such a script in practice for an extended time. The primary motivation is to minimize the number of nuisance alerts that may be caused by a variety of network problems or hiccups without unduly prolonging the time it takes to get notified.

Monitoring Availability: The Robust Version

> **SCENARIO**
> *In addition to checking whether the server can be reached and the SQL Server instance is accepting client connections, you want to be notified when a database becomes unusable or one of the SQL Server support services becomes unresponsive on any SQL Server instances in your environment.*

Let's see how you can make the script in Listing 11-11 more robust and comprehensive for monitoring SQL Server availability.

Improving the Availability Monitoring

There's plenty of room for improvement. In a nutshell, you need to be able to monitor multiple servers, you need more comprehensive availability checking, you need the script to be more customizable, you want to minimize the number of nuisance alerts, and you want better alert logging.

Monitoring Multiple SQL Server Instances

The script `alertAvailability.pl` in Listing 11-11 monitors only one SQL Server instance. To monitor multiple SQL Server instances, you can call the script multiple times in a batch file, each monitoring a separate instance. Although this is a workable solution, it quickly becomes difficult to manage as the number of instances increases.

Enabling More Availability Checks

For a DBA, the availability of the database service to the customers is more than a server that can be pinged and a SQL Server instance that accepts client connections. You have to ensure that the databases are usable and that the SQL Server Agent is running. Optionally, you may want to check that the SQL Mail is functioning, if you support SQL Mail in your environment.

Customizing Availability Checks

You need to be able to specify which of the availability checks should be performed for a given SQL Server instance. It's reasonable to expect that you always want to maintain the server reachability and the connectivity to the SQL Server instance. But it doesn't make sense to insist that all the databases be usable on every instance. A database may be in the middle of a restore on a standby server and therefore can't be queried. Also, a database may be taken offline on purpose. In either case, you don't want to be alerted because the database isn't available.

Keeping the Number of Alerts Under Control

To avoid being flooded with alerts on the availability of the same instance, you can set a minimum alert interval so that another alert for the same instance won't be sent for at least this amount of time.

Logging Alerts

Having a history of all the alerts that the script has sent is useful in reviewing the availability of the SQL Server instances. It's also useful for troubleshooting purposes. Every time the script sends an alert, it should record an entry in a log file.

Creating a Robust Script for Monitoring Availability

The script monitorAvailability.pl in Listing 11-13 incorporates the previous improvements.

Listing 11-13. Monitoring SQL Server Availability: The Robust Version

```
use strict;
use Win32::OLE;
use Net::Ping;
use SQLDBA::Utility qw( dbaSMTPSend dbaTime2str dbaSaveRef dbaInStrList
                        dbaReadSavedRef dbaIsBetweenTime dbaReadINI );

Main: {
   my $configFile = shift or printUsage();
   (-T $configFile) or
        die "***Err: specified config file $configFile does not exist.";
```

```
    # Read config file into $configRef
    my $configRef = dbaReadINI($configFile);

    # validate config options and set defaults
    $configRef = validateConfig($configRef);

    # read the saved status info from the status file, if available
    my $statusRef = (-T $configRef->{CONTROL}->{STATUSFILE})
                    ? dbaReadSavedRef($configRef->{CONTROL}->{STATUSFILE})
                    : {};
    # merge the config data structure and the status data structure
    my $ref = { Config => $configRef,
                Status => $statusRef };

    # Check availability
    $ref = checkAvailability($ref);

    #  Decide whether to send an alert, and sends the alert, if necessary
    $ref = alertAvailability($ref);

    # Save status to the status file for the next invocation
    dbaSaveRef($configRef->{CONTROL}->{STATUSFILE}, $ref->{Status}, 'ref');
} # Main

###################
sub validateConfig {
    my $configRef = shift or die "***Err: validateConfig() expects a reference.";

    foreach my $server (sort keys %{$configRef}) {
        next if $server =~ /^control$/i;  # skip Control section
        next if $configRef->{$server}->{DISABLED} =~ /^y/i; # skip disabled server

        # only validate AlertInteval option (for demo purpose)
        if (!defined $configRef->{$server}->{ALERTINTERVAL} or
            $configRef->{$server}->{ALERTINTERVAL} !~ /\d+/) {
            $configRef->{$server}->{ALERTINTERVAL} = 20; # default to 20 minutes
        }
    }
    return $configRef;
} # validateConfig
```

```perl
#######################
sub checkAvailability {
    my $ref = shift or die "***Err: checkAvailability() expects a reference.";

    foreach my $server (sort keys %{$ref->{Config}}) {
        next if $server =~ /^control$/i;  # skip Control section
        next if $ref->{Config}->{$server}->{DISABLED} =~ /^y/i; # skip the disabled

        # strip off the Server: prefix if necessary
        my ($instance) = $server =~ /^SERVER\s*:\s*(.+)$/i;
        # These two structures are to shorten the expressions
        # in the rest of the function
        my $statusRef = $ref->{Status}->{$server};
        my $configRef = $ref->{Config}->{$server};

        CHECK_HEALTH: {
            # Ping the server
            if ($configRef->{CHECKPING} =~ /^y/i and       # ping enabled
                !isPingOK($instance)) {                     # but failed to ping
                $statusRef->{Ping}->{OK} = 0;               # flag it as no good
                $statusRef->{Ping}->{LastFailed} = dbaTime2str();
                $statusRef->{BadStatusCounter}++;  # increment bad status counter
                $statusRef->{ErrMsg} = 'Failed to ping ' . $instance;
                last CHECK_HEALTH;
            }
            else {
                $statusRef->{Ping}->{OK} = 1;               # ping is good
            }
            # login to the instance
            if ($configRef->{CHECKCONNECTION} =~ /^y/i and # enabled
                !isSQLConnectOK($instance)) {               # but failed to connect
                $statusRef->{SQLConnect}->{OK} = 0;         # flag it as no good
                $statusRef->{SQLConnect}->{LastFailed} = dbaTime2str();
                $statusRef->{BadStatusCounter}++;    # increment the bad status cntr
                $statusRef->{ErrMsg} = 'Failed to connect to ' . $instance;
                last CHECK_HEALTH;
            }
            else {
                $statusRef->{SQLConnect}->{OK} = 1;      # SQL connect is good
            }
            #check DB status
            if ($configRef->{CHECKDATABASES} =~ /^y/i) {  # enabled
                my $DBStatusRef = getDBStatus($ref, $server);
                if (!$DBStatusRef->{OK}) {                  # but some db is no good
```

```
                    $statusRef->{DB}->{OK} = 0;            # flag it as no good
                    $statusRef->{DB}->{LastFailed} = dbaTime2str();
                    $statusRef->{BadStatusCounter}++; # increment the bad status cntr
                    $statusRef->{ErrMsg} = $DBStatusRef->{DBMsg};
                    $statusRef->{DB}->{DBMsg} = $DBStatusRef->{DBMsg};
                    last CHECK_HEALTH;
                }
                else {
                    $statusRef->{DB}->{OK} = 1;    # all databases are good
                }
            }
            else {
                $statusRef->{DB}->{OK} = 1; # if not enabled, default db to good
            }
            # Check SQLAgent
            if ($configRef->{CHECKSQLAGENT} =~ /^y/i and  # enabled
                !isSQLAgentOK($instance)) {                # but not running
                $statusRef->{SQLAgent}->{OK} = 0;          # flag it as no good
                $statusRef->{SQLAgent}->{LastFailed} = dbaTime2str();
                $statusRef->{BadStatusCounter}++;  # increment bad status counter
                $statusRef->{ErrMsg} = "SQLAgent on $instance is not running";
                last CHECK_HEALTH;
            }
            else {
                $statusRef->{SQLAgent}->{OK} = 1;    # SQLAgent is good
            }
            # Check SQL Mail
            if ($configRef->{CHECKSQLMAIL} =~ /^y/i and  # enabled
                !isSQLMailOK($instance)) {                # but not working
                $statusRef->{SQLMail}->{OK} = 0;          # flag it as no good
                $statusRef->{SQLMail}->{LastFailed} = dbaTime2str();
                $statusRef->{BadStatusCounter}++;   # increment bad status counter
                $statusRef->{ErrMsg} = "SQLMail on $instance is not running";
                last CHECK_HEALTH;
            }
            else {
                $statusRef->{SQLMail}->{OK} = 1; # SQLMail is good
            }
        }   # CHECK_HEALTH

        # Now update the overall status
        if ( $statusRef->{Ping}->{OK}        and
             $statusRef->{SQLConnect}->{OK} and
             $statusRef->{SQLAgent}->{OK}    and
```

```
                $statusRef->{SQLMail}->{OK}      and
                $statusRef->{DB}->{OK}) {
            $statusRef->{OK} = 1;                  # overall status flag is good
            $statusRef->{BadStatusCounter} = 0;   # reset the bad status counter
        }
        else {
            $statusRef->{OK} = 0;   # flag the overall status as bad
        }
    }
    return $ref;
} # checkAvailability


###############
sub isPingOK {
    my $server = shift or die "***Err: IsPingOK() expects a server name.";
    $server =~ s/\\.+$//;  # remove the instance name, if any

    my $p = Net::Ping->new("icmp");  # ICMP ping
    my $r = $p->ping($server, 2);     # 2 second timeout
    $p->close();
    return $r;
} # IsPingOK


#######################
sub isSQLConnectOK {
    my $server = shift or die "***Err: IsSQLConnectOK() expects a server name.";

    my $conn = Win32::OLE->new('ADODB.Connection') or return 0;
    $conn->{ConnectionTimeout} = 2;    # 2 second timeout is hard coded
    $conn->Open("Driver={SQL Server};Server=$server;Trusted_Connection=yes");
    my $state = $conn->{State};
    $conn->Close();
    return $state;
} # isSQLConnectOK


#####################
sub isSQLAgentOK {
    my $server = shift or die "***Err: isSQLAgentOK() expects a server name.";

    my ($serverName, $instanceName) = $server =~ /^([^\\]+)\\([^\\]+)$/i;
    my $conn = Win32::OLE->new('ADODB.Connection') or return 0;
    $conn->{ConnectionTimeout} = 2;
    $conn->Open("Driver={SQL Server};Server=$server;Trusted_Connection=yes");
```

```perl
   my $rc = 0;
   my $sql = q/EXEC master..xp_cmdshell 'net start'/;
   my $rs = $conn->Execute($sql);
   if ($rs) {
      while ( !$rs->{EOF} ) {
         my $info = $rs->Fields('output')->{Value};
            if (! $instanceName) {
               $rc = 1 if $info =~ /(SQLExec|SQLServerAgent)/i;
            }
            else {
               $rc = 1 if $info =~ /SQLAgent\$$instanceName/i;
            }
         $rs->MoveNext();
      }
      $rs->Close;
   }
   $conn->Close;
   return $rc if $rc;
} # isSQLAgentOK


####################
sub isSQLMailOK {
   my $server = shift or die "***Err: isSQLMailOK() expects a server name.";

   my $conn = Win32::OLE->new('ADODB.Connection') or return 0;
   $conn->{ConnectionTimeout} = 2;
   $conn->Open("Driver={SQL Server};Server=$server;Trusted_Connection=yes");

   my $rc = 0;
   my $sql = q/ DECLARE @rc int
               SET NOCOUNT ON
               CREATE TABLE #tmp (a varchar(125) null)
               INSERT #tmp EXEC @rc = master..xp_findnextmsg
               SELECT 'output' = @rc/;
   my $rs = $conn->Execute($sql);
   if ($rs) {
      while ( !$rs->{EOF} ) {
         $rc = $rs->Fields('output')->{Value};
         $rs->MoveNext();
      }
      $rs->Close;
   }
   $conn->Close();
   return !$rc;
```

```perl
} # isSQLMailOK


####################
sub getDBStatus {
   my ($ref, $server) = @_;   # $server is expected to have SERVER: prefix
   my $configRef = $ref->{Config}->{$server};
   my $DBStatusRef = $ref->{Status}->{$server}->{DB};


   my ($instance) = $server =~ /^SERVER\s*:\s*(.+)$/i;


   my $conn = Win32::OLE->new('ADODB.Connection');
   $conn->{ConnectionTimeout} = 2;
   my $connStr = "Driver={SQL Server};Server=$instance; ";
      $connStr .= "Database=master;Trusted_Connection=yes";
   $conn->Open($connStr);
   if (!$conn->{State}) {
      $DBStatusRef->{OK} = 0;
      $DBStatusRef->{DBMsg} = "Failed to connect to $instance";
      return $DBStatusRef;
   }


   # get the database names first
   my @DB = ();
   my $sql = q/SELECT name FROM master..sysdatabases
                  WHERE name NOT IN ('pubs', 'model', 'NorthWind')
                     AND name NOT LIKE '%test%' /;


   my $rs = $conn->Execute($sql);
   if ($rs) {
      while ( !$rs->{EOF} ) {
         @DB = (@DB, $rs->Fields('name')->{Value});
         $rs->MoveNext();
      }
      $rs->Close;
   }
   else {
      $DBStatusRef->{OK} = 0;
      $DBStatusRef->{DBMsg} = "Problem executing $sql";
      return $DBStatusRef;
   }


   my $badDB = undef;
   foreach my $db (@DB) {
      $sql = qq/SET QUOTED_IDENTIFIER ON
```

```
                    SELECT count(*) FROM \"$db\"..sysobjects
                      WHERE name = 'sysobjects'/;
        # construct a list of databases that cannot be queried
        unless ($rs = $conn->Execute($sql)) {
            my $dbErr = 'Msg: ' . Win32::OLE->LastError();
            # check whether Offline mode is excluded from alerting
            next if ($dbErr =~ /Database.+is\s+offline/is and
                     dbaInStrList($db, $configRef->{EXCLUDEOFFLINE}));
            # check whether Loading mode is excluded from alerting
            next if ($dbErr =~ /Database.+is\s+in.+\s+restore/is and
                     dbaInStrList($db, $configRef->{EXCLUDELOADING}));
            $badDB .= " $db";
        }
    }
    if ($badDB) {
        $DBStatusRef->{OK} = 0;
        $DBStatusRef->{DBMsg} = "Problem querying database(s):$badDB";
        return $DBStatusRef;
    }
    $conn->Close();
    $DBStatusRef->{OK} = 1;
    return $DBStatusRef;
} # getDBStatus


#####################
sub alertAvailability {
    my $ref = shift or die "***Err: alertAvailability() expects a reference.";

    foreach my $server (sort keys %{$ref->{Config}}) {
        next if $server =~ /^control$/i;
        next if $ref->{Config}->{$server}->{DISABLED} =~ /^y/i;

        my ($instance) = $server =~ /^SERVER\s*:\s*(.+)$/i;
        # these two variables are to shorten the expressions
        my $statusRef = $ref->{Status}->{$server};
        my $configRef = $ref->{Config}->{$server};

        my @receivers = split (/[;,\s]+/, $configRef->{DBAPAGER});
        # if the pagers are not specified for the server, use the DutyPager
        # as the default
        @receivers = ($ref->{Config}->{CONTROL}->{DUTYPAGER}) unless @receivers;
```

```
        # if there is a problem for more than two consecutive times,
        # and it is not quiet time,
        # and it's been longer than the AlertInterval since an alert was last sent
        # send an alert
        if ($statusRef->{OK} == 0 and      # status flag is good
            $statusRef->{BadStatusCounter} > 2 and # bad status counter > 2
            !dbaIsBetweenTime($ref->{Config}->{QuietTime}) and # not quiet time
            (time() - $statusRef->{LastAlertSentTime})  # minutes since last alert
                        > ($configRef->{ALERTINTERVAL})*60 ) {

            if (dbaSMTPSend($configRef->{SMTPServer},
                        \@receivers,
                        $configRef->{SenderAccount},
                        undef,
                        $statusRef->{ErrMsg})) { # send msg in the mail header
                $statusRef->{AlertSent} = 1;       # send was good
                $statusRef->{LastAlertSentTime} = time();
                $statusRef->{LastAlertSentTimeStr} = dbaTime2str();
                $statusRef->{BadStatusCounter} = 0;  # reset bad status counter

                open(LOG, ">>$ref->{Config}->{CONTROL}->{ALERTLOGFILE}");
                printf LOG "%s  %s. Sent to %s\n", dbaTime2str(),
                            $statusRef->{ErrMsg}, $statusRef->{DBAPAGER};
                close(LOG);
            }
        }
    }
    return $ref;
} # alertAvailability


##################
sub printUsage {
    print << '--Usage--';
Usage:
   cmd>perl monitorAvailability.pl <Config File>
        <Config File>  file to specify config options for monitoring availability
--Usage--
    exit;
}
```

You can configure the behavior of the script monitorAvailability.pl in
Listing 11-13 by setting configuration options in a configuration file. Listing 11-14
is an example for two SQL Server instances, SQL1 and SQL1\APOLLO.

Listing 11-14. A Sample Configuration File for monitorAvailability.pl

[Control]
AlertLogFile=Alert.log
StatusFile=status.log
DutyPager=74321@myTel.com
SMTPServer=mail.linchi.com
SMTPSender=dba@linchi.com

[Server:SQL1]
Disabled=no
DBAPager=71234@myTel.com

CheckPing=yes
CheckConnection=yes
CheckSQLAgent=yes
CheckDatabases= yes
CheckSQLMail=no
QuietTime=18-8
AlertInterval=20

[Server:SQL1\APOLLO]
Disabled=no
DBAPager=75114@myTel.com

CheckPing=yes
CheckConnection=yes
CheckSQLAgent=yes
CheckDatabases=yes
CheckSQLMail=yes
QuietTime=24-6
AlertInterval=15
ExcludeLoading=RDM,UDM
ExcludeOffline=Survey

Table 11-5 describes the options you can specify in the Control section of a configuration file passed to monitorAvailability.pl.

Table 11-5. Options in the `Control` *Section for Availability Monitoring*

OPTION	DESCRIPTION
`AlertLogFile`	Every time an alert is sent, a log entry is written to the text file specified by this option.
`StatusFile`	The script persists the status data structure for the availability monitoring to this file.
`DutyPager`	This specifies the email address. Alerts goes to this address if the `DBAPager` option for the server isn't specified.
`SMTPServer`	This is the SMTP server that all the outgoing notification messages use.
`SMTPSender`	This is the SMTP account to identify the sender of the alert messages.

Under the section heading for each SQL Server instance, you can specify the options described in Table 11-6. All options are optional.

Table 11-6. Options for Each SQL Server Instance for Availability Monitoring

OPTION	DESCRIPTION
`Disabled`	If this is set to yes, this SQL Server instance won't be checked for availability.
`DBAPager`	All notifications will be sent to this email address.
`CheckPing`	The script pings the server for reachability only if the option is set to yes.
`CheckConnection`	The script performs the connectivity check on the SQL Server instance only if the option is set to yes.
`CheckDatabases`	The script queries each database to verify whether the database is usable only if the option is set to yes.
`CheckSQLAgent`	The script tries to determine whether the `SQLServerAgent` is online only if the option is set to yes.
`CheckSQLMail`	The script checks whether SQL Mail is responsive only if the option is set to yes.

Table 11-6. Options for Each SQL Server Instance for Availability Monitoring (Continued)

OPTION	DESCRIPTION
QuietTime	This option expects two values in the format of hh-hh, where hh is between 1 and 24, inclusive. This option specifies that between these two hours, no alerts should be sent.
AlertInterval	This option expects an integer that specifies the number of minutes that must elapse before another alert on this SQL Server instance can be sent.
ExcludeLoading	This option expects a comma-separated list of database names. If any of these databases is in the loading mode, the database usability check won't flag it as unusable.
ExcludeOffline	This option expects a comma-separated list of database names. If any of these databases is offline, the database won't be flagged as unusable.

You can run the script monitorAvailability.pl from the command line as follows if the options are specified in the file config.txt in the current directory:

```
cmd>perl monitorAvailability.pl config.txt
```

Examining the Script monitorAvailability.pl

The main body of this script is nearly identical to that of the script in Listing 11-3. It consists of the following steps:

1. The script monitorAvailability.pl first reads the configuration options from the configuration file supplied on the command line and reads the status information—saved by the previous invocation of the script—from the status file specified with the option StatusFile in the configuration file. The script then combines the data structure for the configuration options and the data structure for the status information into a single data structure referenced by $ref. The script uses the data structure $ref throughout the rest of the script.

2. The script updates the status data structure $ref->{Status} with the function checkAvailability(), which performs the specified availability checks for each of the SQL Server instances listed in the configuration file.

3. Next, the function `alertAvailability()` inspects the updated `$ref` data structure, applies the notification rules to decide whether to send any alert, and actually sends the alert if one is deemed necessary. This function also updates the `$ref` data structure to record the information related to sending the alert.

4. Finally, the script calls the SQLDBA::Utility function `dbaSaveRef()` to save the status data structure `$ref->{Status}` to be used when the script runs the next time. Note that the key information to save for each SQL Server instance is the number of consecutively failed availability checks and the last time an alert is sent. These two pieces of information are used to help the script make better notification decisions.

Before moving on to a different topic, the next two sections cover two interesting issues in the design of the availability monitoring script `monitorAvailability.pl` in Listing 11-13.

Deciding What Error Conditions to Alert

First, in the function `checkAvailability()`, the code that performs the availability check resides inside a labeled block:

```
CHECK_HEALTH: {
    ...
}
```

As soon as an availability problem is detected, the script exits the `CHECK_HEALTH` code block without performing any more availability checks. It's clear that for each SQL Server instance only one availability error message is recorded and eventually sent in the alert. This raises an obvious question: What should be sent to the DBA when there are multiple availability error conditions? The function `checkAvailability()` has a simple design: The following error conditions are checked sequentially, and the first error condition encountered is sent; the rest are ignored:

1. Can the script ping the server?

2. Can the script connect to the SQL Server instance?

3. Can the script query the databases?

4. Is SQL Server Agent running?

5. Is SQL Mail running?

This has worked well in practice. But if you're wary of the danger that an important error condition is masked by a less important error, you may decide to notify the DBA of all the important errors instead of only one of them. This doesn't always make sense because there's often natural dependency among the error conditions. Obviously, when one error implies another, only the first one should trigger an alert. For example, when you can't ping a server, it's only annoying to also tell the DBA that you can't log into the SQL Server instance.[4]

However, it does make sense to send two alerts when the SQL Server Agent stops running and a database becomes unusable at the same time. Each of the two availability problems has different implications for the DBA, and there's no apparent dependency between them.

Detecting Database Availability

The second point of interest is how to detect that a database has become unusable. The work happens in the function getDBStatus(). To determine whether the query has run into any problem, the function checks the ADO resultset and the error condition returned by executing the following query from the master database:

```
SET QUOTED_IDENTIFIER ON
SELECT count(*) FROM "<db>"..sysobjects
WHERE name = 'sysobjects'
```

where <db> is the name of the database to be checked. When the SQL Server instance fails to execute this query, the resultset from the ADO Execute method is undefined.

Things become more interesting when you need to exclude a database that's offline or in the loading mode from triggering an alert. To avoid having to explicitly deal with various versions of SQL Server, this script inspects the error message

---

4. This is usually true in a TCP/IP network, which is almost universally used these days.

returned from executing the query to determine whether the error is caused by the database being offline or in the loading mode. It helps to review the following code fragment from the function getDBStatus():

```
my $badDB = undef;
foreach my $db (@DB) {
    $sql = qq/SET QUOTED_IDENTIFIER ON
              SELECT count(*) FROM \"$db\"..sysobjects
              WHERE name = 'sysobjects'/;
    # construct a list of databases that cannot be queried
    unless ($rs = $conn->Execute($sql)) {
        my $dbErr = 'Msg: ' . Win32::OLE->LastError();
        # check whether Offline mode is excluded from alerting
        next if ($dbErr =~ /Database.+is\s+offline/is and
                dbaInStrList($db, $configRef->{EXCLUDEOFFLINE}));
        # check whether Loading mode is excluded from alerting
        next if ($dbErr =~ /Database.+is\s+in.+\s+restore/is and
                dbaInStrList($db, $configRef->{EXCLUDELOADING}));
        $badDB .= " $db";
    }
}
```

In this case, the script examines the error message returned from Win32::OLE->LastError(). Alternatively, you can inspect the ADO errors collection for the same error message patterns. Either would work. But it's easier to work with Win32::OLE->LastError() because there's no need to iterate through a Component Object Model (COM) collection, which is what you must do with the ADO Errors collection.

Monitoring SQL Server Cluster: The Basic Version

SCENARIO
Some of your SQL Server instances are running in a Microsoft failover cluster. You want to be notified when the SQL Server cluster has experienced a significant state change.

With the errorlog monitoring script monitorErrorlogs.pl in Listing 11-3 and the availability monitoring script monitorAvailability.pl in Listing 11-13, your toolset is comprehensive in terms of monitoring SQL Server exceptions. Well, at least that's true if you're monitoring stand-alone SQL Server instances.

When a SQL Server instance runs in a failover cluster, however, these scripts won't notify you when an instance has failed over to a different node or when a node has just gone down. There will be no critical errors in the errorlog for the errorlog monitoring script to catch, and the script `monitorAvailability.pl` won't report any outage if the instance comes up online quickly before the script runs the next time or when only one node isn't up.

Monitoring the Cluster Events

In addition to monitoring the SQL Server errorlog and the SQL Server availability, what should a DBA monitor when a SQL Server instance runs in a failover cluster? In other words, what changes in a cluster are significant enough that the DBA should be notified? This section discusses a script to monitor the following five cluster-specific events:

- The cluster isn't accessible.

- A cluster node is evicted from the cluster.

- The status of a cluster node isn't up.

- The status of a cluster group isn't online.

- A group has moved from one node to another.

Now, how do you detect these changes in a cluster? You can get information on the first four events in the previous list by simply querying the cluster. To ascertain whether a group has moved to a different node, you can resort to the tried-and-true trick of taking two snapshots of the current state of the cluster and then performing a comparison to see whether there's any difference between the two.

Choosing a Tool to Monitor the Cluster

There are two techniques to get a snapshot of the current state of the cluster nodes or groups. One is to parse the output of the command-line utility `cluster.exe`. If the name of the cluster is NYCLUSTER, after issuing the command, you'll obtain a result similar to the one shown in Listing 11-15.

Listing 11-15. Getting Cluster Node Status

```
cmd>cluster NYCLUSTER node

Listing status for all available nodes:

Node                      Node ID       Status
------------------------- ------------- ---------------------
NYCLSQLNODE1              1             Up
NYCLSQLNODE2              2             Up
```

This result is intuitive, which shows that both nodes of the cluster are up. If the status of any of the nodes isn't Up, the DBA should know. Likewise, in the following example, after issuing the command, you'll get a cluster group status report similar to what's shown in Listing 11-16.

Listing 11-16. Getting Cluster Group Status

```
cmd>cluster NYCLUSTER group

Listing status for all available resource groups:

Group               Node            Status
------------------- --------------- ---------
Cluster Group       NYCLSQLNODE1    Online
SQL Server          NYCLSQLNODE1    Online
```

In this case, the cluster has two groups. They're both online and currently both running on node NYCLSQLNODE1. The DBA should be notified if a group status isn't Online.

NOTE *The command-line utility* cluster.exe *comes with Windows 2000. You don't need to install anything.*

Another technique to get the status of a cluster is to use the COM automation interface provided by the Cluster Automation Object. This is a more robust approach because the programming interface is better defined and better documented than the output format of cluster.exe. With the latter, you have to study its various outputs to identify the text patterns, and there's no guarantee that the output format will remain the same when a new version of cluster.exe is released. Using the Cluster Automation Server becomes a necessity if the script needs to explore aspects of a cluster beyond simple node or group status. Although cluster.exe gives almost any information you want with respect to a cluster, the text output can be too messy to parse.

You'll see how to parse the output of cluster.exe, primarily to learn that you can take advantage of another command-line utility in your Perl scripts. The next section uses the Cluster Automation Server to retrieve information from a cluster.

Creating a Script to Monitor the Cluster Events

In addition, to highlight the key points, the script in Listing 11-17 monitors only one cluster with all the configuration options specified on the command line. This is similar to the improvements you've made to the SQL Server errorlog monitoring and SQL Server availability in the previous sections. This section is a sneak preview. The "Monitoring SQL Server Cluster: The Robust Version" section adds more features to monitor multiple SQL Server clusters and improve its robustness.

Listing 11-17 shows the script alertCluster.pl to monitor the events of the SQL Server cluster identified previously.

Listing 11-17. Monitoring SQL Server Cluster: The Basic Version

```
use strict;
use SQLDBA::Utility qw( dbaSMTPSend dbaTime2str dbaSaveRef dbaSetDiff
                        dbaReadSavedRef dbaSetCommon );
use Getopt::Std;

Main: {
   my %opts;
   getopts('C:s:r:a:m:', \%opts);

   ($opts{C} and $opts{a} and $opts{s} and $opts{m} and $opts{r}) or
          printUsage();

   my $configRef = {
          Cluster          => $opts{C},
          SenderAccount    => $opts{a},
          StatusFile       => $opts{s},
          SMTPServer       => $opts{m},
          DBAPager         => $opts{r}
   };
```

```perl
    # read saved status from the status file, if any
    my $statusRef = (-T $configRef->{StatusFile}) ?
                        dbaReadSavedRef($configRef->{StatusFile}) : {};
      # use a single reference in the rest of the script
      my $ref = { Config => $configRef,
                  SavedStatus => $statusRef };


    # get current status
    $ref = getStatus($ref);


    # check the current status and compare it with the saved one
    $ref = checkStatus($ref);


    #  Decide whether to send an alert
    $ref = alertStatus($ref);


    # Save status to the status file for the next time
    dbaSaveRef($configRef->{StatusFile}, $ref->{CurrentStatus}, 'ref');
} # Main


##################
sub printUsage {
    print << '--Usage--';
Usage:
  cmd>perl alertCluster.pl -C <cluster> -s <statusFile> -r <dbaPager>
                                     -a <senderAccount> -m <SMTPServer>

      -C <cluster>     Name of the cluster to be moitored
      -s <statusFile>  Name of the file to record the cluster status
      -r <dbaPager>    pager email address
      -a <sendAccount> Account of the sender on the SMTP server
      -m <SMTPServer>  SMTP server
--Usage--
    exit;
}


################
sub getStatus {
   my $ref = shift or
      die "***Err: getStatus() expects a reference.";

   my $statusRef;
   my $cluster = $ref->{Config}->{Cluster};
```

```perl
    # get node names and status with cluster node
    my $msg = `cluster $cluster node`;    # backtick operator
    my @status = split /[\n\r\f]+/, $msg;
    # skip to the result row
    1 while (shift @status) !~ /----/;    # the header

    # now @status only has the result rows
    unless (@status) {
        $msg =~ s/\s+/ /g;
        $msg =~ s/\s*$//;
        $statusRef->{OK} = 0;
        $statusRef->{AlertStatus}->{FailedQuery}->{Times} =
                $ref->{SavedStatus}->{AlertStatus}->{FailedQuery}->{Times} + 1;
        $statusRef->{AlertStatus}->{FailedQuery}->{Msg} =
                "cluster $cluster node. $msg.";
        $ref->{CurrentStatus} = $statusRef;
        return $ref;
    }

    foreach (@status) {
        my ($node, $status) = $_ =~ /^\s*(\w+)\s+\d+\s+(.+)/;
        $status =~ s/\s*$//;
        $statusRef->{ClusterStatus}->{Nodes}->{$node}->{Status} = $status;
    }

    # get group names and status with cluster group
    $msg = `cluster $cluster group`;     # backtick operator
    @status = split /[\n\r\f]+/, $msg;
    # skip to the result row
    1 while (shift @status) !~ /^----/; # the header

    unless (@status) {
        $msg =~ s/\s+/ /g;
        $msg =~ s/\s*$//;
        $statusRef->{OK} = 0;
        $statusRef->{AlertStatus}->{FailedQuery}->{Times} =
                $ref->{SavedStatus}->{AlertStatus}->{FailedQuery}->{Times} + 1;
        $statusRef->{AlertStatus}->{FailedQuery}->{Msg} =
                        "cluster $cluster group. $msg.";
        $ref->{CurrentStatus} = $statusRef;
        return $ref;
    }
```

```perl
    my $node_re = join('|', keys %{$statusRef->{ClusterStatus}->{Nodes}});
    foreach (@status) {
        my ($group, $node, $status) = $_ =~ /^\s*(.+)\s+($node_re)\s+(.+)/;
        $group =~ s/\s*$//;
        $statusRef->{ClusterStatus}->{Groups}->{$group}->{Status} = $status;
        $statusRef->{ClusterStatus}->{Groups}->{$group}->{Node} = $node;
    }
    $statusRef->{OK} = 1;
    $ref->{CurrentStatus} = $statusRef;
    return $ref;
}  # getStatus


##################
sub checkStatus {
    my ($ref) = shift or die "***Err: checkStatus() expects a reference.";
    my $savedRef = $ref->{SavedStatus}->{ClusterStatus};
    my $currentRef = $ref->{CurrentStatus}->{ClusterStatus};
    my $alertStatusRef;

    my @diff = ();
    my @savedNodes = keys %{$savedRef->{Nodes}};
    my @currentNodes = keys %{$currentRef->{Nodes}};
    my @savedGroups = keys %{$savedRef->{Groups}};
    my @currentGroups = keys %{$currentRef->{Groups}};

    # check if a node is not UP
    foreach my $node (@currentNodes) {
        if ($currentRef->{Nodes}->{$node}->{Status} !~ /^Up$/i) {
            $alertStatusRef->{NodeNotUp}->{Msg} .= "$node,";
            $ref->{CurrentStatus}->{OK} = 0;
        }
    }

    # check if a group is not online
    foreach my $group (@currentGroups) {
        my $status = $currentRef->{Groups}->{$group}->{Status};
        if ($status !~ /^Online$/i) {
            $alertStatusRef->{GroupNotOnline}->{Msg} .= "$group,";
            $ref->{CurrentStatus}->{OK} = 0;
        }
    }

    # check if a node is evicted
    if (@diff = dbaSetDiff(\@savedNodes, \@currentNodes)) {
```

```perl
        my $nodes = join(',', map {"'" . $_ ."'"} @diff);
        $alertStatusRef->{NodeEvicted}->{Msg} = $nodes;
        $ref->{CurrentStatus}->{OK} = 0;
    }

    # check if a group is moved to another node
    foreach my $group (dbaSetCommon(\@currentGroups, \@savedGroups)) {
        my $oldNode = $savedRef->{Groups}->{$group}->{Node};
        my $newNode = $currentRef->{Groups}->{$group}->{Node};
        if ($oldNode ne $newNode ) {
            $alertStatusRef->{GroupMoved}->{Msg} .= "$group: $oldNode->$newNode,";
            $ref->{CurrentStatus}->{OK} = 0;
        }
    }
    $ref->{CurrentStatus}->{AlertStatus} = $alertStatusRef;
    return $ref;
} # checkStatus


################
sub alertStatus {
    my $ref = shift or die "***Err: alertStatus() expects a reference.";
    return $ref if $ref->{CurrentStatus}->{OK};

    my $alertStatusRef = $ref->{CurrentStatus}->{AlertStatus};
    my @receivers = ( $ref->{Config}->{DBAPager} );

    foreach my $alertType (sort keys %{$alertStatusRef}) {
      next if (    $alertType eq 'AccessFailed'
                and $alertStatusRef->{AccessFailed}->{Times} <= 2);
      # tidy up the message
      $alertStatusRef->{$alertType}->{Msg} =~ s/,$//;
      $alertStatusRef->{$alertType}->{Msg}
                    = 'Cluster ' . $ref->{Config}->{Cluster} .
                      " $alertType: " . $alertStatusRef->{$alertType}->{Msg};
      # send via SMTP
      if (dbaSMTPSend($ref->{Config}->{SMTPServer},
                    \@receivers,
                    $ref->{Config}->{SenderAccount},
                    undef,
                    $alertStatusRef->{$alertType}->{Msg})) {
        $ref->{CurrentStatus}->{AlertSent}->{$alertType}->{OK} = 1;
        $ref->{CurrentStatus}->{AlertSent}->{$alertType}->{AlertSentTimeStr}
                       = dbaTime2str();
        printf "%s  %s. Sent to %s\n", dbaTime2str(),
```

```
                $alertStatusRef->{$alertType}->{Msg},
                $ref->{Config}->{DBAPager};
    }
    else {
        $ref->{CurrentStatus}->{AlertSent}->{$alertType}->{OK} = 0;
        $ref->{CurrentStatus}->{AlertSent}->{$alertType}->{AlertSentTimeStr}
                    = undef;
    }
  }
  return $ref;
} # alertStatus
```

Table 11-7 describes the command-line arguments accepted by the script
alertScript.pl in Listing 11-17.

Table 11-7. Command-Line Parameters for the Script in Listing 11-17

PARAMETER	DESCRIPTION
-C <Cluster name>	Specifies the name of the cluster to be monitored
-s <Status file>	Specifies the file to which the cluster status data structure will be saved and from which the saved status information will be read
-r <Recipient>	Specifies the email address of the alert recipient
-a <SMTP account>	Specifies the account of the SMTP email sender
-m <SMTP server>	Specifies the SMTP mail server

Studying the Cluster Alert Script

The first thing to notice about the script alertCluster.pl in Listing 11-17 is that it
really has nothing particular to do with SQL Server. In fact, it's devoid of any specific SQL Server knowledge. The script can monitor any Microsoft cluster server
irrespective of whether it includes a SQL Server virtual server.

Furthermore, when a cluster group includes a SQL Server virtual server and
the SQL Server is offline, the group will be marked partially offline or offline,
which will cause the script in Listing 11-17 to send a notification. If the SQL
Server availability is also being monitored—for instance, with the script in
Listing 11-13—the DBA will then receive two alerts, one from the cluster monitoring script and one from the availability monitoring script.

These redundant alerts may or may not be palatable to you. There are two schools of thought when it comes to deciding what to monitor and how to notify: the minimalist school and the paranoid school. The minimalist wants to keep the notification to the bare minimum without compromising the effectiveness, and the paranoid welcomes redundancy, treating redundant alerts as corroborating each other and fearing that skimping on alerts may result in an important alert being missed.

If you belong to the minimalist school, you can modify the following code segment in the function checkStatus() in Listing 11-17 to skip any cluster group containing a SQL Server virtual server:

```
# check if a group is not online
foreach my $group (@currentGroups) {
   my $status = $currentRef->{Groups}->{$group}->{Status};
   if ($status !~ /^Online$/i) {
      $alertStatusRef->{GroupNotOnline}->{Msg} .= "$group,";
      $ref->{CurrentStatus}->{OK} = 0;
   }
}
```

To find whether a cluster group contains a SQL Server virtual server, you need to enumerate the resources in the group and check each resource to determine whether its resource type is SQL Server service.

Another question about the script alertCluster.pl in Listing 11-17 is why it doesn't check the status of any cluster resources. From experiments with monitoring the status changes at the resource level in addition to the node level and the group level, I found that monitoring the resources of a cluster all too often results in overly redundant alerts and significantly complicates the coding of the script.

In addition, note the following:

- In a Microsoft failover cluster, any status change of an important resource almost always bubbles up to the group level.

- Critical resources such as SQL Server and SQL Server Agent are already being monitored, independent of the cluster in which they're running.

All these factors considered, there's little added value to monitor the resources in a cluster when the nodes and the groups are already being monitored.

Finally, notice how the error conditions are collected and alerts are decided. Listing 11-18 shows an example of the current status data structure. The function checkStatus() is responsible for populating this data structure.

Listing 11-18. A Sample Cluster Status Data Structure—Single Cluster

```
$ref->{CurrentStatus} = {
   OK => '0',
   ClusterStatus => {
      Nodes => {
             NYCLSQLNODE1 => { 'Status' => 'Up' },
             NYCLSQLNODE2 => { 'Status' => 'Paused' }
      }
      Groups => {
          'ClusterGroup' => {     # group named ClusterGroup
                Status => 'Online',
                Node    => 'NYCLSQLNODE2'
          },
           'MSSQL01' => {         # group named MSSQL01
                Status => 'Online',
                Node'=> 'NYCLSQLNODE1'
          },
           'MSSQL02' => {         # group named 'MSSQL02'
                Status => 'Partially Online',
                Node => 'NYCLSQLNODE1'
          }
      }
   },
   AlertStatus => {
      GroupNotOnline => {
            Msg => 'Cluster NYCLUSTER GroupNotOnline: MSSQL02'
      },
      NodeNotUp => {
            Msg => 'Cluster NYCLUSTER NodeNotUp: NYCLSQLNODE2'
      }
   }
};
```

In the hash record of $ref->{CurrentStatus}, there are three keys: OK, ClusterStatus, and AlertStatus. The hash key OK is an overall indicator of the cluster status. If it's set to 1, the cluster is in a good condition; there's no need to look at any more detail, and no alert is necessary. If it's set to 0, the function alertStatus() will go through the hash record

$ref->{CurrentStatus}->{AlertStatus} to send out an alert for each of the following keys, if its value is defined as follows:

- FailedQuery

- NodeNotUp

- NodeEvicted

- GroupNotOnline

- GroupMoved

In Listing 11-18, by inspecting the information in the hash record $ref->{CurrentStatus}->{ClusterStatus}, the script alertCluster.pl found two events: GroupNotOnline and NodeNotUp. Thus, there are two keys under $ref->{CurrentStatus}->{AlertStatus}, GroupNotOnline and NodeNotUp, to record these two events. The messages associated with these two keys will be sent.

Notice that the keys correspond to the five cluster events this section sets out to monitor. Given the nature of these events, it's possible that more than one of them are detected and recorded in the data structure. For instance, in a cluster, a group can be taken offline while another group is moved to a different node and one node is offline. As a result, the DBA may receive multiple alerts in a row, each on a different cluster event.

To determine whether a node is evicted or a group is moved, the script must compare the current cluster status with the previous cluster status. The previous cluster status is read from the status file and kept in the hash record $ref->{Saved-Status}. Its structure is the same as that of the current cluster status. The code fragment to find whether a node is evicted from the cluster is as follows:

```
# check if a node is evicted
if (@diff = dbaSetDiff(\@savedNodes, \@currentNodes)) {
    my $nodes = join(',', map {"'" . $_ ."'"} @diff);
    $alertStatusRef->{NodeEvicted}->{Msg} = $nodes;
    $ref->{CurrentStatus}->{OK} = 0;
}
```

If you're familiar with the Microsoft failover clustering, the script in Listing 11-17 is almost trivial. However, parsing the output of the utility cluster.exe deserves some explanation. The output of the command cluster node is easy to parse because it neatly conforms to a space-separated, three-column format after skipping the initial header and heading. None of the three columns allow space in its values.

The output of the command `cluster group`, however, can be tricky to parse. Even though its output still consists of three columns, a group name in the first column may contain any number of spaces. Fortunately, because the other two columns can't contain any space, you can get the last two columns first and leave the remainder—whatever it may be—to be the first column.

Monitoring SQL Server Clusters: The Robust Version

> **SCENARIO**
> *Instead of monitoring a single cluster, you need to monitor multiple SQL Server clusters.*

Monitoring multiple SQL Server clusters introduces a host of issues that you must consider. This topic reviews these issues and provides a Perl scripting solution to monitor the important state changes of multiple SQL Server clusters. The solution builds on the script `alertCluster.pl` in Listing 11-17.

Improving SQL Server Cluster Monitoring

The cluster monitoring script `alertCluster.pl` is more a proof of concept than a polished and full-featured implementation for production use. The script `alertCluster.pl` is lacking in the following areas: monitoring multiple clusters, managing configurations, and customizing cluster monitoring. Let's examine what can be improved in these areas in turn.

Monitoring Multiple Clusters

The script `alertCluster.pl` is implemented specifically for monitoring a single cluster. To monitor multiple clusters, you have to put this script in a batch file, calling it once for each cluster. This works with a small number of clusters and becomes unmanageable as the number of clusters increases. Instead of trying to make an inherently single-cluster monitoring tool cope with multiple clusters, you'd be better off with a tool that accommodates multiple clusters by design.

Managing Configurations

Specifying all the configuration options on the command line severely limits the number of options you can practically have. Centrally specifying the options in a configuration file is a better way to go.

Customizing Cluster Monitoring

It's cute to parse the output of the command-line utility `cluster.exe` for the cluster status information. However, when you want to customize the script to accommodate additional monitoring requirements, you often need to retrieve cluster information beyond the simple node and group status, and this approach becomes cumbersome. In most cases, you have to wade through a lot of irrelevant data in the text output to get to that specific piece of information. In addition, because the names for many common cluster constructs such as groups, resources, and resource types can have arbitrary characters including spaces, parsing the output can become rather unsightly. The script will be much easier to customize if you use Cluster Automation Server, which allows you to directly go to an object or a property with the information you want.

NOTE *If you're running Windows 2000, the Cluster Automation Server (`MSCLUS.DLL`) is part of Windows 2000, and you don't need to install anything. The best place to find information on programming with the Cluster Automation Server is the Windows Platform Software Development Kit (SDK). The information is also available at the MSDN site (`http://msdn.microsoft.com`).*

Creating a Script to Monitor Multiple SQL Server Clusters

With improvements in these areas, the script `monitorClusters.pl` in Listing 11-19 monitors multiple SQL Server clusters for the following seven cluster-related events:

- The cluster isn't accessible.

- A node is evicted from the cluster.

- The status of a node isn't up.

- The status of a group isn't online.

- A group moves from one node to another.

- A group isn't running on its preferred owner node.

- A group has been removed from the cluster.

The first five events are the same as the ones monitored by the script
alertCluster.pl in Listing 11-17. The requirement for monitoring whether a
group is running on its preferred owner node is a practical one. When you have
multiple SQL Server instances running in a cluster, a given instance is often
configured to run on a specific node—its preferred owner node—under normal
circumstances for performance and administrative purposes. Even though the
instance works on any node, you want to make sure it's on the preferred owner
node, if at all possible.

The script monitorClusters.pl in Listing 11-19 monitors multiple SQL Server
clusters for these seven events.

Listing 11-19. Monitoring SQL Server Clusters: The Robust Version

```perl
use strict;
use SQLDBA::Utility qw( dbaSMTPSend dbaTime2str dbaSaveRef dbaSetDiff
                        dbaReadSavedRef dbaSetCommon dbaInSet
                        dbaIsBetweenTime dbaReadINI );
use Win32::OLE qw(in);

Main: {
   my $configFile = shift;
   $configFile or printUsage();
   (-T $configFile) or
        die "***Err: specified config file $configFile does not exist.";

   # Read config file into $configRef
   my $configRef = dbaReadINI($configFile);

   # validate config options and set defaults
   $configRef = validateConfig($configRef);

   # read saved status information from the status file
   my $savedStatusRef =
        (-T $configRef->{CONTROL}->{STATUSFILE}) ?
         dbaReadSavedRef($configRef->{CONTROL}->{STATUSFILE}) : {};

   # merge the config data structure and the status data structure
   my $ref = { Config => $configRef,
               SavedStatus => $savedStatusRef };

   # get current status
   $ref = getStatus($ref);
```

```
    # check the current status and compare it with the saved one
    $ref = checkStatus($ref);

    #  Decide whether to send an alert, and send the alert, if any
    $ref = alertStatus($ref);

    # Save status to the status file
    dbaSaveRef($configRef->{CONTROL}->{STATUSFILE},
              $ref->{CurrentStatus}, 'ref');
} # Main


######################
sub validateConfig {
   my $configRef = shift or die "***Err: validateConfig() expects a reference.";

   foreach my $cluster (sort keys %{$configRef}) {
      next if $cluster =~ /^control$/i;
      next if $configRef->{$cluster}->{DISABLED} =~ /^y/i;

      if (!defined $configRef->{$cluster}->{ALERTINTERVAL} or
          $configRef->{$cluster}->{ALERTINTERVAL} !~ /\d+/) {
          $configRef->{$cluster}->{ALERTINTERVAL} = 15;  # set the default
      }
   }
   return $configRef;
} # validateConfig


#################
sub getStatus {
   my $ref = shift or die "***Err: getStatus() expects a reference.";

   my %nodeState  = ( -1 => 'Unkown',
                       0 => 'Up',
                       1 => 'Down',
                       2 => 'Paused',
                       3 => 'Joining' );
   my %groupState = ( -1 => 'Unkown',
                       0 => 'Online',
                       1 => 'Offline',
                       2 => 'Failed',
                       3 => 'PartialOnline',
                       4 => 'Pending' );

   foreach my $cluster (sort keys %{$ref->{Config}}) {
```

```perl
next if $cluster =~ /^CONTROL/i;
next if $ref->{Config}->{$cluster}->{DISABLED} =~ /^y/i;

my $statusRef;
my $savedStatusRef = $ref->{SavedStatus}->{$cluster};
my ($clusterName) = $cluster =~ /^CLUSTER\s*:\s*(.+)$/i;

my $clusRef = Win32::OLE->new('MSCluster.Cluster');
unless ($clusRef) {
   my $err = Win32::OLE->LastError();
   $statusRef->{OK} = 0;
   $statusRef->{AlertStatus}->{FailedQuery}->{Times} =
           $savedStatusRef->{AlertStatus}->{FailedQuery}->{Times} + 1;
   $statusRef->{AlertStatus}->{FailedQuery}->{Msg} =
           "Failed new('MSCluster.Cluster'). $err.";
   $ref->{CurrentStatus}->{$cluster} = $statusRef;
   return $ref;
};

$clusRef->Open($clusterName);
if (my $err = Win32::OLE->LastError()) {
   print "***unable to open $cluster. $err\n";
   $statusRef->{OK} = 0;
   $statusRef->{AlertStatus}->{FailedQuery}->{Times} =
           $savedStatusRef->{AlertStatus}->{FailedQuery}->{Times} + 1;
   $statusRef->{AlertStatus}->{FailedQuery}->{Msg} =
           "Failed open($clusterName). $err.";
   $ref->{CurrentStatus}->{$cluster} = $statusRef;
   next;
}

# loop throught the Nodes collection
foreach my $node (in ($clusRef->Nodes)) {
   next unless $node;
   $statusRef->{ClusterStatus}->{Nodes}->{$node->{Name}}->{Status}
                   = $nodeState{$node->{State}};
}

# loop through the ResourceGroups collection
foreach my $group (in ($clusRef->ResourceGroups)) {
   next unless $group;
   my $grpRef = $statusRef->{ClusterStatus}->{Groups}->{$group->{Name}};
   $grpRef->{Status} = $groupState{ $group->{State} };
   $grpRef->{Node} = $group->{OwnerNode}->{Name};
```

```
            # loop through the PreferredOwnerNodes collection
            foreach my $preferredNode (in ($group->{PreferredOwnerNodes})) {
                next unless $preferredNode;
                push @{$grpRef->{PreferredOwnerNodes}},
                    $preferredNode->{Name};
            }
            $statusRef->{ClusterStatus}->{Groups}->{$group->{Name}} = $grpRef;
        }


        $statusRef->{OK} = 1;
        $ref->{CurrentStatus}->{$cluster} = $statusRef;
    }
    return $ref;
}  # getStatus


###################
sub checkStatus {
    my ($ref) = shift or die "***Err: checkStatus() expects a reference.";

    foreach my $cluster (sort keys %{$ref->{Config}}) {
        next if $cluster =~ /^CONTROL/i;
        next if $ref->{Config}->{$cluster}->{DISABLED} =~ /^y/i;

        my ($clusterName) = $cluster =~ /^CLUSTER\s*:\s*(.+)$/i;
        my $savedRef = $ref->{SavedStatus}->{$cluster}->{ClusterStatus};
        my $curRef = $ref->{CurrentStatus}->{$cluster}->{ClusterStatus};
        my $alertRef;

        my @diff = ();
        my @savedNodes = keys %{$savedRef->{Nodes}};
        my @currentNodes = keys %{$curRef->{Nodes}};
        my @savedGroups = keys %{$savedRef->{Groups}};
        my @currentGroups = keys %{$curRef->{Groups}};

        # check if a node is not Up
        foreach my $node (@currentNodes) {
            if ($curRef->{Nodes}->{$node}->{Status} !~ /^Up$/i) {
                $alertRef->{NodeNotUp}->{Msg} .= "$node,";
                $ref->{CurrentStatus}->{$cluster}->{OK} = 0;
            }
        }

        # check if a group is not online
        foreach my $group (@currentGroups) {
```

```perl
            my $status = $curRef->{Groups}->{$group}->{Status};
            if ($status !~ /^Online$/i) {
                $alertRef->{GroupNotOnline}->{Msg} .= "$group,";
                $ref->{CurrentStatus}->{$cluster}->{OK} = 0;
            }
        }

        # check preferred owner nodes for each group
        if ($ref->{Config}->{$cluster}->{CHECKPREFERREDOWNERNODES} =~ /^y/i) {
            foreach my $group (@currentGroups) {
                if (defined $curRef->{Groups}->{$group}->{PreferredOwnerNodes}) {
                    unless (dbaInSet($curRef->{Groups}->{$group}->{Node},
                            $curRef->{Groups}->{$group}->{PreferredOwnerNodes})) {
                        $alertRef->{GroupNotOnOwnerNode}->{Msg} .= "$group,";
                        $ref->{CurrentStatus}->{$cluster}->{OK} = 0;
                    }
                }
            }
        }

        # check if a node is evicted
        if (@diff = dbaSetDiff(\@savedNodes, \@currentNodes)) {
            my $nodes = join(',', map {"'" . $_ ."'"} @diff);
            $alertRef->{NodeEvicted}->{Msg} = $nodes;
            $ref->{CurrentStatus}->{$cluster}->{OK} = 0;
        }

        # check if a group is moved to another node
        foreach my $group (dbaSetCommon(\@currentGroups, \@savedGroups)) {
            my $oldNode = $savedRef->{Groups}->{$group}->{Node};
            my $newNode = $curRef->{Groups}->{$group}->{Node};
            if ($oldNode ne $newNode ) {
                $alertRef->{GroupMoved}->{Msg} .= "$group: $oldNode->$newNode,";
                $ref->{CurrentStatus}->{$cluster}->{OK} = 0;
            }
        }
        $ref->{CurrentStatus}->{$cluster}->{AlertStatus} = $alertRef;
    }
    return $ref;
} # checkStatus


##################
sub alertStatus {
    my $ref = shift or die "***Err: alertStatus() expects a reference.";
```

```
foreach my $cluster (sort keys %{$ref->{Config}}) {
    next if $ref->{CurrentStatus}->{$cluster}->{OK};

    next if $cluster =~ /^CONTROL/i;
    next if $ref->{Config}->{$cluster}->{DISABLED} =~ /^y/i;
    my ($clusterName) = $cluster =~ /^CLUSTER\s*:\s*(.+)$/i;

    my $alertRef = $ref->{CurrentStatus}->{$cluster}->{AlertStatus};
    my $currentRef = $ref->{CurrentStatus}->{$cluster};
    my $savedRef = $ref->{SavedStatus}->{$cluster};
    my @receivers = ( $ref->{Config}->{$cluster}->{DBAPAGER} );

    foreach my $alertType (sort keys %{$alertRef}) {
        # try twice before quitting
        next if (      $alertType eq 'AccessFailed'
                   and $alertRef->{AccessFailed}->{Times} <= 2);
        # was an alert sent recently
        next if (time() -
                $savedRef->{AlertSent}->{$alertType}->{AlertSentTime})
                  < ($ref->{Config}->{$cluster}->{ALERTINTERVAL})*60;
        # don't alert if it's in the quiet time period
        next if dbaIsBetweenTime($ref->{Config}->{$cluster}->{QUIETTIME});

        # tidy up the message
        $alertRef->{$alertType}->{Msg} =~ s/,$//;
        $alertRef->{$alertType}->{Msg}
                    = 'Cluster ' . $clusterName .
                      " $alertType: " . $alertRef->{$alertType}->{Msg};
        # send via SMTP
        if (dbaSMTPSend($ref->{Config}->{CONTROL}->{SMTPSERVER},
                        \@receivers,
                        $ref->{Config}->{CONTROL}->{SMTPSENDER},
                        $alertRef->{$alertType}->{Msg})) {

            $currentRef->{AlertSent}->{$alertType}->{OK} = 1;
            $currentRef->{AlertSent}->{$alertType}->{AlertSentTimeStr}
                        = dbaTime2str();
            $currentRef->{AlertSent}->{$alertType}->{AlertSentTime}
                        = time();
            $currentRef->{AlertSent}->{$alertType}->{Msg}
                        = $alertRef->{$alertType}->{Msg};
            # log it to a file
            if (open(LOG, ">>$ref->{Config}->{CONTROL}->{ALERTLOGFILE}")) {
```

```
                printf LOG "%s  %s. Sent to %s\n", dbaTime2str(),
                        $alertRef->{$alertType}->{Msg},
                        $ref->{Config}->{$cluster}->{DBAPAGER};
                close(LOG);
            }
        }
        else {
            $currentRef->{AlertSent}->{$alertType}->{OK} = 0;
            $currentRef->{AlertSent}->{$alertType}->{AlertSentTimeStr}
                        = undef;
            $currentRef->{AlertSent}->{$alertType}->{AlertSentTime}
                        = undef;
        }
    }
    $ref->{CurrentStatus}->{$cluster} = $currentRef;
  }
  return $ref;
} # alertStatus


#################
sub printUsage {
    print << '--Usage--';
Usage:
  cmd>perl monitorClusters.pl <Config File>
      <Config File>   file to specify config options for monitoring clusters
--Usage--
    exit;
}
```

All the configuration options that the script `monitorClusters.pl` accepts are specified in a configuration file. Assuming the configuration file is `config.txt` in the current directory, you can run the script from the command line as follows:

```
cmd>perl monitorCluster.pl config.txt
```

You should schedule to run the script once every few minutes.

Listing 11-20 is a sample configuration file for monitoring two clusters, NYCLSQL01 and NYCLSQL02.

Listing 11-20. A Sample Configuration File for monitorClusters.pl

[Control]
AlertLogFile=d:\dba\clusters\Alert.log
StatusFile=d:\dba\clusters\status.log
SMTPServer=mail.linchi.com
SMTPSender=sql@linchi.com

[Cluster:NYCLSQL01]
Disabled=no
DBAPager=72001@myTel.com
QuietTime=20-8
AlertInterval=15
CheckPreferredOwnerNodes=yes

[Cluster:NYCLSQL02]
Disabled=no
DBAPager=74321@myTel.com
QuietTime=24-6
AlertInterval=30
CheckPreferredOwnerNodes=no

Table 11-8 describes each of these configuration options. For brevity, this table contains both the options in the Control section and the options for each cluster.

Table 11-8. Options for monitorClusters.pl

OPTION	DESCRIPTION
AlertLogFile	A log entry is made to this text file every time an alert is sent.
StatusFile	This is the file where the cluster status data structure will be saved. The monitorClusters.pl script reads from this file the next time it runs.
SMTPServer	The SMTP mail server.
SMTPSender	This is the SMTP account to identify the sender of the alert.
Disabled	When this is set to yes, the script doesn't monitor the cluster.
DBAPager	All alerts for this cluster will be sent to this address.

Table 11-8. Options for `monitorClusters.pl` *(Continued)*

OPTION	DESCRIPTION
QuietTime	This option accepts two values in the format of hh-hh, where hh is between 1 and 24, inclusive. When this is specified, no alerts for this cluster will be sent between these two hours.
AlertInterval	This option specifies the minimum amount of time in minutes that must elapse before another alert for this cluster can be sent again.
CheckPreferredOwnerNodes	This is a toggle with values yes or no. When it's set to no, the script won't check whether a group is running on its preferred owner node.

Studying the Script monitorClusters.pl

The overall flow of this script is similar to that of the basic version of the cluster monitoring script alertCluster.pl in Listing 11-18, but several salient differences are worth noting.

One such notable difference is between the data structures used by these two scripts. Although the data structure for a given cluster in Listing 11-19 is nearly identical to the data structure used in Listing 11-17, the former has one more level in the overall data structure to explicitly accommodate multiple clusters. Listing 11-21 shows the data structure for the cluster NYCLSQL01 and illustrates the addition of the level immediately below $ref->{CurrentStatus} in the data structure hierarchy.

Listing 11-21. A Sample Cluster Status Data Structure—Multiple Clusters

```
$ref->{CurrentStatus}->{'CLUSTER:NYCLSQL01'} = {
    OK => '0',
    ClusterStatus => {
        Nodes => {
                NYCLSQL01NODE1 => { Status => 'Up' },
                NYCLSQL01NODE2 => { Status => 'Up' }
        }
        Groups => {
            MSSQL01 => {
                PreferredOwnerNodes => [ 'NYCLSQL01NODE1' ],
                Status => 'Online',
                Node => 'NYCLSQLNODE2'
            },
```

```
                    MSSQL02 => {
                        PreferredOwnerNodes => [ 'NYCLSQL01NODE1' ],
                        Status => 'Partial Online',
                        Node => 'NYCLSQL01NODE1'
                    },
                    ClusterGroup => {
                        Status => 'Online',
                        Node => 'NYCLSQL01NODE2'
                    }
                },
            }
        AlertStatus => {
            GroupNotOnPreferredOwnerNode => {
                Msg => 'Cluster NYCLSQL01 GroupNotOnPreferredOwnerNode: MSSQL01'
            },
            GroupNotOnline => {
                Msg => 'Cluster NYCLSQL01 GroupNotOnline: MSSQL02'
            }
        },
    };
```

Let's compare this data structure with that in Listing 11-17. They're identical with the exception of the additional keys under the individual group to capture the list of preferred owner nodes.

From a programming standpoint, instead of referencing the group MSSQL01 on the cluster NYCLSQL01 as follows:

```
$statusRef->{ClusterStatus}->{Groups}->{MSSQL01}
```

where $statusRef is set to $ref->{CurrentStatus}), you now reference it as follows:

```
$statusRef->{'CLUSTER:NYCLSQL01'}->{ClusterStatus}->{Groups}->{MSSQL01}
```

Literally, all you need to do to accommodate multiple clusters is to add another layer of reference (for example, {'CLUSTER:NYCLSQL01'}) in all the references and add a loop to go through all the clusters wherever appropriate. This again demonstrates the power of Perl's reference-based dynamic data structure in creating a hierarchical model and the ease with which you can manipulate the hierarchy.

The second salient difference between the script monitorClusters.pl in Listing 11-19 and the script in Listing 11-17 is how they implement the function getStatus(). This function retrieves the node and group status information to populate the current status data structure ($ref->{CurrentStatus} in Listing 11-17 and $ref->{CurrentStatus}->{'CLUSTER:NYCLSQL01'} for the cluster NYCLSQL01 in Listing 11-20). In the script monitorClusters.pl, the function getStatus() employs the Cluster Automation Server to retrieve the status information of the nodes and the status information of the groups in a cluster. The function getStatus() first invokes the Cluster Automation Server as follows to obtain the Cluster object:

```
my $clusRef = Win32::OLE->new('MSCluster.Cluster');
```

Contrast this with the use of the command-line utility cluster.exe in the script alertCluster.pl in Listing 11-17.

The following code fragment in the function getStatus() in Listing 11-19 gets the preferred owner nodes for each group:

```
# loop through the PreferredOwnerNodes collection
foreach my $preferredNode (in ($group->{PreferredOwnerNodes})) {
   next unless $preferredNode;
   push @{$grpRef->{PreferredOwnerNodes}},
      $preferredNode->{Name};
}
```

PreferredOwnerNodes is a property of the Group object, which is a member of the ResourceGroup collection. You can get ResourceGroup from the Cluster object. The preferred owner information would be rather cumbersome to obtain if you rely on parsing the text output of cluster.exe.

Summary

Setting up and maintaining a SQL Server monitoring infrastructure is a never-ending job because it has to accommodate systems and operational changes, and most significantly it has to adapt to organizational changes. Just when you think you've finally hammered in that last nail, you discover that you overlooked a peculiar but still important scenario, you can't ignore an issue as you previously thought, or the evolved environment has given rise to new monitoring requirements. This is true regardless of whether you're customizing a third-party monitoring package or writing your own home-grown monitoring scripts.

The scripts in this chapter demonstrate that writing your own scripts in Perl to effectively monitor SQL Server instances and SQL Server clusters isn't only feasible but that it can also be easily accomplished. These Perl scripts offer ultimate flexibility in meeting new requirements or addressing unanticipated twists in the existing requirements. Furthermore, they were not created in vacuum but have grown out of acute real-world needs. Scripts similar to the ones discussed in this chapter have been used to successfully monitor substantial SQL Server installations.

Experience suggests that the script for monitoring SQL Server errorlogs, the script for monitoring SQL Server availability, and the script for monitoring SQL Server clusters together comprise a comprehensive set of tools for monitoring exceptions in SQL Server environments.

The next chapter, which is the final chapter of this book, focuses on using Perl to simplify managing SQL Server instances in the enterprise environment.

CHAPTER 12

Managing SQL Servers in the Enterprise

MANAGING A LARGE SQL SERVER environment is significantly different from managing a small one. What's a large SQL Server environment? You can look at it from several dimensions:

- Number of SQL Servers or SQL Server instances

- Number of databases

- Number of Database Administrators (DBAs)

- Number of applications supported by the databases

If you manage one or two dozen SQL Server instances, you may not consider your environment large. However, if the number is 50, 100, or more, then the nature of SQL Server administration changes significantly. Although the impact of a large number of databases on database administration isn't as dramatic as that of a large number of SQL Server instances, it nevertheless rapidly increases the complexity of your environment. When you have a group of DBAs looking after the SQL Server environment, the issues of coordination and communication become critical. One of the key implications of SQL Server administration in a large environment as opposed to a small environment is that the need for tools that facilitate the administration of many SQL Servers becomes acute.

Unfortunately, most of the SQL Server tools have been designed with a single-server-centric view. In other words, they're designed to work on a single server. But wait! You may contend that tools such as SQL Server Enterprise Manager and other similar Graphical User Interface (GUI) tools already work with many servers.

It's true that their GUIs present you a tree-view of as many SQL Server instances as you care to register. However, when it comes to performing any DBA work, you don't work on a group of servers at once; you still administer each server individually.

When you have a large number of SQL Server instances, a significant class of DBA tasks emerges that are inherently multiserver oriented. This chapter samples some of these multiserver tasks and presents Perl scripts that help you perform these tasks, not on one server at a time but on multiple servers at once.

The focus of this chapter isn't on one or two substantial issues that require lengthy scripting. Instead, the chapter focuses on a series of discrete multiserver tasks where you can write quick Perl scripts to significantly ease your life as a DBA. As you'll see, these Perl scripts are relatively short yet effective.

> **NOTE** *This isn't the only chapter that deals with issues that are multiserver in nature. Chapter 6, Chapter 9, Chapter 10, and Chapter 11 all include scripts you can use to work on all the SQL Server instances in your environment.*

You're probably asking "So what are these multiserver scenarios you keep mentioning?" To whet your appetite, the following is a sample list:

- Finding all the SQL Server instances that have a particular database

- Finding where a Windows account is used to run SQL Server services

- Finding the space usage of a database on all the SQL Server instances that have this database

- Removing obsolete database backup files that litter your servers

- Finding all the databases with transaction logs larger than 5 gigabytes (GB)

- Finding the disk usage of all the instances in a SQL Server cluster

This chapter assumes you already have a Windows initialization (INI) file that lists all your SQL Server instances in the section headings. The scripts rely on the function dbaReadINI() from the SQLDBA::Utility module to retrieve the SQL Server instance names. The chapter begins with a script that's the multiserver version of osql.exe. It then proceeds to scripts that extract useful information such as configured SQL Server TCP ports, the locations of all the errorlogs, the status of SQL Server services, the up time of the SQL Server computers, and the SQL Server memory configurations. The chapter also covers the issues of archiving the SQL Server system tables and registry entries. It ends with a script that helps you purge the old SQL Server backup files from your environment.

Querying Live Databases vs. Querying a DBA Repository

One of the must-haves in managing a large SQL Server environment is a DBA repository that keeps track of all the server and database information. This can be another SQL Server database that stores the information about all the servers and databases in your environment.

A DBA repository should have two types of information:

- One type is the system information that you can extract from your servers and databases. You can schedule a daily job to scan all your servers and databases to collect the system information such as database names, sizes, collations, object schemas, and server configurations and to store the collected information in the repository database. In addition, you can schedule batch jobs to summarize the information in your repository. Your management often likes to see summary information such as weekly and monthly space consumption.

- The other type of information you should keep in the DBA repository can't be collected automatically. This includes such information as the application name of a database, the client contacts, the primary DBA of the database, the physical location of the server, and so on.

It's important to realize that the presence of a comprehensive and up-to-date DBA repository doesn't void the need to directly query the servers for many reasons.

You may want to query the live databases just to make sure that the repository is up-to-date or to retrieve the most current information. Alternatively, perhaps the repository hasn't been designed to accommodate what you're looking to find.

Running Queries on Multiple Servers

SCENARIO
You need to run a T-SQL query not on one SQL Server instance but on all the instances in your environment. In particular, you want to avoid manually running the same query on each SQL Server instance repeatedly.

You can use the Perl script msql.pl to be presented in Listing 12-1. The m in msql.pl stands for multiple servers. This script mimics osql.exe, but it runs a Transact-SQL (T-SQL) query or a T-SQL script on all the SQL Server instances specified in an INI file or on the command line.

Before diving into the code, the following cases show that the need for a multiserver version of osql.exe is common and real:

- You're suddenly asked to take over the support for a project. You want to quickly find the databases for the project.

- You want to find all the instances that are at a certain service pack level.

- You want to find all the logins in your environment that don't have a password, or you want to find all the orphaned database users.

- You want to change the password of a SQL Server login globally.

- You want to check the sizes of a database on all the SQL Server instances.

The multiserver version of osql.exe, called msql.pl, accepts all the command-line arguments that osql.exe accepts, and it introduces the following two extensions:

- The script extends the -S option to accept a comma-separated list of SQL Server instances.

- The script accepts a new option, -C. This option expects an INI file that lists SQL Server instances in its section headings.

Programmatically, the msql.pl script loops through the SQL Server instances in the INI file. For each instance, the script invokes osql.exe and passes all the other command-line arguments to osql.exe. Listing 12-1 shows the code of msql.pl.

Listing 12-1. Executing T-SQL Queries on Multiple SQL Server Instances

```
1.  use strict;
2.  use Getopt::Std;
3.  use SQLDBA::Utility qw( dbaReadINI );
4.
5.  my %opts;
6.  # accept all the osql.exe arguments plus -C
7.  getopts('C:U:P:S:H:d:l:t:h:s:w:a:L:c:D:q:Q:m:r:i:o:EeInpb', \%opts);
8.  # store all the server instance names in $optRef->{S}
9.  my $optRef = validateConfig(\%opts);
10.
11. # run osql.exe on each server
12. foreach my $server (sort @{$optRef->{S}}) {
```

```perl
13.     print "Server: $server\n";
14.     my $optStr = ' ';
15.     foreach my $opt (keys %$optRef) {
16.         next if $opt eq 'S';
17.         $optStr .= '-' . $opt . $optRef->{$opt} . ' ';
18.     }
19.     my $osql = "osql -S$server $optStr 2>&1"; # direct STDERR to STDOUT
20.     # run osql.exe and capture result in $rs
21.     my $rs = `$osql`;  # using the backtick operator
22.     print $rs;
23. }
24.
25. #########################
26. sub validateConfig {
27.     my $optRef = shift or die "***Err: validateConfig() expects a reference.";
28.     if (!defined $optRef->{C} and !defined $optRef->{S}) {
29.         die "***Err: either -C or -S must be specified.";
30.     }
31.     # set the value of the options that don't accept arguments to undef
32.     # Getopt::Std assigns a numeric 1 to such an option. Since we concatenate
33.     # the option and its value to construct the osql command line, we can't
34.     # use the number 1.
35.     for my $opt ('E', 'e', 'I', 'n', 'p', 'b') {
36.         $optRef->{$opt} = undef if exists $optRef->{$opt};
37.     }
38.     if ($optRef->{S}) {  # split the instance names into an array
39.         $optRef->{S} = [ split /\s*,\s*/, $optRef->{S} ];
40.     }
41.     # move all the listed server instances to $optRef->{S}, and
42.     # remove $optRef->{C}
43.     if ($optRef->{C}) {
44.         my $configRef = dbaReadINI($optRef->{C});
45.         push @{$optRef->{S}}, keys %$configRef;
46.         delete $optRef->{C};
47.     }
48.     # for these options, we may need to put the double quotes back
49.     foreach my $opt ('q', 'Q', 'i') {
50.         if ($optRef->{$opt}) {
51.             $optRef->{$opt} =~ s/\"/\"\"/;  # escape double quotes
52.             $optRef->{$opt} = '"' . $optRef->{$opt} . '"';
53.         }
54.     }
55.     return $optRef;
56. } # validateConfig;
```

This script is straightforward. The bulk of the code is in the function validateConfig(), which prepares the command-line arguments to pass to osql.exe for each SQL Server.

On line 39, the function validateConfig() splits the comma-separated SQL Server instance names—specified with -S—into an array and assigns its reference to $optRef->{S}. If more SQL Server instances are specified in the section headings of the INI file, which is specified on the command line with -C, validateConfig() merges them into this array on line 45.

In addition, the function put the double quotes back to the values of the options, -q, -Q, and -i, before passing them to osql.exe. Note that the function escapes each embedded double quote with another double quote on line 51.

Let's see how msql.pl can help with some of the typical multiserver cases. Unless otherwise described, the subsequent sections assume that all the SQL Server instances in your environment are listed in the file config.txt as shown in Listing 12-2. In addition, for most cases, only partial results from running msql.pl are printed.

Listing 12-2. A Sample INI File

```
[SQL1\APOLLO]
...
[SQL2]
...
[SQL2\PANTHEON]
...
```

The script msql.pl doesn't care about what configuration options are listed in each section. It only needs to read the SQL Server instance names from the section headings.

Finding a Database

You want to quickly find all the SQL Server instances that have a database named Orders. Place the following T-SQL query in the file findDB.sql:

```
SET NOCOUNT ON

SELECT name
  FROM master..sysdatabases
 WHERE name = 'Orders'
```

Next, run `msql.pl` as follows to find the SQL Server instances with the database
Orders:

```
cmd>perl msql.pl -C config.txt -i findDB.sql -E -n -h-1 -w1024
Server: SQL1\APOLLO
 Orders

Server: SQL2

Server: SQL2\PANTHEON
```

This result shows that the Orders database is found on the SQL Server instance
SQL1\APOLLO.

You may wonder why finding a database is even a problem. Indeed, in a small
environment where you're aware of all the databases, this wouldn't be a problem.
However, in a large environment where there are many SQL Server instances and
many databases—and where the databases may be managed by a group of DBAs
who may not even sit at the same physical location—it's not uncommon to run
into questions such as "One of my clients has just asked me about a database
called PSGD. He believes it runs on one of our servers. Could you find whether we
are managing it and, if yes, its location, size, and so on?"

Unless you've searched all the SQL Server instances in your environment or
searched an up-to-date DBA repository, you wouldn't have any confidence in
answering questions of this nature.

Finding SQL Server Instances with Old Service Packs

You want to find among all your SQL Server instances those with old service packs.
The following T-SQL script in the file `findServicePack.sql` determines whether the
service pack on a SQL Server instance is less than 8.00.760, which is SQL Server
2000 Service Pack 3:

```
USE master
go

SET NOCOUNT ON
IF CAST(SUBSTRING(@@VERSION, PATINDEX('%8.00.%', @@VERSION)+5, 3) as int) < 760
BEGIN
    SELECT SUBSTRING(@@VERSION, PATINDEX('%8.00.%', @@VERSION), 8)
END
```

This is the result of running this T-SQL script with msql.pl:

```
cmd>perl msql.pl -C config.txt -i findServicePack.sql -E -n -h-1 -w1024
Server: SQL1\APOLLO:

Server: SQL2:

Server: SQL2\PANTHEON:
 8.00.690
```

In this case, the instances SQL1\APOLLO and SQL2 are running SQL Server 2000 Service Pack 3 or higher, and SQL2\PANTHEON is running below Service Pack 3.

Finding Null Passwords for SQL Server Logins

You want to find the SQL Server logins with null passwords from all the SQL Server instances in your environment. The following simple T-SQL query finds the logins with null passwords on a SQL Server instance:

```
SET NOCOUNT ON

SELECT name FROM master..syslogins
 WHERE password is NULL
   AND isntname = 0
```

Running the query with msql.pl gives the following result:

```
cmd>perl msql.pl -C config.txt -i findNullPassword.sql -E -n -h-1 -w 1024
Server: SQL1\APOLLO
    apollo
    sa

Server: SQL2
    sa

Server: SQL2\PANTHEON
```

It has found the logins apollo and sa with null password on SQL1\APOLLO and the login sa with null password on SQL2.

Finding Information About a Database

For a given database—for example, Orders—you want to find such information as the locations of its files and its database settings anywhere this database may reside in your environment. The solution is to run sp_helpdb 'Orders' on each SQL Server instance. The following shows only the result for the instance SQL1\APOLLO:

```
cmd>perl msql.pl -C config.txt -Q"sp_helpdb 'Orders'" -E -n -h-1 -w 2048
Server: SQL1\APOLLO:
 name        db_size owner dbid  created     status
 ---------- ------- ------ ----- ----------- ------------------------------------
 Orders      3.31 MB sa    5     Dec  7 2002 Status=ONLINE, Updateability=READ...

 name           fileid filename                              filegroup   size ...
 ---------- ------ ----------------------------------- ---------- -------
 Orders              1 e:\mssql\mssql$apollo\Orders.mdf     PRIMARY     1600 KB ...
 Orders_log          2 e:\mssql\mssql$apollo\Orders_log.LDF NULL        768 KB  ...
 Orders2             3 d:\mssql\mssql$apollo\Orders2.ndf   ReadOnly_FG 1024 KB ...

Server: SQL2:
...
Server: SQL2\PANTHEON:
...
```

Finding the Missing Database Backups

You want to identify all the nontrivial databases in your environment that haven't been backed up for more than five days. Note that it's common that there's no need to back up some databases. For those that do need backing up but whose backups are missing, it's important that they're brought to your attention. One solution is to run the following T-SQL query on each server:

```
SET NOCOUNT ON
SELECT 'ServerName' = @@servername, 'DatabaseName' = d.name
  FROM master..sysdatabases d
 WHERE NOT EXISTS (
        SELECT * FROM msdb..backupset b
         WHERE b.type = 'D'    -- full database backup only
           AND DATEDIFF(day, b.backup_finish_date, GETDATE()) < 5  -- 5 days
           AND b.database_name = d.name)
   AND name NOT IN ('model', 'tempdb', 'pubs', 'Northwind', 'DBA')
```

Save this query to the file `findMissingBackups.sql` and execute it with `msql.pl` to produce the following output:

```
cmd>perl msql.pl -C config.txt -ifindMissingBackups.sql -E -n -h-1 -w 2048
Server: SQL1\APOLLO
  ServerName          DatabaseName
  ------------------- --------------

  SQL1\APOLLO         distribution
  SQL1\APOLLO         master
  SQL1\APOLLO         msdb


Server: SQL2
  ServerName          DatabaseName
  ------------------- --------------

  SQL2                TradeDB
  SQL2                master
```

The databases `distribution`, `master`, and `msdb` haven't been backed for five days on SQL\APOLLO. On SQL2, the `TradeDB` and `master` databases haven't been backed for five days.

From these five multiserver cases, it's clear that the `msql.pl` script can be handy if you have more than a few SQL Server instances in your environment. You can run any T-SQL query with `msql.pl` against all your instances as long as you can run the query with `osql.exe` and you can run the query as if you were running it on a single SQL Server instance.

 NOTE   *In my environment, I maintain an up-to-date INI file for monitoring and inventory purposes. This INI file has all the SQL Server instances—listed in the section headings—that deserve the DBA's attention. When you have such an INI file, using the* `msql.pl` *utility becomes convenient.*

Finding the Configured SQL Server TCP Ports

SCENARIO
You want to find all the configured TCP ports on which the SQL Server instances listen in your entire environment.

For a given instance, you can use Server Network Utility, which is one of the SQL Server client tools, to check the TCP port on which it's configured to listen.

Alternatively, you can review the registry entries that record the port configurations for this instance.

For a named instance (for example, SQL1\APOLLO), you can find the TCP port under the registry value `TcpPort` in the registry key `Microsoft SQL Server/APOLLO/MSSQLServer/SuperSocketNetLib/Tcp` in the Microsoft software root, which is `HKEY_LOCAL_MACHINE/Software/Microsoft`.

For the default instance, the TCP port on which it listens is in the registry value `MSSQLServer/MSSQLServer/ListenOn` in the same Microsoft software root.

Listing 12-3 is a Perl script—`configuredSQLPorts.pl`—that loops through all the instances listed in the section headings of an INI file and, for each instance, retrieves the TCP port from the server by querying its registry entries with the module Win32::TieRegstry. Chapter 2, "Working with Commonly Used Perl Modules," covered this module in detail.

Listing 12-3. Finding All the Configured TCP Ports

```
1.  use strict;
2.  use SQLDBA::Utility qw( dbaReadINI );
3.  use Win32::TieRegistry (Delimiter => '/'); # / is the path separator
4.
5.  # get the config file name
6.  my $configFile = shift or die "***Err: $0 expects a file.";
7.  # read the config file
8.  my $configRef = dbaReadINI($configFile);
9.
10. my $portRef;
11. foreach my $inst (sort keys %$configRef) {
12.     next if $inst =~ /^CONTROL$/i;      # skip the CONTROL section
13.     $inst =~ /^\s*(.+?)(\\(.+))?\s*$/;  # separate server from instance
14.     my ($server, $instance) = ($1, $3);
15.     $instance = $instance || 'MSSQLServer'; # it's the default instance
16.
17.     my $MSRoot = "//$server/LMachine/Software/Microsoft/"; # MS root
18.     # get the root of the named instance
19.     my $namedRoot = $MSRoot . "Microsoft SQL Server/$instance";
20.     # get the root of the default instance
21.     my $defaultRoot = $MSRoot . "MSSQLServer/";
22.
23.     my ($portPath, $verPath, $port, $version);
24.     # get verison of the instance. Port location is version dependent
25.     if ($instance ne 'MSSQLServer') {   # named instance
26.         $verPath = $namedRoot . "/MSSQLServer/CurrentVersion/CurrentVersion";
27.     }
```

```
28.    else {                                    # default instance
29.        $verPath = $defaultRoot . "MSSQLServer/CurrentVersion/CurrentVersion";
30.    }
31.    # get the version of the instance
32.    $version = $Registry->{$verPath};
33.
34.    if ($version =~ /8\.00\./ ) {              # SQL 2000
35.        $portPath .= $namedRoot . "/MSSQLServer/SuperSocketNetLib/Tcp/TcpPort";
36.        $port = $Registry->{$portPath} or
37.            warn "***Warning: couldn't read port for $portPath.";
38.    }
39.    else {                                     # SQL 7
40.        $portPath = $defaultRoot . "MSSQLServer/ListenOn";
41.        $port = $Registry->{$portPath}
42.            or warn "***Warning: couldn't read port for $portPath.";
43.        foreach (split(/\x0/, $port)) { # multiple ports are null separated
44.            if (/SSMSS/i) {
45.                $port = $_;
46.                last;
47.            }
48.        }
49.    }
50.    $portRef->{$server}->{$instance} = $port;
51. }
52.
53. foreach my $srv (sort keys %$portRef) {
54.    print "Server: $srv\n";
55.    foreach my $instance (sort keys %{$portRef->{$srv}}) {
56.        print "\tInstance: $instance, Port: $portRef->{$srv}->{$instance}\n";
57.    }
58. }
```

Running this script against the INI file `config.txt` that lists three SQL Server instances in its section headings produced the following result:

```
cmd>perl configuredSQLPorts.pl config.txt
Server: SQL1
    Instance: MSSQLServer, Port: 1433
    Instance: APOLLO, Port: 4752
Server: SQL2
    Instance: PANTHEON, Port: 4009
```

Let's look at how the script in Listing 12-3 retrieves the configured port information from the Windows registry.

On line 15, when no instance is specified for a server, the default instance is assumed, which is MSSQLServer when you need to explicitly specify the default instance name. Then on line 32, the script retrieves the version number of the instance. The version information is necessary because, as mentioned earlier, the location of the registry value that stores the TCP port number is version dependent.

The port information is read on line 36 for SQL Server 2000 or line 41 for SQL Server 7.0. Prior to reading the port, the script configuredSQLPorts.pl in Listing 12-3 devotes much of the work to preparing the correct registry path to the port registry value.

Note that the code between lines 43 and 48 applies to SQL Server 7.0 because the ListenOn registry value records the configuration information for all the Inter-process Communications (IPC), not just for the TCP port configuration. The value is a null-separated multiple-part string. The part for the TCP port is prefixed with the string SSMSS, hence the code between lines 43 and 48.

When you have a large number of SQL Server instances in your environment, keeping a record of all the configured TCP ports is useful. Some applications may choose or may be forced to explicitly specify the port in the connection string instead of relying on the SQL Server listener service at the UDP port 1434 to automatically determine the port. For these applications, you need to make sure that the ports used by the SQL Server instances don't change. If an instance does change the port it listens on, you need to be able to quickly revert it to its correct port.

Connecting to SQL Server Instances

SQL Server allows a client to connect to its instances in many different ways. Assume that you have the following SQL Server information:

- Server name: SQL1
- SQL Server instance name: APOLLO
- IP address: 172.125.30.165
- Port number: 1674
- Fully qualified domain name of the server: apollo.myTel.com

If you're using osql.exe, you can specify any of the following after the -S option to connect to the SQL Server instance:

- SQL1\APOLLO
- 172.125.30.165,1674
- apollo.myTel.com,1674

You can also configure an alias on the client side using the Client Network Utility, and use the alias after the -S option.

Regardless of how you connect to SQL Server, if you don't specify the port explicitly, you're relying on the SQL Server client to resolve the port for you. The SQL Server client needs to communicate with SQL Server over the User Datagram Protocol (UDP) port 1434 to determine the correct port to use.

Finding SQL Server Errorlogs

| SCENARIO
You want to find the locations of all the errorlogs in your environment.

You can solve this problem in at least three ways. First, you could rely on SQL-DMO and read the ErrorLogPath property of the Registry object. Second, you can use a Perl script to control the command-line utility reg.exe, which is part of the Windows NT/2000 Resource Kit. The third approach, and the one that's adopted in this section, is to continue the method of using the Win32::TieRegistry module to query the appropriate registry keys and values.

The following observations help solve this problem:

- The location of the errorlog for a SQL Server instance is in one of the startup parameters.

- For a named instance, you can find the startup parameters in the registry under the key HKLM\Software\Microsoft\Microsoft SQL Server\<InstanceName>\MSSQLServer\Parameters.

- For the default instance, you can find the startup parameters in the registry under the key HKLM\Software\Microsoft\MSSQLServer\ MSSQLServer\Parameters.

- The errorlog location can be the value of any of the registry values under the Parameters key.

Listing 12-4 is a Perl script, findErrorlogs.pl, that reads the SQL Server names from an INI file expected on the command line, and for each server it finds all the SQL Server instances installed on that server. Depending on whether it's a named instance or the default instance, the script traverses to the correct registry key to read all the startup parameter values. The value that starts with -e is the location of the errorlog for the SQL Server instance.

Listing 12-4. Finding the Errorlogs for All the Servers

```perl
1.   use strict;
2.   use SQLDBA::Utility qw( dbaReadINI );
3.   use Win32::TieRegistry (Delimiter => '/'); # / is the path separator
4.
5.   # get the config file name from the command line
6.   my $configFile = shift or
7.      die "***Err: $0 expects a config file.";
8.   # read the config file
9.   my $configRef = dbaReadINI($configFile);
10.
11.  my %checked;    # used to determine whether a server has been checked
12.  # loop throuhg all the servers
13.  foreach my $server (keys %$configRef) { # loop through the servers
14.     next if $server =~ /^CONTROL$/i;     # skip the CONTROL section
15.     $server =~ /^\s*(.+?)(\\(.+))?\s*$/; # separate server from instance
16.     $server = $1;
17.     next if exists $checked{$server};    # skip if checked already
18.
19.     print "Server: $server\n";
20.     my $rKey = "//$server/LMachine/Software/Microsoft/Microsoft SQL Server/";
21.     my $sqlKey = $Registry->{$rKey};
22.
23.     # now loop through each instance of this server
24.     foreach my $instance (split /\0/, $sqlKey->{'/InstalledInstances'}) {
25.        my $pKey;
26.        if ($instance !~ /^\s*MSSQLServer\s*$/) {     # named instance
27.           $pKey = $sqlKey->{$instance . '/MSSQLServer/Parameters/'};
28.        }
39.        else {                                      # default instance
30.          my $dKey = "//$server/LMachine/Software/Microsoft/MSSQLServer/";
31.           $dKey .= "MSSQLServer/Parameters/";
32.           $pKey = $Registry->{$dKey};
33.        }
34.
35.        # now loop through the startup parameters to find errorlog
36.        foreach my $value (keys %{$pKey}) { # now print the -e parameter
37.           my $val = $pKey->{$value};
38.           if ($val =~ s/^\s*\-e//) {
39.               print "\t$val\n";
40.           }
41.        }
42.     }
43.     $checked{$server} = 1;  # flag the server name in the hash as checked
44. }
```

Using the sample INI file in Listing 12-2, you can run the script in Listing 12-4 as follows:

```
cmd>perl findErrorlogs.pl config.txt
Server: SQL1
    D:\MSSQL$APOLLO\log\ERRORLOG
Server: SQL2
    E:\MSSQL\log\ERRORLOG
    E:\MSSQL$PANTHEON\log\ERRORLOG
```

This finds the errorlogs for all the SQL Server instances installed on both SQL1 and SQL2. In this case, the script reported one errorlog for SQL1 and two errorlogs for SQL2.

Note that because the INI file lists SQL Server instances—not servers—in its section headings, a server may be listed many times if it has multiple SQL Server instances. As a result, the loop that begins on line 13 may run into the same server multiple times. However, for each server, the script in Listing 12-4 enumerates all the SQL Server errorlogs. Therefore, if the script has already checked a server and reported the errorlogs of all its instances, it shouldn't produce the report again when it loops to a different SQL Server instance of the same server.

The script relies on the hash %checked declared on line 11 to record the servers that have already been checked. When the script finishes reporting the errorlogs of a server, it adds the server name to the hash on line 43. On line 17, before the script does anything with a server, it first inspects the hash to see whether the server name is already recorded and skips it if it is.

Another point to note is on line 24. The script obtains all the installed SQL Server instances by retrieving the registry value InstalledInstances in the registry key HKEY_LOCAL_MACHINE/Software/Microsoft/Microsoft SQL Server. The data in this registry value contains multiple strings, separated by null. Each of the strings is the name of an installed SQL Server instance with the default instance being represented by MSSQLServer. Note that the ASCII value of null is 0; thus the strings are split into a list of individual strings with \0 on line 24.

It's convenient to keep a copy of the errorlog locations such as the preceding output. In fact, it's convenient to keep a copy of all the startup parameter values. You can easily modify the script in Listing 12-4 to print the values of all the startup parameters instead of the one that includes the errorlog location.

TIP *The Windows NT/2000 Resource Kit utility* reg.exe *is a versatile tool. You can use this tool to query, manipulate, back up, and restore the registry entries from the command line. In particular, when you know the registry path and want to see all the subentries at a glance, you can use* reg query <Registry Path> /s *to print the entire registry tree under that path. This is a nice complement to the GUI tools such as* Regedt32.exe *and* RegEdit.exe.

Obtaining Server Information with srvinfo.exe

SCENARIO
For each SQL Server in your environment, you want to quickly obtain such basic system information as the number of Central Processing Units (CPUs), the Windows version and the currently applied service pack, the domain of the server, the disk drives plus their capacity and usage, the network cards, the IP addresses, the system up time, and so on.

There are numerous ways to accomplish this task. You can use the Win32::TieRegistry module to get much of the wanted information from the registry on each server and use Win32::Service to get the information on the services. Alternatively, you can rely on the module Win32::Lanman. For completeness, you should know that you can use the Win32::OLE module to invoke Windows Management Instrumentation (WMI) or Active Directory Scripting Interface (ADSI) to retrieve a variety of system information. WMI and ADSI are two important topics not covered in this book.

This section takes a shortcut by using Perl to control the Windows 2000/NT Resource Kit utility srvinfo.exe and filter its output to return only the portion matching the criteria. The srvinfo.exe utility does the hard work of retrieving the system information. All that is left for you to do is to choose what you need from the output of srvinfo.exe.

This is a continuation of demonstrating how you can effectively use Perl to glue or extend other tools.

NOTE *The* srvinfo.exe *utility is one of the most useful command-line utilities on the Windows platform. If you haven't used it, you should drop everything else and try it right away. If you've used it, you've most likely found it indispensable.*

If you're not familiar with srvinfo.exe yet, you may want to carefully review Listing 12-5, which shows an output of running srvinfo.exe against the server SQL1.

Listing 12-5. The Sample Output of srvinfo.exe

```
cmd>srvinfo \\SQL1
Server Name: SQL1
Security: Users
Registered Owner: Linchi Shea
Registered Organization: Linchi Shea
ProductID: 987532-270-XYZ624-ABCDEFG
Original Install Date: Sat Sep 22 21:48:02 2001
Version: 5.0
Build: 2195, Service Pack 3
Current Type: Multiprocessor Free
Product Name: Microsoft Windows 2000
Product Options: Server, Enterprise, Terminal Server
HAL.DLL is  5.00.2195.5201 - Microsoft Corporation - 5.0:2195.81
PDC: \\NYRES.linchi.com
Domain: NYRES.linchi.com
CPU[0]: x86 Family 6 Model 10 Stepping 1: 699 MHz
CPU[1]: x86 Family 6 Model 10 Stepping 1: 699 MHz
CPU[2]: x86 Family 6 Model 10 Stepping 1: 699 MHz
CPU[3]: x86 Family 6 Model 10 Stepping 1: 699 MHz
Registered Owner: Linchi Shea
Hotfixes:
   [ServicePackUninstall]:
   [Q815021]:
   [Q811630]:
   ...
   [Q147222]:
Drive: [FileSys]  [ Size ]  [ Free ]  [ Used ]
   C$    NTFS       2048       233      1815
   D$    NTFS       2048       577      1471
   E$    NTFS       1946       283      1663
```

```
    G$      NTFS        142      139         3
Services:
    [Running]   Alerter
    [Stopped]   Application Management
    [Running]   AVSync Manager
    ...
    [Running]   Microsoft Search
    [Running]   MSSQL$APOLLO
    [Stopped]   MSSQL$PANTHEON
    [Stopped]   MSSQLServer
    [Stopped]   MSSQLServerADHelper
    [Stopped]   MSSQLServerOLAPService
    ...
    [Stopped]   SQLAgent$APOLLO
    [Stopped]   SQLAgent$PANTHEON
    [Stopped]   SQLServerAgent
    ...
    [Running]   Windows Management Instrumentation Driver Extensions
Network Card [0]: Compaq NC3131 Fast Ethernet NIC
Network Card [1]: Compaq NC3131 Fast Ethernet NIC
Network Card [2]: Compaq NC3131 Fast Ethernet NIC
Network Card [3]: Compaq NC3131 Fast Ethernet NIC
Protocols:
    Internet Protocol (TCP/IP)
    Network Monitor Driver
    Remote Access NDIS WAN Driver
    WINS Client(TCP/IP) Protocol
    Layer 2 Tunneling Protocol
    Point to Point Tunneling Protocol
    HP Network Teaming and Configuration
    Message-oriented TCP/IP Protocol (SMB session)
    System Up Time: 2 Days, 12 Hr, 31 Min, 10 Sec
```

As you can see, the output of srvinfo.exe falls into several categories:

- Basic system configurations, including the number of CPUs and their models, the operating system version and service pack, and the domain and the domain controller of the server

- Applied hot fixes

- All the drives, including capacities and usage

- Installed services, including their names and status

- Installed network interface cards

- Installed protocols

- System up time

 CAUTION   *If you run* srvinfo.exe *against Windows NT 4.0 with an older service pack, you may run into an access violation.*

You can simply run srvinfo.exe against all your SQL Server machines. However, the output would be voluminous. Often, you're only interested in certain aspects of your system configurations. Listing 12-6 shows the script grepSrvinfo.pl that allows you to specify a regular expression on the command line to filter for the exact information for which you're looking.

Listing 12-6. Filtering the Output of srvinfo.exe *from All the Servers*

```
1.  use strict;
2.  use Getopt::Std;
3.  use SQLDBA::Utility qw ( dbaReadINI );
4.
5.  Main: {
6.      my %opts;
7.      getopts('c:r:', \%opts); # get command line arguments
8.
9.      # check and normalize command line arguments
10.     my $argsRef = checkArgs(\%opts);
11.
12.     # run srvinfo.exe for each server, and scan the output for regex matches
13.     grepSrvinfo($argsRef);
14. } # Main
15.
16. #####################
17. sub checkArgs {
18.     my $argsRef = shift or die "***Err: checkArgs() expects a reference.";
19.
20.     # check the -c option for config file name.
21.     # -c is mandatory
22.     defined $argsRef->{c} or die "***Err: option -c must be specified.";
23.
24.     # get the server name into @temp
```

```perl
25.    my @temp;
26.    my $configRef = dbaReadINI($argsRef->{c});
27.    foreach my $instance (keys %$configRef) { # get the instance name
28.        $instance =~ /^([^\\]+)(\\.+)?/;
29.        push @temp, $1 unless grep /^$1$/i, @temp;
30.    }
31.    if (@temp) {   # if @temp is not empty
32.        $argsRef->{c} = \@temp; # record server names in the hash
33.    }
34.    else {
35.        die "***Err: didn't find any server in the config file.";
36.    }
37.
38.    # check the -r option for a regular expression
39.    # -r is optional. If not specified, all srvinfo.exe output is printed
40.    # if defined, it must be a valid regular expression
41.    if (defined $argsRef->{r}) {
42.        # check if it's prefixed with qr. If not, add it.
43.        my $re = 'qr' . $argsRef->{r} unless $argsRef->{r} =~ /^\s*qr/;
44.        my $regex = eval $re;
45.        if ($@) {
46.            die "***Err: $argsRef->{r} is not a valid regex.";
47.        }
48.        $argsRef->{r} = $regex;  # convert to compiled regex
49.    }
50.    return $argsRef;
51. } # checkArgs
52.
53. ##########################
54. sub grepSrvinfo {
55.    my $argsRef = shift or die "***Err: grepSrvinfo() expects a reference.";
56.
57.    foreach my $server (sort @{$argsRef->{c}}) { # loop through the servers
58.        print "***\n";
59.        print "*** srvinfo \\\\$server\n";
60.        print "***\n";
61.
62.        # execute srvinfo \\<serverName> and grep the output
63.        my @rs = grep /$argsRef->{r}/, `srvinfo \\\\$server`;
64.        foreach (@rs) {
65.            print "\t$_";
66.        }
67.    }
68. } # grepSrvinfo
```

On line 26 in Listing 12-6, the script grepSrvinfo.pl reads from the INI file all the SQL Server instance names. The INI file is specified on the command line with the -c switch. Because srvinfo.exe works on the server name, not the SQL Server instance name, the script singles out only the server names between lines 27 and 30 and keeps only the server names in the array $argsRef->{c} on line 32.

Between lines 41 and 49, the script validates the regular expression you specify with -r on the command line. The validation is performed using the Perl built-in function eval(). This prevents an invalid regular expression from crashing the whole script.

When everything goes well, the function checkArgs() exits on line 10 in the Main block of the script with a reference to a hash data structure that has a list of server names and a valid regular expression. The following is a sample of the data structure returned from the function checkArgs():

```
$argsRef = {
        'r' => qr/(?-xism:\[\w+\]\s+(MSSQL|SQLAgent|SQLServerAgent))/, # a regex
        'c' => [
                  'SQL1', 'SQL2'    # two server names
               ]
       };
```

In this example, there are two servers, SQL1 and SQL2, in the list, and the regular expression is to filter for the SQL Server services—including those running and those that have been stopped—reported by srvinfo.exe.

The function grepSrvinfo() on line 13 then runs srvinfo.exe against each server in the list and uses the regular expression to keep only the output that matches. This is all done on line 63, where srvinfo.exe is run in the backtick operator.

Now, let's look at several cases where this script can provide you useful information about the servers in your environment. In all the following cases, the results include only two servers, which is sufficient for illustration purposes.

Finding the System Up Time

To find the system up time from all the servers in your environment, you can run the script grepSrvinfo.pl as follows:

```
cmd>perl grepSrvinfo.pl -c config.txt -r "/System\s+Up\s+time/i"
***
*** srvinfo \\SQL1
***
     System Up Time: 0 Days, 1 Hr, 40 Min, 13 Sec


***
*** srvinfo \\SQL2
***
     System Up Time: 10 Days, 4 Hr, 35 Min, 21 Sec
```

Finding the Status of All the SQL Server Services

To find the status of all the SQL Server services in your environment, run the script as follows on a single line:

```
cmd>perl grepSrvinfo.pl -c config.txt
                     -r "/\[\w+\]\s+(MSSQL|SQLAgent|SQLServerAgent)/i"
***
*** srvinfo \\SQL1
***
     [Running]     MSSQL$APOLLO
     [Running]     SQLAgent$APOLLO


***
*** srvinfo \\SQL2
***
     [Stopped]     MSSQL$PANTHEON
     [Stopped]     MSSQLServer
     [Stopped]     MSSQLServerADHelper
     [Stopped]     MSSQLServerOLAPService
     [Stopped]     SQLAgent$PANTHEON
     [Stopped]     SQLServerAgent
```

Finding the Domains of All the SQL Servers

To find the domains of all the SQL Servers in your environment, run the script as follows:

```
cmd>perl grepSrvinfo.pl -c config.txt -r "/^\s*Domain:/i"
***
*** srvinfo \\SQL1
***

    Domain: NYRES


***
*** srvinfo \\SQL2
***

    Domain: NJRES
```

Finding Information About All the Drives

To find the information on all the disk drives on the SQL Servers in your environment, run the script grepSrvinfo.pl as follows:

```
cmd>perl grepSrvinfo.pl -c config.txt -r "/^\s*(Drive:|\w\$\s+\w+\s+\d+)/i"
***
*** srvinfo \\SQL1
***
```

Drive:	[FileSys]	[Size]	[Free]	[Used]
C$	NTFS	2048	232	1816
D$	NTFS	2048	577	1471
E$	NTFS	1946	283	1663
G$	NTFS	142	139	3

```
***
*** srvinfo \\SQL2
***
```

Drive:	[FileSys]	[Size]	[Free]	[Used]
C$	NTFS	4096	1024	3072
D$	NTFS	4096	577	3519

Note that you need Drive: in the regular expression so that the script also prints the headings of the disk usage table.

As you can see, it's powerful to combine Perl, `srvinfo.exe`, and a list of all your SQL Server instances. However, you may have noticed that one important parameter is missing from the output of `srvinfo.exe`. That's the memory configuration of the server.

The next section presents a script to retrieve the information on the memory configurations of all the servers in your environment.

Finding the Memory Configurations

SCENARIO

You want to find how the memory is configured on all your servers.

When it comes to configuring SQL Server, there aren't that many knobs for you to turn. SQL Server works relatively well out of box. However, when you run multiple instances on a server and when you use a large amount of memory (more than 3 gigabytes), you need to keep an eye on your memory configurations. In a large environment, this need becomes especially acute. You can't afford to wait until a problem occurs or waste valuable memory resources because of inappropriate configurations.

What server or SQL Server instance memory configuration parameters are of importance to the SQL Server DBA? The DBA should keep track of the following memory configurations:

- The total amount of physical memory.

- The memory allocation in each SQL Server instance—in other words, the values of the `sp_configure` options `max server memory` and `min server memory`.

- The `awe enabled` option of `sp_configure`, which enables SQL Server 2000 Enterprise Edition or Developer Edition to support Windows 2000 Address Windowing Extensions (AWE).

- The `/3gb` and `/pae` parameters in the `boot.ini` file. The `/3gb` parameter enables Windows 2000 Advanced Server and Windows 2000 Datacenter Server to support a 3GB virtual address space, and the `/pae` parameter enables them to use more than 4GB of physical memory.

A report on these memory configuration parameters for all the SQL Server instances in your environment allows you to determine whether memory is properly configured for a given SQL Server instance, for all the SQL Server instances on a server, and for the SQL Server instances to take advantage of the physical memory beyond 4GB.

Listing 12-7 is the script findMemoryConfig.pl that loops through all the SQL Server instances listed in an INI file and produces a report that includes the information on these memory configuration parameters for each server on the list.

Listing 12-7. Reporting on SQL Server Memory Configurations

```
1.   use strict;
2.   use SQLDBA::Utility qw( dbaReadINI dbaRunQueryADO dbaRunOsql );
3.
4.   my $configFile = shift or die "***Err: $0 expects a config file.";
5.   my $configRef = dbaReadINI($configFile);
6.
7.   # loop through the SQL instances to get their memory configurations
8.   foreach my $server (sort keys %$configRef) {
9.       next if $server =~ /^CONTROL$/i;
10.
11.      # need to determine the SQL version first because some memory
12.      # configurations are version dependent
13.      my $ver = dbaRunOsql($server, 'select @@version',
14.                                    {'-E' => undef, '-d' => 'master'});
15.      next unless $ver =~ /(7.00|8.00)/; # only applies to SQL7 or SQL2000
16.
17.      print "\n***\n***Server: $server\n***\n";
18.      if ($ver =~ /(\d.00.\d+)/) { print " Version: $1\n"; }
19.
20.      # get the total physical memory
21.      my $sql = "EXEC master..xp_msver \'PhysicalMemory\'";
22.      my $result = dbaRunQueryADO($server, $sql, 3);
23.      my $rd = shift @{shift @$result};
24.      print " PhysicalMemory: $rd->{Internal_Value} (MB)\n";
25.
26.      # get SQL instance memory configurations
27.      $sql = <<___ENDSQL;
28.        set nocount on
29.        EXEC sp_configure 'max server memory'
30.        EXEC sp_configure 'min server memory'
31.        if charindex('8.00.', \@\@version) > 0 # only applies to SQL2000
32.            EXEC sp_configure 'awe enabled'
33.   ___ENDSQL
34.
35.      $result = dbaRunQueryADO($server, $sql, 3);
36.      printf " %-30s %-11s %-11s %-11s %-11s\n",
37.              'name', 'minimum', 'maximum', 'config_value', 'run_value';
38.      printf " %-30s %-11s %-11s %-11s %-11s\n",
```

```
39.            '-' x 30, '-' x 11, '-' x 11, '-' x 11, '-' x 11;
40.    foreach my $rset (@$result) {
41.        foreach my $r (@$rset) {
42.            printf " %-30s %-11s %-11s %-11s %-11s\n",
43.                    $r->{name}, $r->{minimum}, $r->{maximum},
44.                    $r->{config_value}, $r->{run_value};
45.        }
46.    }
47.
48.    # determine the system drive of the server so that we know
49.    # where to scan the boot.ini file on the server
50.    my $sysDrive = dbaRunOsql($server,
51.                             "EXEC xp_cmdshell 'set systemdrive'",
52.                             {'-E' => undef, '-d' => 'master'});
53.    if ($sysDrive =~ /\n\s*SystemDrive=(\w):/i) {
54.        $sysDrive = $1;
55.
56.        # get boot.ini memory parameters /3gb and /pae
57.        $server =~ s/\\.+//;
58.        my $bootini = "\\\\$server\\$sysDrive\$\\boot.ini";
59.        print "\n boot.ini configurations:\n";
60.        open(BOOT, $bootini) or warn " ***Err: couldn't open $bootini.";
61.        while (<BOOT>) {
62.            print " $_" if /multi\(\d+\)disk/i;
63.        }
64.        close(BOOT);
65.    }
66.    else {
67.        warn "***Err: couldn't get the system drive via xp_cmshell.";
68.    }
69. }
```

In Listing 12-7, after reading in the INI file on line 5, the script findMemoryConfig.pl loops through the SQL Server instances listed in the INI file. The loop starts on line 8. For each SQL Server instance, the script divides the work performed by the script into four sections:

1. Between lines 11 and 18, the script findMemoryConfig.pl determines the version of the SQL Server instance. Because some memory configuration parameters are applicable only to SQL Server 2000, it's important to ascertain the version first.

2. Between lines 20 and 24, the script retrieves the total amount of physical memory on the server through the T-SQL query xp_msver 'PhysicalMemory'. The value is retrieved using the dbaRunQueryADO() function imported from the module SQLDBA::Utility.

3. Between lines 26 and 46, the script retrieves the memory options of sp_configure. The two memory options are max server memory and min server memory. For SQL Server 2000, the script retrieves the setting of awe enabled. Again, the script relies on the dbaRunQueryADO() function to retrieve the option values from the SQL Server instance.

4. The final section of the script retrieves the content of the boot.ini file from the server. The key step is to determine on which drive the boot.ini file resides. Note that this file always resides on the system drive. The script queries the SQL Server instance with xp_cmdshell 'set systemdrive' and parses the result to identify the system drive.

Listing 12-8 shows a sample result of running the findMemoryConfig.pl script. As usual, the config.txt file has all the SQL Server instances listed in its section headings.

Listing 12-8. Sample Output of findMemoryConfig.pl

```
cmd>perl findmemoryConfig.pl config.txt
***
***Server: SQL1
***

Version: 8.00.760
PhysicalMemory: 4096 (MB)
name                         minimum     maximum     config_value run_value
---------------------------- ----------- ----------- ----------- -----------
max server memory (MB)       4           2147483647  2147483647  2147483647
min server memory (MB)       0           2147483647  0           0
awe enabled                  0           1           0           0

boot.ini configurations:
default=multi(0)disk(0)rdisk(0)partition(2)\WINNT
multi(0)disk(0)rdisk(0)partition(2)\WINNT="Microsoft Windows 2000 ... /3GB /pae

***
***Server: SQL2
***

Version: 8.00.679
```

```
PhysicalMemory: 8192 (MB)
name                       minimum     maximum     config_value run_value
-------------------------- ----------- ----------- ------------ -----------
max server memory (MB)     4           2147483647  5120         5120
min server memory (MB)     0           2147483647  5120         5120
awe enabled                0           1           0            0


boot.ini configurations:
default=multi(0)disk(0)rdisk(0)partition(2)\WINNT
multi(0)disk(0)rdisk(0)partition(2)\WINNT="Microsoft Windows 2000 ... /3GB /pae
```

Note that the SQL Server version and the max/min server memory options are specific to the SQL Server instance. The physical memory and the boot.ini file are attributes of the server as a whole. In Listing 12-8, both SQL Server instances are configured with the /3gb and /pae parameters. On SQL1, this was apparently a mistake because the server only has a total physical memory of 4GB. The default instance on SQL2 is configured to use a fixed amount memory of 5120MB (or 5GB) because both the max server memory and the min server memory are set to the same value.

Having such a memory configuration report for all the SQL Server instances in your environment is nice. It would be even better to expand the script in Listing 12-7 to include checking some best-practice rules so that it can help detect inappropriate memory configurations.

Archiving the SQL Server System Tables

SCENARIO
You want to preserve a history of the SQL Server system tables.

The SQL Server system tables, including the system tables in the master database and the system tables in all user databases, store critical system information about the SQL Server configurations, the database configurations, and the object schema. In addition, they contain information on such SQL Server components as replications and SQL Server Agent scheduled jobs.

SQL Server DBAs use the system tables constantly, but in most cases indirectly. When you generate and archive the scripts for your database objects, you're archiving the information from the system tables. When you save the information about your replication setup, you're archiving the information from the system tables. When you check the backup history of your databases, you're reviewing the information from the system tables.

There's no need to reiterate the importance of keeping a history of the snapshots of your SQL Server environment. You can do so in many different ways. One way is to keep a history of the re-engineered database scripts such as the object schema scripts, the scheduled job scripts, and the replication setup scripts. You can also keep a history of your database and server configurations.

Eventually, you'll come to a situation where you need the information about certain aspects of your environment at a certain point in time in the recent past. However, to your great dismay, you discover that the information isn't available because no setup was in place to take the snapshot of those aspects of your environment.

The danger of selectively preserving information is that you may not have the information when you need it. You can eliminate this danger by preserving all the information, if possible. Having been burnt a few times, I've come to appreciate the importance of keeping a comprehensive repository of the system information by archiving all the system tables.

Instead of selectively preserving the SQL Server system information, you can choose to archive all the system information by archiving all the system tables indiscriminately. Some of the information in the archived system tables won't be as immediately usable as reverse-engineered T-SQL scripts or the result of sp_configure. But when you've archived every system table, you're assured that whatever system you may need is there. When you're in a disaster situation, this assurance is extremely comforting.

Listing 12-9 is the Perl script archiveSysTables.pl that bulk copies out all the system tables from all the SQL Server instances listed in an INI file. The script allows you to specify for how many days the bulk copied files should be preserved. This helps contain the storage consumption of the archived system tables.

Listing 12-9. Archiving All the SQL Server System Tables

```
use strict;
use SQLDBA::Utility qw( dbaRunQueryADO dbaReadINI dbaTime2str dbaStr2time );
use Data::Dumper;

my $configFile = shift or die "***Err: $0 expects an INI file.";
(-T $configFile) or die "***Err: $0 couldn't find $configFile.";

Main: {
    my $configRef = dbaReadINI($configFile);
    $configRef = validateConfig($configRef);

    # bulk copy out all the system tables
    bcpSysTables($configRef);
    # purge the old directories, if any
    purgeOldDir($configRef);
} # Main
```

```perl
#######################
sub bcpSysTables {
   my ($configRef) = @_;

   foreach my $server (sort keys %$configRef) {
      next if $server =~ /^CONTROL$/i;
      next if $configRef->{$server}->{DISABLED} =~ /^y/i;

      print "\n****\n";
      print "**** Bulk copy system tables from $server\n";
      print "****\n\n";

      # get the complete list of the system table names
      my $tableRef = getSysTableNames($configRef, $server, 'SystemTables');

      my $dir;
      # create a directory with today's date string
      $dir = createDir($configRef, $server);
      if ($dir and -d $dir) {                   # directory created and exists
         # loop through each system table to export it
         foreach my $table (@$tableRef) {
            # construct the bulk copy statement using trusted connection
            my $bcpcmd = "bcp $table out $dir\\$table\.txt -c -S$server -T";
            print "\n-- $bcpcmd\n";  # debug print
            system($bcpcmd);            # execute bcp
         }
      }
   }
} #bcpSysTables


#######################
sub validateConfig {
   my $configRef = shift or
      die "***Err: validateConfig() expects a reference.";

   # The path to the archive folder root must be specified
   defined $configRef->{CONTROL}->{REPOSITORYFILESHARE} or
      die "***Err: RepositoryFileShare is not specified.";

   # set default configurations
   $configRef->{CONTROL}->{KEEPDAYS} ||= 10;  # default to 10 days
   $configRef->{CONTROL}->{KEEPMINIMUMNUMBER} ||= 10;  # default to 10 days
   return $configRef;
} # validateConfig
```

```perl
############################
sub getSysTableNames {
   my ($ref, $server) = @_;
   my $excludedDB = '';

   # construct the excluded DB conditions for the WHERE clause
   my @excludedDBs = split(/\s*[,;]\s*/, $ref->{$server}->{EXCLUDEDB});
   for (@excludedDBs) { $_ = q/'/ . $_ . q/'/; }  # add single quotes
   if (@excludedDBs) {
      $excludedDB = ' AND name NOT IN (' . join(/,/, @excludedDBs) . ')';
   }

   # construct the SQL script to get all the system tables
   my $sql =<<"TSQL__";
     SET NOCOUNT ON

     CREATE TABLE \#name (name varchar(255))

     DECLARE \@db sysname,
             \@name sysname,
             \@sql varchar(255)

     DECLARE name_cr CURSOR
     FOR SELECT RTRIM(name)
          FROM master..sysdatabases
          WHERE name NOT IN ('model', 'tempdb', 'pubs', 'Northwind')
          $excludedDB
     FOR READ ONLY

     OPEN name_cr
     FETCH name_cr INTO \@db
     WHILE \@\@FETCH_STATUS = 0
     BEGIN
       SELECT \@sql = 'select ''' + \@db + '..'' + name
         FROM ' + \@db + '..sysobjects
        WHERE type = ''S''
          AND id < 100
          AND NOT name LIKE ''MS%'''

       INSERT \#name
       EXEC (\@sql)

       FETCH name_cr INTO \@db
     END
```

```
        CLOSE name_cr
        DEALLOCATE name_cr

        SELECT * FROM \#name
TSQL__

    my @list;
    # get the first resultset (there is only one result in this case)
    my $rs = dbaRunQueryADO($server, $sql, 3);
    foreach my $r (@{shift @$rs}) {   # loop through the first resultset
        push @list, $r->{name};         # add the system table name to the list
    }
    \@list;    # return the list of system table names
} #getSysTableNames


####################
sub createDir {
    my ($ref, $server, $source) = @_;

    my $serverDir = $server;
    $serverDir =~ s/\\/\_/g;

    my($sec, $min, $hour, $mday, $mon, $year, $wday, $yday, $isdst)
                    = localtime();
    my $timeStr = sprintf("%04d-%02d-%02d", $year+1900, ++$mon, $mday);

    my $dir =  $ref->{CONTROL}->{REPOSITORYFILESHARE} .
                "\\$serverDir\\$source\\$timeStr";
    # create the directory if not exists
    `md $dir` unless (-d $dir);

    if (-d $dir) {
        return $dir;
    }
    else {
        return 0;
    }
} #createDir


######################
sub purgeOldDir {
    my ($configRef, $source) = @_;
```

```
    foreach my $server (sort keys %$configRef) {
       next if $server =~ /^CONTROL$/i;
       next if $configRef->{$server}->{DISABLED} =~ /^y/i;

       my $serverDir = $server;
       $serverDir =~ s/\\/\_/g;  # change backslash to underscore

       my $dir = $configRef->{CONTROL}->{REPOSITORYFILESHARE} .
                   "\\$serverDir\\$source";
       opendir DIR, "$dir" or
          do {print "***Err: could not open directory $dir"; return; };
       # only get the folders whose names are date strings
       my @dirs = grep {/\d\d\d\d-\d\d-\d\d/} readdir DIR;
       close(DIR);

       my %r_dirs;   # used to help sort by date/time
       map { $r_dirs{dbaStr2time($_)} = $_ } @dirs;

       my $i = scalar @dirs;  # get the total dir count
       foreach my $d (sort keys %r_dirs) {  # sort by date/time
          # exit if the dir count is at or below the min threshold
          last if ($i <= $configRef->{CONTROL}->{KEEPMINIMUMNUMBER});
          # remove the dir if it's older than the KeepDays threshold
          if ((time() - $d) > $configRef->{CONTROL}->{KEEPDAYS}*24*3600) {
             print "Removing $dir\\$r_dirs{$d}. It's more than ",
                     "$configRef->{$server}->{KeepDays} days old.\n";
             # remove the directory
             `rd \/s \/q $dir\\$r_dirs{$d}` if (-d "$dir\\$r_dirs{$d}");
             $i--;
          }
       }
    }
 }
} #purgeOldDir
```

The script archiveSysTables.pl in Listing 12-9 accepts an INI file, an example of which is shown in Listing 12-10.

Listing 12-10. A Sample INI File for archiveSysTables.pl

```
[CONTROL]
RepositoryFileShare=\\DBASRV1\DBARepository
KeepDays=20
KeepMinimumNumber=20

[SQL1]
Disabled=no
ExcludeDB=CDReports,CTSummary

[SQL1\APOLLO]
Disabled=no
ExcludeDB=

[SQL2]
Disabled=yes
ExcludeDB=
```

Table 12-1 briefly describes the configuration options in this INI file.

Table 12-1. Configuration Options for archiveSysTables.pl

OPTION	DESCRIPTION
RepositoryFileShare	Specifies a folder to store the files of the exported system tables. The exported files aren't directly stored in this directory but in the various subfolders.
KeepDays	Specifies the number of days in which the exported files must be kept.
KeepMinimumNumber	Specifies the minimum number of copies of the exported system tables you want to keep. Note that the KeepDays option doesn't guarantee that you'll at least have that many copies. This option takes precedence over KeepDays.
ExcludeDB	Specifies a comma-separated list of databases whose system tables you don't care to preserve.

Save the configurations in Listing 12-10 to the file `config.txt` and run the script in Listing 12-9 with `config.txt` as follows:

```
cmd>perl archiveSysTables.pl config.txt
```

You have instructed the script to perform the following:

- Bulk copy out all the system tables from the SQL Server instances SQL1 and SQL1\APOLLO. Note that SQL2 is disabled in `config.txt`.

- For SQL1, the system tables will be bulk copied to the directory `\\DBASRV1\DBARepository\SQL1\SystemTables\2003-04-12`, if you run the script on April 12, 2003. For SQL1\APOLLO, the script will bulk copy all the system tables to the directory `\\DBASRV1\DBARepository\SQL1_APOLLO\SystemTables\2003-04-12`.

- For each SQL Server instance listed in the INI file, if the number of subdirectories under the `SystemTables` directory is more than 20—the value of the `KeepMinimumNumber` option in the `Control` section of the INI file—the script removes the older subdirectories to keep the number at 20.

In summary, all the system tables are exported to their respective subdirectories under the directory specified with the option `RepositiryFileShare`. In the `RepositoryFileShare` directory, there's a subdirectory for each SQL Server instance listed in the INI file. Under the directory that bears the name of the instance, there's a `SystemTables` directory whose subdirectories are all named with date strings. The intension is to run the script `archiveSysTables.pl` in Listing 12-9 once a day. Each time it runs, the current date string is assigned to a new subdirectory under the `SystemTables` directory.

Listing 12-11 is an example directory structure that the script `archiveSysTables.pl` maintains for the instances SQL1 and SQL1\APOLLO.

Listing 12-11. Sample Directory Structure to Store the Bulk Copied System Tables

```
\\DBASRV1\DBARepository\SQL1\SystemTables\2003-03-31\
                            ...
                            TradeDB..sysindexes.txt
                            ...
                            master..sysobjects.txt
                            ...
                            \2003-04-01\
                            ...
                            TradeDB..sysindexes.txt
                            ...
                            master..sysobjects.txt
                            ...
                        ...
\\DBASRV1\DBARepository\SQL1_APOLLO\SystemTables\2003-03-31\
                            ...
                            GSSDB..sysindexes.txt
                            ...
                            master..sysobjects.txt
                            ...
                            \2003-04-01\
                            ...
                            GSSDB..sysindexes.txt
                            ...
                            master..sysobjects.txt
                            ...
                        ...
```

The script in Listing 12-11 is relatively straightforward. The script controls the bulk copy process and manages the directory structures and the exported files.

Note the design decision to use the qualified system table name as the name of the exported text file. This allows the function getSysTableNames() to retrieve the names of all the system tables on a given SQL Server instance and returns them in a single list regardless of which database the script is working with at the time. This also allows the script to export all the system tables on a given day to the same directory without running into any system table name clash.

On an ordinary day, there's little need for accessing these exported system tables because there's almost always a better way to get to whatever system information you want to obtain than to interrogate the exported system tables. And in a well-planned environment, you probably never need to access these exported system tables.

However, no environment is ideal and not everything can be well planned in advance. The exported system tables have helped me several times. In one case, a server failed with a completely ruined disk subsystem. It turned out that I only needed to recover one of the databases. A quick text search in the exported files `msdb..backupset.txt` and `msdb..backupmediafamily.txt` revealed in which directory the most recent backup files of the database were located.

In another case, the troubleshooting team wanted to know whether a SQL Server configuration parameter was changed in the last few days. Again, a quick search in the folders corresponding to the past few days' archives of `master..sysconfigures.txt` and `master..syscurconfigs.txt` provided the answer.

NOTE *You should treat the exported system tables as your last line of defense. Don't rely on them. Instead, devote efforts to maintain a robust and up-to-date DBA repository that keeps information in a more readily accessible format.*

Archiving the SQL Server Registry Entries

SCENARIO
You want to preserve a history of the complete SQL Server system information.

The preceding section, "Archiving the SQL Server System Tables," gives you a means to preserve all the SQL Server system tables in your environment. Unfortunately, not all the SQL Server system information is in the system tables. To be complete, you also need to preserve the SQL Server registry entries.

This section continues the same philosophy of the preceding section. That is, instead of selectively preserving SQL Server registry entries, it preserves all the SQL Server registry entries for fear of missing anything that you may find useful later.

The SQL Server registry entries include such important configuration information as the SQL Server startup parameters, the network library configurations, the SQL Server service accounts, and SQL Server Agent error log location.

Conceptually, the script archiveSQLReg.pl in Listing 12-12 is similar to the script archiveSysTables.pl in Listing 12-9. Rather than bulk copying out the system tables, archiveSQLReg.pl exports the SQL Server registry entries to the text files using the Windows 2000/NT Resource Kit utility regdump.exe and manages the exported files in exactly the same way archiveSysTables.pl manages the bulk copies of the system tables.

Listing 12-12. Archiving the SQL Server Registry Entries

```
use strict;
use SQLDBA::Utility qw( dbaReadINI dbaTime2str dbaStr2time );

my $configFile = shift or die "***Err: $0 expects an INI file.";
(-T $configFile) or die "***Err: $0 couldn't find $configFile.";

Main: {
   my $configRef = dbaReadINI($configFile);
   $configRef = validateConfig($configRef);

   # export the SQL Server registry entries
   exportSQLReg($configRef);
   # purge the old directories, if any
   purgeOldDir($configRef, 'RegistryEntries');
} # Main


########################
sub exportSQLReg {
   my ($configRef) = @_;

   foreach my $server (sort keys %$configRef) {
      next if $server =~ /^CONTROL$/i;
      next if $configRef->{$server}->{DISABLED} =~ /^y/i;

      print "\n****\n";
      print "**** Export SQL registry entries for $server\n";
      print "****\n\n";

      my ($dir, $instance, $regPath, $outPath, $regdmp);
      $dir = createDir($configRef, $server, 'RegistryEntries');

      # check it's a named instance or the default instance
      if ($server =~ /^([^\\]+)(\\(.+))?$/i) {
         ($server, $instance) = ($1, $3);
      }
```

```perl
if ($dir and -d $dir) {                  # directory created and exists
   # 1. Export the entries under HKLM\Software\Microsoft
   #   1.a If it's the default instance, export entries in \MSSQLServer
   #   1.b If it's a named instancem export entries in
   #                                \Microsoft SQL Server\<InstanceName>
   $outPath = "$dir\\SoftwareEntries.log";
   if ($instance) {  # a named instance
      $regPath = "HKEY_LOCAL_MACHINE\\Software\\Microsoft\\" .
                 "Microsoft SQL Server\\$instance";
   }
   else {            # the default instance
      $regPath = "HKEY_LOCAL_MACHINE\\Software\\Microsoft\\MSSQLServer";
   }
   # construct the regdmp.exe command line
   $regdmp = "regdmp -m \\\\$server -o 2048 \"$regPath\" > $outPath";
   print "\n-- $regdmp\n";  # debug print
   system($regdmp);         # execute regdmp.exe


   # 2. Export the entries under HKLM\System\CurrentControlSet\Services
   #   2.a For default instance, export entries in \MSSQLServer and
   #                                                \SQLServerAgent
   #   2.b For a named instancem, export entries in \MSSQL$<Instance>
   #                                                \SQLAgent$<Instance>
   $outPath = "$dir\\SystemEntries.log";
   my ($mssqlPath, $sqlAgentPath);
   if ($instance) {  # a named instance
      $mssqlPath = "HKEY_LOCAL_MACHINE\\System\\CurrentControlSet\\" .
                 "Services\\MSSQL\$$instance";
      $sqlAgentPath = "HKEY_LOCAL_MACHINE\\System\\CurrentControlSet\\" .
                 "Services\\SQLAgent\$$instance";
   }
   else {            # the default instance
      $mssqlPath = "HKEY_LOCAL_MACHINE\\System\\CurrentControlSet\\" .
                 "Services\\MSSQLServer";
      $sqlAgentPath = "HKEY_LOCAL_MACHINE\\System\\CurrentControlSet\\" .
                 "Services\\SQLServerAgent";
   }
   # construct the regdmp.exe command line for MSSQL service
   $regdmp = "regdmp -m \\\\$server -o 2048 \"$mssqlPath\" > $outPath";
   print "\n-- $regdmp\n";  # debug print
   system($regdmp);         # execute regdmp.exe


   # construct the regdmp.exe command line for SQLAgent service
```

```
        $regdmp = "regdmp -m \\\\$server -o 2048 \"$sqlAgentPath\" >> $outPath";
        print "\n-- $regdmp\n";   # debug print
        system($regdmp);          # execute regdmp.exe
      }
    }
} #exportSQLReg


######################
sub validateConfig{
# See the same function in 12-9
}  # validateConfig


##################
sub createDir {
# See the same function in Listing 12-9
} #createDir


#####################
sub purgeOldDir {
# See the same function in Listing 12-9
} #purgeOldDir
```

Similar to archiveSysTables.pl, you run this script as follows:

```
cmd>perl archiveSQLReg.pl config.txt
```

where config.txt is the same INI file accepted by archiveSysTables.pl. See
Table 12-1 for a brief description of its options.

For the default SQL Server instance, the following three registry keys under
HKEY_LOCAL_MACHINE are important:

- Software\Microsoft\MSSQLServer

- System\CurrentControlSet\Services\MSSQLServer

- System\CurrentControlSet\Services\SQLServerAgent

For a named instance, the three HKEY_LOCAL_MACHINE registry keys are as
follows:

- Software\Microsoft\MSSQL$<InstanceName>

- System\CurrentControlSet\Services\MSSQL$<InstanceName>

- System\CurrentControlSet\Services\SQLServer$<InstanceName>

The bulk of the script in Listing 12-12 involves preparing the correct registry path and the correct output directory for the `regdmp.exe` command line. For a named instance, say SQL1\APOLLO, if you execute `archiveSQLReg.pl` on April 14, 2003, the `regdmp.exe` command line generated by `archiveSQLReg.pl` to archive everything under the registry path HKEY_LOCAL_MACHINE\Software\Microsoft\MSSQL$APOLLO is as follows (all should be on the same line):

```
regdmp -m \\SQL1 -o 2048 "HKEY_LOCAL_MACHINE\Software\Microsoft\MSSQL$APOLLO"
    > \\DBASRV1\Repository\SQL1\RegistryEntries\2003-04-14\SoftwareEntries.log
```

After the script has executed this `regdmp.exe` command, the file `SoftwareEntries.log` has all the keys and values under the specified registry path.

NOTE   *You need to be a member of the local administrators group to execute the script* `archiveSQLReg.pl` *because it accesses parts of the registry.*

The scripts `archiveSysTables.pl` and `archiveSQLReg.pl` together enable you to preserve a history of comprehensive system information for the SQL Server installations in your environment.

With this comprehensive system information securely stashed away, you now have the peace of mind that you can answer any question thrown at you. For some of the questions, it may take some digging in these archived system tables and registry entries. But it's comforting to know that the information is available.

Purging Old Obsolete Backup Files

SCENARIO
You want to scan for and remove old obsolete backup files that litter your servers.

In a large SQL Server environment with many servers and many DBAs, the problem of old obsolete database backup files or log backup files littering your disk drives and eating away space isn't phantom.

It's a common practice that during an upgrade or new release, the DBA would make a few database backups and plan to remove them in a few days. But sometimes the files that are supposed to be transient live a much longer life than they should.

It's not an easy task to clean up these old backup files that could be in any directories on any server. The cleanup is further complicated by the fact that the files could assume any names, bound only by the whim of the DBA at the time of their creation. You can impose standards and procedures to mitigate the problem. But it's unrealistic to expect that the standards and procedures be followed by every DBA at all time. To remove them, you need to look for them everywhere on the server.

It's easy to scan for files and find their ages. But the key question is this: How do you determine an old file is a database or transaction log backup file? You certainly can't rely on any file-naming convention. When different DBAs are involved, the file-naming convention is at best unreliable.

Fortunately, you can enlist the help from SQL Server to check each file with the T-SQL statement RESTORE FILELISTONLY or RESTORE HEADERONLY. If the file isn't a SQL Server 7.0 or SQL Server 2000 backup file, you would get an error if you apply either of these two statements to the file.

The strategy is therefore to scan all the directories on each server (excluding some obvious directories such as the system directory) for the files that are older than the age threshold and then test each old file using the RESTORE FILELISTONLY statement to determine whether it's a SQL Server backup file. The script purgeOldBackupFiles.pl in Listing 12-13 implements this strategy.

Listing 12-13. Purging Old Backup Files

```
1.   use strict;
2.   use SQLDBA::Utility qw( dbaReadINI );
3.   use Getopt::Std;
4.   use Win32::OLE;
5.
6.   # Make these variables global for the function scriptDel() to use
7.   my (%opts, $conn);
8.
9.   getopts('c:S:a:', \%opts); # get command-line arguments
10.  unless (defined $opts{c} and defined $opts{S} and defined $opts{a}) {
11.     printUsage();
12.  }
13.
14.  # establish the ADO connection to SQL instance to verify file format
15.  $conn = Win32::OLE->new('ADODB.Connection') or
16.     die "***Err: Win32::OLE->new() failed.";
17.  $conn->{ConnectionTimeout} = 4;     # set connection timeout to 4 sec
18.  $conn->Open("Provider=sqloledb;Server=$opts{S};Trusted_Connection=yes");
19.  ! Win32::OLE->LastError() or die Win32::OLE->LastError();
```

```
20.
21.  Main: {
22.      my $configRef = dbaReadINI($opts{c});
23.
24.      # loop through all the servers
25.      foreach my $server (sort keys %$configRef) {
26.          $server =~ /^([^\\]+)\\/ and $server = $1;
27.
28.          # get all the drive letters for the server
29.          my @srvinfo = `srvinfo \\\\$server`;
30.          my @drives;
31.          foreach my $line (@srvinfo) {
32.              if ($line =~ /\s*(\w)\$\s+\w+\s+\d+/) { # e.g. C$  NTFS  234
33.                  push @drives, $1;
34.              }
35.          }
36.          unless (@drives) {
37.              warn "***Err: problem getting drive info from srvinfo.exe.";
38.          }
39.
40.          # check each drive and all its subdirectories
41.          foreach my $dr (@drives) {
42.              my $dir = "\\\\$server\\$dr\$";
43.              print "Checking $dir ...\n";
44.
45.              # now recursively check each file in the directory
46.              # and all its sub-directories
47.              walkDir($dir);
48.          }
49.      }
50.  } # Main
51.
52.  # close the ADO connection
53.  $conn->Close();
54.
55.  ################
56.  sub walkDir {
57.      my $dir = shift or die "***Err: walkDir() expects a reference.";
58.
59.      opendir(DIR, $dir) or die "***Err: can't open $dir.";
60.      my @list = readdir(DIR);
61.      foreach my $dirfile (@list) {
62.          next if $dirfile =~ /^(\.\.|\.)$/;  # skip . and ..
63.
```

```
64.          # now the real work of working with the file
65.          if (-f "$dir\\$dirfile") {
67.              # check the file and generate del command if the file
68.              # meets the criteria
69.              scriptDel("$dir\\$dirfile");
70.          }
71.
72.          if (-d "$dir\\$dirfile") {
73.              # skip these before recursively call walkDir() again
74.              next if $dirfile =~ /system\s+volume\s+information/i;
75.              next if $dirfile =~ /(documents and settings|recycler)/i;
76.              next if $dirfile =~ /(winnt|program files|platform sdk|binn)/i;
77.
78.              print "\tChecking $dir\\$dirfile\n";
79.              walkDir("$dir\\$dirfile");
80.          }
81.      }
82.      close(DIR);
83. } # walkDir
84.
85. #################
86. sub scriptDel {
87.      my $file = shift or die "***Err: scriptDel() expects a file.";
88.      my $size = 0;
89.
90.      # if the file is older than the age threshold
91.      if (-M $file > $opts{a} ) {
92.          # skip the file if it has any of these file extension
93.          return if /\.(mdf|ndf|ldf|exe|dll|htm|html|ini|gif|sql|bat)$/i;
94.
95.          # construct the RESTORE FILELISTONLY statement
96.          my $sql = "RESTORE FILELISTONLY FROM disk=\'$file\'";
97.          if (my $rs = $conn->Execute($sql)) {      # if it returns a recordset
98.              while (!$rs->{EOF}) {
99.                  # if LogicalName has a value, this is a backup file
100.                 if ($rs->Fields('LogicalName')->{Value}) {
101.                     print "del \"$file\"\n";
102.                     last;
103.                 }
104.             } # while
105.         } # Execute()
106.     } # -M
107. } # scriptDel
108.
```

```
109. ###################
110. sub printUsage {
111.    print <<__Usage__;
112. usage:
113.    cmd>perl $0 -c <config file> -S <Server> -a <Age>
114.
115.       -c accepts an INI file name
116.       -S accepts the name of the SQL Server which runs RESTORE FILELISTONLY
117.       -a sets the age threshold in days
118. __Usage__
119.    exit;
120. }
```

On the command line, the script in Listing 12-13 accepts an INI file that lists the SQL Server instances in the section headings and a SQL Server 2000 instance that's used to help test whether a file is a SQL Server backup file. The script also accepts a file age threshold. It doesn't check any file newer than this age threshold.

Assume that you have the servers SQL1 and SQL2 listed in the file config.txt and that you've decided to use the SQL Server instance SQL1\APOLLO to run the RESTORE FILELISTONLY test. You can then run the script purgeOldBackupFiles.pl as shown in Listing 12-14 to generate a batch file of the Windows del commands. The batch file deletes from these two servers the SQL Server backup files that are older than 10 days.

Listing 12-14. Sample Result of Running purgeOldBackupFiles.pl

```
cmd>perl purgeOldBackupFiles.pl -c config.txt -S SQL1\APOLLO -a 10
Checking \\SQL1\C$ ...
...
Checking \\SQL1\D$ ...
    Checking \\SQL1\D$\SQLData
    Checking \\SQL1\D$\SQLDBA
    Checking \\SQL1\D$\SQLDBA\logs
    Checking \\SQL1\D$\SQLDBA\scripts
    Checking \\SQL1\D$\SQLDumps

del "\\SQL1\D$\SQLDumps\NuityDB_200304082100.BAK"
del "\\SQL1\D$\SQLDumps\AuthorsDB_old.bkp"

    Checking \\SQL1\D$\SQLFTP
Checking \\SQL1\E$ ...
...
```

```
Checking \\SQL2\C$ ...

...
    Checking \\SQL2\D$\MSSQL
    Checking \\SQL2\D$\MSSQL\Backup
    Checking \\SQL2\D$\SQLDumps
Checking \\SQL2\F$ ...
```

In this example, the script `purgeOldBackupFiles.pl` scanned the drives and directories on both SQL1 and SQL2 for SQL Server backup files older than 10 days. It found two such files on SQL1 and therefore constructed two Windows `del` commands. Note that the output in Listing 12-14 isn't in the proper batch file format because it includes the informational messages showing the directory paths that the script has scanned. If you remove all the lines that begin with the string `Checking`, what you have left is a batch file that you can run to delete the old backup files.

Several points are worth noting about the script `purgeOldBackupFiles.pl` in Listing 12-13. First, before the `Main` block in the script, between lines 15 and 19, the script opens an ActiveX Data Objects (ADO) connection to the SQL Server instance specified on the command line. Later in the script, when it traverses the drives and directories on each server, the script uses this same connection to test whether a file is a SQL Server backup file. The function `scriptDel()` between lines 96 and 105 performs this test.

Second, the script enumerates the drives on a server by parsing the result of `srvinfo.exe` between lines 29 and 38. You obtain the result of `srvinfo.exe` with the backtick operator as follows:

```
29.        my @srvinfo = `srvinfo \\\\$server`;
```

Using the Win32::Lanman Module

Note that, alternatively, you can choose to use the Win32::Lanman module to get a complete list of drives on a remote server:

```
use Win32::Lanman;
Win32::Lanman::NetServerDiskEnum("\\\\SQL1",\@drives);
```

The enumerated drives are in the array `@drives`. Chapter 2, "Working with Commonly Used Perl Modules," covered the Win32::Lanman module.

Third, the script in Listing 12-13 traverses recursively down the directory tree on a drive with the function walkDir() defined between lines 56 and 83. This function is similar to the find() function exported from the module File::Find, which was discussed in Chapter 2, "Working with Commonly Used Perl Modules." The walkDir() function takes a directory as its parameter. It relies on the two Perl built-in functions, opendir() and readdir(), to find the subdirectories and the files in the directories. The opendir() function creates a handle to a directory, and the readdir() function accepts the directory handle and returns all the entries in that directory. For each file, walkDir() calls the function scriptDel() to test the file and generate a del command if the file meets the criteria. For each subdirectory, walkDir() calls itself to recursively move down to the lower-level directories in the directory tree.

Note that walkDir() doesn't blindly traverse a directory tree. Before it calls itself on a subdirectory, it first checks whether the directory is considered unlikely to have any SQL Server backup files and therefore should be excluded from further examination. Lines 74, 75, and 76 in Listing 12-13 exclude the directories whose names match the regular expressions. For your environment, you should modify these regular expressions to effectively prune the search and therefore increase the performance.

Finally, on line 91, the function scriptDel() checks each file to see whether it's older than the age threshold specified on the command line with the option -a. A file is ignored if it's newer than the age threshold. On line 93, the function further prunes its search by skipping any file with an extension such as exe, dll, mdf, ldf, and bat. The RESTORE FILELISTONLY statement for a file is constructed on line 96:

```
96.        my $sql = "RESTORE FILELISTONLY FROM disk=\'$file\'";
```

On line 97 in Listing 12-13, the script then executes this statement on the SQL Server instance using the ADO connection opened at the beginning of the script (see lines 15 through 19). The SQL Server instance is specified with the -S option on the command line. If the ADO Execute() method returns the expected resultset, the file is confirmed to be a SQL Server backup file, and the script prints a Windows del command on line 101.

In my own environment, this script has helped me find many gigabytes of lost space. You'll probably find it useful as well.

Summary

This chapter sampled a range of multiserver scenarios that demand you to administer a group of SQL Server instances as a single unit. Of course, nothing prevents you from the common habit of working on one server a time. But that would be inefficient for most scenarios in this chapter and downright boring for some.

There are many more real-world scenarios that are multiserver in nature. When you find yourself repeating certain SQL Server administrative procedures or routines on different servers, you know you've encountered a multiserver scenario. If you're well versed in T-SQL, you may be tempted to consider a pure T-SQL solution. Unfortunately, T-SQL doesn't have adequate features to gracefully administer multiple servers. The most likely T-SQL solution is to rely on linked servers to communicate with other SQL Server instances. Experiment with T-SQL on some of the multiserver scenarios in this chapter, and you'll soon discover that it alone isn't the right tool.

This chapter once again highlights the need to extend existing tools and to take advantage of multiple tools in managing SQL Server in a large environment. In keeping multiple tools working together, Perl gives you the adhesive glue.

Perl Resources

ONE OF THE PROBLEMS WITH learning and keeping up with Perl isn't where to find resources—Perl is heavily documented and discussed. The problem is that there's an overwhelming amount of Perl resources listed in the Perl documentation, in published books and articles, on the Web, and in discussion lists and newsgroups.

This appendix compiles a manageable collection of Perl resources that are relevant to the topics covered in this book.

This appendix comes in four sections. The first section highlights the pages in the Perl documentation that are important for any Perl beginner. The second section reviews the Perl books that I highly recommend. Then, the third section lists the Perl Web sites and discussion lists you may want to visit regularly. The final section includes all the Perl modules used in the scripts discussed in this book.

Perl Online Documentation

In case it isn't obvious, no matter how good any of the other resources may be, the Perl online documentation is the most important Perl resource. The documentation is divided into *pages* (also known as *manpages*, a clearly Unix legacy). You can read these pages in two ways. You can read them with the ActivePerl online documentation in Hypertext Markup Language (HTML). The title of each page appears in the left pane; click the title and the content will appear in the right pane. Alternatively, you can run perldoc <page title> on the command line to read the page text in the command prompt.

At the minimum, the Perl beginner should become comfortable with the information presented in the following pages:

perlsyn—Perl Syntax: This page covers the syntax of the Perl language.

perldata—Perl Data Types: This page covers the basic data types such as scalars, arrays, and hashes. It also discusses important topics such as Perl contexts and file handles.

perlsub—Perl Subroutines: This page covers the creation and use of Perl subroutines (or simply routines or functions). Pay particular attention to how Perl passes parameters to functions.

perlrequick—Perl Regular Expressions Quick Start: This pages covers the bare essentials of Perl's powerful regular expressions. It's a must that you understand what's discussed in this page. After this page, you can move on to the page "perlretut—Perl Regular Expressions Tutorial."

perlreftut—Mark's Very Short Tutorial About References: Perl luminary Mark-Jason Dominus wrote this tutorial. After you've finished this page, if you're more comfortable learning by example, you can move on to the page "perllol—Manipulating Arrays of Arrays in Perl" and then to the page "perldsc—Perl Data Structures Cookbook."

perlmod—Perl Modules: This is relatively advanced material. But because you need to use Perl modules all the time, it's important to at least understand the implications of using a module.

perlfaq—Frequently Asked Questions About Perl: This page consists of perlfaq1 through perlfaq9. These nine pages contain Perl Frequently Asked Questions (FAQ). You'll inevitably ask questions on the Perl lists or newsgroups. Before you do that, make sure you've read these FAQ pages.

Perl Books

The following are recommended Perl books:

Programming Perl, Third Edition **by Larry Wall, Tom Christiansen, and Jon Orwant (O'Reilly, 2000)**: This is *the* Perl book written by none other than Perl creator Larry Wall. If you're serious about programming Perl and you can only buy one Perl book, this should be that book. However, if you're new to Perl, you may find it difficult to start with this book.

Perl Cookbook **by Tom Christiansen and Nathan Torkington (O'Reilly, 1998)**: I highly recommend this book to anyone who plans to write Perl scripts. This book is filled with practical Perl scripting gems that even an experienced Perl programmer will find useful from time to time. While you're programming or learning to program Perl, you'll find yourself constantly going back to this book for help.

Learning Perl on Win32 Systems **by Randal L. Schwartz, Erik Olsen, and Tom Christiansen (O'Reilly, 1997)**: This is a smooth and properly paced Perl tutorial book—an excellent Perl primer. If you're new to Perl, this is a good book to start.

Win32 Perl Programming: The Standard Extensions, Second Edition **by Dave Roth (New Riders, 2001)**: This book is about using Perl's Win32 standard extensions to address the Windows NT/2000 administrative issues such as network management, user management, database access with Open Database Connectivity (ODBC), and OLE Automation. The book isn't for Perl beginners. Regardless of whether you're a network administrator, as long as you're serious about Perl scripting on the Win32 platform, you should get a copy of this book.

Win32 Perl Scripting: **The Administrator's Handbook by Dave Roth (New Riders, 2000)**: This book goes well with Dave's other book, *Win32 Perl programming: The Standard Extensions, Second Edition* (New Riders, 2001). This is a code-heavy book consisting primarily of sample scripts with complementary discussions. I think this is a good book to keep.

ActivePerl with ASP and ADO **by Tobias Martinsson (John Wiley & Sons, 2000)**: For a SQL Server Database Administrator (DBA), this book's coverage of programming ADO with ActivePerl is well worth the money. Although ADO is just another Component Object Model (COM) accessible via the OLE Automation module Win32::OLE, you need to become familiar with its unique characteristics to use it proficiently.

Data Munging with Perl **by David Cross (Manning Publications Company, 2001)**: This book focuses on using Perl's string functions, regular expressions, and modules to recognize patterns in data, parse and filter data, and transform data. This book complements Chapter 4, "Migrating Data," well.

Effective Perl Programming: Writing Better Programs with Perl **by Joseph N. Hall and Randal L. Schwartz (Addison-Wesley, 1997)**: This isn't a book for the Perl beginner. However, this book is worth reading if you want to polish your Perl skills. The book is filled with Perl scripting best practices that can make a real difference to the quality of your Perl scripts.

Perl for System Administration **by David N. Blank-Edelman (O'Reilly, 2000)**: This book is interesting for its general coverage of applying Perl to solve system administrative problems. Although it has a chapter on SQL database administration, what it discusses isn't really what a SQL Server DBA would consider database administration. Of all the chapters, Chapter 9, "Log Files," is of the most value.

Mastering Regular Expressions, Second Edition **by Jeffery E. F. Friedl (O'Reilly, 2002)**: This book is on everyone's recommended reading list when it comes to regular expressions. This is indeed an excellent book. But if you're a Perl beginner, it isn't the book for you. It would be more cost effective for you to come back to this book once you've gained some level of comfort with Perl's regular expressions.

Perl for Oracle DBAs **by Andy Duncan and Jared Still (O'Reilly, 2002)**: I'd be remiss if I didn't mention this recently published book, which holds the bragging rights of the first book dedicated to managing databases with Perl. Perhaps because of the significant difference between the Oracle DBA tools and the SQL Server DBA tools, the SQL Server DBA may find the scripts covered in the book of little value or not compelling enough in the SQL Server world.

Perl Web Sites, Mailing Lists, and Newsgroups

There are numerous Perl Web sites, mailing lists, and newsgroups. I've singled out the ones I regularly visit. As an ActivePerl user, I found the mailing lists hosted and archived by ActiveState to be of the most value. These mailing lists provide excellent peer support, which is an essential part of learning and using Perl:

http://www.perl.com: This is *the* Perl site. You should visit this site regularly to keep up with what's happening within the Perl community.

http://www.activestate.com: If you use Perl only on the Win32 platform, this is probably the most important site to visit. This is the home page of ActiveState, which distributes ActivePerl. Because I use ActivePerl exclusively, I visit this site regularly to get new releases. This site also holds the default package repository for the Programmer's Package Manager (PPM). In addition, you can search the archive of several important Win32 Perl mailing lists at this site.

http://www.cpan.org: This is the primary gateway to the Comprehensive Perl Archive Network (CPAN), which holds a large collection of Perl materials including scripts, modules, documentation, and Perl source code. Although CPAN is physically distributed on many servers (currently documented at about 200 machines) across the globe, this address is all you need to access CPAN.

http://www.roth.net: Dave Roth maintains this site. It holds a package repository that allows you to install Dave's Win32 modules via PPM. You can download from this site many interesting sample scripts for administrating Windows NT/2000 and browse to other Perl sites through its links.

http://msdn.microsoft.com: This is the Microsoft Developer Network (MSDN) Web site. It's not a site dedicated to Perl. In fact, it contains almost nothing on Perl. However, because many Perl Win32 modules are the wrappers around some Microsoft Application Programming Interfaces (APIs) including the Win32 API, it's important to become familiar with or at least know how to access the documentation of these APIs.

Lists: ActivePerl, perl-win32-users, perl-win32-admin: You can subscribe to these lists via http://www.activestate.com/support. These lists are specific to Win32 and are often very active. If you have an ActivePerl question, chances are good that you'll receive an answer quickly on one of these lists. You can learn a great deal about programming Perl on the Win32 platform just by lurking on these lists. ActiveState hosts and archives these lists. I've been able to find answers to many of my Perl questions by searching the ActiveState archive.

Newsgroup: comp.lang.perl.misc: This Perl newsgroup is active and has been around for a long time. It's for all things Perl on any platform. You should include this newsgroup when you search the newsgroup archive for Perl information.

http://www.google.com: Although this isn't specific to Perl, a Google search is one of the quickest ways to research a Perl issue. More often than not, you'll find the answer to your question in either Google Web search or Google advanced newsgroup search. Google is quick and to the point, and it's truly indispensable.

Perl Modules

This section lists all the modules used in the Perl scripts discussed in this book. Chapter 2, "Working with Commonly Used Perl Modules," reviews many of these modules. Most of them ship with ActivePerl.

For details of these modules, including the list of the functions they export, you should consult their accompanying documentation. You can read their documentation via the Perl online documentation in the HTML format or via typing `perldoc <module name>` at the command prompt.

Carp: This module ships with ActivePerl 5.6.1 and is part of the Perl standard distribution. You can use the Carp functions in place of the `die()` and `warn()` functions to report where the code that calls the function runs into problem.

Data::Dumper: This module ships with ActivePerl 5.6.1. Whenever you need to deal with Perl nested data structures, you'll find this module indispensable. It's used heavily in this book to persist data structures and to debug code. The version used is 2.102.

File::Compare: This module ships with ActivePerl 5.6.1. It exposes functions to compare two files. The version used is 1.1002.

File::Find: This module ships with ActivePerl 5.6.1. Your script can use this module to recursively traverse a directory tree and perform a function, which you define, on each file.

Getopt::Std: This module ships with ActivePerl 5.6.1. It permits single-character switches and switch clustering on the command line. The version used is 1.02.

Net::Ping: This module ships with ActivePerl 5.6.1. A script can use this module to ping a machine. The version used is 2.02.

Net::SMTP: This module ships with ActivePerl 5.6.1. It implements the Simple Mail Transfer Protocol (SMTP). A script can use this module to talk to an SMTP server and send email messages. The version used is 2.15.

Parse::RecDescent: You can find this powerful module on CPAN. This module exposes functions that read grammars and generate recursive descent parsers. The version used is 1.80.

SQLDBA::ParseSQL: This is part of the SQLDBA Toolkit that you can download from the Apress Web site (http://www.apress.com). The module exports functions to help parse T-SQL scripts, primarily to remove the complications caused by Transact-SQL (T-SQL) comments, quoted strings, and quoted identifiers. The current version is 1.0.

SQLDBA::ScriptSQL: This is part of the SQLDBA Toolkit that you can download from the Apress Web site (http://www.apress.com). The module exports functions to script SQL Server tables and their conversion. The current version is 1.0.

SQLDBA::Security: This is part of the SQLDBA Toolkit that you can download from the Apress Web site (http://www.apress.com). The module exports functions to retrieve SQL Server–related security information. The current version is 1.0.

SQLDBA::SQLDMO: This is part of the SQLDBA Toolkit that you can download from the Apress Web site (http://www.apress.com). This module exports functions that use SQL-DMO to retrieve SQL Server schema information. The current version is 1.0.

SQLDBA::Utility: This is a custom-built utility module I wrote to gather a collection of utility functions that are frequently used by the scripts throughout this book. The version used is 1.0.

Time::Local: This module ships with ActivePerl 5.6.1. It exports functions to convert a string to epoch seconds.

Win32: This module ships with ActivePerl 5.6.1. This module exports many Windows API functions, many of which have been built into the Perl core. For the ones built into the Perl core, you don't need to explicitly use Win32. The version used is 0.18.

Win32:;EventLog: This module ships with ActivePerl 5.6.1. It provides an object-oriented interface to accessing and manipulating Windows event logs. The version used is 0.072.

Win32::Lanman: This powerful module ships with ActivePerl 5.6.1. It exposes a comprehensive set of the Windows NT/2000 networking API functions and a host of functions for manipulating registries and services among other things. You definitely want to become familiar with this module. The version used is 1.100.

Win32::NetAdmin: This module ships with ActivePerl 5.6.1. It exposes the Windows network API for controlling the administration of groups and users. The version used is 0.08.

Win32::ODBC: This module ships with ActivePerl 5.6.1. It provides a convenient interface to call the underlying ODBC functions. To use this module, the SQL Server ODBC driver must have been installed on the machine. For additional information and more samples on this module, please visit the module author's Web site at `http://www.roth.net`. The version used is 0.032.

Win32::OLE: This module ships with ActivePerl 5.6.1. This is the gateway to all things OLE Automation from Perl. This module is indispensable. The version used is 0.1502.

Win32::OLE::Const: This module ships with ActivePerl 5.6.1 and is part of the Win32::OLE distribution. The module exports the symbolic contacts held in a type library.

Win32::Perms: Dave Roth authored this module, which is available from `http://www.roth.com`. You can use the module to manage the permissions on Win32 objects such as files, shares, directories, and registry keys. The version used is 20020605.

Win32::Service: This module ships with ActivePerl 5.6.1. It provides the functions to manipulate Win32 system services. The version used is 0.05.

Win32::TieRegistry: This module ships with ActivePerl 5.6.1. It exposes the Windows registry to a Perl hash-like interface, enabling you to manipulate the registry as if you were manipulating hashes. The version used is 0.24.

APPENDIX B

Getting Started
with Perl

THE FIRST THREE CHAPTERS of this book were devoted to making you comfortable
with basic Perl programming scenarios. However, it wasn't possible to systematically cover all the basic language concepts; furthermore, the scripts presented in
these chapters implicitly assume that you were already familiar with them. If you
had difficulty following some of the scripts in the first three chapters, I strongly
recommend you consult some of the excellent tutorial books—for example,
Learning Perl on Win32 Systems by Randal L. Schwartz, Erik Olsen, and Tom
Christiansen (O'Reilly, 1997)—listed in Appendix A, "Perl Resources."

If you're in a hurry, you may want to spend a few minutes on this appendix,
which covers the Perl bare essentials. This appendix doesn't intend to replace any
general Perl tutorials. Rather, its intent is to complement the first three chapters.

Installing Perl

If you're more interested in using Perl to solve SQL Server administrative problems
than getting to know the ins and outs of Perl itself, you may want to skip compiling
Perl yourself from the source code. On the Win32 platform, the easiest and
quickest way to get Perl installed and start using it is to download the latest Perl
binary distribution from the ActiveState Web site (http://www.activestate.com).

The ActiveState Perl binary distribution comes in a Microsoft Installer (MSI)
package. After you have downloaded the MSI file to your hard drive, double-click
the file to start the installation. The installation wizard will guide you through the
setup, following the common installation prompts and procedures familiar to SQL
Server Database Administrators (DBAs).

After the installation is complete, to verify that you have Perl installed, you can
open a command prompt and type the following:

```
cmd>perl -v
```

This should display the Perl version and the ActiveState binary build number.
To further verify that you can execute Perl statements, you can run the following at
the command prompt:

```
cmd>perl -e "print 'Hello, world!';"
```

If this prints *Hello, world!* on the command line, you're done with your Perl installation.

 NOTE   *By default, ActivePerl installs in* %SystemDrive%:\perl, *where* %SystemDrive% *is usually the C drive. You can choose to install Perl on any drive or directory. Assuming that you have installed Perl in* C:\perl, *Perl installation will add* C:\perl\bin, *where* perl.exe *resides, to the* PATH *environment variable.*

Running Perl Scripts

You prepare a Perl script in a plain-text file, often with the file extension .pl. You can use any of your favorite text editors. Let's say you have created a single line Perl script as follows:

```
print "Hello, world!\n";
```

and have placed it in the file test.pl in the directory d:\scripts. If you have Active-Perl installed, you can run the test.pl script in one of several ways.

Running perl.exe

First, you can open a command prompt and execute the following:

```
cmd>perl d:\scripts\test.pl
Hello, world!
```

Or, if you have made d:\scripts your current directory, you can simply type the following:

```
cmd>perl test.pl
Hello, world!
```

Using File Type Association

The second method of running a Perl script is to rely on the file type association established during the ActivePerl installation. By default, when you install ActivePerl, it associates the file extension .pl with the file type Perl and specifies the installed Perl executable as the program to open files of this type. In other words, you can simply type the following to run the script:

```
cmd>d:\scripts\test.pl
Hello, world!
```

or if d:\scripts is your current directory, you can run the script as follows:

```
cmd>test.pl
Hello, world!
```

To verify the file type and the association with the Perl executable, you can type the following at the command prompt (this is what displays on my computer):

```
cmd>assoc .pl
.pl=Perl
cmd>ftype perl
perl="D:\Perl\bin\perl.exe"%1" %*
```

Doubling-Clicking the Perl Script File

Another method of running a Perl script is simply to double-click its filename from the NT Explorer. However, this approach doesn't allow you to supply any command-line arguments. Also, the command prompt closes immediately after the completion of the script, making it impossible to review the output sent to the screen.

NOTE *It's possible to have multiple* perl\bin *directories listed on the* PATH *environment variable. When you execute a Perl script on the command line without fully qualifying* perl.exe *or when you double-click the Perl script file, the first* perl.exe *found on the* PATH *will execute the script. If you have installed multiple versions, make sure you type* perl -v *on the command line to ascertain the version you're using.*

Personally, I prefer to explicitly include perl.exe on the command line. If you depend on the file association to find perl.exe, it can take some time to locate perl.exe when you run the Perl script for the first time.

Getting to Know the Perl Bare Essentials

This section covers the Perl bare essentials. It only scratches the surface of Perl.

Introducing Values, Data Types, and Variables

Perl has three basic data types: scalars, arrays, and hashes. A value in Perl is a scalar, an array, or a hash.

If you're familiar with "conventional" programming languages such as Basic, Pascal, or C, this classification of data types may appear to be rather weird. Be patient! The wisdom of this design will become apparent when you actually start using Perl.

Like most programming languages, you usually refer to values in Perl by name—that is, by variable name. For a scalar value, the variable name always starts with a $ sign. For an array value, the variable name starts with an @ sign. For a hash value, the variable name starts with a % sign.

It's important to remember that the first character of a variable name is always the sign that identifies the data type of the value to which it refers. Therefore, the variable name should start with a $ sign if it refers to a specific value in an array because it's a scalar. However, it should have an @ sign if it refers to a subarray.

The following are some examples of variable names:

```
$tableName                      # possibly a string value
$tableSize                      # possibly a numeric value
$tableNames[1]                  # the second value of the array @tableNames
$tableSizes{'authors'}          # the value of the key 'authors' in the
                                  hash %tableSizes
@tableNames[1,2]                # the array consisting of the second and
                                  third value in the array @tableNames
@tableSizes{'authors', 'titles'} # the array consisting of the values of the
                                  keys 'authors' and 'titles' in the hash
                                  %tableSizes
```

The value of the last example is the same as ($tableSizes{'authors'}, $tableSizes{'titles'}); it's an array.

Note that the variable names of different data types live in different namespaces. Thus, it's perfectly legal—though not necessarily a good choice—to have a scalar named `$tableName` and an array named `@tableName` without colliding into each other.

In a variable name, you can always put a pair of braces around the alphanumeric name—that is, the complete variable name minus the data type prefix ($, @, or %):

```
${tableName}      # the same as $tableName
```

This is useful when you have string appended to the value of a variable such as the following:

```
print "$tableName = ${tableSize}MB\n";
```

This may print something like the following:

```
authors = 2MB
```

where the value of the variable `$tableName` is `authors` and the value of the variable `$tableSize` is 2. Note that there's no space between the value of 2 and the string MB.

NOTE *To go beyond the bare essentials, when you put a pair of braces around the alphanumeric variable name, you can replace it with an expression that returns a reference to the variable. In addition, if you don't have* use strict 'refs'*, you can replace it with an expression that returns a string matching the alphanumeric name.*

Understanding Scalars, Arrays, and Hashes

Scalars are single values and are the foundation of Perl's values. The values of an array consist of a list of scalars indexed by numeric positions. A hash is a list of scalars indexed by strings.

Scalars

There are three kinds of scalar values—numbers, strings, and references. You'll see references later in this appendix. Let's study several examples of numeric or strings scalars:

```
$size = '10240';        # read the size from a text file. Thus, the number is
                        # a string. Assume it's in kilobytes.
$size = $size / 1024;   # convert the size to megabytes
$sizeMB = $size . "MB"; # append MB to the size
```

In the first example, $size is assigned a value extracted from a text file. This value is a string. Then, in the second example, it's used as a number. In the third example, it's concatenated with the string MB; therefore, it's used again as a string.

Being able to convert a value from a number to a string and vice versa without going through any hassle is an inherent design of Perl. Remember that Perl was created to extract information from text files and then perform further processing to produce the desired reports. The numbers in a text file are plain strings. But you want to use them as real numbers during the processing.

The need to convert strings to numbers and numbers to strings is ubiquitous. Perl spares you the pain of having to jump through the hoops to perform these conversions; it performs the conversions for you in most places when you expect them.

Arrays

An *array* is a collection of values you can access through their numeric indexes. An array has the following properties:

- Its indexes are zero based. Thus, the first element of an array has the index of zero, and the second element has the index of one.

- An array can dynamically grow or shrink.

- The array elements are scalars.

- The array elements are ordered by their indexes.

Arrays are central to Perl programming, and Perl provides a large number of operators to manipulate arrays. The following are some common examples:

```
@tbs = ('authors', 'titles', 'stores'); # initialize @tbs with a list of values
@tbs = @rc[1,3];                         # assign @tbs the second and fourth
                                         # values of the array @rc. This is to
                                         # slice the array @rc.
@tbs = (@tbs, 'titleauthor');            # add a new element to the tail of @tbs
@tbs = ('titleauthor', @tbs);            # add a new element to the head of @tbs
@tbs = push @tbs, 'titleauthor';         # add a new element to the tail of @tbs
                                         # same as (@tbs, 'titleauthor')
$tb = pop @tbs;                          # remove the last element from @tbs and
                                         # return it
@tbs = unshift @tbs, 'titleauthor';      # add a new element to the head of @tbs
$tb = shift @tbs;                        # remove the first element from @tbs and
                                         # return it
@tbs = splice(@tbs, 2, 3, @new);         # replace 3 elements starting at index
                                         # position 2 with the elements of array
                                         # @new, and return the resultant array.
```

Note that $tbs[2] and @tbs[2] are different. The former returns the third element of the array @tbs, and the latter returns an array consisting of a single element, which is the third element of the array @tbs.

A data structure is only as useful as the means you have to manipulate it. Perl provides an extensive number of operators to create and manipulate arrays. It's no exaggeration to say that almost all the Perl constructs implicitly accept or work with arrays. For instance, the command-line arguments are stored in the pre-defined array @ARGV, and a Perl routine—in other words, function—accepts parameters in an array.

NOTE *The only requirement imposed on the elements of an array is that they're scalars. It's perfectly legal to mix numbers, strings, and references in the same array.*

One of the most important operations on an array is to enumerate its elements and perform actions for each enumerated element. The simplest method is to use the foreach statement. The following example iterates through each element of the array @tbs and prints the element:

```
foreach $tb (@tbs) {
    print "$tb\n";
}
```

During each iteration, an element of the array @tbs is assigned to the variable $tb. The code segment exits after the last element has been assigned to $tb and $tb has been printed. To be more precise, $tb isn't really assigned a copy of the element in @tbs; when you change the value of $tb, you are changing the value of the element in the array.

Hashes

It's unique among the programming languages for Perl to elevate hashes to the level of one of its three fundamental data types. But this is one reason why Perl is a powerful language; although you have to spend considerable efforts constructing data structures similar to a hash in other languages, Perl offers it to you for free.

A *hash* is similar to an array in that it has a list of indexed values. However, a hash has the following distinct properties:

- The hash values are indexed with strings. Note that the array values are indexed with numbers.

- The hash values aren't ordered.

- The hash values are scalars.

- The hash can dynamically grow and shrink.

It's most intuitive to consider a hash as consisting of a collection of key/value pairs, where the keys are strings and the values are scalars. Similar to the operations on arrays, Perl provides a large number of operators to manipulate hashes. The following are some common examples:

```
%tbSize = ('authors', 23, 'titles', 15); # initialize %tbSize two keys
                                          # ('authors' and 'titles') and
                                          # their are 23 and 15, respectively
%tbSize = ( 'authors' => 23,              # same as the previous example, but
            'titles'  => 15);             # with the intuitive arrow notation.
@tbs = keys %tbSize;                      # returns all the keys of %tbSize. @tbs
                                          # has the value of ('authors', 'titles')
@sizes = values %tbSize;                  # returns all the values of %tbSize
                                          # @sizes has the value of (23, 15)
$tbSize{'store'} = 34;                    # add a new entry to %tbSize, if the key
                                          # 'store' doesn't already exist. If the
                                          # key already exists, this updates its
                                          # value.
delete $tbSize{'titles'}                  # delete the hash entry of the key
                                          # 'titles'
```

The most common idiom for iterating through a hash is as follows with the foreach statement:

```
foreach $tb (keys %tbSize) {
   print "The size of $tb is $tbSize{$tb}\n";
}
```

This code segment loops through all the keys of the hash %tbSize. For each key, it prints a string showing the table name—which is the hash key and the size— that's the corresponding hash value. For the hash in the previous example, this code segment prints the following:

```
The size of authors is 23
The size of titles is 15
```

Because a hash isn't ordered, it's possible that the script prints the line for titles before the line for authors. If you want to control the order of the keys, you can sort the keys as follows:

```
foreach $tb (sort keys %tbSize) {
   print "The size of $tb is $tbSize{$tb}\n";
}
```

This guarantees that the code prints authors before it does titles.

NOTE *As mentioned, Perl's choice of fundamental data types in terms of scalars, arrays, and hashes may appear to be rather unorthodox. But it turns out to be an elegant design in that you can easily model surprisingly many problems with these data types. Throwing references in the mix, you can use them to model arbitrarily complex problems.*

Understanding Scalar Context and List Context

Perl has two basic contexts: scalar and list. You should remember the following key points with regard to the Perl contexts:

- The same Perl operation or value may be interpreted differently depending on the context around it.

- An operation provides the context for the interpretation of its arguments.

- The left argument (that is, the left side) of an assignment provides the context for the right argument. Assignment to a scalar evaluates the right argument in scalar context, and assignment to a list, an array, or a hash evaluates the right argument in list context.

You can find the behavior of a Perl built-in operator with respect to its context in the Perl online documentation.

When you strike up a conversation in English, your conversation is greatly simplified because the parties have a shared understanding of the context. Likewise, this type of context sensitivity simplifies Perl programming.

The following is an example of how the context affects the behavior of the <> operator:

```
$line = <FH>;        # reads in a single line from the filehandle FH
@lines = <FH>;       # reads in all the lines from the filehandle FH
```

Determining True or False

Because Perl often performs automatic and implicit conversion between numbers and strings, the question of what is true or false isn't as simple as it is in a language such as Basic or C.

The following values are false when Perl evaluates them to determine whether they're true or false:

- Unquoted numbers: 0, 0.0, and 0.00 or any number of zero's after the decimal place

- Quoted single-digit zero '0' or "0" and the quoted empty string '' (two consecutive single quotes) or "" (two consecutive double quotes)

- The undef value

Any other defined value is true.

While on the topic of "true" and "false," I should mention a special scalar context called *Boolean context*, which is "simply any place where an expression is being evaluated to see whether it's true or false."[1]

Note that in Perl you can place any expression in Boolean context to evaluate its truth value.

---

1. *Programming Perl* by Larry Wall, Tom Christiansen, and Jon Orwant (O'Reilly, 2000)

Grouping Statements into Code Blocks

If you add a semicolon to the end of any valid Perl expression, it becomes a statement. This is the so-called *simple* statement.

You can group one or more statements to form a code block. Often, a code block is enclosed in a pair of braces. Code blocks can be nested.

For example, each pair of the braces in the following three examples specifies a code block:

```
# 1st example
while( 1==1) {
    ...
}

# 2nd example
{
  $table = 'authors';
  print "$table\n";
}

# 3rd example
C_BLOCK: {
  $table = 'authors';
  print "$table\n";
}
```

In the first example, the `while` statement expects a block. The second example is a block that contains two statements. The block isn't labeled. In the third example, the block is labeled as `C_BLOCK`.

One of the most common reasons you want to group statements in a block is to contain the variables declared in the block, in other words, to provide a scope for the variable names. The section "Declaring Variables" later in this appendix briefly discusses the concept of variable scope.

The other common reason for grouping individual statements into a block is for control flow. Thus, you can say the following:

```
if (...)
   BLOCK
else
   BLOCK
```

where `BLOCK` represents a Perl code block in a pair of braces. The label for a block is optional. About the only occasion I find a label useful is when you want to branch to a specific layer from within multiple nested loops. You'll learn more about Perl loops shortly.

> **NOTE** *In fact, you can label any Perl statement. You can also use Perl's* goto *operator to jump to a labeled statement. However, you should avoid this style of Perl scripting.*

You may use a labeled code block for its visual effects. In many scripts in this book, I grouped all the statements in the main body of the script in a code block labeled as Main, similar to the following:

```
Main: {
    # the main flow the script here
    ...
} # Main
```

This label and the braces don't serve any functional purpose, but they make the main body of the script stand out when there are many functions defined in the same script.

Creating Compound Statements

Adding a semicolon to an expression makes a simple statement. You can also add control flow elements to construct compound statements. A compound statement often specifies the conditional execution of a Perl code block or a loop over a code block. The following are some examples of compound statements:

```
if (EXPR) BLOCK           # if EXPR is true, execute BLOCK
unless (EXPR) BLOCK       # if EXPR is not true, execute BLOCK
until (EXPR) BLOCK        # execute BLOCK until EXPR becomes true
while (EXPR) BLOCK        # execute BLOCK as long as EXPR is true
foreach VAR (LIST) BLOCK  # for each value in the LIST, run the code
```

Note that EXPR in these sample statements can be any valid Perl expression enclosed in a pair of parentheses, and BLOCK is a code block enclosed in a pair of braces. The following are examples of Perl compound statements:

```
# Example 1: run the code block if $times is greater than 3
if ($times > 3) {
    updateAlert($ref);
    sendAlert($ref);
}


# Example 2: run the code block if $times is not greater than 3
unless ($times > 3) {
    updateAlert($ref);
}


# Example 3: repeatedly run the code block as long as $times is greater than 3
while ($times > 3) {
    ...    # do something here
}


# Example 4: iterate through each element in the array @tables.
#            Each iteration sets $table to the element and run the code block.
foreach $table (@tables) {
    ... # do something
}
```

NOTE   *In these compound statements, when Perl expects a* BLOCK, *it expects code in a pair of braces. Even if you only have a single statement inside a* BLOCK, *it still has to be in a pair of braces.*

It's important to note that you can optionally include the so-called modifier in a simple statement. You can add these modifiers before the terminating semicolon:

- if EXPR

- unless EXPR

- while EXPR

- until EXPR

- foreach EXPR

Using these modifiers, you can make a simple statement behave like a compound statement. The following are three examples of simple statements that include the modifiers:

```
updateAlert($ref) unless $times > 3;
print $msg if $OK;
do { ... } while $cnt < 5;
```

Remember that these aren't compound statements. Each of these examples is still a single statement terminated with a semicolon.

Declaring Variables

If you write a throwaway script that has only a couple of lines, you may not need to declare your variables. By default, Perl doesn't insist that you declare anything at all; you can just start using Perl variables whenever you need to use them.

However, if you're writing any nontrivial script, you should declare your variables to save you a lot of grief later. The use strict 'vars', or simply use strict, declaration forces you to declare all the variables before they're used. The most obvious advantage of declaring variables is that the Perl compiler can help you catch a typo in the variable name. Mistakes such as misspelling a variable name have the potential to waste you hours.

TIP *Always include* use strict; *at the beginning of your script.*

Note that declaring variables is more than helping you catch a typo. It also helps you restrict a variable to a specific scope. This seemingly simple concept of *scoping* is in fact a rather complex one and shouldn't really be part of a bare essential introduction.

However, because the my operator is ubiquitous in the scripts throughout this book, it's important to understand its implications. The following three examples illustrate the my operator:

```
my $table;
my $table = 'authors';
foreach my $i (@tables) { ... }
```

The first example declares the variable $table to be visible in the rest of the current block. Until the variable is assigned a defined value, it remains undefined.

The second example has the same effect as the first example except that the variable is initialized to the string authors.

In the third example, the variable $i is declared to be visible in the code block delimited with the braces and is initialized with a value from the array @tables upon each iteration through the array.

Comparing Values

Perl differentiates between comparing numeric values and comparing string values because the meaning of their comparison is clearly different. For instance, a "numerical less than" is different from a "string-wise less than."

For numeric comparison, the operators are <, <=, >, >=, and ==. For string-wise comparison, the operators are lt, le, gt, ge, eq, and ne. Table B-1 documents their respective meanings.

Table B-1. Operators for Comparing Values

NUMERIC	STRING	DESCRIPTION
<	lt	Less than
<=	le	Less than or equal to
>	gt	Greater than
>=	ge	Greater than or equal to
==	eq	Equal to
!=	ne	Not equal to

The operators in the first four rows in Table B-1 are often called *relational operators*, and the operators in the last two rows are called *equality operators*.

NOTE *It's important you use the numeric operators to compare numbers and string-wise operators to compare strings. Because Perl converts numbers to strings and strings to numbers automatically, when you use a numeric operator to compare two strings or use a string-wise operator to compare two numbers, you may not get an error. But the result is rarely what you expect. For instance, the result of* '23' > '0123' *is different from the result of* '23' gt '0123'.

Interpolating Variables

In Perl, you can use either double quotation marks or single quotation marks to quote a string. If you embed a scalar variable or an array variable inside a double-quoted string, Perl replaces the variable with its value when it evaluates the string, and this is called *variable interpolation.*

Assume that the value of the variable $tb is the string authors and the variable @tbs has the value ('authors', 'titles'). The following examples illustrate this powerful feature:

```
$rc = 'Name: $tb';  # $rc is assigned the string 'Name: $tb' (without quotes)
$rc = "Name: $tb";  # $rc is assigned the string 'Name: auhtors' (without quotes)
$rc = 'Name: @tbs'; # $rc is assigned the string 'Name: @tbs' (without quotes)
$rc = "Name: @tbs"; # $rc is assigned the string 'Name: authors titles' (without
                    # quotes.)
```

NOTE   *The backslash sign (\) is always special. You can use it to escape an embedded single quote or another backslash, even inside single quotes.*

Using Functions or Routines

In Perl, *functions* and *routines* are synonyms. Conceptually, they're not different from functions you find in any other programming languages. You pass some parameters to a function and expect it to carry out some actions or return some results. The following sections highlight the basics you need to know to declare and call a function.

Declaring a Function

To declare a function named myFunc, you place the following code segment anywhere in the script:

```
sub myFunc {
   # define your function here

   ...
}
```

You can place this *anywhere* in your script because Perl goes through a script twice, once to compile it and then to execute it. A function is compiled at the compile time. By the time it's called during the run-time, Perl already knows about the function no matter where in the script it's declared.

Perl groups all the parameters passed to a function in a flat list and stores the list in the predefined array variable @_. Thus, the following idiom is common:

```
sub myFunc {
    my (@params) = @_;
    # do something with @params

    ...
}
```

In this case, all the parameters are assigned to the array variable @params. It's then up to your function to interpret the individual elements of the array. Note that the declaration of @params in my() makes it private to the function.

A function returns the value of its last expression to the caller. This value can be a list or a scalar. You can also use the return() function to return a value explicitly. Personally, I prefer to always use return() in a function. It's more readable to be explicit.

Listing B-1 is a complete example of a function declaration.

Listing B-1. Declaring a Function

```
1.   sub getName {
2.     my ($db, $owner, $tb) = @_;
3.     my $tbName = $tb or die "***Err: getName() expects a table name.";
4.
5.     if ($db) {
6.         $tbName = "$db.$owner.$tbName";
7.     }
8.     elsif ($owner) {
9.         $tbName = "$owner.$tbName";
10.    }
11.    return $tbName;
12. }
```

The function getName() in Listing B-1 accepts three parameters, representing a database name, an owner name, and a table name, respectively. It returns a three-part table name, conforming to the Transact-SQL (T-SQL) syntax.

Let's dissect the code in Listing B-1:

On line 2, the parameters stored in the variable @_ are assigned to the variables $db, $owner, and $tb. You can pass more parameters to the functions, and they'll all be stored in @_. But this function simply ignores anything after the third element in @_.

On line 3, $tb is assigned to the variable $tbName. The line also tests $tb. If it's defined and isn't an empty string or '0', the function accepts it as a valid table name. Otherwise, the function aborts the whole script with die().

On line 5, the function tests whether a valid database name is passed. If it is, it constructs a three-part table name regardless of whether the owner is passed.

On lines 8 and 9, having ascertained that the database name is missing, the function tries to construct a two-part name with the owner name and the table name.

Finally, on line 11, the function returns the table name, possibly qualified with the database name and/or the owner name to the caller.

Calling a Function

The following are some examples of calling a function in Perl. Note that the parameters are always passed in a list:

```
$tb = getName('pubs', undef, 'authors'); # return a value to $tb
myFunc(@some_values);                     # throw away the returned value, if any
&myFunc(@some_value);                     # same as the previous example. The &
                                          # prefix is optional.
```

The most important point to remember about calling a function is that the parameters passed are in a single list. Thus, for example, if you call a function as follows:

```
myFunc(@values1, @values2);
```

the elements in both @values1 and @values2 will be in @_. The function only sees @_, and it won't be able to tell which elements are from @values1 and which are from @values2.

If you call a function as follows:

```
myFunc();
```

the @_ array will be an empty list.

To pass anything other than a simple list of scalars to a function, you'll have to resort to a reference (introduced later in the section "Understanding References"). With references, you can pass anything to a function.

Quoting Strings

From the section "Interpolating Variables," you know that a string may behave differently depending on whether you quote it with the double quotation marks or the single quotation marks. Apparently, these two types of quotation marks alone don't afford enough convenience to the demanding Perl developers. Perl provides many more ways to quote strings. You choose one that best suits your need for the particular occasion.

It's important for the beginner to become familiar with the different ways you can quote strings in Perl.

The following are examples of different ways to quote strings in Perl:

```
$tb = "authors";         # doule quotes. Good for variable interpolation
$tb = 'authors';         # single quotes. Good if you don't want interpolation
$tb = q/authors/;        # same as single quote
$tb = qq/auhtors/;       # same as double quotes
@tbs = qw/authors titles/; # same as ('authors', 'titles')
```

In the last example, the qw operator is a shortcut to avoid individually quoting each word. This saves you many single quotes if you have to specify many words.

NOTE *The single-quoted string* 'authors\n' *is different from the double-quoted string* "authors\n". *In the former,* \n *are two characters— a backslash followed by the letter n. In the latter,* \n *is interpolated to a single newline character.*

If you need to quote a large block of text, it's convenient to use Perl's *here* document syntax, which allows you to quote multiple lines of text with an arbitrary string on a separate line. The following examples quote the SQL statement with the string --SQL--:

```
1. $sql = <<--SQL--;
2. SELECT * FROM authors
3.  WHERE au_id = '312-34-456'
4. --SQL--
```

The double less-than sign (<<) introduces the opening quote string (--SQL--), and the closing quote string must exactly match the opening quote string and be on a separate line, starting from the first column. In the previous example, note that line 1 is a complete statement by itself with the terminating semicolon. The following example assigns exactly the same string to the variable $sql:

```
$sql = "SELECT * FROM authors
 WHERE au_id = '312-34-456'";
```

If the text is large, the terminating semicolon will be far away from the beginning of the statement, making it less intuitive to tell where the statement starts and where it ends.

Understanding References

References are pointers. However, they don't point to a memory byte/word location in that you can't apply the memory address operations on them like you can on the pointers of the C programming language.

They're actually scalars that point to other scalars, arrays, or hashes. Because an array has scalars as its elements, having a reference as its element enables an array to point to another scalar, array, or hash. Similarly, because a value of a hash is a scalar, having a reference as its value enables a hash to point to another scalar, array, or hash.

Storing references in arrays or in hashes is Perl's way of creating arbitrarily complex data structures.

Let's review the most basic reference-related operations. The following examples show how you can obtain a reference and how you can get the value of the scalar, array, or hash pointed to by the reference (in other words, dereference a reference):

```
# to obtain a reference to a named varaible, apply backslash to the variable

$scalarRef = \$tb;     # apply \ to a scalar to obtain the reference to the scalar
$arrayRef = \@thbs;    # apply \ to an array to obtain the reference to the array
$hashRef = \%tbSize;   # apply \ to a hash to obtain the reference to the hash

# to get the value pointed to by the reference, apply the type prefix to
# the reference

$newTb = $$scalarRef;     # $newTb has the value of $tb
@newTbs = @$arrayRef;     # @newTbs has the elements of @tbs
%newTbSize = %$hashRef;   # %newTbSize has the key/value pairs of %tbSize
```

Actually, what follows the type prefix ($, @, or %) doesn't have to be a reference variable. It can be a block of code that returns the reference of the proper type. For instance, $$scalarRef is the same as ${$scalarRef}, which is the same as the following:

```
${  ... # any code
    $scalarRef; }
```

This brace notation can become rather convoluted when you have more than one level of references involving arrays and/or hashes. For instance, assume that $ref is a reference pointing to a hash, whose 'authors' key has the value that's again a reference pointing to an array. If you have $ref and you want to return the value of second element in the array, how do you do it?

Let's do it in steps like you'd peel an onion:

```
%hash = %{$ref};           # returns the hash
$value = $hash{'authors'}  # returns the value of the 'authors' key.
                           # It's a refernce.
@array = @$value           # returns the array
$array[1]                  # returns the second element in the array
```

There are a lot of intermediate variables. Fortunately, you don't have to introduce these intermediate variables. Let's try the "peeling an onion" approach again, but without the intermediate variables, as shown in Listing B-2.

Listing B-2. Returning a Value in a Data Structure

```
%{$ref}                   # returns the hash
${$ref}{'authors'}        # returns a reference to the array
@{${$ref}{'authors'}}     # returns the array
${${$ref}{'authors'}}[1]  # returns the second element of the array
```

As a beginner, you'll find this last expression difficult to understand. Well, you're not alone! Even an experienced Perl programmer may have difficulty deciphering the expression or being able to correctly write such an expression. The syntax doesn't facilitate understanding at all.

For this common problem, Perl has an arrow notation that visually simplifies the expression returning a value within an arbitrary data structure constructed with references.

Briefly, you can use the arrow notation with either a reference to an array or a reference to a hash. Listing B-3 shows how to use the arrow notation to return a hash value or an array element.

Listing B-3. Returning a Hash Value or an Array Element with the Arrow Notation

```
$hashRef->{'authors'}
$arrayRef->[1]
```

If $ref is a reference to an array, $ref->[1] gives you the value of the second element in the array. If $ref is a reference to a hash, $ref->{'authors'} gives you the value of the key 'authors' in the hash. The most important thing about the arrow notation is that you can chain the arrows as in the following example, which returns the same value as the last example in Listing B-2 does:

```
$ref->{'authors'}->[1]
```

You read this notation left to right. First, $ref is a reference, and ->{'authors'} that follows indicates that it's a reference to a hash. Thus, $ref->{'authors'} gets the value of the hash key 'authors'. Second, the expression $ref->{'authors'} returns a reference, which happens to be a reference to an array. Finally, $ref->{'authors'}->[1] returns the second element of the array.

NOTE *The concept of references may not be considered as bare essential material. However, references are of great importance in Perl and are used throughout this book. It's necessary for you to understand references to grasp the scripts presented in this book. The first three chapters of this book contain more expositions and examples of references. Furthermore, the resources listed in Appendix A, "Perl Resources," discuss references in detail.*

Introducing Perl Regular Expressions

Given the importance of hashes and references in Perl, it isn't an exaggeration to say that if you don't understand hashes and references, you aren't programming Perl. This also applies to Perl regular expressions: If you don't understand Perl regular expressions, you aren't programming Perl.

Regular expressions are tightly integrated into the Perl language. Numerous Perl language constructs work with regular expressions seamlessly.

Using Regular Expressions

Before learning how to write regular expressions, it's useful to see how you can use them. The following are the common scenarios where you use Perl regular expressions. In these examples, PATTERN represents a regular expression:

```
# The =~ operator
if ($str =~ /PATTERN/) { ... }  # if the value of $str matches PATTERN
$str =~ s/PATTERN/REPLACEMENT/; # replace the part of $str that matches PATTERN
                                # with the string specified with REPLACEMENT


# The split and grep functions
@rc = split /PATTERN/, $str;    # split the string $str into a list of substrings.
                                # In $str, these substrings are separated by
                                # strings that match PATTERN
@rc = grep /PATTERN/, @strs;    # get all the elements of @strs that match PATTERN
```

A common Perl idiom is to perform pattern matching on the predefined variable $_. In the previous examples, if you don't specify $str at all, Perl assumes you're trying to find a substring in $_ that matches the PATTERN. Table B-2 shows the use of $_ with regular expressions.

Table B-2. Pattern Matching on $_

STATEMENT	THE EQUIVALENT
/PATTERN/;	$_ =~ /PATTERN/;
s/PATTERN/REPLACEMENT/;	$_ =~ s/PATTERN/REPLACEMENT/;
@rc = split /PATTERN/;	@rc = split /PATTERN/, $_;

Now you'll learn how to write Perl regular expressions by example. You'll start with building simple regular expressions and then move on to more complex patterns.

Writing Simple Regular Expressions

The simplest regular expression is a literal string. Thus, to check whether $tb contains the string authors, you can write the following:

```
if ($tb =~ /authors/) {
   print "yes";
}
```

Note that a pattern matches a string if the pattern completely matches part of the string. Thus, $tb =~ /authors/ succeeds if $tb contains the string authors. In addition, the script in the previous example exhibits the following behavior:

- It prints yes when $tb is assigned any of the following strings: my_authors, authors2, authors, and authorsbook. In other words, it prints yes if the string authors is anywhere in $tb.

- It doesn't print yes when $tb is assigned either of the following strings: Authors and MyAuthors. In other words, it prints yes when the variable $tb contains authors in all lowercase.

If you want to perform case-insensitive pattern matching, you can use the /i modifier. Thus, the pattern /authors/i will match the string authors regardless of the case of each letter in the string.

NOTE *In addition to /i, Perl regular expressions support several other modifiers to alter the behavior of a regular expression. The section "Modifying Patterns" introduces these modifiers.*

If you want to match authors exactly, you can write the script as follows:

```
if ($tb =~ /^authors$/) {
   print "yes";
}
```

This script prints yes only if the variable $tb is assigned the exact string authors. The ^ and $ characters in this example are called *anchor metacharacters*. They don't match any explicitly written characters in the string. Rather, the anchor ^ matches at the beginning of the string, and the anchor $ matches at the end of the string.

Matching Multiple Alternatives

A common requirement is to match one of several choices. For instance, if you want to check whether the variable $tb contains either authors or titles, you can write the script as follows:

```
if ($tb =~ /authors|titles/) {
   print "yes";
}
```

In this case, the vertical bar (|) separates the alternatives. Perl first tries to see whether $tb contains the string authors. If $tb doesn't, Perl then checks whether $tb contains the string titles. When there are multiple alternative patterns, Perl tries each one from left to right, and it quits as soon as it finds the first match.

Using Metacharacters

The anchors ^ and $ in the previous section are examples of metacharacters. They don't match any character literally in a string. Rather, they alter the behavior of a regular expression. Perl has the following metacharacters:

```
{}[]()^$.|*+?\
```

The meanings of these metacharacters will become clear as you move through this appendix. To literally match a metacharacter, you must escape it with a backslash in the regular expression. For instance, the following code matches the string [authors]:

```
if ($tb =~ /\[authors\]/) {
    print "yes";
}
```

Understanding Character Classes

In a regular expression, if you see some characters inside a pair of square brackets and the square brackets aren't escaped with backslashes, you're looking at an example of the so-called *character class*. In the following two examples, the first regular expression includes a character class, and the second one doesn't:

```
# Example 1
/[Aa]uthors/;    # Matches either Authors or authors

# Example 2
/\[authors\]/;  # Matches [authors]
```

Like you can specify a pattern to match one of several alternative strings, a character class specifies possible characters for a single character position you want to match in the regular expression. For example, the following script matches a string whose first character is either an @ sign or a # sign, followed by the string authors:

```
if ($tb =~ /[@#]authors/) {  # the first character is either @ or #
    print "yes";
}
```

In this example, [@#] specifies a character class.

Four characters are special inside a character class and must be escaped if you want to match them literally. The special characters are -,], \, ^, and $. Table B-3 explains their special meanings.

NOTE *In Perl, the character # usually indicates that the rest of the line is a comment and can be ignored. If you want to keep # as a literal #, you need to escape it with a backslash. Thus, you say \#. In a character class, however, you can use # as is without prefixing it with a backslash.*

Table B-3. Special Characters for Character Classes

CHARACTER	MEANING
-	This is the range operator that allows you to specify all the letters between two letters or all the digits between two digits. For example, the character class [0-6] means [0123456], and [a-f] means [abcdef].
]	This is the closing square bracket for the character class.
\	The backslash sign is always special. It escapes other characters.
^	This sign negates a character class. For example, the character class [^0-5] means any character other than 0, 1, 2, 3, 4, or 5. Furthermore, [^#@] means any character other than # or @.
$	This may indicate a scalar variable. Perl regular expressions allow variable interpolation. For example, if the value of the variable $x is aA, the pattern /[$x]uthors/ matches authors or Authors.

Because some character classes are used so often, Perl provides special abbreviations—or shortcuts—for them. You'll run into these shortcuts all the time when you work with Perl regular expressions. Table B-4 summarizes the common character class shortcuts.

Table B-4. Shortcuts for the Common Character Classes

SHORTCUT	ASCII EQUIVALENT	DESCRIPTION
\s	[\t\n\r\f]	Whitespace
\w	[a-zA-Z0-9_]	Word character
\d	[0-9]	Digit
.	[^\n]	Any character except \n
\S	[^ \t\n\r\f]	Nonwhitespace
\W	[^a-zA-Z0-9_]	Nonword character
\D	[^0-9]	Nondigit

Composing Complex Regular Expressions

To write more complex regular expressions, you need several more constructs that can organize simple expressions into complex ones. These constructs are all expressed in terms of the Perl metacharacters.

Grouping with Parentheses

Except in the simplest cases, you need to use parentheses to clearly delineate alternative patterns. The following are examples of grouping alternatives with parentheses:

```
/authors|titles/       # no need for parentheses in this case
/(authors|titles)/     # same as the previous example
/tb_(authors|titles)/  # matches either tb_authors or tb_titles. Without the
                         parentheses, it would match tb_authors or titles.
```

The parentheses in these regular expressions don't match any parentheses in a string. Remember, parentheses are metacharacters in Perl regular expressions. If you want to find a parenthesis in a string, you need to escape the parenthesis with a backslash in the regular expression. In other words, you specify either \(or \).

Later, you'll see that you can also use parentheses inside a regular expression to remember the matched substrings to be used later in the script.

Using Quantifiers

One of the most important methods to construct complex regular expressions is to apply quantifiers to simpler regular expressions. You can apply a quantifier to a single character, a character class, or a grouping of alternatives.

Table B-5 describes the quantifiers you can use in Perl regular expressions. Some of the quantifiers have been flagged as *greedy*, which means that Perl will try to match the pattern to which the quantifier is applied the maximum number of times.

Table B-5. Regular Expression Quantifiers

QUANTIFIER	DESCRIPTION
*	Matches 0 or more times (greedy).
+	Matches 1 or more times (greedy).
?	Matches 0 or 1 time (greedy).
{COUNT}	Matches exactly COUNT times. COUNT is an integer.
{MIN,}	Match at least MIN times (greedy). MIN is an integer.
{MIN,MAX}	Matches at least MIN times and at most MAX times (greedy).
*?	Matches 0 or more times (non greedy).
+?	Matches 1 or more times (non greedy).
??	Matches 0 or 1 time (non greedy).

Character classes, character class shortcuts, grouping, alternatives, and quantifiers work together to enable you to specify some rather interesting regular expressions. It's best to illustrate the behavior of these quantifiers with examples:

```
/\w+/                    # Matches one or more 'word' character ([0-9a-zA-Z_])
/[a-zA-Z].*/             # the first character must be a letter, followed by 0 or
                         # more non-newline characters
/(\w+\.)?\w+/            # Matches a 'word' or two 'words' separated with a dot
/CREATE\s+PROC(EDURE)?/  # Matches CREATE PROC or CREATE PROCEDURE. There can be
                         # one or more whitespaces between the two words.
/\d{3}-\d{4}/            # Match exactly three digits, followed by a hyphen, then
                         # four more digits. A US telephone number is an example.
/CREATE\s+PROC(EDURE)??/ # Matches CREATE PROC or CREATE PROCEDURE. There can
                         # one or more whitespaces between the two words.
```

All the quantifiers with the exception of the last two examples make Perl match the patterns as many times as possible. Thus, /\w+/ matches as many "word" characters as it can match. Assume that the variable $sql has the string 'CREATE PROCEDURE spAdd'. Because the regular expression /CREATE\s+PROC(EDURE)?/ matches both the string CREATE PROC and the string CREATE PROCEDURE and the quantifier is greedy, the pattern matches CREATE PROCEDURE, not CREATE PROC.

However, in the last example, the quantifier ? is appended with another ? character, making the quantifier not greedy. In this case, the pattern matches CREATE PROC instead of CREATE PROCEDURE.

Whether you should use a quantifier in its greedy version or its nongreedy version depends on what you're trying to accomplish. If you're trying to pattern match a T-SQL CREATE PROCEDURE statement, you probably should use the greedy version, because it's unlikely that you want to match CREATE PROC when you can match CREATE PROCEDURE.

When you need to capture and use the matched substring, the greediness of a quantifier may significantly alter the behavior of a script.

Understanding Assertions

To enable you to express patterns more specifically, Perl regular expressions support a collection of zero-width assertions. They're zero width because they don't match any character in the string. Rather, they help position the pattern in the string. These assertions are also known as *anchors*.

Table B-6 describes the common assertions.

Table B-6. Common Zero-Width Assertions

ASSERTION	DESCRIPTION
^	Matches the beginning of the string.
$	Matches the end of a string when the $ sign is at the end of a regular expression.
\b	Matches any word boundary. The word boundary is the position between \w and \W.
\B	Matches any position that isn't a word boundary.
\z	Matches the end of the string.
\Z	Matches the end of the string if there isn't a newline at the end of the string. If there's a newline at the end of the string, this assertion matches the position before the last newline.

You've seen the assertions ^ and $ already. The following are four examples using the other assertions:

```
/\bauthors\b/    # Matches authors, #authors, or authors tmp. But doesn't match
                 # tb_authors, authors2
/\Bauthors/      # Matches tb_authors, tb_authors2, or tmpauthors. But doesn't
                 # match authors, tmp authros, #authors, or @authors
/authors\z/      # Matches authors, tb_authors, or #authors. But doesn't
                 # match authors2 or "authors\n" (without quotes).
/authors\Z/      # Matches authors, tb_authors, #authors, or "authors\n"
                 # (without quotes). But does't match "authors\n\n"
```

The \B assertion is the opposite of \b, and it matches any position between two \w characters. In addition, it also matches between two \W\W characters. For example, it matches between @$.

Note that \z matches the end of a string no matter what comes before it. \Z also matches the end of the string. However, if there's a newline at the end of the string, it doesn't include the newline. Instead, it matches right before the newline. If there's no newline at the end of the string, \z and \Z behave the same.

Modifying Patterns

Perl allows you to modify the behavior of a regular expression by placing a single character immediately following the last pattern delimiters of //. Table B-7 describes the most common modifiers.

Table B-7. Pattern Modifiers

MODIFIER	DESCRIPTION
/i	Makes the pattern match case insensitive.
/s	Lets the wildcard . match any character including an embedded newline character.
/m	Lets the anchors ^ match after an embedded newline and lets the anchor $ match before an embedded newline.
/x	Allows whitespace and comments inside the pattern. They're ignored during the pattern match.

If this is the first time you've read about the pattern modifiers, the description in Table B-7 may not all make sense. Several examples should help flatten your learning curve significantly:

```
/authors/i     # Matches authors, Authors, MyAuthors, authorS2, or any combination
               # of lower or upper case characters
/authors./     # Matches authors followed by any character other than a newline.
               # It doesn't match "Table: authors\n" (without the quotes)
/authors./s    # Matches "Table: authors\n" (without the quotes) because the
               # wildcard . matches the newline when the /s modifier is specified.
/^authors$/    # Matches authors, but not "Table:\nauthors\ntitles\n" (without
               # the quotes)
/^authors$/m   # Matches "Table:\nauthors\ntitles\n" (without the quotes). More
               # precisely, it matches the string authors between the two
               # newlines.
```

The /x modifier deserves special attention. You use it to make your regular expression more legible. With this modifier, you can break the regular expression into multiple lines, add spaces and tabs, and include comments after the # character. For example, to parse a three-part SQL Server table identifier, you write the regular expression as follows:

```
/\w+\.\w+\.\w+|\w+\.\w+|\w+/
```

With the /x modifier, you can rewrite the expression as follows:

```
/
  \w+\.\w+\.\w+  |     # three-part name (DBName.Owner.TableName), or
  \w+\.\w+       |     # two-part name (Owner.TableName), or
  \w+                  # one-part name (TableName)
/x
```

NOTE *If you use the /x modifier and still want to match a whitespace, you need to specify the whitespace explicitly. Thus,* /CREATE PROCEDURE/x *doesn't match the string* CREATE PROCEDURE. *You need to specify the regular expression as* /CREATE\s+PROCEDURE/x.

Using More Advanced Features

It's beyond the scope of this brief tutorial to cover all the advanced features of Perl regular expressions. However, some of the advanced features are also essential. Leaving them out would leave a big hole in your regular expression knowledge.

This section completes the tutorial by discussing two such features: capturing the matched strings and using the /g modifier.

Capturing with Parentheses

If you can only use a regular expression to check whether there's a match, it's useful but not useful enough. When you use a regular expression to look for a match in a string, often you want to do something with the matched substring later in the script.

Perl provides the built-in variables $1, $2, up to $n—where n is an integer—to record the substrings matched by the first pair of parentheses, the second pair of parentheses, and up to the *n*th pair parentheses, respectively. To count the parentheses in a regular expression, you go from left to right by counting the opening parentheses only.

Some examples should help clarify this useful feature. The following code segment demonstrates how to capture the unqualified table name in a three-part name:[2]

```
$tb = 'pubs.dbo.authors';
if ($tb =~ /\w+\.\w*\.(\w+)/) {
    print "Table name: $1\n";
}
```

There's only one pair of parentheses in this regular expression. The pattern inside the parentheses matches the unqualified table name in a three-part name stored in the variable $tb. If there's a match, the variable $1 remembers the unqualified table name. This example prints the string authors.

Assume that you know $tb may contain an unqualified table name all by itself. To capture the table name, you can rewrite the code as follows:

```
$tb = 'authors';
if ($tb =~ /(\w+\.\w*\.)?(\w+)/) {
    print "Table name: $2\n";
}
```

---

2. The regular expression in this code segment isn't meant to match all the variations of a three-part name permitted by T-SQL.

This example still prints the string authors. But the string is captured with the variable $2, corresponding to the second pair of parentheses.

Furthermore, let's still assume that $tb may contain an unqualified table name. Now, if the database name and the owner name are present, you want to capture them in addition to capturing the table name. For this scenario, you can rewrite the code as follows:

```
$tb = 'pubs..authors';
if ($tb =~ /((\w+)\.(\w*)\.)?(\w+)/) {
    print "DB name: $2, Owner name: $3, Table name: $4\n";
}
```

This code segment prints the following:

```
DB name: pubs, Owner name:, Table name: authors
```

Note that the database name is captured with $2, the owner name $3, and the table name $4. In this code segment, the first pair of parentheses is for grouping purposes. It enables the quantifier ? to mark the grouping optional. Although it captures the concatenation of the database name and the owner name in $1, it isn't useful in this case.

NOTE *Perl regular expressions do allow you flag a pair of parentheses for grouping only without capturing the matched substring. Check the Perl online documentation page* perlre *and* perlretut *for non-capturing groupings.*

Using the /g Modifier

The /g modifier is the so-called *global match modifier*. It modifies the pattern match operator m//, telling it to find as many matches as possible. You typically use the m// operator on the right side of the =~ operator. The left side of the =~ operator specifies the string in which you apply the regular expression to find the pattern.

The exact behavior of the /g modifier depends on the context. In list context, it returns all the substrings captured with parentheses or all the substrings that match the entire pattern when there are no parentheses.

NOTE *It's a common idiom to omit the letter* m *in the* m// *operator. However, if you use a symbol rather than the forward slash to delimit the regular expression, you must include the letter* m.

The following example demonstrates the behavior of the /g modifier in list context:

```
$tb = 'SQL1.pubs.dbo.authors';
@names = $tb =~ /(\w+)\./g;
```

Note that in this code segment, the pattern matches three substrings: 'SQL1.', 'pub.', and 'dbo.' (without the quotes). The @names array has three elements: ('SQL1', 'pubs', 'dbo'). Contrast this result with the value returned from the match operator when the /g modifier isn't specified.[3]

Remove the parentheses, and the code segment is as follows:

```
$tb = 'SQL1.pubs.dbo.authors';
@names = $tb =~ /\w+\./g;
```

The @names array now has three elements: ('SQL1.', 'pubs.', 'dbo.'). When the regular expression doesn't have any embedded parentheses, the /g modifier treats the entire regular expression as if it's enclosed in a pair of parentheses.

In scalar context, you can repeatedly execute the match operator with the /g modifier to find one matched substring a time. If you keep executing the match operator with the /g modifier—in other words, m//g—you'll find all the matches. Every time m//g runs, it returns true when there's a match and false when there's no match.

It's common to place m//g in a while condition to work on all the matches for a given pattern and string. For example, to find all the CREATE PROCEDURE statements in a script stored in the variable $sql, you can execute following:[4]

```
while ($sql =~ /\bcreate\s+proc(edure)?\s+([^\s]+)/ig) {
   @sp = (@sp, $2);
}
```

---

3. Hint: Without the /g modifier, the match operator returns a list with a single element, which is ('SQL1').

4. To simplify the exposition, the pattern inside the second pair of parentheses assumes that the name of the stored procedure doesn't contain any whitespace.

This code segment populates the array @sp with the names of all the stored procedures defined in $sql.

When you specify the /g modifier, Perl remembers where in the string the last successful match took place. That's why it's able to skip the matched substrings and look for only the next new match.

Summary

This appendix highlighted several aspects of Perl that are important to master. They won't turn you into a Perl expert, but they should help get you started.

Learning Perl is a never-ending process. Not only is the language itself comprehensive, but it also is evolving in terms of new modules. In addition, the next major version of Perl is expected to introduce many useful new features.

However, the good thing about Perl is that you don't have to wait until you've learned a substantial part of the language to start using it. As soon as you've picked up the basics, you can start using the scripts written by others, modifying them to solve your own problems. You'll find it effective to study the concepts and techniques in existing scripts while you're using them.

Soon, you'll start writing your own scripts and incorporating more advanced features.

Index

Numbers and Symbols

$ identifier
for scalar data types, 11

$@ predefined variable, 51

$/ predefined variable, 51

$| predefined variable, 51

$_ predefined variable, 51

$/ special variable
in Perl, 335

$0 predefined variable, 51

$1 predefined variable, 51

$configRef data structure
generating for the configuration options, 530

$currentRef configuration file
example of, 531–532

$diffRef data structure
populating, 532

$hours element
of dates and times, 42

$isdst element
of dates and times, 42

$mday element
of dates and times, 42

$min element
of dates and times, 42

$<N> predefined variable, 51

$parser->query()
data structure returned for the SELECT statement from, 85–87

$ref->{Config} hash record
command-line arguments kept in, 618

$ref->{CurrentStatus} hash record
keys in, 647

$ref->{Status} data structure
code sample of, 620

$ref->{Status} hash record
keys of, 620

$rowRef
example of hash referenced by, 270

$savedRef data structure
populating with the dbaReadSavedRef() function, 532

$sec element
of dates and times, 42

$spCallRef
example of returned by getSPCall() function, 242

$summaryRef data structure
code example of, 455–456

$wday element
of dates and times, 42

$yday element
of dates and times, 42

$year element
of dates and times, 42

% identifier
prefixing hash variables with, 13–15
representing a hash with, 11

%ENV predefined variable, 51

%opts
testing with various command-line scenarios, 45

... predefined variable, 51

/ (forward slash)
as a delimiter, 5–6

/g modifier
using to get all matched strings into an array, 336

E

open() function

  file access modes, 17–18

  using, 17

opendir() function

  using, 72–74

Orders database

  finding, 668–669

osql.exe

  executing a T-SQL script via, 124–127

Owner key

  returned by dbaScriptSP() function, 152

owner name

  three possibilities for, 394

P

PAG lock

  description and resource, 304

page ID

  converting a byte-swapped hex string to, 255–258

page IDs and rows

  mapping between, 271–273

page removals and page splits

  observing, 275–278

PageFID

  reference to file number of a page, 263

pages

  mapping to from table rows, 258–261

PageType

  for identifying the type of page, 263

Parse::RecDescent module, 33

  writer of, 78

parsing

  for stored procedure calls, 226–229

pattern-matched exceptions

  setting options for, 598–599

  understanding, 593, 605–607

patterns

  finding array elements that match, 16

  finding in a string, 5–6

performance counter logs

  importing into a database, 182–187

  preparing for bulk copy import, 184–185

performance data

  exporting to a file for charting, 187–192

  preparing in CSV format for charting, 188–191

Performance Logs and Alerts tool

  introduced in Windows 2000, 182

Perl

  basic data types in, 11–13

  case sensitivity of, 2

  introduction to the basics of, 1–29

  logical operators, 102

  solutions to some SQL Server monitoring problems, 561–661

  using its text processing features to analyze SQL code, 329–375

  using the \s+ whitespace to separate T-SQL reserved words, 398–399

  using to analyze log files, 434

Perl Cookbook (O'Reilly, 1998)

  for various issues of working with modules, 37

Perl data structure

  dumping, 44–46

Perl function

  for converting a byte-swapped hex string to a page ID, 257–258

Perl modules

  defined, 31

  reference for working with, 37

  reviewing the documentation for, 34–35

  using in a Perl script, 33–37

  verifying installation of, 33–34

  working with commonly used, 31–87

U